CHOPPER - THE MAKING OF A MEGA-CITY REBEL

Marlon 'Chopper' Shakespeare wasn't prepared to be just another unemployed nobody living in Mega-City One. As a teen, the young rebel set out to become the best wall-scrawler (graffiti artist) in the Big Meg, but was eventually caught by Judge Dredd whilst going up against his arch-rival, the mysterious 'Phantom'.

(See *UnAmerican Graffiti*, originally published in *2000 AD* Progs 206-207 and collected in *Judge Dredd: The Complete Case Files 04*).

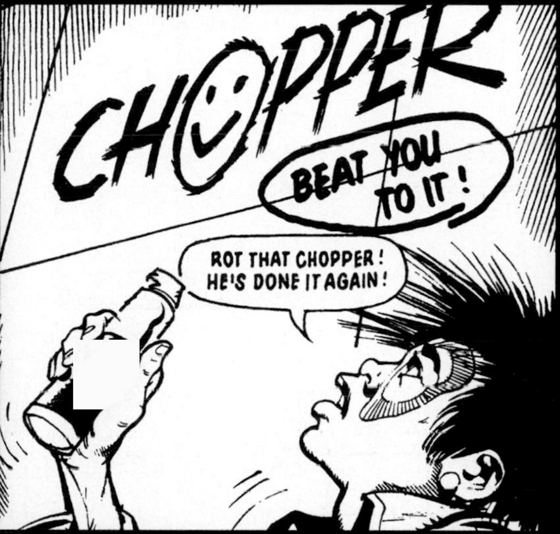
CHOPPER
BEAT YOU TO IT!
ROT THAT CHOPPER! HE'S DONE IT AGAIN!

Having survived his time in the Iso-Cubes, Chopper returned slightly older and even more determined to stand out from the crowd. Only this time he had traded in his spray cans for a flying surfboard. Entering Supersurf 7, Chopper proved to have the skills to be the very best skysurfer the world had ever seen. He also found his way back on the wrong side of the law.

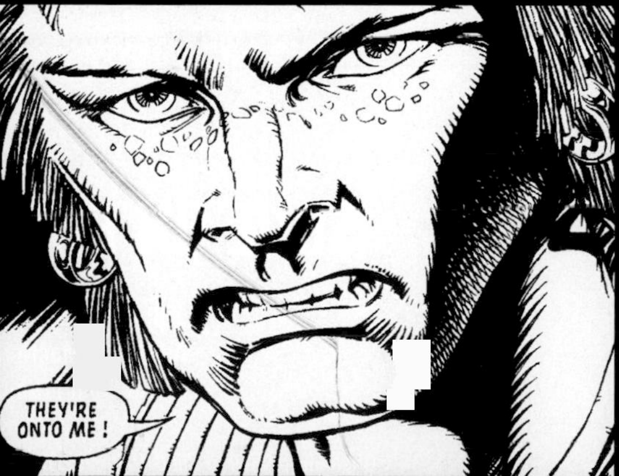
THEY'RE ONTO ME!

(*Midnight Surfer*, originally published in *2000 AD* Progs 424-429 and collected in *Judge Dredd: The Complete Case Files 09*).

On the eve of Supersurf 10 in Oz, Chopper managed to escape custody and set out on a treacherous journey in order to take the world championship title back from the 'Wizard of Oz', Jug McKenzie.
After being narrowly defeated by Jug, a deflated Chopper avoided being shot by Dredd (with a little help from McKenzie & Oz lawman Judge Bruce), escaping out into the Radlands – where he could remain free...

(*Oz* originally published in *2000 AD* Progs 545-570 and collected in *Judge Dredd: The Complete Case Files 11*).

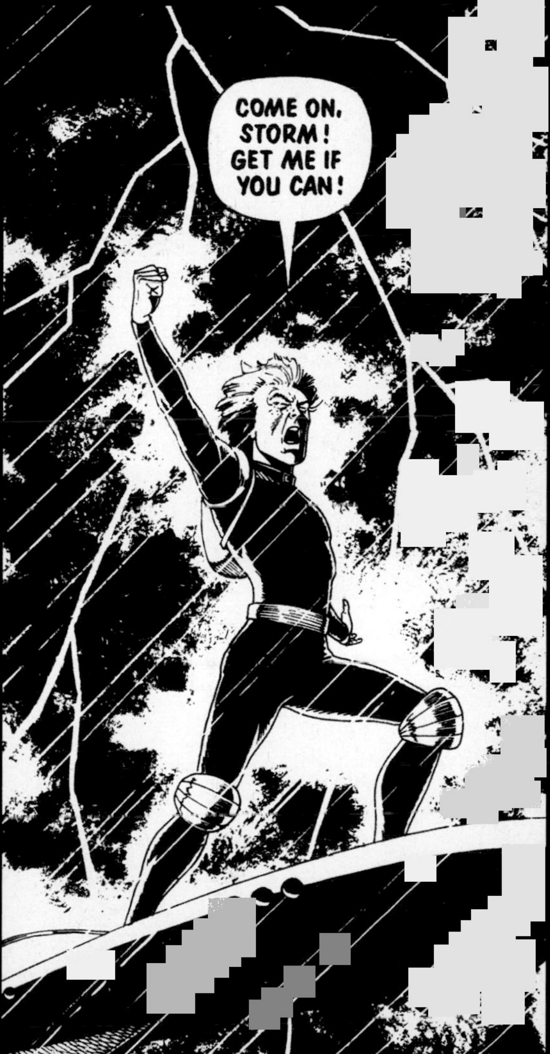
COME ON, STORM! GET ME IF YOU CAN!

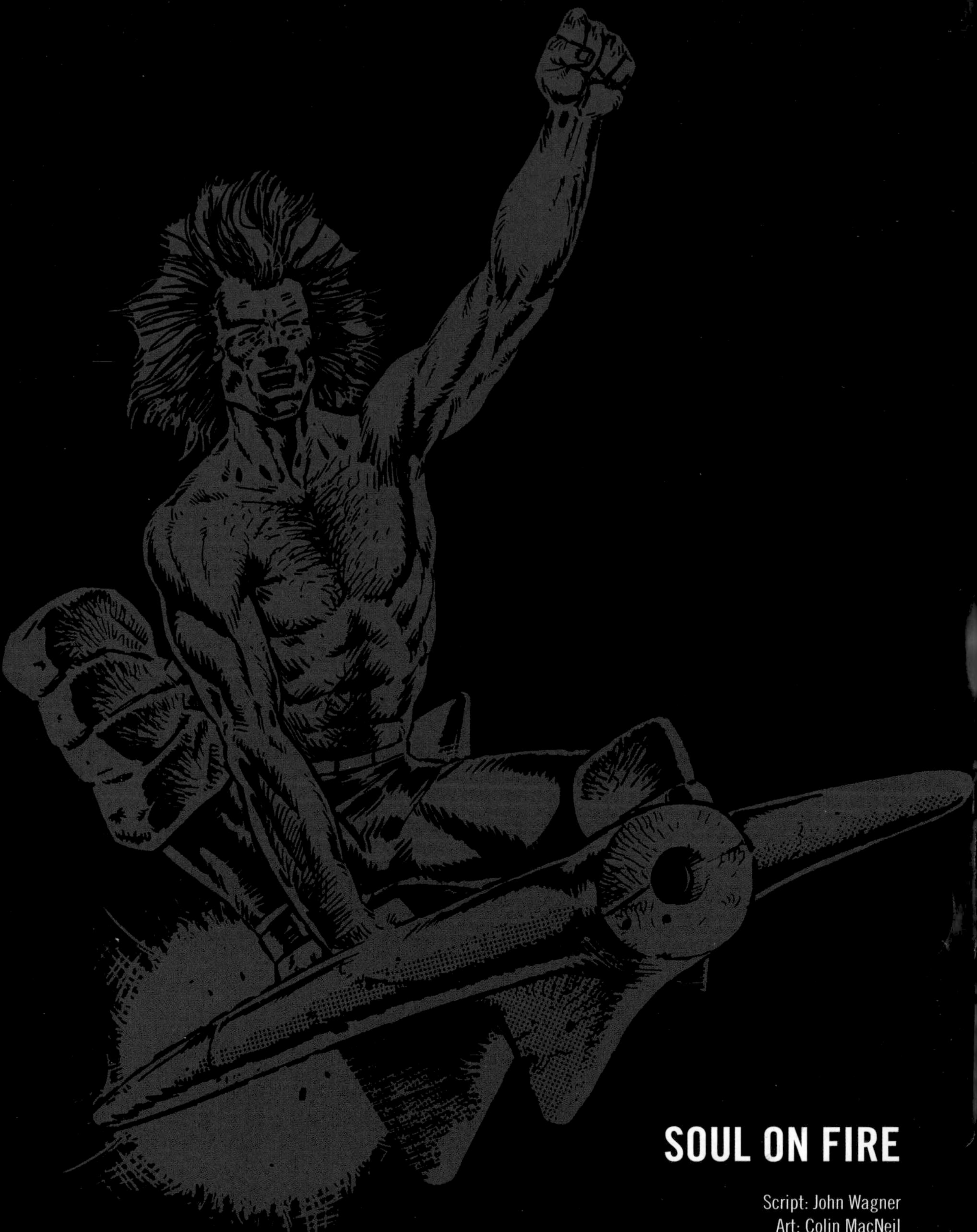

SOUL ON FIRE

Script: John Wagner
Art: Colin MacNeil
Letters: Tom Frame

Originally printed in *2000 AD* Progs 594-597

CHOPPER
SURF'S UP

CHOPPER CREAT... ...H & CAM KENNEDY

CHOPPER
SURF'S UP

JOHN WAGNER ★ GARTH ENNIS ★ ALAN MCKENZIE
Writer

COLIN MACNEIL ★ JOHN MCCREA ★ JOHN HIGGINS ★ MARTIN EMOND ★ PATRICK GODDARD
Artists

GLENN FABRY
Cover Art

Originally serialised in *2000 AD* Progs 594-597, 654-665, 964-971, 1387-1394, *The Judge Dredd Megazine* 1.01-1.06, 2.36, *Judge Dredd* Poster Prog 4. Copyright © 1988, 1989, 1990, 1993, 1994, 1995 2004, 2010 Rebellion A/S. All Rights Reserved. *Chopper* and all related characters, their distinctive likenesses and related elements featured in this publication are trademarks of Rebellion A/S. *2000 AD* is a registered trademark. No portion of this book may be reproduced without the express permission of the publisher. Names, character, places and incidents featured in the publication are either the product of the author's imagination or used fictitiously. Any resemblance to actual persons, living or dead (except for satirical purposes) is entirely coincidental.

Published by Rebellion, Riverside House, Osney Mead, Oxford, OX2 0ES, UK.
www.rebellion.co.uk

ISBN: 978-1-907519-27-7
Printed in Malta by Gutenberg Press
Manufactured in the EU by LPPS Ltd., Wellingborough, NN8 3PJ, UK.
First published: December 2010
10 9 8 7 6 5 4 3 2 1

Printed on FSC Accredited Paper

A CIP catalogue record for this book is available from the British Library.

For information on other *2000 AD* graphic novels, or if you have any comments on this book, please email books@2000ADonline.com

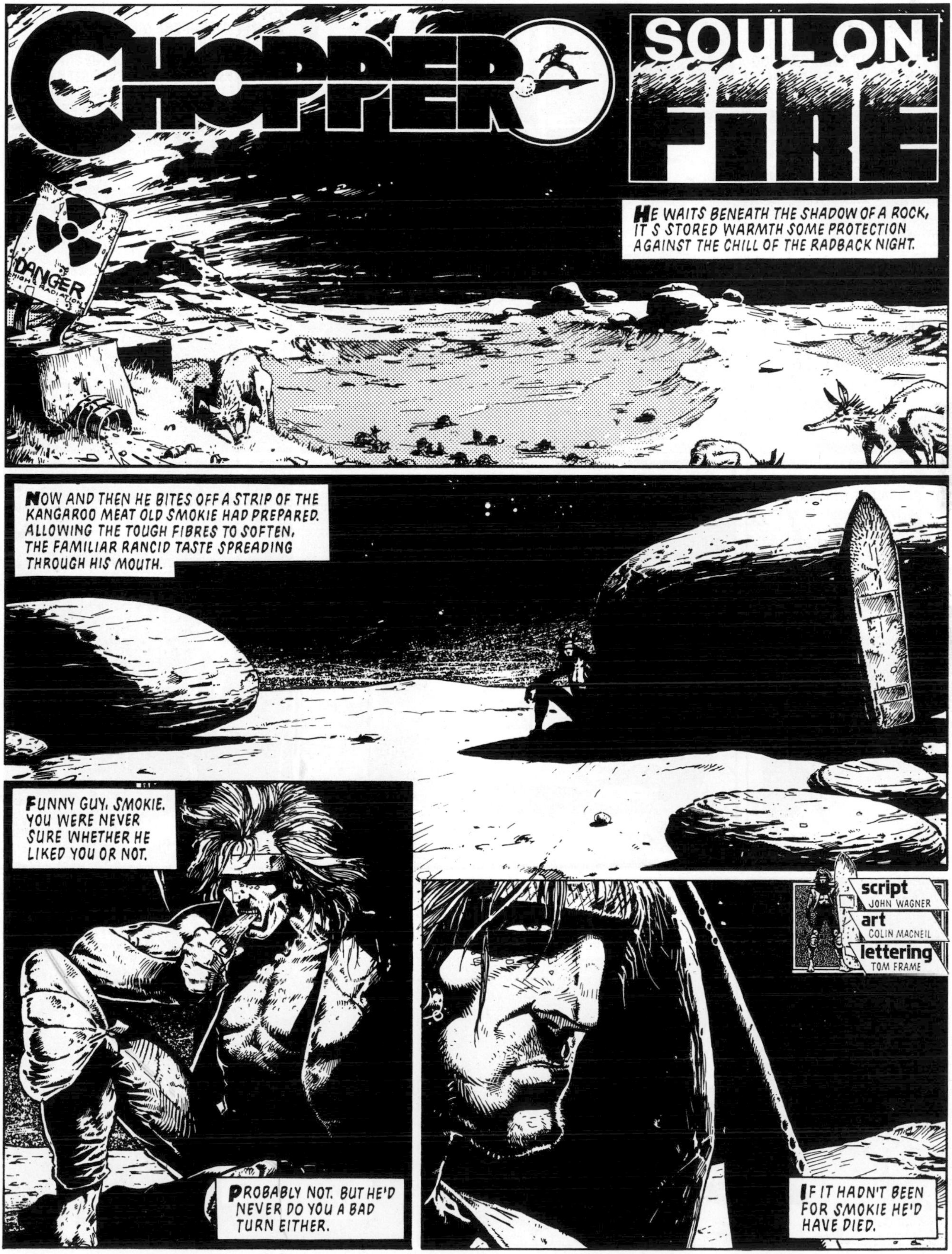
CHOPPER
SOUL ON FIRE
DANGER
HIGH RADIATION
HE WAITS BENEATH THE SHADOW OF A ROCK, IT S STORED WARMTH SOME PROTECTION AGAINST THE CHILL OF THE RADBACK NIGHT.
NOW AND THEN HE BITES OFF A STRIP OF THE KANGAROO MEAT OLD SMOKIE HAD PREPARED. ALLOWING THE TOUGH FIBRES TO SOFTEN, THE FAMILIAR RANCID TASTE SPREADING THROUGH HIS MOUTH.
FUNNY GUY, SMOKIE. YOU WERE NEVER SURE WHETHER HE LIKED YOU OR NOT.
PROBABLY NOT. BUT HE'D NEVER DO YOU A BAD TURN EITHER.
script JOHN WAGNER
art COLIN MACNEIL
lettering TOM FRAME
IF IT HADN'T BEEN FOR SMOKIE HE'D HAVE DIED.

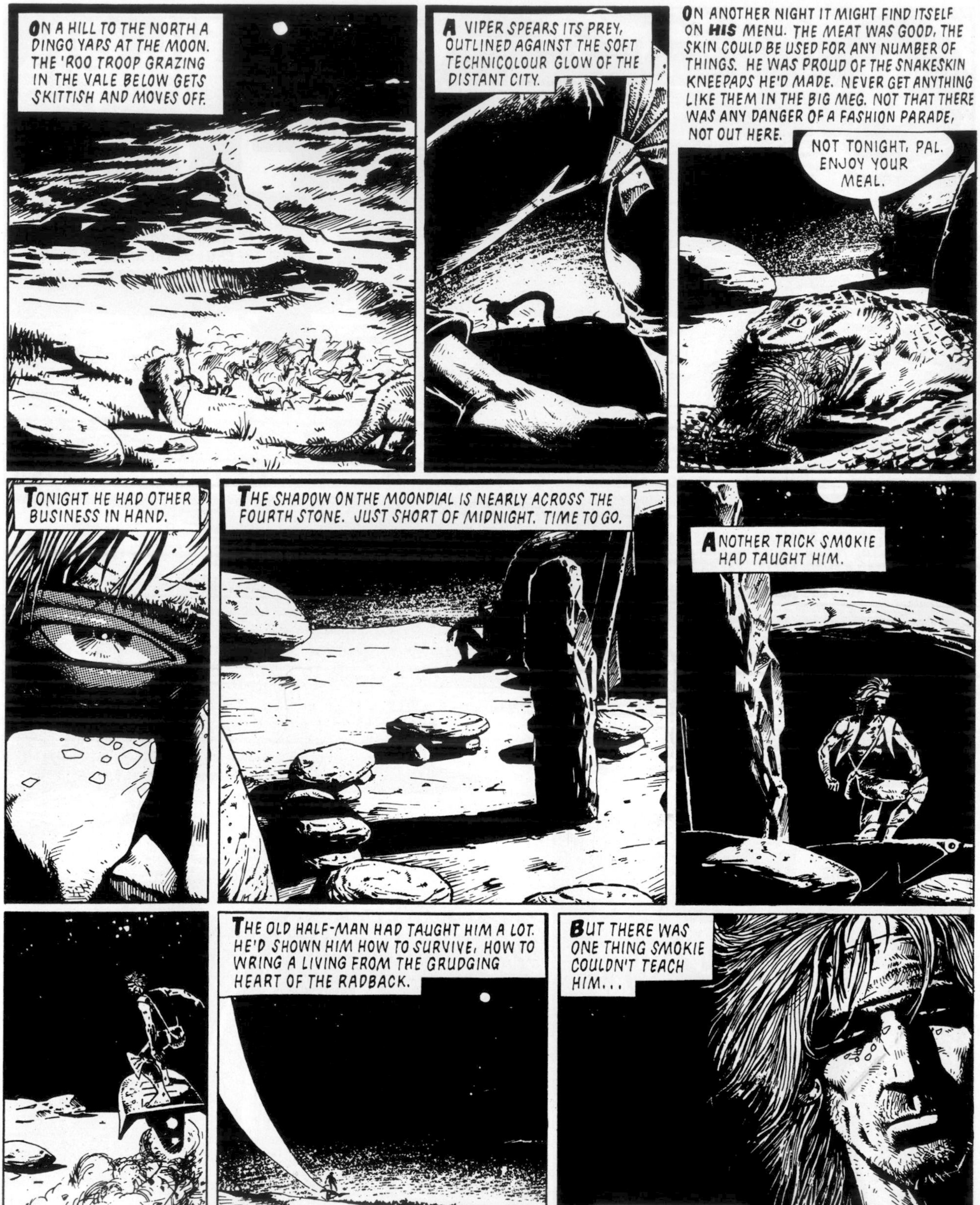
ON A HILL TO THE NORTH A DINGO YAPS AT THE MOON. THE 'ROO TROOP GRAZING IN THE VALE BELOW GETS SKITTISH AND MOVES OFF.
A VIPER SPEARS ITS PREY, OUTLINED AGAINST THE SOFT TECHNICOLOUR GLOW OF THE DISTANT CITY.
ON ANOTHER NIGHT IT MIGHT FIND ITSELF ON HIS MENU. THE MEAT WAS GOOD, THE SKIN COULD BE USED FOR ANY NUMBER OF THINGS. HE WAS PROUD OF THE SNAKESKIN KNEEPADS HE'D MADE. NEVER GET ANYTHING LIKE THEM IN THE BIG MEG. NOT THAT THERE WAS ANY DANGER OF A FASHION PARADE, NOT OUT HERE.
NOT TONIGHT, PAL. ENJOY YOUR MEAL.
TONIGHT HE HAD OTHER BUSINESS IN HAND.
THE SHADOW ON THE MOONDIAL IS NEARLY ACROSS THE FOURTH STONE. JUST SHORT OF MIDNIGHT. TIME TO GO.
ANOTHER TRICK SMOKIE HAD TAUGHT HIM.
THE OLD HALF-MAN HAD TAUGHT HIM A LOT. HE'D SHOWN HIM HOW TO SURVIVE, HOW TO WRING A LIVING FROM THE GRUDGING HEART OF THE RADBACK.
BUT THERE WAS ONE THING SMOKIE COULDN'T TEACH HIM...
...AND THAT WAS HOW TO LIVE WITH FAILURE.

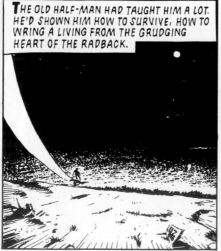

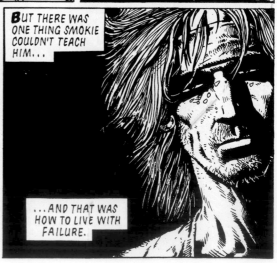

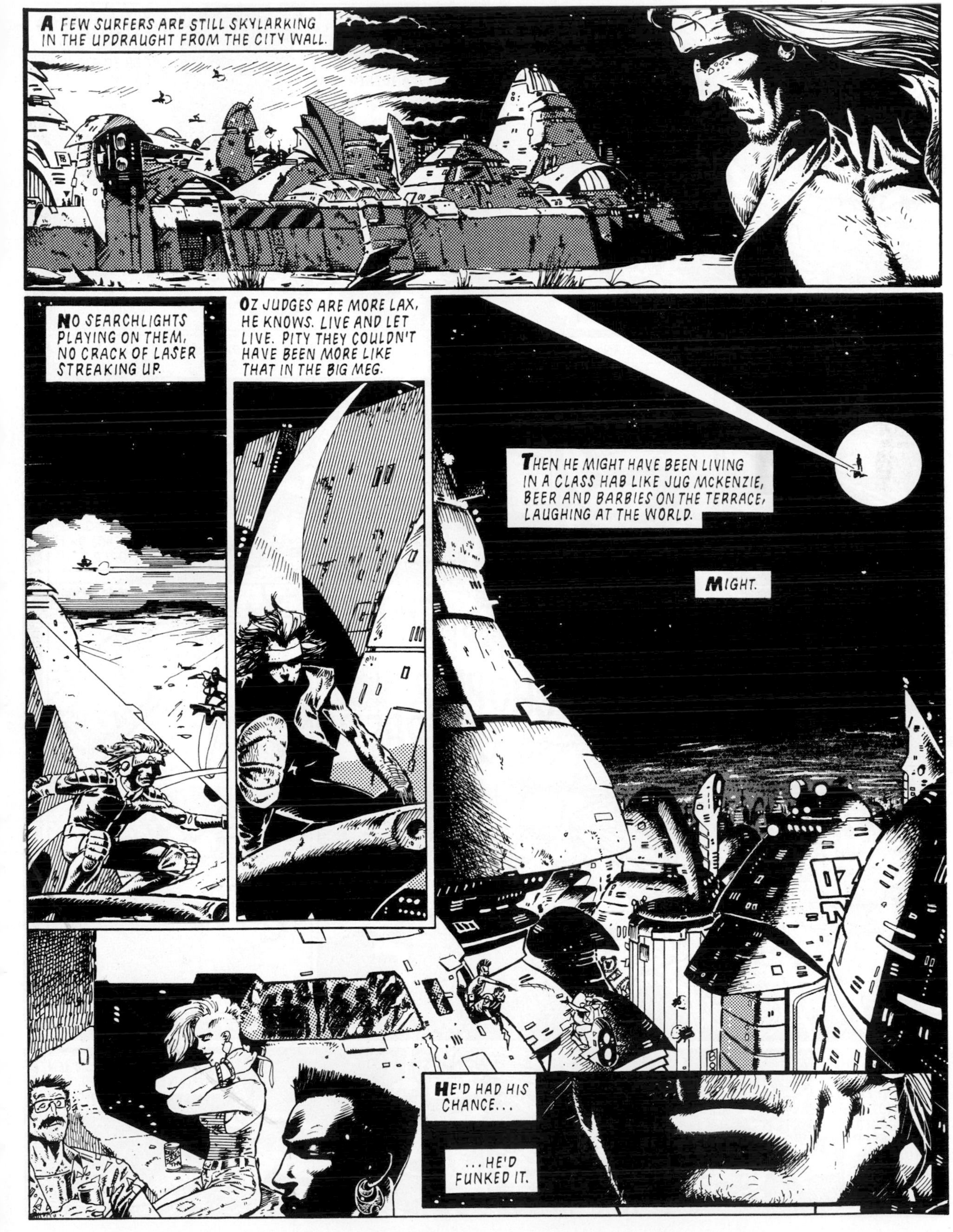
A FEW SURFERS ARE STILL SKYLARKING IN THE UPDRAUGHT FROM THE CITY WALL.
NO SEARCHLIGHTS PLAYING ON THEM, NO CRACK OF LASER STREAKING UP.
OZ JUDGES ARE MORE LAX, HE KNOWS. LIVE AND LET LIVE. PITY THEY COULDN'T HAVE BEEN MORE LIKE THAT IN THE BIG MEG.
THEN HE MIGHT HAVE BEEN LIVING IN A CLASS HAB LIKE JUG MCKENZIE, BEER AND BARBIES ON THE TERRACE, LAUGHING AT THE WORLD.
MIGHT.
HE'D HAD HIS CHANCE...
...HE'D FUNKED IT.

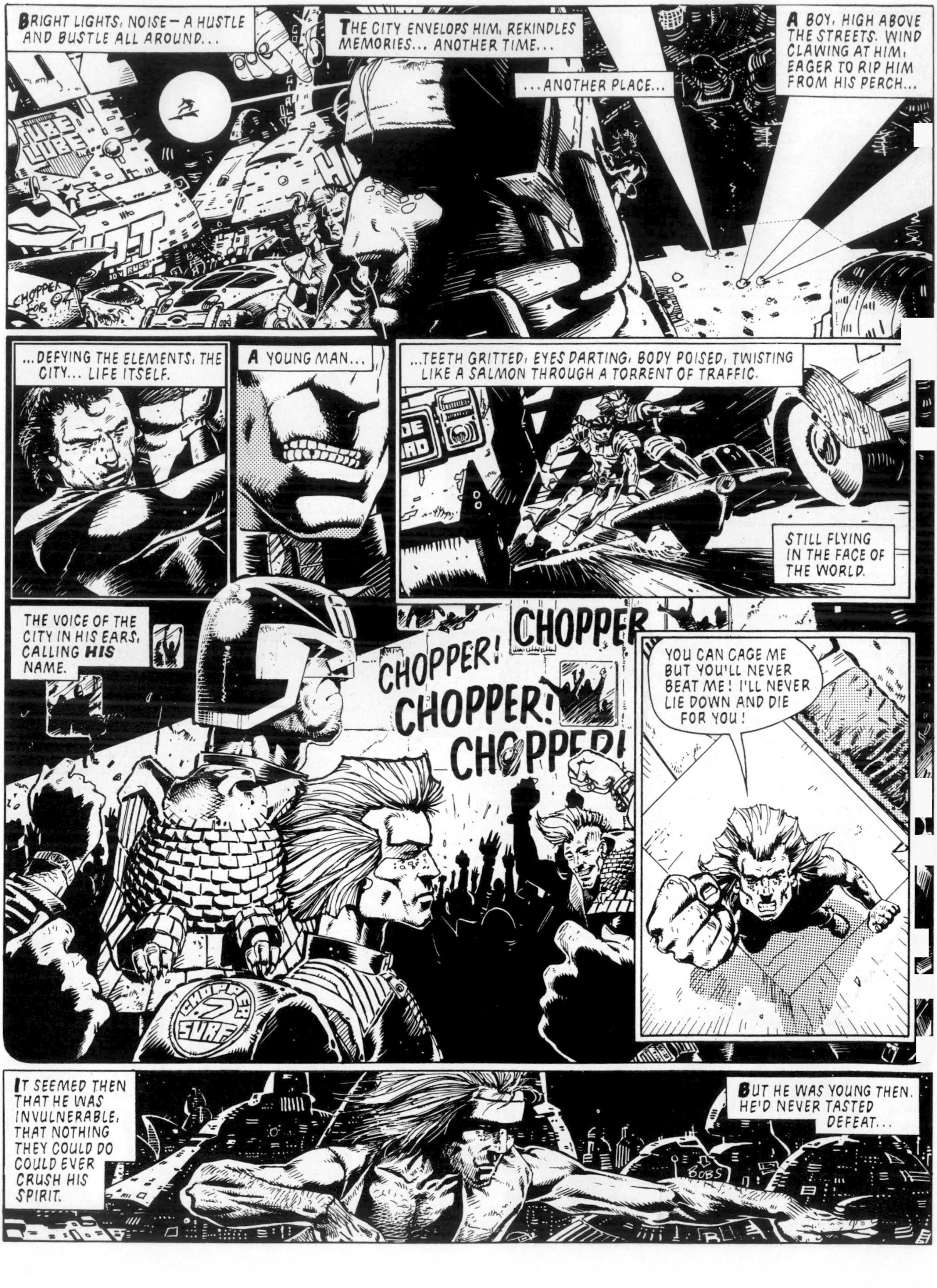
BRIGHT LIGHTS; NOISE — A HUSTLE AND BUSTLE ALL AROUND...
THE CITY ENVELOPS HIM, REKINDLES MEMORIES... ANOTHER TIME...
...ANOTHER PLACE...
A BOY, HIGH ABOVE THE STREETS. WIND CLAWING AT HIM, EAGER TO RIP HIM FROM HIS PERCH...
TUBE LUBE
...DEFYING THE ELEMENTS, THE CITY... LIFE ITSELF.
A YOUNG MAN...
...TEETH GRITTED, EYES DARTING, BODY POISED, TWISTING LIKE A SALMON THROUGH A TORRENT OF TRAFFIC.
STILL FLYING IN THE FACE OF THE WORLD.
THE VOICE OF THE CITY IN HIS EARS, CALLING **HIS** NAME.
CHOPPER
CHOPPER!
CHOPPER!
CHOPPER!
YOU CAN CAGE ME BUT YOU'LL NEVER BEAT ME! I'LL NEVER LIE DOWN AND DIE FOR YOU!
CHOPPER 2 SURF
IT SEEMED THEN THAT HE WAS INVULNERABLE, THAT NOTHING THEY COULD DO COULD EVER CRUSH HIS SPIRIT.
BUT HE WAS YOUNG THEN. HE'D NEVER TASTED DEFEAT...
BOBS

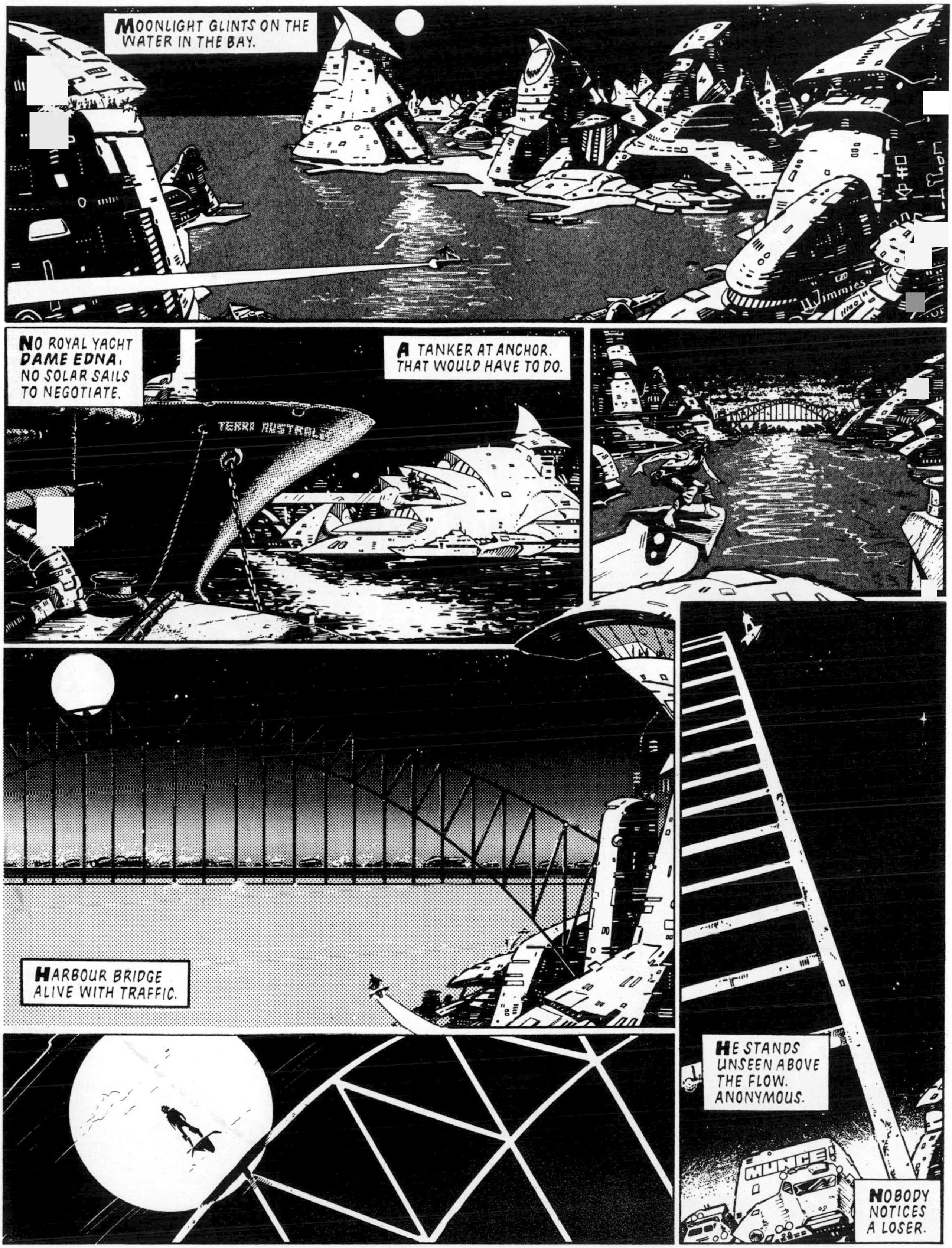
MOONLIGHT GLINTS ON THE WATER IN THE BAY.
Jimmies
NO ROYAL YACHT DAME EDNA, NO SOLAR SAILS TO NEGOTIATE.
A TANKER AT ANCHOR. THAT WOULD HAVE TO DO.
HARBOUR BRIDGE ALIVE WITH TRAFFIC.
HE STANDS UNSEEN ABOVE THE FLOW. ANONYMOUS.
NOBODY NOTICES A LOSER.

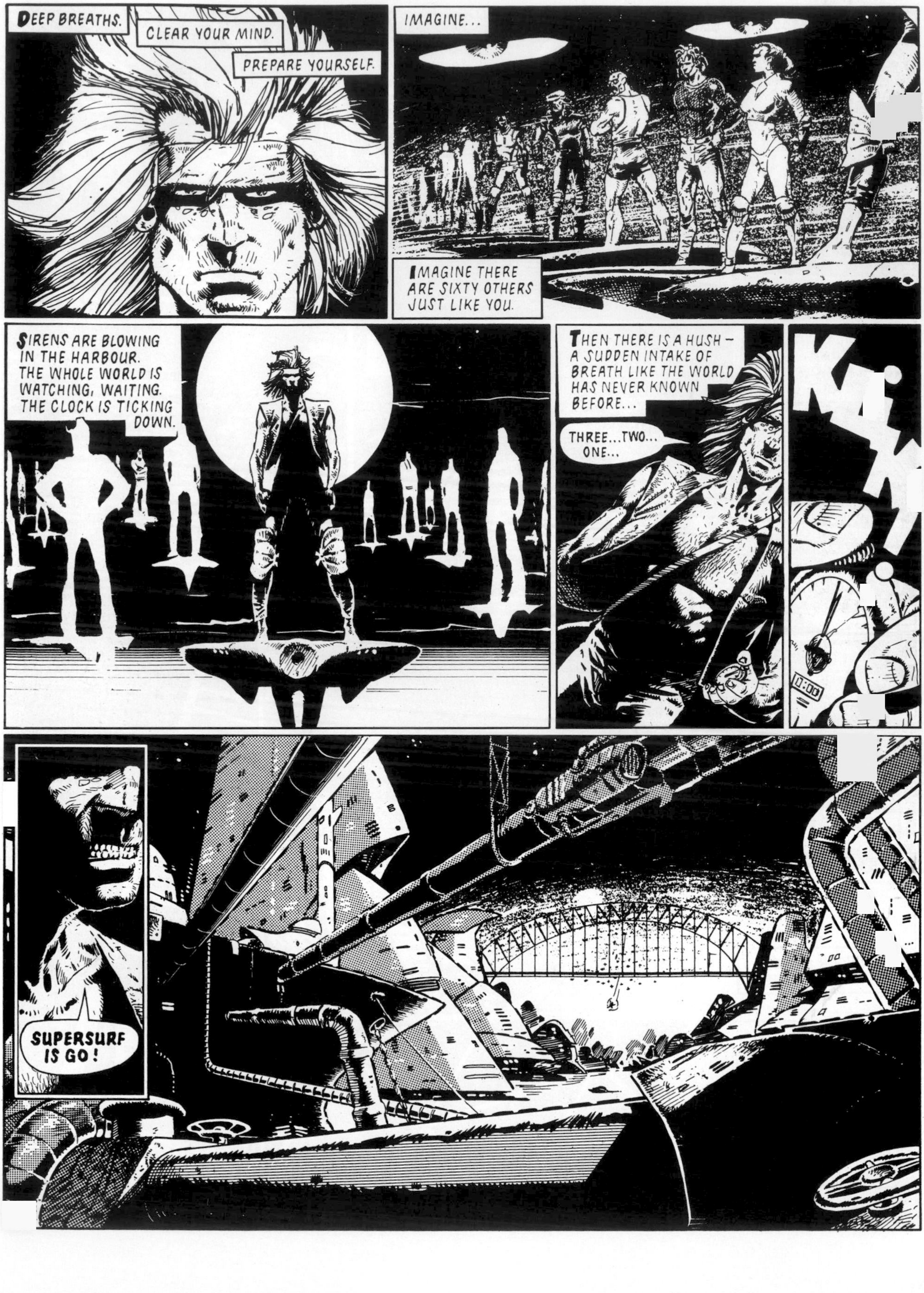
DEEP BREATHS.
CLEAR YOUR MIND.
PREPARE YOURSELF.
IMAGINE...
IMAGINE THERE ARE SIXTY OTHERS JUST LIKE YOU.
SIRENS ARE BLOWING IN THE HARBOUR. THE WHOLE WORLD IS WATCHING, WAITING. THE CLOCK IS TICKING DOWN.
THEN THERE IS A HUSH – A SUDDEN INTAKE OF BREATH LIKE THE WORLD HAS NEVER KNOWN BEFORE...
THREE...TWO... ONE...
10:00
SUPERSURF IS GO!

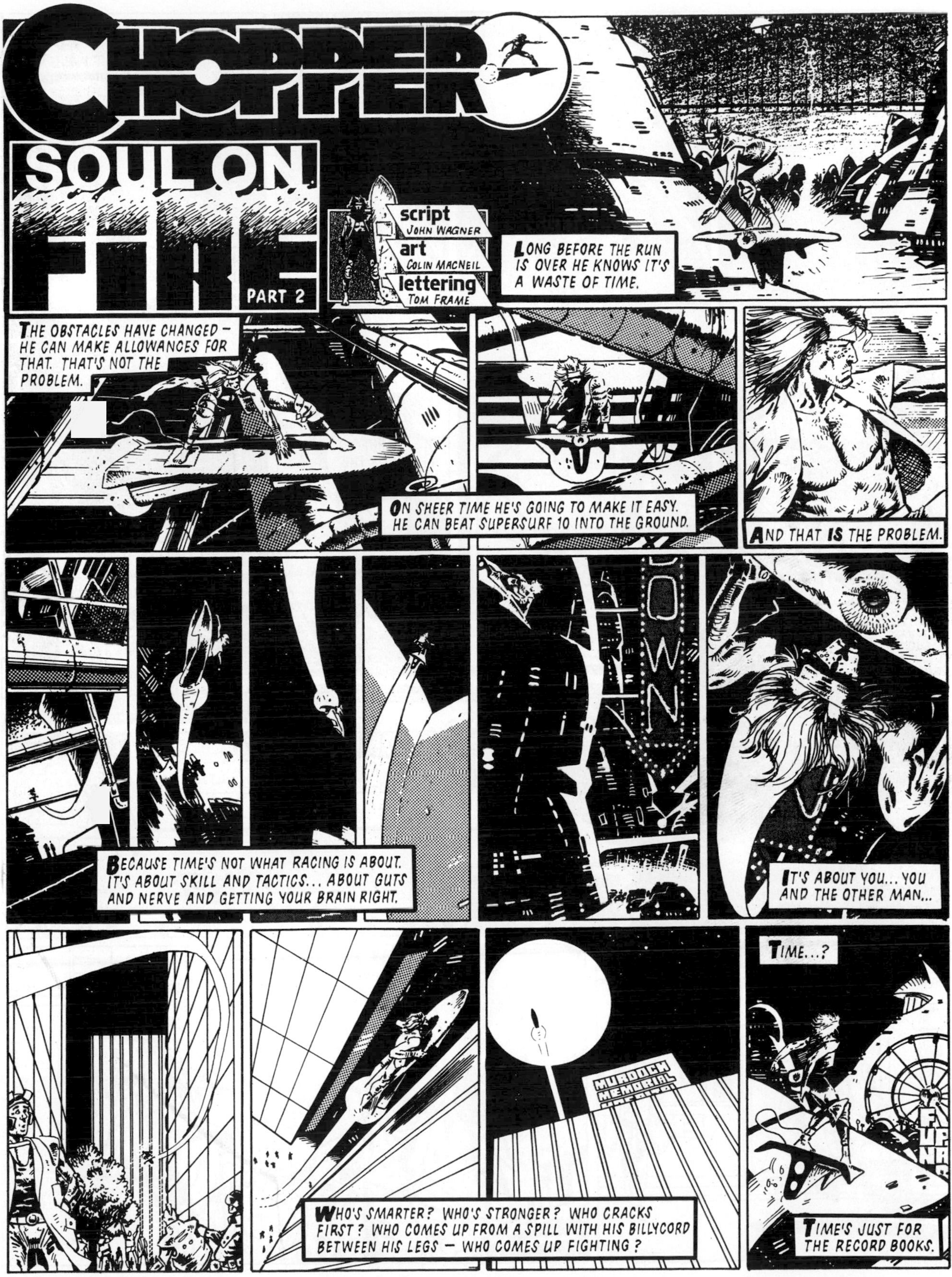
CHOPPER
SOUL ON FIRE
PART 2
script JOHN WAGNER
art COLIN MACNEIL
lettering TOM FRAME
LONG BEFORE THE RUN IS OVER HE KNOWS IT'S A WASTE OF TIME.
THE OBSTACLES HAVE CHANGED — HE CAN MAKE ALLOWANCES FOR THAT. THAT'S NOT THE PROBLEM.
ON SHEER TIME HE'S GOING TO MAKE IT EASY. HE CAN BEAT SUPERSURF 10 INTO THE GROUND.
AND THAT IS THE PROBLEM.
DOWN
BECAUSE TIME'S NOT WHAT RACING IS ABOUT. IT'S ABOUT SKILL AND TACTICS... ABOUT GUTS AND NERVE AND GETTING YOUR BRAIN RIGHT.
IT'S ABOUT YOU... YOU AND THE OTHER MAN...
MURDOCH MEMORIAL
WHO'S SMARTER? WHO'S STRONGER? WHO CRACKS FIRST? WHO COMES UP FROM A SPILL WITH HIS BILLYCORD BETWEEN HIS LEGS — WHO COMES UP FIGHTING?
TIME...?
TIME'S JUST FOR THE RECORD BOOKS.

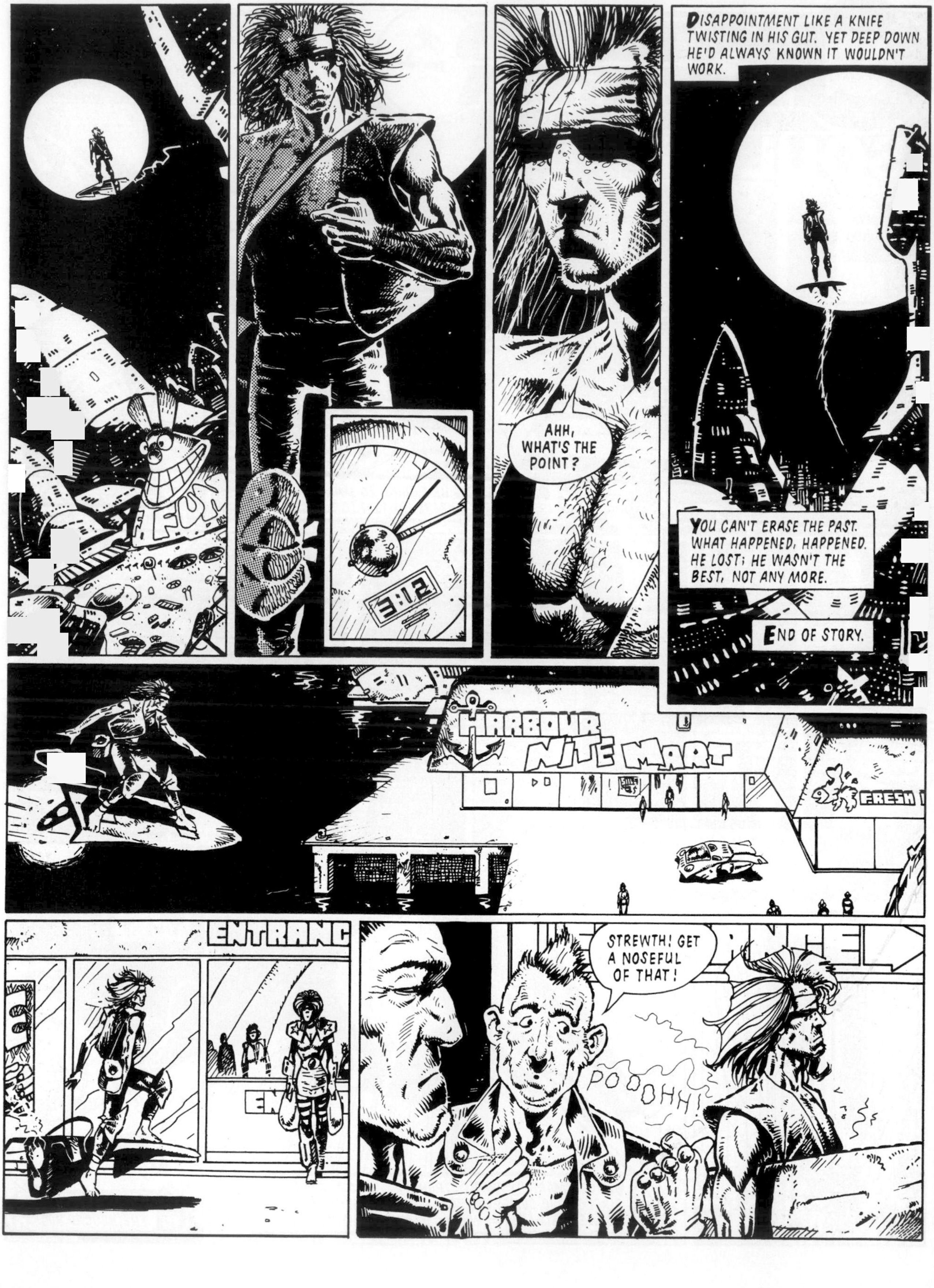
AHH, WHAT'S THE POINT?
DISAPPOINTMENT LIKE A KNIFE TWISTING IN HIS GUT. YET DEEP DOWN HE'D ALWAYS KNOWN IT WOULDN'T WORK.
YOU CAN'T ERASE THE PAST. WHAT HAPPENED, HAPPENED. HE LOST; HE WASN'T THE BEST, NOT ANY MORE.
END OF STORY.
HARBOUR NITE MART
FRESH
ENTRANC
STREWTH! GET A NOSEFUL OF THAT!
POOOHH!

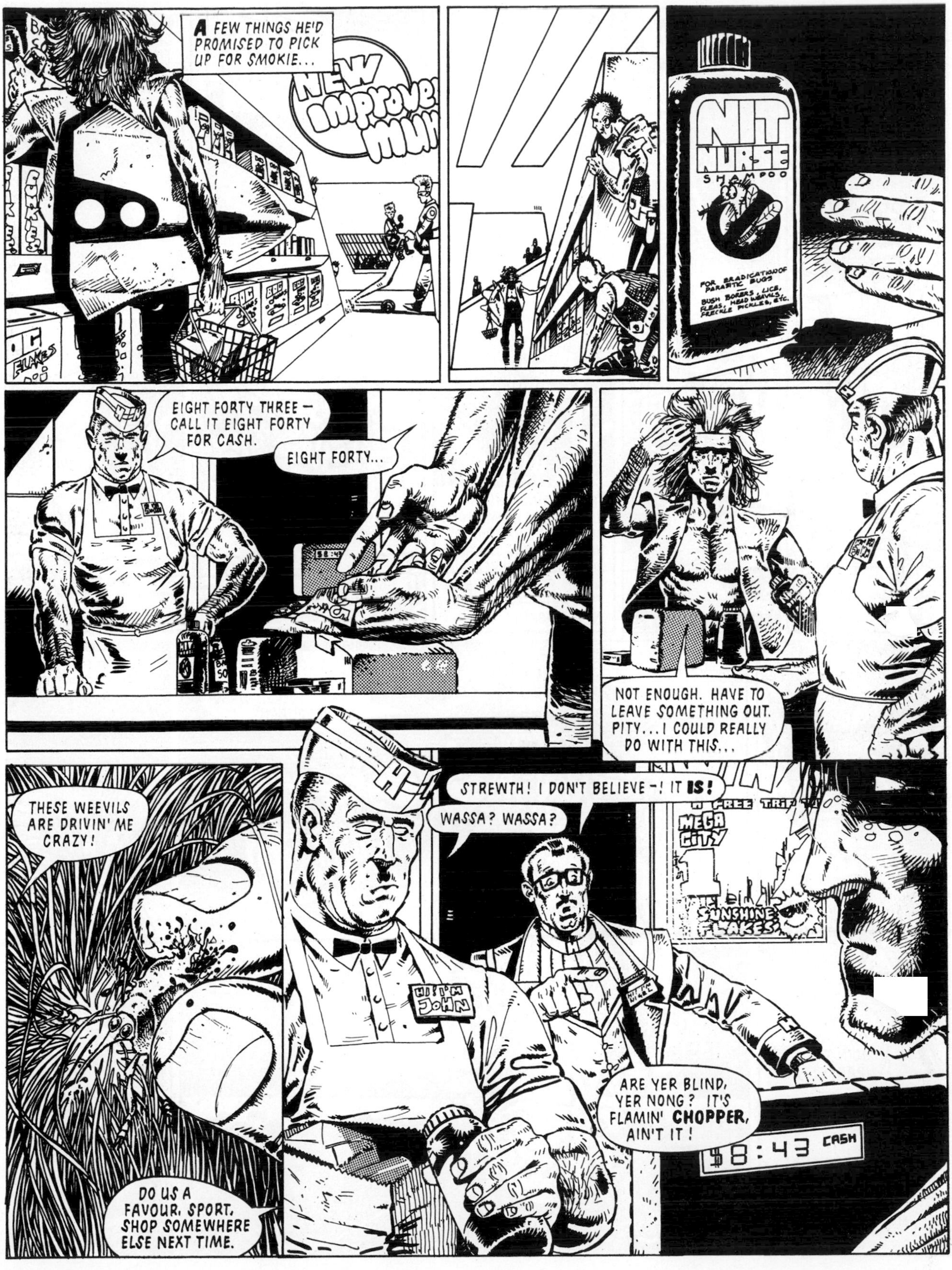
A FEW THINGS HE'D PROMISED TO PICK UP FOR SMOKIE...
NIT NURSE SHAMPOO
FOR ERADICATION OF PARASITIC BUGS
BUSH BORERS, LICE, FLEAS, HEAD WEEVILS, FRECKLE PICKLES, ETC.
EIGHT FORTY THREE — CALL IT EIGHT FORTY FOR CASH.
EIGHT FORTY...
NOT ENOUGH. HAVE TO LEAVE SOMETHING OUT. PITY... I COULD REALLY DO WITH THIS...
THESE WEEVILS ARE DRIVIN' ME CRAZY!
DO US A FAVOUR, SPORT. SHOP SOMEWHERE ELSE NEXT TIME.
STREWTH! I DON'T BELIEVE-! IT IS!
WASSA? WASSA?
HI! I'M JOHN
MEGA CITY 1
SUNSHINE FLAKES
ARE YER BLIND, YER NONG? IT'S FLAMIN' CHOPPER, AIN'T IT!
$8:43 CASH

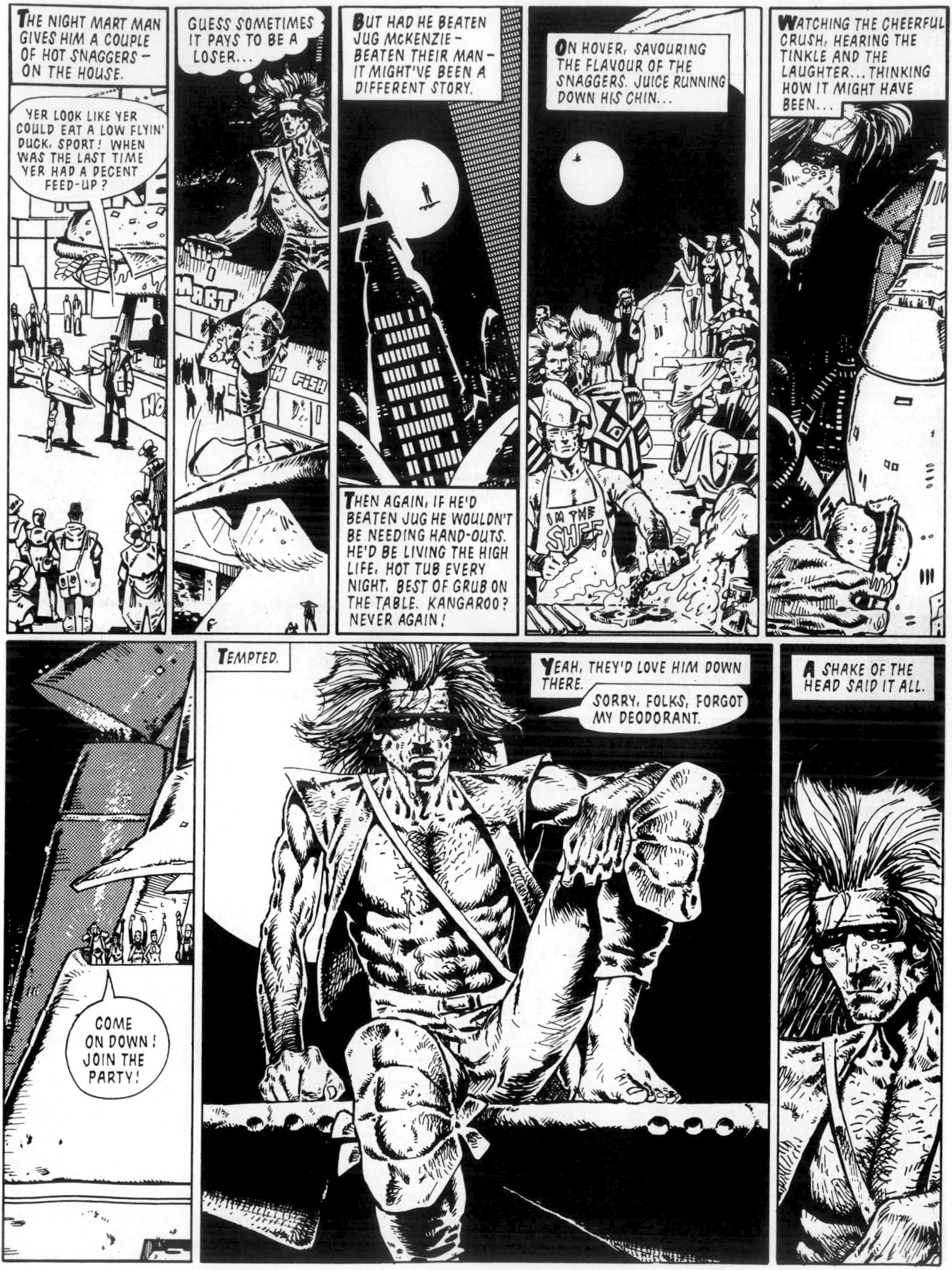

THE NIGHT MART MAN GIVES HIM A COUPLE OF HOT SNAGGERS — ON THE HOUSE.
YER LOOK LIKE YER COULD EAT A LOW FLYIN' DUCK, SPORT! WHEN WAS THE LAST TIME YER HAD A DECENT FEED-UP?
GUESS SOMETIMES IT PAYS TO BE A LOSER...
MART
BUT HAD HE BEATEN JUG McKENZIE — BEATEN THEIR MAN — IT MIGHT'VE BEEN A DIFFERENT STORY.
THEN AGAIN, IF HE'D BEATEN JUG HE WOULDN'T BE NEEDING HAND-OUTS. HE'D BE LIVING THE HIGH LIFE. HOT TUB EVERY NIGHT. BEST OF GRUB ON THE TABLE. KANGAROO? NEVER AGAIN!
ON HOVER, SAVOURING THE FLAVOUR OF THE SNAGGERS. JUICE RUNNING DOWN HIS CHIN...
I'M THE SHEF!
WATCHING THE CHEERFUL CRUSH, HEARING THE TINKLE AND THE LAUGHTER... THINKING HOW IT MIGHT HAVE BEEN...
COME ON DOWN! JOIN THE PARTY!
TEMPTED.
YEAH, THEY'D LOVE HIM DOWN THERE.
SORRY, FOLKS, FORGOT MY DEODORANT.
A SHAKE OF THE HEAD SAID IT ALL.

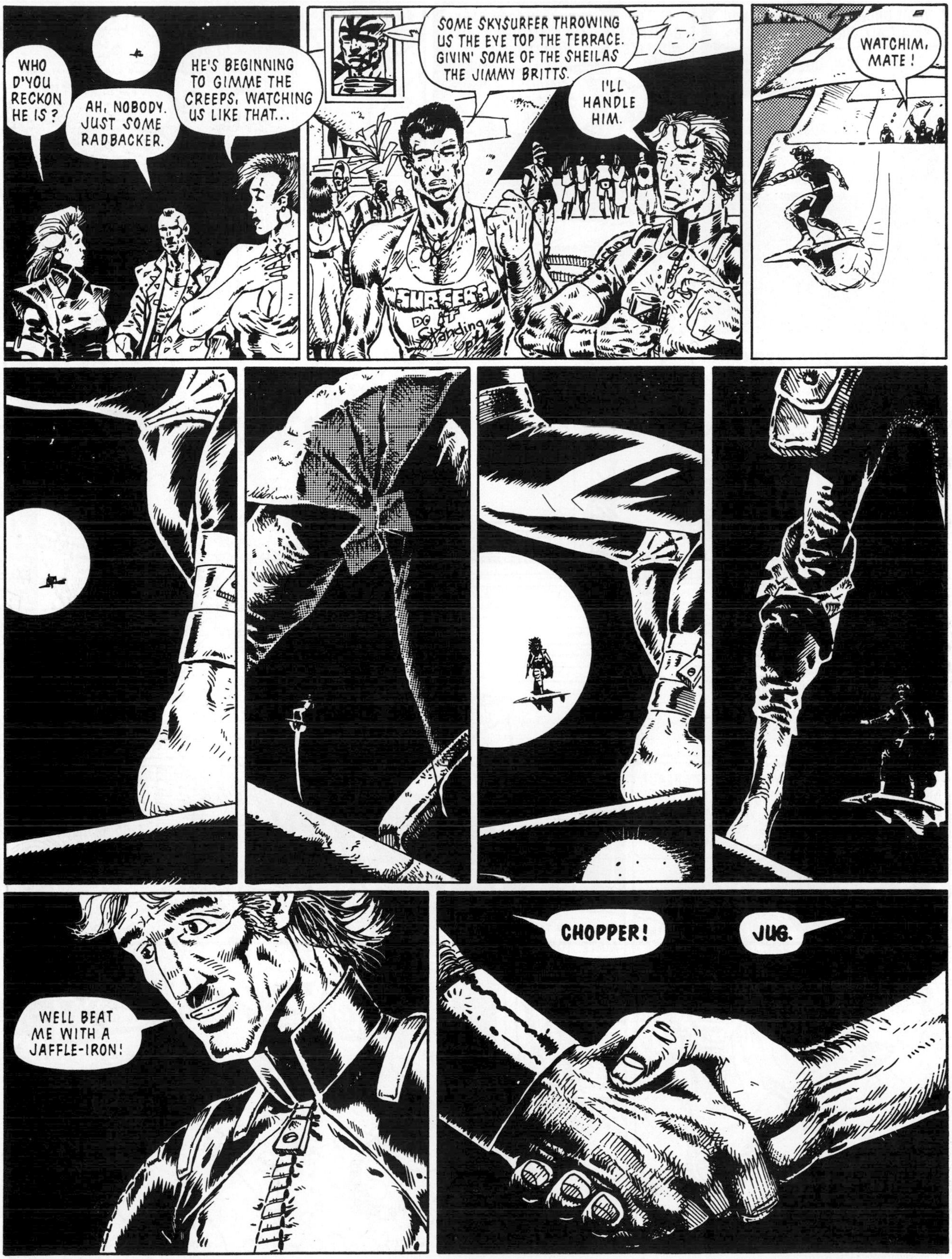
WHO D'YOU RECKON HE IS?
AH, NOBODY. JUST SOME RADBACKER.
HE'S BEGINNING TO GIMME THE CREEPS, WATCHING US LIKE THAT...
SOME SKYSURFER THROWING US THE EYE TOP THE TERRACE. GIVIN' SOME OF THE SHEILAS THE JIMMY BRITTS.
I'LL HANDLE HIM.
SURFERS DO IT Standing Up!
WATCHIM, MATE!
WELL BEAT ME WITH A JAFFLE-IRON!
CHOPPER!
JUG.

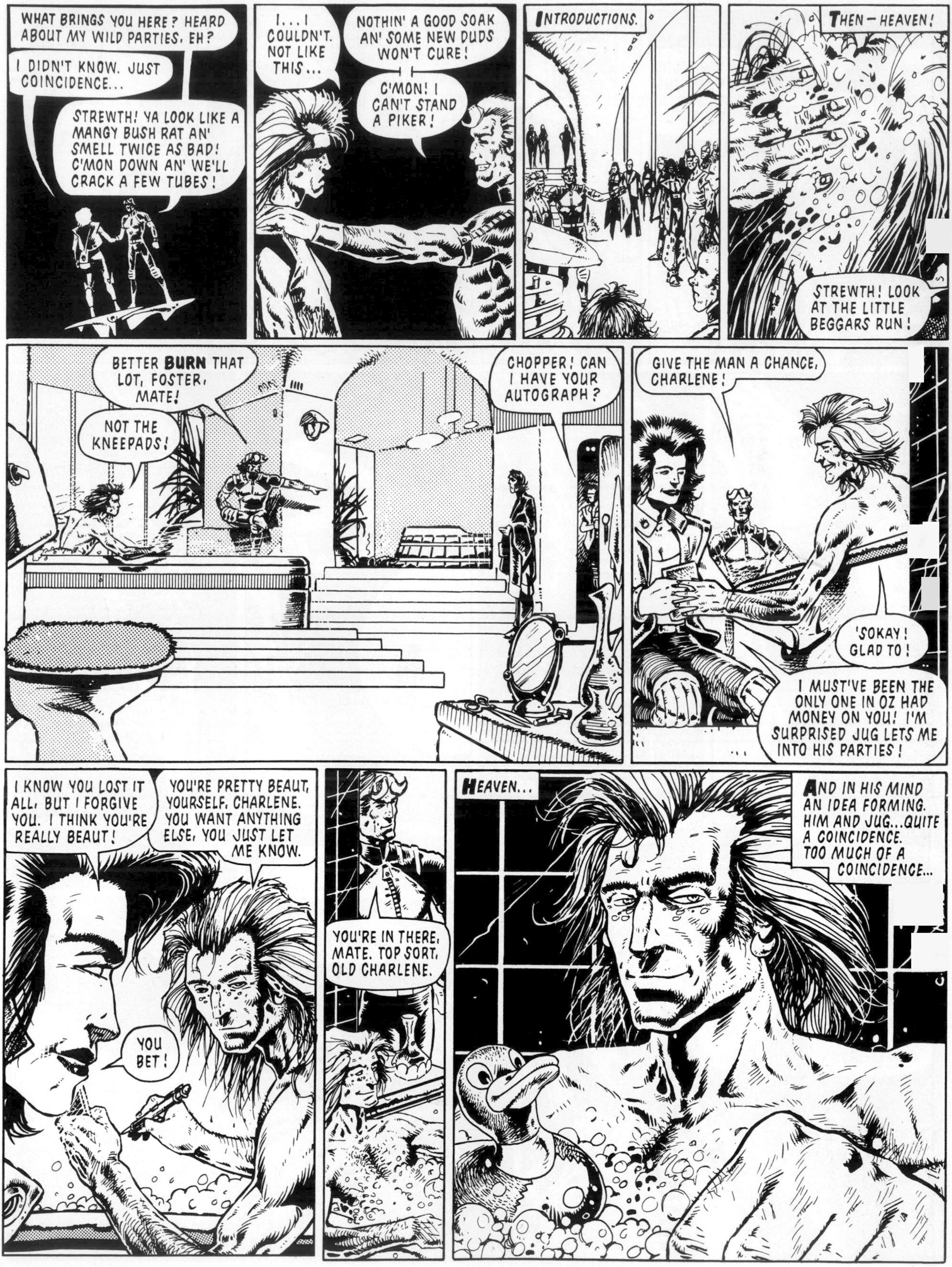
WHAT BRINGS YOU HERE? HEARD ABOUT MY WILD PARTIES, EH?
I DIDN'T KNOW. JUST COINCIDENCE...
STREWTH! YA LOOK LIKE A MANGY BUSH RAT AN' SMELL TWICE AS BAD! C'MON DOWN AN' WE'LL CRACK A FEW TUBES!
I... I COULDN'T. NOT LIKE THIS...
NOTHIN' A GOOD SOAK AN' SOME NEW DUDS WON'T CURE!
C'MON! I CAN'T STAND A PIKER!
INTRODUCTIONS.
THEN — HEAVEN!
STREWTH! LOOK AT THE LITTLE BEGGARS RUN!
BETTER BURN THAT LOT, FOSTER, MATE!
NOT THE KNEEPADS!
CHOPPER! CAN I HAVE YOUR AUTOGRAPH?
GIVE THE MAN A CHANCE, CHARLENE!
'SOKAY! GLAD TO!
I MUST'VE BEEN THE ONLY ONE IN OZ HAD MONEY ON YOU! I'M SURPRISED JUG LETS ME INTO HIS PARTIES!
I KNOW YOU LOST IT ALL, BUT I FORGIVE YOU. I THINK YOU'RE REALLY BEAUT!
YOU'RE PRETTY BEAUT, YOURSELF, CHARLENE. YOU WANT ANYTHING ELSE, YOU JUST LET ME KNOW.
YOU BET!
YOU'RE IN THERE, MATE. TOP SORT, OLD CHARLENE.
HEAVEN...
AND IN HIS MIND AN IDEA FORMING. HIM AND JUG... QUITE A COINCIDENCE. TOO MUCH OF A COINCIDENCE...

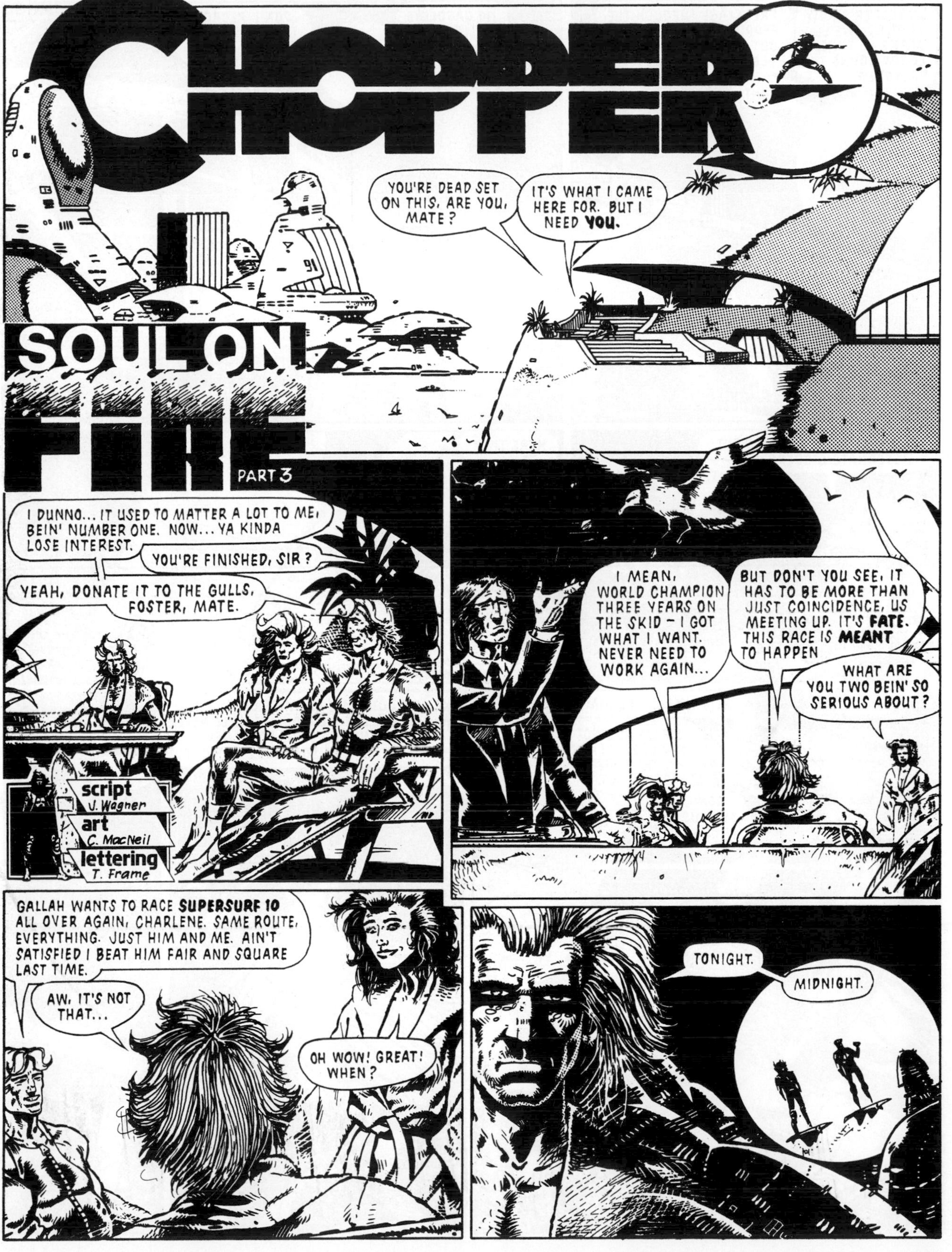
CHOPPER
YOU'RE DEAD SET ON THIS, ARE YOU, MATE?
IT'S WHAT I CAME HERE FOR. BUT I NEED YOU.
SOUL ON FIRE
PART 3
I DUNNO... IT USED TO MATTER A LOT TO ME, BEIN' NUMBER ONE. NOW... YA KINDA LOSE INTEREST.
YOU'RE FINISHED, SIR?
YEAH, DONATE IT TO THE GULLS, FOSTER, MATE.
script V. Wagner
art C. MacNeil
lettering T. Frame
I MEAN, WORLD CHAMPION THREE YEARS ON THE SKID – I GOT WHAT I WANT. NEVER NEED TO WORK AGAIN...
BUT DON'T YOU SEE, IT HAS TO BE MORE THAN JUST COINCIDENCE, US MEETING UP. IT'S FATE. THIS RACE IS MEANT TO HAPPEN
WHAT ARE YOU TWO BEIN' SO SERIOUS ABOUT?
GALLAH WANTS TO RACE SUPERSURF 10 ALL OVER AGAIN, CHARLENE. SAME ROUTE, EVERYTHING. JUST HIM AND ME. AIN'T SATISFIED I BEAT HIM FAIR AND SQUARE LAST TIME.
AW, IT'S NOT THAT...
OH WOW! GREAT! WHEN?
TONIGHT.
MIDNIGHT.

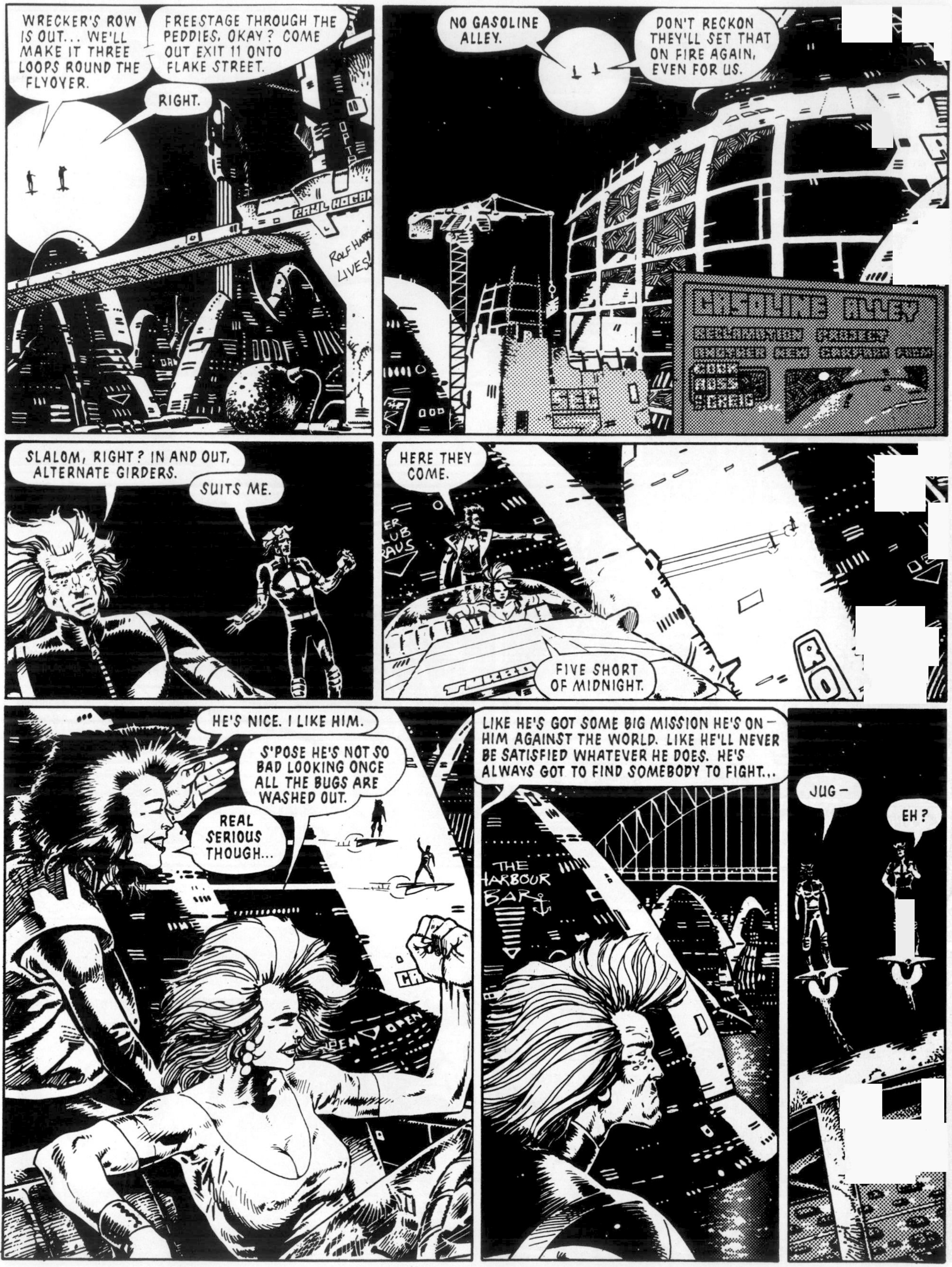
WRECKER'S ROW IS OUT... WE'LL MAKE IT THREE LOOPS ROUND THE FLYOVER.
FREESTAGE THROUGH THE PEDDIES. OKAY? COME OUT EXIT 11 ONTO FLAKE STREET.
RIGHT.
PAUL HOGAN
NO GASOLINE ALLEY.
DON'T RECKON THEY'LL SET THAT ON FIRE AGAIN, EVEN FOR US.
GASOLINE ALLEY
SLALOM, RIGHT? IN AND OUT, ALTERNATE GIRDERS.
SUITS ME.
HERE THEY COME.
FIVE SHORT OF MIDNIGHT.
HE'S NICE. I LIKE HIM.
S'POSE HE'S NOT SO BAD LOOKING ONCE ALL THE BUGS ARE WASHED OUT.
REAL SERIOUS THOUGH...
LIKE HE'S GOT SOME BIG MISSION HE'S ON — HIM AGAINST THE WORLD. LIKE HE'LL NEVER BE SATISFIED WHATEVER HE DOES. HE'S ALWAYS GOT TO FIND SOMEBODY TO FIGHT...
THE HARBOUR BAR
JUG—
EH?

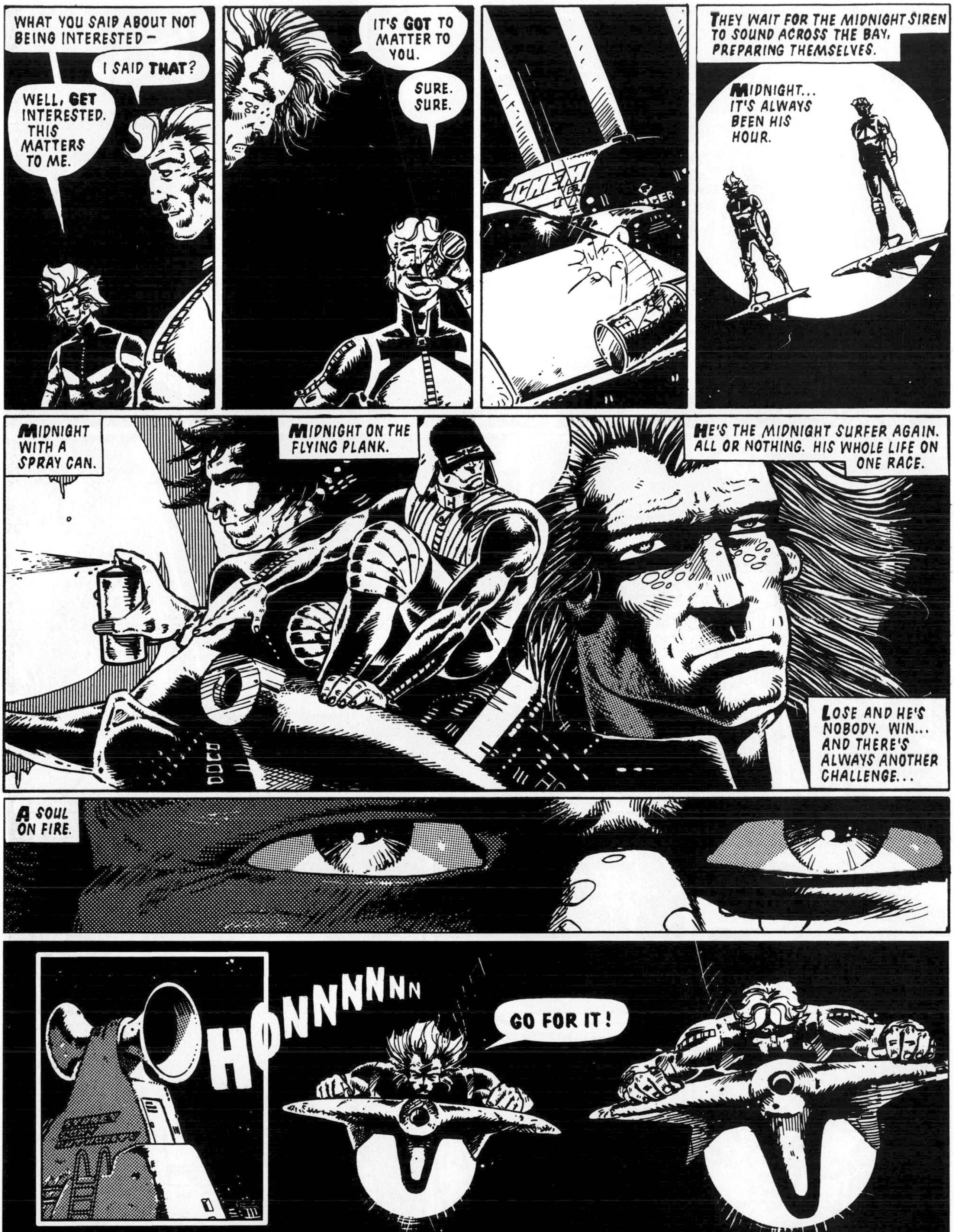
WHAT YOU SAID ABOUT NOT BEING INTERESTED –
I SAID THAT?
WELL, GET INTERESTED. THIS MATTERS TO ME.
IT'S GOT TO MATTER TO YOU.
SURE. SURE.
THEY WAIT FOR THE MIDNIGHT SIREN TO SOUND ACROSS THE BAY, PREPARING THEMSELVES.
MIDNIGHT... IT'S ALWAYS BEEN HIS HOUR.
MIDNIGHT WITH A SPRAY CAN.
MIDNIGHT ON THE FLYING PLANK.
HE'S THE MIDNIGHT SURFER AGAIN. ALL OR NOTHING. HIS WHOLE LIFE ON ONE RACE.
LOSE AND HE'S NOBODY. WIN... AND THERE'S ALWAYS ANOTHER CHALLENGE...
A SOUL ON FIRE.
HONNNNNNN
GO FOR IT!

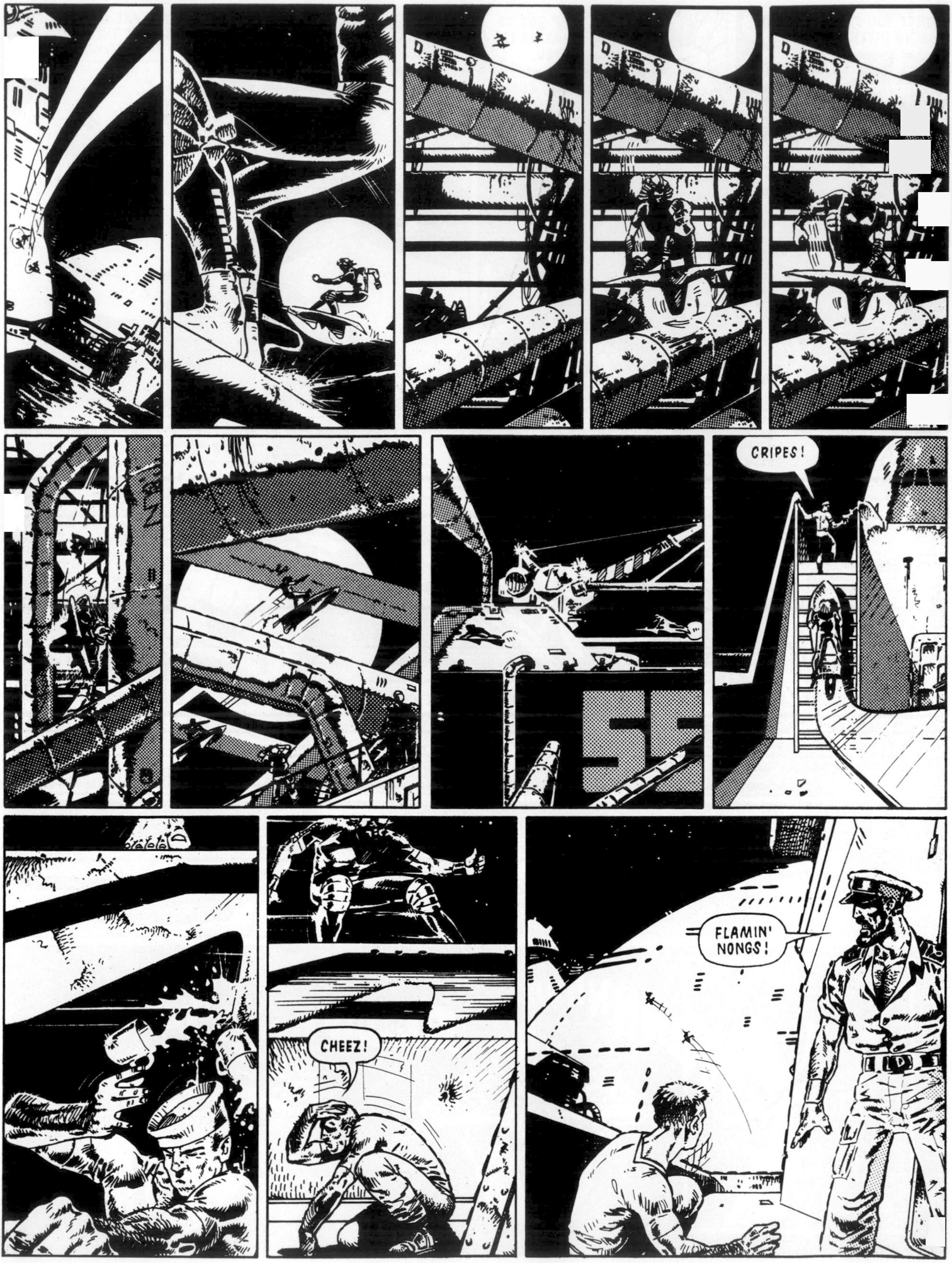
CRIPES!
CHEEZ!
FLAMIN' NONGS!

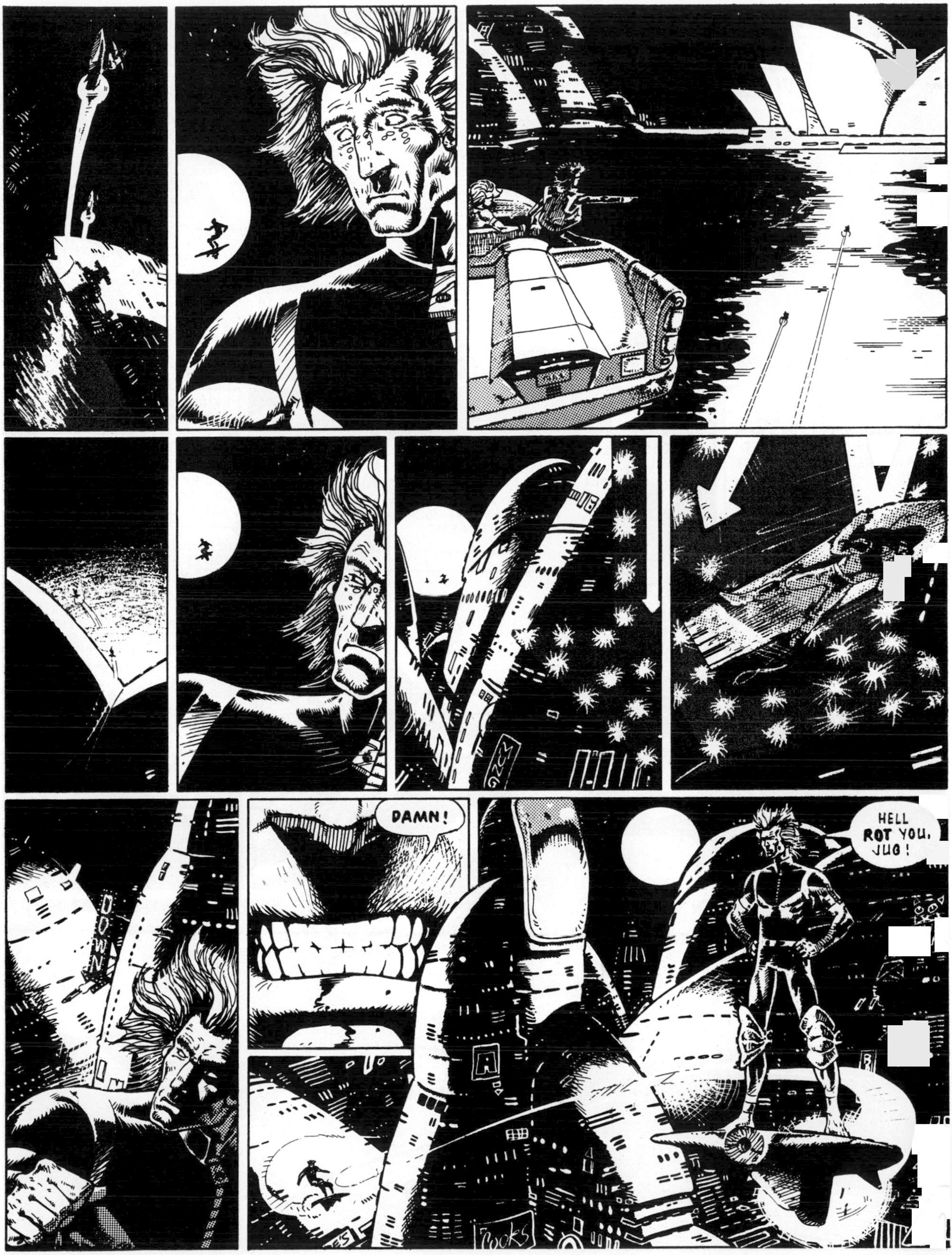
DAMN!
HELL ROT YOU, JUG!

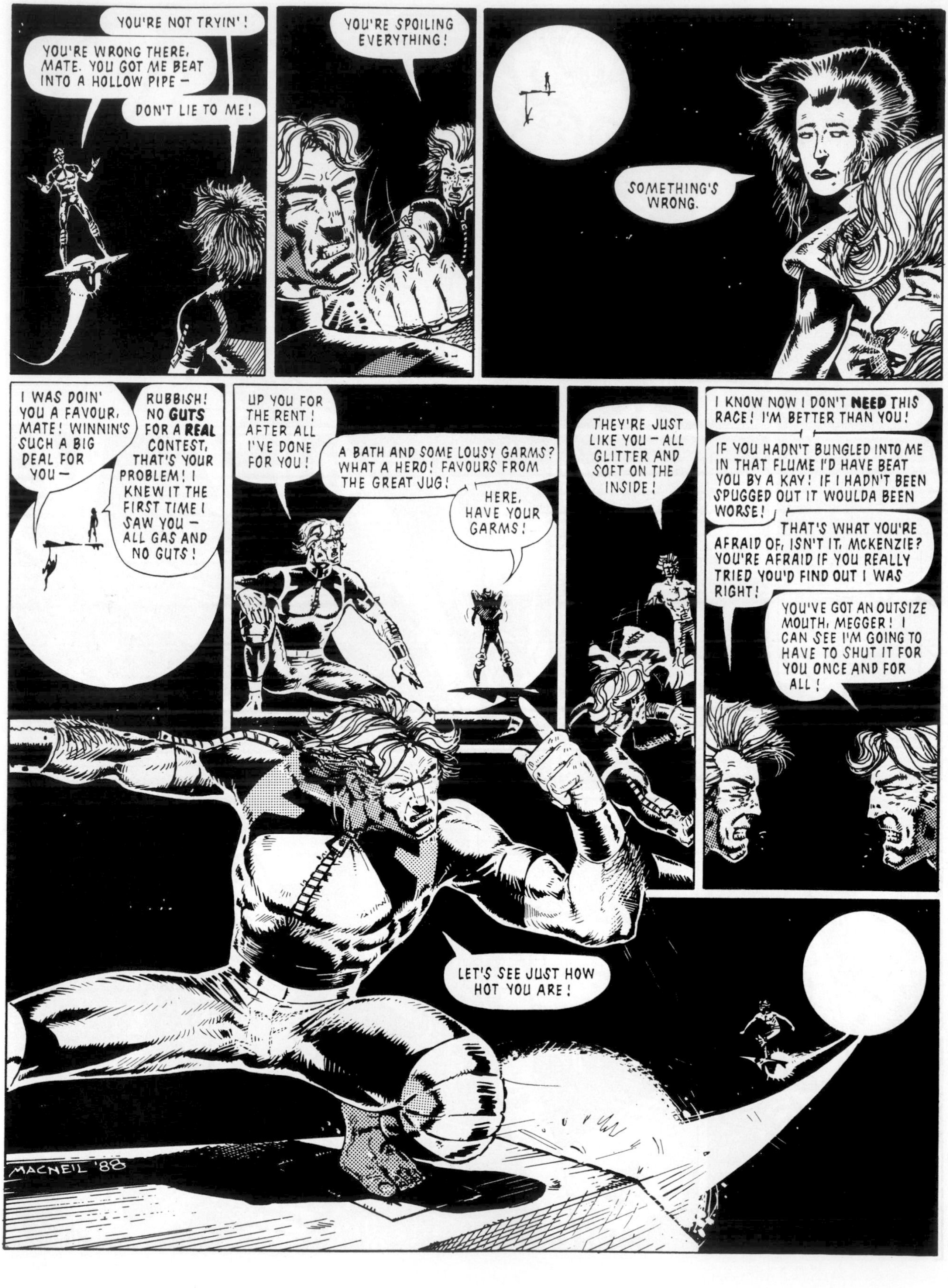
YOU'RE NOT TRYIN'!
YOU'RE WRONG THERE, MATE. YOU GOT ME BEAT INTO A HOLLOW PIPE —
DON'T LIE TO ME!
YOU'RE SPOILING EVERYTHING!
SOMETHING'S WRONG.
I WAS DOIN' YOU A FAVOUR, MATE! WINNIN'S SUCH A BIG DEAL FOR YOU —
RUBBISH! NO GUTS FOR A REAL CONTEST, THAT'S YOUR PROBLEM! I KNEW IT THE FIRST TIME I SAW YOU — ALL GAS AND NO GUTS!
UP YOU FOR THE RENT! AFTER ALL I'VE DONE FOR YOU!
A BATH AND SOME LOUSY GARMS? WHAT A HERO! FAVOURS FROM THE GREAT JUG!
HERE, HAVE YOUR GARMS!
THEY'RE JUST LIKE YOU — ALL GLITTER AND SOFT ON THE INSIDE!
I KNOW NOW I DON'T NEED THIS RACE! I'M BETTER THAN YOU!
IF YOU HADN'T BUNGLED INTO ME IN THAT FLUME I'D HAVE BEAT YOU BY A KAY! IF I HADN'T BEEN SPUGGED OUT IT WOULDA BEEN WORSE!
THAT'S WHAT YOU'RE AFRAID OF, ISN'T IT, McKENZIE? YOU'RE AFRAID IF YOU REALLY TRIED YOU'D FIND OUT I WAS RIGHT!
YOU'VE GOT AN OUTSIZE MOUTH, MEGGER! I CAN SEE I'M GOING TO HAVE TO SHUT IT FOR YOU ONCE AND FOR ALL!
LET'S SEE JUST HOW HOT YOU ARE!
MACNEIL '88

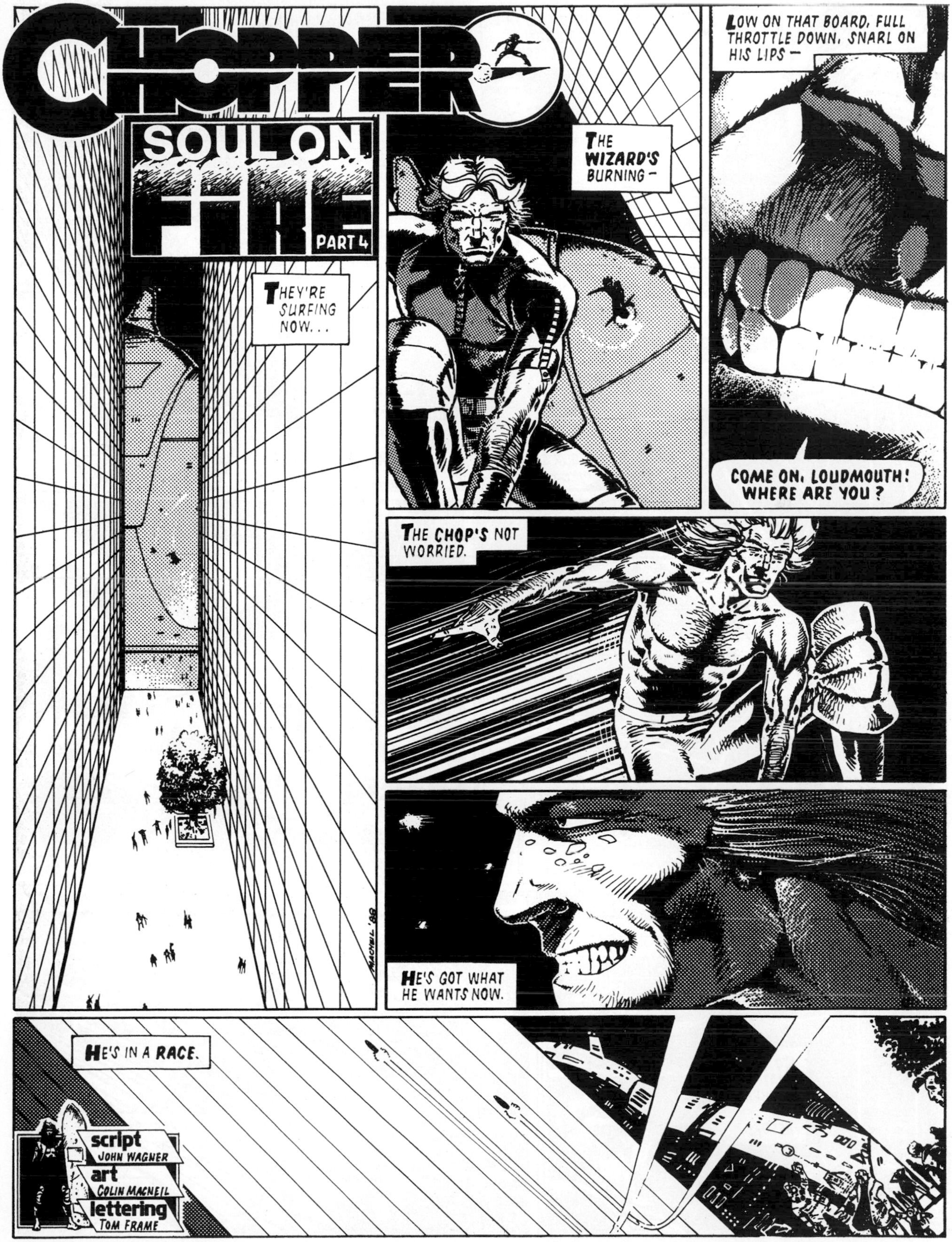
CHOPPER
SOUL ON FIRE
PART 4
THEY'RE SURFING NOW...
THE WIZARD'S BURNING –
LOW ON THAT BOARD, FULL THROTTLE DOWN, SNARL ON HIS LIPS –
COME ON, LOUDMOUTH! WHERE ARE YOU ?
THE CHOP'S NOT WORRIED.
HE'S GOT WHAT HE WANTS NOW.
HE'S IN A RACE.
script JOHN WAGNER
art COLIN MACNEIL
lettering TOM FRAME

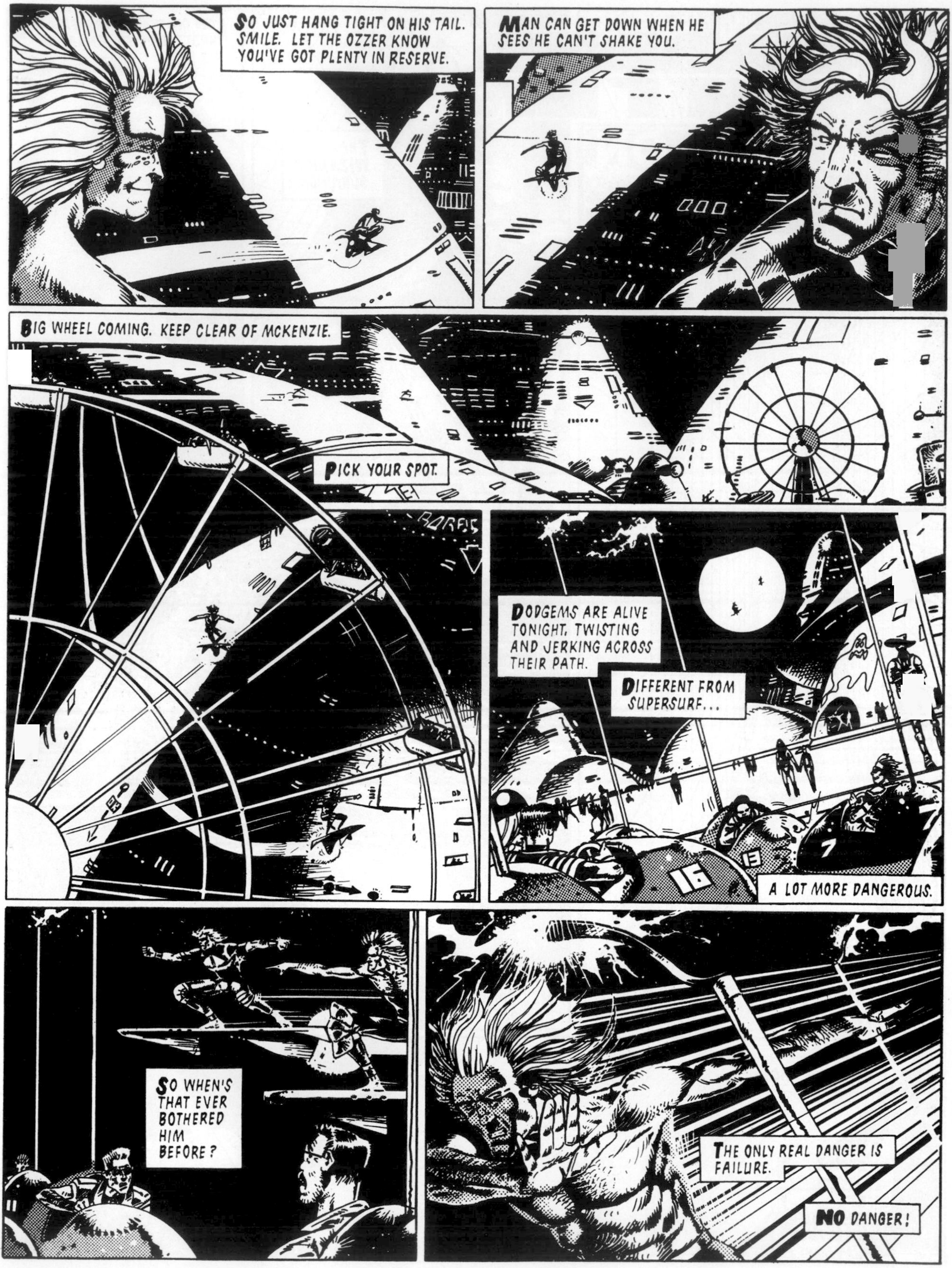
SO JUST HANG TIGHT ON HIS TAIL. SMILE. LET THE OZZER KNOW YOU'VE GOT PLENTY IN RESERVE.
MAN CAN GET DOWN WHEN HE SEES HE CAN'T SHAKE YOU.
BIG WHEEL COMING. KEEP CLEAR OF MCKENZIE.
PICK YOUR SPOT.
DODGEMS ARE ALIVE TONIGHT, TWISTING AND JERKING ACROSS THEIR PATH.
DIFFERENT FROM SUPERSURF...
A LOT MORE DANGEROUS.
SO WHEN'S THAT EVER BOTHERED HIM BEFORE?
THE ONLY REAL DANGER IS FAILURE.
NO DANGER!

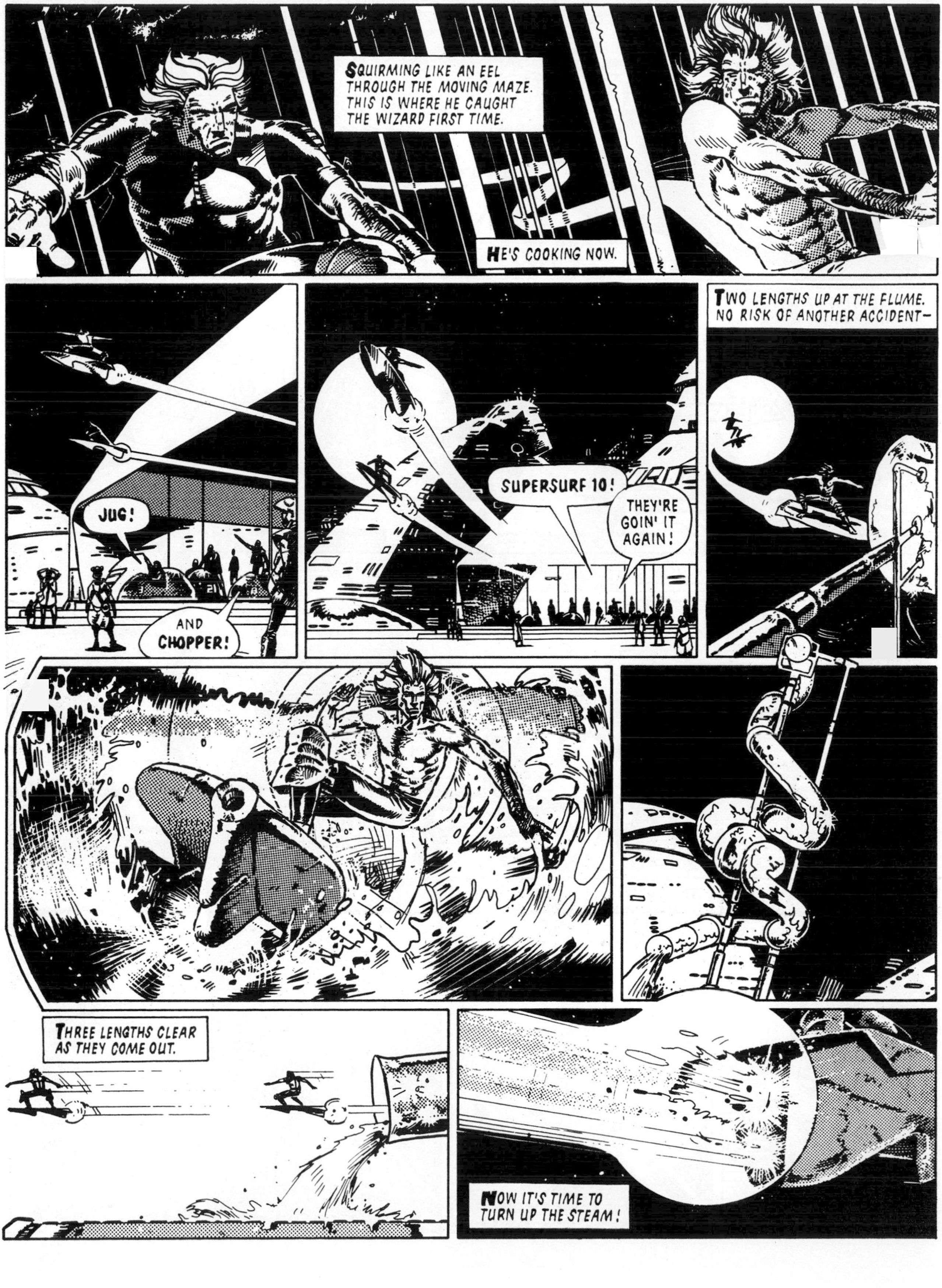
SQUIRMING LIKE AN EEL THROUGH THE MOVING MAZE. THIS IS WHERE HE CAUGHT THE WIZARD FIRST TIME.
HE'S COOKING NOW.
JUG!
AND CHOPPER!
SUPERSURF 10!
THEY'RE GOIN' IT AGAIN!
TWO LENGTHS UP AT THE FLUME. NO RISK OF ANOTHER ACCIDENT—
THREE LENGTHS CLEAR AS THEY COME OUT.
NOW IT'S TIME TO TURN UP THE STEAM!

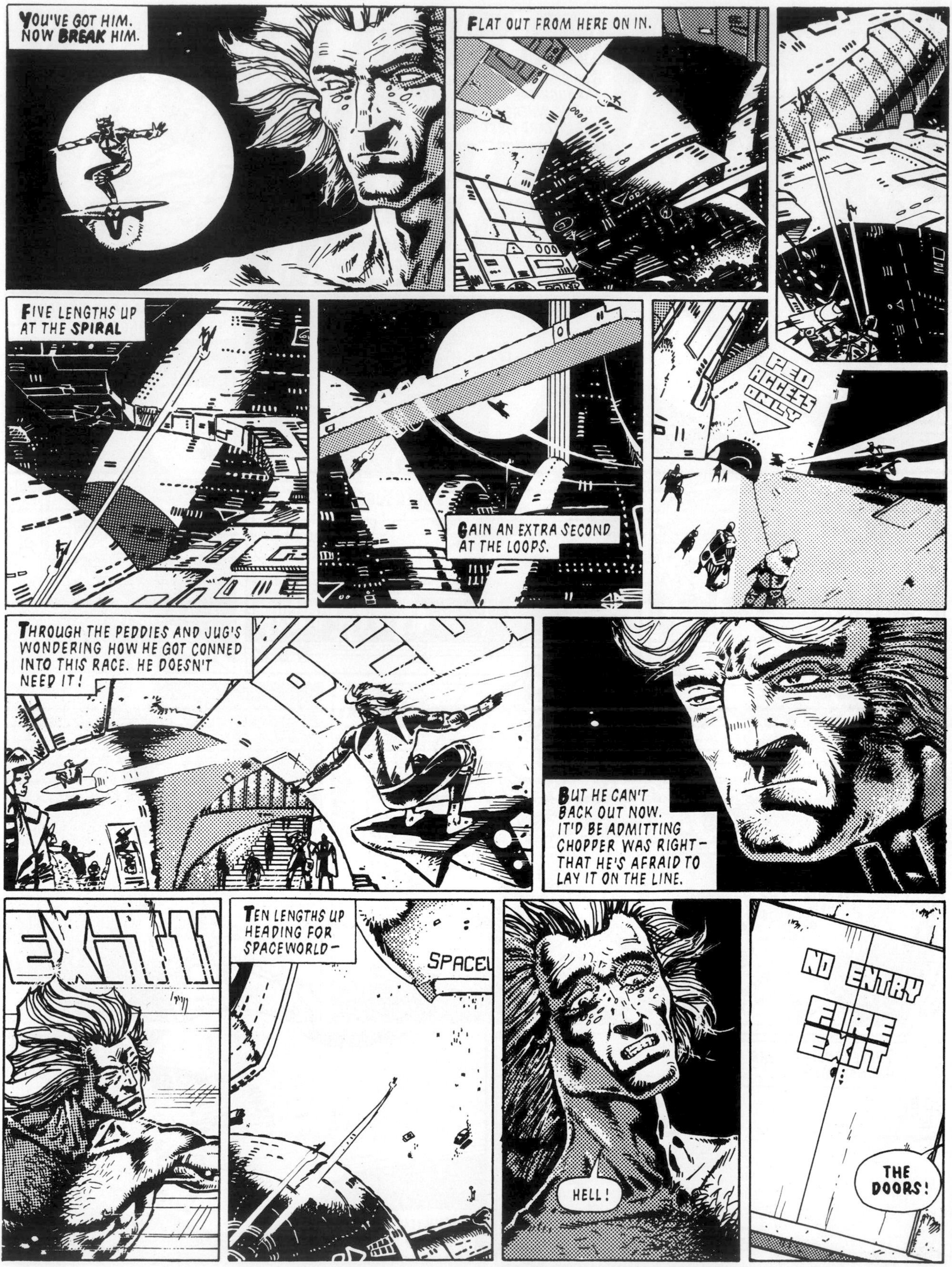
YOU'VE GOT HIM. NOW BREAK HIM.
FLAT OUT FROM HERE ON IN.
FIVE LENGTHS UP AT THE SPIRAL
GAIN AN EXTRA SECOND AT THE LOOPS.
PED ACCESS ONLY
THROUGH THE PEDDIES AND JUG'S WONDERING HOW HE GOT CONNED INTO THIS RACE. HE DOESN'T NEED IT!
BUT HE CAN'T BACK OUT NOW. IT'D BE ADMITTING CHOPPER WAS RIGHT— THAT HE'S AFRAID TO LAY IT ON THE LINE.
TEN LENGTHS UP HEADING FOR SPACEWORLD—
HELL!
NO ENTRY
FIRE EXIT
THE DOORS!

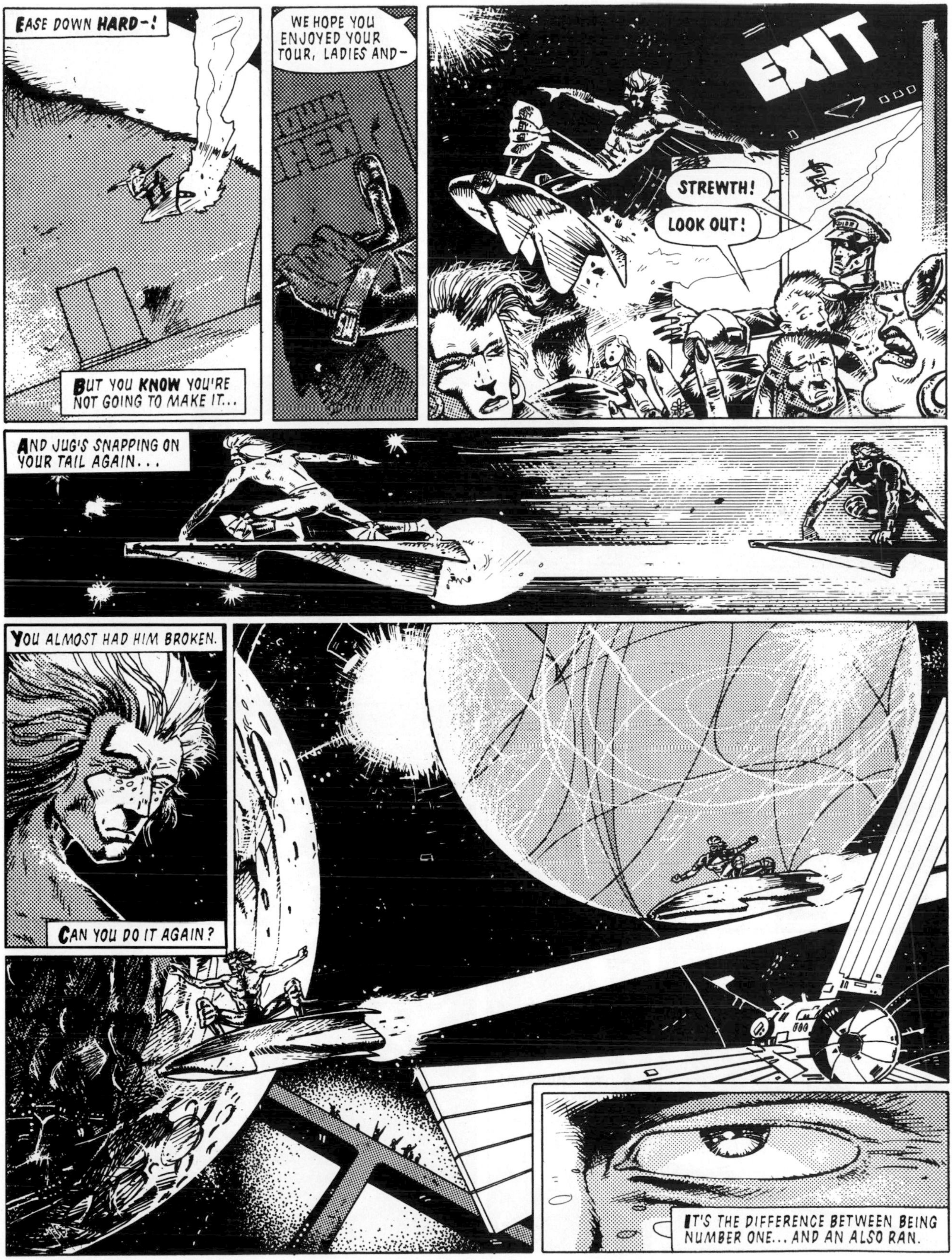
EASE DOWN HARD-!
BUT YOU KNOW YOU'RE NOT GOING TO MAKE IT...
WE HOPE YOU ENJOYED YOUR TOUR, LADIES AND-
EXIT
STREWTH!
LOOK OUT!
AND JUG'S SNAPPING ON YOUR TAIL AGAIN...
YOU ALMOST HAD HIM BROKEN.
CAN YOU DO IT AGAIN?
IT'S THE DIFFERENCE BETWEEN BEING NUMBER ONE... AND AN ALSO RAN.

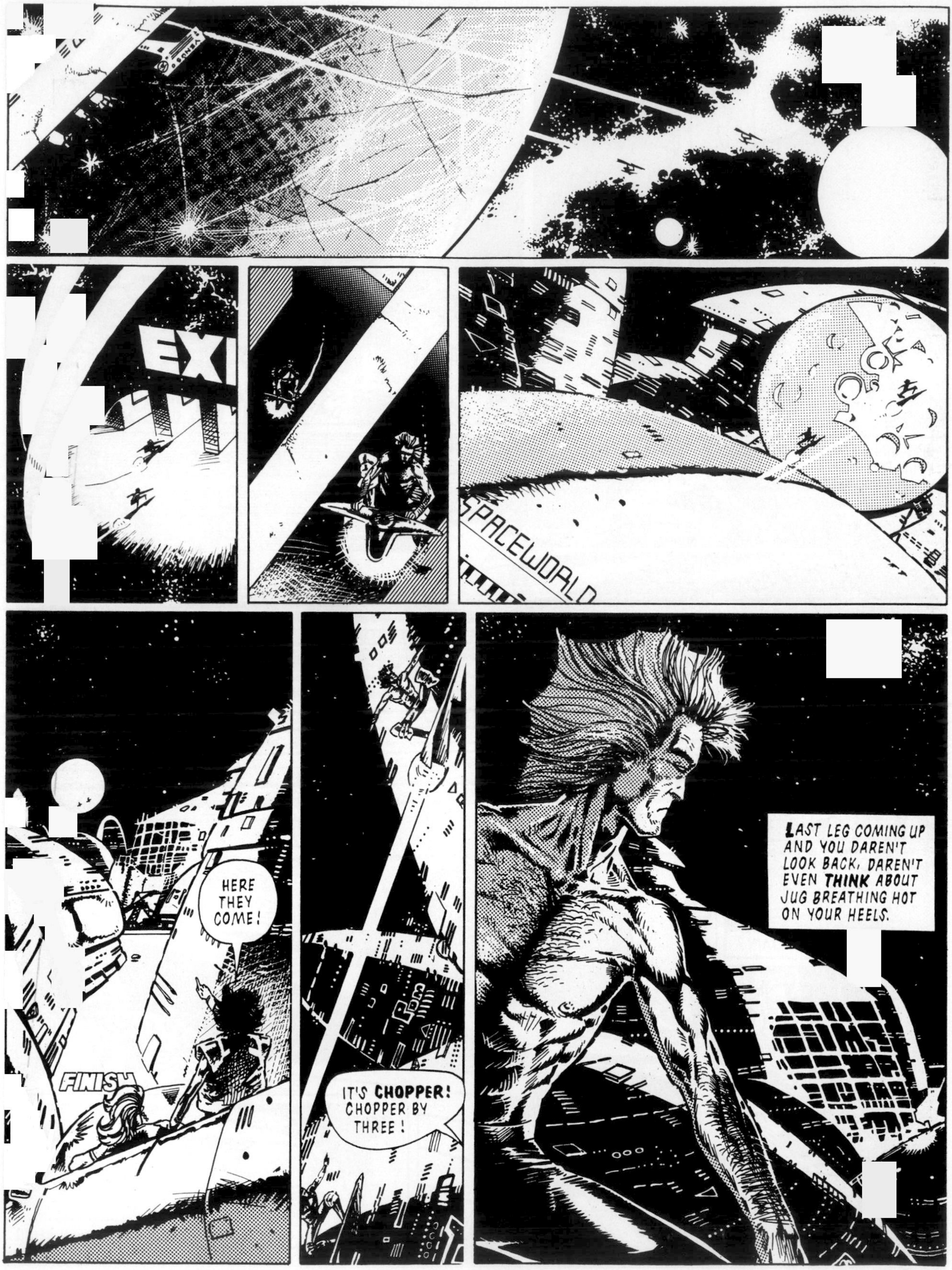
SPACEWORLD
HERE THEY COME!
FINISH
IT'S CHOPPER! CHOPPER BY THREE!
LAST LEG COMING UP AND YOU DAREN'T LOOK BACK, DAREN'T EVEN THINK ABOUT JUG BREATHING HOT ON YOUR HEELS.

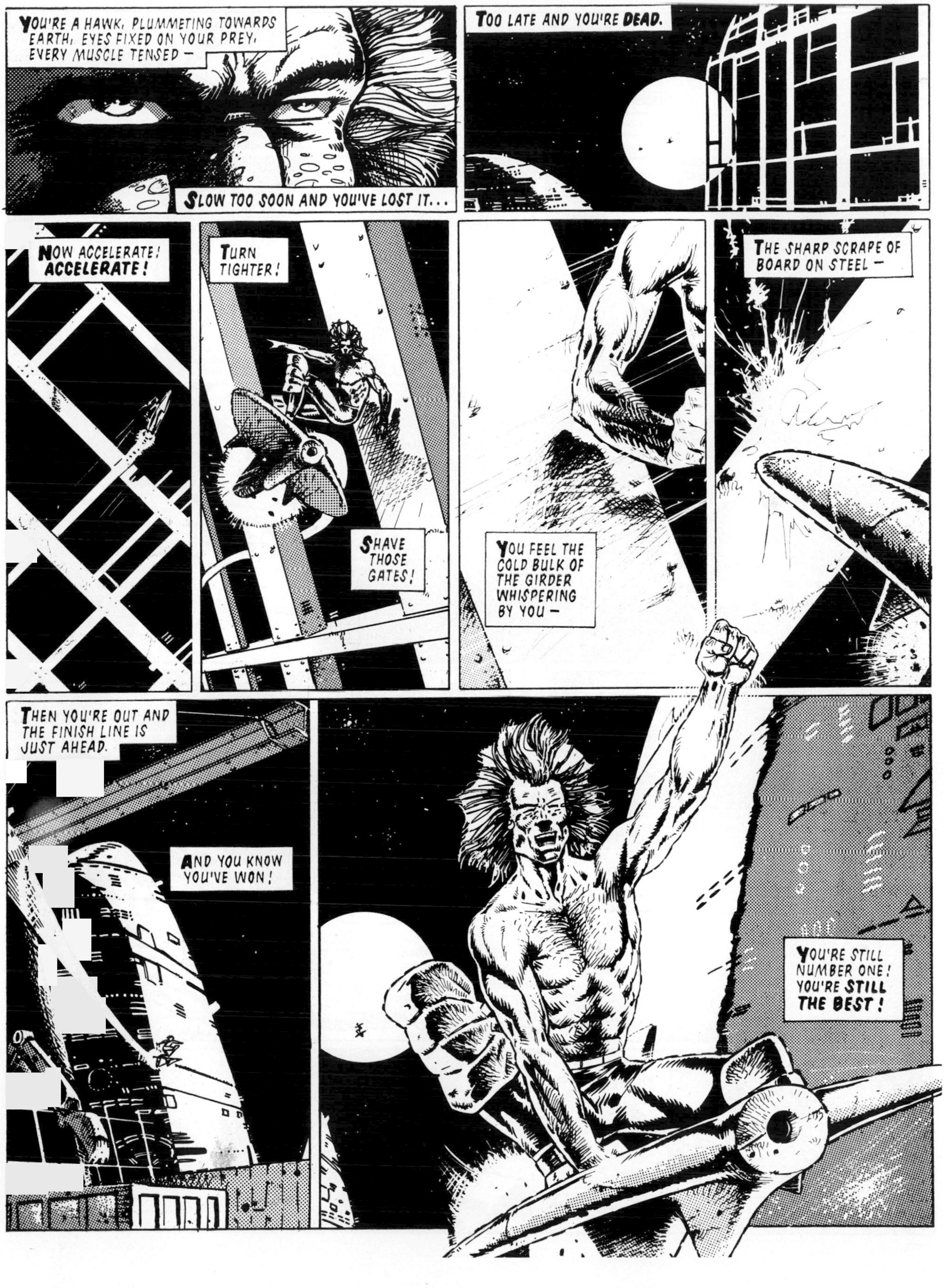

YOU'RE A HAWK, PLUMMETING TOWARDS EARTH, EYES FIXED ON YOUR PREY, EVERY MUSCLE TENSED –
SLOW TOO SOON AND YOU'VE LOST IT...
TOO LATE AND YOU'RE DEAD.
NOW ACCELERATE! ACCELERATE!
TURN TIGHTER!
SHAVE THOSE GATES!
YOU FEEL THE COLD BULK OF THE GIRDER WHISPERING BY YOU –
THE SHARP SCRAPE OF BOARD ON STEEL –
THEN YOU'RE OUT AND THE FINISH LINE IS JUST AHEAD.
AND YOU KNOW YOU'VE WON!
YOU'RE STILL NUMBER ONE! YOU'RE STILL THE BEST!

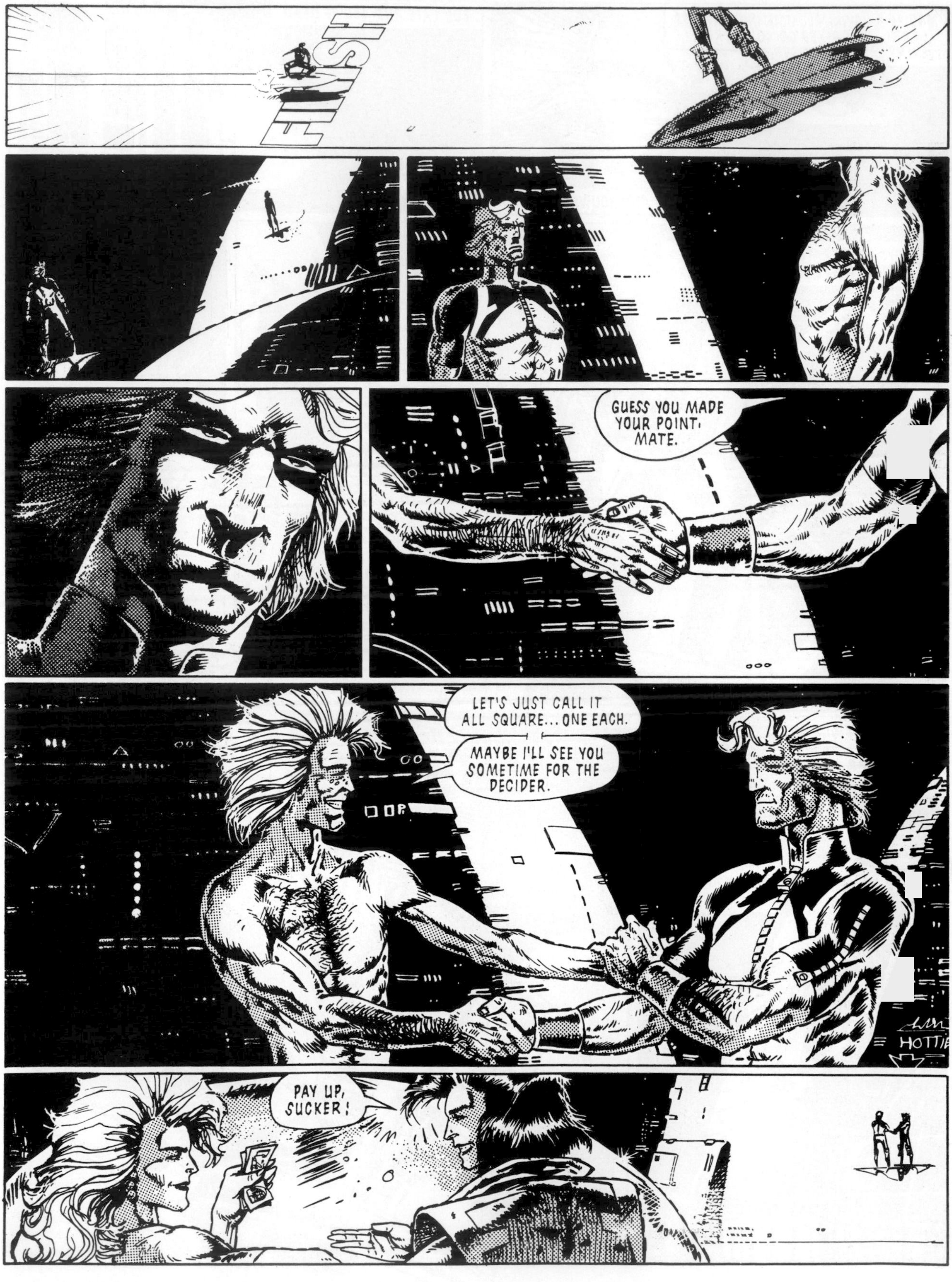
FINISH
GUESS YOU MADE YOUR POINT, MATE.
LET'S JUST CALL IT ALL SQUARE... ONE EACH.
MAYBE I'LL SEE YOU SOMETIME FOR THE DECIDER.
PAY UP, SUCKER!

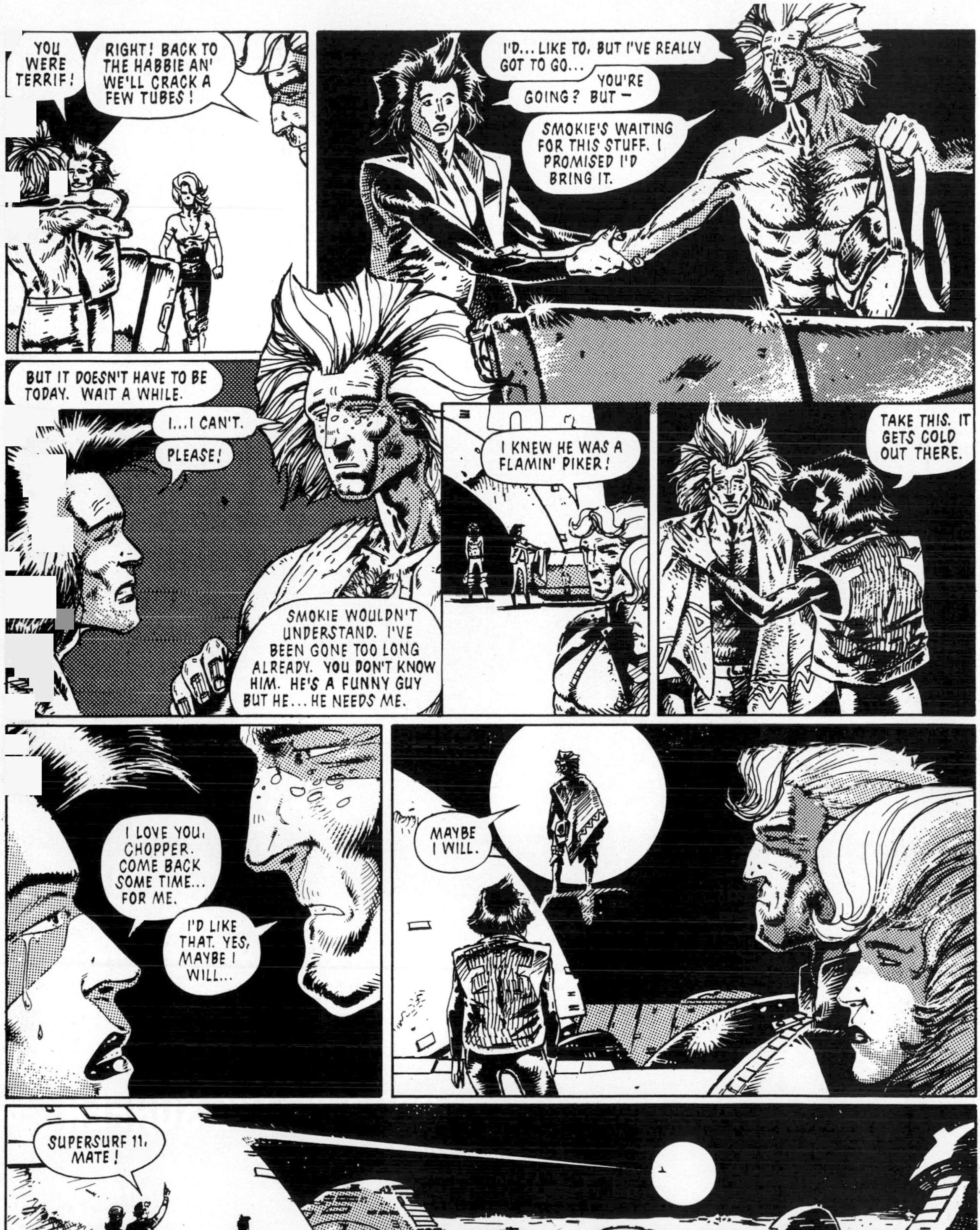
YOU WERE TERRIF!
RIGHT! BACK TO THE HABBIE AN' WE'LL CRACK A FEW TUBES!
I'D... LIKE TO, BUT I'VE REALLY GOT TO GO...
YOU'RE GOING? BUT —
SMOKIE'S WAITING FOR THIS STUFF. I PROMISED I'D BRING IT.
BUT IT DOESN'T HAVE TO BE TODAY. WAIT A WHILE.
I...I CAN'T.
PLEASE!
SMOKIE WOULDN'T UNDERSTAND. I'VE BEEN GONE TOO LONG ALREADY. YOU DON'T KNOW HIM. HE'S A FUNNY GUY BUT HE... HE NEEDS ME.
I KNEW HE WAS A FLAMIN' PIKER!
TAKE THIS. IT GETS COLD OUT THERE.
I LOVE YOU, CHOPPER. COME BACK SOME TIME... FOR ME.
I'D LIKE THAT. YES, MAYBE I WILL...
MAYBE I WILL.
SUPERSURF 11, MATE!
THE END.

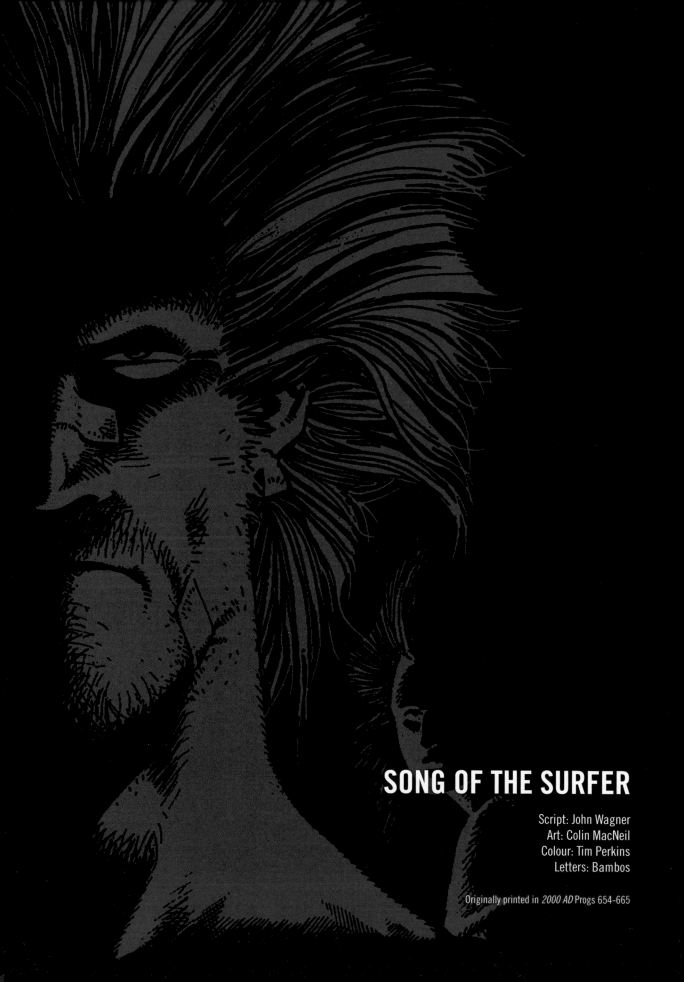

SONG OF THE SURFER

Script: John Wagner
Art: Colin MacNeil
Colour: Tim Perkins
Letters: Bambos

Originally printed in *2000 AD* Progs 654-665

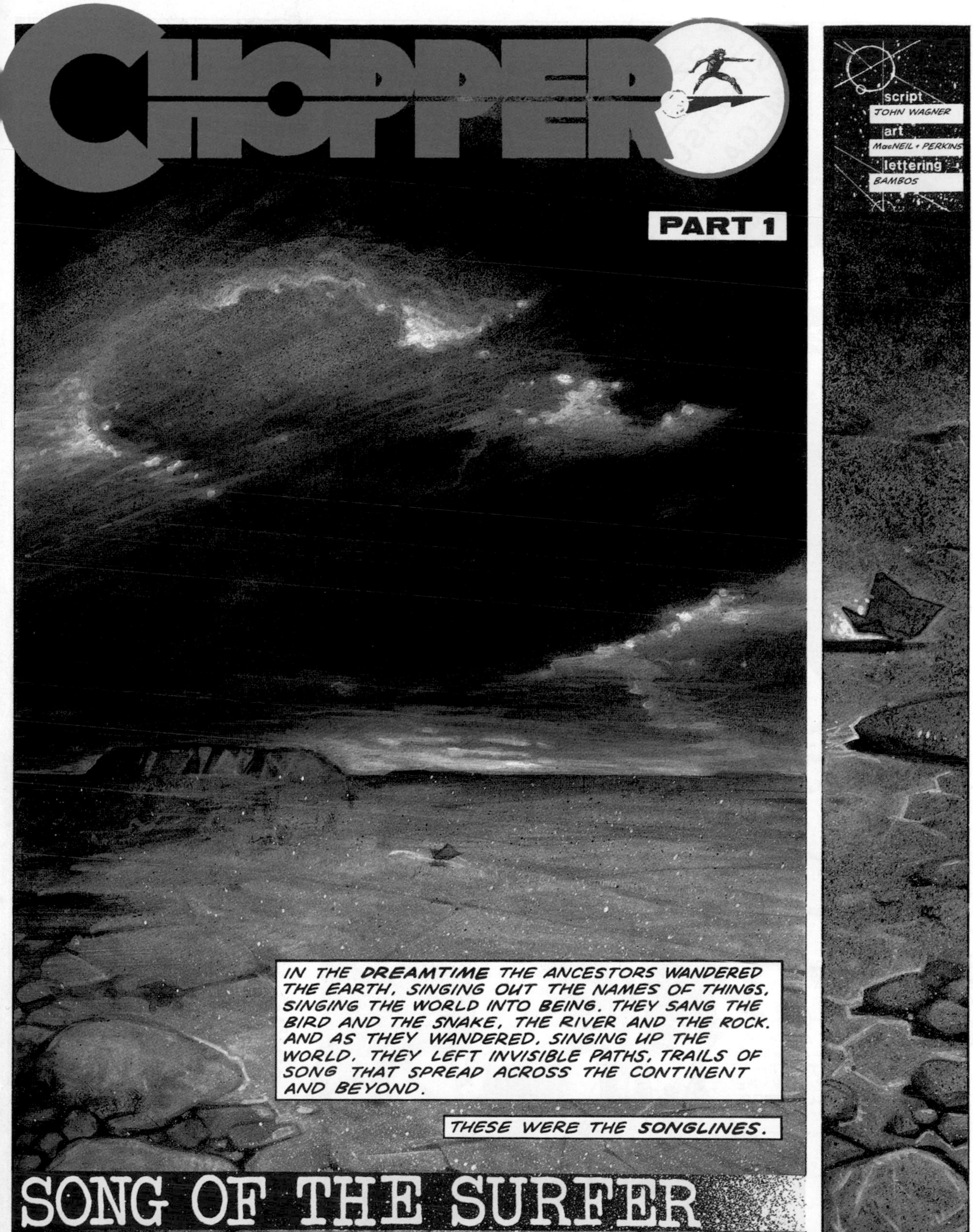
CHOPPER
script
JOHN WAGNER
art
MacNEIL + PERKINS
lettering
BAMBOS
PART 1
IN THE DREAMTIME THE ANCESTORS WANDERED THE EARTH, SINGING OUT THE NAMES OF THINGS, SINGING THE WORLD INTO BEING. THEY SANG THE BIRD AND THE SNAKE, THE RIVER AND THE ROCK. AND AS THEY WANDERED, SINGING UP THE WORLD, THEY LEFT INVISIBLE PATHS, TRAILS OF SONG THAT SPREAD ACROSS THE CONTINENT AND BEYOND.
THESE WERE THE SONGLINES.
SONG OF THE SURFER
MACNEIL '89

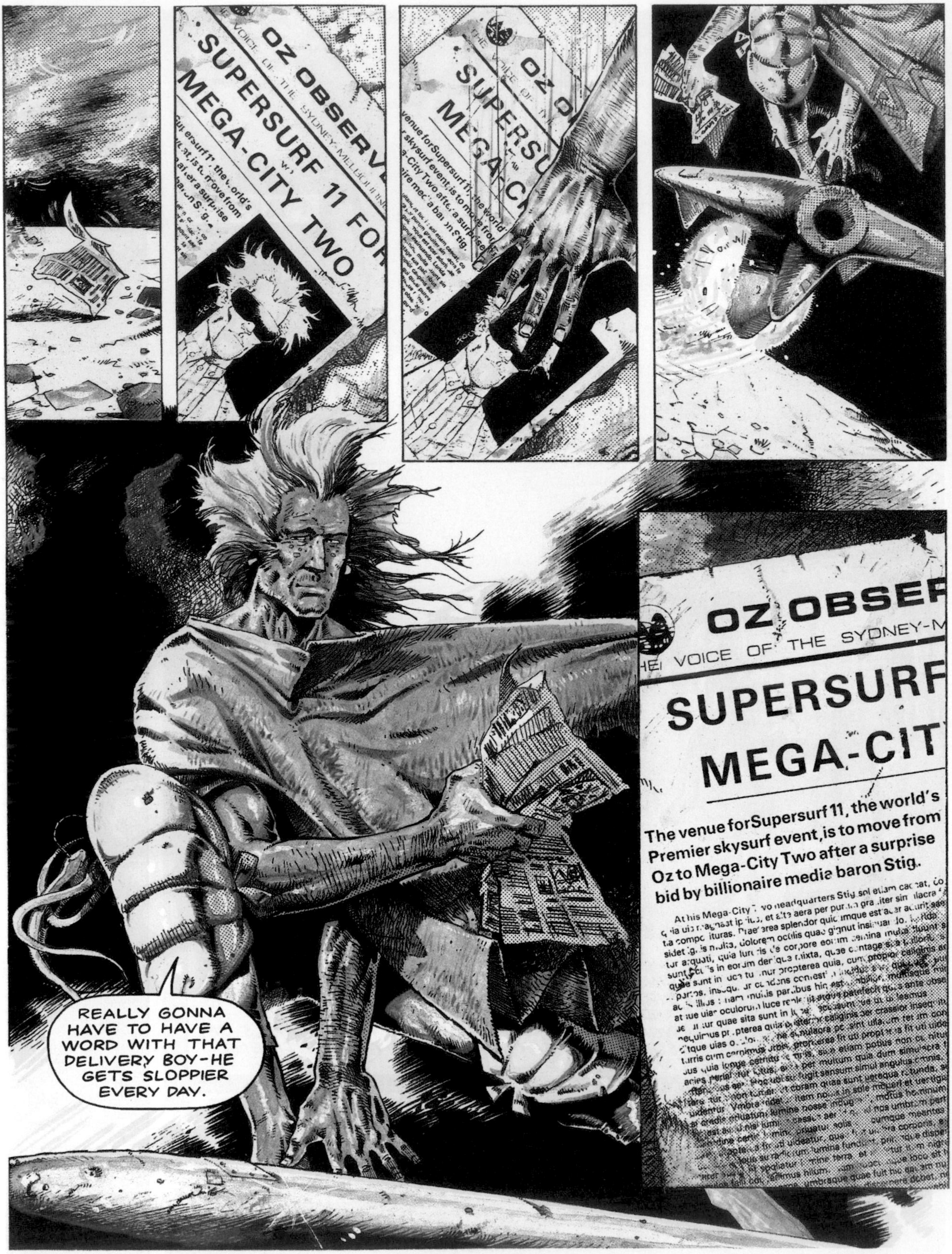
OZ OBSERVE
SUPERSURF 11 FOR
MEGA-CITY TWO
OZ OBSER
THE VOICE OF THE SYDNEY-M
SUPERSURF
MEGA-CIT
The venue forSupersurf 11, the world's Premier skysurf event, is to move from Oz to Mega-City Two after a surprise bid by billionaire media baron Stig.
REALLY GONNA HAVE TO HAVE A WORD WITH THAT DELIVERY BOY-HE GETS SLOPPIER EVERY DAY.

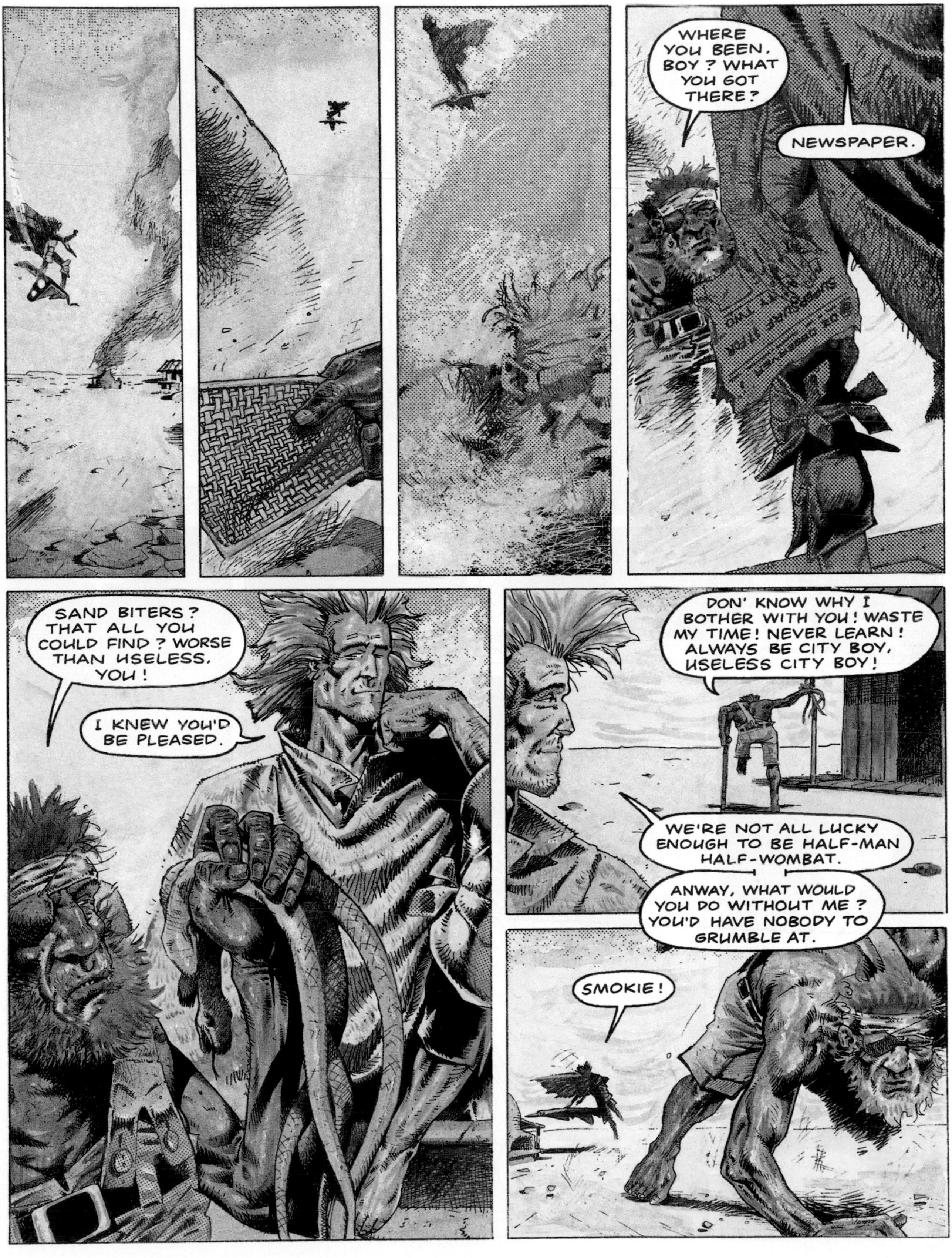
WHERE YOU BEEN, BOY? WHAT YOU GOT THERE?
NEWSPAPER.
SAND BITERS? THAT ALL YOU COULD FIND? WORSE THAN USELESS, YOU!
I KNEW YOU'D BE PLEASED.
DON' KNOW WHY I BOTHER WITH YOU! WASTE MY TIME! NEVER LEARN! ALWAYS BE CITY BOY, USELESS CITY BOY!
WE'RE NOT ALL LUCKY ENOUGH TO BE HALF-MAN HALF-WOMBAT.
ANWAY, WHAT WOULD YOU DO WITHOUT ME? YOU'D HAVE NOBODY TO GRUMBLE AT.
SMOKIE!

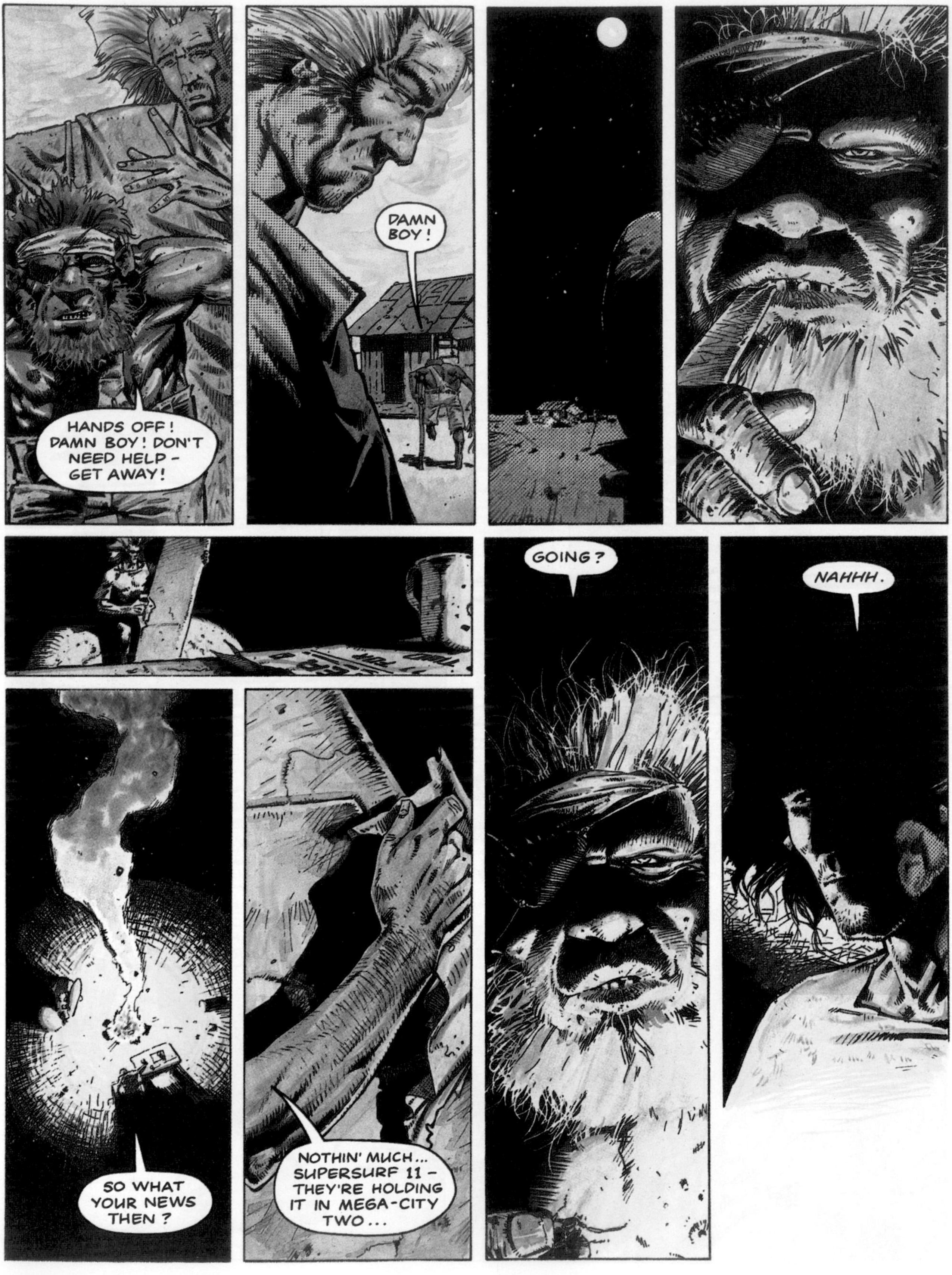
HANDS OFF! DAMN BOY! DON'T NEED HELP - GET AWAY!
DAMN BOY!
GOING?
NAHHH.
SO WHAT YOUR NEWS THEN?
NOTHIN' MUCH... SUPERSURF 11 - THEY'RE HOLDING IT IN MEGA-CITY TWO...

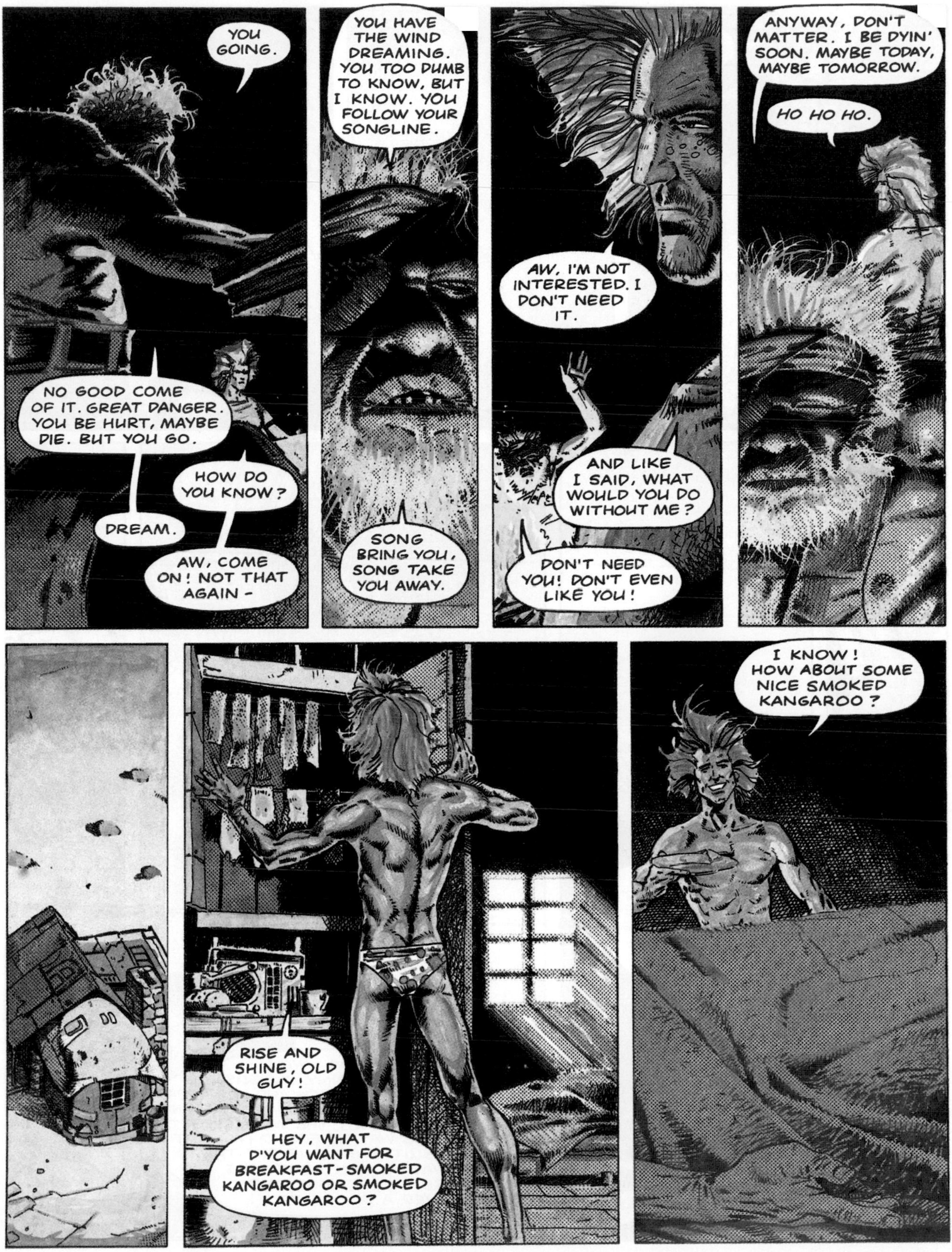
YOU GOING.
NO GOOD COME OF IT. GREAT DANGER. YOU BE HURT, MAYBE DIE. BUT YOU GO.
HOW DO YOU KNOW?
DREAM.
AW, COME ON! NOT THAT AGAIN -
YOU HAVE THE WIND DREAMING. YOU TOO DUMB TO KNOW, BUT I KNOW. YOU FOLLOW YOUR SONGLINE.
SONG BRING YOU, SONG TAKE YOU AWAY.
AW, I'M NOT INTERESTED. I DON'T NEED IT.
AND LIKE I SAID, WHAT WOULD YOU DO WITHOUT ME?
DON'T NEED YOU! DON'T EVEN LIKE YOU!
ANYWAY, DON'T MATTER. I BE DYIN' SOON. MAYBE TODAY, MAYBE TOMORROW.
HO HO HO.
RISE AND SHINE, OLD GUY!
HEY, WHAT D'YOU WANT FOR BREAKFAST- SMOKED KANGAROO OR SMOKED KANGAROO?
I KNOW! HOW ABOUT SOME NICE SMOKED KANGAROO?

SMOKIE! HEY!

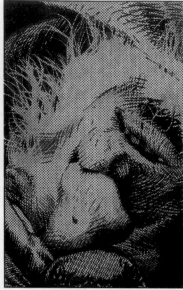

CRAFTY OLD DEVIL...YOU DID AND ALL...

DON'T REALLY KNOW HOW YOU'D LIKE THIS DONE, SMOKIE. S'POSE I OUGHTA SAY A FEW WORDS...

SMOKIE WAS...WELL, HE WAS A FUNNY OLD GUY. HE NEVER TOOK MUCH AND HE NEVER GAVE MUCH IN RETURN. HE LIVED AND DIED AND HE LEFT THE WORLD PRETTY MUCH THE WAY HE FOUND IT. THAT DON'T SUIT EVERYONE BUT THAT'S THE WAY HE WANTED IT SO I GUESS BY HIS LIGHTS HE LIVED A GOOD LIFE...

AMEN.

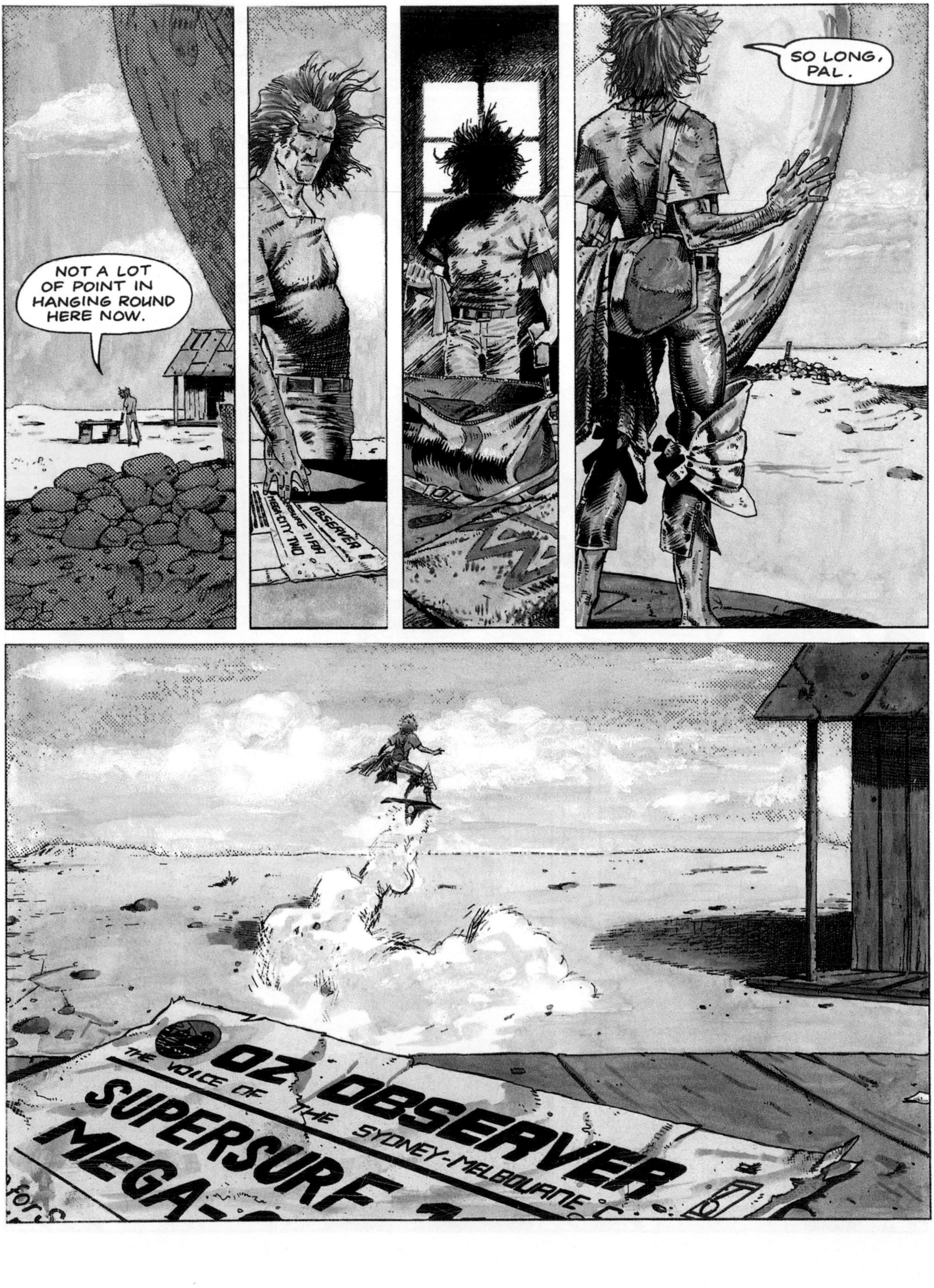
NOT A LOT OF POINT IN HANGING ROUND HERE NOW.
OBSERVER
SO LONG, PAL.
OZ OBSERVER
THE VOICE OF THE SYDNEY-MELBOURNE
SUPERSURF
MEGA-

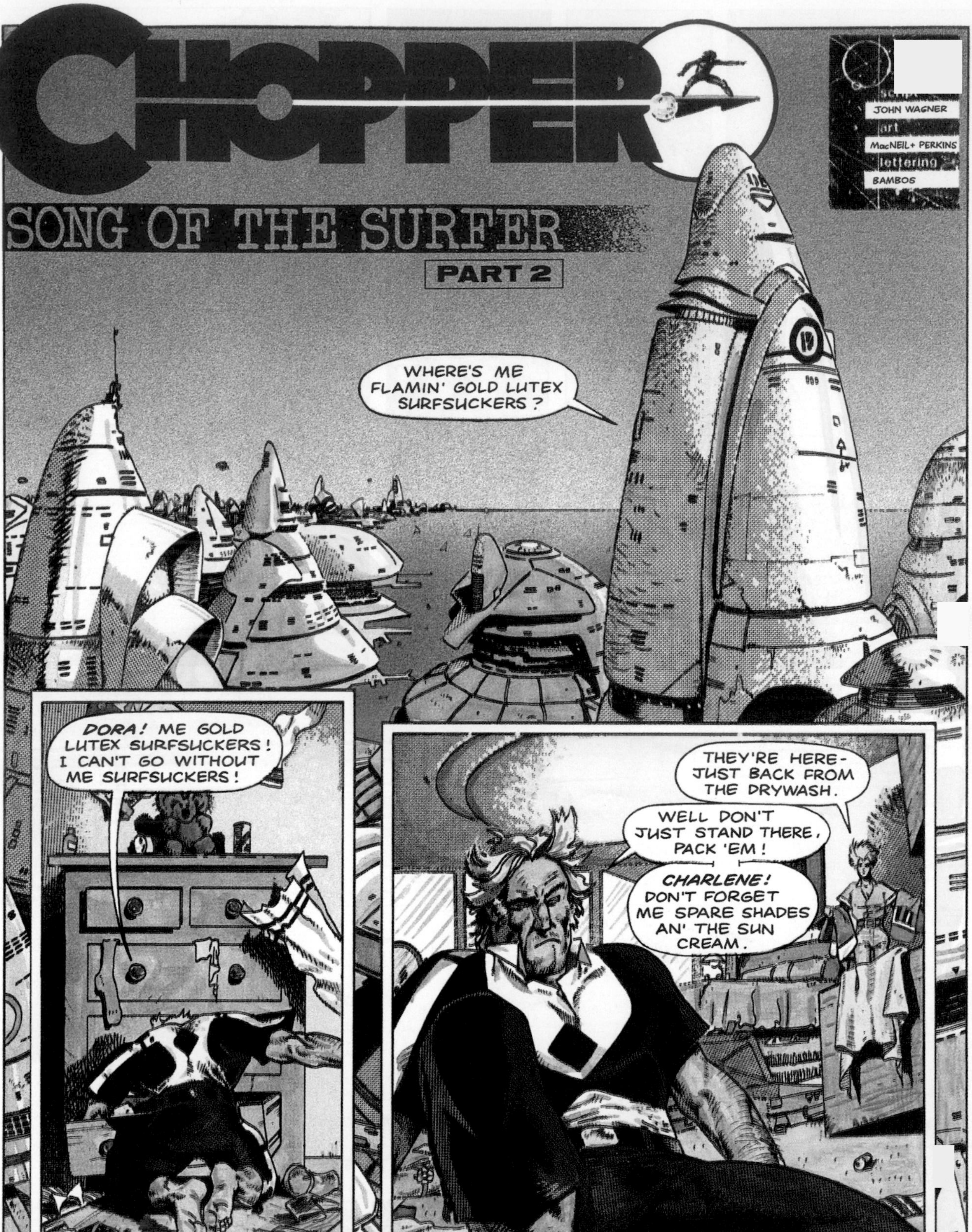
CHOPPER
JOHN WAGNER
art
MacNEIL+ PERKINS
lettering
BAMBOS
SONG OF THE SURFER
PART 2
WHERE'S ME FLAMIN' GOLD LUTEX SURFSUCKERS?
DORA! ME GOLD LUTEX SURFSUCKERS! I CAN'T GO WITHOUT ME SURFSUCKERS!
THEY'RE HERE- JUST BACK FROM THE DRYWASH.
WELL DON'T JUST STAND THERE, PACK 'EM!
CHARLENE! DON'T FORGET ME SPARE SHADES AN' THE SUN CREAM.

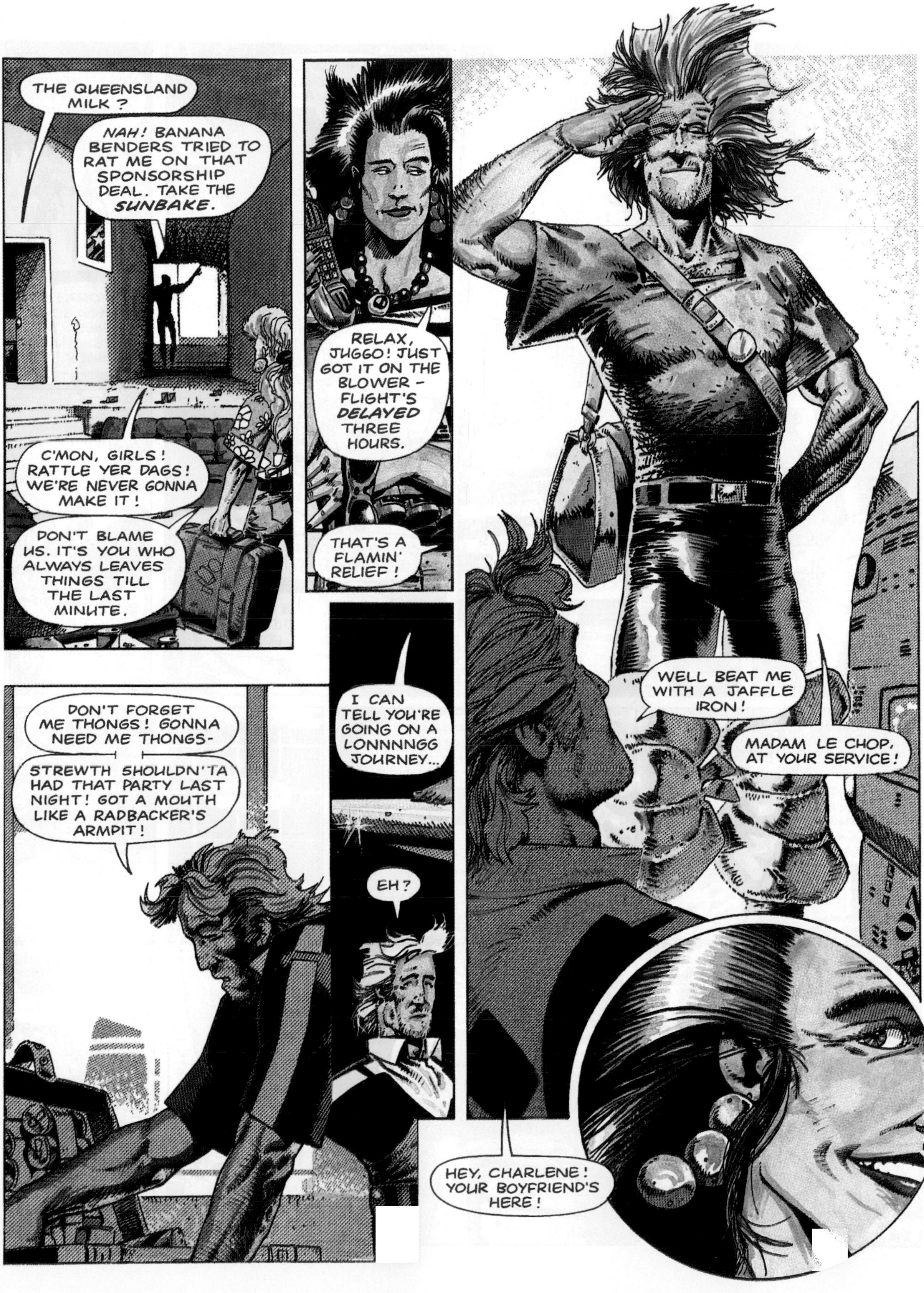
THE QUEENSLAND MILK ?
NAH! BANANA BENDERS TRIED TO RAT ME ON THAT SPONSORSHIP DEAL. TAKE THE SUNBAKE.
C'MON, GIRLS! RATTLE YER DAGS! WE'RE NEVER GONNA MAKE IT!
DON'T BLAME US. IT'S YOU WHO ALWAYS LEAVES THINGS TILL THE LAST MINUTE.
RELAX, JUGGO! JUST GOT IT ON THE BLOWER - FLIGHT'S DELAYED THREE HOURS.
THAT'S A FLAMIN' RELIEF!
DON'T FORGET ME THONGS! GONNA NEED ME THONGS-
STREWTH SHOULDN'TA HAD THAT PARTY LAST NIGHT! GOT A MOUTH LIKE A RADBACKER'S ARMPIT!
I CAN TELL YOU'RE GOING ON A LONNNNGG JOURNEY...
EH?
WELL BEAT ME WITH A JAFFLE IRON!
MADAM LE CHOP, AT YOUR SERVICE!
HEY, CHARLENE! YOUR BOYFRIEND'S HERE!

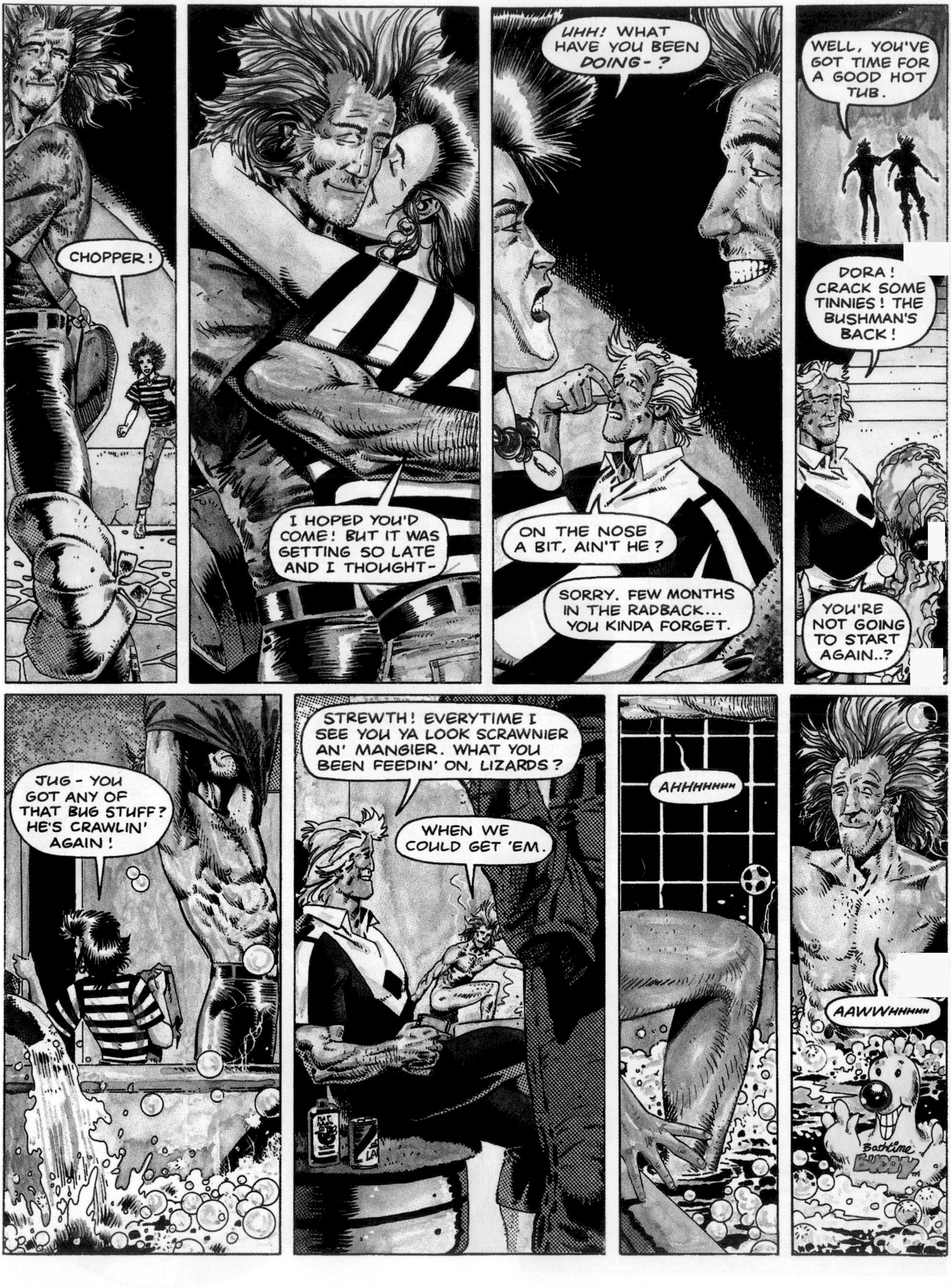
CHOPPER!
I HOPED YOU'D COME! BUT IT WAS GETTING SO LATE AND I THOUGHT-
UHH! WHAT HAVE YOU BEEN DOING-?
ON THE NOSE A BIT, AIN'T HE?
SORRY. FEW MONTHS IN THE RADBACK... YOU KINDA FORGET.
WELL, YOU'VE GOT TIME FOR A GOOD HOT TUB.
DORA! CRACK SOME TINNIES! THE BUSHMAN'S BACK!
YOU'RE NOT GOING TO START AGAIN..?
JUG - YOU GOT ANY OF THAT BUG STUFF? HE'S CRAWLIN' AGAIN!
STREWTH! EVERYTIME I SEE YOU YA LOOK SCRAWNIER AN' MANGIER. WHAT YOU BEEN FEEDIN' ON, LIZARDS?
WHEN WE COULD GET 'EM.
AHHHHHHH
AAWWHHHHH
Bathtime BUDDY

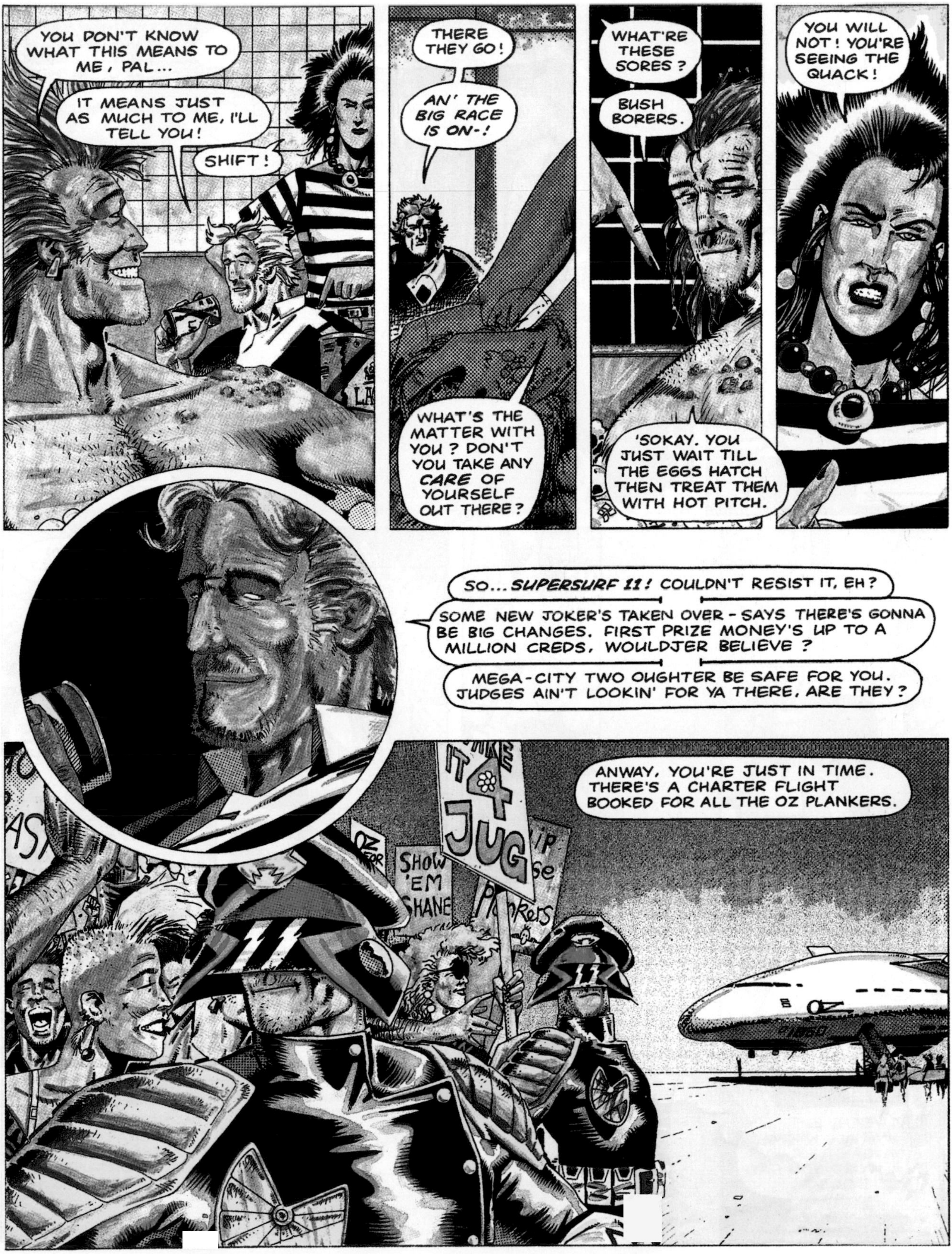
YOU DON'T KNOW WHAT THIS MEANS TO ME, PAL...
IT MEANS JUST AS MUCH TO ME, I'LL TELL YOU!
SHIFT!
THERE THEY GO!
AN' THE BIG RACE IS ON-!
WHAT'S THE MATTER WITH YOU? DON'T YOU TAKE ANY CARE OF YOURSELF OUT THERE?
WHAT'RE THESE SORES?
BUSH BORERS.
'SOKAY. YOU JUST WAIT TILL THE EGGS HATCH THEN TREAT THEM WITH HOT PITCH.
YOU WILL NOT! YOU'RE SEEING THE QUACK!
SO... SUPERSURF 11! COULDN'T RESIST IT, EH?
SOME NEW JOKER'S TAKEN OVER - SAYS THERE'S GONNA BE BIG CHANGES. FIRST PRIZE MONEY'S UP TO A MILLION CREDS, WOULDJER BELIEVE?
MEGA-CITY TWO OUGHTER BE SAFE FOR YOU. JUDGES AIN'T LOOKIN' FOR YA THERE, ARE THEY?
ANWAY, YOU'RE JUST IN TIME. THERE'S A CHARTER FLIGHT BOOKED FOR ALL THE OZ PLANKERS.
SHOW 'EM SHANE
JUG
Plankers
OZ

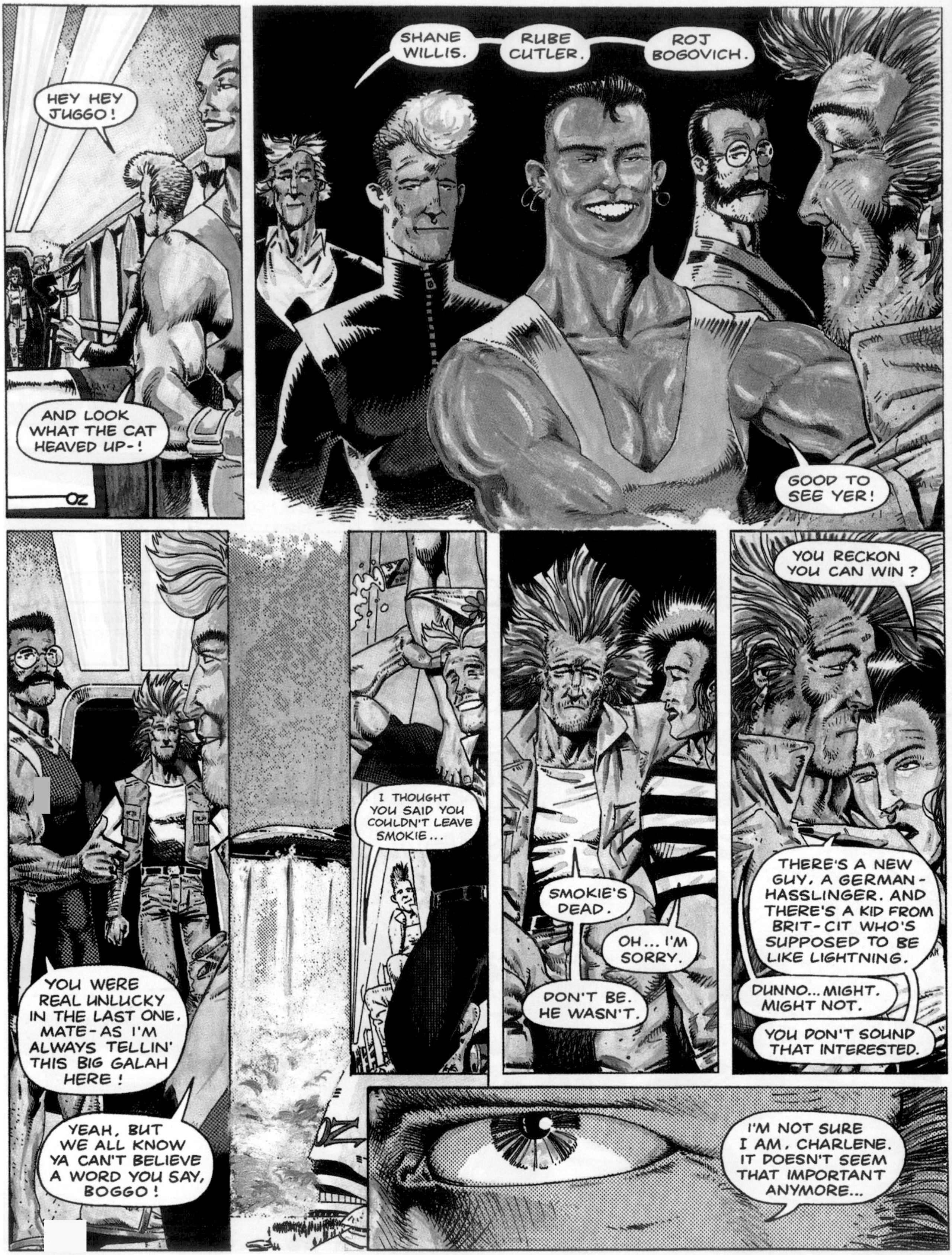
HEY HEY JUGGO!
AND LOOK WHAT THE CAT HEAVED UP-!
OZ
SHANE WILLIS.
RUBE CUTLER.
ROJ BOGOVICH.
GOOD TO SEE YER!
YOU WERE REAL UNLUCKY IN THE LAST ONE, MATE-AS I'M ALWAYS TELLIN' THIS BIG GALAH HERE!
YEAH, BUT WE ALL KNOW YA CAN'T BELIEVE A WORD YOU SAY, BOGGO!
I THOUGHT YOU SAID YOU COULDN'T LEAVE SMOKIE...
SMOKIE'S DEAD.
OH... I'M SORRY.
DON'T BE. HE WASN'T.
YOU RECKON YOU CAN WIN?
THERE'S A NEW GUY, A GERMAN - HASSLINGER. AND THERE'S A KID FROM BRIT-CIT WHO'S SUPPOSED TO BE LIKE LIGHTNING.
DUNNO... MIGHT. MIGHT NOT.
YOU DON'T SOUND THAT INTERESTED.
I'M NOT SURE I AM, CHARLENE. IT DOESN'T SEEM THAT IMPORTANT ANYMORE...

THAT'S JUST THE WAY JUG USED TO TALK — AND LOOK AT HIM NOW, EXCITED AS A PUPPY. YOU'LL FEEL DIFFERENT SOON.

SURE.

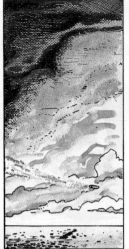

SMOKIE SAID I'M JUST FOLLOWING THE *SONGLINES*. I DON'T KNOW IT, BUT THAT'S WHAT I'M DOING.

THE SONGLINES... I HEARD OF THEM. THEY'RE... SORT OF *DREAM TRACKS* - ANCIENT TRAILS OF SONG LEFT BY THE ABORIGINAL ANCESTORS...

SOMETHING LIKE THAT, I DON'T REALLY UNDERSTAND IT THAT MUCH...

HE SAID THAT EACH ONE OF US IS DESCENDED FROM A PARTICULAR ANCESTOR, EACH OF US HAS OUR OWN *'DREAMING'*.. THAT'S WHAT HE CALLED IT.

SMOKIE HAD A WOMBAT DREAMING. THAT MEANT THAT HE BELONGED TO THE WOMBAT ANCESTOR, AND THE SONGLINES WERE HIS LINK WITH HIS PAST, WITH THE EARTH ITSELF...

BUT THE ANCESTORS DIDN'T HAVE TO BE ANIMALS — THEY COULD BE RIVERS OR ROCKS OR TREES — ANYTHING.

HE SAID I HAD A *WIND* DREAMING.

WIND DREAMING... LIKE... A CHILD OF THE WIND.

THAT'S NICE.

ANYWAY, ACCORDING TO SMOKIE I'M JUST FOLLOWING THE WINDSONG.

ME, I RECKON, WELL... I'VE GOT NOTHING BETTER TO DO.

ANYWAY — YOU'RE HERE. THAT'S REASON ENOUGH.

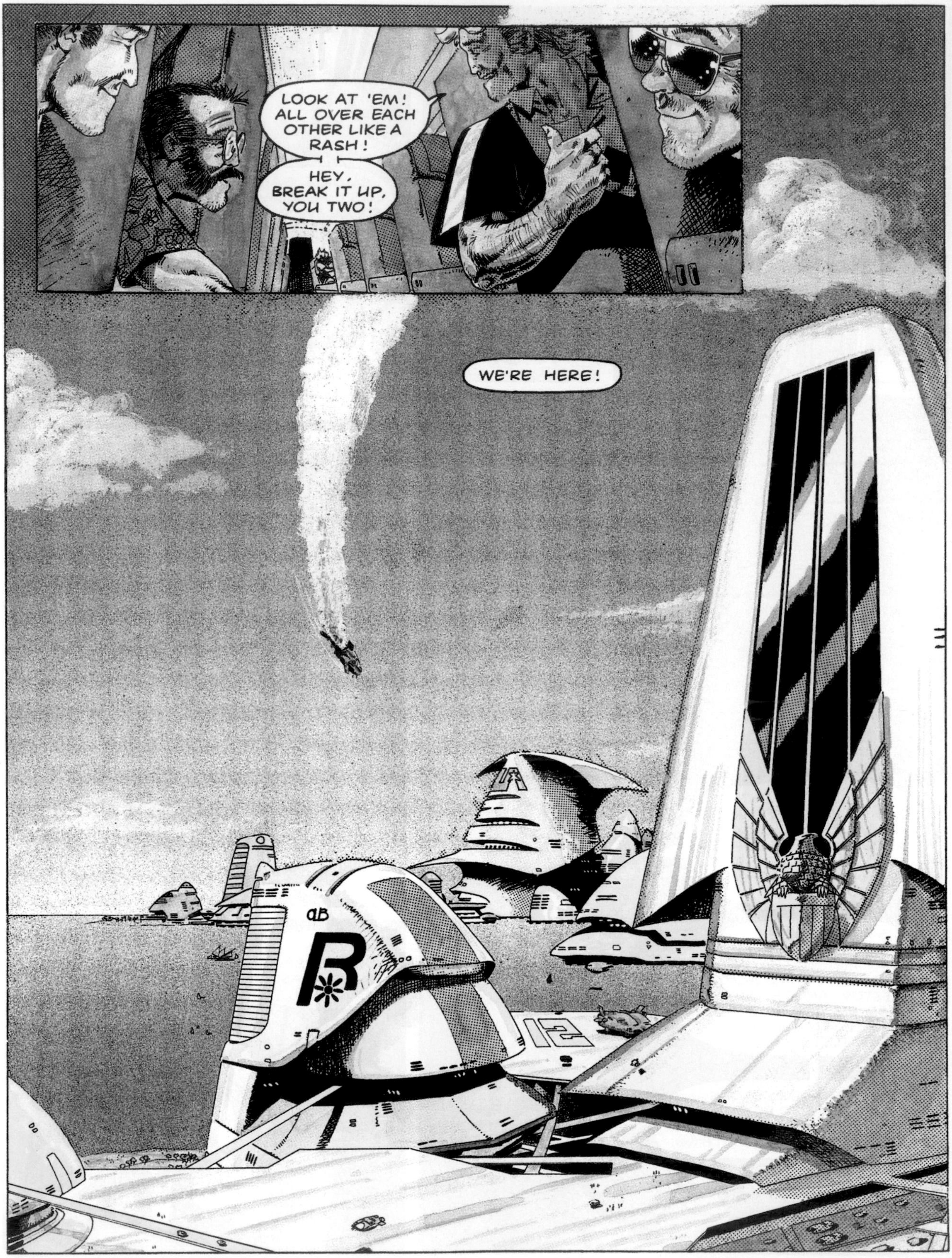
LOOK AT 'EM! ALL OVER EACH OTHER LIKE A RASH!
HEY, BREAK IT UP, YOU TWO!
WE'RE HERE!

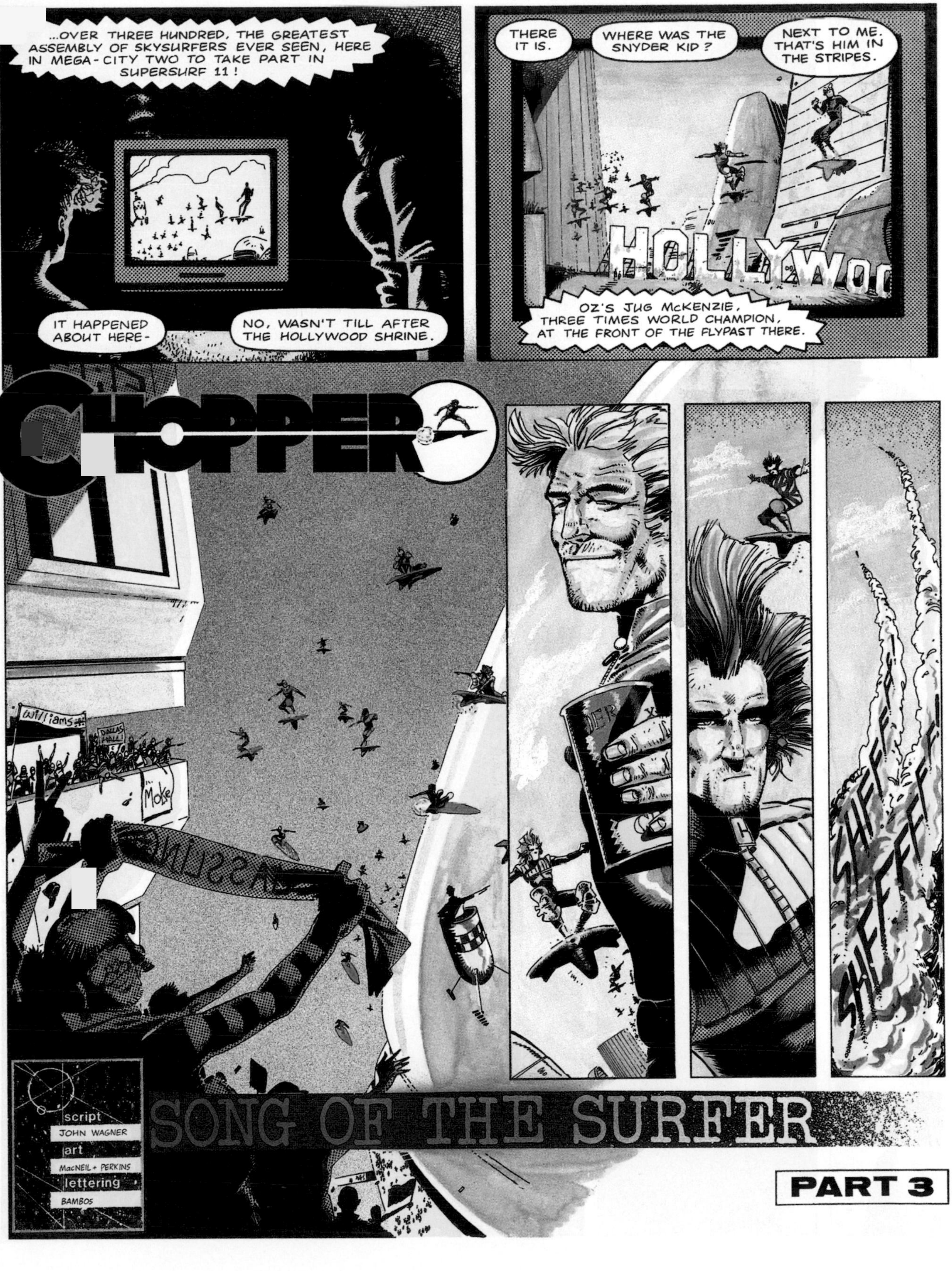
...OVER THREE HUNDRED, THE GREATEST ASSEMBLY OF SKYSURFERS EVER SEEN, HERE IN MEGA-CITY TWO TO TAKE PART IN SUPERSURF 11!
IT HAPPENED ABOUT HERE-
NO, WASN'T TILL AFTER THE HOLLYWOOD SHRINE.
THERE IT IS.
WHERE WAS THE SNYDER KID?
NEXT TO ME. THAT'S HIM IN THE STRIPES.
HOLLYWOO
OZ'S JUG McKENZIE, THREE TIMES WORLD CHAMPION, AT THE FRONT OF THE FLYPAST THERE.
CHOPPER
williams
DALLAS HALL
Moke
SHEFFF!
SHEFFFF!
SHEFF!
script
JOHN WAGNER
art
MacNEIL + PERKINS
lettering
BAMBOS
SONG OF THE SURFER
PART 3

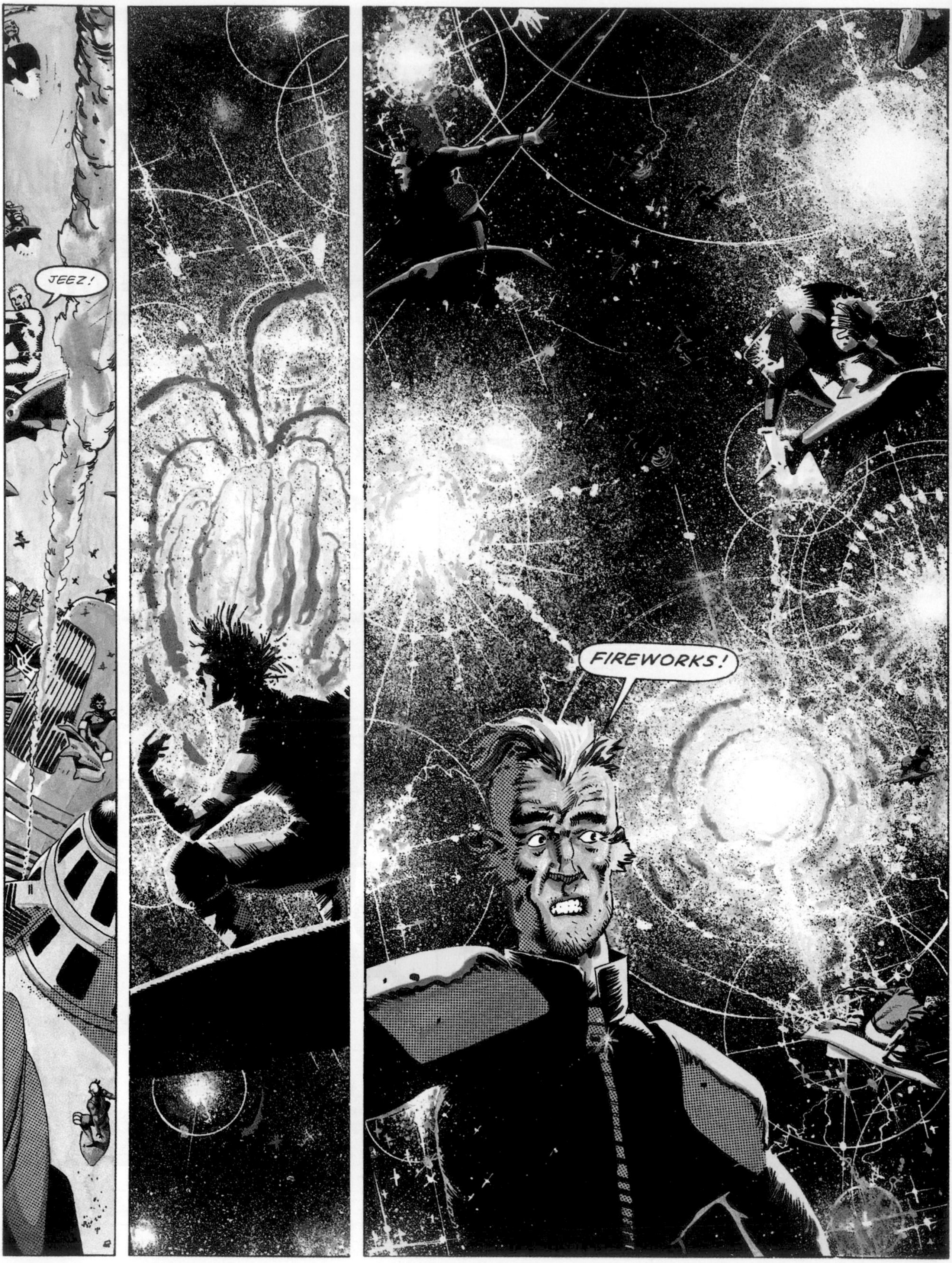
JEEZ!
FIREWORKS!

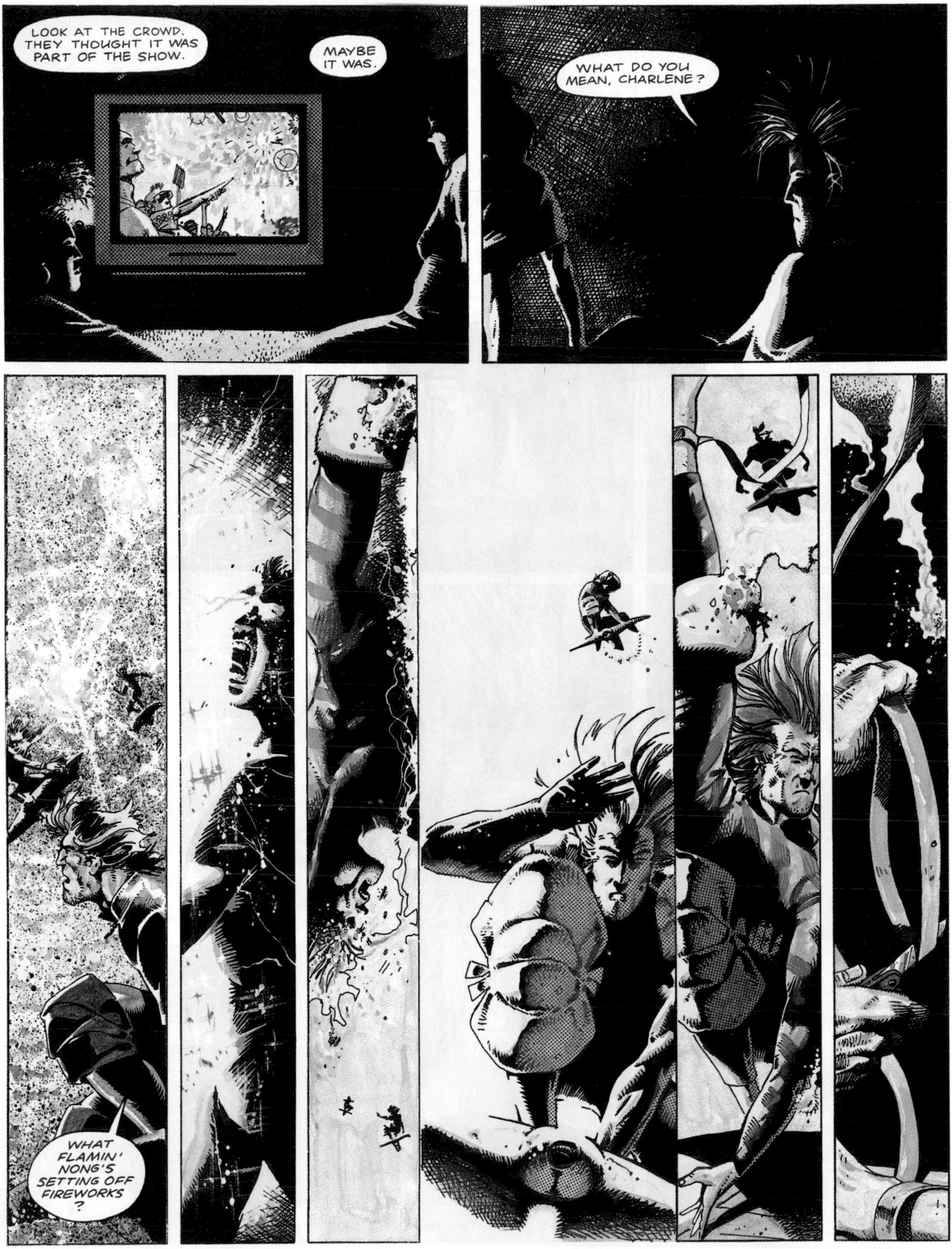
LOOK AT THE CROWD. THEY THOUGHT IT WAS PART OF THE SHOW.
MAYBE IT WAS.
WHAT DO YOU MEAN, CHARLENE?
WHAT FLAMIN' NONG'S SETTING OFF FIREWORKS ?

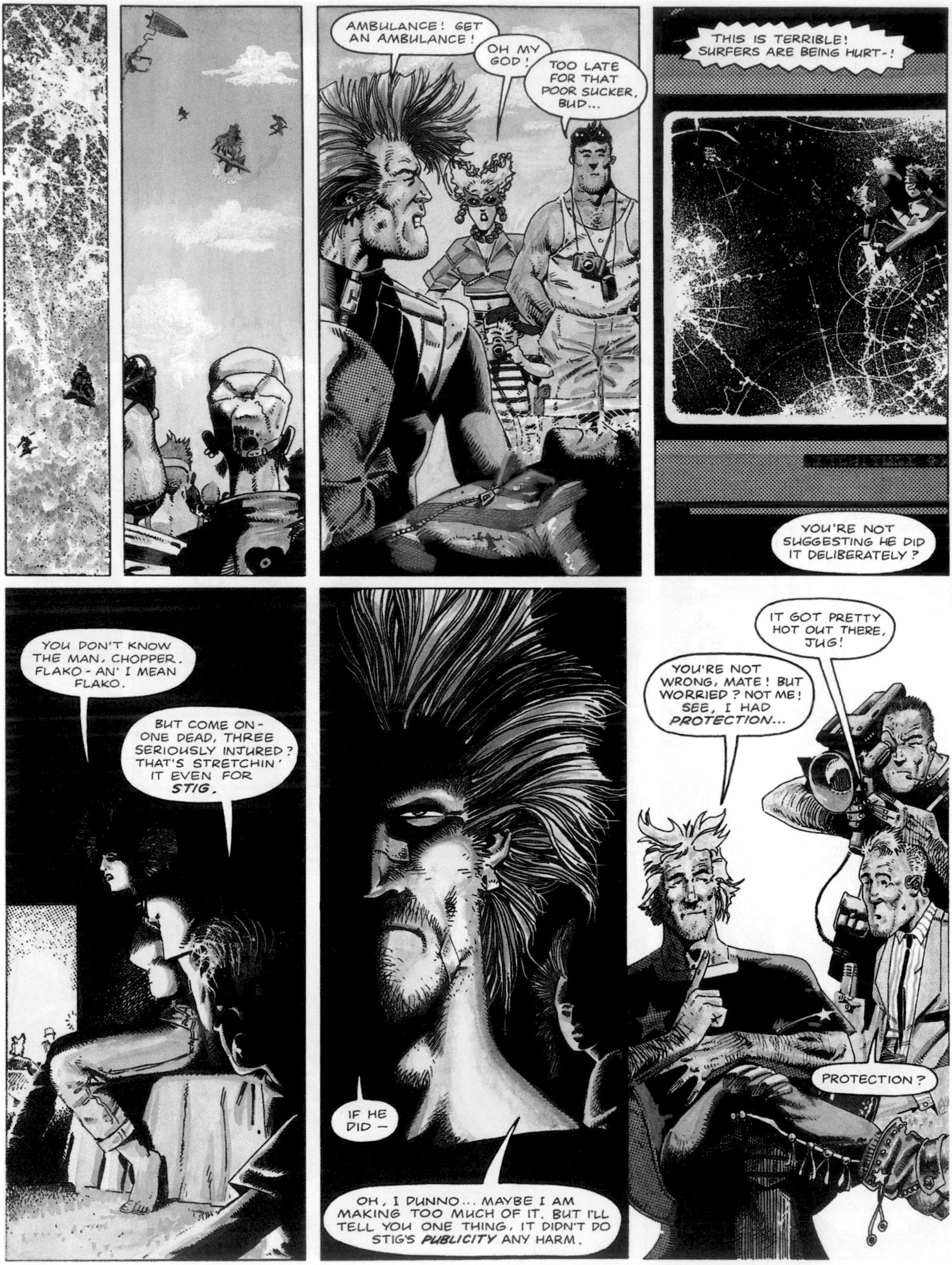
AMBULANCE! GET AN AMBULANCE!
OH MY GOD!
TOO LATE FOR THAT POOR SUCKER, BUD...
THIS IS TERRIBLE! SURFERS ARE BEING HURT-!
YOU'RE NOT SUGGESTING HE DID IT DELIBERATELY?
YOU DON'T KNOW THE MAN, CHOPPER. FLAKO - AN' I MEAN FLAKO.
BUT COME ON - ONE DEAD, THREE SERIOUSLY INJURED? THAT'S STRETCHIN' IT EVEN FOR STIG.
IF HE DID -
OH, I DUNNO... MAYBE I AM MAKING TOO MUCH OF IT. BUT I'LL TELL YOU ONE THING, IT DIDN'T DO STIG'S PUBLICITY ANY HARM.
IT GOT PRETTY HOT OUT THERE, JUG!
YOU'RE NOT WRONG, MATE! BUT WORRIED? NOT ME! SEE, I HAD PROTECTION...
PROTECTION?

SUNBAKE!

IT'S ALL A CIRCUS, ISN'T IT, DORA?

ONCE IT WAS JUST A RACE...NO MONEY, JUST MAN AGAINST MAN AND THAT WAS ENOUGH. NOW... EVERYBODY'S OUT TO SCREW WHAT THEY CAN GET.

JUG... JUG'S OFF THE BOIL, CHOPPER...

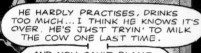

HE HARDLY PRACTISES, DRINKS TOO MUCH...I THINK HE KNOWS IT'S OVER. HE'S JUST TRYIN' TO MILK THE COW ONE LAST TIME.

AND YOU CAN'T BLAME HIM. HE'S GIVEN A HELLUVA LOT TO THIS SPORT.

SO MAYBE I DIDN'T BEAT THE REAL JUG McKENZIE THAT NIGHT...

I DON'T KNOW...I...I GUESS NOT...

YOU DIDN'T SEE 8 AND 9, DID YOU?

DIDN'T SHOW IT IN THE CUBES - 'SPECIALLY NOT MINE.

HE WAS AT HIS BEST THEN, WHEN HE WAS JUST COMING UP...

YOU AND HIM IN 8 - THAT WOULDA BEEN SOME RACE.

SHAKESPEARE? MARLON SHAKESPEARE?

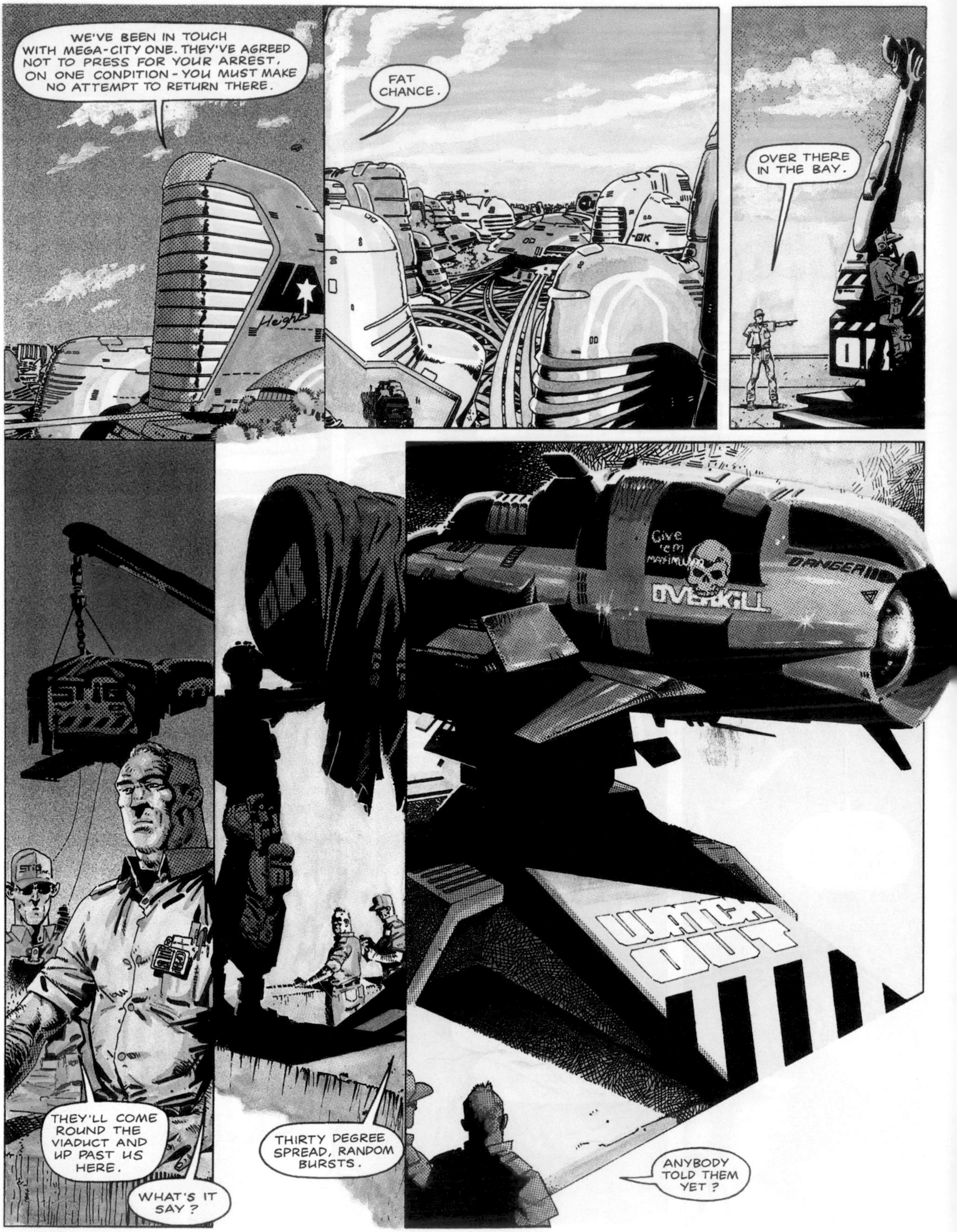
WE'VE BEEN IN TOUCH WITH MEGA-CITY ONE. THEY'VE AGREED NOT TO PRESS FOR YOUR ARREST, ON ONE CONDITION - YOU MUST MAKE NO ATTEMPT TO RETURN THERE.
FAT CHANCE.
OVER THERE IN THE BAY.
THEY'LL COME ROUND THE VIADUCT AND UP PAST US HERE.
WHAT'S IT SAY?
THIRTY DEGREE SPREAD, RANDOM BURSTS.
Give 'em MAXIMUM
DANGER
OVERKILL
ANYBODY TOLD THEM YET?

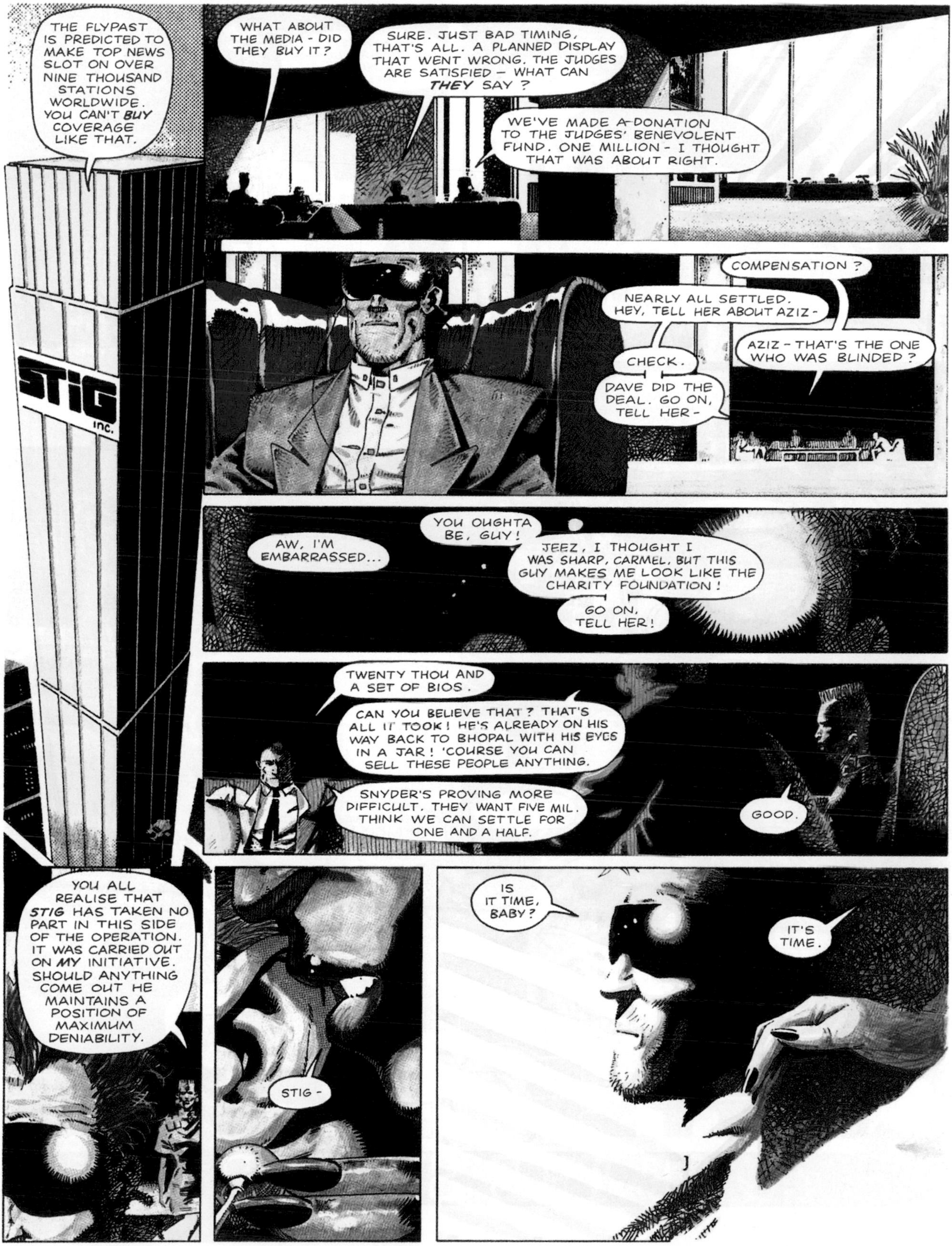
THE FLYPAST IS PREDICTED TO MAKE TOP NEWS SLOT ON OVER NINE THOUSAND STATIONS WORLDWIDE. YOU CAN'T BUY COVERAGE LIKE THAT.
STIG INC.
WHAT ABOUT THE MEDIA - DID THEY BUY IT?
SURE. JUST BAD TIMING, THAT'S ALL. A PLANNED DISPLAY THAT WENT WRONG. THE JUDGES ARE SATISFIED — WHAT CAN THEY SAY?
WE'VE MADE A DONATION TO THE JUDGES' BENEVOLENT FUND. ONE MILLION - I THOUGHT THAT WAS ABOUT RIGHT.
COMPENSATION?
NEARLY ALL SETTLED. HEY, TELL HER ABOUT AZIZ -
CHECK.
DAVE DID THE DEAL. GO ON, TELL HER -
AZIZ - THAT'S THE ONE WHO WAS BLINDED?
AW, I'M EMBARRASSED...
YOU OUGHTA BE, GUY!
JEEZ, I THOUGHT I WAS SHARP, CARMEL, BUT THIS GUY MAKES ME LOOK LIKE THE CHARITY FOUNDATION!
GO ON, TELL HER!
TWENTY THOU AND A SET OF BIOS.
CAN YOU BELIEVE THAT? THAT'S ALL IT TOOK! HE'S ALREADY ON HIS WAY BACK TO BHOPAL WITH HIS EYES IN A JAR! 'COURSE YOU CAN SELL THESE PEOPLE ANYTHING.
SNYDER'S PROVING MORE DIFFICULT. THEY WANT FIVE MIL. THINK WE CAN SETTLE FOR ONE AND A HALF.
GOOD.
YOU ALL REALISE THAT STIG HAS TAKEN NO PART IN THIS SIDE OF THE OPERATION. IT WAS CARRIED OUT ON MY INITIATIVE. SHOULD ANYTHING COME OUT HE MAINTAINS A POSITION OF MAXIMUM DENIABILITY.
STIG -
IS IT TIME, BABY?
IT'S TIME.

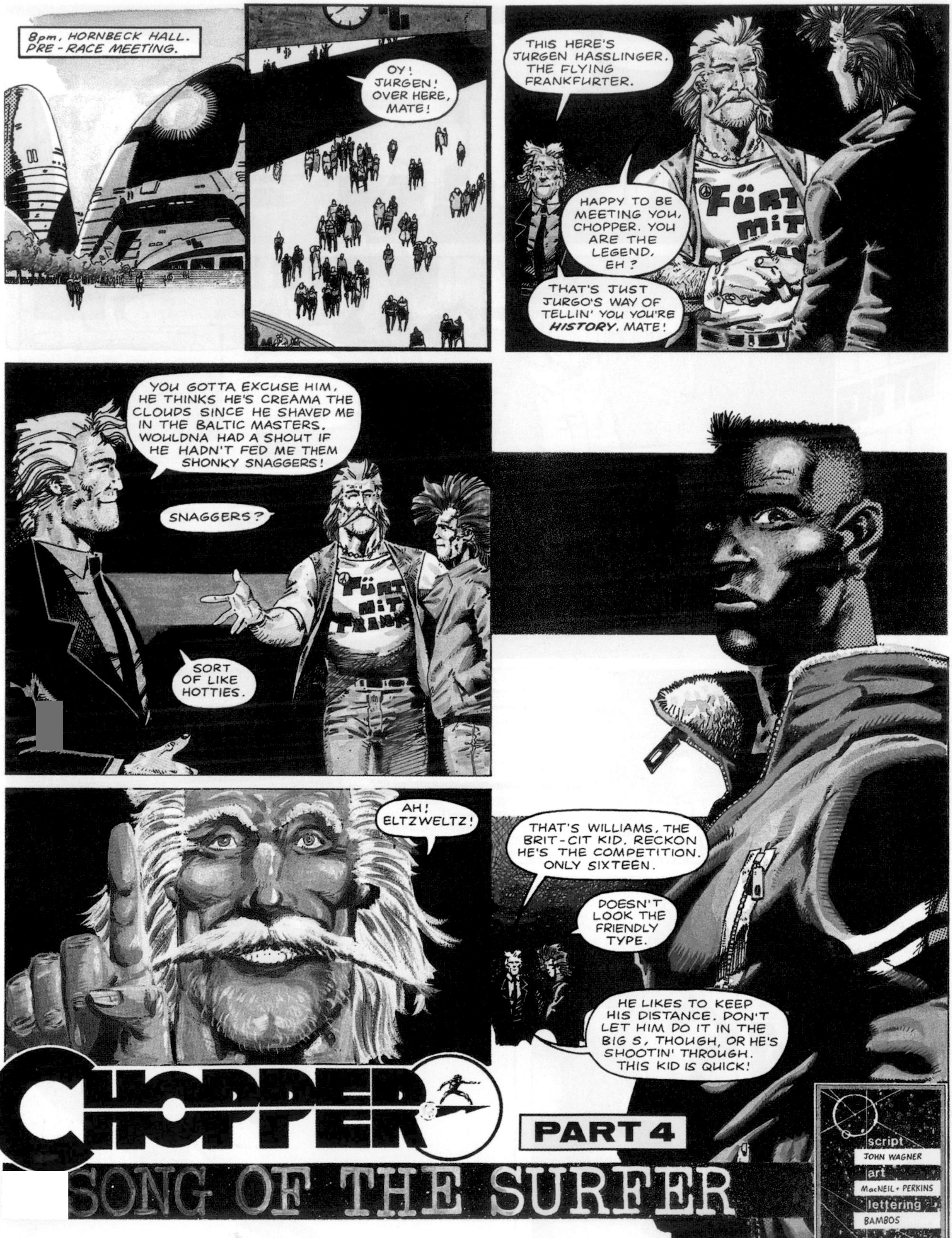
8pm, HORNBECK HALL. PRE-RACE MEETING.
OY! JURGEN! OVER HERE, MATE!
THIS HERE'S JURGEN HASSLINGER, THE FLYING FRANKFURTER.
HAPPY TO BE MEETING YOU, CHOPPER. YOU ARE THE LEGEND, EH?
THAT'S JUST JURGO'S WAY OF TELLIN' YOU YOU'RE HISTORY, MATE!
FÜRT MIT
YOU GOTTA EXCUSE HIM. HE THINKS HE'S CREAMA THE CLOUDS SINCE HE SHAVED ME IN THE BALTIC MASTERS. WOULDNA HAD A SHOUT IF HE HADN'T FED ME THEM SHONKY SNAGGERS!
SNAGGERS?
SORT OF LIKE HOTTIES.
FÜRT MIT FRANK
AH! ELTZWELTZ!
THAT'S WILLIAMS, THE BRIT-CIT KID. RECKON HE'S THE COMPETITION. ONLY SIXTEEN.
DOESN'T LOOK THE FRIENDLY TYPE.
HE LIKES TO KEEP HIS DISTANCE. DON'T LET HIM DO IT IN THE BIG S, THOUGH, OR HE'S SHOOTIN' THROUGH. THIS KID IS QUICK!
CHOPPER
PART 4
SONG OF THE SURFER
script
JOHN WAGNER
art
MacNEIL + PERKINS
lettering
BAMBOS

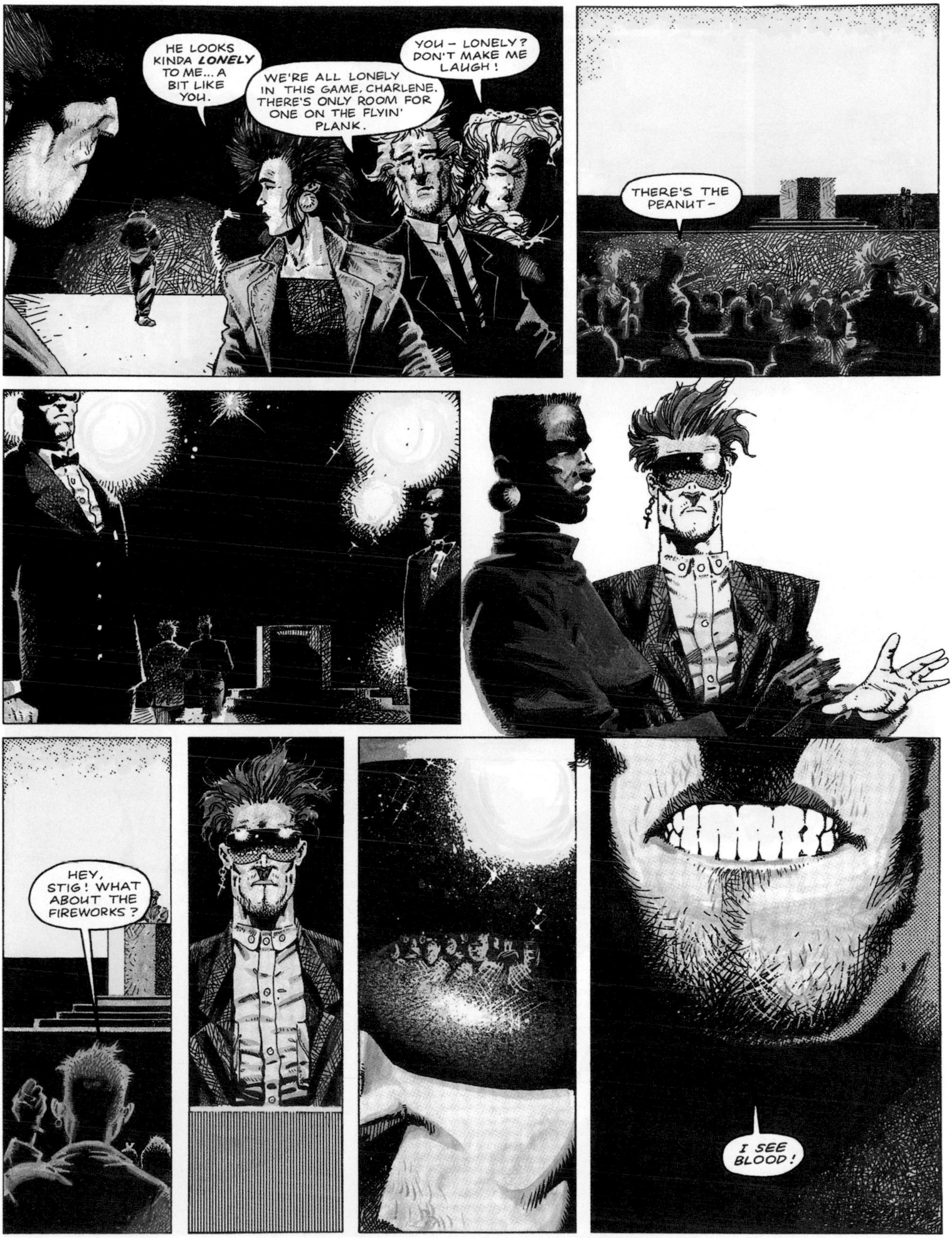
HE LOOKS KINDA **LONELY** TO ME... A BIT LIKE YOU.
WE'RE ALL LONELY IN THIS GAME, CHARLENE. THERE'S ONLY ROOM FOR ONE ON THE FLYIN' PLANK.
YOU - LONELY? DON'T MAKE ME LAUGH!
THERE'S THE PEANUT-
HEY, STIG! WHAT ABOUT THE FIREWORKS?
I SEE BLOOD!

I SEE THE HOT FLASH OF LASERS - I HEAR THE WHUMP OF CANNON, THE CRACK OF THE SNIPER'S BULLET!
I SEE BODIES - YOUR BODIES - PARTING LIKE RIPE SEED PODS!
I SEE STREETS SPLASHED IN CRIMSON - I HEAR CHILDREN CRYING AND WOMEN, STRONG WOMEN SCREAMING!
I AM A VISIONARY - A DREAMER! HEAR ME! I KNOW! I HAVE SEEN THE FUTURE - AND IT IS RED!
STREWTH!
TOLD YOU HE WAS FLAKO -!
YOU HEROES OUT THERE - HEROES? YOU'RE NOTHING! YOUR DAY IS PAST! YOU'RE JUST RACERS - SPORTSMEN! AND THE PEOPLE DON'T WANT SPORT ANYMORE... THEY WANT BLOOD!
AND TOGETHER WE SHALL GIVE IT TO THEM! OH, YES! WE'LL PAINT A MASTERWORK OF CARNAGE ACROSS THE SKY!
AND WHEN IT IS OVER ONE OF YOU WILL BE A HERO - A TRUE HERO, FORGED IN THE HEAT OF BATTLE! AND FOR A SHORT WHILE YOU WILL BE THE MOST FAMOUS HUMAN BEING ON THIS EARTH!
IS THAT NOT WORTH MAKING SACRIFICES FOR?

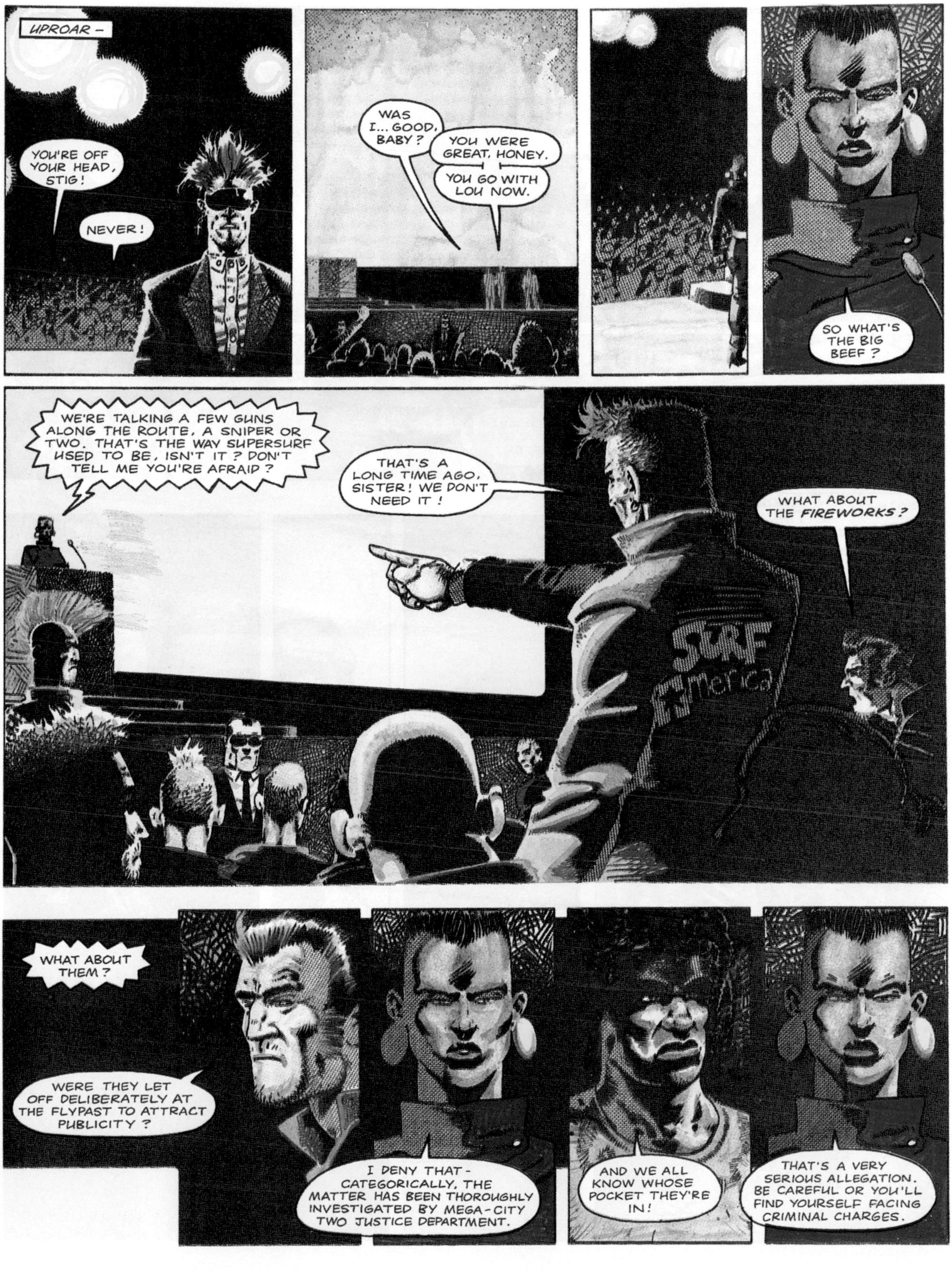
UPROAR –
YOU'RE OFF YOUR HEAD, STIG!
NEVER!
WAS I... GOOD, BABY?
YOU WERE GREAT, HONEY.
YOU GO WITH LOU NOW.
SO WHAT'S THE BIG BEEF?
WE'RE TALKING A FEW GUNS ALONG THE ROUTE, A SNIPER OR TWO. THAT'S THE WAY SUPERSURF USED TO BE, ISN'T IT? DON'T TELL ME YOU'RE AFRAID?
THAT'S A LONG TIME AGO, SISTER! WE DON'T NEED IT!
WHAT ABOUT THE FIREWORKS?
SURF America
WHAT ABOUT THEM?
WERE THEY LET OFF DELIBERATELY AT THE FLYPAST TO ATTRACT PUBLICITY?
I DENY THAT – CATEGORICALLY. THE MATTER HAS BEEN THOROUGHLY INVESTIGATED BY MEGA-CITY TWO JUSTICE DEPARTMENT.
AND WE ALL KNOW WHOSE POCKET THEY'RE IN!
THAT'S A VERY SERIOUS ALLEGATION. BE CAREFUL OR YOU'LL FIND YOURSELF FACING CRIMINAL CHARGES.

STEWARDS ARE NOW PASSING OUT ENTRY FORMS. THEY CONTAIN A DISCLAIMER ABSOLVING STIG INC FROM ANY DEATHS OR INJURIES CAUSED BEFORE OR DURING SUPERSURF 11. SIGN AND RETURN THEM BY MIDNIGHT TOMORROW.

YOU MAY, OF COURSE, CHOOSE NOT TO TAKE PART. THAT IS YOUR DECISION.

TOO RIGHT IT IS! SCRATCH ME, LADY!

THAT'S A PITY. LOOKS LIKE WE'LL BE HAVING A NEW WORLD CHAMPION!

DON'T KID YOURSELF! THERE'S NOT ONE OF US GOING ALONG WITH A BLOODBATH!

YOU AIN'T GOT A RACE, SISTER!

...ully acknowledge the r... ...solve Stig Inc and associate... ...y responsibility for injury... ...the preperations for or in... ...persurf Eleven.

Sonny William...

YOU CRAZY, MAN!

COMPETITOR NUMBER ONE— SONNY WILLIAMS, BRIT-CIT!

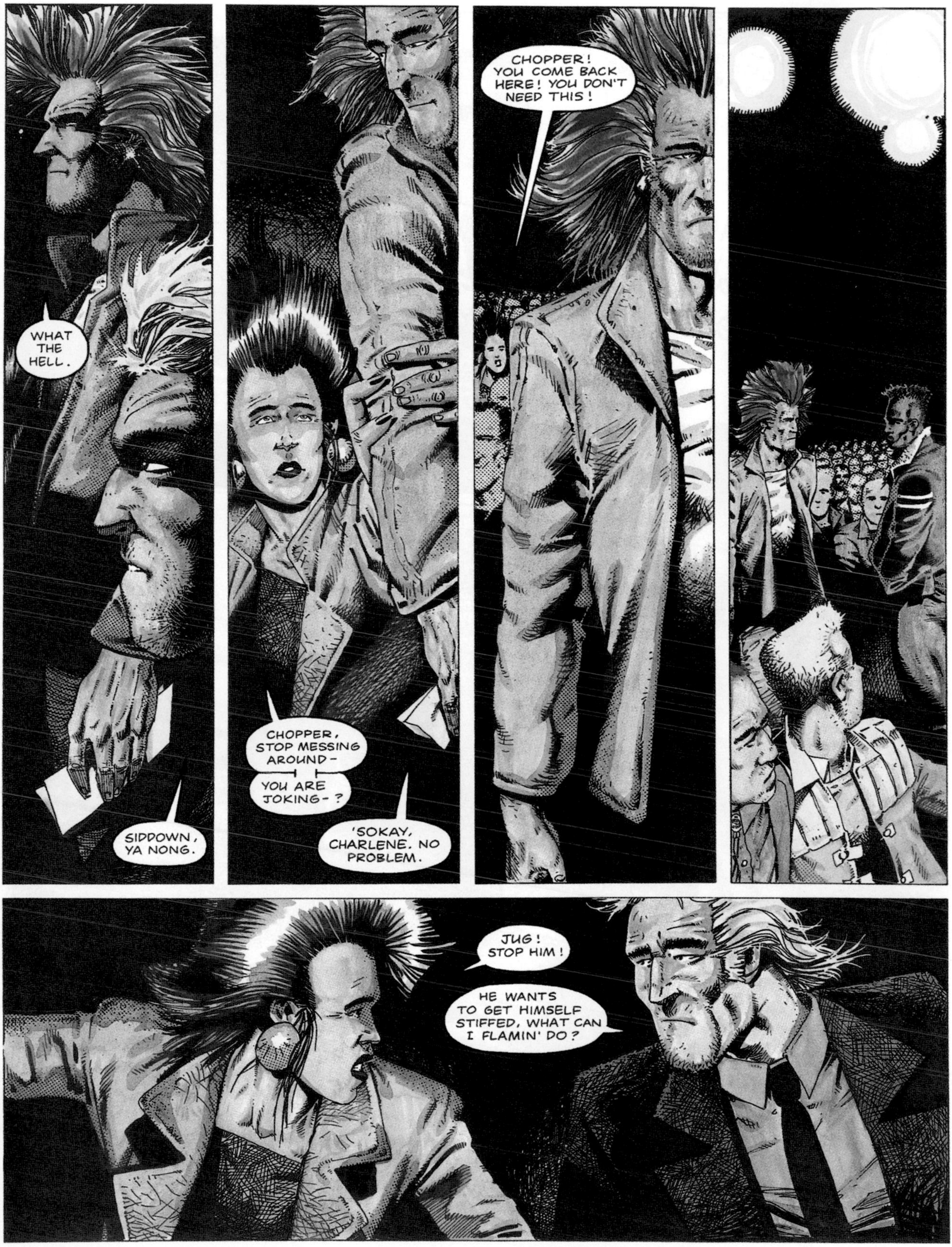
WHAT THE HELL.
SIDDOWN, YA NONG.
CHOPPER, STOP MESSING AROUND–
YOU ARE JOKING–?
'SOKAY, CHARLENE. NO PROBLEM.
CHOPPER! YOU COME BACK HERE! YOU DON'T NEED THIS!
JUG! STOP HIM!
HE WANTS TO GET HIMSELF STIFFED, WHAT CAN I FLAMIN' DO?

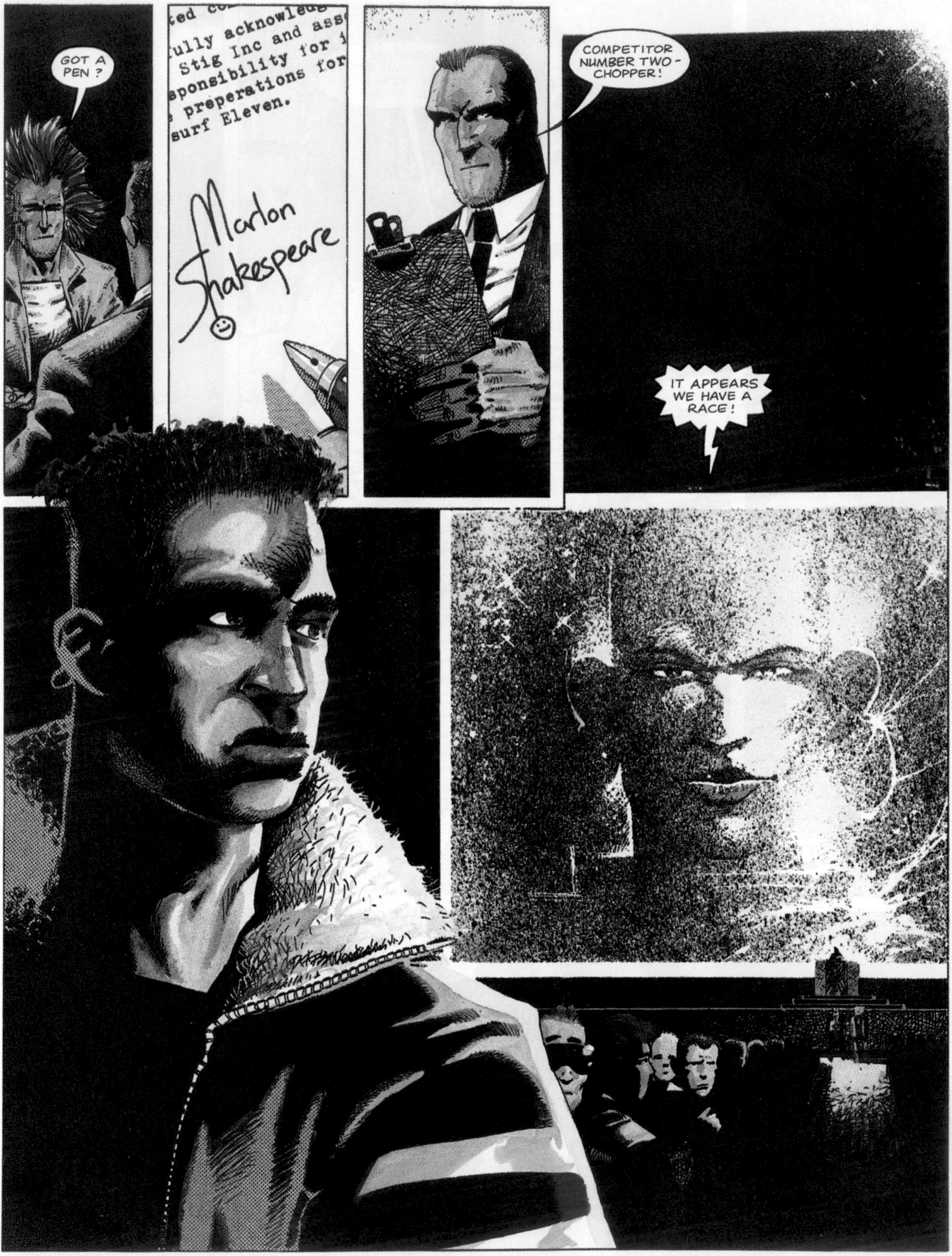
GOT A PEN ?
ted co
ully acknowledg
Stig Inc and ass
sponsibility for i
preperations for
surf Eleven.
Marlon Shakespeare
COMPETITOR NUMBER TWO - CHOPPER!
IT APPEARS WE HAVE A RACE!

IT'S BECAUSE OF WHAT DORA SAID, ISN'T IT?

EH?

SHE TOLD YOU JUG WAS OFF FORM WHEN YOU BEAT HIM. NOW YOU FEEL YOU'VE GOT IT ALL TO DO AGAIN.

IT'S NOT THAT...

I DUNNO...

THEN WHY?

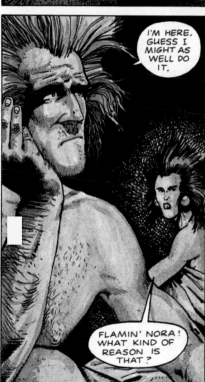

I'M HERE, GUESS I MIGHT AS WELL DO IT.

FLAMIN' NORA! WHAT KIND OF REASON IS THAT?

CHARLENE —

"I'VE GOT A RAZOR, I MIGHT AS WELL SLIT ME THROAT! OH, HERE'S A GUN! I THINK I'LL JUST SHOOT MESELF!"

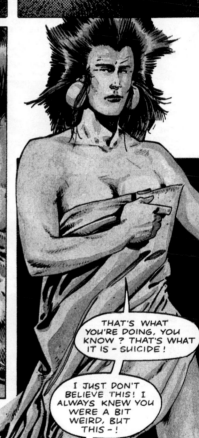

THAT'S WHAT YOU'RE DOING, YOU KNOW? THAT'S WHAT IT IS - SUICIDE!

I JUST DON'T BELIEVE THIS! I ALWAYS KNEW YOU WERE A BIT WEIRD, BUT THIS —!

JUG - EVEN JUG'S GOT ENOUGH SENSE TO PULL OUT! WHY CAN'T YOU?

CHOPPER

script
JOHN WAGNER

art
MacNEIL • PERKINS

lettering
BAMBOS

SONG OF THE SURFER

PART 5

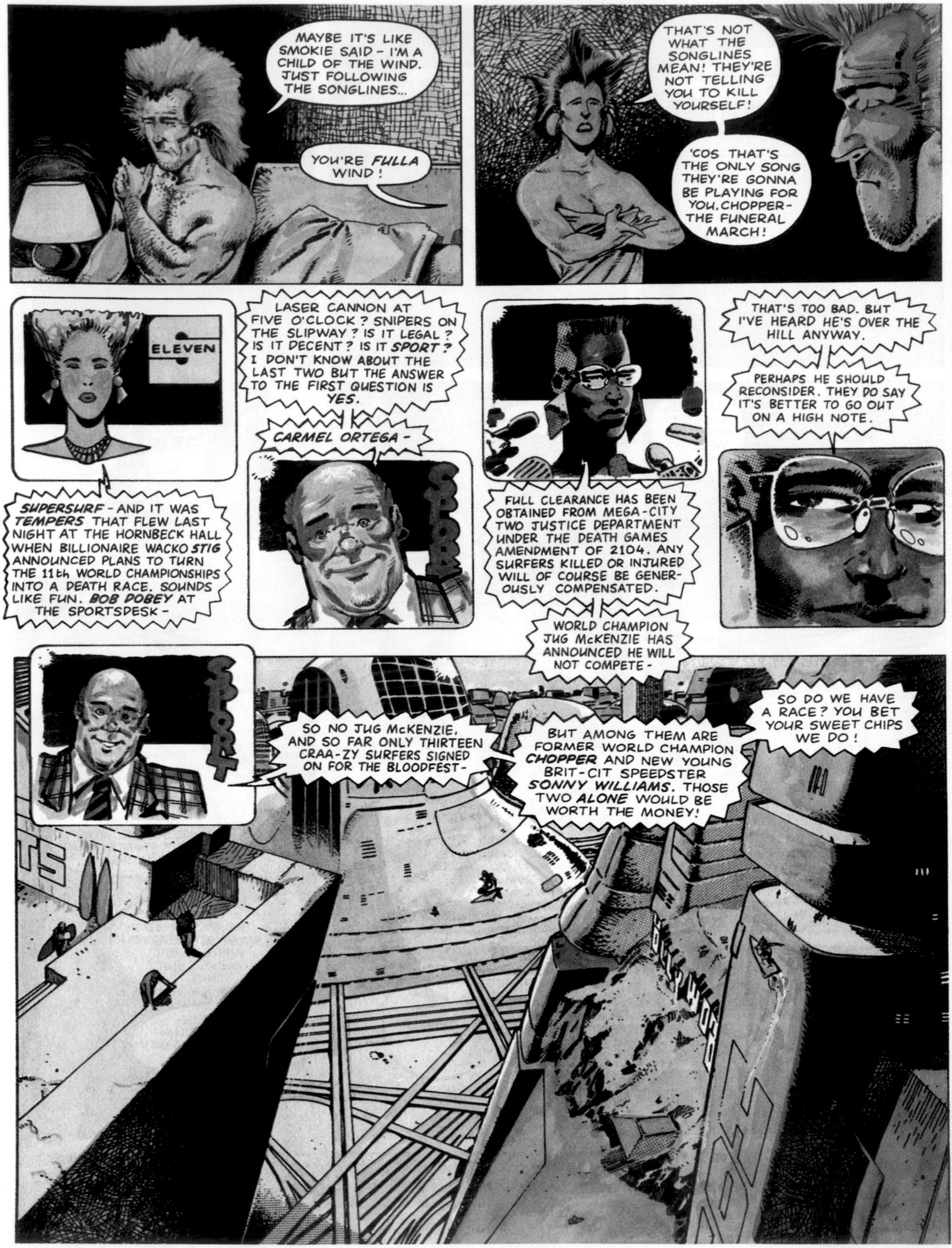
MAYBE IT'S LIKE SMOKIE SAID - I'M A CHILD OF THE WIND. JUST FOLLOWING THE SONGLINES...
YOU'RE FULLA WIND!
THAT'S NOT WHAT THE SONGLINES MEAN! THEY'RE NOT TELLING YOU TO KILL YOURSELF!
'COS THAT'S THE ONLY SONG THEY'RE GONNA BE PLAYING FOR YOU, CHOPPER - THE FUNERAL MARCH!
ELEVEN
SUPERSURF - AND IT WAS TEMPERS THAT FLEW LAST NIGHT AT THE HORNBECK HALL WHEN BILLIONAIRE WACKO STIG ANNOUNCED PLANS TO TURN THE 11th WORLD CHAMPIONSHIPS INTO A DEATH RACE. SOUNDS LIKE FUN. BOB DOBEY AT THE SPORTSDESK -
LASER CANNON AT FIVE O'CLOCK? SNIPERS ON THE SLIPWAY? IS IT LEGAL? IS IT DECENT? IS IT SPORT? I DON'T KNOW ABOUT THE LAST TWO BUT THE ANSWER TO THE FIRST QUESTION IS YES.
CARMEL ORTEGA -
SPORT
FULL CLEARANCE HAS BEEN OBTAINED FROM MEGA-CITY TWO JUSTICE DEPARTMENT UNDER THE DEATH GAMES AMENDMENT OF 2104. ANY SURFERS KILLED OR INJURED WILL OF COURSE BE GENEROUSLY COMPENSATED.
WORLD CHAMPION JUG McKENZIE HAS ANNOUNCED HE WILL NOT COMPETE -
THAT'S TOO BAD. BUT I'VE HEARD HE'S OVER THE HILL ANYWAY.
PERHAPS HE SHOULD RECONSIDER. THEY DO SAY IT'S BETTER TO GO OUT ON A HIGH NOTE.
SPORT
SO NO JUG McKENZIE, AND SO FAR ONLY THIRTEEN CRAA-ZY SURFERS SIGNED ON FOR THE BLOODFEST -
BUT AMONG THEM ARE FORMER WORLD CHAMPION CHOPPER AND NEW YOUNG BRIT-CIT SPEEDSTER SONNY WILLIAMS. THOSE TWO ALONE WOULD BE WORTH THE MONEY!
SO DO WE HAVE A RACE? YOU BET YOUR SWEET CHIPS WE DO!

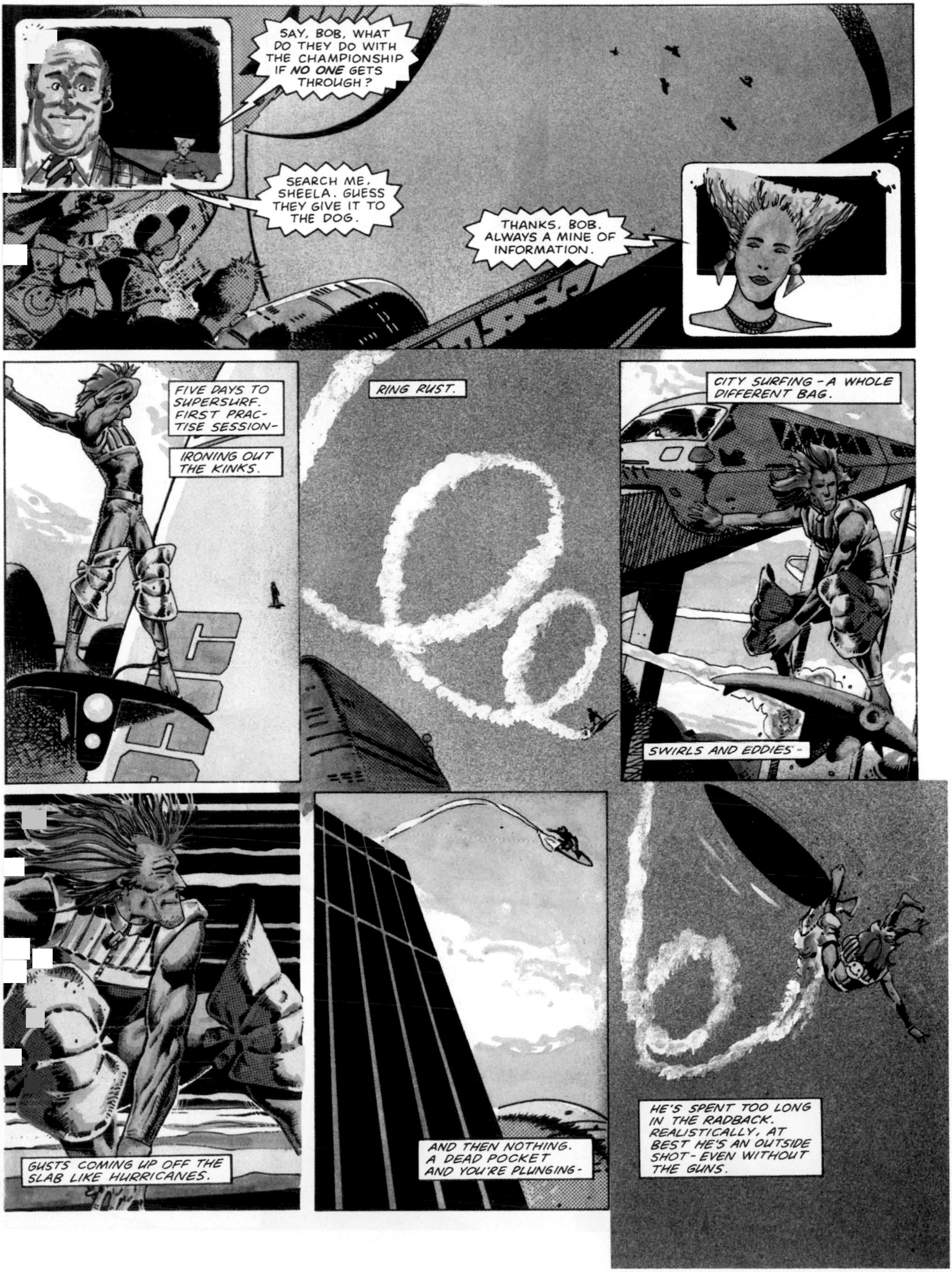
SAY, BOB, WHAT DO THEY DO WITH THE CHAMPIONSHIP IF NO ONE GETS THROUGH?
SEARCH ME, SHEELA. GUESS THEY GIVE IT TO THE DOG.
THANKS, BOB. ALWAYS A MINE OF INFORMATION.
FIVE DAYS TO SUPERSURF. FIRST PRAC-TISE SESSION-
IRONING OUT THE KINKS.
RING RUST.
CITY SURFING - A WHOLE DIFFERENT BAG.
SWIRLS AND EDDIES -
GUSTS COMING UP OFF THE SLAB LIKE HURRICANES.
AND THEN NOTHING. A DEAD POCKET AND YOU'RE PLUNGING -
HE'S SPENT TOO LONG IN THE RADBACK. REALISTICALLY, AT BEST HE'S AN OUTSIDE SHOT - EVEN WITHOUT THE GUNS.

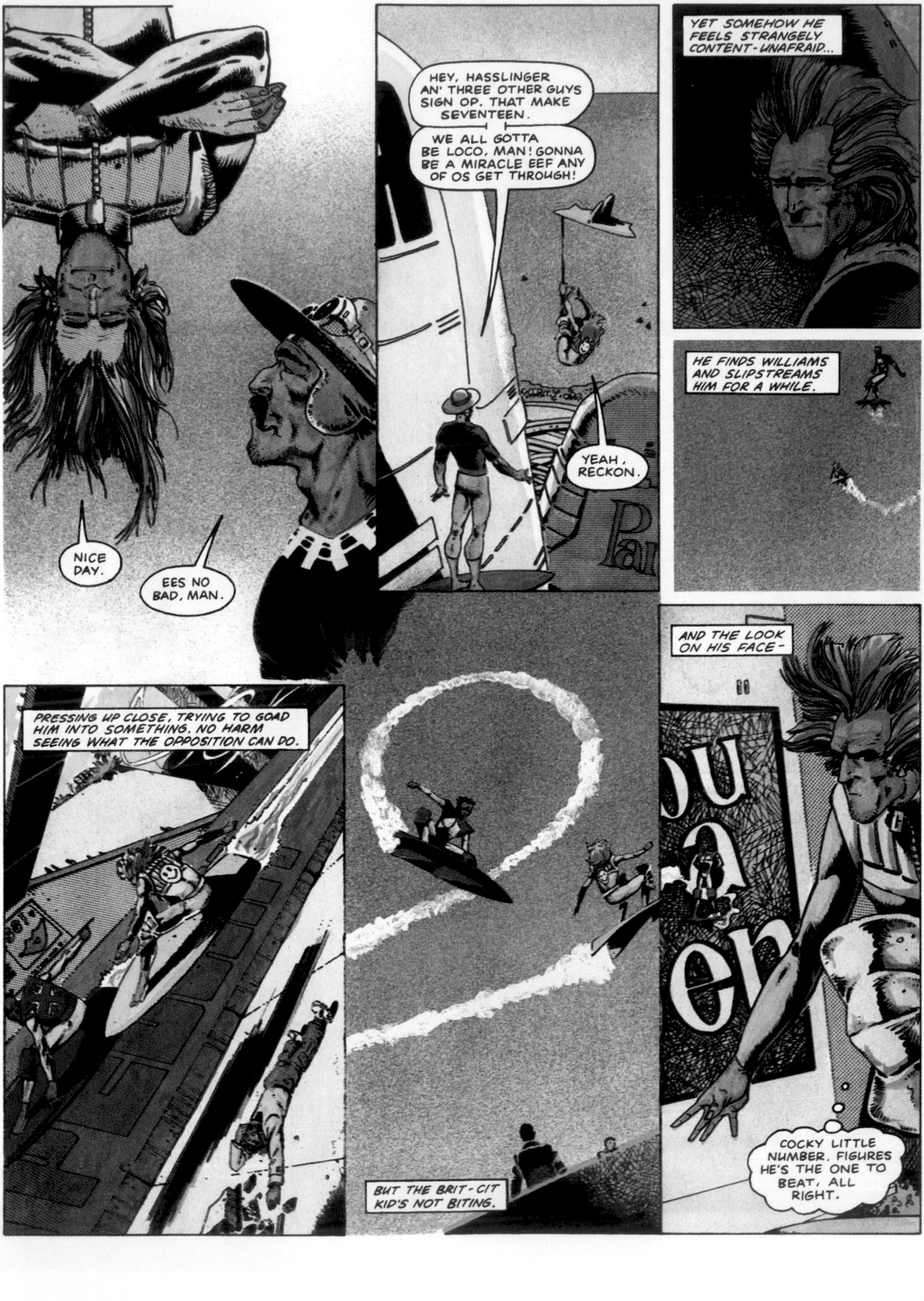
NICE DAY.
EES NO BAD, MAN.
HEY, HASSLINGER AN' THREE OTHER GUYS SIGN OP. THAT MAKE SEVENTEEN.
WE ALL GOTTA BE LOCO, MAN! GONNA BE A MIRACLE EEF ANY OF OS GET THROUGH!
YEAH, RECKON.
YET SOMEHOW HE FEELS STRANGELY CONTENT- UNAFRAID...
HE FINDS WILLIAMS AND SLIPSTREAMS HIM FOR A WHILE.
PRESSING UP CLOSE, TRYING TO GOAD HIM INTO SOMETHING. NO HARM SEEING WHAT THE OPPOSITION CAN DO.
BUT THE BRIT-CIT KID'S NOT BITING.
AND THE LOOK ON HIS FACE-
COCKY LITTLE NUMBER. FIGURES HE'S THE ONE TO BEAT, ALL RIGHT.

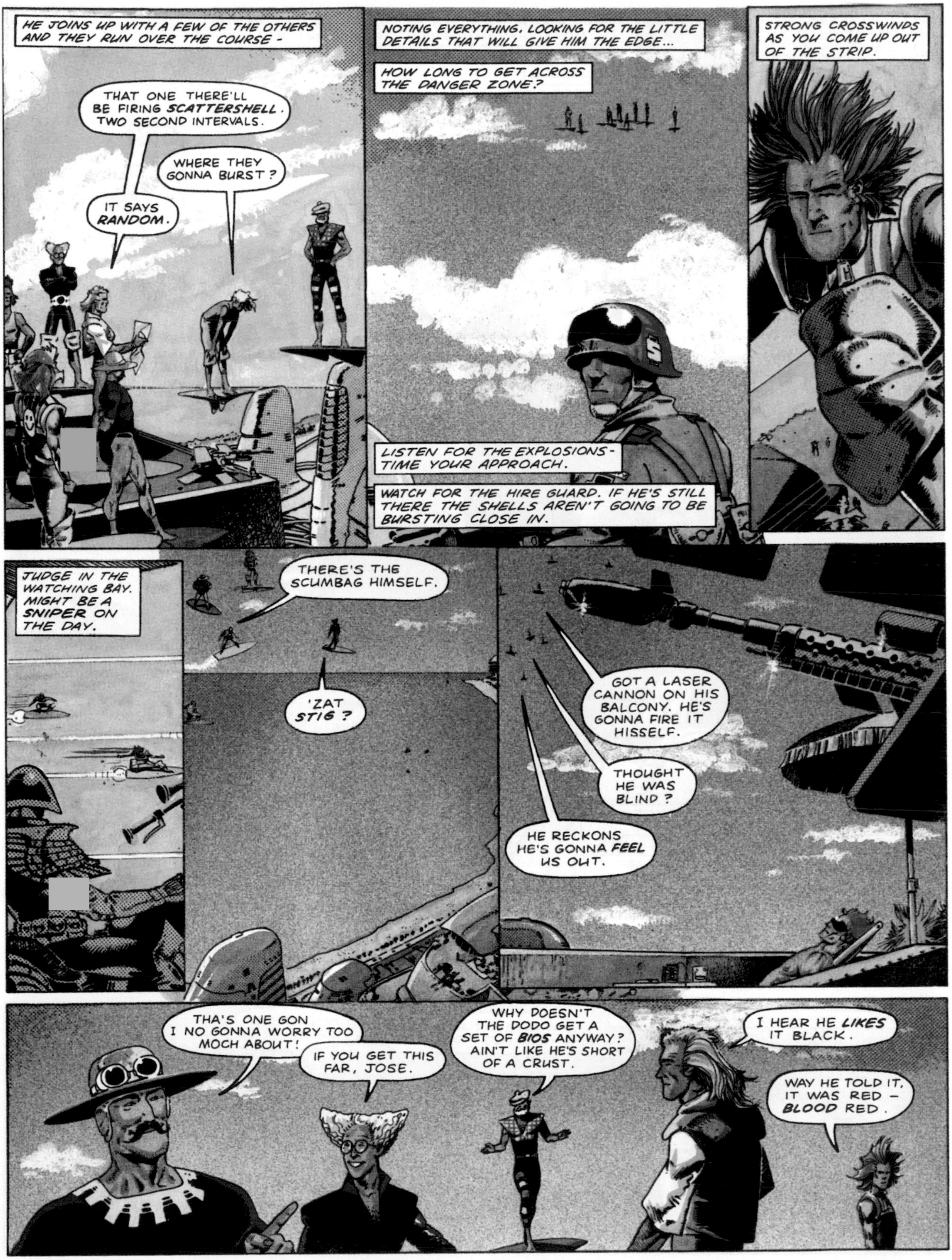

HE JOINS UP WITH A FEW OF THE OTHERS AND THEY RUN OVER THE COURSE -
THAT ONE THERE'LL BE FIRING SCATTERSHELL. TWO SECOND INTERVALS.
WHERE THEY GONNA BURST?
IT SAYS RANDOM.
NOTING EVERYTHING, LOOKING FOR THE LITTLE DETAILS THAT WILL GIVE HIM THE EDGE...
HOW LONG TO GET ACROSS THE DANGER ZONE?
LISTEN FOR THE EXPLOSIONS - TIME YOUR APPROACH.
WATCH FOR THE HIRE GUARD. IF HE'S STILL THERE THE SHELLS AREN'T GOING TO BE BURSTING CLOSE IN.
STRONG CROSSWINDS AS YOU COME UP OUT OF THE STRIP.
JUDGE IN THE WATCHING BAY. MIGHT BE A SNIPER ON THE DAY.
THERE'S THE SCUMBAG HIMSELF.
'ZAT STIG?
GOT A LASER CANNON ON HIS BALCONY. HE'S GONNA FIRE IT HISSELF.
THOUGHT HE WAS BLIND?
HE RECKONS HE'S GONNA FEEL US OUT.
THA'S ONE GON I NO GONNA WORRY TOO MOCH ABOUT!
IF YOU GET THIS FAR, JOSE.
WHY DOESN'T THE DODO GET A SET OF BIOS ANYWAY? AIN'T LIKE HE'S SHORT OF A CRUST.
I HEAR HE LIKES IT BLACK.
WAY HE TOLD IT, IT WAS RED - BLOOD RED.

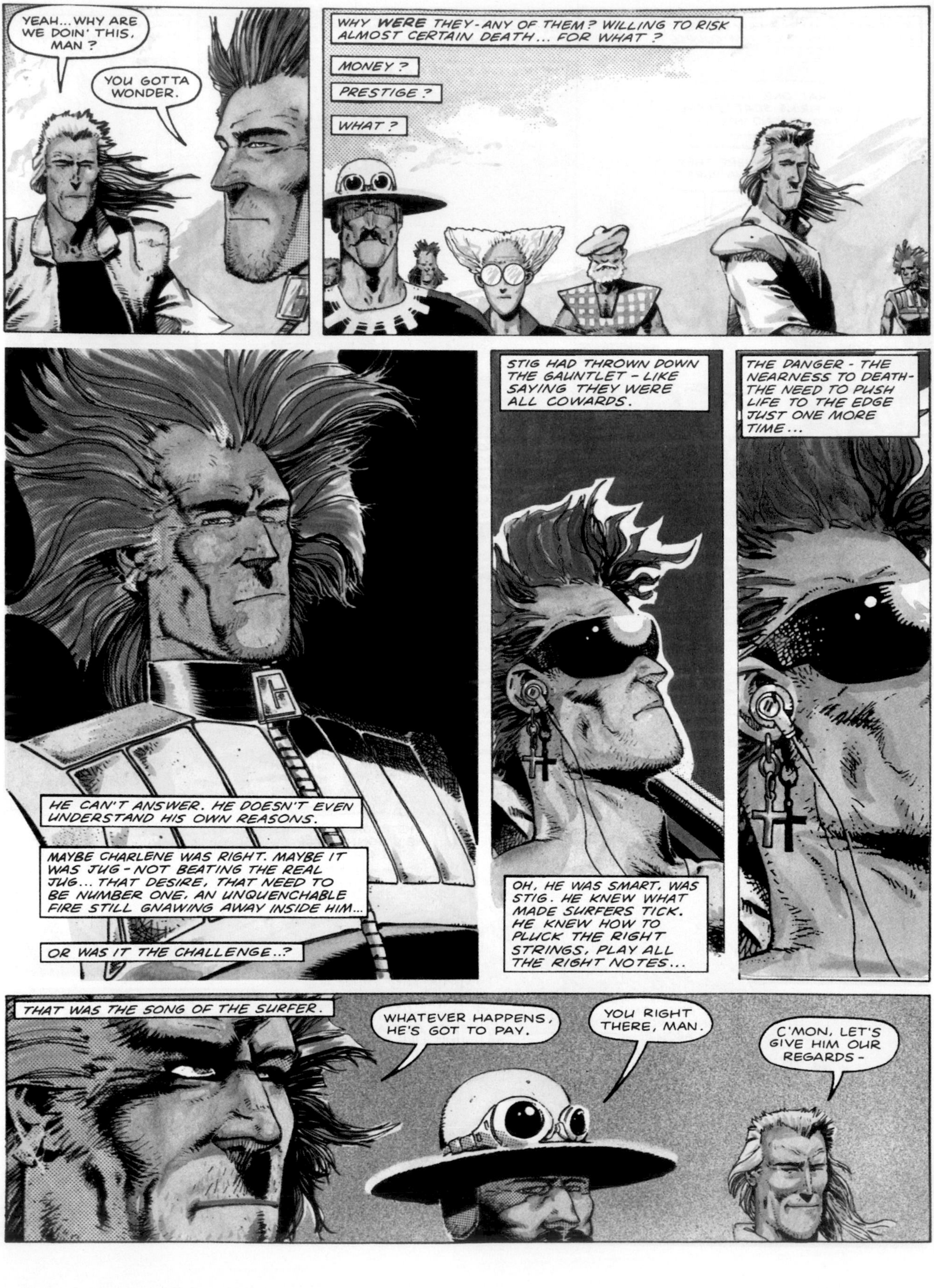
YEAH... WHY ARE WE DOIN' THIS, MAN ?
YOU GOTTA WONDER.
WHY WERE THEY - ANY OF THEM? WILLING TO RISK ALMOST CERTAIN DEATH... FOR WHAT ?
MONEY ?
PRESTIGE ?
WHAT ?
HE CAN'T ANSWER. HE DOESN'T EVEN UNDERSTAND HIS OWN REASONS.
MAYBE CHARLENE WAS RIGHT. MAYBE IT WAS JUG - NOT BEATING THE REAL JUG... THAT DESIRE, THAT NEED TO BE NUMBER ONE, AN UNQUENCHABLE FIRE STILL GNAWING AWAY INSIDE HIM...
OR WAS IT THE CHALLENGE..?
STIG HAD THROWN DOWN THE GAUNTLET - LIKE SAYING THEY WERE ALL COWARDS.
OH, HE WAS SMART, WAS STIG. HE KNEW WHAT MADE SURFERS TICK. HE KNEW HOW TO PLUCK THE RIGHT STRINGS, PLAY ALL THE RIGHT NOTES...
THE DANGER - THE NEARNESS TO DEATH - THE NEED TO PUSH LIFE TO THE EDGE JUST ONE MORE TIME...
THAT WAS THE SONG OF THE SURFER.
WHATEVER HAPPENS, HE'S GOT TO PAY.
YOU RIGHT THERE, MAN.
C'MON, LET'S GIVE HIM OUR REGARDS -

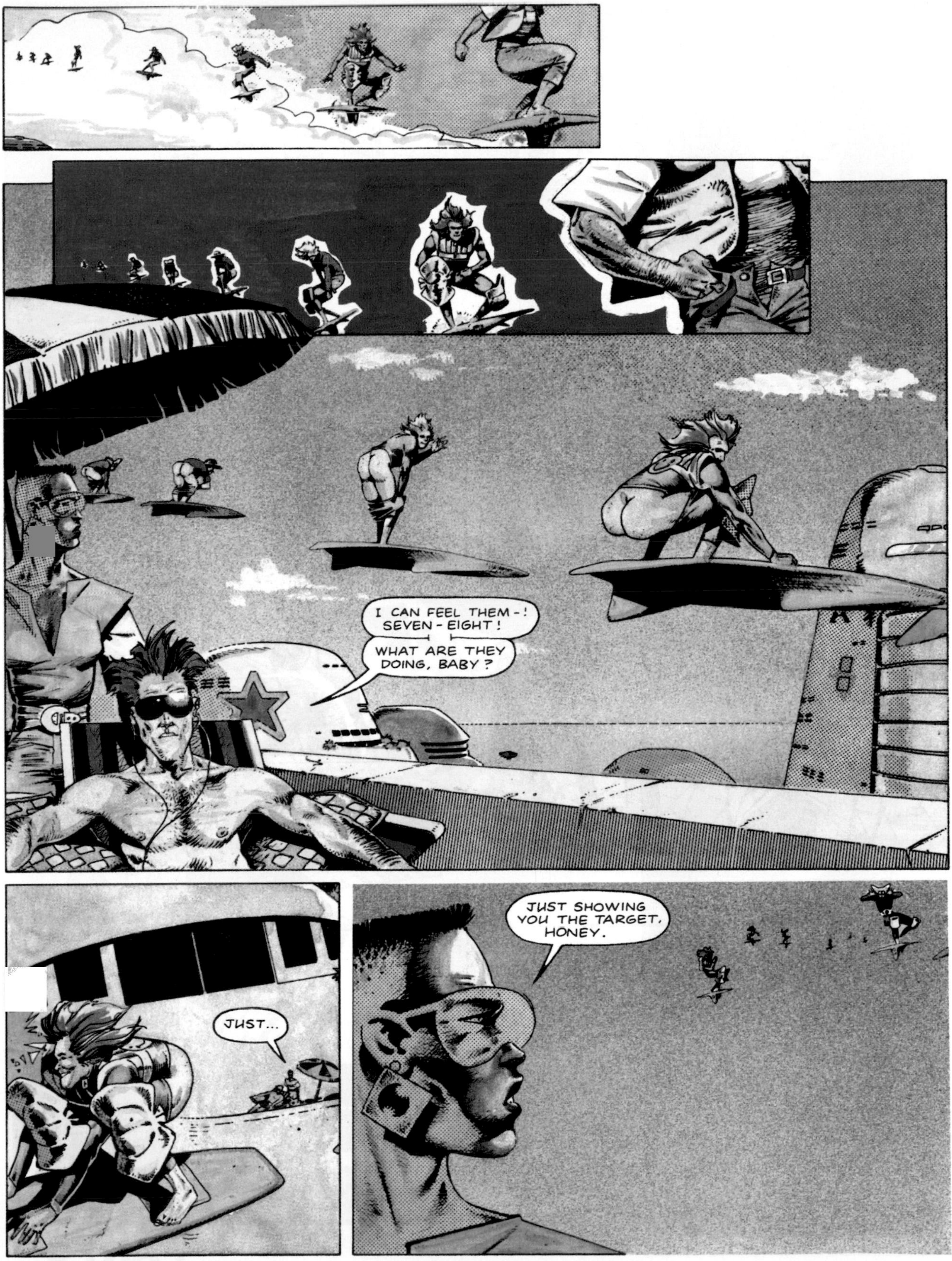
I CAN FEEL THEM-! SEVEN-EIGHT!
WHAT ARE THEY DOING, BABY?
JUST...
JUST SHOWING YOU THE TARGET, HONEY.

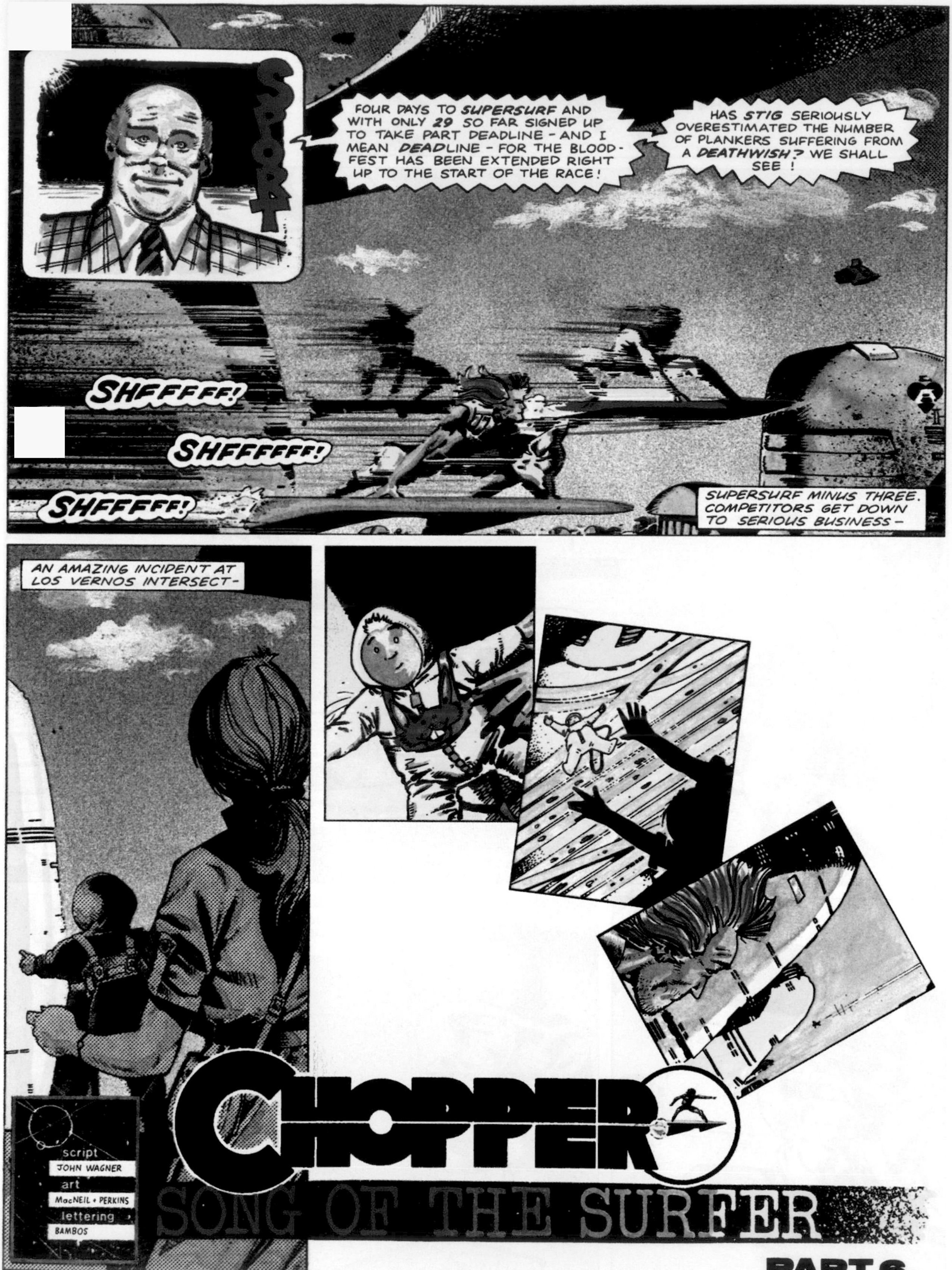
SPORT
FOUR DAYS TO SUPERSURF AND WITH ONLY 29 SO FAR SIGNED UP TO TAKE PART DEADLINE - AND I MEAN DEADLINE - FOR THE BLOOD-FEST HAS BEEN EXTENDED RIGHT UP TO THE START OF THE RACE!
HAS STIG SERIOUSLY OVERESTIMATED THE NUMBER OF PLANKERS SUFFERING FROM A DEATHWISH? WE SHALL SEE!
SHFFFFFF!
SHFFFFFFF!
SHFFFFFF!
SUPERSURF MINUS THREE. COMPETITORS GET DOWN TO SERIOUS BUSINESS-
AN AMAZING INCIDENT AT LOS VERNOS INTERSECT-
CHOPPER
SONG OF THE SURFER
script
JOHN WAGNER
art
MacNEIL + PERKINS
lettering
BAMBOS

PART 6

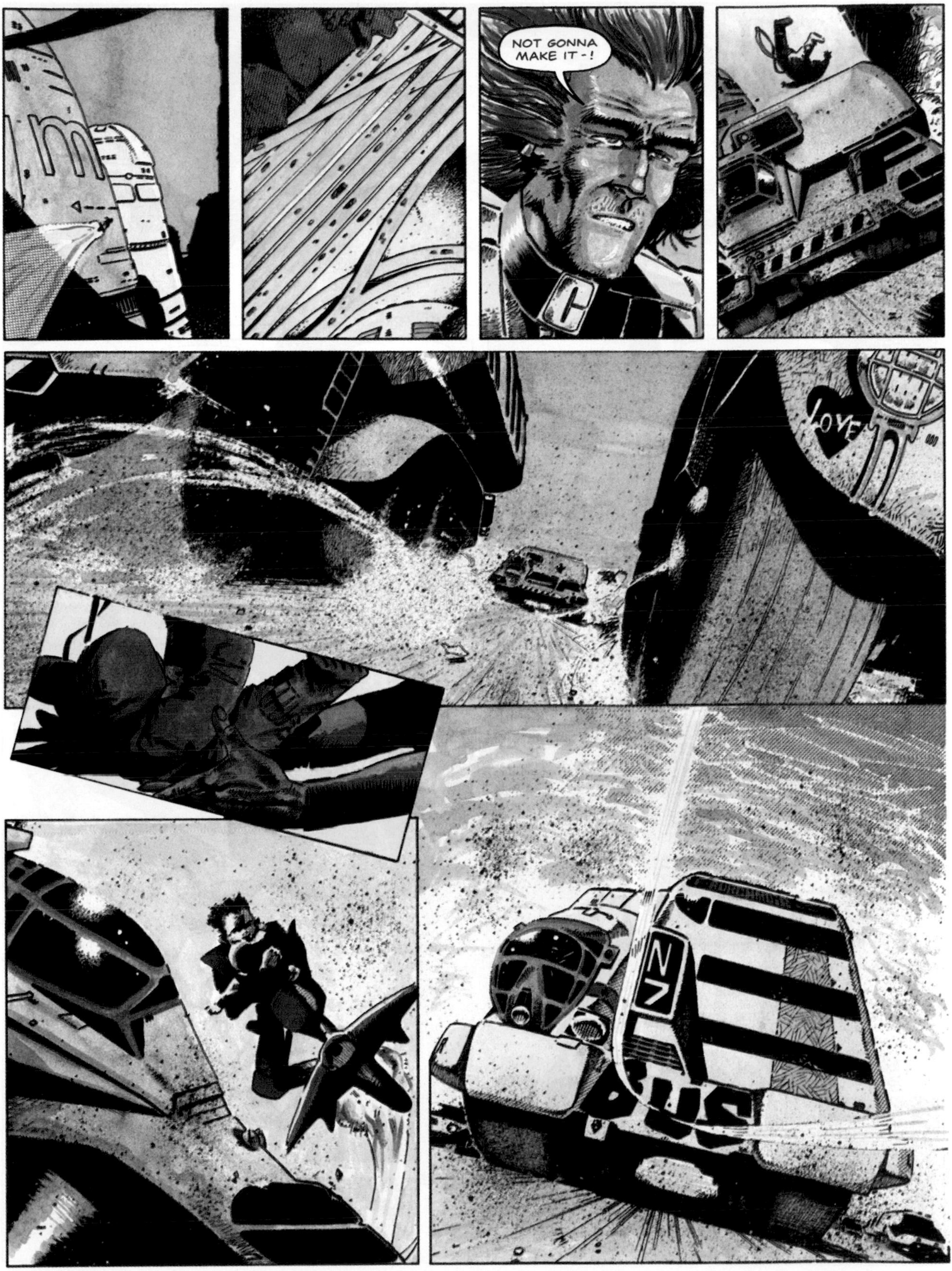
NOT GONNA MAKE IT -!
LOVE
N7
BUS

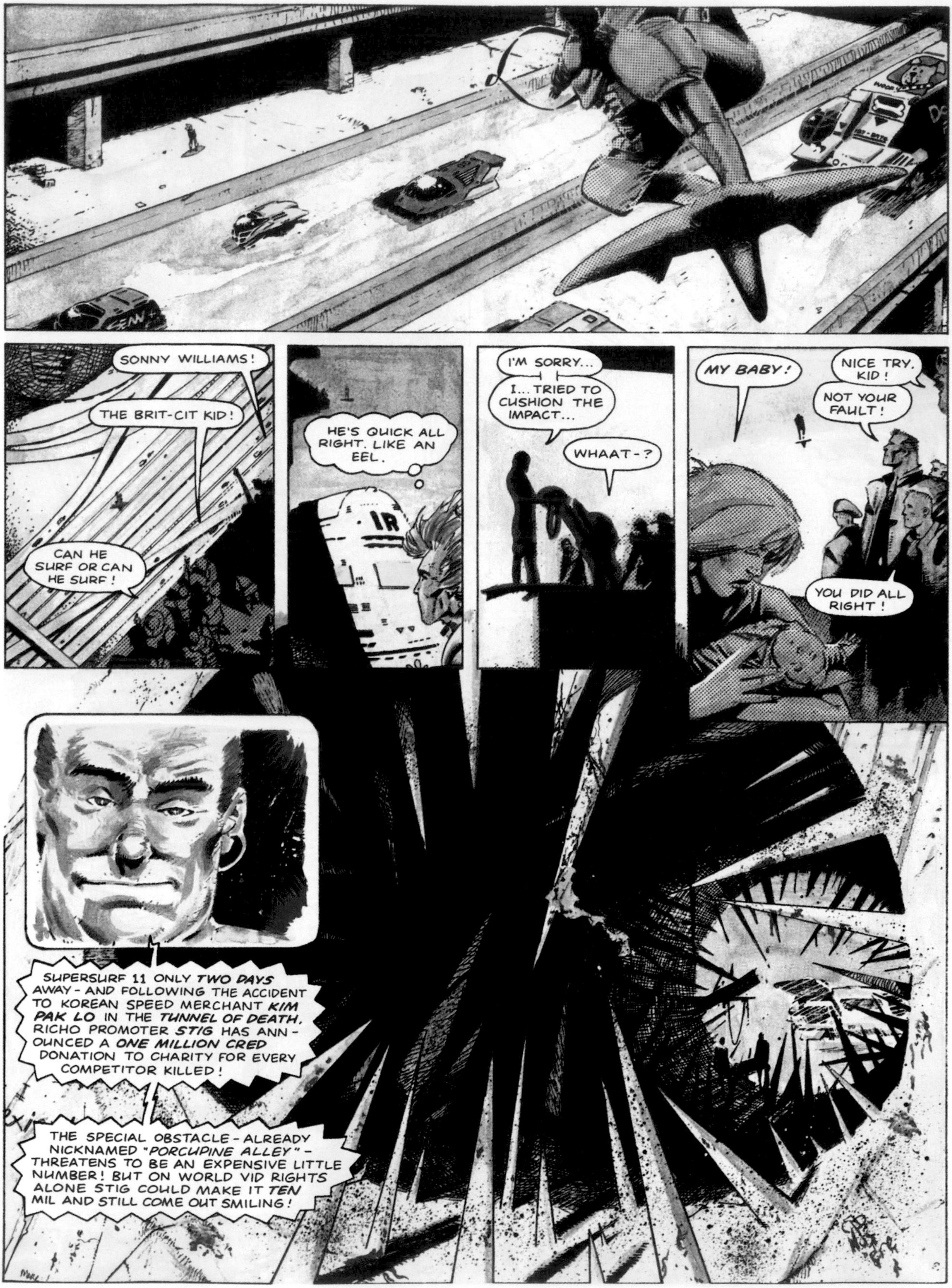
SONNY WILLIAMS!
THE BRIT-CIT KID!
CAN HE SURF OR CAN HE SURF!
HE'S QUICK ALL RIGHT. LIKE AN EEL.
I'M SORRY...
I... TRIED TO CUSHION THE IMPACT...
WHAAT-?
MY BABY!
NICE TRY, KID!
NOT YOUR FAULT!
YOU DID ALL RIGHT!
SUPERSURF 11 ONLY TWO DAYS AWAY - AND FOLLOWING THE ACCIDENT TO KOREAN SPEED MERCHANT KIM PAK LO IN THE TUNNEL OF DEATH, RICHO PROMOTER STIG HAS ANNOUNCED A ONE MILLION CRED DONATION TO CHARITY FOR EVERY COMPETITOR KILLED!
THE SPECIAL OBSTACLE - ALREADY NICKNAMED "PORCUPINE ALLEY" - THREATENS TO BE AN EXPENSIVE LITTLE NUMBER! BUT ON WORLD VID RIGHTS ALONE STIG COULD MAKE IT TEN MIL AND STILL COME OUT SMILING!

JUG MCKENZIE, PEOPLE ARE SAYING YOU'RE A YELLOWBELLY, THAT YOU HAVEN'T GOT THE *GUTS* FOR A REAL FIGHT —

DRONGOS CAN SAY WHAT THEY LIKE — I AIN'T BROWNIN' ME DUFFIES.

NOW JACK OFF BEFORE I OICK YA, YER GRUBBY BAS —

HE'S NOT WORTH IT, JUG!

AND ON THE *DAY BEFORE* THE BIG OFF THE NUMBER OF COMPETITORS HAS NOW RISEN TO *34*, INCLUDING TEXAS CITY'S *DALLAS HALL*, THIRD IN LAST YEAR'S SUPERSURF!

CHOPPER — WILLIAMS — HASSLINGER — HALL — WE'VE GOT A RACE ALL RIGHT! AND THE MESSAGE FROM THE SURFING WORLD IS: JUG MCKENZIE — WE DON'T NEED YOU!

TWELVE HOURS TO SUPERSURF —

WHAT'S GOIN' ON?

GUESS!

AW, COME ON, CHARLENE —

I FIGURED YOU'D COME TO YOUR SENSES. I SHOULDA KNOWN BETTER! WELL, IF YOU THINK I'M GOING TO HANG AROUND AND WATCH YOU COMMIT SUICIDE YOU'RE WAY WRONG!

I LOVE YOU, CHOPPER. I'M ASKING YOU — *BEGGING* YOU, ONE LAST TIME — GIVE IT UP!

YOU KNOW I *CAN'T*...

WELL, SCREW YOU, MATE!

CHARLENE!

SCUMBAG! I DON'T MATTER A DAMN TO YOU, DO I? YOU DON'T CARE ABOUT ANYTHING EXCEPT YOUR STUPID RACE!

THAT'S NOT TRUE—

HAVE YOU EVEN *THOUGHT* WHAT I'M GOING TO DO WHEN YOU'RE GONE? DO YOU KNOW WHAT THIS IS GOING TO DO TO ME?

YOU SAY YOU LOVE ME BUT YOU DON'T! YOU CAN'T OR YOU WOULDN'T DO IT!

WELL, I WANT YOU TO KNOW YOU'RE NOT JUST KILLING YOURSELF OUT THERE..!

SLAM!

CHARLENE—!

DAMN!

DAMN! DAMN! DAMN!

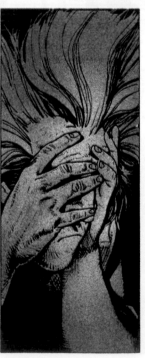

SNIK!

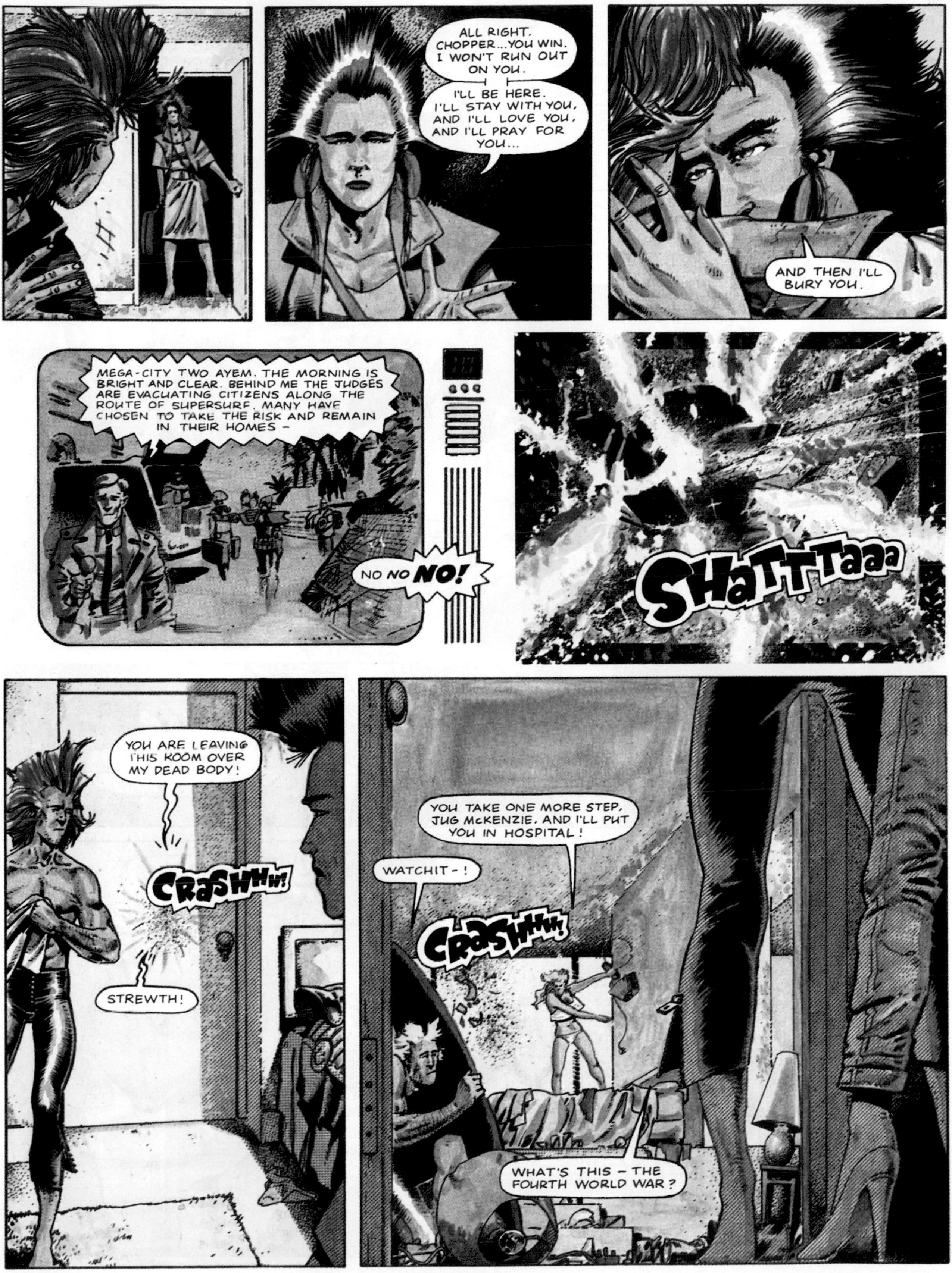
ALL RIGHT. CHOPPER...YOU WIN. I WON'T RUN OUT ON YOU.
I'LL BE HERE. I'LL STAY WITH YOU, AND I'LL LOVE YOU, AND I'LL PRAY FOR YOU...
AND THEN I'LL BURY YOU.
MEGA-CITY TWO AYEM. THE MORNING IS BRIGHT AND CLEAR. BEHIND ME THE JUDGES ARE EVACUATING CITIZENS ALONG THE ROUTE OF SUPERSURF. MANY HAVE CHOSEN TO TAKE THE RISK AND REMAIN IN THEIR HOMES –
NO NO NO!
SHATTTaaa
YOU ARE LEAVING THIS ROOM OVER MY DEAD BODY!
CRASHHH!
STREWTH!
YOU TAKE ONE MORE STEP, JUG McKENZIE, AND I'LL PUT YOU IN HOSPITAL!
WATCHIT –!
CRASHHHH!
WHAT'S THIS – THE FOURTH WORLD WAR?

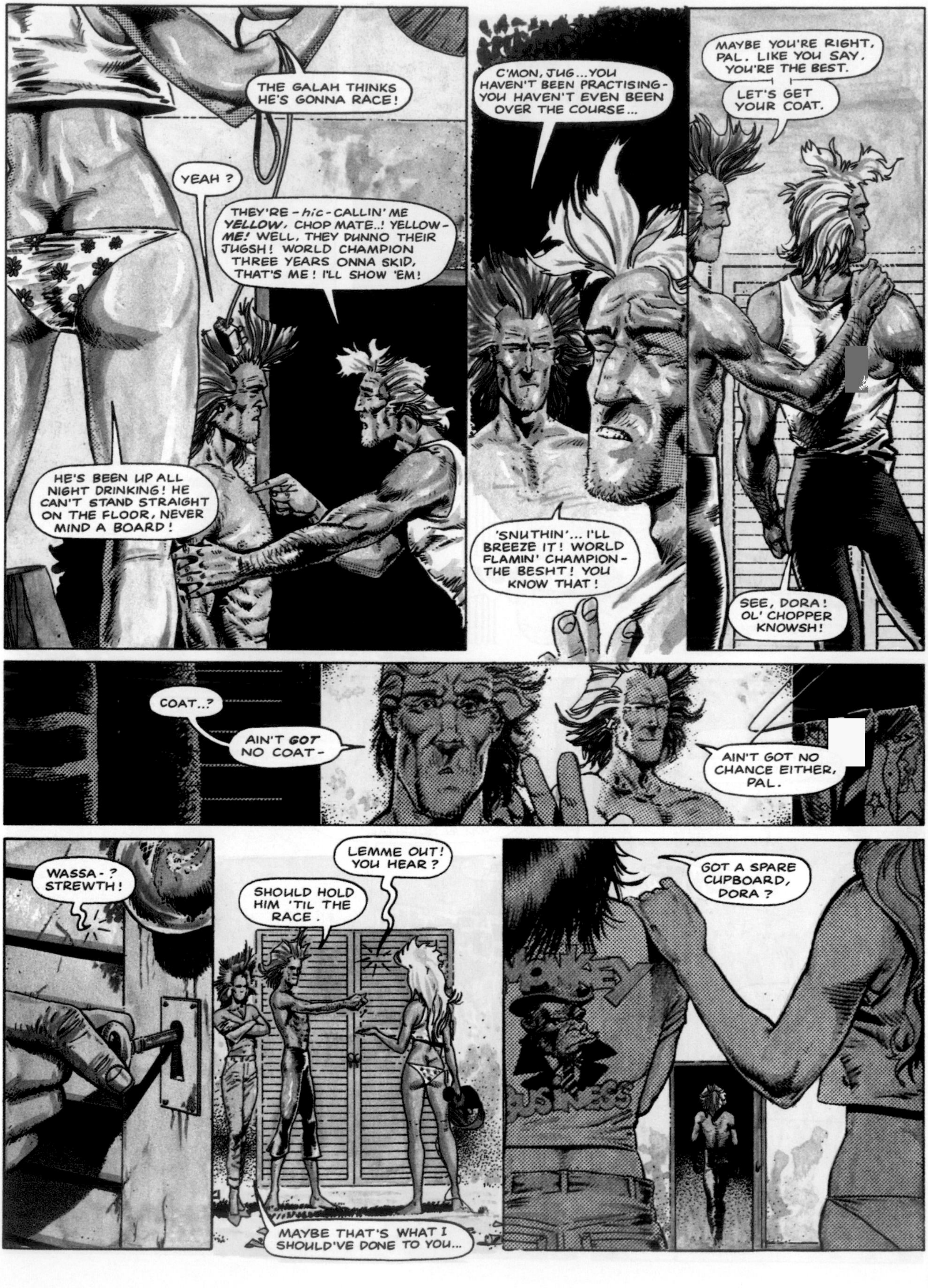
THE GALAH THINKS HE'S GONNA RACE!
YEAH ?
THEY'RE - hic - CALLIN' ME YELLOW, CHOP MATE..! YELLOW - ME! WELL, THEY DUNNO THEIR JUGSH! WORLD CHAMPION THREE YEARS ONNA SKID, THAT'S ME! I'LL SHOW 'EM!
HE'S BEEN UP ALL NIGHT DRINKING! HE CAN'T STAND STRAIGHT ON THE FLOOR, NEVER MIND A BOARD!
C'MON, JUG... YOU HAVEN'T BEEN PRACTISING - YOU HAVEN'T EVEN BEEN OVER THE COURSE...
'SNUTHIN'... I'LL BREEZE IT! WORLD FLAMIN' CHAMPION - THE BESHT! YOU KNOW THAT!
MAYBE YOU'RE RIGHT, PAL. LIKE YOU SAY, YOU'RE THE BEST.
LET'S GET YOUR COAT.
SEE, DORA! OL' CHOPPER KNOWSH!
COAT..?
AIN'T GOT NO COAT -
AIN'T GOT NO CHANCE EITHER, PAL.
WASSA - ? STREWTH!
LEMME OUT! YOU HEAR ?
SHOULD HOLD HIM 'TIL THE RACE.
MAYBE THAT'S WHAT I SHOULD'VE DONE TO YOU...
GOT A SPARE CUPBOARD, DORA ?

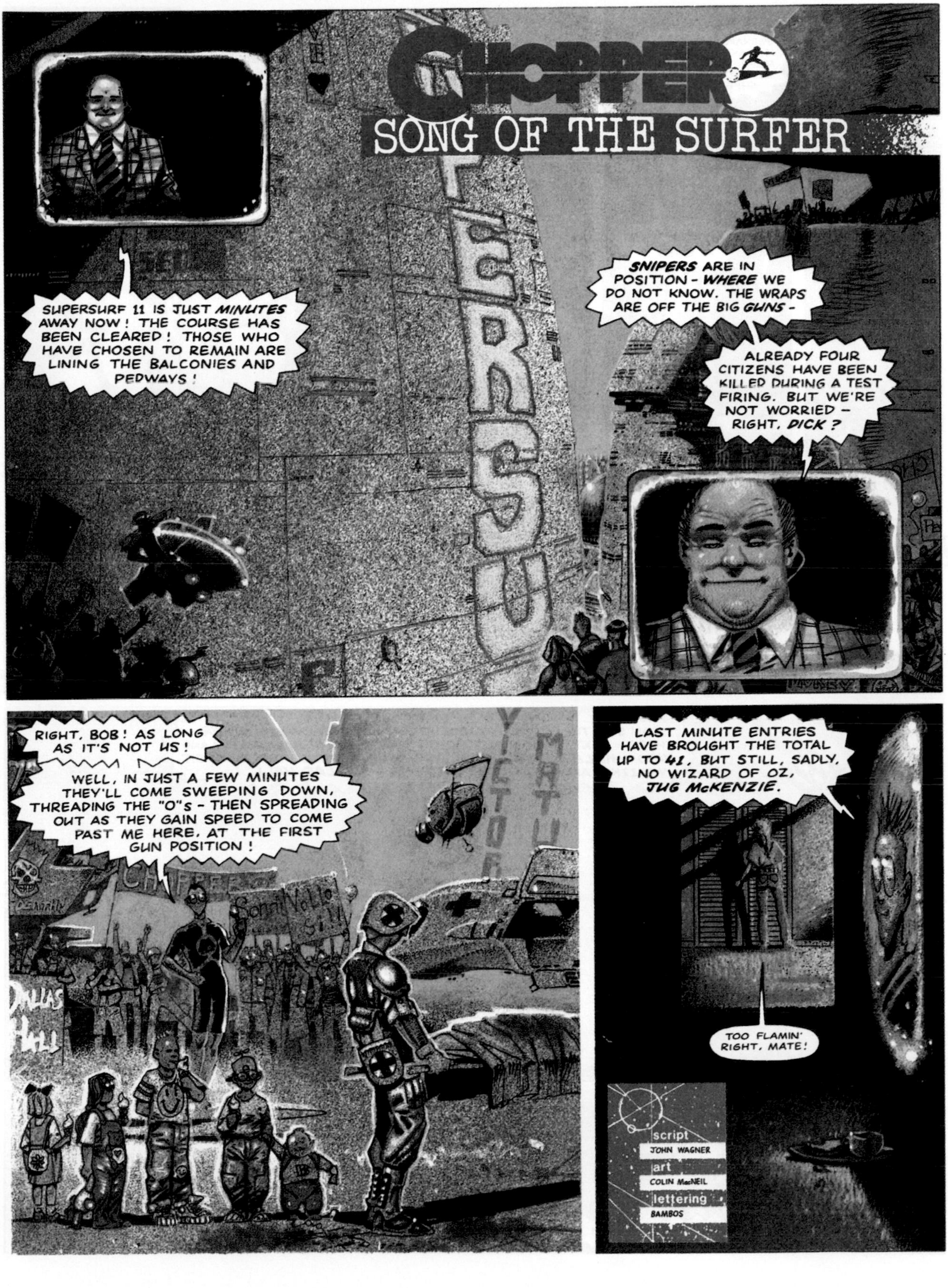
CHOPPER
SONG OF THE SURFER
SUPERSURF 11 IS JUST MINUTES AWAY NOW! THE COURSE HAS BEEN CLEARED! THOSE WHO HAVE CHOSEN TO REMAIN ARE LINING THE BALCONIES AND PEDWAYS!
SNIPERS ARE IN POSITION - WHERE WE DO NOT KNOW. THE WRAPS ARE OFF THE BIG GUNS -
ALREADY FOUR CITIZENS HAVE BEEN KILLED DURING A TEST FIRING. BUT WE'RE NOT WORRIED - RIGHT, DICK?
RIGHT, BOB! AS LONG AS IT'S NOT US!
WELL, IN JUST A FEW MINUTES THEY'LL COME SWEEPING DOWN, THREADING THE "O"s - THEN SPREADING OUT AS THEY GAIN SPEED TO COME PAST ME HERE, AT THE FIRST GUN POSITION!
LAST MINUTE ENTRIES HAVE BROUGHT THE TOTAL UP TO 41, BUT STILL, SADLY, NO WIZARD OF OZ, JUG McKENZIE.
TOO FLAMIN' RIGHT, MATE!
script
JOHN WAGNER
art
COLIN MacNEIL
lettering
BAMBOS

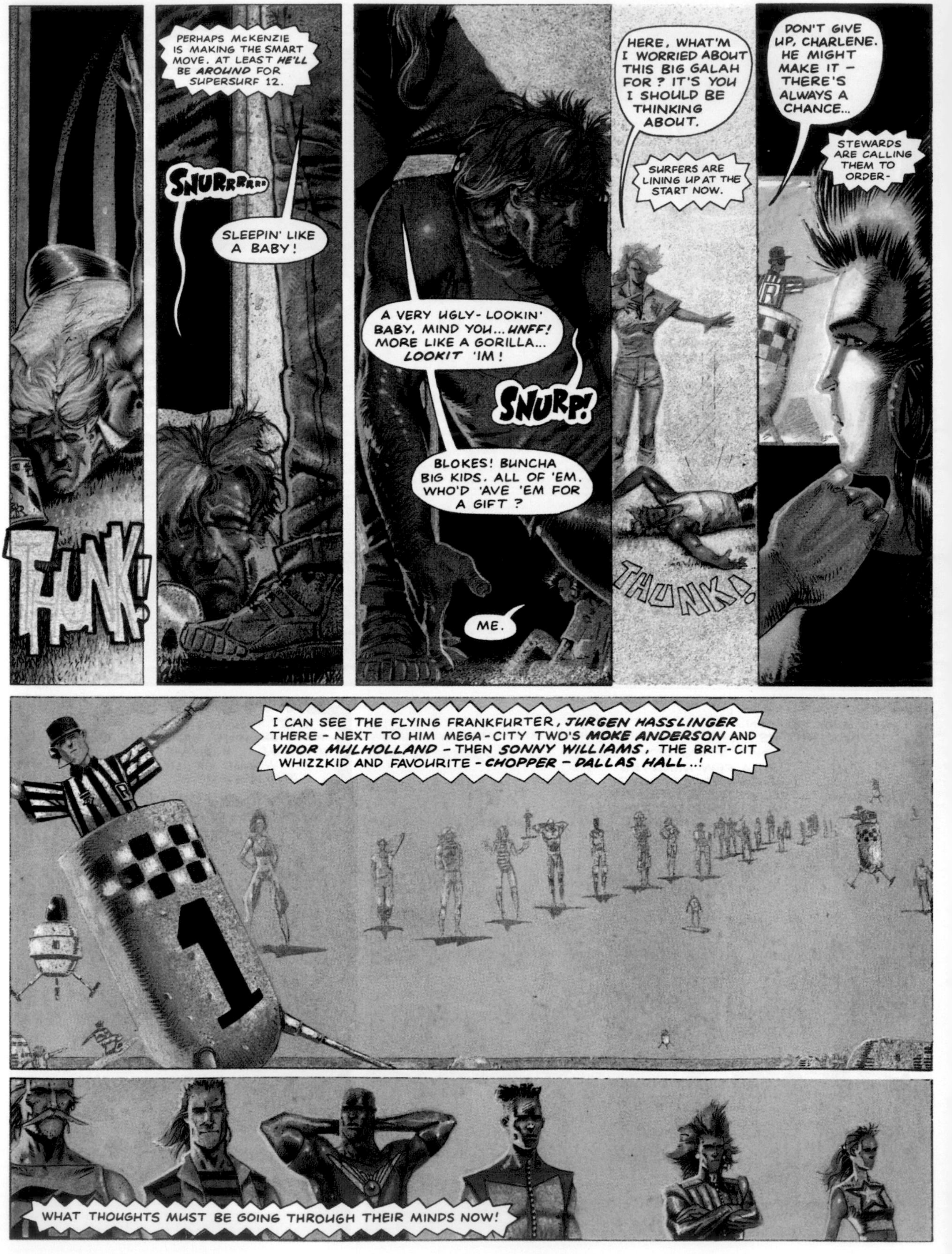
THUNK!
PERHAPS McKENZIE IS MAKING THE SMART MOVE. AT LEAST HE'LL BE AROUND FOR SUPERSURF 12.
SNURRRRRR
SLEEPIN' LIKE A BABY!
A VERY UGLY-LOOKIN' BABY, MIND YOU... UNFF! MORE LIKE A GORILLA... LOOKIT 'IM!
SNURP!
BLOKES! BUNCHA BIG KIDS. ALL OF 'EM. WHO'D 'AVE 'EM FOR A GIFT?
ME.
HERE, WHAT'M I WORRIED ABOUT THIS BIG GALAH FOR? IT'S YOU I SHOULD BE THINKING ABOUT.
SURFERS ARE LINING UP AT THE START NOW.
THUNK!
DON'T GIVE UP, CHARLENE. HE MIGHT MAKE IT — THERE'S ALWAYS A CHANCE...
STEWARDS ARE CALLING THEM TO ORDER-
I CAN SEE THE FLYING FRANKFURTER, JURGEN HASSLINGER THERE - NEXT TO HIM MEGA-CITY TWO'S MOKE ANDERSON AND VIDOR MULHOLLAND - THEN SONNY WILLIAMS, THE BRIT-CIT WHIZZKID AND FAVOURITE - CHOPPER - DALLAS HALL..!
1
WHAT THOUGHTS MUST BE GOING THROUGH THEIR MINDS NOW!

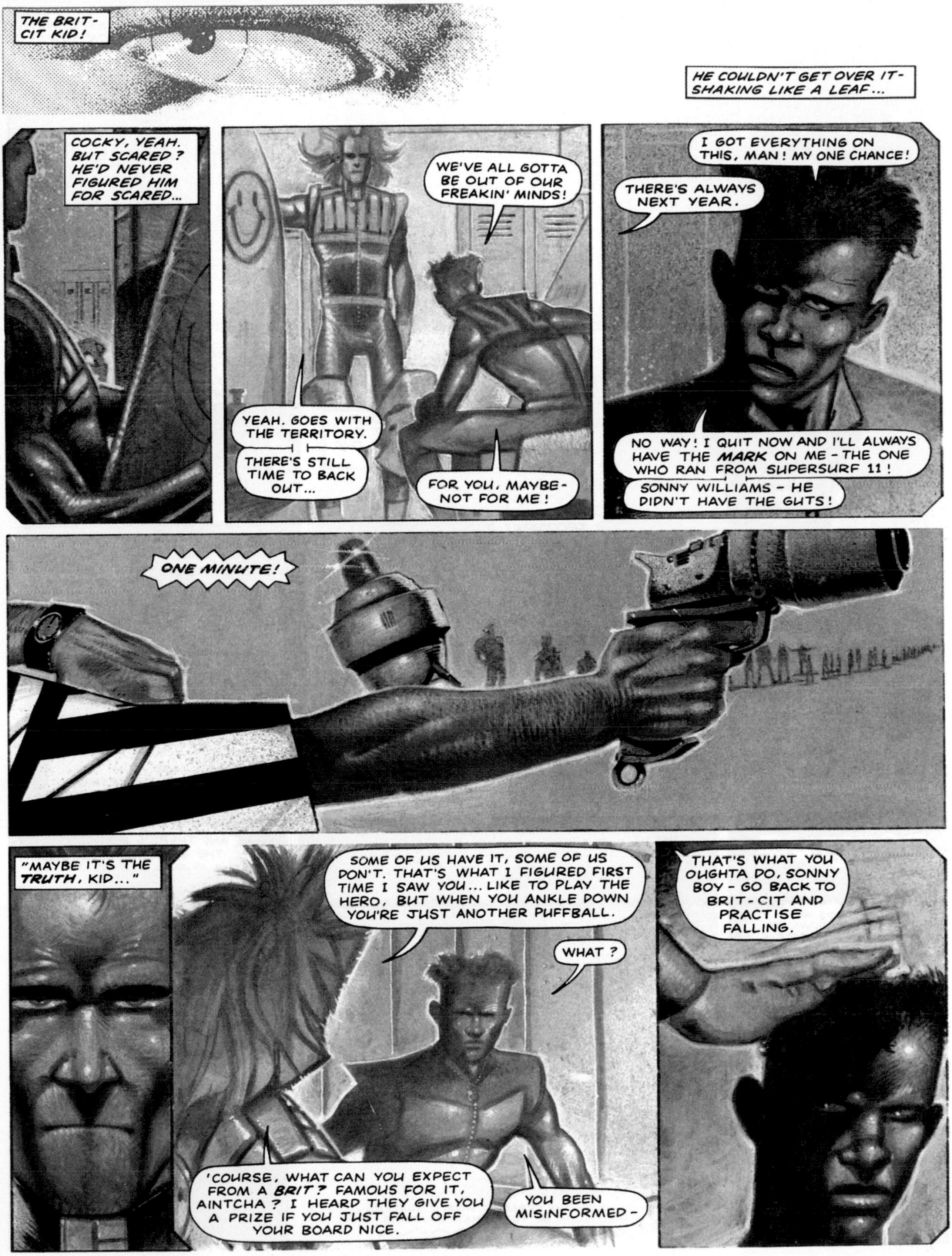
THE BRIT-CIT KID!
HE COULDN'T GET OVER IT-SHAKING LIKE A LEAF...
COCKY, YEAH. BUT SCARED? HE'D NEVER FIGURED HIM FOR SCARED...
WE'VE ALL GOTTA BE OUT OF OUR FREAKIN' MINDS!
YEAH. GOES WITH THE TERRITORY.
THERE'S STILL TIME TO BACK OUT...
FOR YOU, MAYBE-NOT FOR ME!
I GOT EVERYTHING ON THIS, MAN! MY ONE CHANCE!
THERE'S ALWAYS NEXT YEAR.
NO WAY! I QUIT NOW AND I'LL ALWAYS HAVE THE MARK ON ME - THE ONE WHO RAN FROM SUPERSURF 11!
SONNY WILLIAMS - HE DIDN'T HAVE THE GUTS!
ONE MINUTE!
"MAYBE IT'S THE TRUTH, KID..."
SOME OF US HAVE IT, SOME OF US DON'T. THAT'S WHAT I FIGURED FIRST TIME I SAW YOU... LIKE TO PLAY THE HERO, BUT WHEN YOU ANKLE DOWN YOU'RE JUST ANOTHER PUFFBALL.
WHAT?
'COURSE, WHAT CAN YOU EXPECT FROM A BRIT? FAMOUS FOR IT, AINTCHA? I HEARD THEY GIVE YOU A PRIZE IF YOU JUST FALL OFF YOUR BOARD NICE.
YOU BEEN MISINFORMED-
THAT'S WHAT YOU OUGHTA DO, SONNY BOY - GO BACK TO BRIT-CIT AND PRACTISE FALLING.

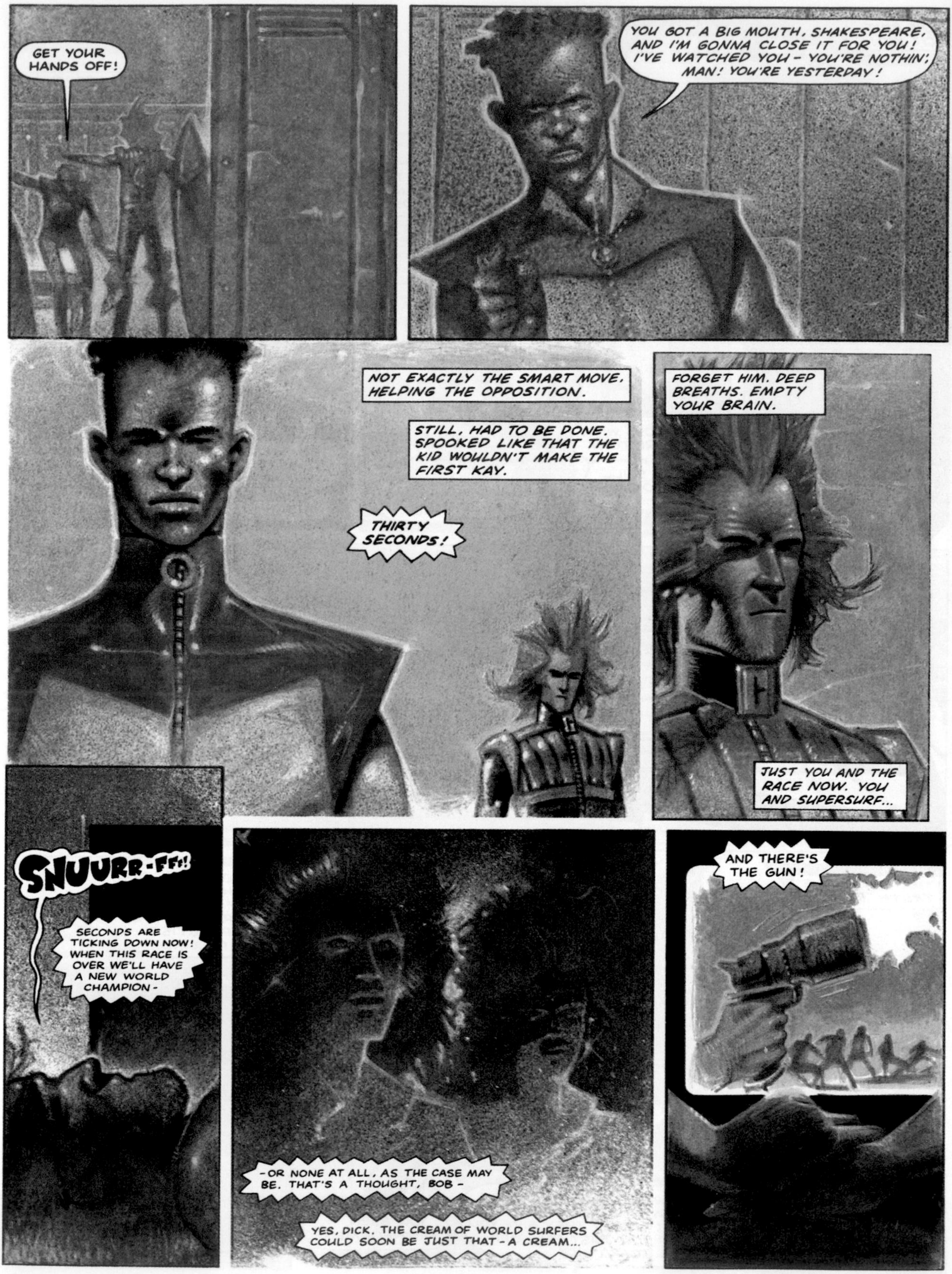
GET YOUR HANDS OFF!
YOU GOT A BIG MOUTH, SHAKESPEARE, AND I'M GONNA CLOSE IT FOR YOU! I'VE WATCHED YOU - YOU'RE NOTHIN', MAN! YOU'RE YESTERDAY!
NOT EXACTLY THE SMART MOVE, HELPING THE OPPOSITION.
STILL, HAD TO BE DONE. SPOOKED LIKE THAT THE KID WOULDN'T MAKE THE FIRST KAY.
THIRTY SECONDS!
FORGET HIM. DEEP BREATHS. EMPTY YOUR BRAIN.
JUST YOU AND THE RACE NOW. YOU AND SUPERSURF...
SNUURR-FFT!
SECONDS ARE TICKING DOWN NOW! WHEN THIS RACE IS OVER WE'LL HAVE A NEW WORLD CHAMPION -
-OR NONE AT ALL, AS THE CASE MAY BE. THAT'S A THOUGHT, BOB -
YES, DICK. THE CREAM OF WORLD SURFERS COULD SOON BE JUST THAT - A CREAM...
AND THERE'S THE GUN!

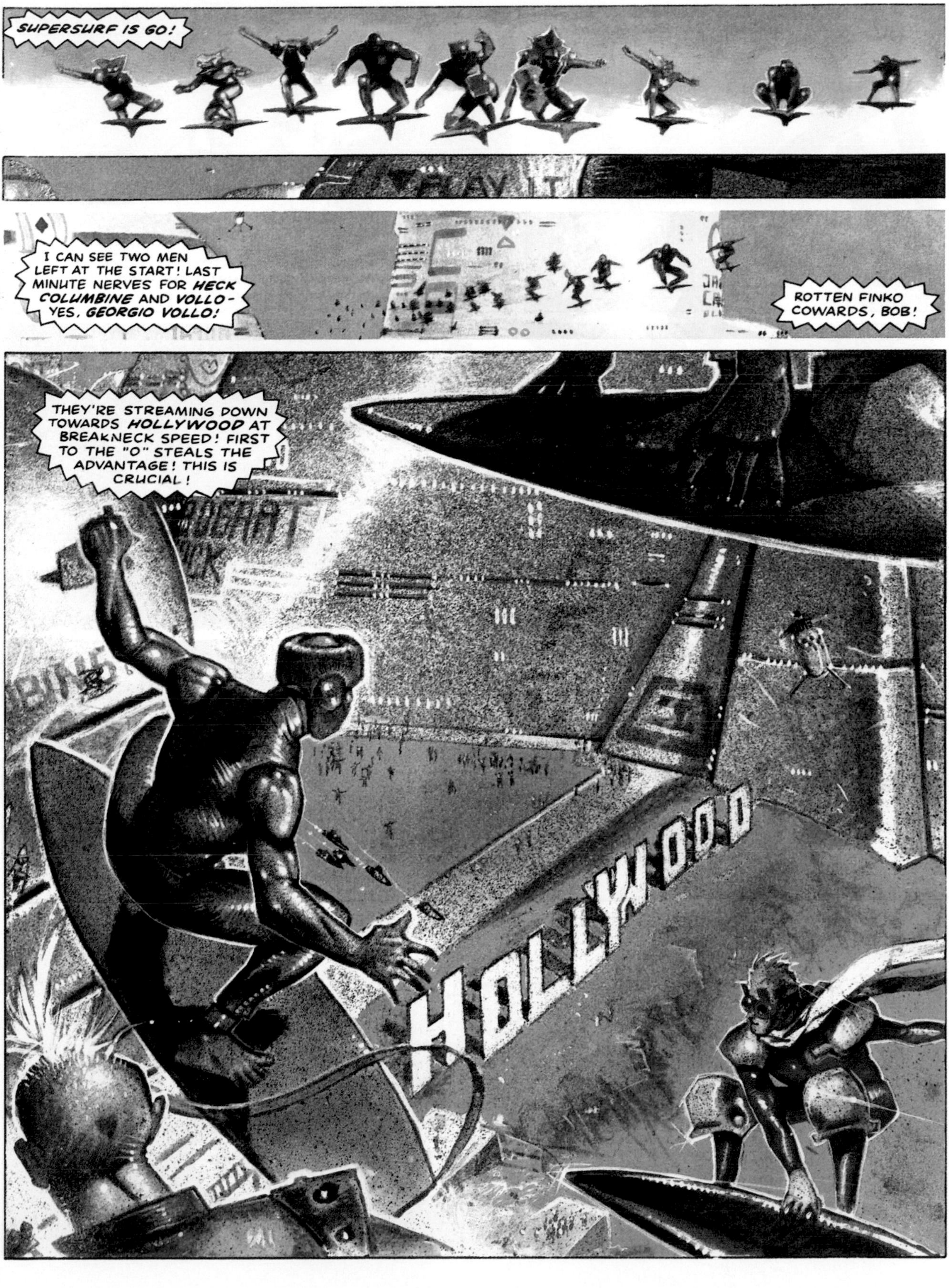
SUPERSURF IS GO!
I CAN SEE TWO MEN LEFT AT THE START! LAST MINUTE NERVES FOR HECK COLUMBINE AND VOLLO- YES, GEORGIO VOLLO!
ROTTEN FINKO COWARDS, BOB!
THEY'RE STREAMING DOWN TOWARDS HOLLYWOOD AT BREAKNECK SPEED! FIRST TO THE "O" STEALS THE ADVANTAGE! THIS IS CRUCIAL!
HOLLYWOOD

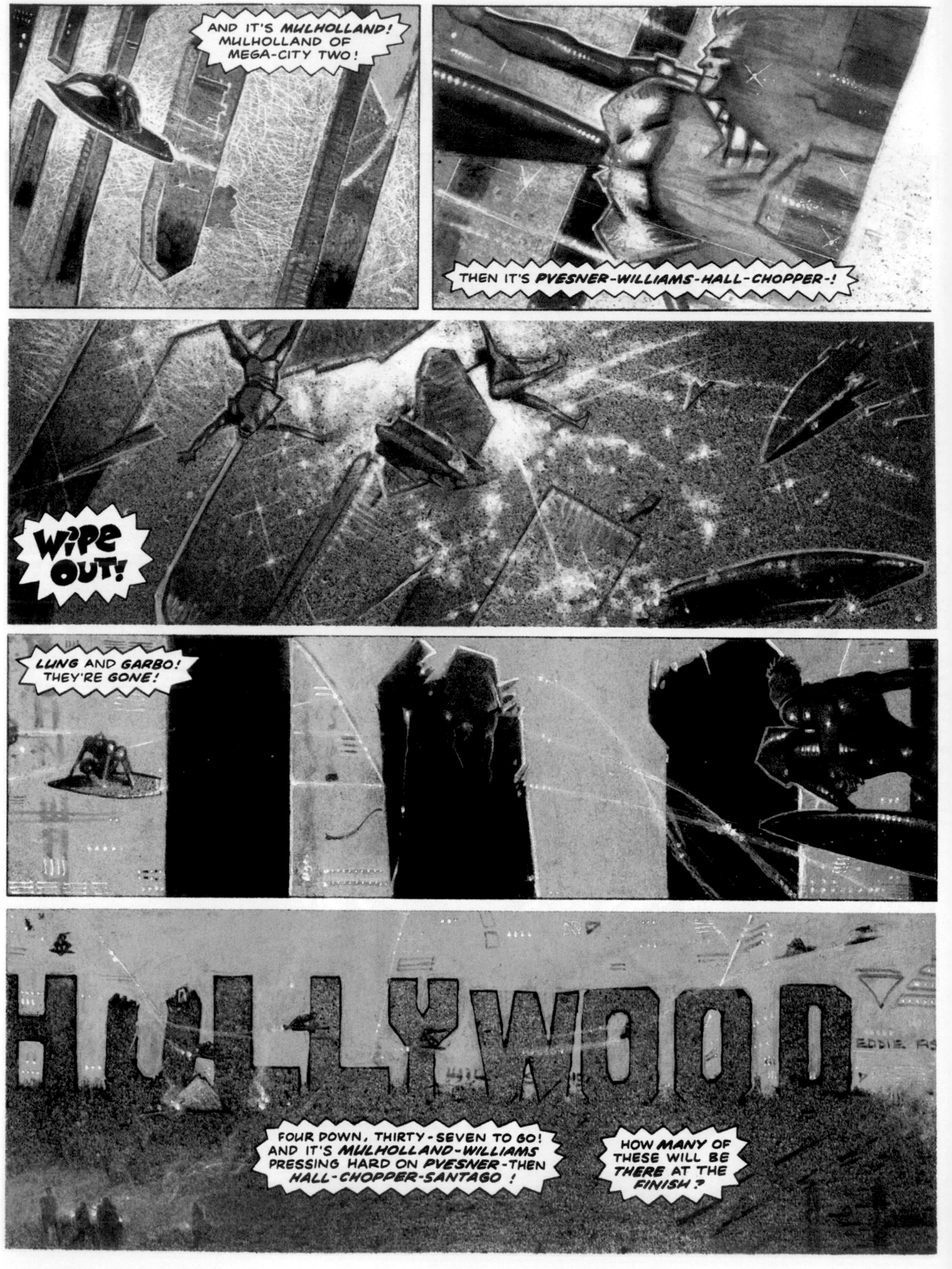
AND IT'S MULHOLLAND! MULHOLLAND OF MEGA-CITY TWO!
THEN IT'S PVESNER-WILLIAMS-HALL-CHOPPER-!
WIPE OUT!
LUNG AND GARBO! THEY'RE GONE!
FOUR DOWN, THIRTY-SEVEN TO GO! AND IT'S MULHOLLAND-WILLIAMS PRESSING HARD ON PVESNER-THEN HALL-CHOPPER-SANTAGO!
HOW MANY OF THESE WILL BE THERE AT THE FINISH?

THEY'RE THROUGH THE "O"s AND HEADING FOR HARDLUCK HEIGHTS AND IT'S STILL *MUL-HOLLAND* OF MEGA-CITY TWO — THEN BRIT-CIT'S *SONNY WILLIAMS*—!

THESE TWO THEN *DALLAS HALL* AND *PVESNER* TOGETHER, *CHOPPER* PRESSING THEM HARD!

BEHIND THEM ANOTHER PILE-UP AT HOLLYWOOD! *NEGRI'S* OFF — AND *DIDIER*!

BUT THEY'RE ALL RIGHT! THEY'RE PULLING THEMSELVES BACK ON!

HERE ON THE HEIGHTS THE FIRST GUN HAS OPENED UP! *ROD ZUSHLAG* — YOU'RE ON AUTOMATIC HERE?

UH, RIGHT, DICK. UH, TWO SECOND INTERVALS, RANDOM SPREAD.

CHOPPER

script JOHN WAGNER
art COLIN MacNEIL
lettering BAMBOS

SONG OF THE SURFER

UH, WE'RE FIRING *SPLINTER SHELL*, SO WE, UH, SHOULD BAG A FEW.

GET SOME SPECTATORS AT LEAST.

OKAY, ROD. BE LUCKY.

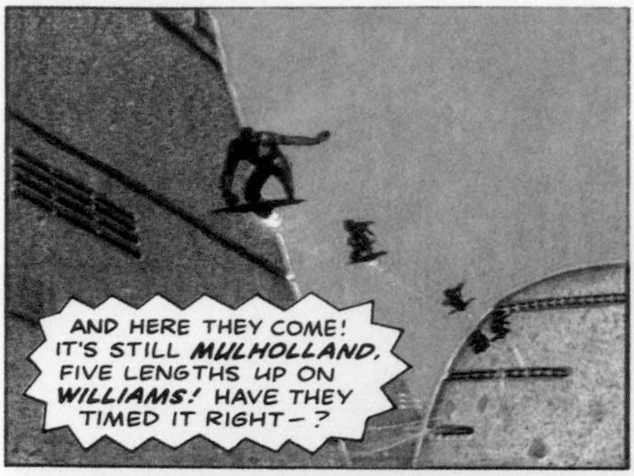
AND HERE THEY COME! IT'S STILL MULHOLLAND, FIVE LENGTHS UP ON WILLIAMS! HAVE THEY TIMED IT RIGHT—?
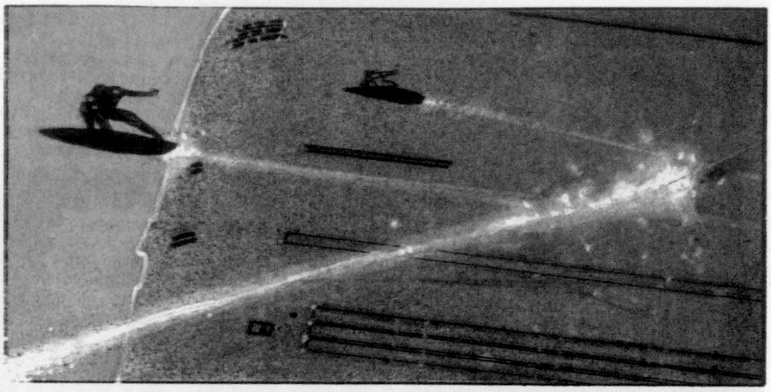
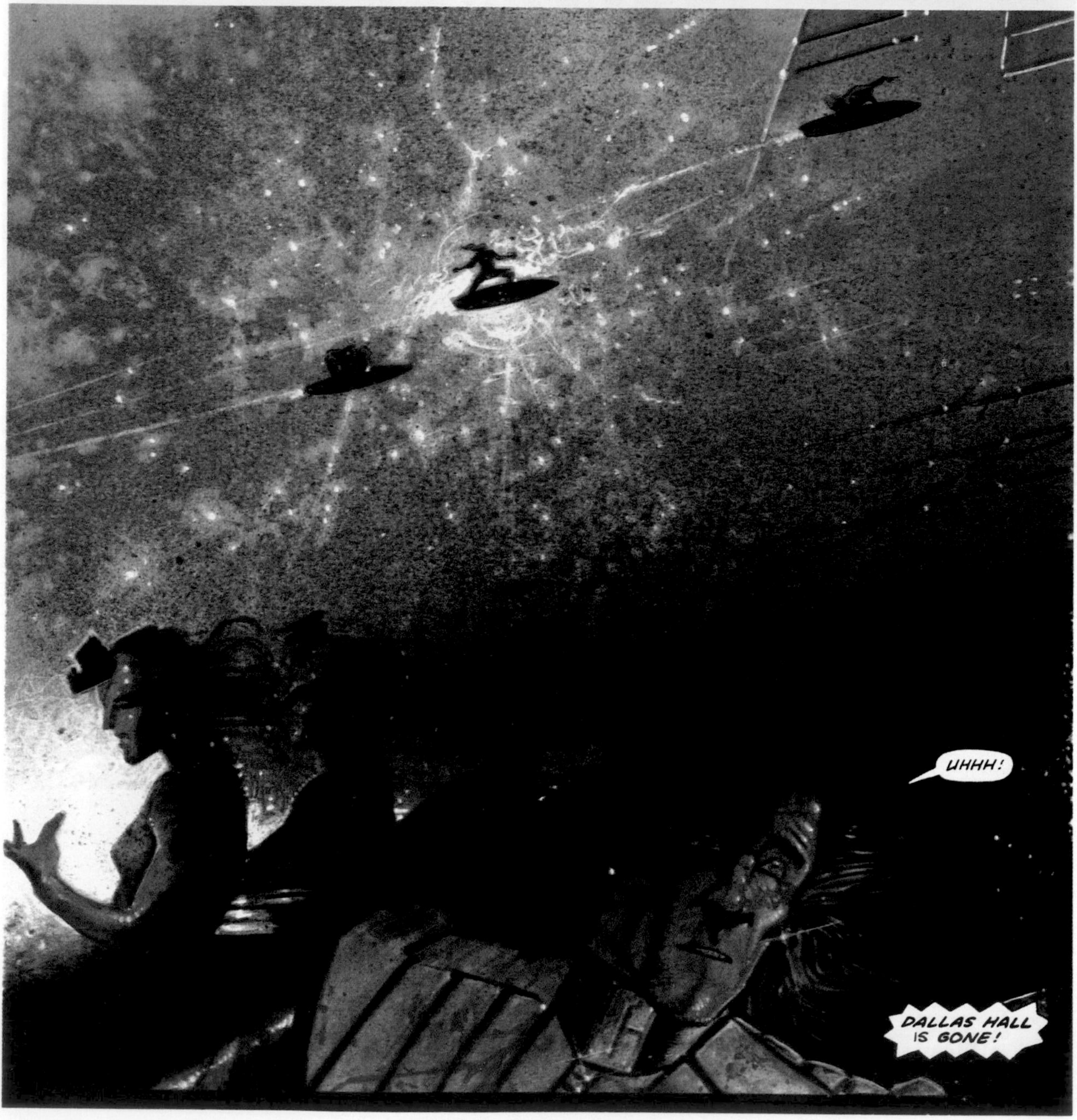
UHHH!
DALLAS HALL IS GONE!

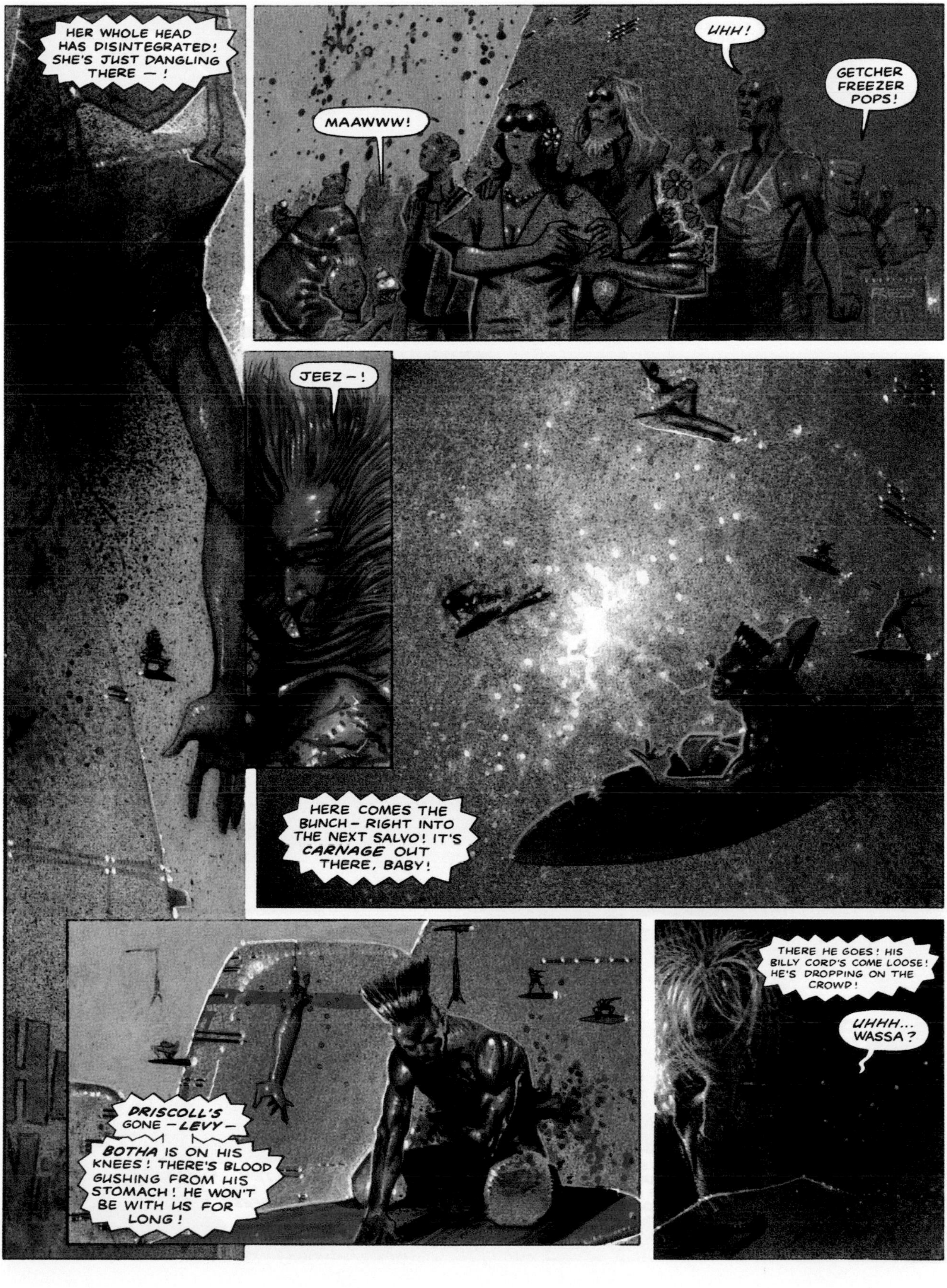
HER WHOLE HEAD HAS DISINTEGRATED! SHE'S JUST DANGLING THERE — !
MAAWWW!
UHH!
GETCHER FREEZER POPS!
JEEZ — !
HERE COMES THE BUNCH — RIGHT INTO THE NEXT SALVO! IT'S CARNAGE OUT THERE, BABY!
DRISCOLL'S GONE — LEVY —
BOTHA IS ON HIS KNEES! THERE'S BLOOD GUSHING FROM HIS STOMACH! HE WON'T BE WITH US FOR LONG!
THERE HE GOES! HIS BILLY CORD'S COME LOOSE! HE'S DROPPING ON THE CROWD!
UHHH... WASSA?

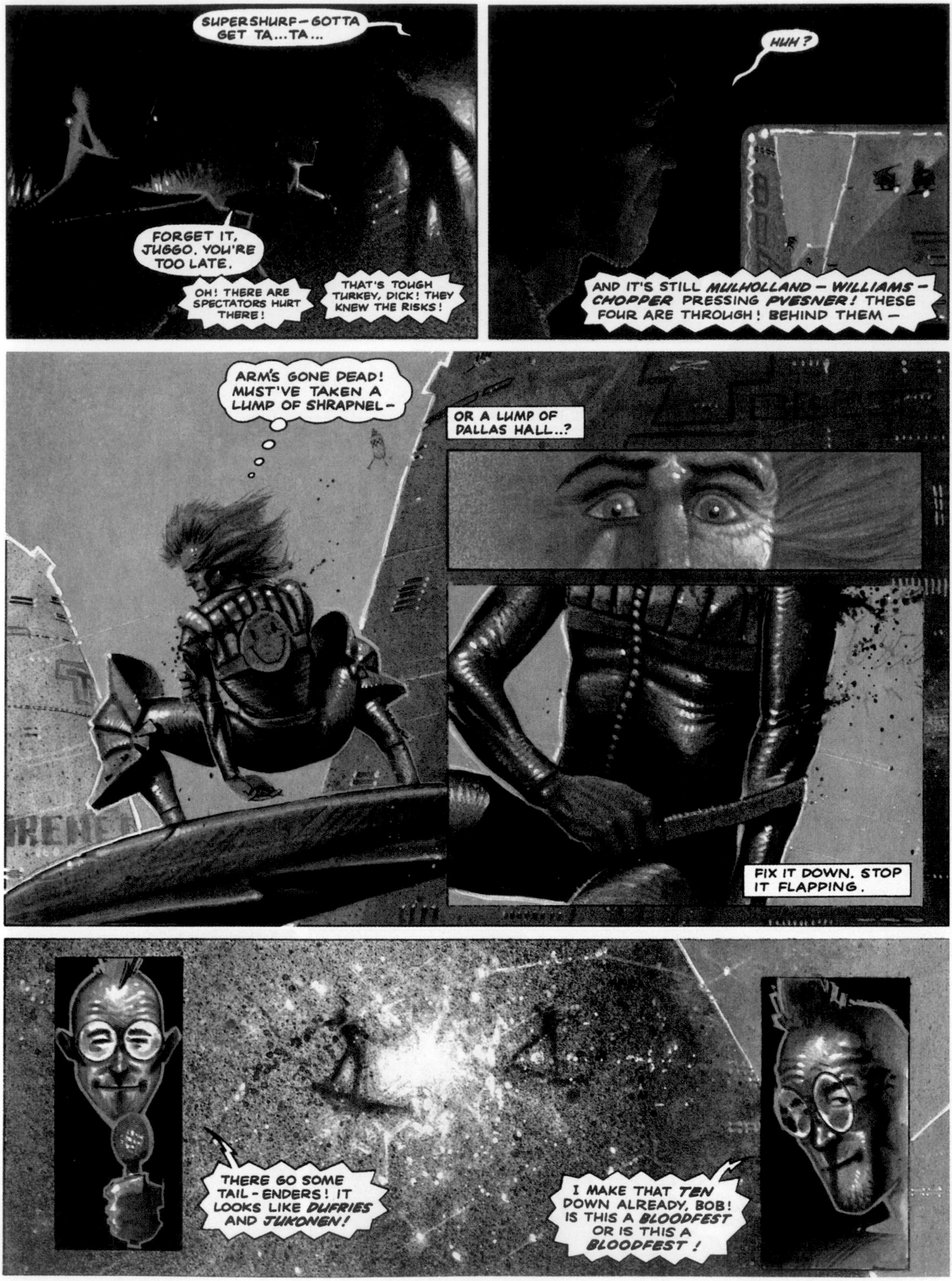
SUPERSHURF—GOTTA GET TA...TA...
FORGET IT, JUGGO. YOU'RE TOO LATE.
OH! THERE ARE SPECTATORS HURT THERE!
THAT'S TOUGH TURKEY, DICK! THEY KNEW THE RISKS!
HUH?
AND IT'S STILL MULHOLLAND — WILLIAMS — CHOPPER PRESSING PVESNER! THESE FOUR ARE THROUGH! BEHIND THEM —
ARM'S GONE DEAD! MUST'VE TAKEN A LUMP OF SHRAPNEL—
OR A LUMP OF DALLAS HALL..?
FIX IT DOWN. STOP IT FLAPPING.
THERE GO SOME TAIL-ENDERS! IT LOOKS LIKE DUFRIES AND JUKONEN!
I MAKE THAT TEN DOWN ALREADY, BOB! IS THIS A BLOODFEST OR IS THIS A BLOODFEST!

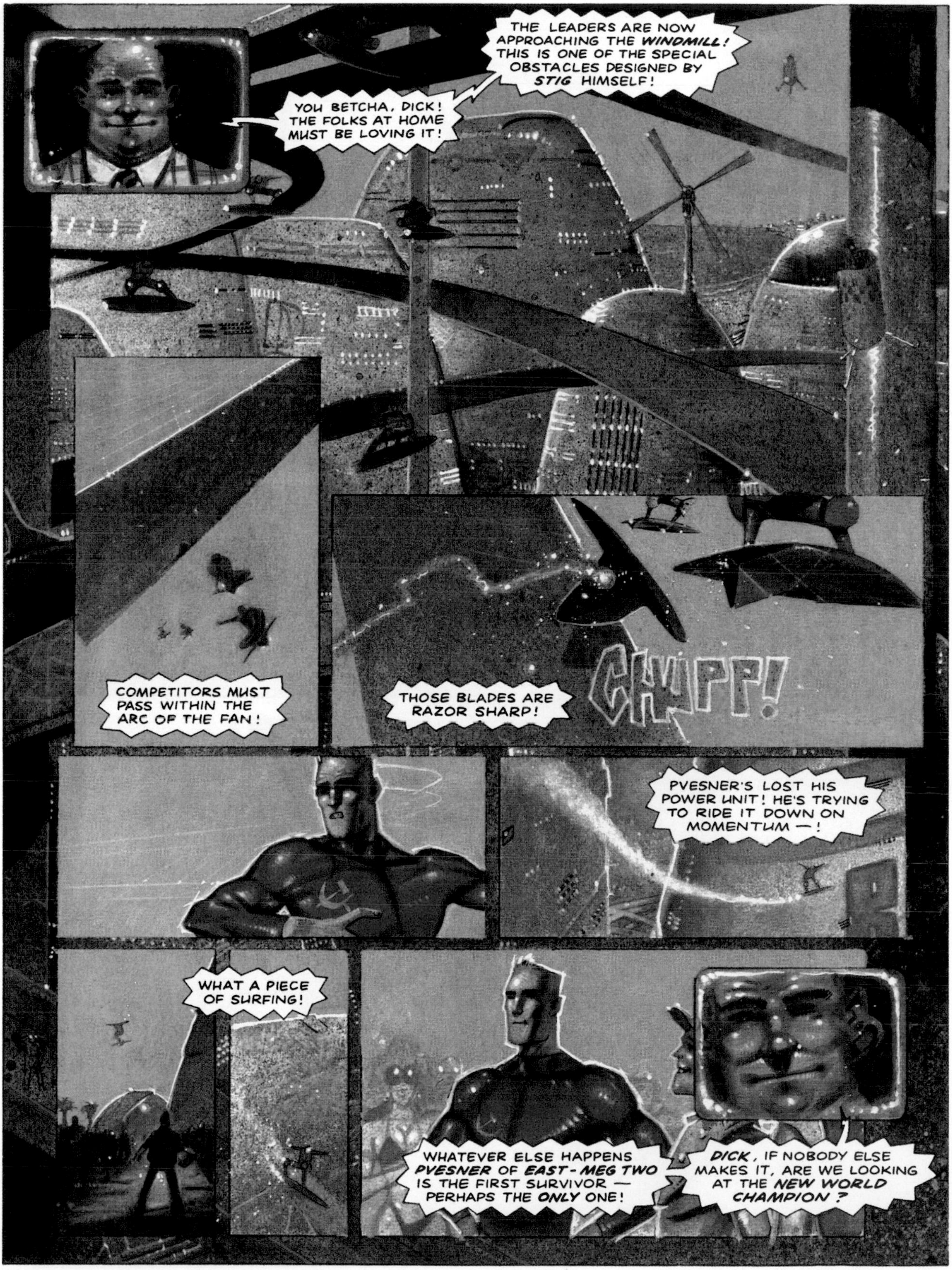
THE LEADERS ARE NOW APPROACHING THE WINDMILL! THIS IS ONE OF THE SPECIAL OBSTACLES DESIGNED BY STIG HIMSELF!
YOU BETCHA, DICK! THE FOLKS AT HOME MUST BE LOVING IT!
COMPETITORS MUST PASS WITHIN THE ARC OF THE FAN!
THOSE BLADES ARE RAZOR SHARP!
CHUPP!
PVESNER'S LOST HIS POWER UNIT! HE'S TRYING TO RIDE IT DOWN ON MOMENTUM —!
WHAT A PIECE OF SURFING!
WHATEVER ELSE HAPPENS PVESNER OF EAST-MEG TWO IS THE FIRST SURVIVOR — PERHAPS THE ONLY ONE!
DICK, IF NOBODY ELSE MAKES IT, ARE WE LOOKING AT THE NEW WORLD CHAMPION?

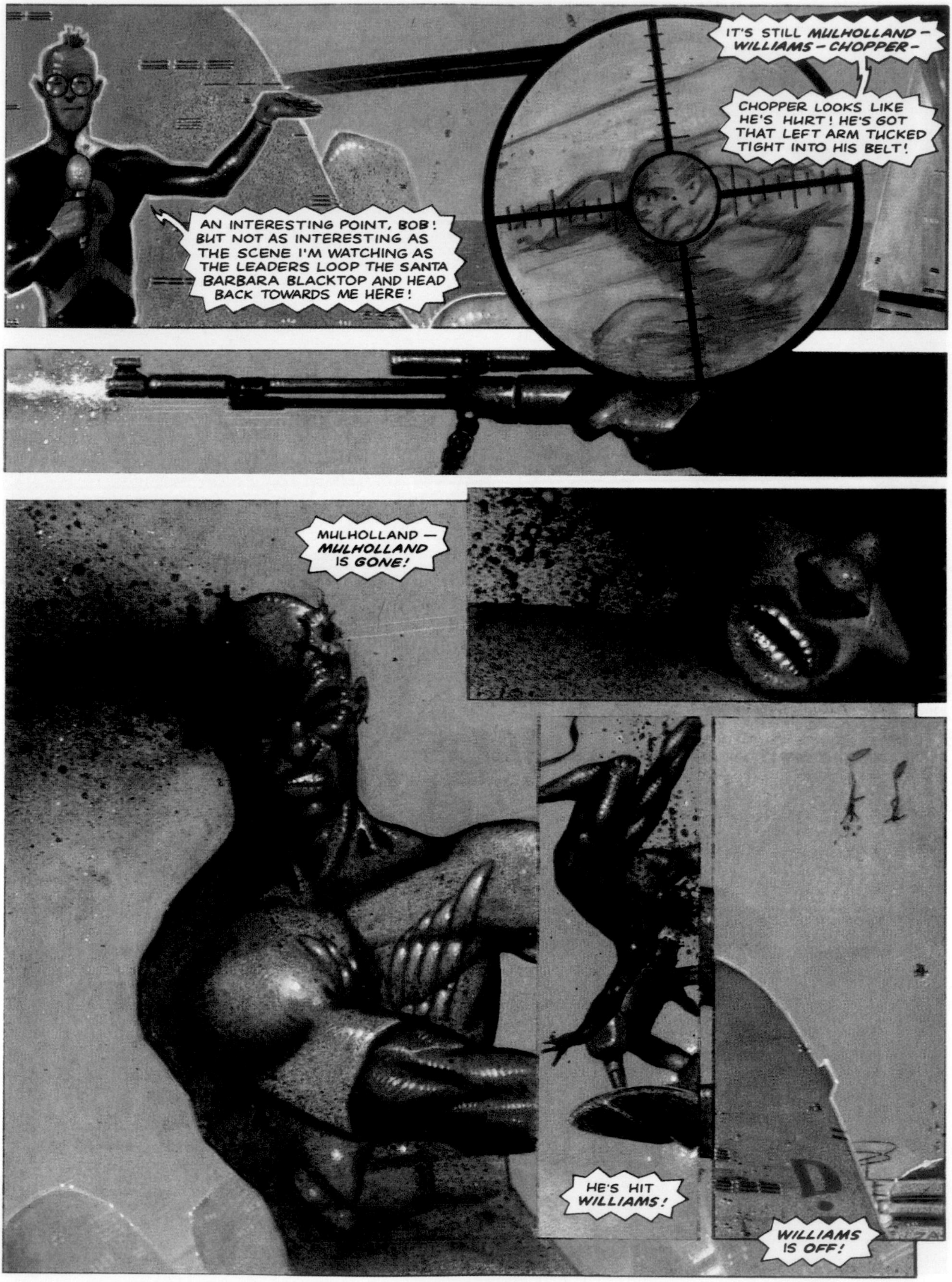
AN INTERESTING POINT, BOB! BUT NOT AS INTERESTING AS THE SCENE I'M WATCHING AS THE LEADERS LOOP THE SANTA BARBARA BLACKTOP AND HEAD BACK TOWARDS ME HERE!
IT'S STILL MULHOLLAND — WILLIAMS — CHOPPER —
CHOPPER LOOKS LIKE HE'S HURT! HE'S GOT THAT LEFT ARM TUCKED TIGHT INTO HIS BELT!
MULHOLLAND — MULHOLLAND IS GONE!
HE'S HIT WILLIAMS!
WILLIAMS IS OFF!

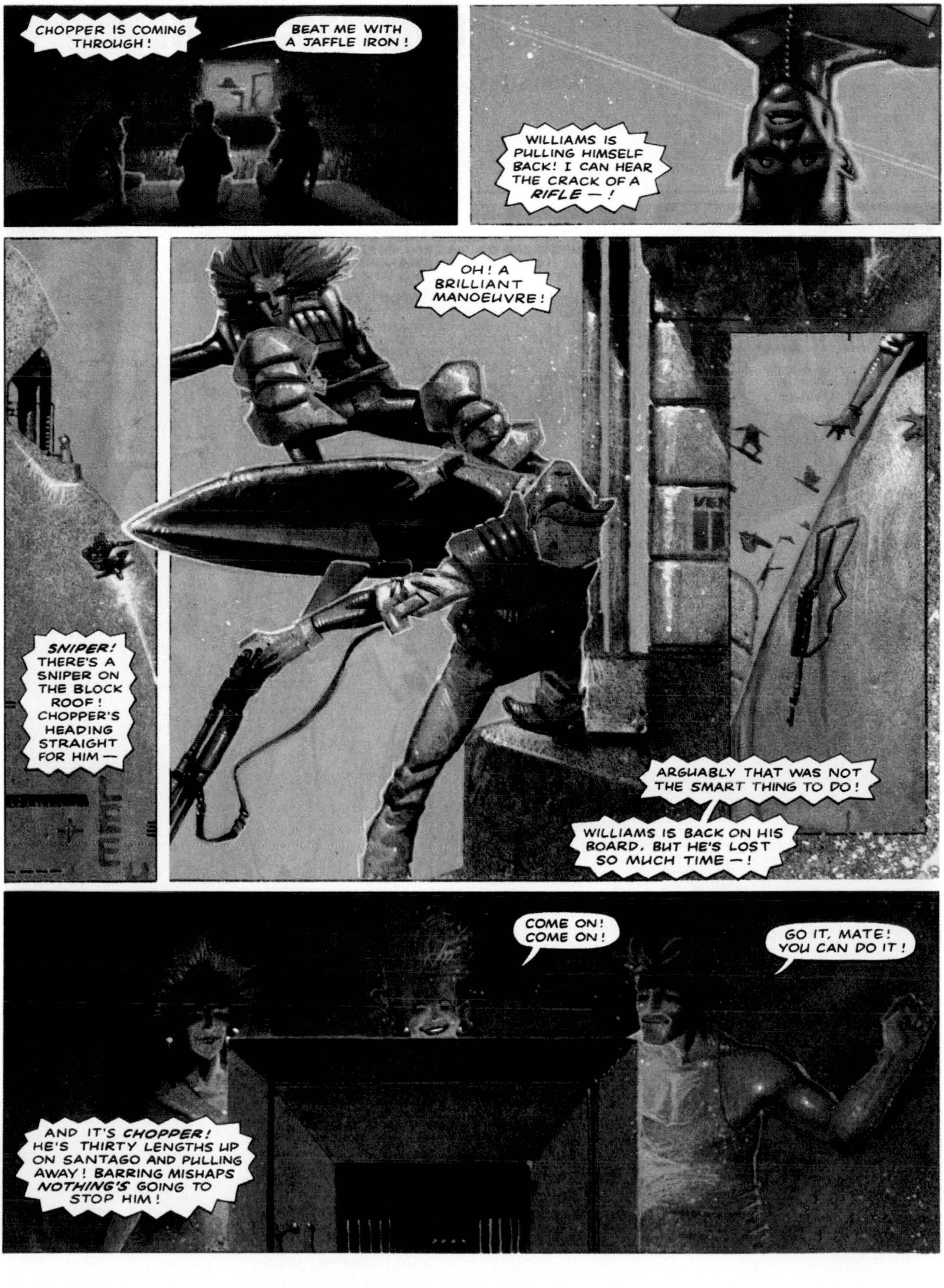
CHOPPER IS COMING THROUGH!
BEAT ME WITH A JAFFLE IRON!
WILLIAMS IS PULLING HIMSELF BACK! I CAN HEAR THE CRACK OF A *RIFLE*—!
SNIPER! THERE'S A SNIPER ON THE BLOCK ROOF! CHOPPER'S HEADING STRAIGHT FOR HIM—
OH! A BRILLIANT MANOEUVRE!
ARGUABLY THAT WAS NOT THE SMART THING TO DO!
WILLIAMS IS BACK ON HIS BOARD, BUT HE'S LOST SO MUCH TIME—!
AND IT'S *CHOPPER!* HE'S THIRTY LENGTHS UP ON SANTAGO AND PULLING AWAY! BARRING MISHAPS *NOTHING'S* GOING TO STOP HIM!
COME ON! COME ON!
GO IT, MATE! YOU CAN DO IT!

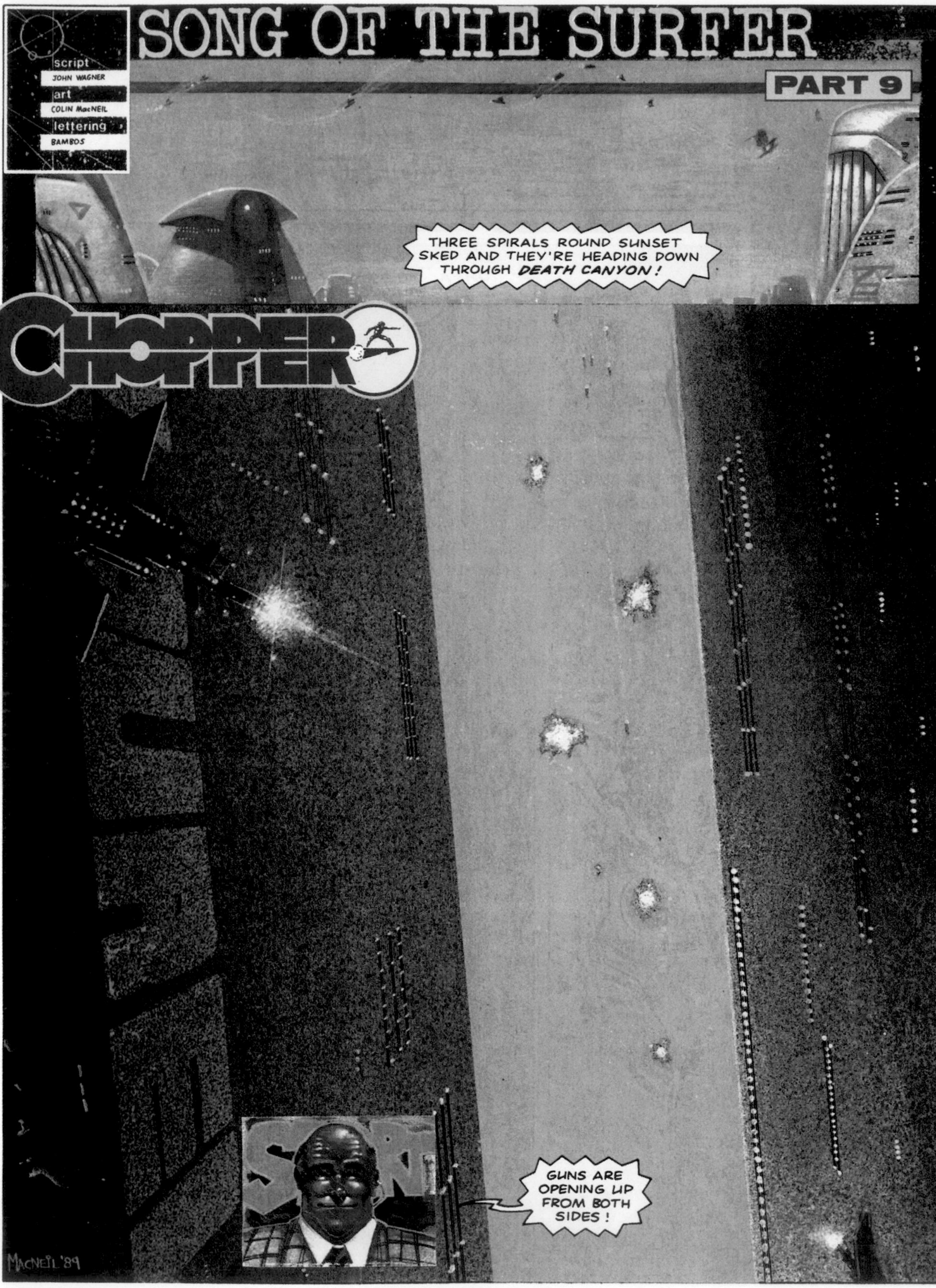
SONG OF THE SURFER
script
JOHN WAGNER
art
COLIN MacNEIL
lettering
BAMBOS
PART 9
THREE SPIRALS ROUND SUNSET SKED AND THEY'RE HEADING DOWN THROUGH *DEATH CANYON!*
CHOPPER
GUNS ARE OPENING UP FROM BOTH SIDES!
MACNEIL '89

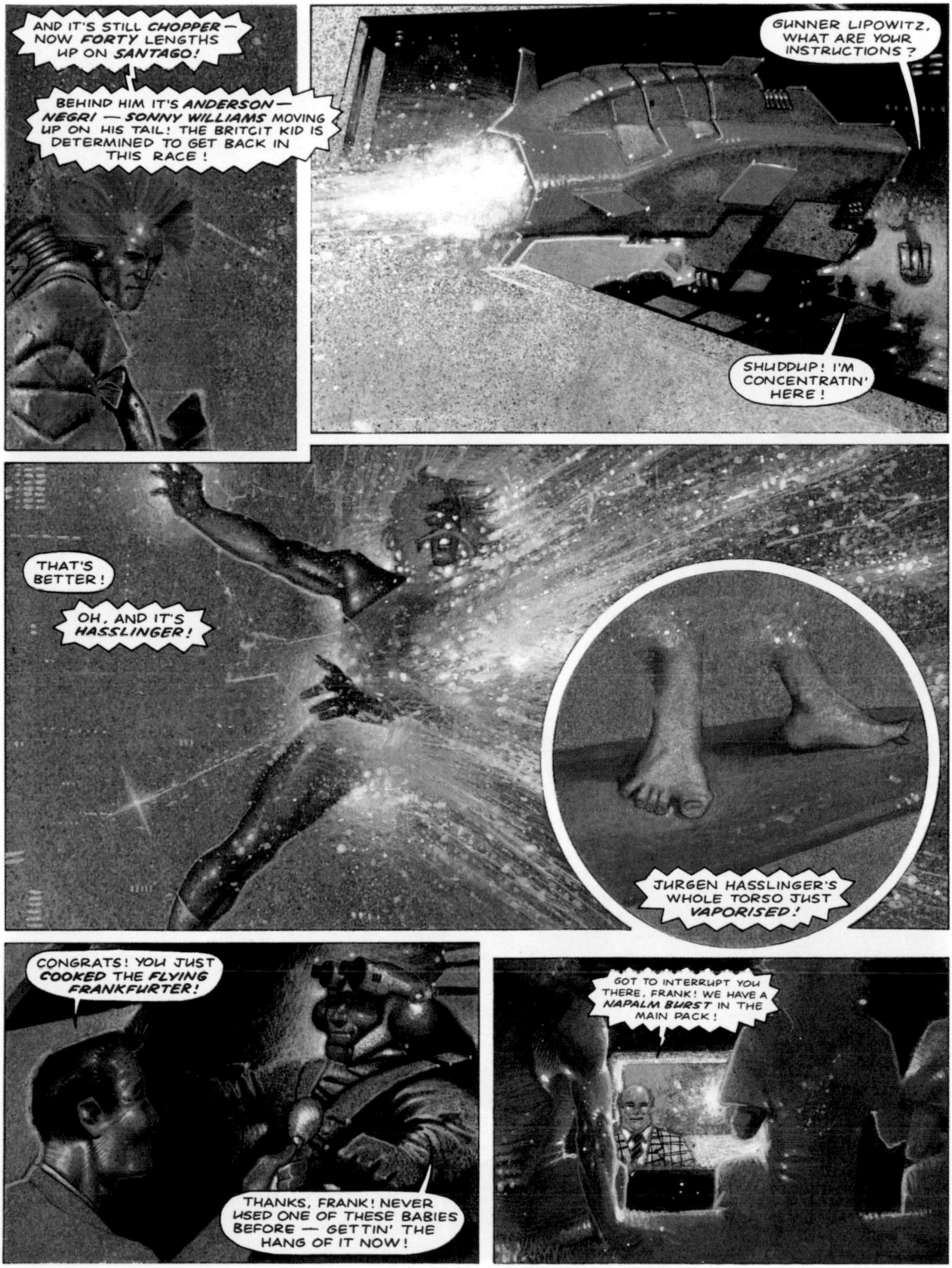
AND IT'S STILL CHOPPER — NOW FORTY LENGTHS UP ON SANTAGO!
BEHIND HIM IT'S ANDERSON — NEGRI — SONNY WILLIAMS MOVING UP ON HIS TAIL! THE BRITCIT KID IS DETERMINED TO GET BACK IN THIS RACE!
GUNNER LIPOWITZ, WHAT ARE YOUR INSTRUCTIONS?
SHUDDUP! I'M CONCENTRATIN' HERE!
THAT'S BETTER!
OH, AND IT'S HASSLINGER!
JURGEN HASSLINGER'S WHOLE TORSO JUST VAPORISED!
CONGRATS! YOU JUST COOKED THE FLYING FRANKFURTER!
THANKS, FRANK! NEVER USED ONE OF THESE BABIES BEFORE — GETTIN' THE HANG OF IT NOW!
GOT TO INTERRUPT YOU THERE, FRANK! WE HAVE A NAPALM BURST IN THE MAIN PACK!

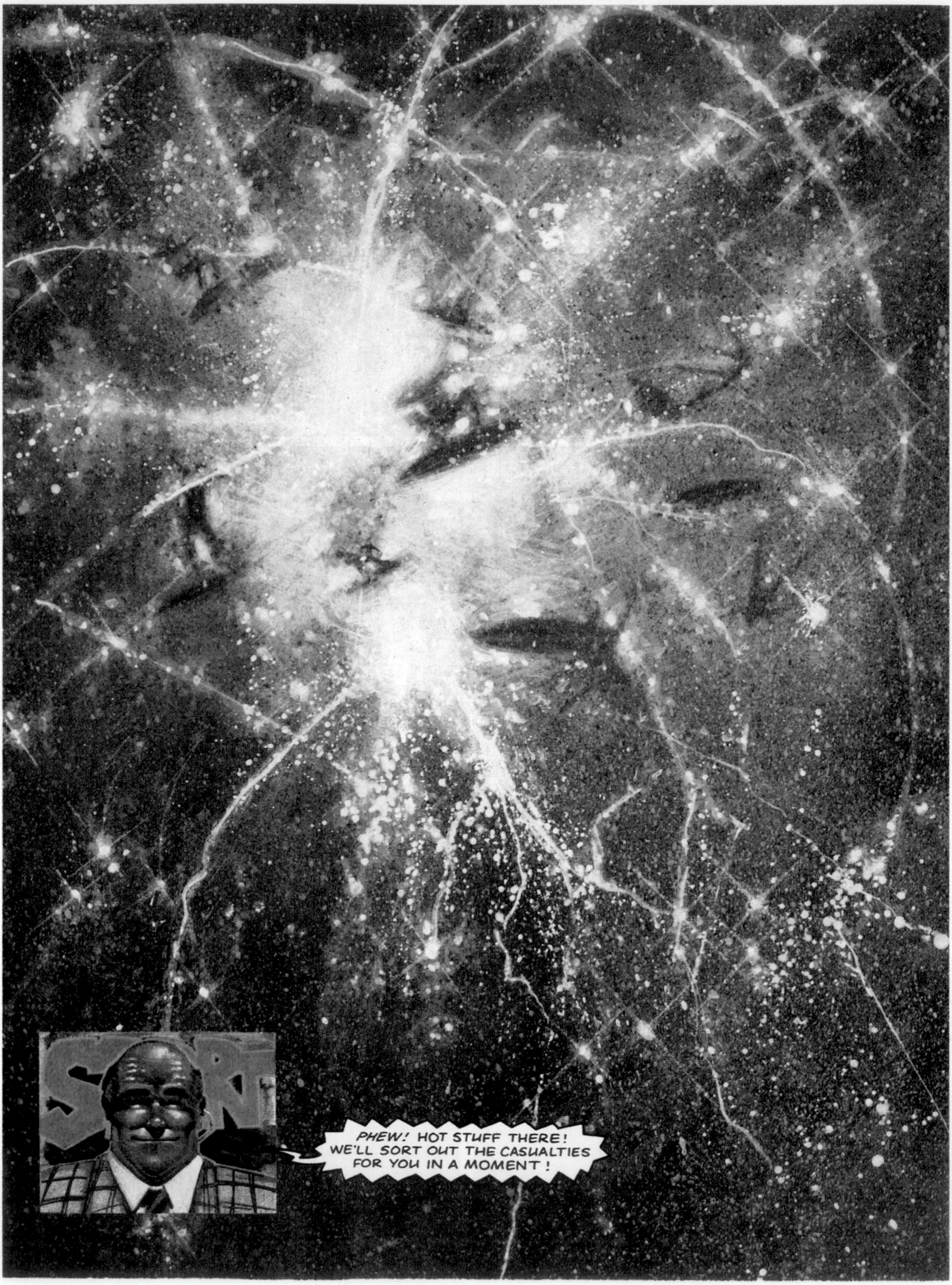
PHEW! HOT STUFF THERE! WE'LL SORT OUT THE CASUALTIES FOR YOU IN A MOMENT!

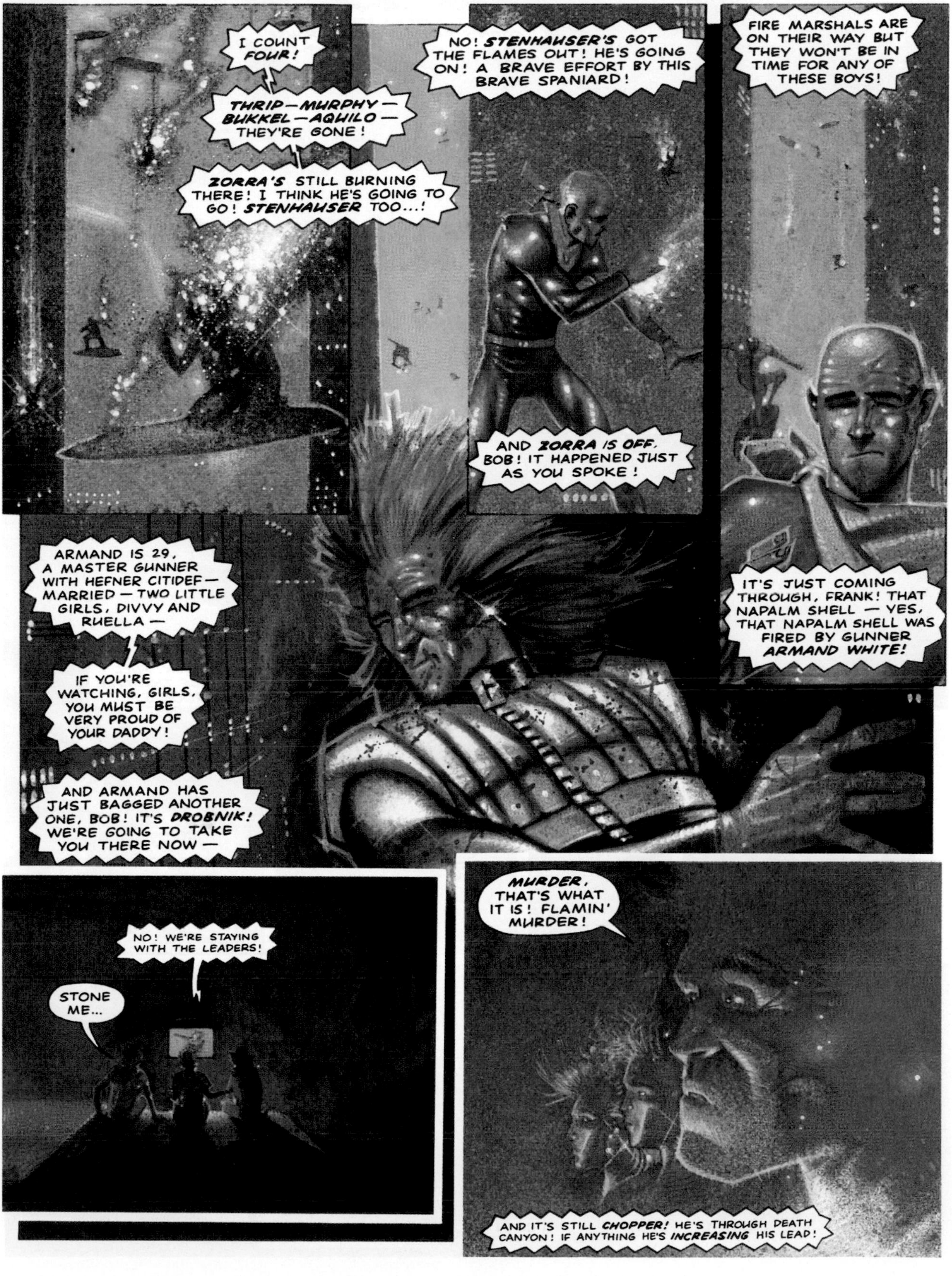
I COUNT FOUR!
THRIP—MURPHY—BUKKEL—AQUILO—THEY'RE GONE!
ZORRA'S STILL BURNING THERE! I THINK HE'S GOING TO GO! STENHAUSER TOO...!
NO! STENHAUSER'S GOT THE FLAMES OUT! HE'S GOING ON! A BRAVE EFFORT BY THIS BRAVE SPANIARD!
AND ZORRA IS OFF, BOB! IT HAPPENED JUST AS YOU SPOKE!
FIRE MARSHALS ARE ON THEIR WAY BUT THEY WON'T BE IN TIME FOR ANY OF THESE BOYS!
ARMAND IS 29, A MASTER GUNNER WITH HEFNER CITIDEF—MARRIED—TWO LITTLE GIRLS, DIVVY AND RUELLA—
IF YOU'RE WATCHING, GIRLS, YOU MUST BE VERY PROUD OF YOUR DADDY!
AND ARMAND HAS JUST BAGGED ANOTHER ONE, BOB! IT'S DROBNIK! WE'RE GOING TO TAKE YOU THERE NOW—
IT'S JUST COMING THROUGH, FRANK! THAT NAPALM SHELL — YES, THAT NAPALM SHELL WAS FIRED BY GUNNER ARMAND WHITE!
NO! WE'RE STAYING WITH THE LEADERS!
STONE ME...
MURDER, THAT'S WHAT IT IS! FLAMIN' MURDER!
AND IT'S STILL CHOPPER! HE'S THROUGH DEATH CANYON! IF ANYTHING HE'S INCREASING HIS LEAD!

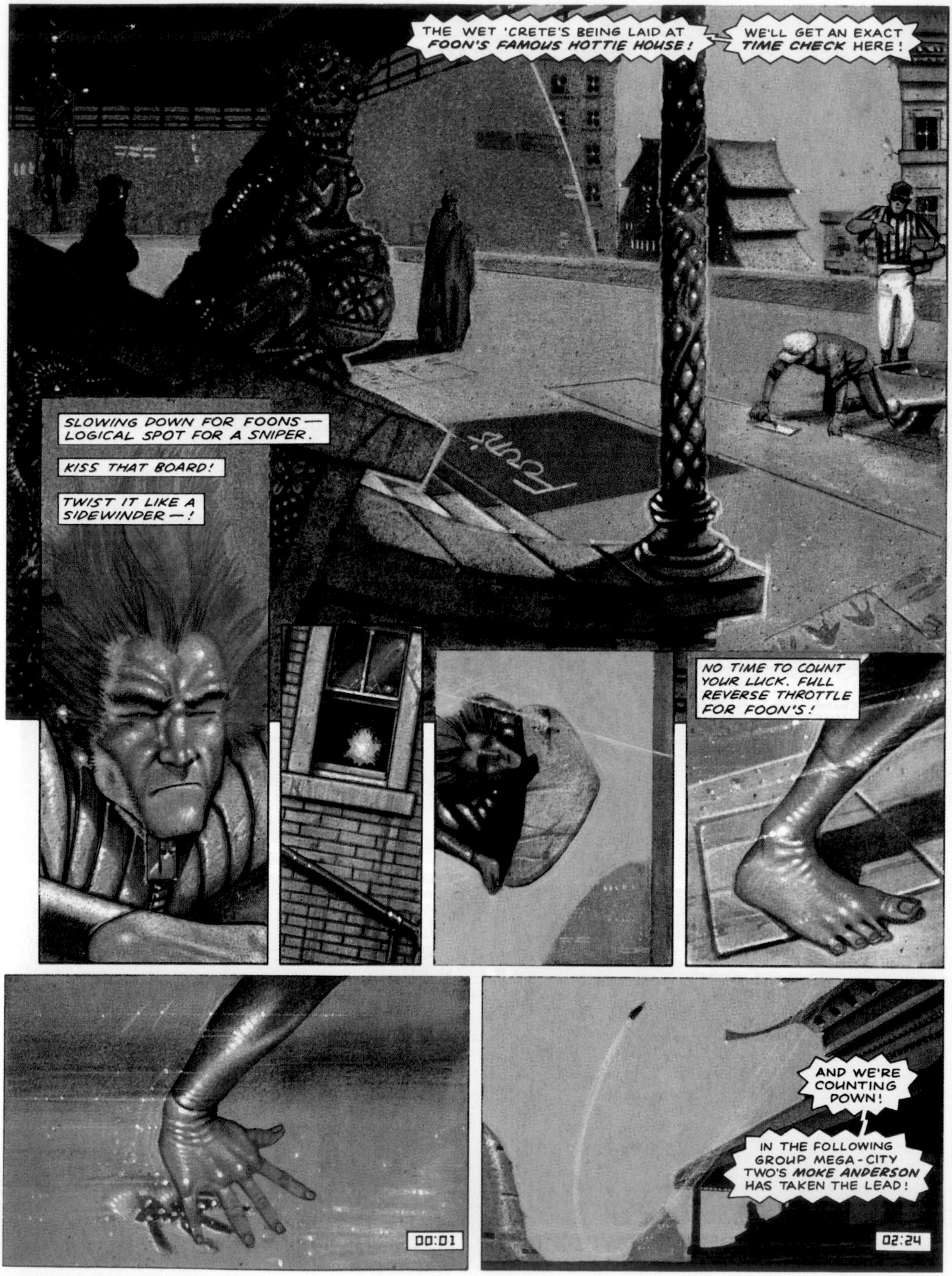
THE WET 'CRETE'S BEING LAID AT FOON'S FAMOUS HOTTIE HOUSE!
WE'LL GET AN EXACT TIME CHECK HERE!
SLOWING DOWN FOR FOONS — LOGICAL SPOT FOR A SNIPER.
KISS THAT BOARD!
TWIST IT LIKE A SIDEWINDER —!
NO TIME TO COUNT YOUR LUCK. FULL REVERSE THROTTLE FOR FOON'S!
00:01
AND WE'RE COUNTING DOWN!
IN THE FOLLOWING GROUP MEGA-CITY TWO'S MOKE ANDERSON HAS TAKEN THE LEAD!
02:24

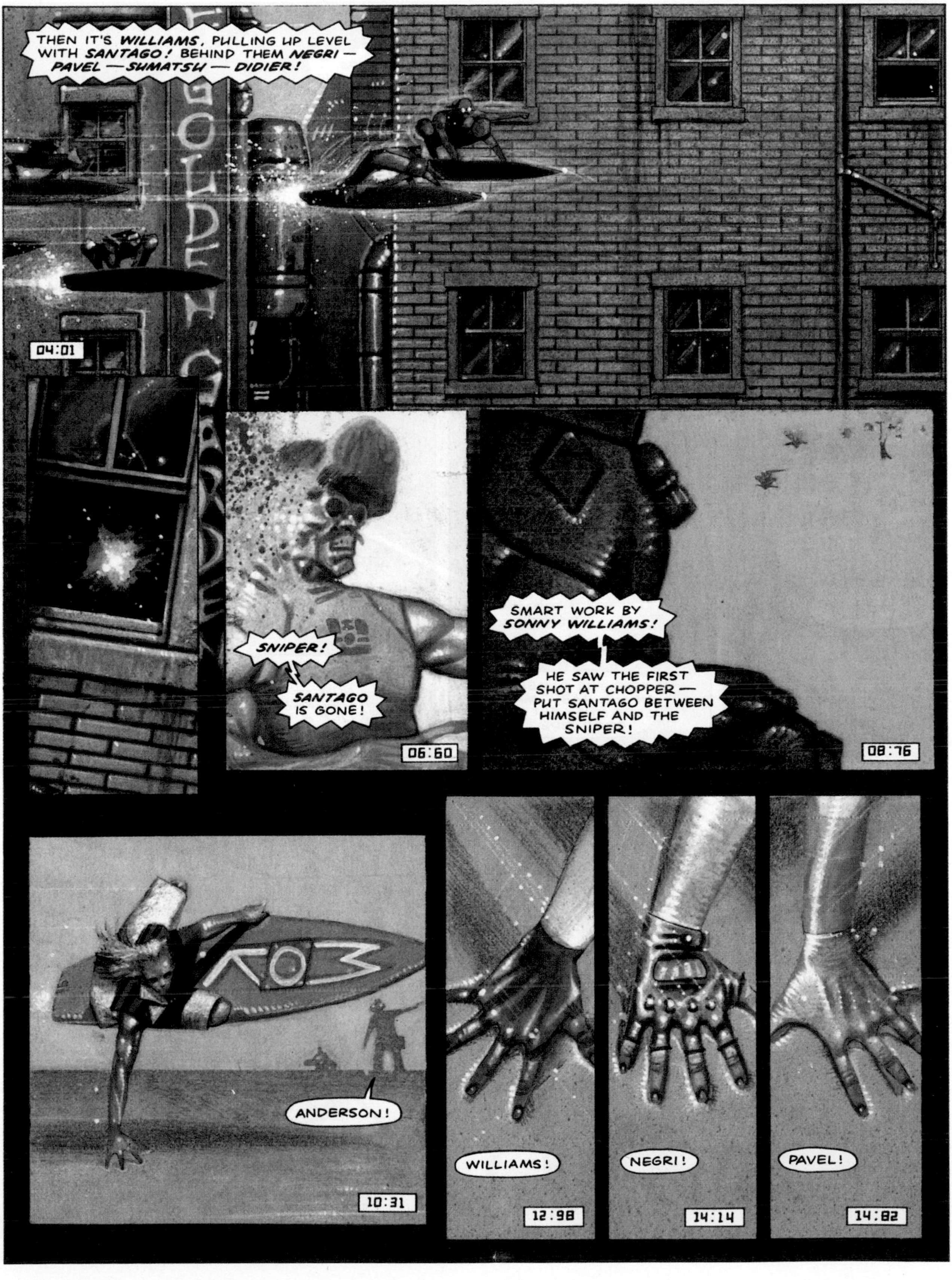
THEN IT'S WILLIAMS, PULLING UP LEVEL WITH SANTAGO! BEHIND THEM NEGRI— PAVEL—SUMATSU—DIDIER!
04:01
SNIPER!
SANTAGO IS GONE!
06:60
SMART WORK BY SONNY WILLIAMS!
HE SAW THE FIRST SHOT AT CHOPPER— PUT SANTAGO BETWEEN HIMSELF AND THE SNIPER!
08:76
ANDERSON!
10:31
WILLIAMS!
12:98
NEGRI!
14:14
PAVEL!
14:82

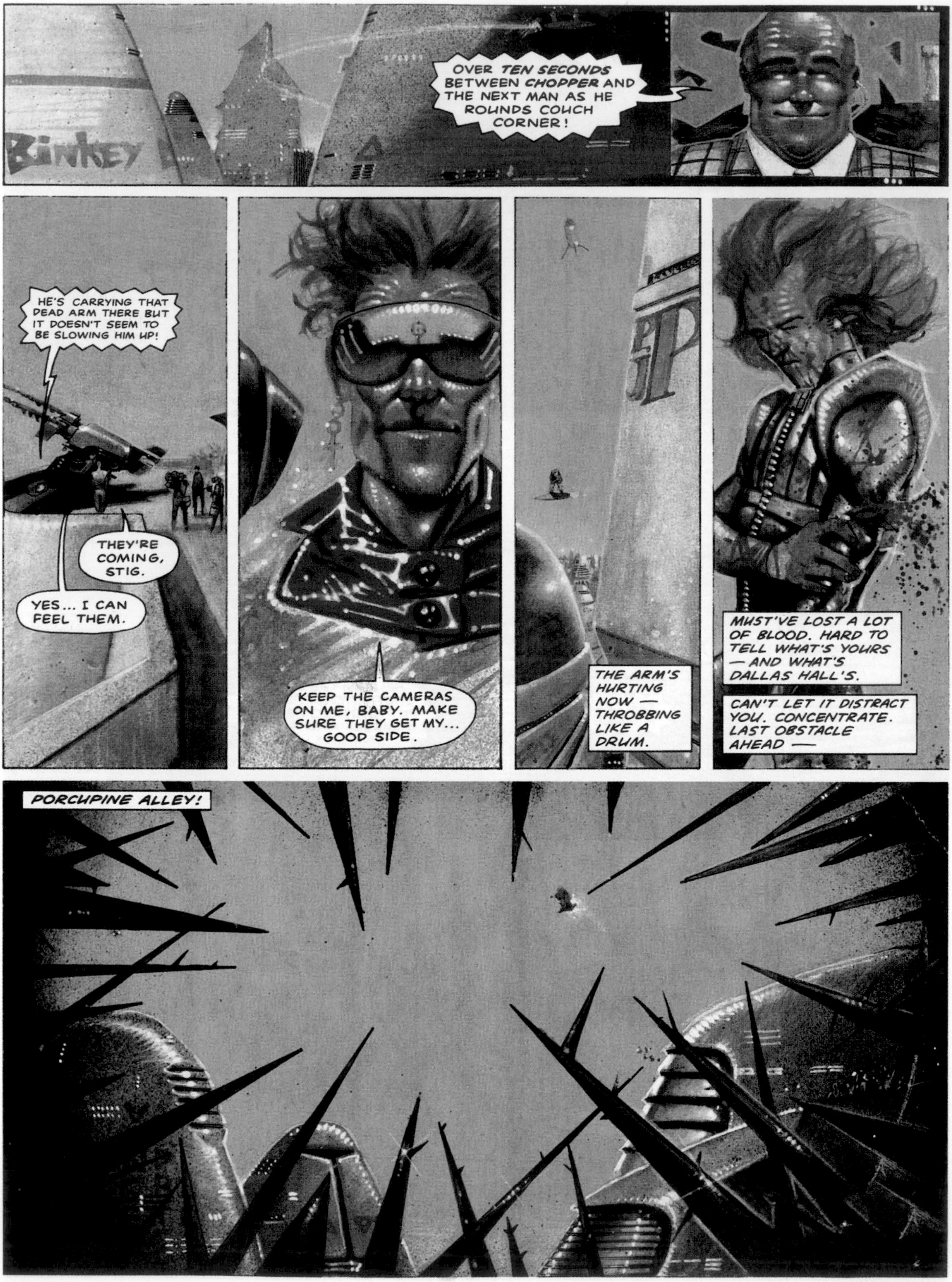
BINKEY
OVER TEN SECONDS BETWEEN CHOPPER AND THE NEXT MAN AS HE ROUNDS COUCH CORNER!
HE'S CARRYING THAT DEAD ARM THERE BUT IT DOESN'T SEEM TO BE SLOWING HIM UP!
THEY'RE COMING, STIG.
YES... I CAN FEEL THEM.
KEEP THE CAMERAS ON ME, BABY. MAKE SURE THEY GET MY... GOOD SIDE.
THE ARM'S HURTING NOW — THROBBING LIKE A DRUM.
MUST'VE LOST A LOT OF BLOOD. HARD TO TELL WHAT'S YOURS — AND WHAT'S DALLAS HALL'S.
CAN'T LET IT DISTRACT YOU. CONCENTRATE. LAST OBSTACLE AHEAD —
PORCUPINE ALLEY!

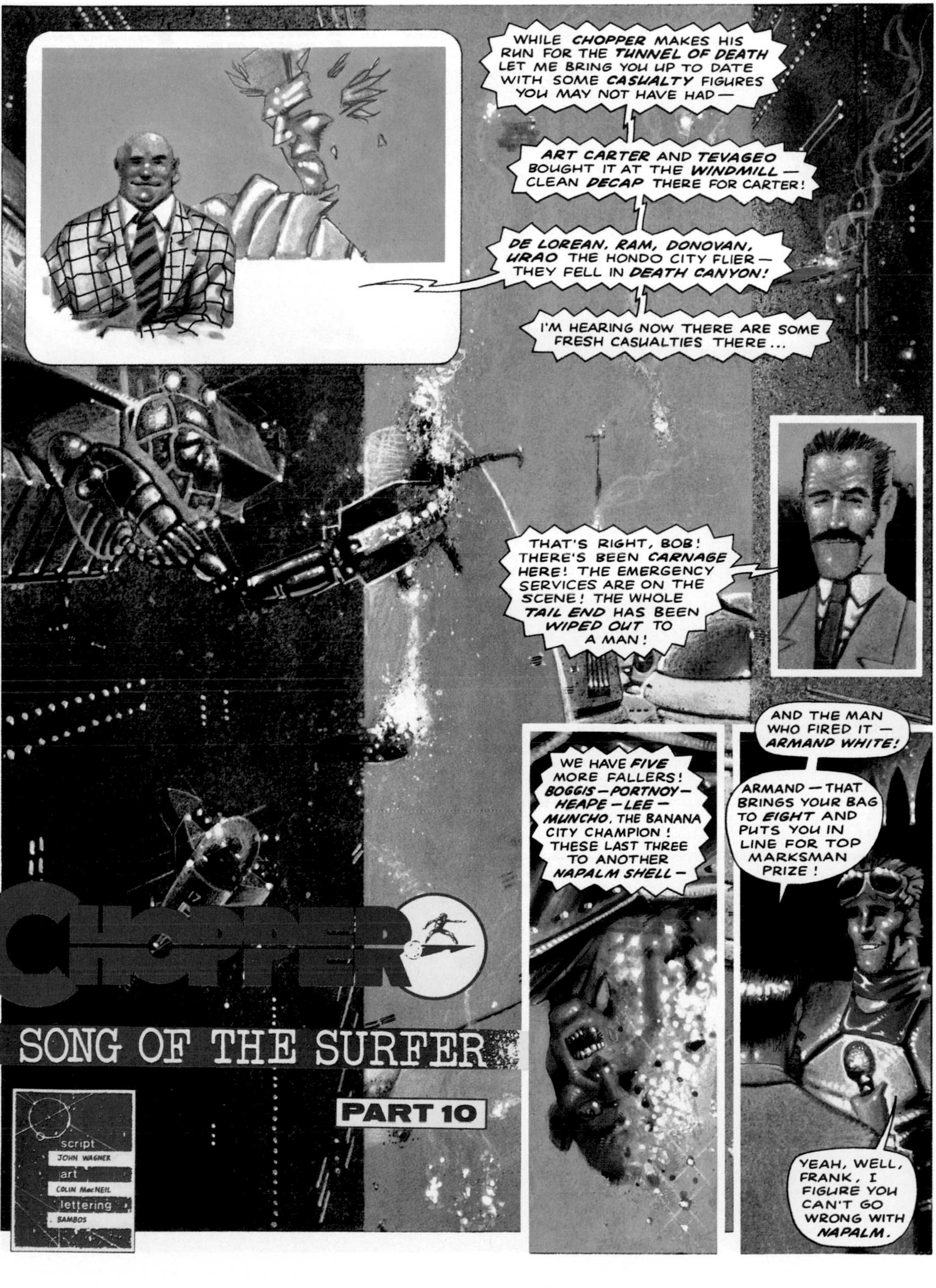
WHILE CHOPPER MAKES HIS RUN FOR THE TUNNEL OF DEATH LET ME BRING YOU UP TO DATE WITH SOME CASUALTY FIGURES YOU MAY NOT HAVE HAD —
ART CARTER AND TEVAGEO BOUGHT IT AT THE WINDMILL — CLEAN DECAP THERE FOR CARTER!
DE LOREAN, RAM, DONOVAN, URAO THE HONDO CITY FLIER — THEY FELL IN DEATH CANYON!
I'M HEARING NOW THERE ARE SOME FRESH CASUALTIES THERE...
THAT'S RIGHT, BOB! THERE'S BEEN CARNAGE HERE! THE EMERGENCY SERVICES ARE ON THE SCENE! THE WHOLE TAIL END HAS BEEN WIPED OUT TO A MAN!
CHOPPER
SONG OF THE SURFER
PART 10
script
JOHN WAGNER
art
COLIN MacNEIL
lettering
BAMBOS
WE HAVE FIVE MORE FALLERS! BOGGIS — PORTNOY — HEAPE — LEE — MUNCHO, THE BANANA CITY CHAMPION! THESE LAST THREE TO ANOTHER NAPALM SHELL —
AND THE MAN WHO FIRED IT — ARMAND WHITE!
ARMAND — THAT BRINGS YOUR BAG TO EIGHT AND PUTS YOU IN LINE FOR TOP MARKSMAN PRIZE!
YEAH, WELL, FRANK, I FIGURE YOU CAN'T GO WRONG WITH NAPALM.

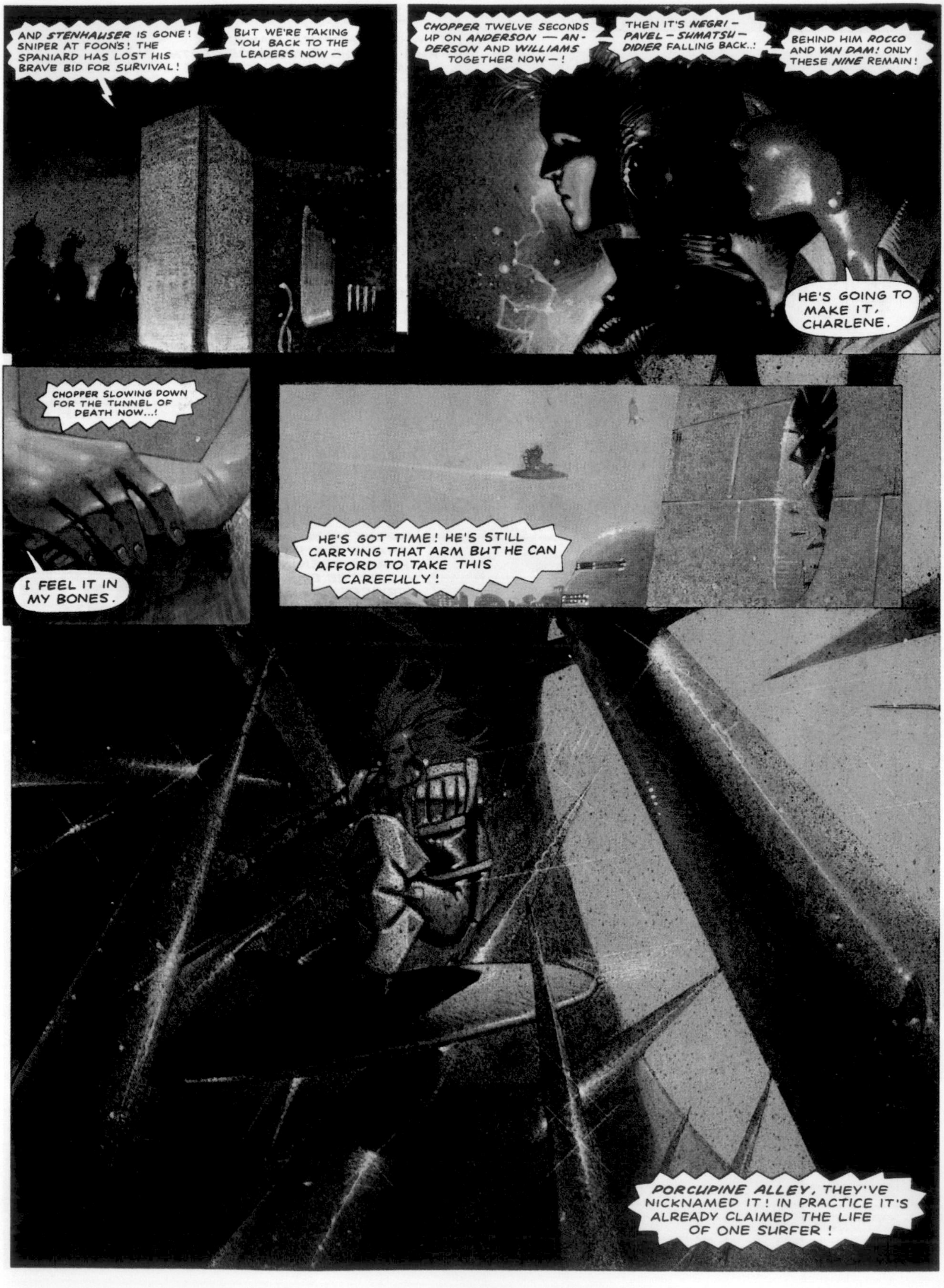
AND STENHAUSER IS GONE! SNIPER AT FOON'S! THE SPANIARD HAS LOST HIS BRAVE BID FOR SURVIVAL!
BUT WE'RE TAKING YOU BACK TO THE LEADERS NOW —
CHOPPER TWELVE SECONDS UP ON ANDERSON — ANDERSON AND WILLIAMS TOGETHER NOW —!
THEN IT'S NEGRI — PAVEL — SUMATSU — DIDIER FALLING BACK..!
BEHIND HIM ROCCO AND VAN DAM! ONLY THESE NINE REMAIN!
HE'S GOING TO MAKE IT, CHARLENE.
CHOPPER SLOWING DOWN FOR THE TUNNEL OF DEATH NOW...!
I FEEL IT IN MY BONES.
HE'S GOT TIME! HE'S STILL CARRYING THAT ARM BUT HE CAN AFFORD TO TAKE THIS CAREFULLY!
PORCUPINE ALLEY, THEY'VE NICKNAMED IT! IN PRACTICE IT'S ALREADY CLAIMED THE LIFE OF ONE SURFER!

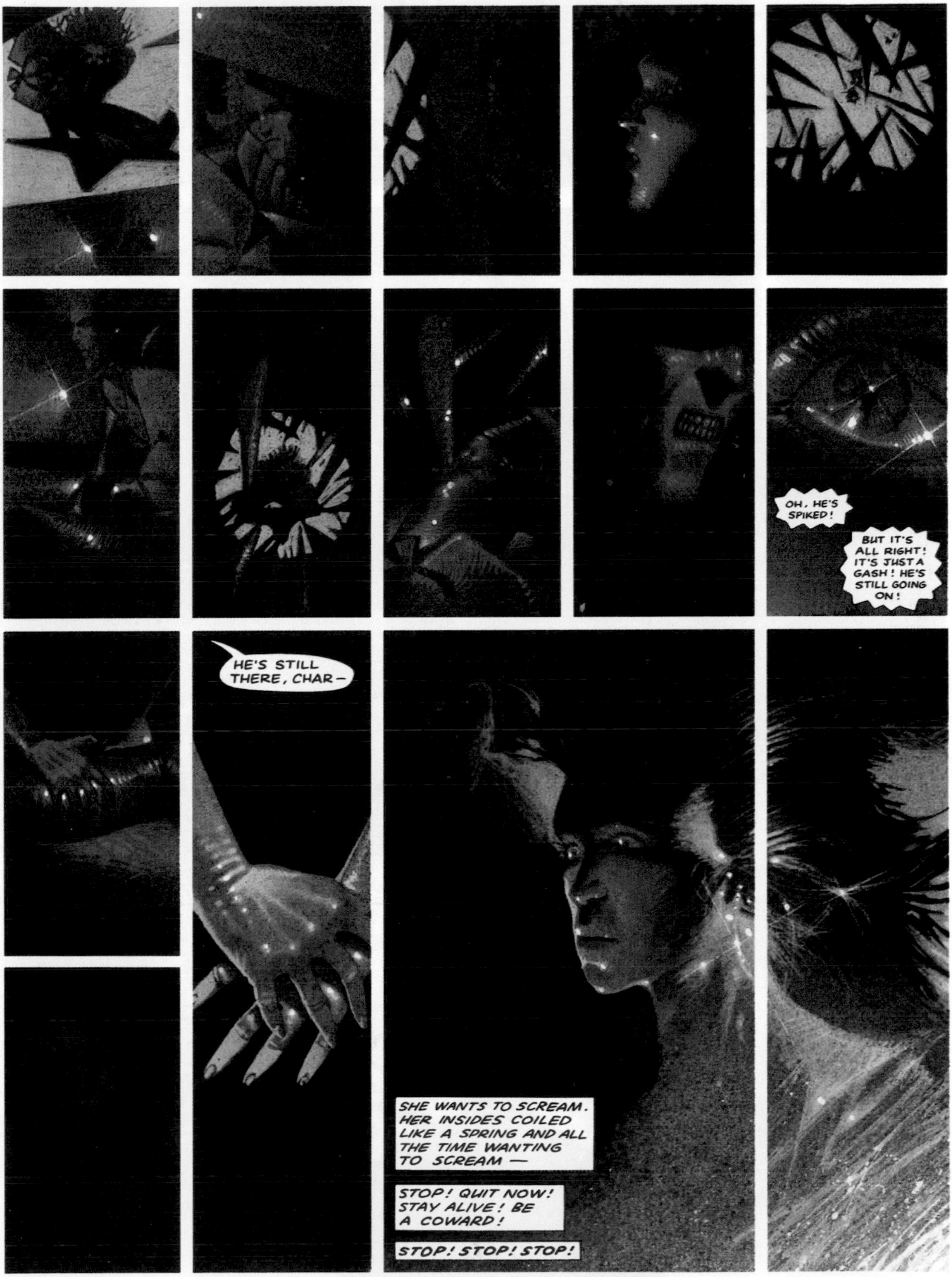
OH, HE'S SPIKED!
BUT IT'S ALL RIGHT! IT'S JUST A GASH! HE'S STILL GOING ON!
HE'S STILL THERE, CHAR—
SHE WANTS TO SCREAM. HER INSIDES COILED LIKE A SPRING AND ALL THE TIME WANTING TO SCREAM —
STOP! QUIT NOW! STAY ALIVE! BE A COWARD!
STOP! STOP! STOP!

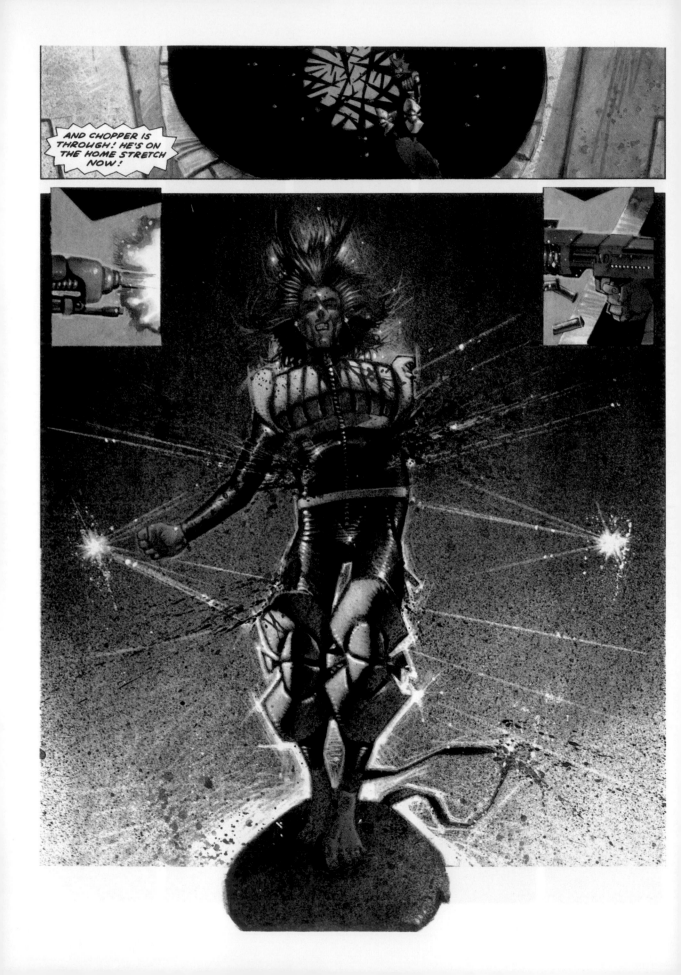

AND CHOPPER IS THROUGH! HE'S ON THE HOME STRETCH NOW!

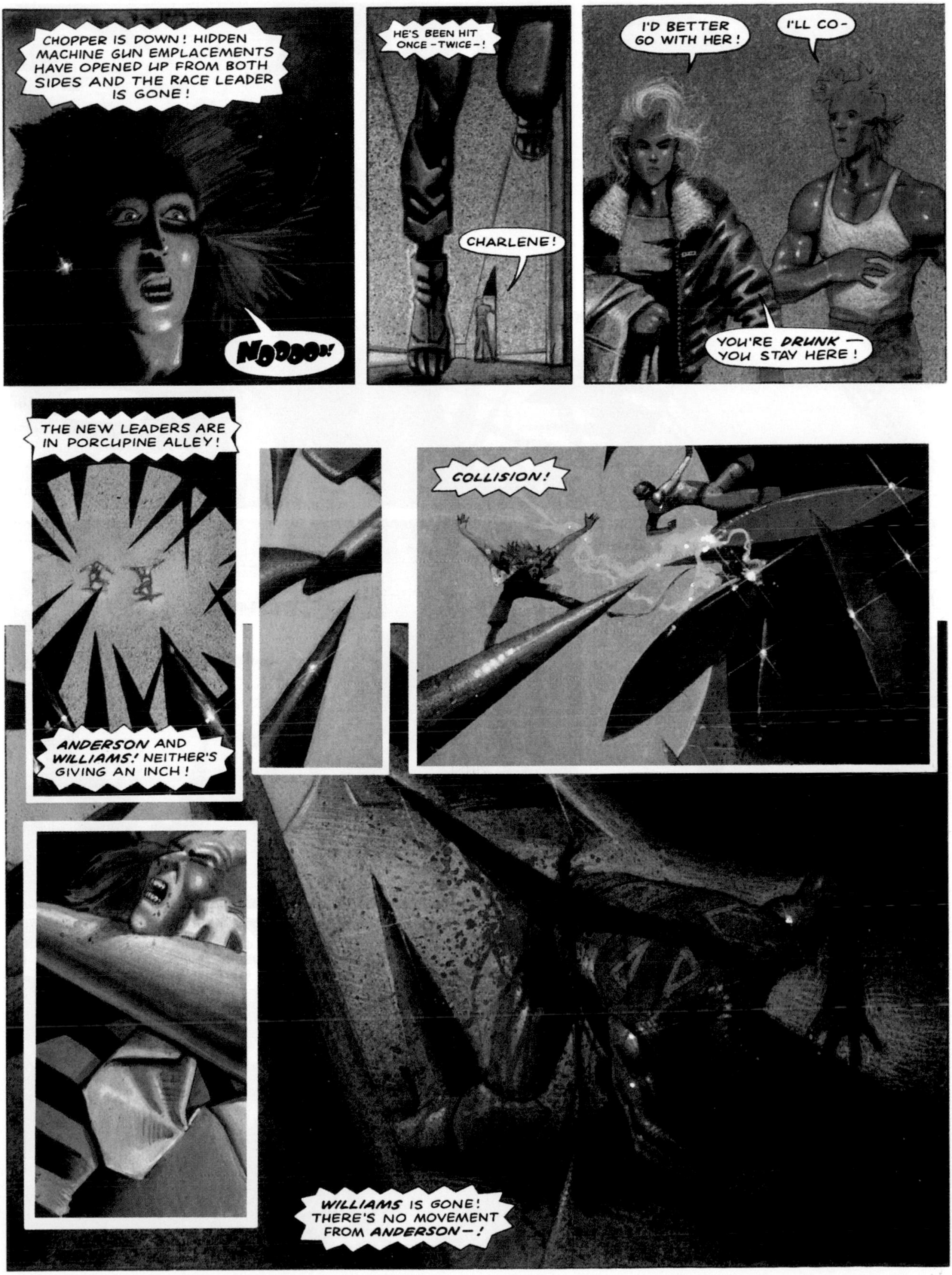
CHOPPER IS DOWN! HIDDEN MACHINE GUN EMPLACEMENTS HAVE OPENED UP FROM BOTH SIDES AND THE RACE LEADER IS GONE!
NOOOOO!
HE'S BEEN HIT ONCE-TWICE-!
CHARLENE!
I'D BETTER GO WITH HER!
I'LL CO-
YOU'RE DRUNK — YOU STAY HERE!
THE NEW LEADERS ARE IN PORCUPINE ALLEY!
ANDERSON AND WILLIAMS! NEITHER'S GIVING AN INCH!
COLLISION!
WILLIAMS IS GONE! THERE'S NO MOVEMENT FROM ANDERSON-!

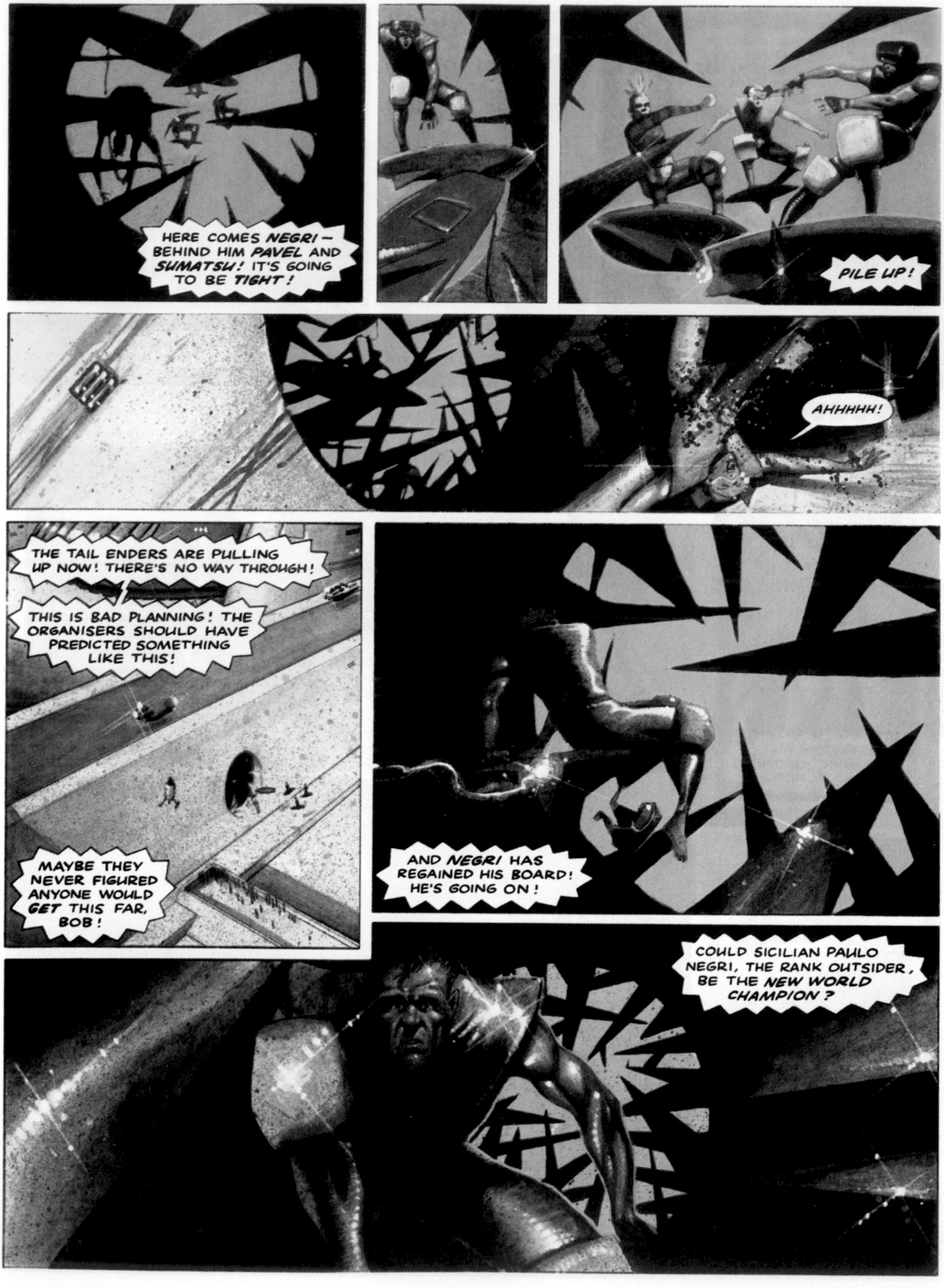
HERE COMES NEGRI — BEHIND HIM PAVEL AND SUMATSU! IT'S GOING TO BE TIGHT!
PILE UP!
AHHHHH!
THE TAIL ENDERS ARE PULLING UP NOW! THERE'S NO WAY THROUGH!
THIS IS BAD PLANNING! THE ORGANISERS SHOULD HAVE PREDICTED SOMETHING LIKE THIS!
MAYBE THEY NEVER FIGURED ANYONE WOULD GET THIS FAR, BOB!
AND NEGRI HAS REGAINED HIS BOARD! HE'S GOING ON!
COULD SICILIAN PAULO NEGRI, THE RANK OUTSIDER, BE THE NEW WORLD CHAMPION?

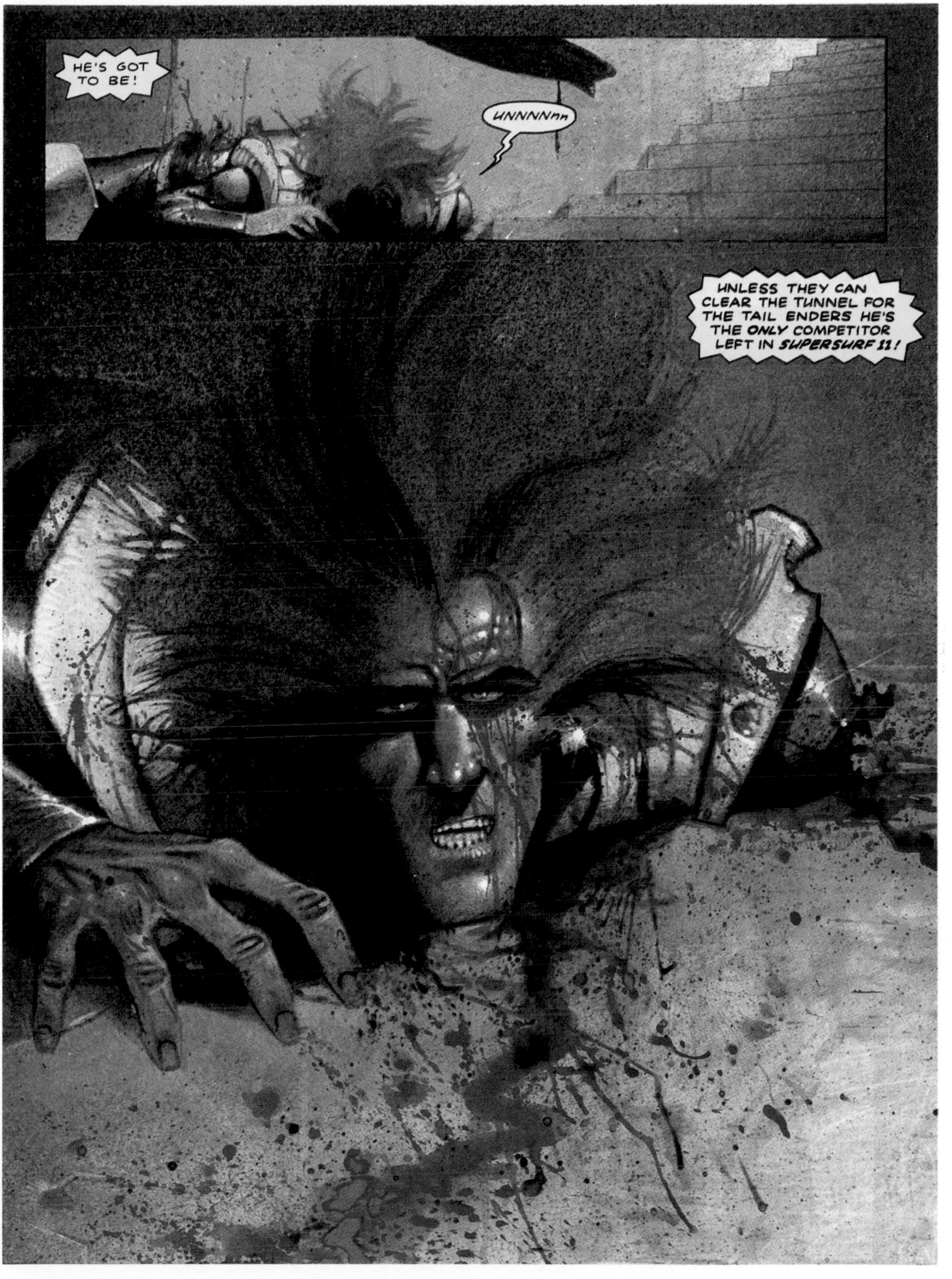
HE'S GOT TO BE!
UNNNNnn
UNLESS THEY CAN CLEAR THE TUNNEL FOR THE TAIL ENDERS HE'S THE ONLY COMPETITOR LEFT IN SUPERSURF 11!

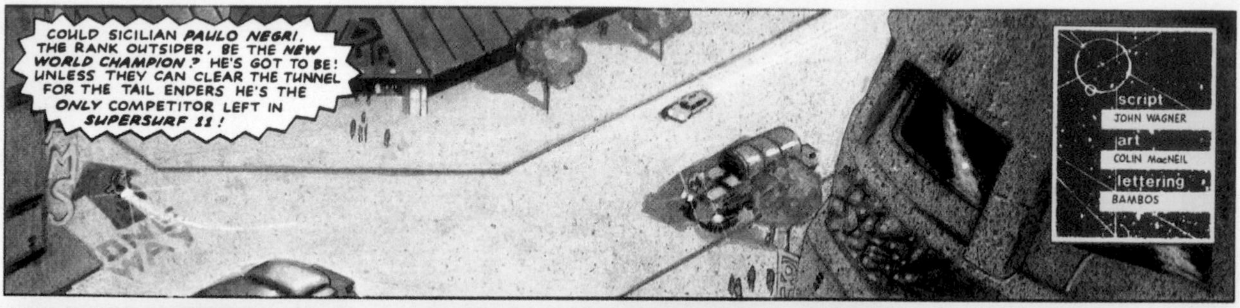
COULD SICILIAN PAULO NEGRI, THE RANK OUTSIDER, BE THE NEW WORLD CHAMPION? HE'S GOT TO BE! UNLESS THEY CAN CLEAR THE TUNNEL FOR THE TAIL ENDERS HE'S THE ONLY COMPETITOR LEFT IN SUPERSURF 11!
script
JOHN WAGNER
art
COLIN MacNEIL
lettering
BAMBOS

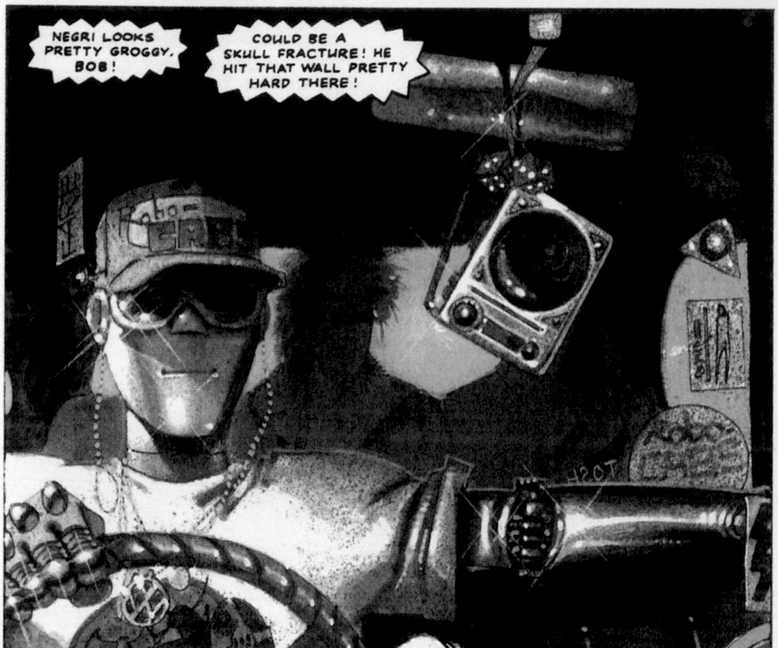
NEGRI LOOKS PRETTY GROGGY, BOB!
COULD BE A SKULL FRACTURE! HE HIT THAT WALL PRETTY HARD THERE!
SOME RACE! GORE CITY! BEATS THE SATURDAY NIGHT EXECUTIONS EVERY TIME!

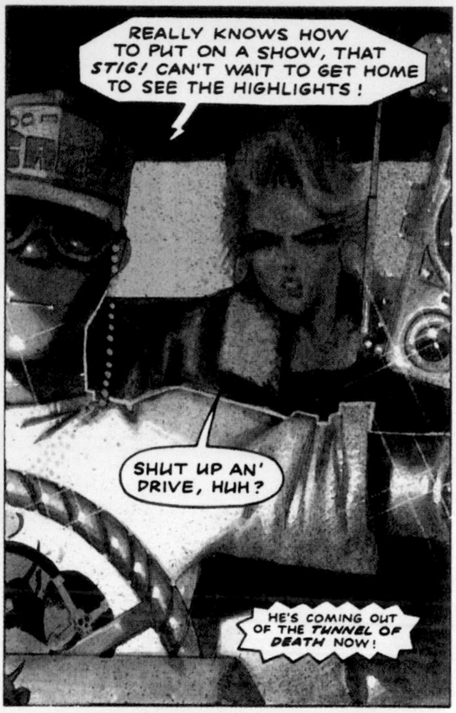
REALLY KNOWS HOW TO PUT ON A SHOW, THAT STIG! CAN'T WAIT TO GET HOME TO SEE THE HIGHLIGHTS!
SHUT UP AN' DRIVE, HUH?
HE'S COMING OUT OF THE TUNNEL OF DEATH NOW!

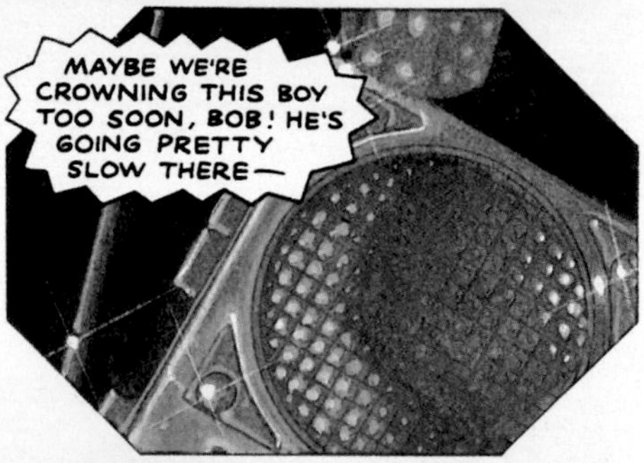
MAYBE WE'RE CROWNING THIS BOY TOO SOON, BOB! HE'S GOING PRETTY SLOW THERE—

CHOPPER

SONG OF THE SURFER

PART 11

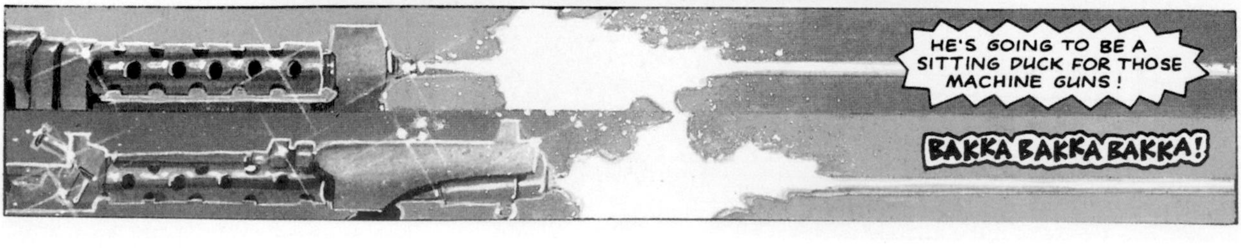
HE'S GOING TO BE A SITTING DUCK FOR THOSE MACHINE GUNS!
BAKKA BAKKA BAKKA!

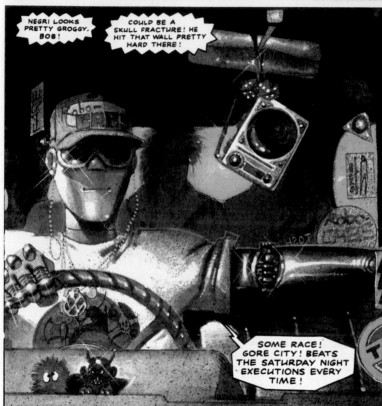

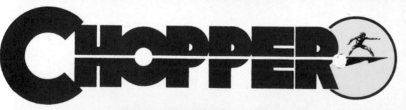

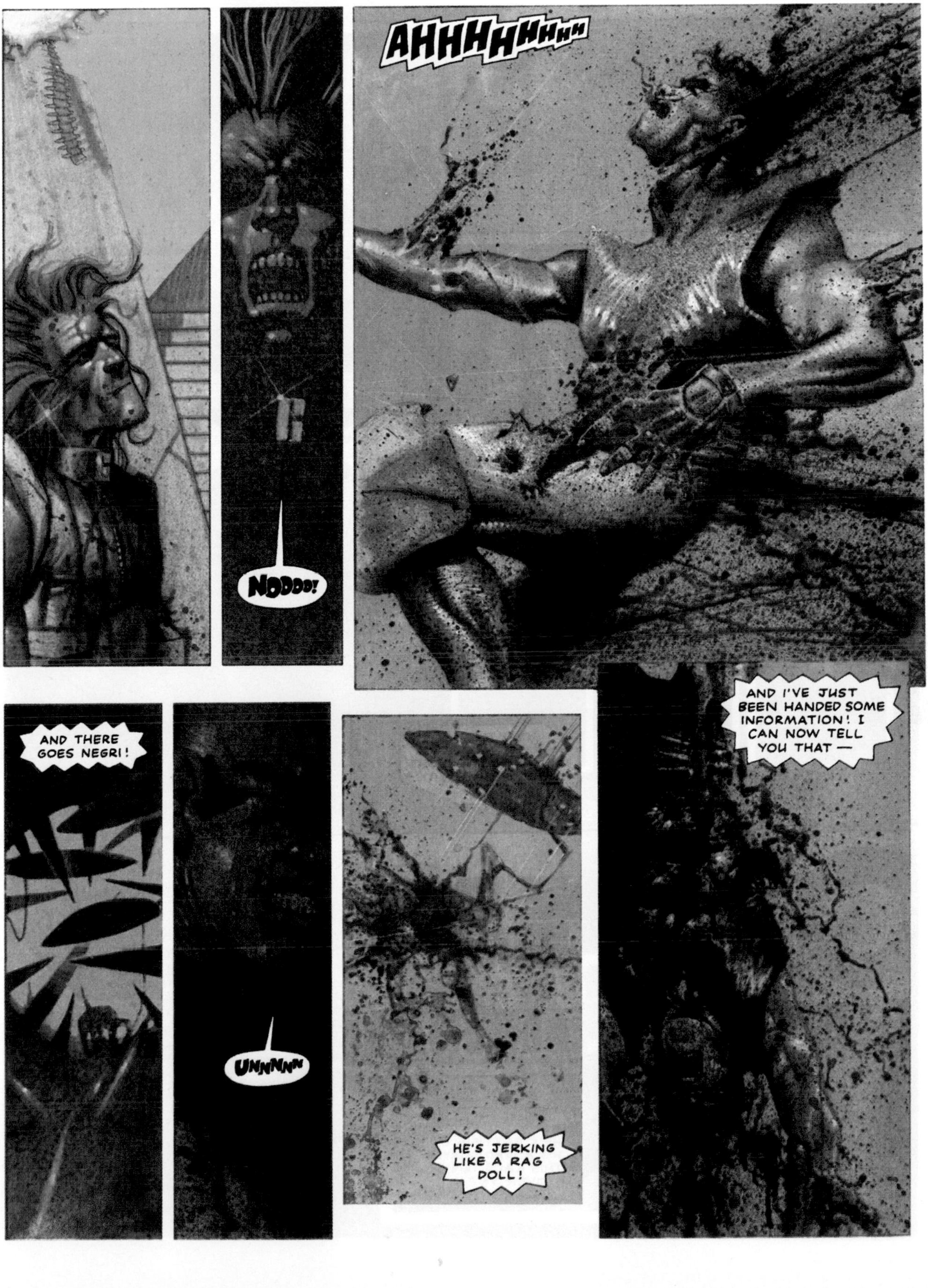
NOOOO!
AHHHHHHHH
AND THERE GOES NEGRI!
UNNNNN
HE'S JERKING LIKE A RAG DOLL!
AND I'VE JUST BEEN HANDED SOME INFORMATION! I CAN NOW TELL YOU THAT —

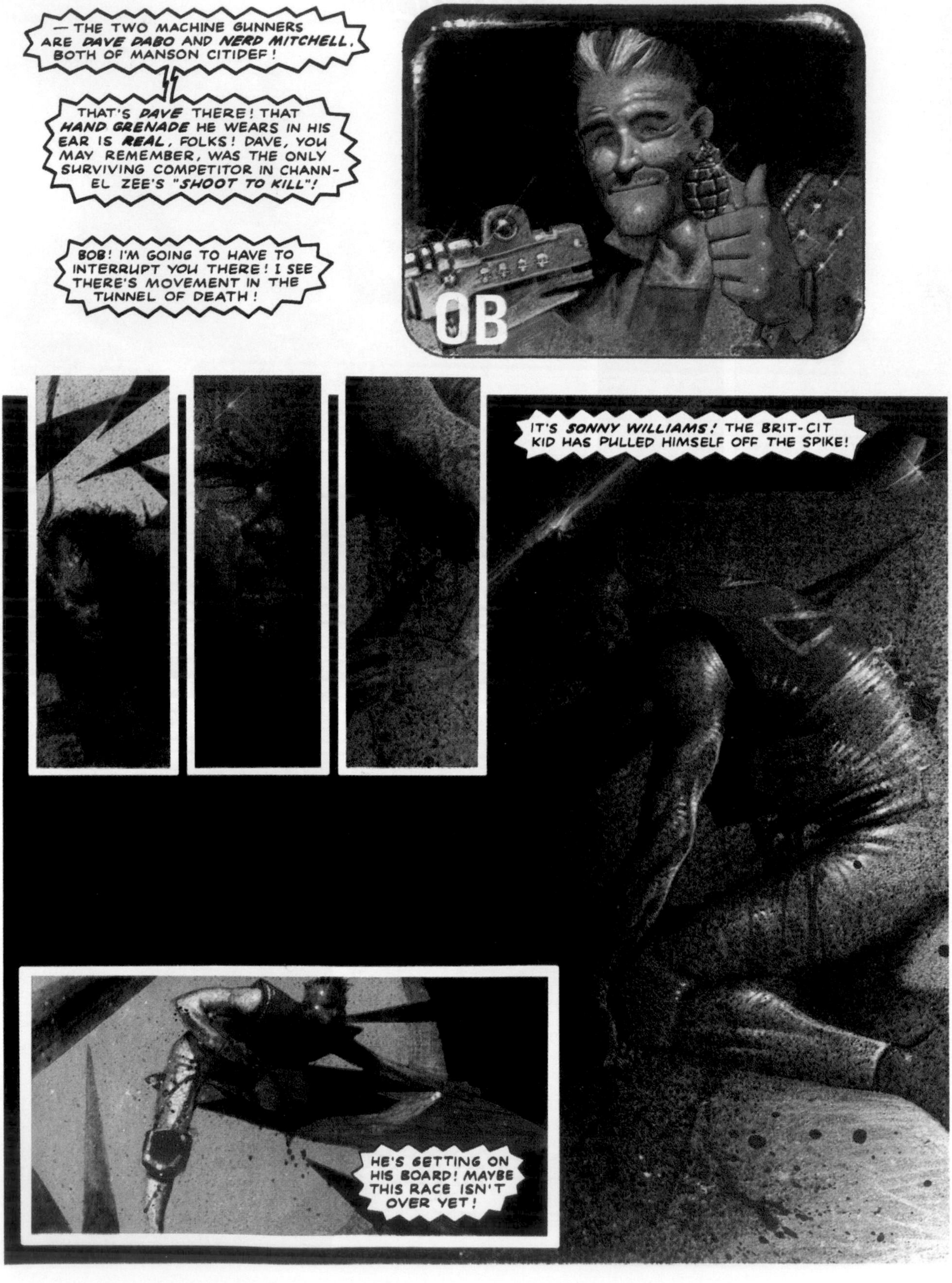
—THE TWO MACHINE GUNNERS ARE DAVE DABO AND NERD MITCHELL, BOTH OF MANSON CITIDEF!
THAT'S DAVE THERE! THAT HAND GRENADE HE WEARS IN HIS EAR IS REAL, FOLKS! DAVE, YOU MAY REMEMBER, WAS THE ONLY SURVIVING COMPETITOR IN CHANNEL ZEE'S "SHOOT TO KILL"!
BOB! I'M GOING TO HAVE TO INTERRUPT YOU THERE! I SEE THERE'S MOVEMENT IN THE TUNNEL OF DEATH!
OB
IT'S SONNY WILLIAMS! THE BRIT-CIT KID HAS PULLED HIMSELF OFF THE SPIKE!
HE'S GETTING ON HIS BOARD! MAYBE THIS RACE ISN'T OVER YET!

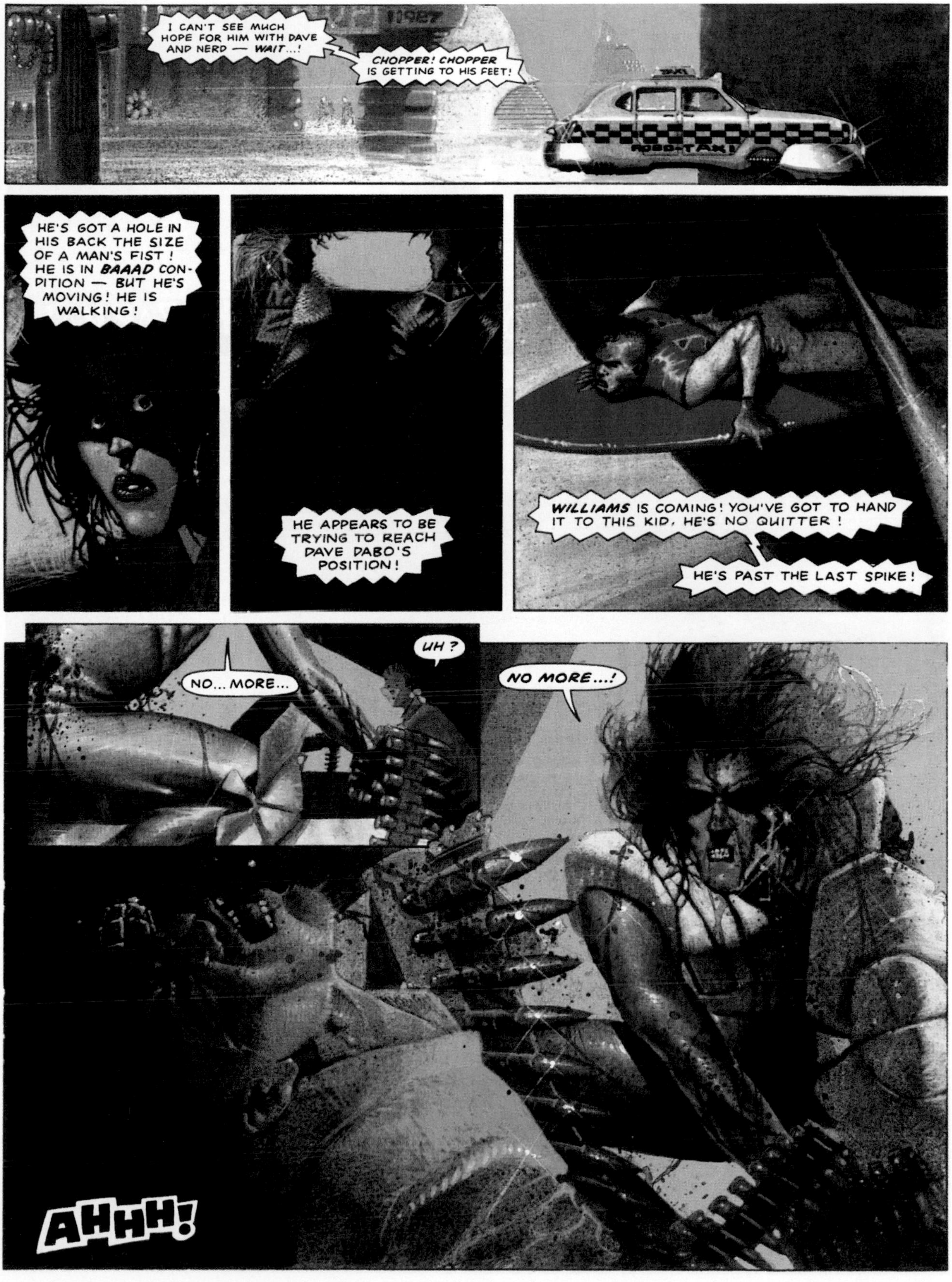
I CAN'T SEE MUCH HOPE FOR HIM WITH DAVE AND NERD — WAIT...!
CHOPPER! CHOPPER IS GETTING TO HIS FEET!
ROBO-TAXI
HE'S GOT A HOLE IN HIS BACK THE SIZE OF A MAN'S FIST! HE IS IN BAAAD CONDITION — BUT HE'S MOVING! HE IS WALKING!
HE APPEARS TO BE TRYING TO REACH DAVE DABO'S POSITION!
WILLIAMS IS COMING! YOU'VE GOT TO HAND IT TO THIS KID, HE'S NO QUITTER!
HE'S PAST THE LAST SPIKE!
NO... MORE...
UH?
NO MORE...!
AHHH!

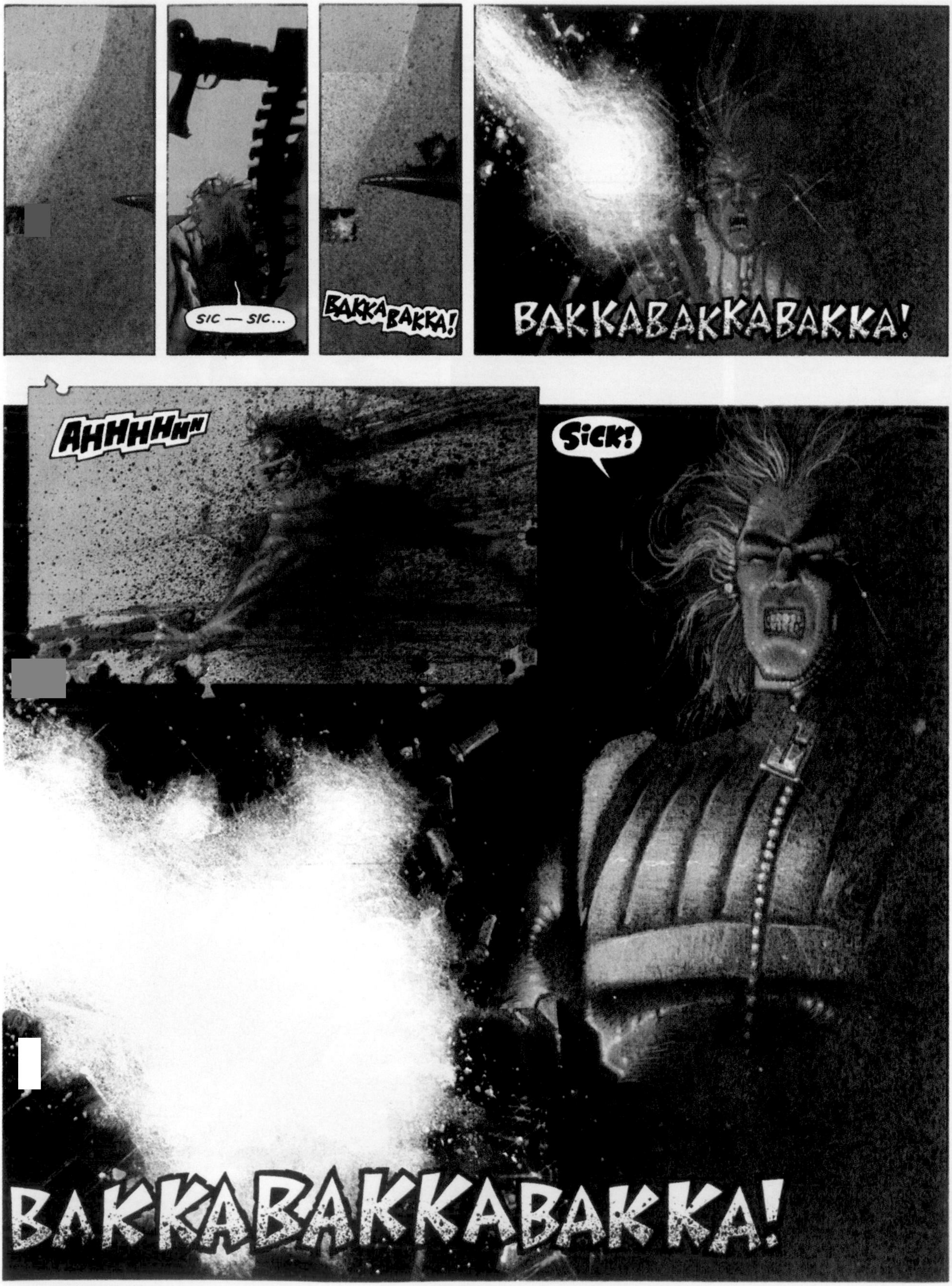
SIC — SIC...
BAKKA BAKKA!
BAKKABAKKABAKKA!
AHHHHHH
SICK!
BAKKABAKKABAKKA!

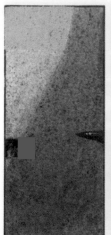

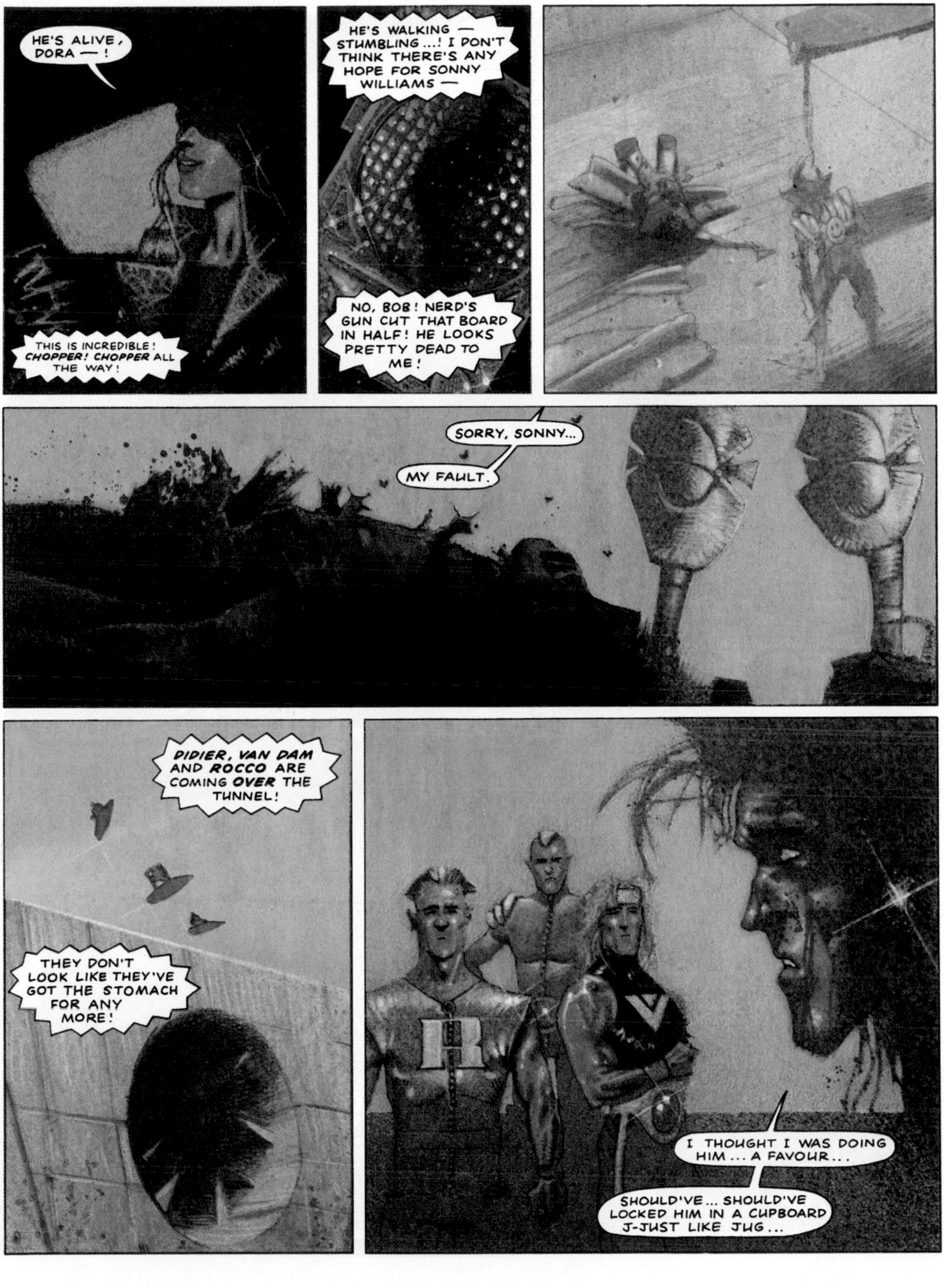
HE'S ALIVE, DORA — !
THIS IS INCREDIBLE! CHOPPER! CHOPPER ALL THE WAY!
HE'S WALKING — STUMBLING...! I DON'T THINK THERE'S ANY HOPE FOR SONNY WILLIAMS —
NO, BOB! NERD'S GUN CUT THAT BOARD IN HALF! HE LOOKS PRETTY DEAD TO ME!
SORRY, SONNY...
MY FAULT.
DIDIER, VAN DAM AND ROCCO ARE COMING OVER THE TUNNEL!
THEY DON'T LOOK LIKE THEY'VE GOT THE STOMACH FOR ANY MORE!
I THOUGHT I WAS DOING HIM ... A FAVOUR ...
SHOULD'VE... SHOULD'VE LOCKED HIM IN A CUPBOARD J-JUST LIKE JUG...

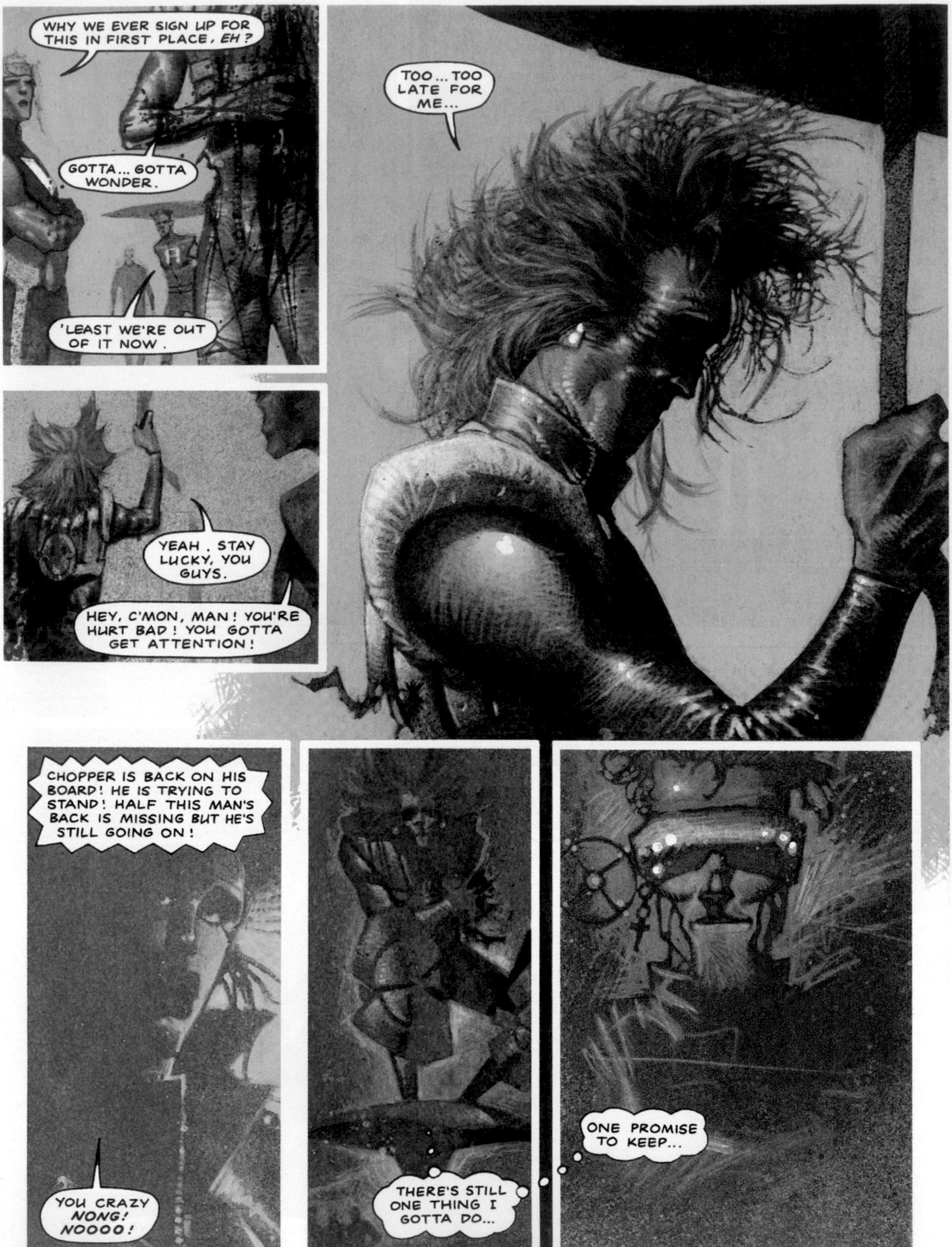
WHY WE EVER SIGN UP FOR THIS IN FIRST PLACE, EH?
GOTTA... GOTTA WONDER.
'LEAST WE'RE OUT OF IT NOW.
YEAH. STAY LUCKY, YOU GUYS.
HEY, C'MON, MAN! YOU'RE HURT BAD! YOU GOTTA GET ATTENTION!
TOO... TOO LATE FOR ME...
CHOPPER IS BACK ON HIS BOARD! HE IS TRYING TO STAND! HALF THIS MAN'S BACK IS MISSING BUT HE'S STILL GOING ON!
YOU CRAZY NONG! NOOOO!
THERE'S STILL ONE THING I GOTTA DO...
ONE PROMISE TO KEEP...

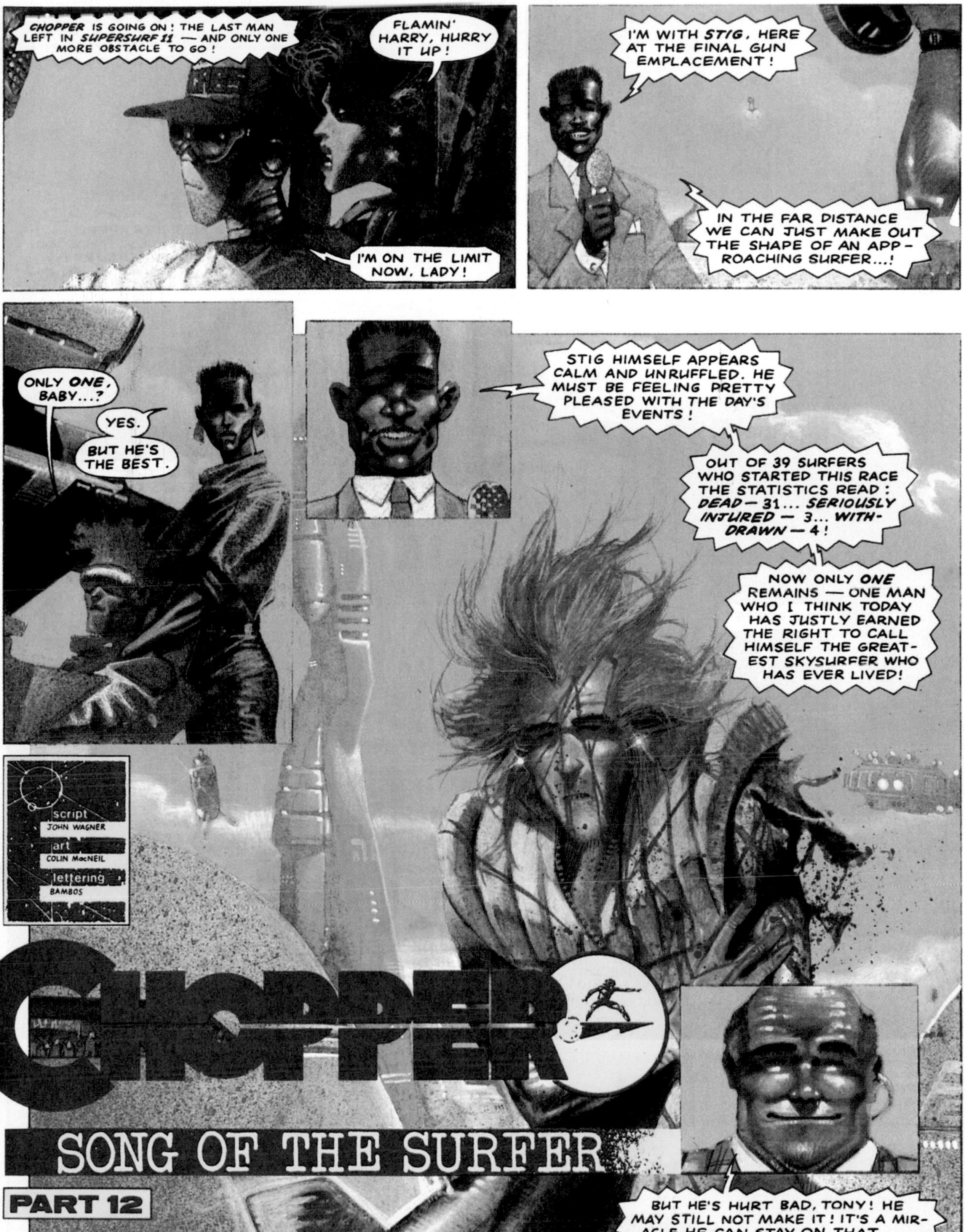

CHOPPER IS GOING ON! THE LAST MAN LEFT IN SUPERSURF 11 — AND ONLY ONE MORE OBSTACLE TO GO!
FLAMIN' HARRY, HURRY IT UP!
I'M ON THE LIMIT NOW, LADY!
I'M WITH STIG, HERE AT THE FINAL GUN EMPLACEMENT!
IN THE FAR DISTANCE WE CAN JUST MAKE OUT THE SHAPE OF AN APP-ROACHING SURFER...!
ONLY ONE, BABY...?
YES.
BUT HE'S THE BEST.
STIG HIMSELF APPEARS CALM AND UNRUFFLED. HE MUST BE FEELING PRETTY PLEASED WITH THE DAY'S EVENTS!
OUT OF 39 SURFERS WHO STARTED THIS RACE THE STATISTICS READ: DEAD — 31... SERIOUSLY INJURED — 3... WITH-DRAWN — 4!
NOW ONLY ONE REMAINS — ONE MAN WHO I THINK TODAY HAS JUSTLY EARNED THE RIGHT TO CALL HIMSELF THE GREAT-EST SKYSURFER WHO HAS EVER LIVED!
script JOHN WAGNER
art COLIN MacNEIL
lettering BAMBOS
CHOPPER
SONG OF THE SURFER
PART 12
BUT HE'S HURT BAD, TONY! HE MAY STILL NOT MAKE IT! IT'S A MIR-ACLE HE CAN STAY ON THAT BOARD AS IT IS!

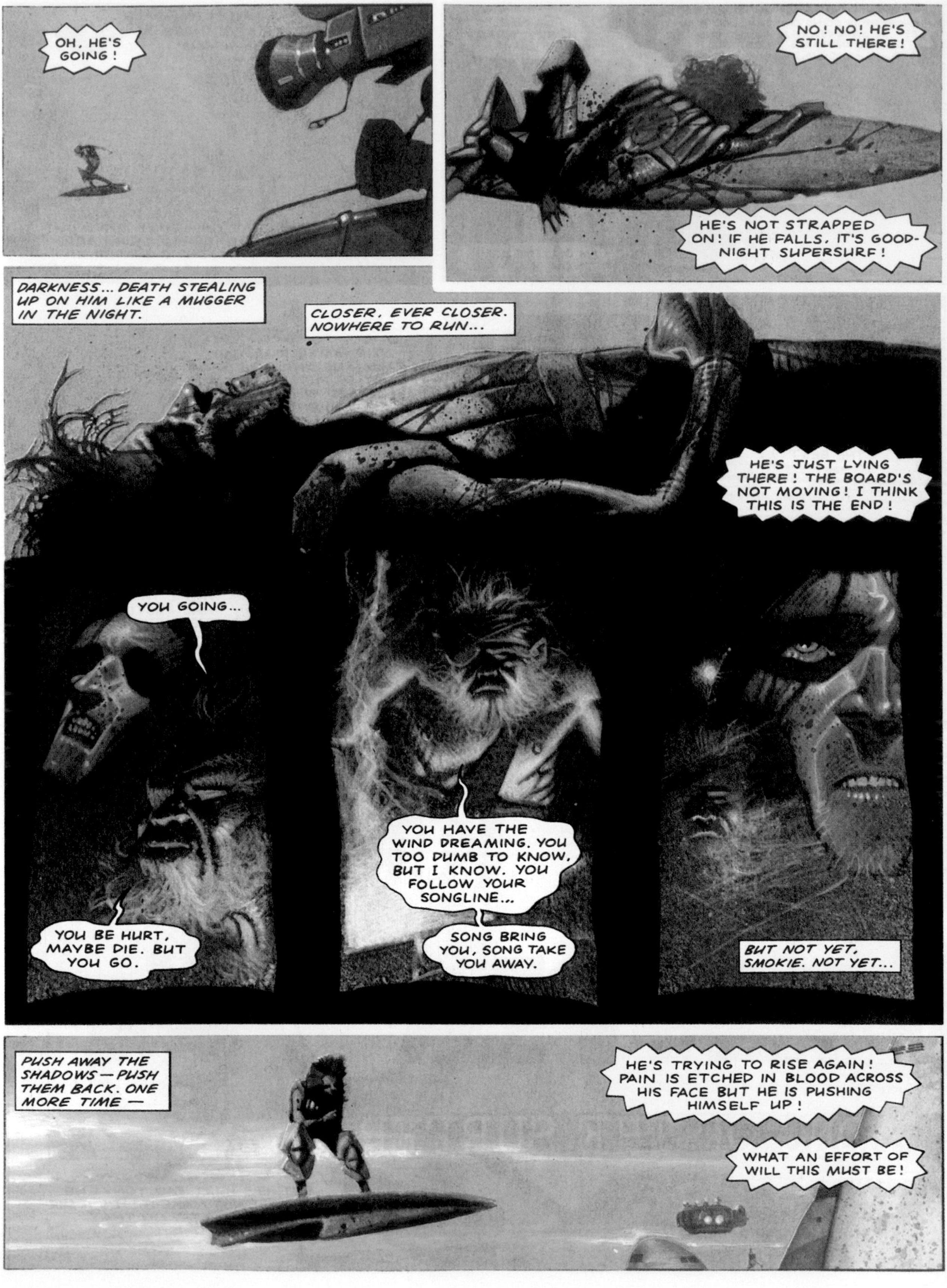
OH, HE'S GOING!
NO! NO! HE'S STILL THERE!
HE'S NOT STRAPPED ON! IF HE FALLS, IT'S GOOD-NIGHT SUPERSURF!
DARKNESS... DEATH STEALING UP ON HIM LIKE A MUGGER IN THE NIGHT.
CLOSER, EVER CLOSER. NOWHERE TO RUN...
HE'S JUST LYING THERE! THE BOARD'S NOT MOVING! I THINK THIS IS THE END!
YOU GOING...
YOU BE HURT, MAYBE DIE. BUT YOU GO.
YOU HAVE THE WIND DREAMING. YOU TOO DUMB TO KNOW, BUT I KNOW. YOU FOLLOW YOUR SONGLINE...
SONG BRING YOU, SONG TAKE YOU AWAY.
BUT NOT YET, SMOKIE. NOT YET...
PUSH AWAY THE SHADOWS — PUSH THEM BACK. ONE MORE TIME —
HE'S TRYING TO RISE AGAIN! PAIN IS ETCHED IN BLOOD ACROSS HIS FACE BUT HE IS PUSHING HIMSELF UP!
WHAT AN EFFORT OF WILL THIS MUST BE!

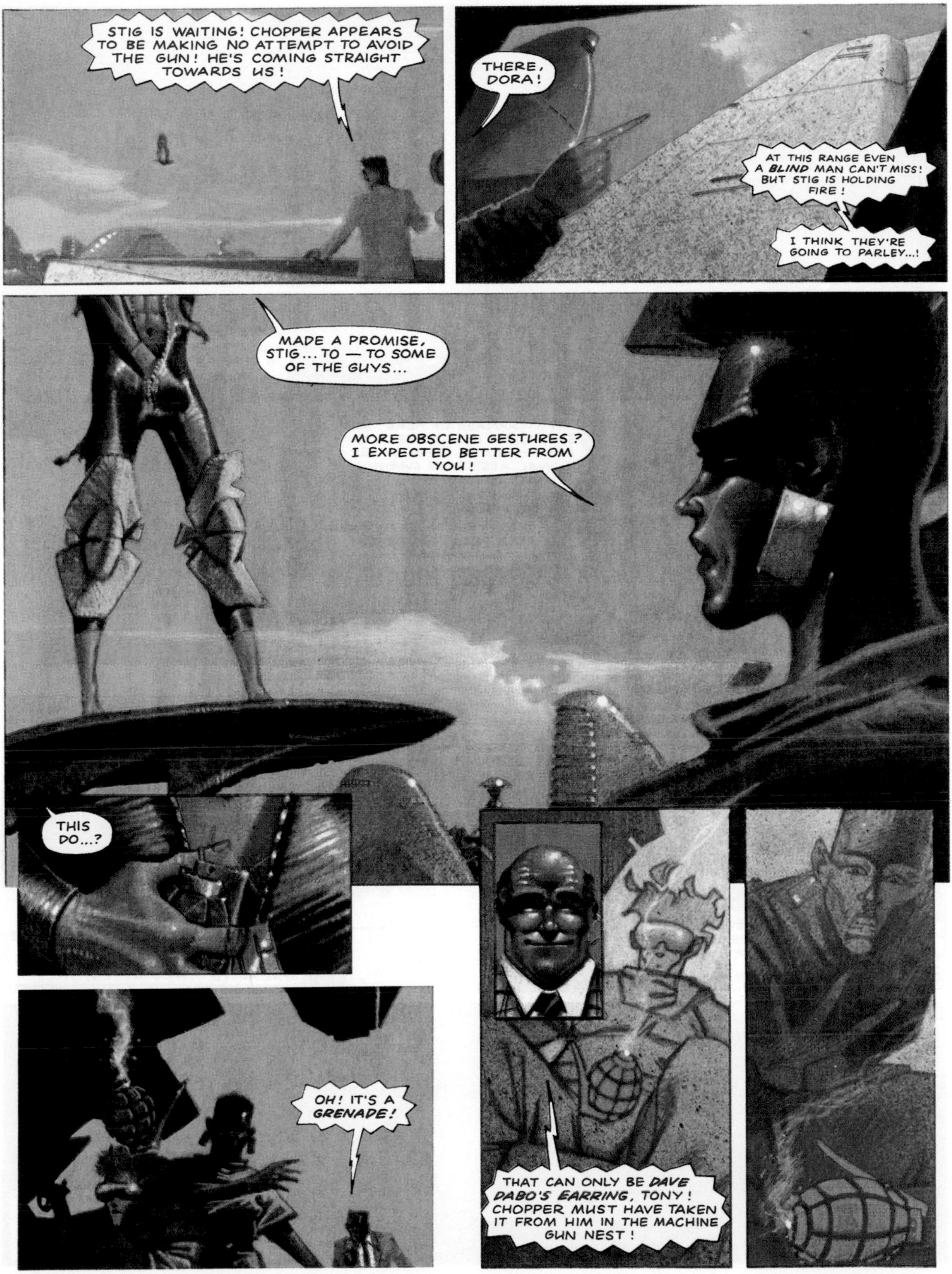
STIG IS WAITING! CHOPPER APPEARS TO BE MAKING NO ATTEMPT TO AVOID THE GUN! HE'S COMING STRAIGHT TOWARDS US!
THERE, DORA!
AT THIS RANGE EVEN A BLIND MAN CAN'T MISS! BUT STIG IS HOLDING FIRE!
I THINK THEY'RE GOING TO PARLEY...!
MADE A PROMISE, STIG... TO — TO SOME OF THE GUYS...
MORE OBSCENE GESTURES? I EXPECTED BETTER FROM YOU!
THIS DO...?
OH! IT'S A GRENADE!
THAT CAN ONLY BE DAVE DABO'S EARRING, TONY! CHOPPER MUST HAVE TAKEN IT FROM HIM IN THE MACHINE GUN NEST!

AJEEEEE:!

WELL, *THERE'S* A TURN-UP!

IT'S CARNAGE UP HERE, BOB! SUPERSURF ORGANISER *STIG* IS DEAD — ALONG WITH HIS PER-SONAL ASSISTANT *CARMEL!* AND I THINK —

YES! THE TIP OF MY *OWN* LEFT FOOT HAS BEEN *BLOWN OFF!*

THEY CERTAINLY CAN'T CALL YOU AN ARMCHAIR COMMENTATOR, TONY!

BUT WE'RE WITH THE LEADER NOW! THE ONLY MAN LEFT IN SUPER-SURF 11!

HE IS WEAK! HE IS SWAYING ON THAT BOARD! BUT HE IS HEADING TOWARDS THE *FINISH LINE!*

DARKNESS... STEALING UP ON HIM AGAIN.

PAIN GONE. JUST A NUMBNESS — AN ALMOST PLEASANT NUMBNESS — SPREADING THROUGH HIM...

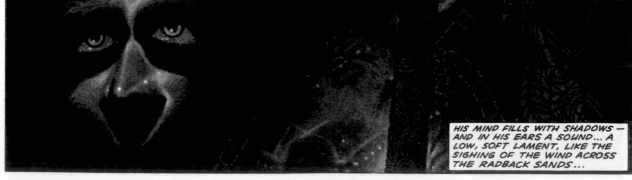

HIS MIND FILLS WITH SHADOWS — AND IN HIS EARS A SOUND... A LOW, SOFT LAMENT, LIKE THE SIGHING OF THE WIND ACROSS THE RADBACK SANDS...

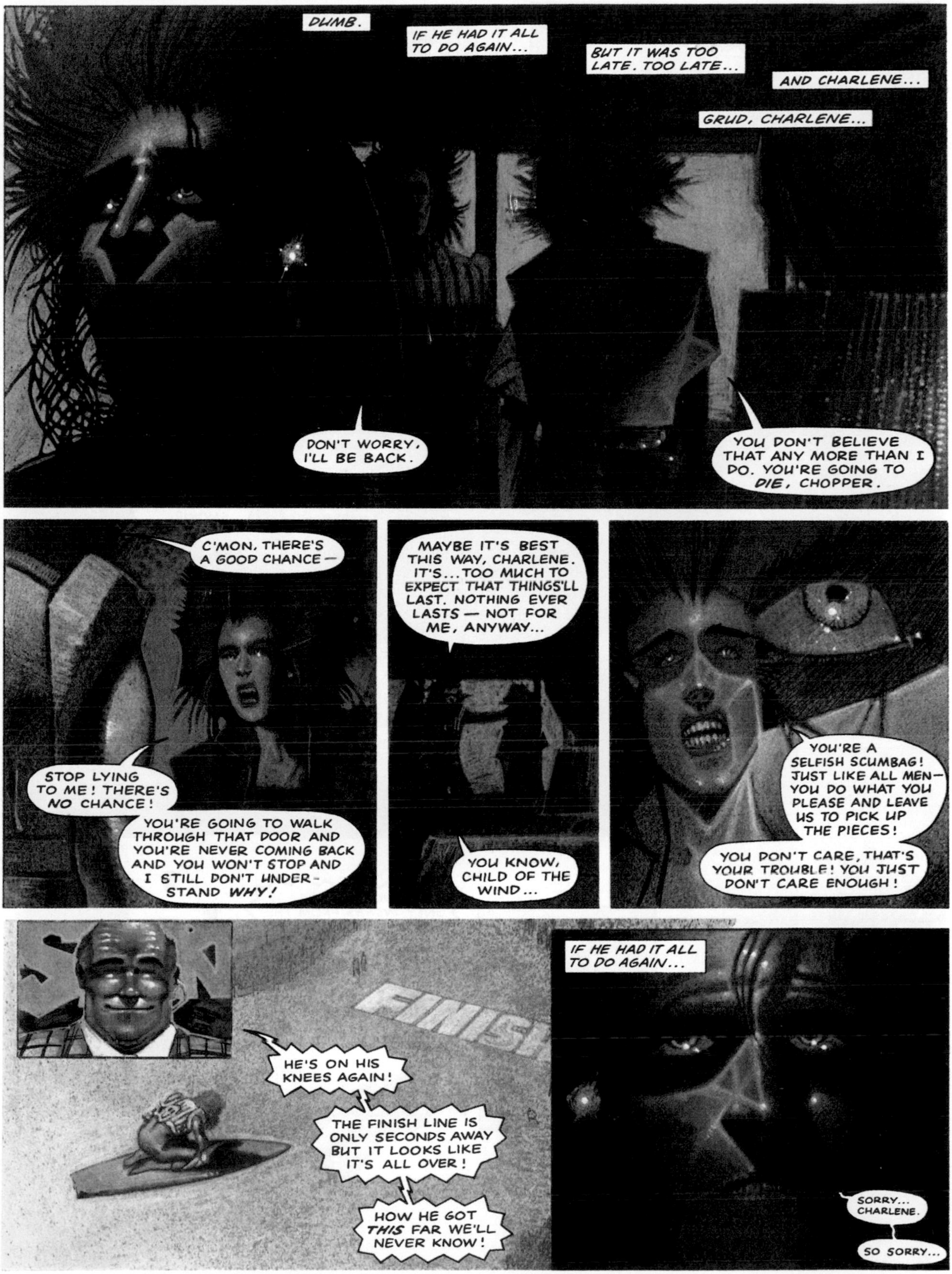
DUMB.
IF HE HAD IT ALL TO DO AGAIN...
BUT IT WAS TOO LATE. TOO LATE...
AND CHARLENE...
GRUD, CHARLENE...
DON'T WORRY, I'LL BE BACK.
YOU DON'T BELIEVE THAT ANY MORE THAN I DO. YOU'RE GOING TO *DIE*, CHOPPER.
C'MON, THERE'S A GOOD CHANCE—
STOP LYING TO ME! THERE'S *NO* CHANCE!
YOU'RE GOING TO WALK THROUGH THAT DOOR AND YOU'RE NEVER COMING BACK AND YOU WON'T STOP AND I STILL DON'T UNDER-STAND *WHY!*
MAYBE IT'S BEST THIS WAY, CHARLENE. IT'S... TOO MUCH TO EXPECT THAT THINGS'LL LAST. NOTHING EVER LASTS — NOT FOR ME, ANYWAY...
YOU KNOW, CHILD OF THE WIND...
YOU'RE A SELFISH SCUMBAG! JUST LIKE ALL MEN— YOU DO WHAT YOU PLEASE AND LEAVE US TO PICK UP THE PIECES!
YOU DON'T CARE, THAT'S YOUR TROUBLE! YOU JUST DON'T CARE ENOUGH!
FINISH
HE'S ON HIS KNEES AGAIN!
THE FINISH LINE IS ONLY SECONDS AWAY BUT IT LOOKS LIKE IT'S ALL OVER!
HOW HE GOT *THIS* FAR WE'LL NEVER KNOW!
IF HE HAD IT ALL TO DO AGAIN...
SORRY... CHARLENE.
SO SORRY...

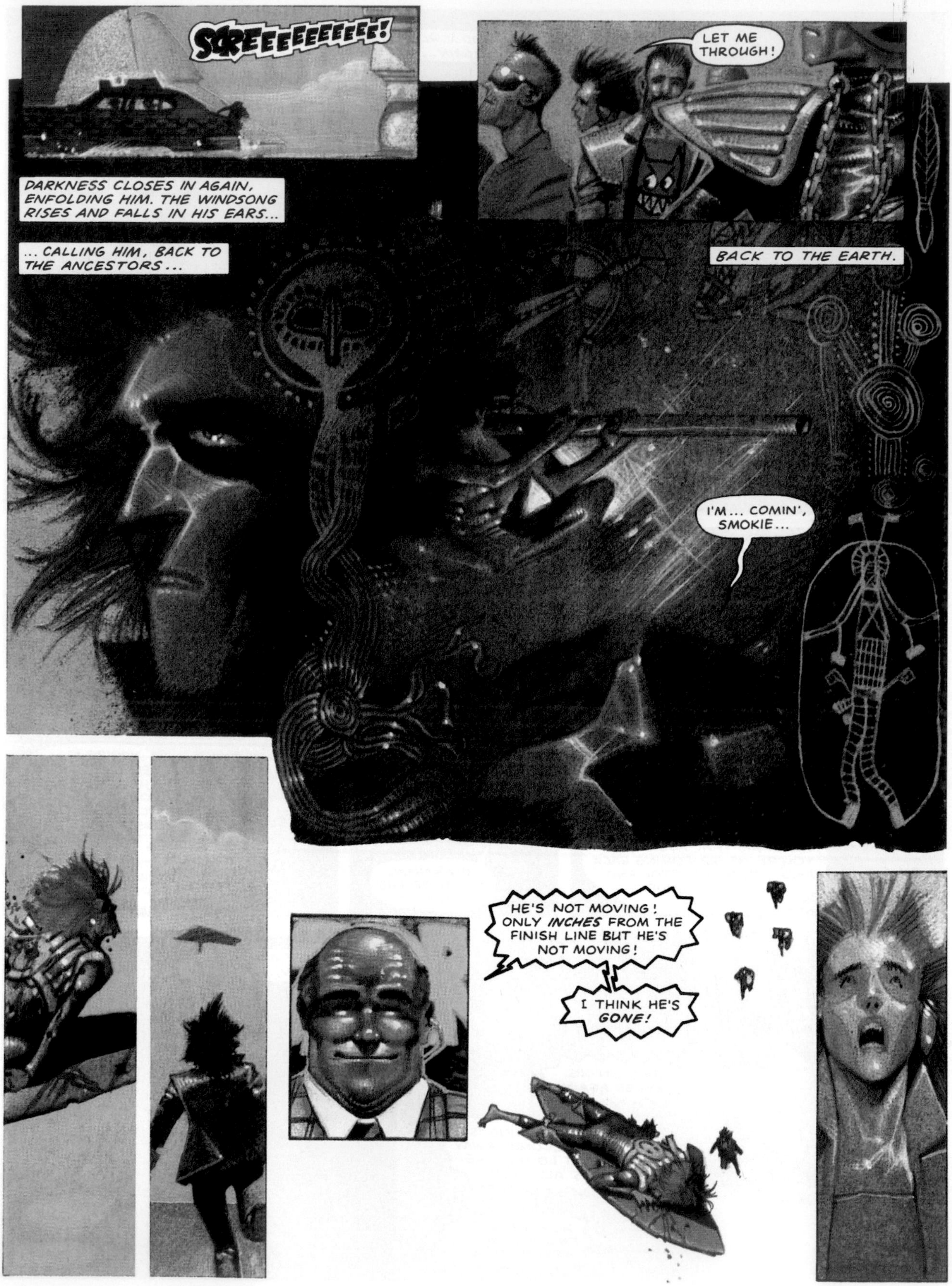
SCREEEEEEEEEE!
LET ME THROUGH!
DARKNESS CLOSES IN AGAIN, ENFOLDING HIM. THE WINDSONG RISES AND FALLS IN HIS EARS...
... CALLING HIM, BACK TO THE ANCESTORS...
BACK TO THE EARTH.
I'M... COMIN', SMOKIE...
HE'S NOT MOVING! ONLY INCHES FROM THE FINISH LINE BUT HE'S NOT MOVING!
I THINK HE'S GONE!

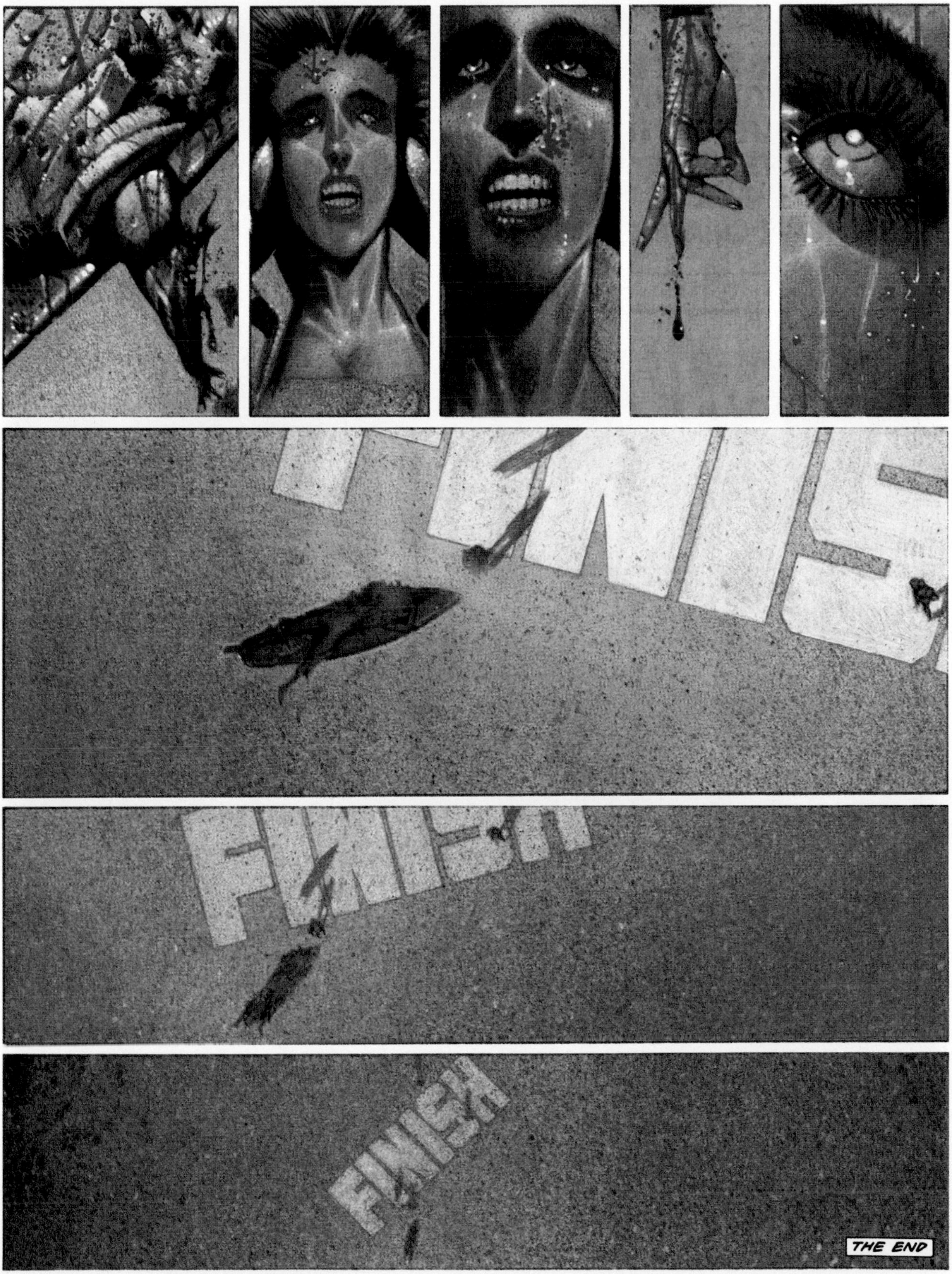
FINISH
FINISH
THE END

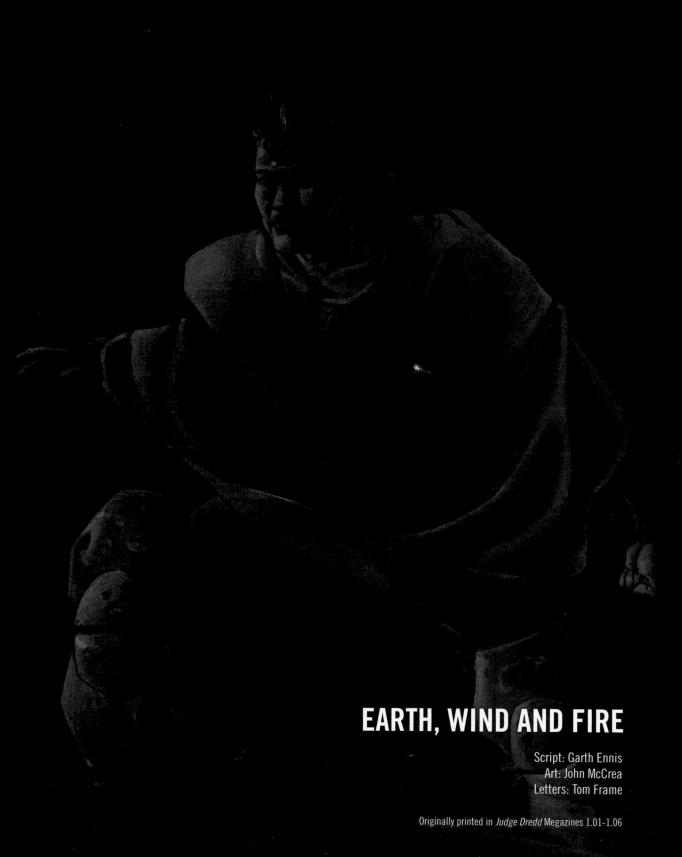

EARTH, WIND AND FIRE

Script: Garth Ennis
Art: John McCrea
Letters: Tom Frame

Originally printed in *Judge Dredd* Megazines 1.01-1.06

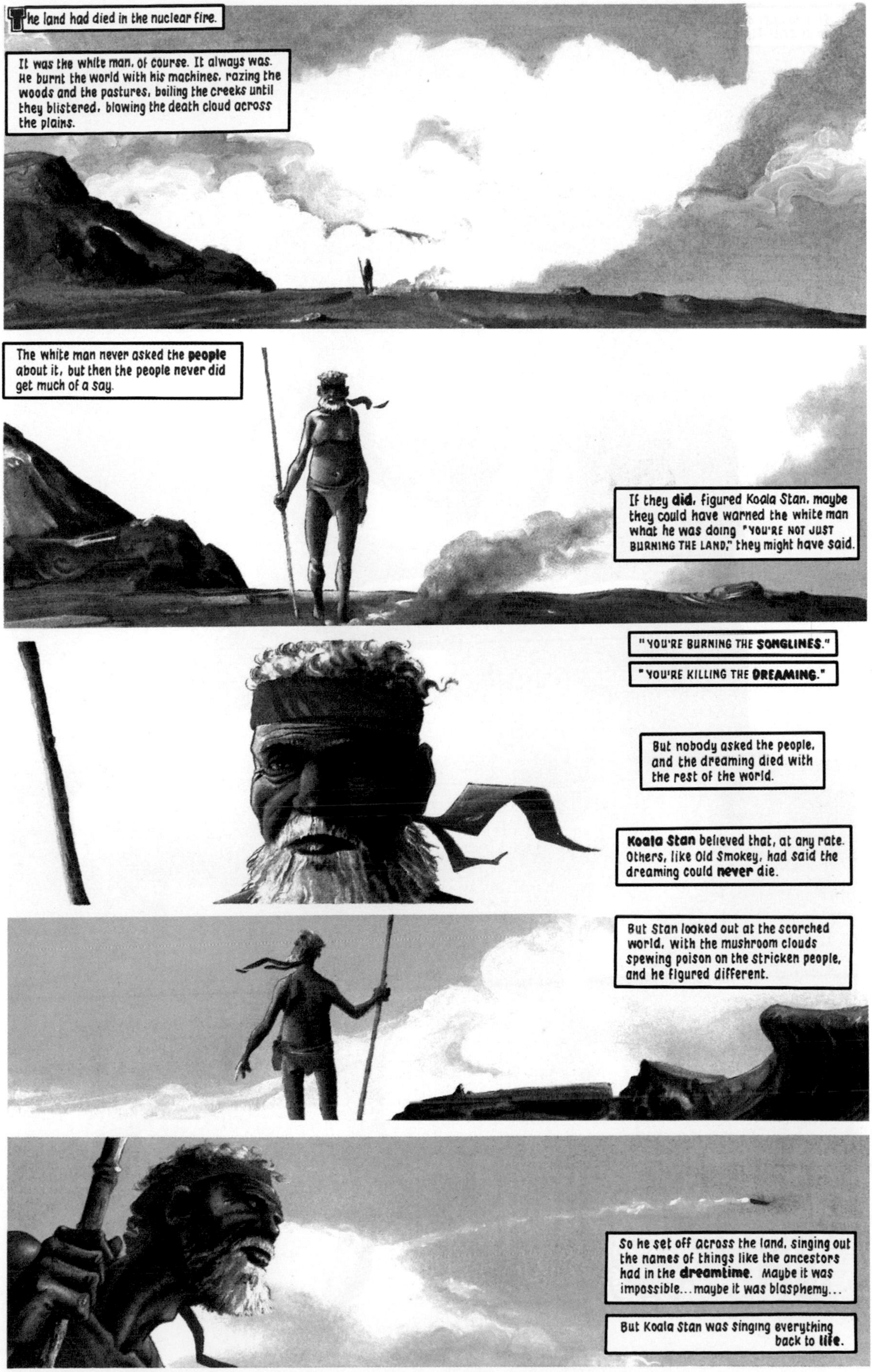
The land had died in the nuclear fire.
It was the white man, of course. It always was. He burnt the world with his machines, razing the woods and the pastures, boiling the creeks until they blistered, blowing the death cloud across the plains.
The white man never asked the **people** about it, but then the people never did get much of a say.
If they **did**, figured Koala Stan, maybe they could have warned the white man what he was doing "YOU'RE NOT JUST BURNING THE LAND," they might have said.
"YOU'RE BURNING THE **SONGLINES**."
"YOU'RE KILLING THE **DREAMING**."
But nobody asked the people, and the dreaming died with the rest of the world.
Koala Stan believed that, at any rate. Others, like Old Smokey, had said the dreaming could **never** die.
But Stan looked out at the scorched world, with the mushroom clouds spewing poison on the stricken people, and he figured different.
So he set off across the land, singing out the names of things like the ancestors had in the **dreamtime**. Maybe it was impossible... maybe it was blasphemy...
But Koala Stan was singing everything back to **life**.

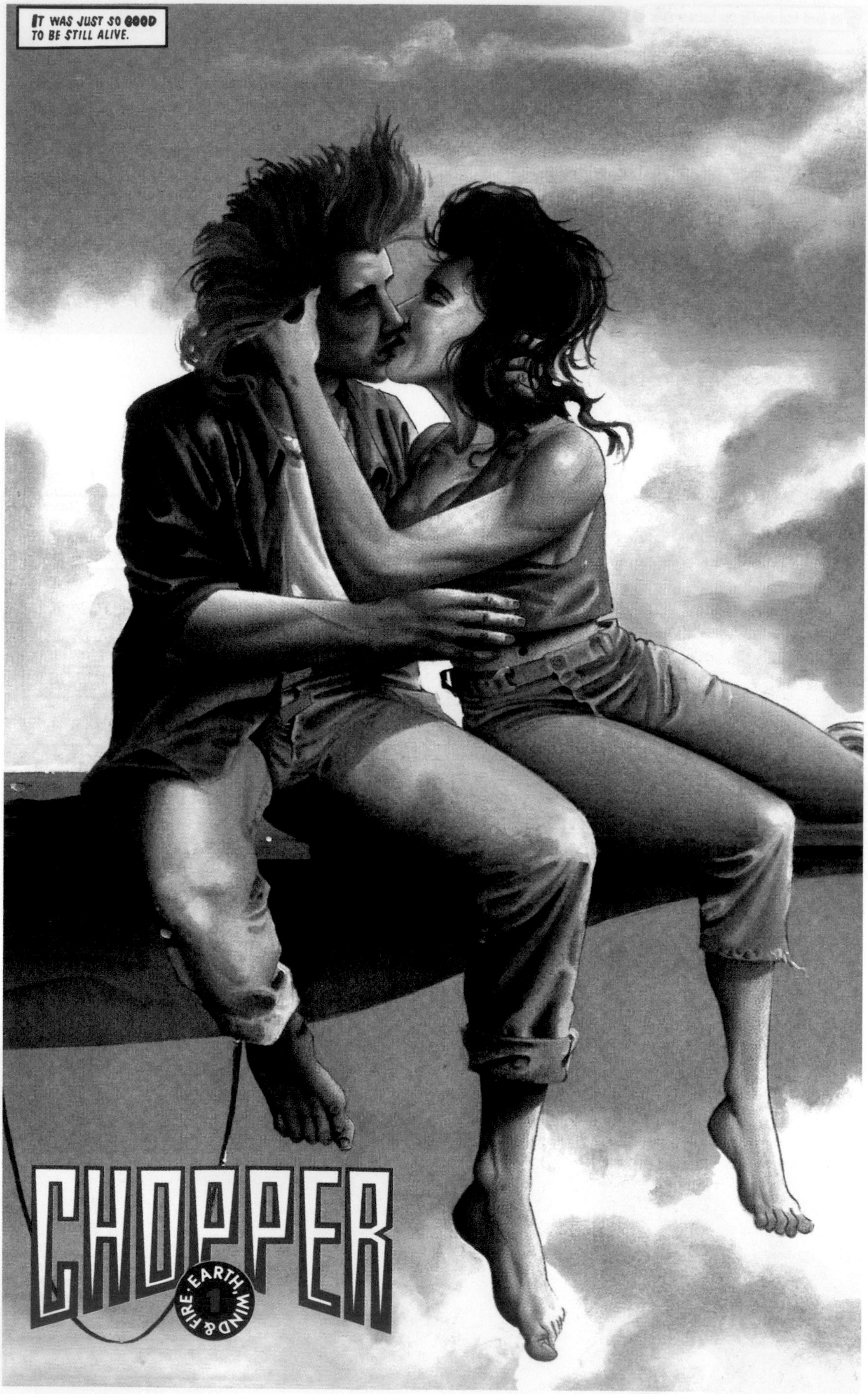
IT WAS JUST SO GOOD TO BE STILL ALIVE.
CHOPPER
EARTH, WIND & FIRE 1

HE DIDN'T DESERVE TO BE ALIVE, HE KNEW. AND HE CERTAINLY DIDN'T DESERVE **CHARLENE.**

HE'D BETRAYED HER IN MEGA-CITY TWO... SHE'D LOVED HIM, CARED FOR HIM, AND ALL HE COULD DO IN RETURN WAS GET HIMSELF BUTCHERED IN A STUPID, POINTLESS SURF RACE. SHE'D HAD EVERY RIGHT TO LEAVE HIM.

WHEN HE WOKE UP IN THE HOSPITAL, SHE WAS THE FIRST THING HE SAW.

HE'D CRIED HIS EYES OUT.

BUT THE RACE WAS OVER NOW. THE WIND SONG THAT NEARLY BLEW HIM ALL THE WAY TO HELL HAD DIED AWAY, AND THEY'D COME BACK TO OZ... TO DRONGO SPRINGS, DEEP IN THE RADBACK.

IN MEMORY
THOSE WHO DI
IN SUPERSURF
DALLAS HALL
VIDOR MULHOLLA
SONY WILLIAMS
JURGEN HASSLI
ART CARTER
PAULO NE

HE WASN'T A FIGHTER ANYMORE. HE WASN'T **SOMEBODY,** WASN'T KING SURFER, WASN'T A SOUL ON FIRE, WASN'T THE GREATEST SKYSURFER WHO EVER LIVED.

HE WAS JUST CHOPPER, AND HE WAS AT HOME WITH HIS LOVER AND HIS FRIENDS.

HE WAS AT **PEACE.**

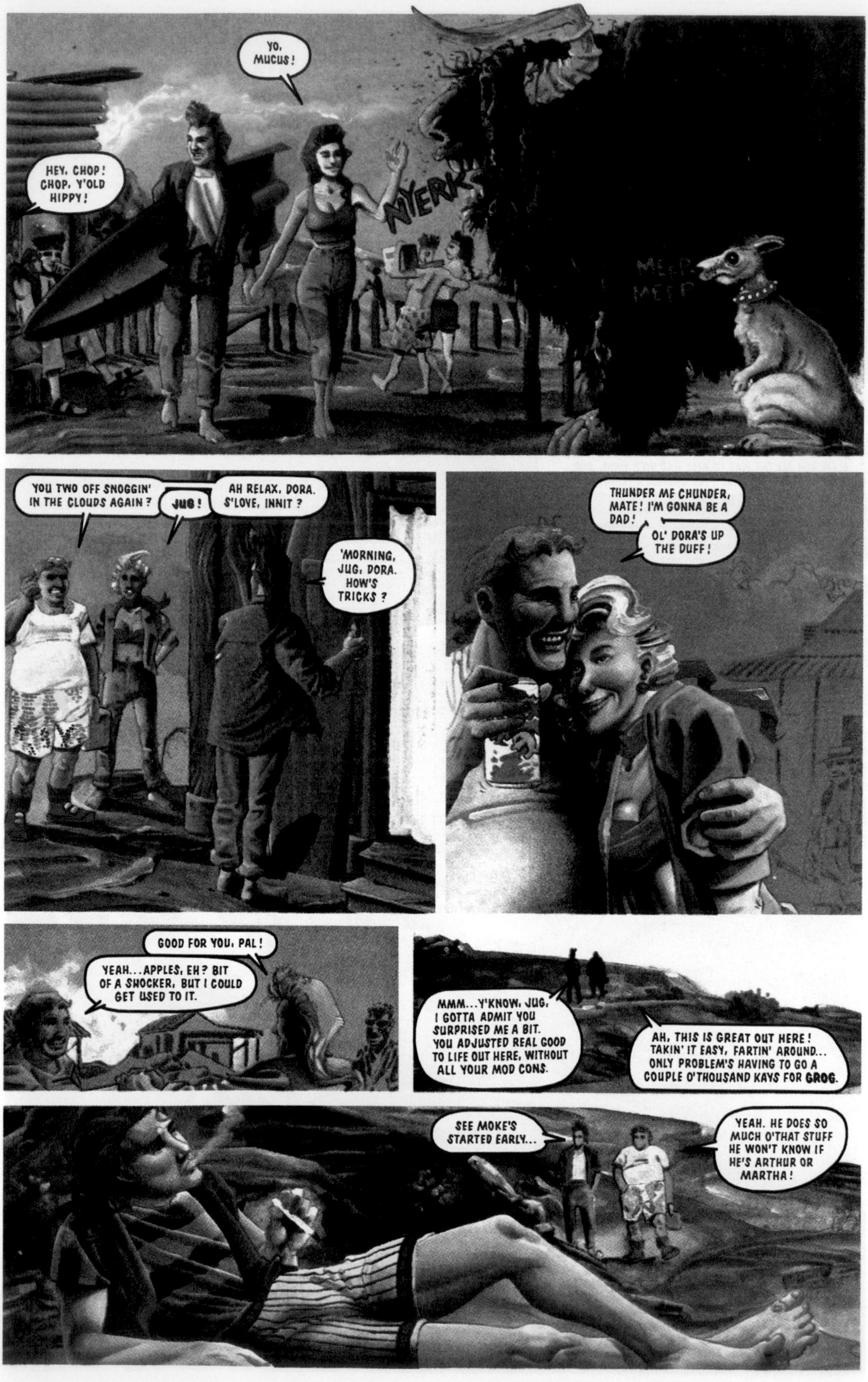
HEY, CHOP! CHOP, Y'OLD HIPPY!
YO, MUCUS!
NYERK
MEEP MEEP
YOU TWO OFF SNOGGIN' IN THE CLOUDS AGAIN?
JUG!
AH RELAX, DORA. S'LOVE, INNIT?
'MORNING, JUG, DORA. HOW'S TRICKS?
THUNDER ME CHUNDER, MATE! I'M GONNA BE A DAD!
OL' DORA'S UP THE DUFF!
GOOD FOR YOU, PAL!
YEAH... APPLES, EH? BIT OF A SHOCKER, BUT I COULD GET USED TO IT.
MMM... Y'KNOW, JUG, I GOTTA ADMIT YOU SURPRISED ME A BIT. YOU ADJUSTED REAL GOOD TO LIFE OUT HERE, WITHOUT ALL YOUR MOD CONS.
AH, THIS IS GREAT OUT HERE! TAKIN' IT EASY, FARTIN' AROUND... ONLY PROBLEM'S HAVING TO GO A COUPLE O'THOUSAND KAYS FOR GROG.
SEE MOKE'S STARTED EARLY...
YEAH. HE DOES SO MUCH O'THAT STUFF HE WON'T KNOW IF HE'S ARTHUR OR MARTHA!

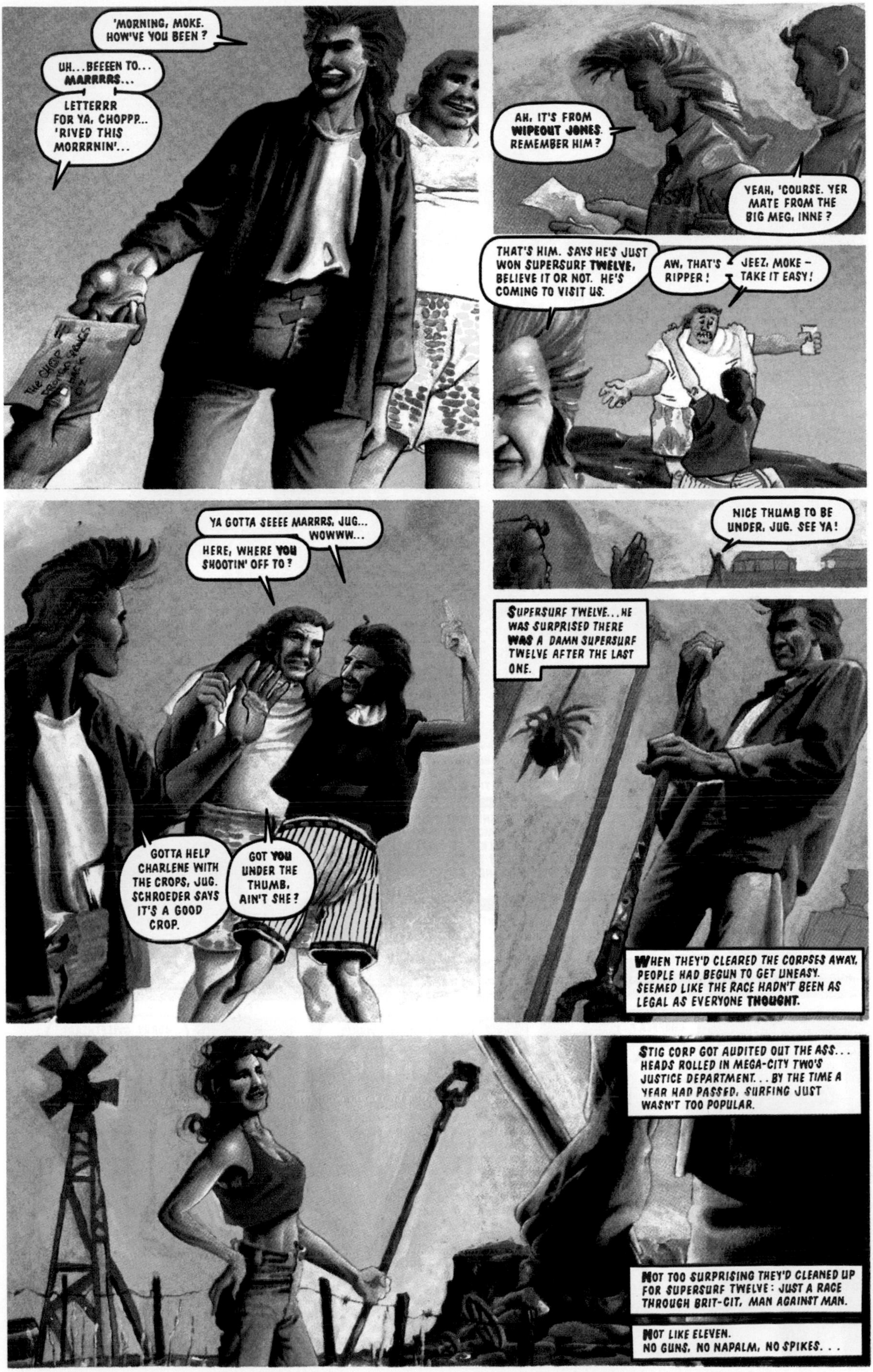
'MORNING, MOKE. HOW'VE YOU BEEN?
UH... BEEEEN TO... MARRRRS...
LETTERRR FOR YA, CHOPPP... 'RIVED THIS MORRRNIN'...
AH, IT'S FROM WIPEOUT JONES. REMEMBER HIM?
YEAH, 'COURSE. YER MATE FROM THE BIG MEG, INNE?
THAT'S HIM. SAYS HE'S JUST WON SUPERSURF TWELVE, BELIEVE IT OR NOT. HE'S COMING TO VISIT US.
AW, THAT'S RIPPER!
JEEZ, MOKE – TAKE IT EASY!
YA GOTTA SEEEE MARRRS, JUG... WOWWW...
HERE, WHERE YOU SHOOTIN' OFF TO?
GOTTA HELP CHARLENE WITH THE CROPS, JUG. SCHROEDER SAYS IT'S A GOOD CROP.
GOT YOU UNDER THE THUMB, AIN'T SHE?
NICE THUMB TO BE UNDER, JUG. SEE YA!
SUPERSURF TWELVE... HE WAS SURPRISED THERE WAS A DAMN SUPERSURF TWELVE AFTER THE LAST ONE.
WHEN THEY'D CLEARED THE CORPSES AWAY, PEOPLE HAD BEGUN TO GET UNEASY. SEEMED LIKE THE RACE HADN'T BEEN AS LEGAL AS EVERYONE THOUGHT.
STIG CORP GOT AUDITED OUT THE ASS... HEADS ROLLED IN MEGA-CITY TWO'S JUSTICE DEPARTMENT... BY THE TIME A YEAR HAD PASSED, SURFING JUST WASN'T TOO POPULAR.
NOT TOO SURPRISING THEY'D CLEANED UP FOR SUPERSURF TWELVE: JUST A RACE THROUGH BRIT-CIT, MAN AGAINST MAN.
NOT LIKE ELEVEN.
NO GUNS, NO NAPALM, NO SPIKES...

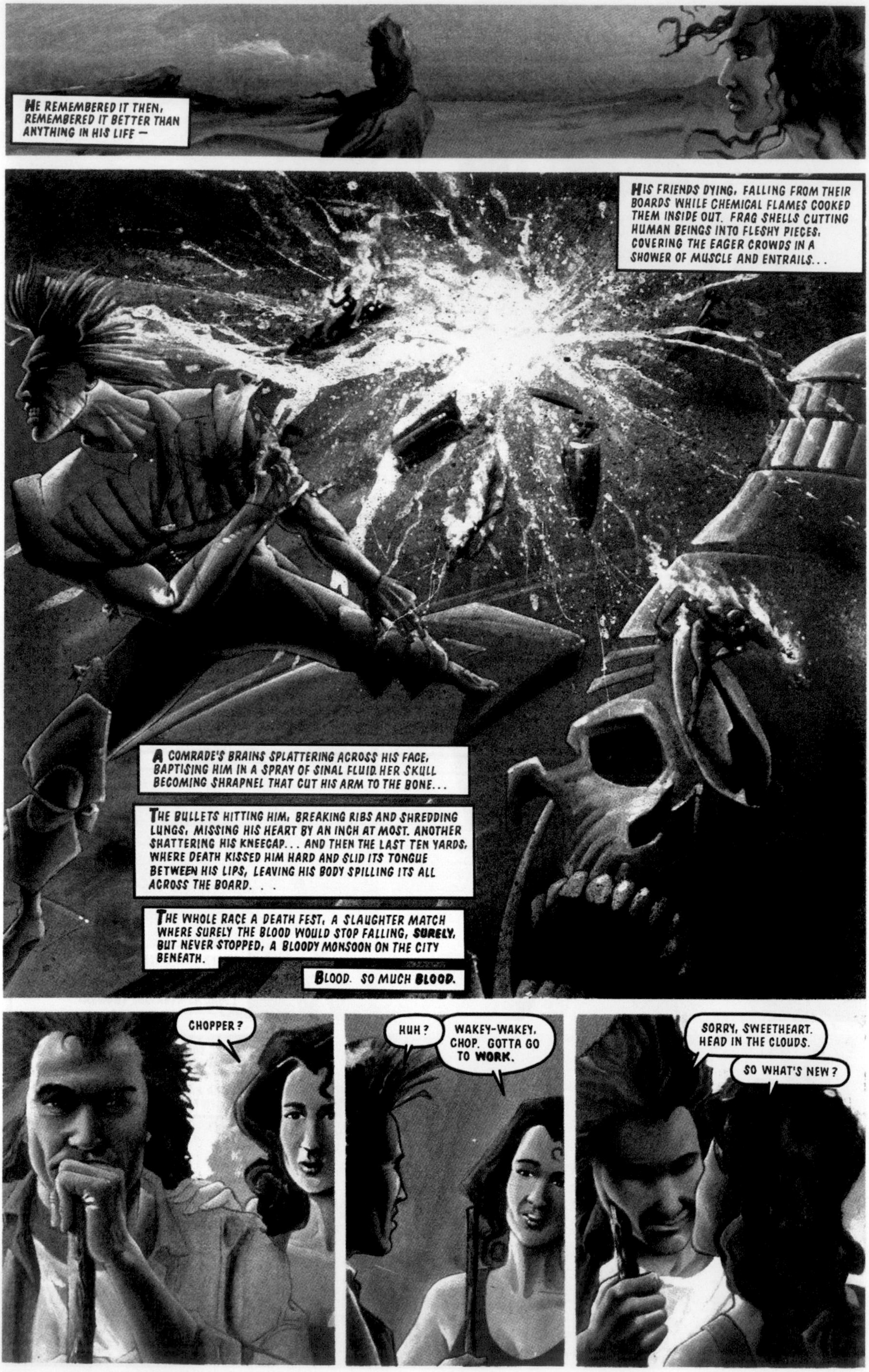
HE REMEMBERED IT THEN, REMEMBERED IT BETTER THAN ANYTHING IN HIS LIFE —
HIS FRIENDS DYING, FALLING FROM THEIR BOARDS WHILE CHEMICAL FLAMES COOKED THEM INSIDE OUT. FRAG SHELLS CUTTING HUMAN BEINGS INTO FLESHY PIECES, COVERING THE EAGER CROWDS IN A SHOWER OF MUSCLE AND ENTRAILS. . .
A COMRADE'S BRAINS SPLATTERING ACROSS HIS FACE, BAPTISING HIM IN A SPRAY OF SINAL FLUID. HER SKULL BECOMING SHRAPNEL THAT CUT HIS ARM TO THE BONE. . .
THE BULLETS HITTING HIM, BREAKING RIBS AND SHREDDING LUNGS, MISSING HIS HEART BY AN INCH AT MOST. ANOTHER SHATTERING HIS KNEECAP. . . AND THEN THE LAST TEN YARDS, WHERE DEATH KISSED HIM HARD AND SLID ITS TONGUE BETWEEN HIS LIPS, LEAVING HIS BODY SPILLING ITS ALL ACROSS THE BOARD. . .
THE WHOLE RACE A DEATH FEST, A SLAUGHTER MATCH WHERE SURELY THE BLOOD WOULD STOP FALLING, SURELY, BUT NEVER STOPPED, A BLOODY MONSOON ON THE CITY BENEATH.
BLOOD. SO MUCH BLOOD.
CHOPPER?
HUH?
WAKEY-WAKEY, CHOP. GOTTA GO TO WORK.
SORRY, SWEETHEART. HEAD IN THE CLOUDS.
SO WHAT'S NEW?

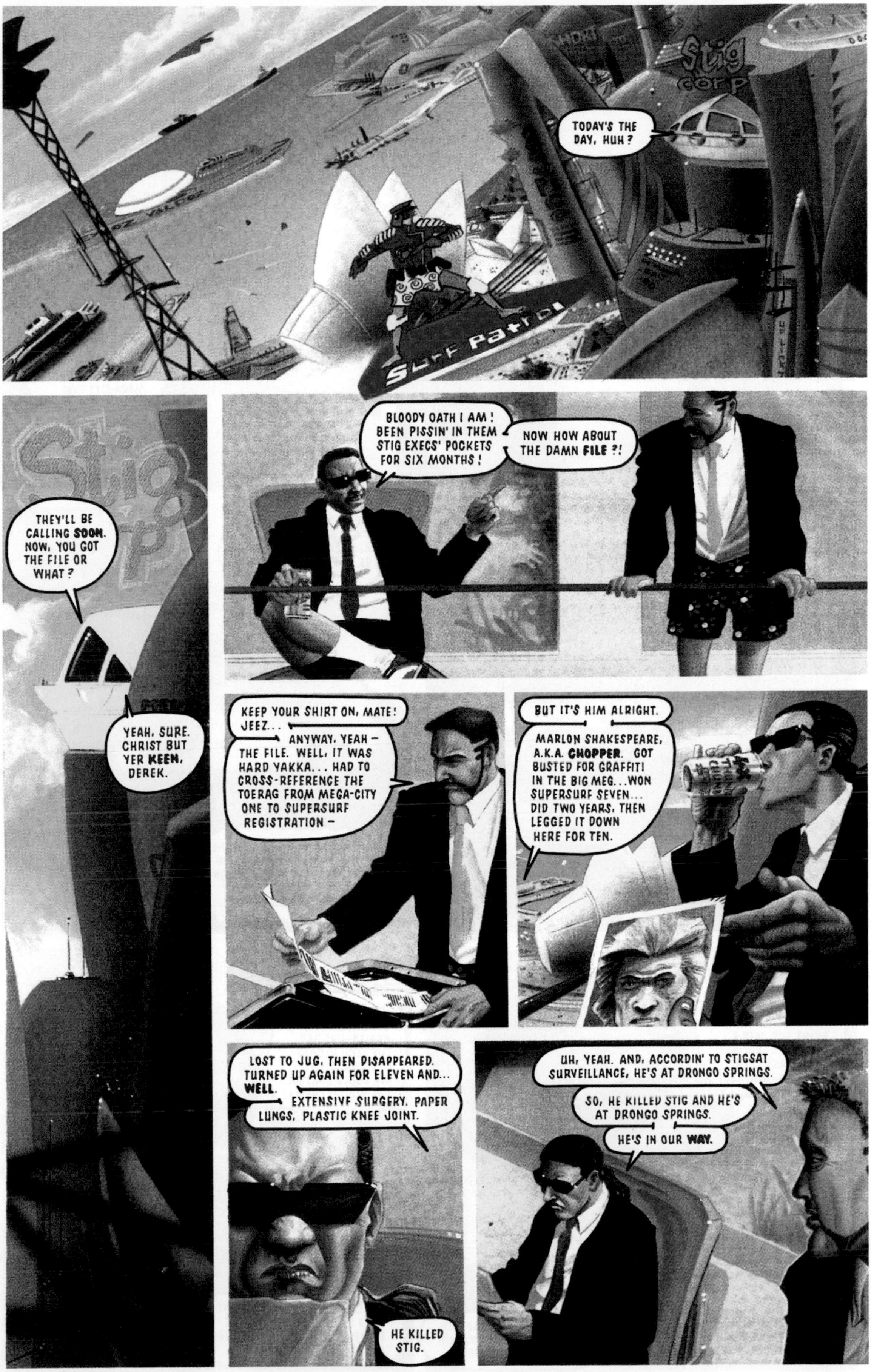
TODAY'S THE DAY, HUH?
THEY'LL BE CALLING SOON. NOW, YOU GOT THE FILE OR WHAT?
YEAH, SURE. CHRIST BUT YER KEEN, DEREK.
BLOODY OATH I AM! BEEN PISSIN' IN THEM STIG EXECS' POCKETS FOR SIX MONTHS!
NOW HOW ABOUT THE DAMN FILE?!
KEEP YOUR SHIRT ON, MATE! JEEZ...
ANYWAY, YEAH — THE FILE. WELL, IT WAS HARD YAKKA... HAD TO CROSS-REFERENCE THE TOERAG FROM MEGA-CITY ONE TO SUPERSURF REGISTRATION —
BUT IT'S HIM ALRIGHT.
MARLON SHAKESPEARE, A.K.A. CHOPPER. GOT BUSTED FOR GRAFFITI IN THE BIG MEG...WON SUPERSURF SEVEN... DID TWO YEARS, THEN LEGGED IT DOWN HERE FOR TEN.
LOST TO JUG, THEN DISAPPEARED. TURNED UP AGAIN FOR ELEVEN AND... WELL.
EXTENSIVE SURGERY. PAPER LUNGS, PLASTIC KNEE JOINT.
HE KILLED STIG.
UH, YEAH. AND, ACCORDIN' TO STIGSAT SURVEILLANCE, HE'S AT DRONGO SPRINGS.
SO, HE KILLED STIG AND HE'S AT DRONGO SPRINGS.
HE'S IN OUR WAY.

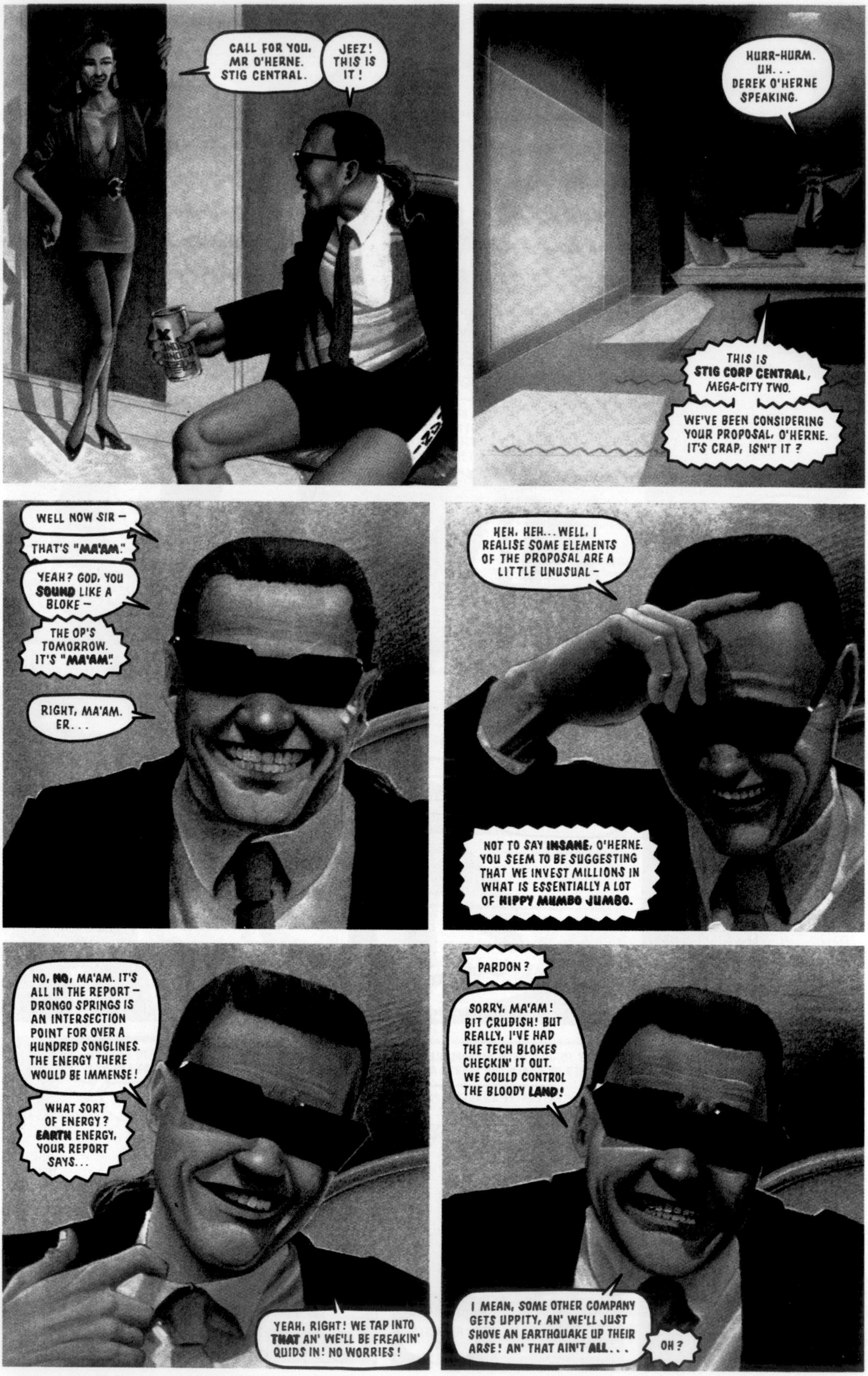
CALL FOR YOU, MR O'HERNE. STIG CENTRAL.
JEEZ! THIS IS IT!
HURR-HURM. UH... DEREK O'HERNE SPEAKING.
THIS IS STIG CORP CENTRAL, MEGA-CITY TWO.
WE'VE BEEN CONSIDERING YOUR PROPOSAL, O'HERNE. IT'S CRAP, ISN'T IT?
WELL NOW SIR —
THAT'S "MA'AM."
YEAH? GOD, YOU SOUND LIKE A BLOKE —
THE OP'S TOMORROW. IT'S "MA'AM".
RIGHT, MA'AM. ER...
HEH, HEH... WELL, I REALISE SOME ELEMENTS OF THE PROPOSAL ARE A LITTLE UNUSUAL —
NOT TO SAY INSANE, O'HERNE. YOU SEEM TO BE SUGGESTING THAT WE INVEST MILLIONS IN WHAT IS ESSENTIALLY A LOT OF HIPPY MUMBO JUMBO.
NO, NO, MA'AM. IT'S ALL IN THE REPORT — DRONGO SPRINGS IS AN INTERSECTION POINT FOR OVER A HUNDRED SONGLINES. THE ENERGY THERE WOULD BE IMMENSE!
WHAT SORT OF ENERGY? EARTH ENERGY, YOUR REPORT SAYS...
YEAH, RIGHT! WE TAP INTO THAT AN' WE'LL BE FREAKIN' QUIDS IN! NO WORRIES!
PARDON?
SORRY, MA'AM! BIT CRUDISH! BUT REALLY, I'VE HAD THE TECH BLOKES CHECKIN' IT OUT. WE COULD CONTROL THE BLOODY LAND!
I MEAN, SOME OTHER COMPANY GETS UPPITY, AN' WE'LL JUST SHOVE AN EARTHQUAKE UP THEIR ARSE! AN' THAT AIN'T ALL...
OH?

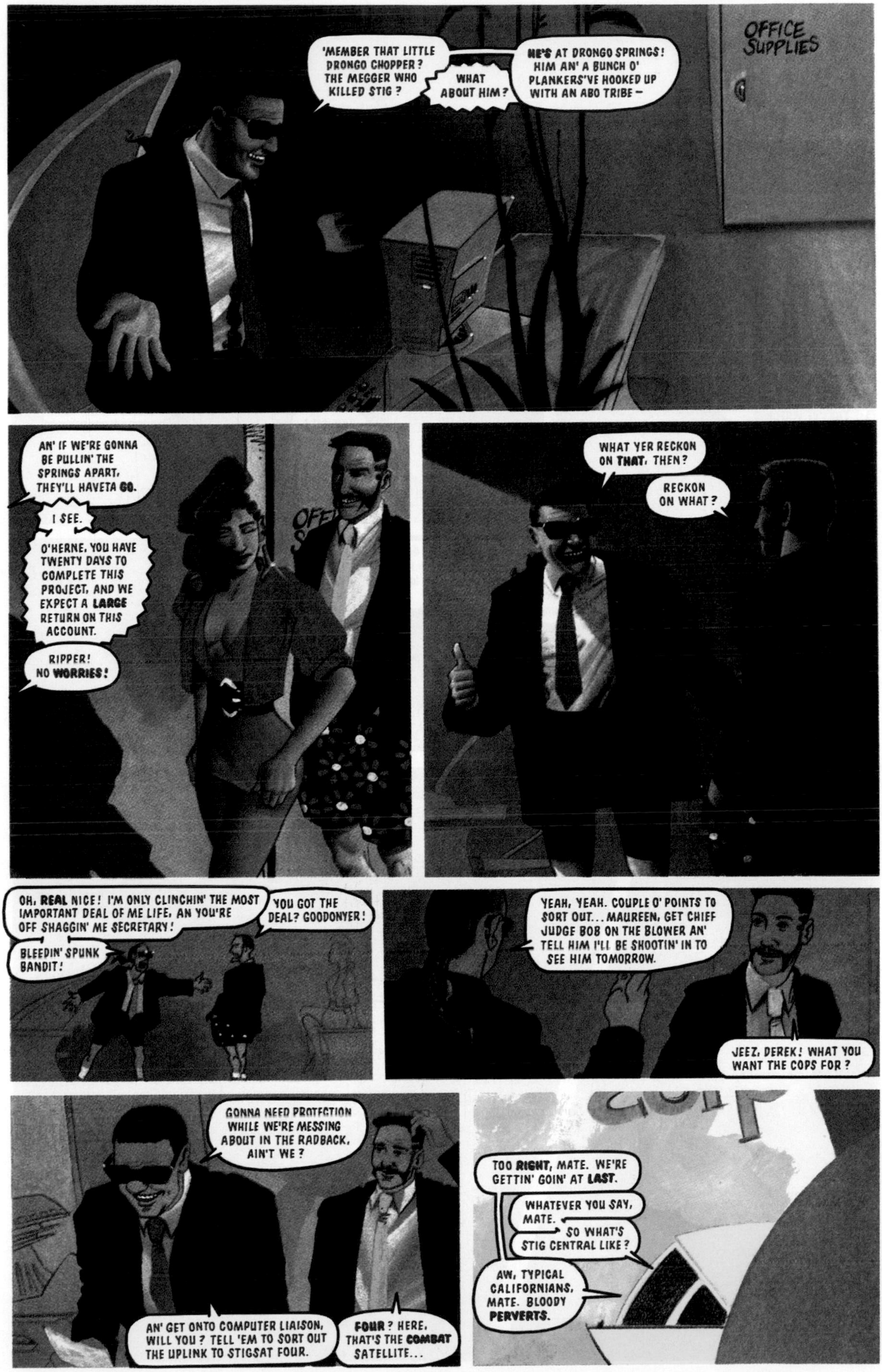
'MEMBER THAT LITTLE DRONGO CHOPPER? THE MEGGER WHO KILLED STIG?
WHAT ABOUT HIM?
HE'S AT DRONGO SPRINGS! HIM AN' A BUNCH O' PLANKERS'VE HOOKED UP WITH AN ABO TRIBE –
OFFICE SUPPLIES
AN' IF WE'RE GONNA BE PULLIN' THE SPRINGS APART, THEY'LL HAVETA GO.
I SEE.
O'HERNE, YOU HAVE TWENTY DAYS TO COMPLETE THIS PROJECT, AND WE EXPECT A LARGE RETURN ON THIS ACCOUNT.
RIPPER! NO WORRIES!
WHAT YER RECKON ON THAT, THEN?
RECKON ON WHAT?
OH, REAL NICE! I'M ONLY CLINCHIN' THE MOST IMPORTANT DEAL OF ME LIFE, AN YOU'RE OFF SHAGGIN' ME SECRETARY!
YOU GOT THE DEAL? GOODONYER!
BLEEDIN' SPUNK BANDIT!
YEAH, YEAH. COUPLE O' POINTS TO SORT OUT... MAUREEN, GET CHIEF JUDGE BOB ON THE BLOWER AN' TELL HIM I'LL BE SHOOTIN' IN TO SEE HIM TOMORROW.
JEEZ, DEREK! WHAT YOU WANT THE COPS FOR?
GONNA NEED PROTECTION WHILE WE'RE MESSING ABOUT IN THE RADBACK, AIN'T WE?
AN' GET ONTO COMPUTER LIAISON, WILL YOU? TELL 'EM TO SORT OUT THE UPLINK TO STIGSAT FOUR.
FOUR? HERE, THAT'S THE COMBAT SATELLITE...
TOO RIGHT, MATE. WE'RE GETTIN' GOIN' AT LAST.
WHATEVER YOU SAY, MATE.
SO WHAT'S STIG CENTRAL LIKE?
AW, TYPICAL CALIFORNIANS, MATE. BLOODY PERVERTS.

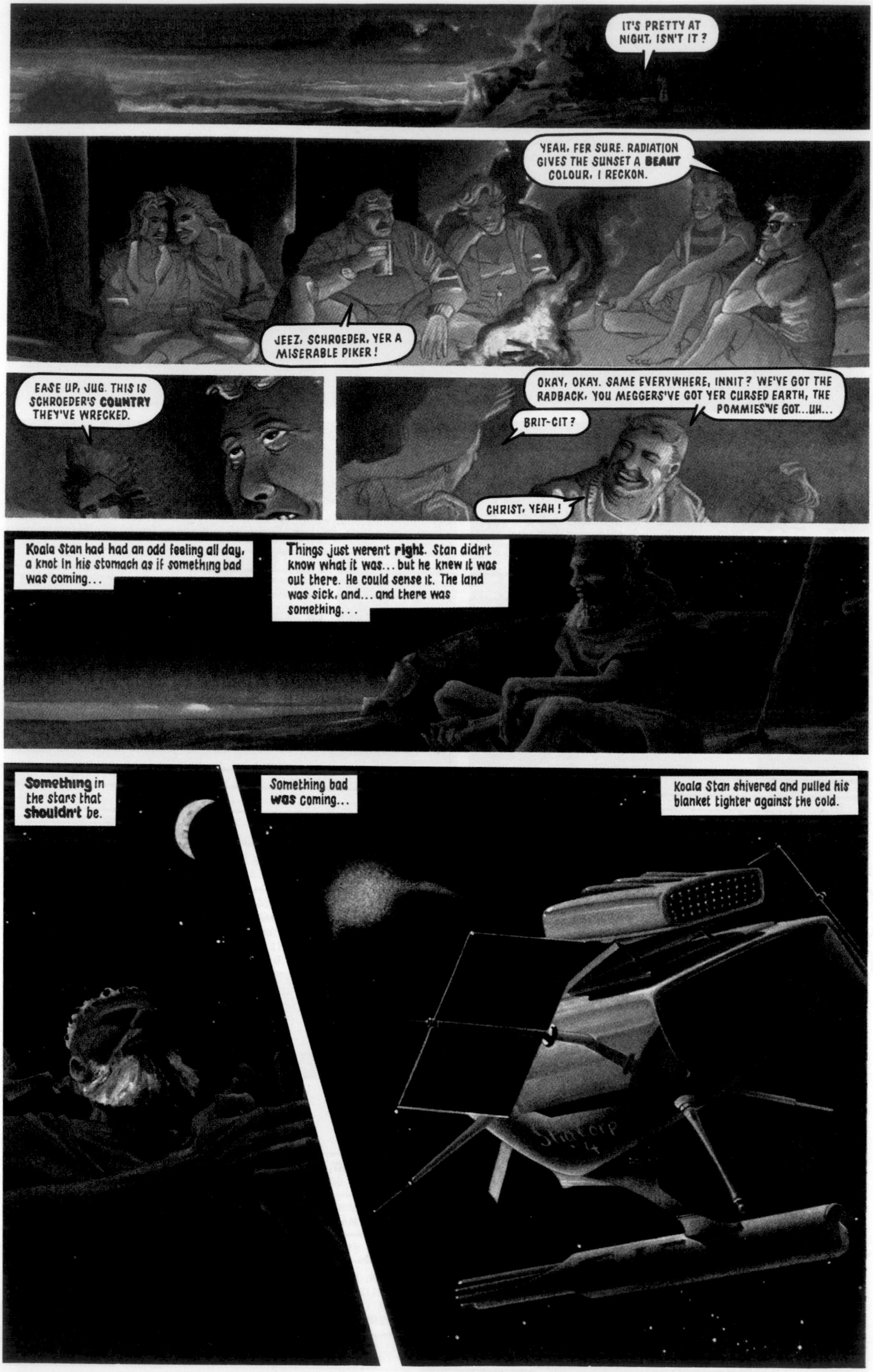
IT'S PRETTY AT NIGHT, ISN'T IT?
YEAH, FER SURE. RADIATION GIVES THE SUNSET A BEAUT COLOUR, I RECKON.
JEEZ, SCHROEDER, YER A MISERABLE PIKER!
EASE UP, JUG. THIS IS SCHROEDER'S COUNTRY THEY'VE WRECKED.
OKAY, OKAY. SAME EVERYWHERE, INNIT? WE'VE GOT THE RADBACK, YOU MEGGERS'VE GOT YER CURSED EARTH, THE POMMIES'VE GOT...UH...
BRIT-CIT?
CHRIST, YEAH!
Koala Stan had had an odd feeling all day, a knot in his stomach as if something bad was coming...
Things just weren't right. Stan didn't know what it was... but he knew it was out there. He could sense it. The land was sick, and... and there was something...
Something in the stars that shouldn't be.
Something bad was coming...
Koala Stan shivered and pulled his blanket tighter against the cold.

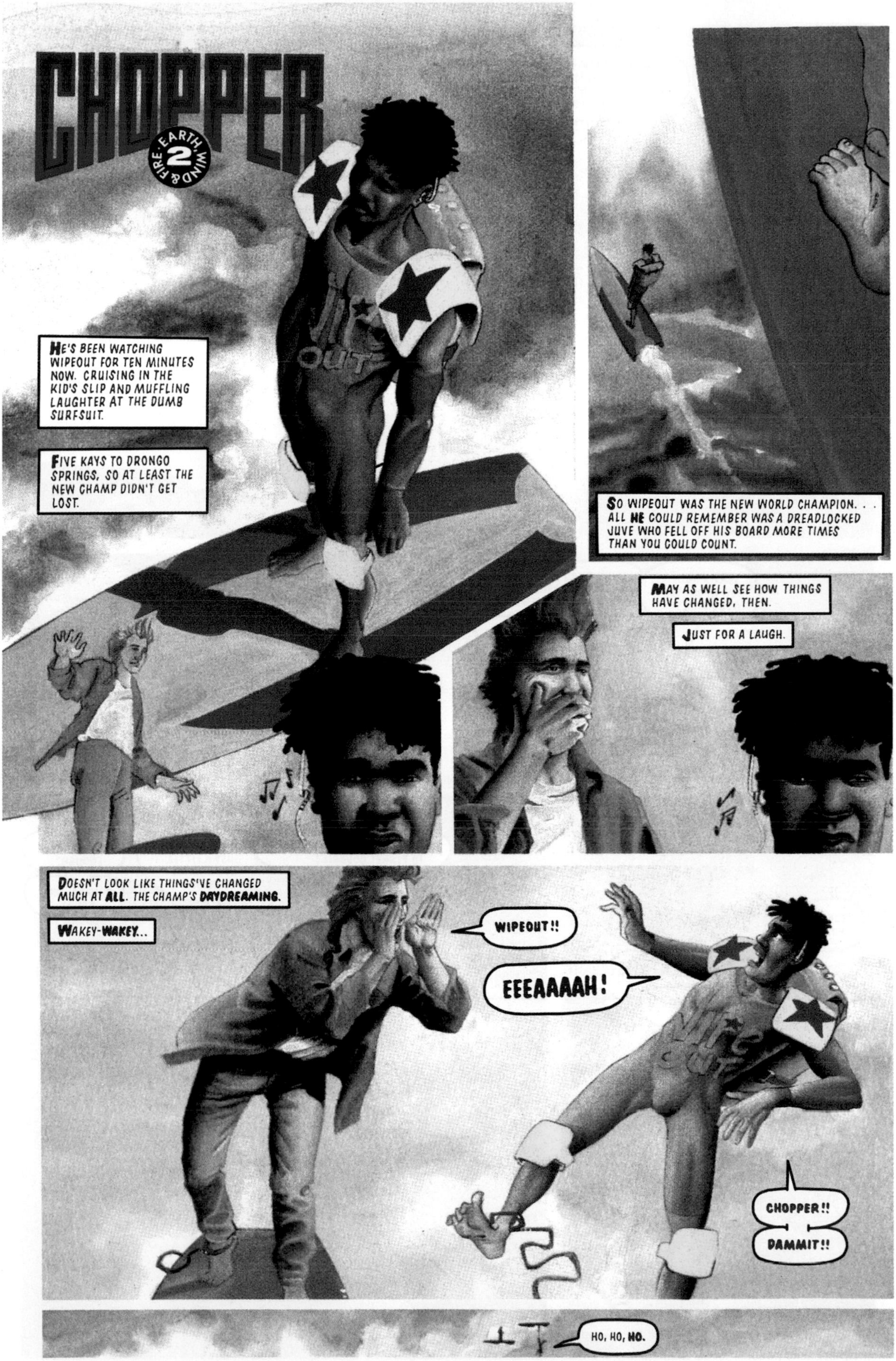
CHOPPER
EARTH, WIND & FIRE 2
HE'S BEEN WATCHING WIPEOUT FOR TEN MINUTES NOW. CRUISING IN THE KID'S SLIP AND MUFFLING LAUGHTER AT THE DUMB SURFSUIT.
FIVE KAYS TO DRONGO SPRINGS, SO AT LEAST THE NEW CHAMP DIDN'T GET LOST.
SO WIPEOUT WAS THE NEW WORLD CHAMPION. . . ALL HE COULD REMEMBER WAS A DREADLOCKED JUVE WHO FELL OFF HIS BOARD MORE TIMES THAN YOU COULD COUNT.
MAY AS WELL SEE HOW THINGS HAVE CHANGED, THEN.
JUST FOR A LAUGH.
DOESN'T LOOK LIKE THINGS'VE CHANGED MUCH AT ALL. THE CHAMP'S DAYDREAMING.
WAKEY-WAKEY...
WIPEOUT!!
EEEAAAAAH!
CHOPPER!!
DAMMIT!!
HO, HO, HO.

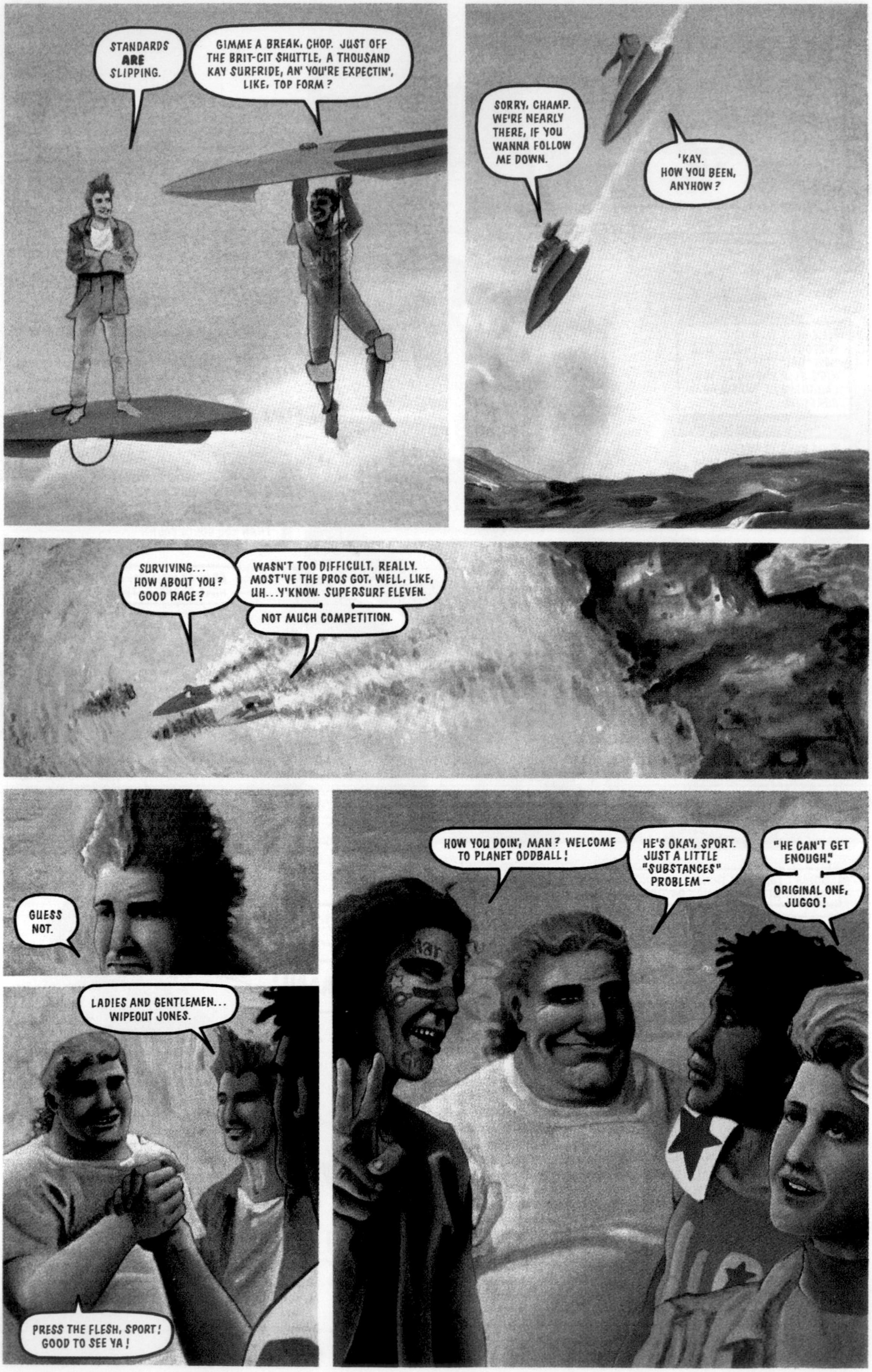
STANDARDS ARE SLIPPING.
GIMME A BREAK, CHOP. JUST OFF THE BRIT-CIT SHUTTLE, A THOUSAND KAY SURFRIDE, AN' YOU'RE EXPECTIN', LIKE, TOP FORM?
SORRY, CHAMP. WE'RE NEARLY THERE, IF YOU WANNA FOLLOW ME DOWN.
'KAY. HOW YOU BEEN, ANYHOW?
SURVIVING... HOW ABOUT YOU? GOOD RACE?
WASN'T TOO DIFFICULT, REALLY. MOST'VE THE PROS GOT, WELL, LIKE, UH...Y'KNOW. SUPERSURF ELEVEN.
NOT MUCH COMPETITION.
GUESS NOT.
LADIES AND GENTLEMEN... WIPEOUT JONES.
PRESS THE FLESH, SPORT! GOOD TO SEE YA!
HOW YOU DOIN', MAN? WELCOME TO PLANET ODDBALL!
HE'S OKAY, SPORT. JUST A LITTLE "SUBSTANCES" PROBLEM —
"HE CAN'T GET ENOUGH."
ORIGINAL ONE, JUGGO!

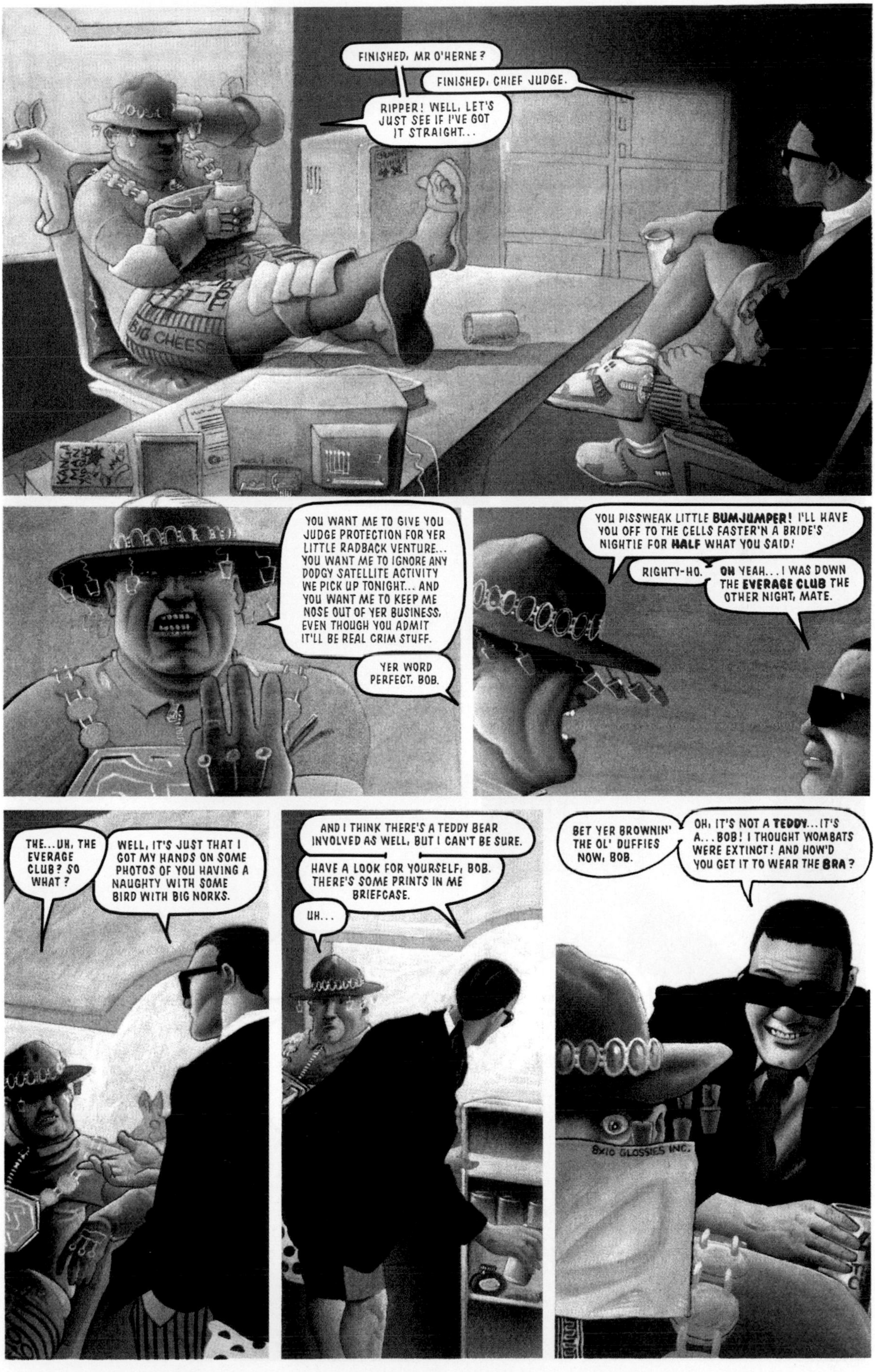
FINISHED, MR O'HERNE?
FINISHED, CHIEF JUDGE.
RIPPER! WELL, LET'S JUST SEE IF I'VE GOT IT STRAIGHT...
BIG CHEESE
YOU WANT ME TO GIVE YOU JUDGE PROTECTION FOR YER LITTLE RADBACK VENTURE... YOU WANT ME TO IGNORE ANY DODGY SATELLITE ACTIVITY WE PICK UP TONIGHT... AND YOU WANT ME TO KEEP ME NOSE OUT OF YER BUSINESS, EVEN THOUGH YOU ADMIT IT'LL BE REAL CRIM STUFF.
YER WORD PERFECT, BOB.
YOU PISSWEAK LITTLE **BUMJUMPER!** I'LL HAVE YOU OFF TO THE CELLS FASTER'N A BRIDE'S NIGHTIE FOR **HALF** WHAT YOU SAID!
RIGHTY-HO.
OH YEAH... I WAS DOWN THE **EVERAGE CLUB** THE OTHER NIGHT, MATE.
THE... UH, THE EVERAGE CLUB? SO WHAT?
WELL, IT'S JUST THAT I GOT MY HANDS ON SOME PHOTOS OF YOU HAVING A NAUGHTY WITH SOME BIRD WITH BIG NORKS.
AND I THINK THERE'S A TEDDY BEAR INVOLVED AS WELL, BUT I CAN'T BE SURE.
HAVE A LOOK FOR YOURSELF, BOB. THERE'S SOME PRINTS IN ME BRIEFCASE.
UH...
BET YER BROWNIN' THE OL' DUFFIES NOW, BOB.
OH, IT'S NOT A **TEDDY**... IT'S A... BOB! I THOUGHT WOMBATS WERE EXTINCT! AND HOW'D YOU GET IT TO WEAR THE **BRA**?
8X10 GLOSSIES INC.

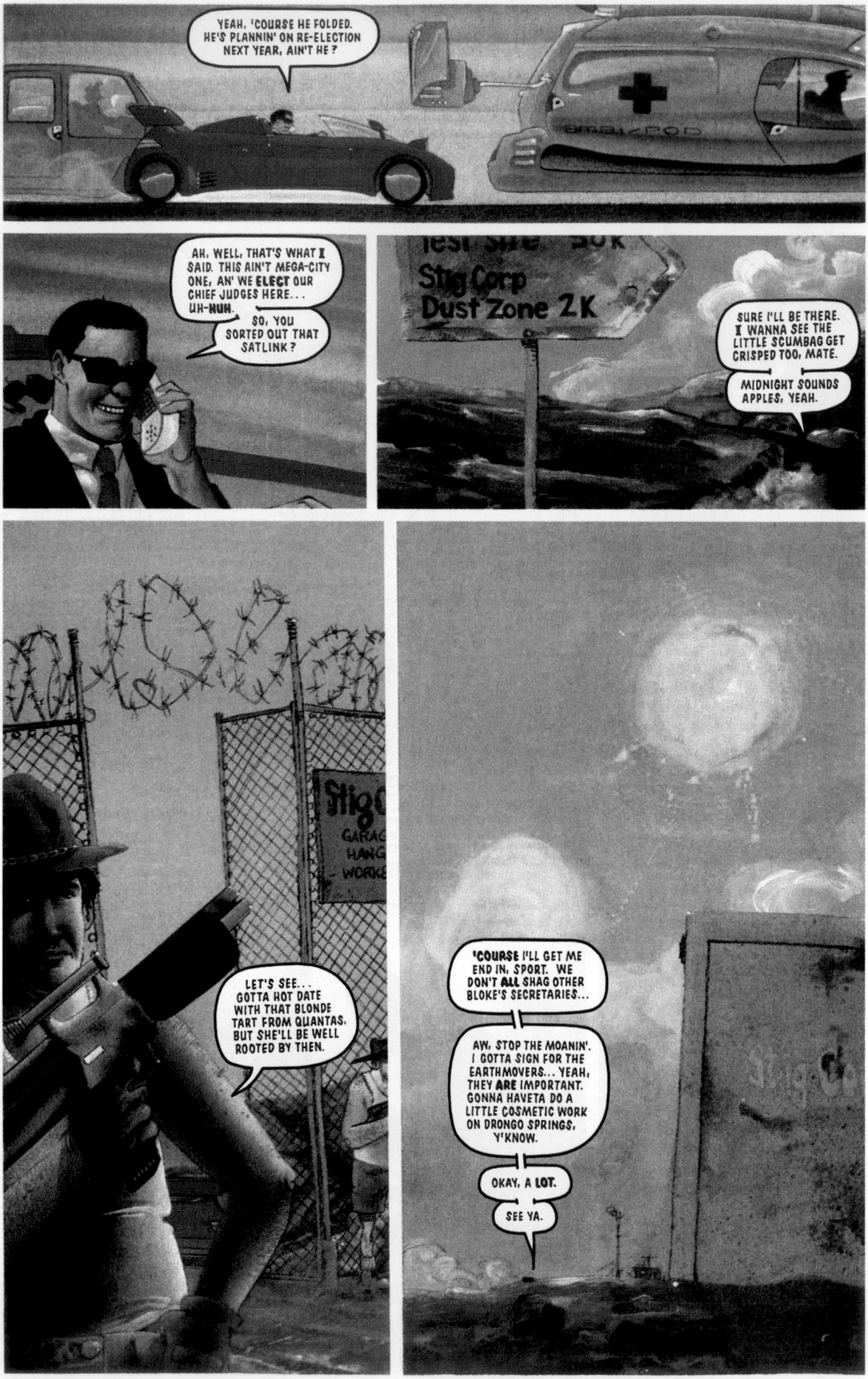
YEAH, 'COURSE HE FOLDED. HE'S PLANNIN' ON RE-ELECTION NEXT YEAR, AIN'T HE?
AH, WELL, THAT'S WHAT I SAID. THIS AIN'T MEGA-CITY ONE, AN' WE **ELECT** OUR CHIEF JUDGES HERE... UH-**HUH**.
SO, YOU SORTED OUT THAT SATLINK?
Stig Corp
Dust Zone 2K
SURE I'LL BE THERE. **I** WANNA SEE THE LITTLE SCUMBAG GET CRISPED TOO, MATE.
MIDNIGHT SOUNDS APPLES, YEAH.
LET'S SEE... GOTTA HOT DATE WITH THAT BLONDE TART FROM QUANTAS, BUT SHE'LL BE WELL ROOTED BY THEN.
'COURSE I'LL GET ME END IN, SPORT. WE DON'T **ALL** SHAG OTHER BLOKE'S SECRETARIES...
AW, STOP THE MOANIN'. I GOTTA SIGN FOR THE EARTHMOVERS... YEAH, THEY **ARE** IMPORTANT. GONNA HAVETA DO A LITTLE COSMETIC WORK ON DRONGO SPRINGS, Y'KNOW.
OKAY, A **LOT**.
SEE YA.

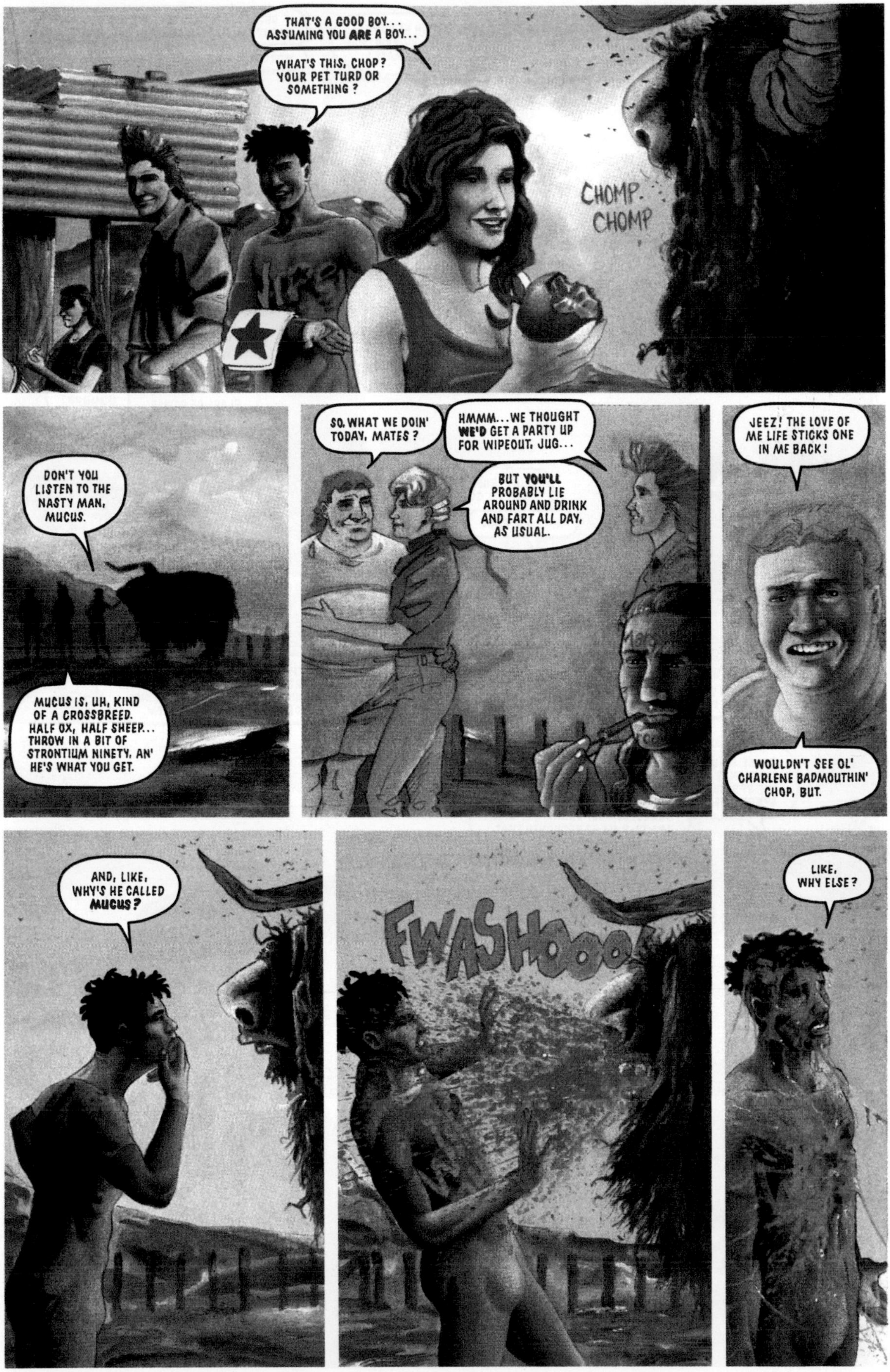

THAT'S A GOOD BOY... ASSUMING YOU **ARE** A BOY...
WHAT'S THIS, CHOP? YOUR PET TURD OR SOMETHING?
CHOMP CHOMP
DON'T YOU LISTEN TO THE NASTY MAN, MUCUS.
MUCUS IS, UH, KIND OF A CROSSBREED. HALF OX, HALF SHEEP... THROW IN A BIT OF STRONTIUM NINETY, AN' HE'S WHAT YOU GET.
SO, WHAT WE DOIN' TODAY, MATES?
HMMM... WE THOUGHT **WE'D** GET A PARTY UP FOR WIPEOUT, JUG...
BUT **YOU'LL** PROBABLY LIE AROUND AND DRINK AND FART ALL DAY, AS USUAL.
JEEZ! THE LOVE OF ME LIFE STICKS ONE IN ME BACK!
WOULDN'T SEE OL' CHARLENE BADMOUTHIN' CHOP, BUT.
AND, LIKE, WHY'S HE CALLED **MUCUS?**
FWASHOOO
LIKE, WHY ELSE?

ALL THE WAY TO OZ SO SOME, LIKE, MUTIE SHEEP CAN COVER ME IN BOOGERS...

PROBABLY JUST MEANS HE LIKES YOU, WIPEOUT.

WATCH HE DON'T START HUMPIN' YOU LATER, MATE !

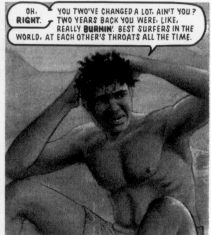

OH, RIGHT.

YOU TWO'VE CHANGED A LOT, AIN'T YOU ? TWO YEARS BACK YOU WERE, LIKE, REALLY **BURNIN'**. BEST SURFERS IN THE WORLD, AT EACH OTHER'S THROATS ALL THE TIME.

TRUE, TRUE. LEMME SEE, NOW...I GOT **FAT**...

AN' I GOT **SHOT**.

MELLOWED OUT A LOT, HUH ? S'POSE THIS PLACE, LIKE, HELPS.

IT'S A...SORT'VE A PLACE OF POWER, IN A WAY.

UUUURP !

ONE OF THE ABORIGINES — SCHROEDER — HE'S AN EXPERT ON IT. HE SAYS IT'S THE POWER IN THE LAND ITSELF... IN THE SONGLINES THE ANCESTORS LEFT BEHIND THEM.

THERE'S HUNDREDS OF THOSE SONGLINES CROSSING THROUGH THE SPRINGS. THE DREAMING'S **STRONG** HERE.

SCHROEDER GOT DRUNK ONE NIGHT AND TOLD ME HE RECKONED THAT WAS WHAT KEPT THE RADIATION AWAY.

SOUNDS LIKE YOU'RE REALLY SORT OF **INTO** IT, CHOP.

SORT OF.

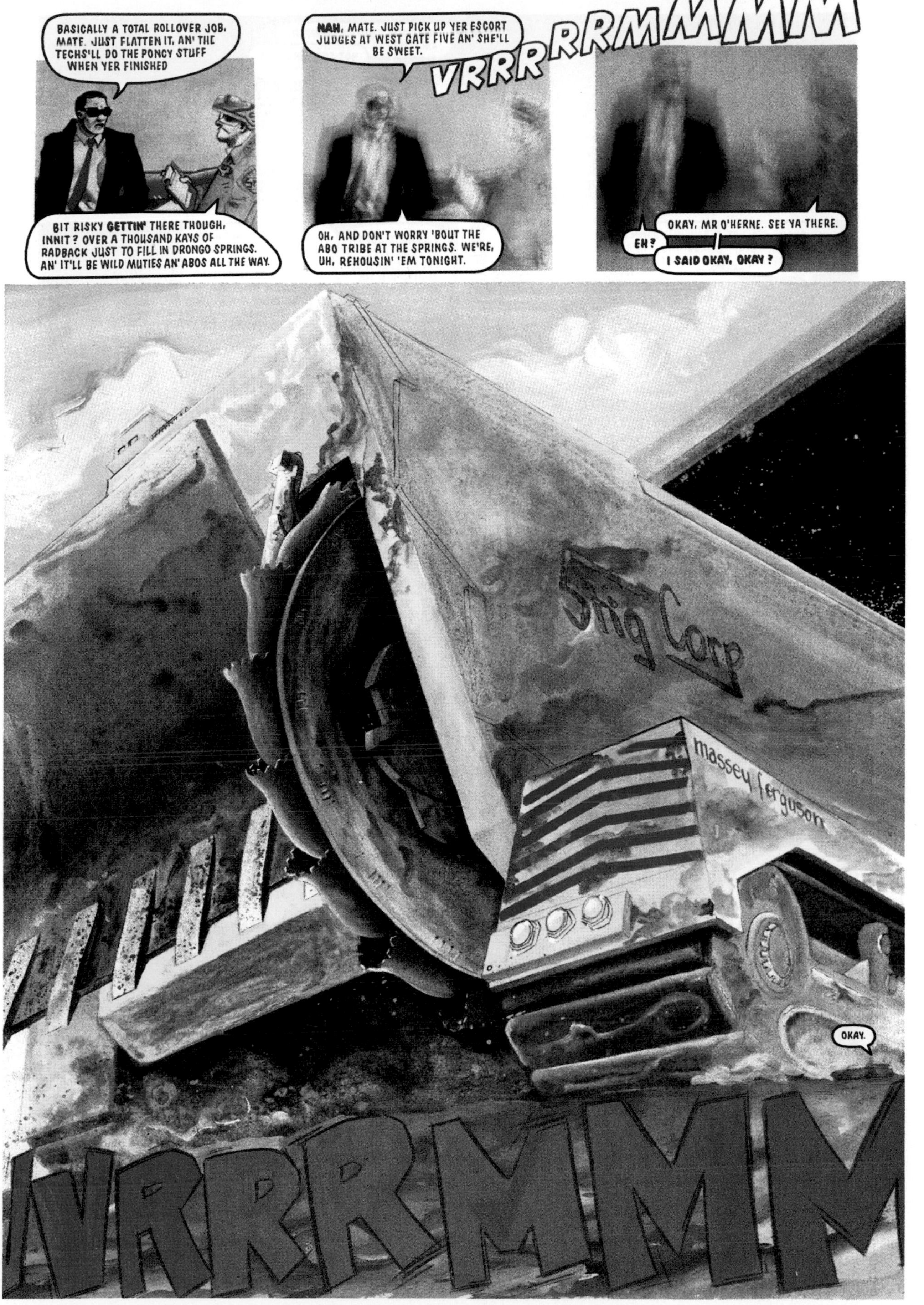
BASICALLY A TOTAL ROLLOVER JOB, MATE. JUST FLATTEN IT, AN' THE TECHS'LL DO THE PONCY STUFF WHEN YER FINISHED
BIT RISKY GETTIN' THERE THOUGH, INNIT? OVER A THOUSAND KAYS OF RADBACK JUST TO FILL IN DRONGO SPRINGS. AN' IT'LL BE WILD MUTIES AN' ABOS ALL THE WAY.
NAH, MATE. JUST PICK UP YER ESCORT JUDGES AT WEST GATE FIVE AN' SHE'LL BE SWEET.
VRRRRRMMMMM
OH, AND DON'T WORRY 'BOUT THE ABO TRIBE AT THE SPRINGS. WE'RE, UH, REHOUSIN' 'EM TONIGHT.
OKAY, MR O'HERNE. SEE YA THERE.
EH?
I SAID OKAY, OKAY?
Stig Corp
massey ferguson
OKAY.
VRRRMMM

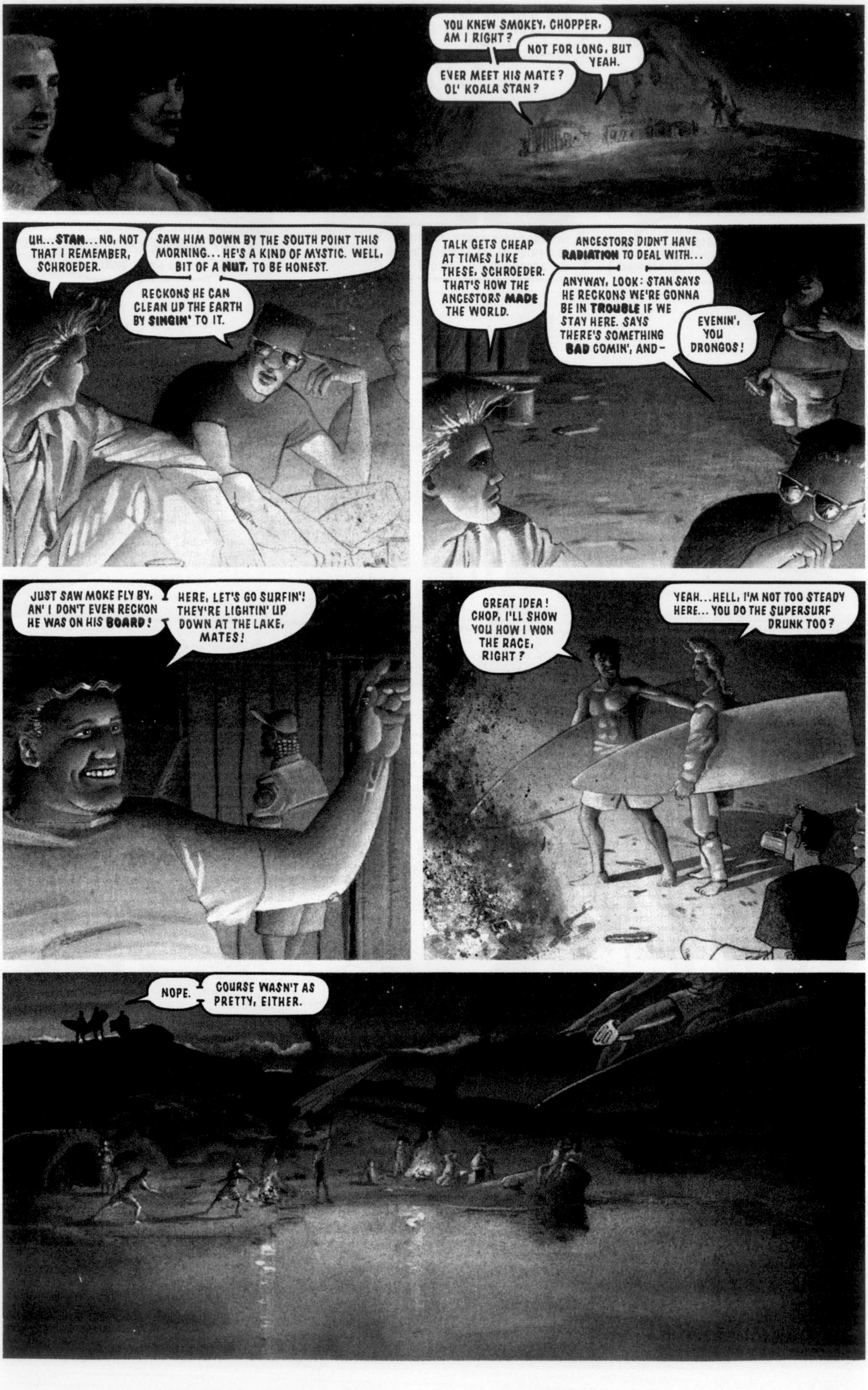
YOU KNEW SMOKEY, CHOPPER. AM I RIGHT?
NOT FOR LONG, BUT YEAH.
EVER MEET HIS MATE? OL' KOALA STAN?
UH...STAN...NO, NOT THAT I REMEMBER, SCHROEDER.
SAW HIM DOWN BY THE SOUTH POINT THIS MORNING... HE'S A KIND OF MYSTIC. WELL, BIT OF A NUT, TO BE HONEST.
RECKONS HE CAN CLEAN UP THE EARTH BY SINGIN' TO IT.
TALK GETS CHEAP AT TIMES LIKE THESE, SCHROEDER. THAT'S HOW THE ANCESTORS MADE THE WORLD.
ANCESTORS DIDN'T HAVE RADIATION TO DEAL WITH...
ANYWAY, LOOK: STAN SAYS HE RECKONS WE'RE GONNA BE IN TROUBLE IF WE STAY HERE. SAYS THERE'S SOMETHING BAD COMIN', AND–
EVENIN', YOU DRONGOS!
JUST SAW MOKE FLY BY. AN' I DON'T EVEN RECKON HE WAS ON HIS BOARD!
HERE, LET'S GO SURFIN'! THEY'RE LIGHTIN' UP DOWN AT THE LAKE, MATES!
GREAT IDEA! CHOP, I'LL SHOW YOU HOW I WON THE RACE, RIGHT?
YEAH...HELL, I'M NOT TOO STEADY HERE... YOU DO THE SUPERSURF DRUNK TOO?
NOPE.
COURSE WASN'T AS PRETTY, EITHER.

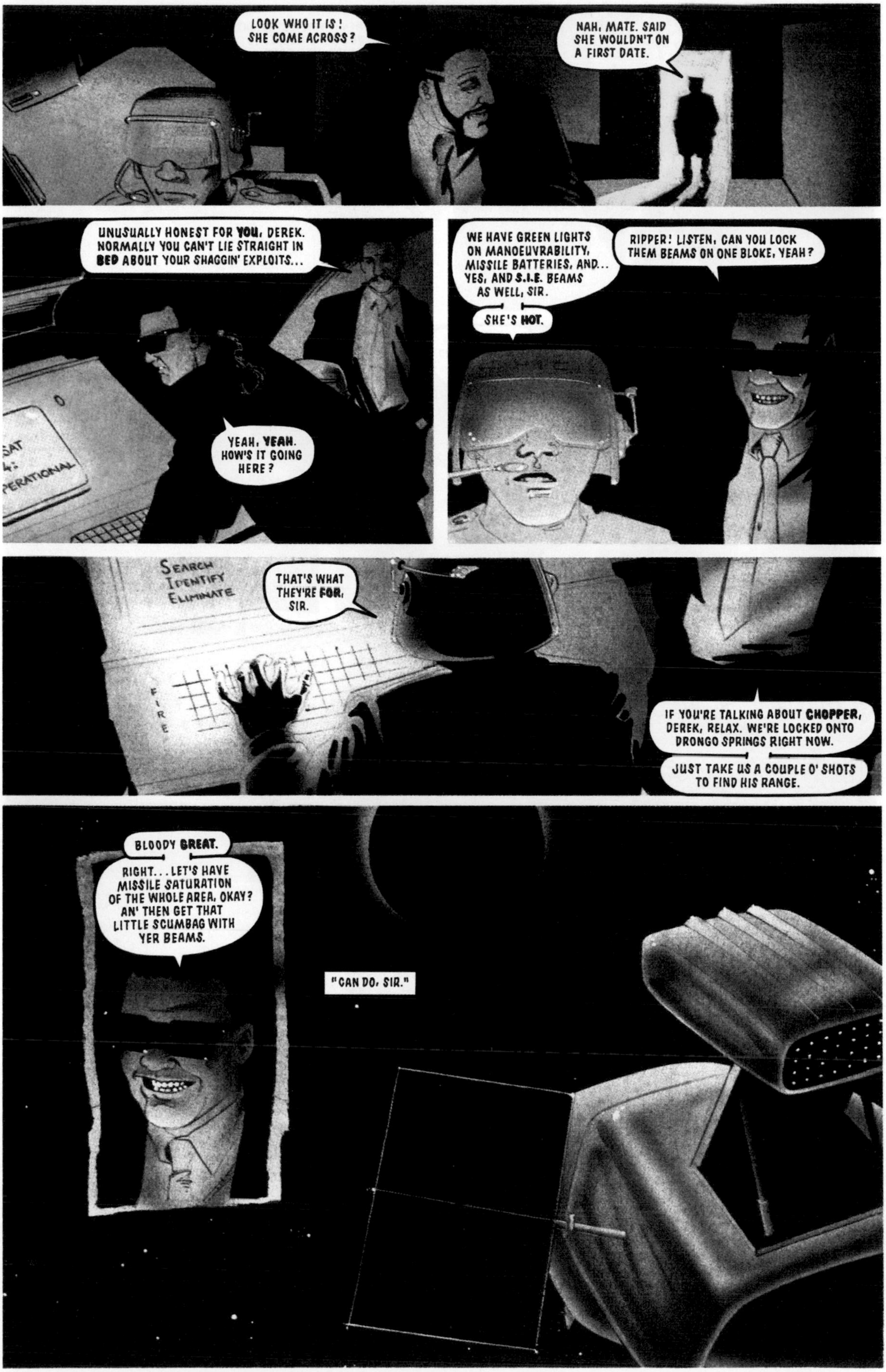
LOOK WHO IT IS! SHE COME ACROSS?
NAH, MATE. SAID SHE WOULDN'T ON A FIRST DATE.
UNUSUALLY HONEST FOR YOU, DEREK. NORMALLY YOU CAN'T LIE STRAIGHT IN BED ABOUT YOUR SHAGGIN' EXPLOITS...
YEAH, YEAH. HOW'S IT GOING HERE?
WE HAVE GREEN LIGHTS ON MANOEUVRABILITY, MISSILE BATTERIES, AND... YES, AND S.I.E. BEAMS AS WELL, SIR.
SHE'S HOT.
RIPPER! LISTEN, CAN YOU LOCK THEM BEAMS ON ONE BLOKE, YEAH?
SEARCH IDENTIFY ELIMINATE
THAT'S WHAT THEY'RE FOR, SIR.
FIRE
IF YOU'RE TALKING ABOUT CHOPPER, DEREK, RELAX. WE'RE LOCKED ONTO DRONGO SPRINGS RIGHT NOW.
JUST TAKE US A COUPLE O' SHOTS TO FIND HIS RANGE.
BLOODY GREAT.
RIGHT... LET'S HAVE MISSILE SATURATION OF THE WHOLE AREA, OKAY? AN' THEN GET THAT LITTLE SCUMBAG WITH YER BEAMS.
"CAN DO, SIR."

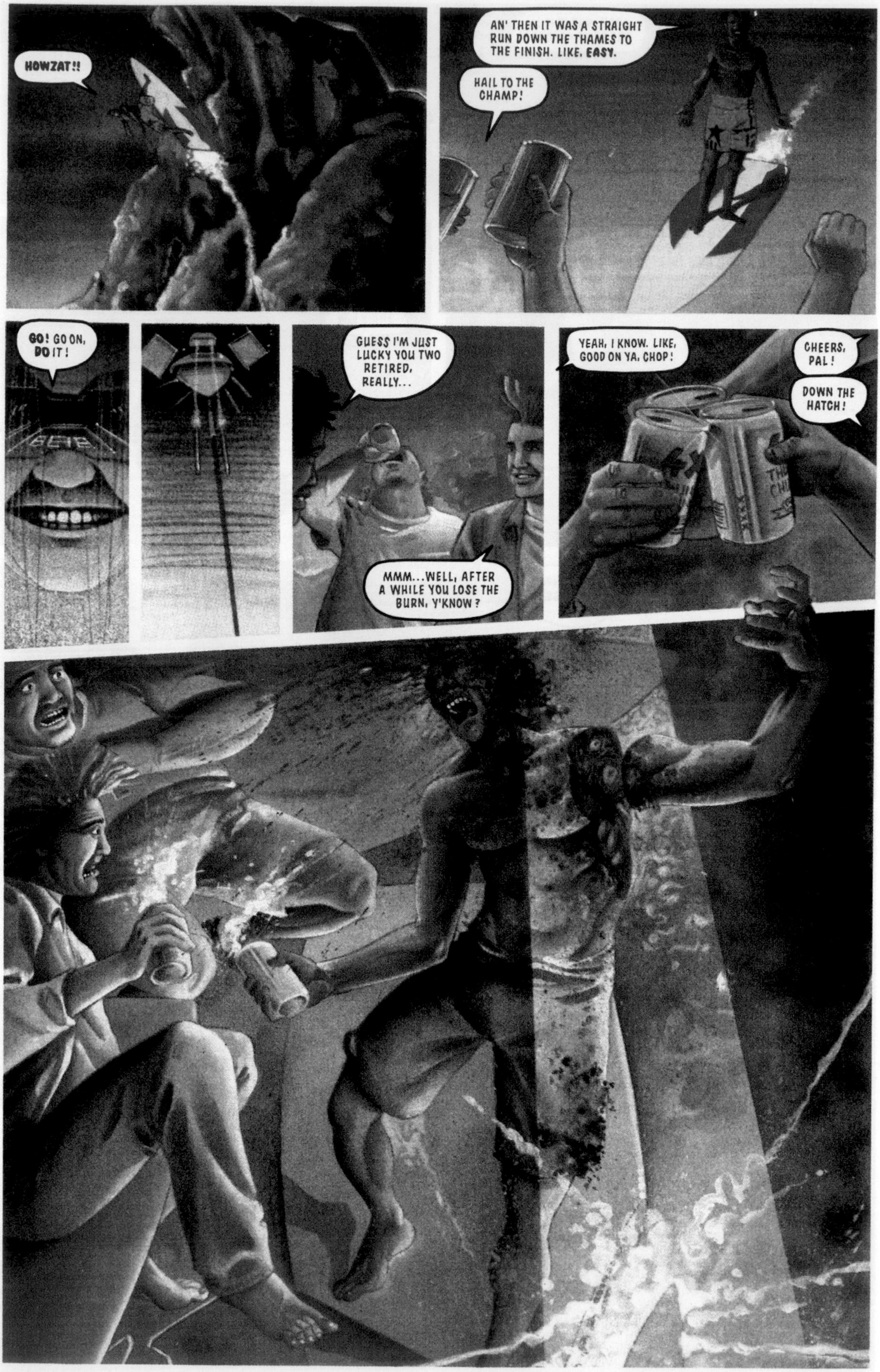
HOWZAT!!
AN' THEN IT WAS A STRAIGHT RUN DOWN THE THAMES TO THE FINISH. LIKE, EASY.
HAIL TO THE CHAMP!
GO! GO ON, DO IT!
GUESS I'M JUST LUCKY YOU TWO RETIRED, REALLY...
MMM...WELL, AFTER A WHILE YOU LOSE THE BURN, Y'KNOW?
YEAH, I KNOW. LIKE, GOOD ON YA, CHOP!
CHEERS, PAL!
DOWN THE HATCH!

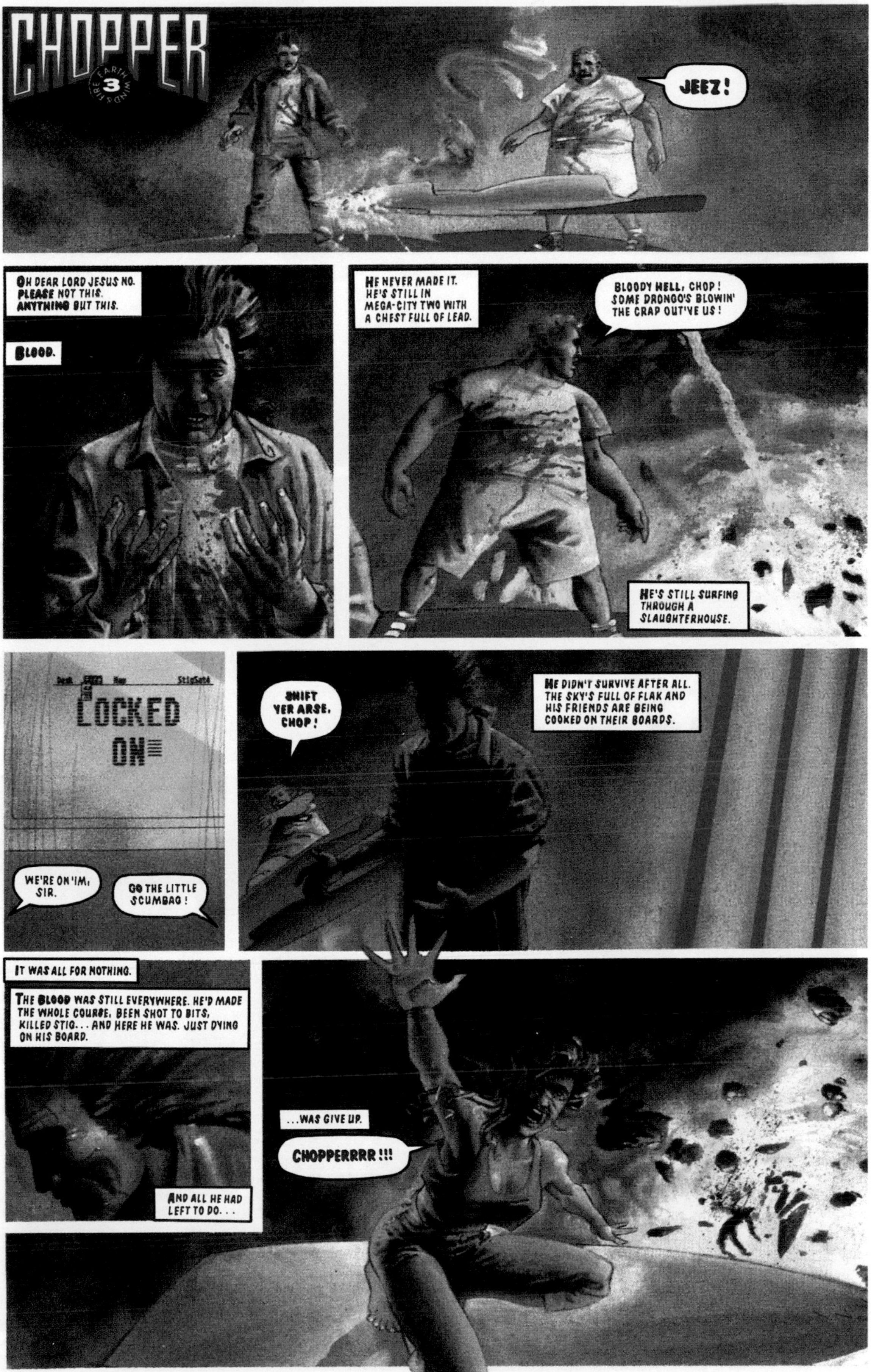
CHOPPER
3
EARTH WIND FIRE
JEEZ!
OH DEAR LORD JESUS NO. PLEASE NOT THIS. ANYTHING BUT THIS.
BLOOD.
HE NEVER MADE IT. HE'S STILL IN MEGA-CITY TWO WITH A CHEST FULL OF LEAD.
BLOODY HELL, CHOP! SOME DRONGO'S BLOWIN' THE CRAP OUT'VE US!
HE'S STILL SURFING THROUGH A SLAUGHTERHOUSE.
LOCKED ON
WE'RE ON 'IM, SIR.
GO THE LITTLE SCUMBAG!
SHIFT YER ARSE, CHOP!
HE DIDN'T SURVIVE AFTER ALL. THE SKY'S FULL OF FLAK AND HIS FRIENDS ARE BEING COOKED ON THEIR BOARDS.
IT WAS ALL FOR NOTHING.
THE BLOOD WAS STILL EVERYWHERE. HE'D MADE THE WHOLE COURSE, BEEN SHOT TO BITS, KILLED STIG... AND HERE HE WAS. JUST DYING ON HIS BOARD.
AND ALL HE HAD LEFT TO DO...
...WAS GIVE UP.
CHOPPERRRR!!!

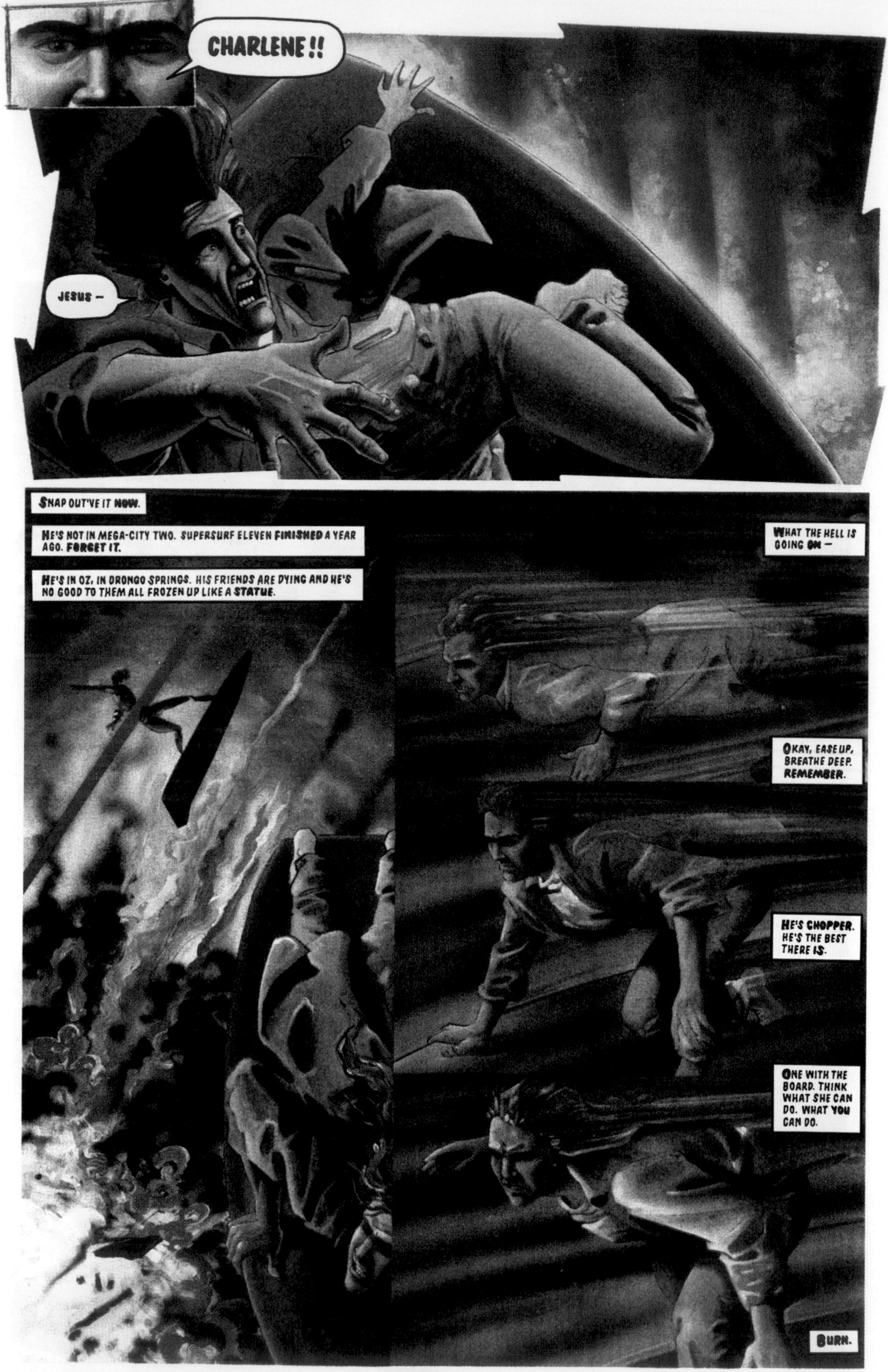
CHARLENE!!
JESUS –
SNAP OUT'VE IT NOW.
HE'S NOT IN MEGA-CITY TWO. SUPERSURF ELEVEN FINISHED A YEAR AGO. FORGET IT.
HE'S IN OZ, IN DRONGO SPRINGS. HIS FRIENDS ARE DYING AND HE'S NO GOOD TO THEM ALL FROZEN UP LIKE A STATUE.
WHAT THE HELL IS GOING ON –
OKAY, EASE UP, BREATHE DEEP. REMEMBER.
HE'S CHOPPER. HE'S THE BEST THERE IS.
ONE WITH THE BOARD. THINK WHAT SHE CAN DO. WHAT YOU CAN DO.
BURN.

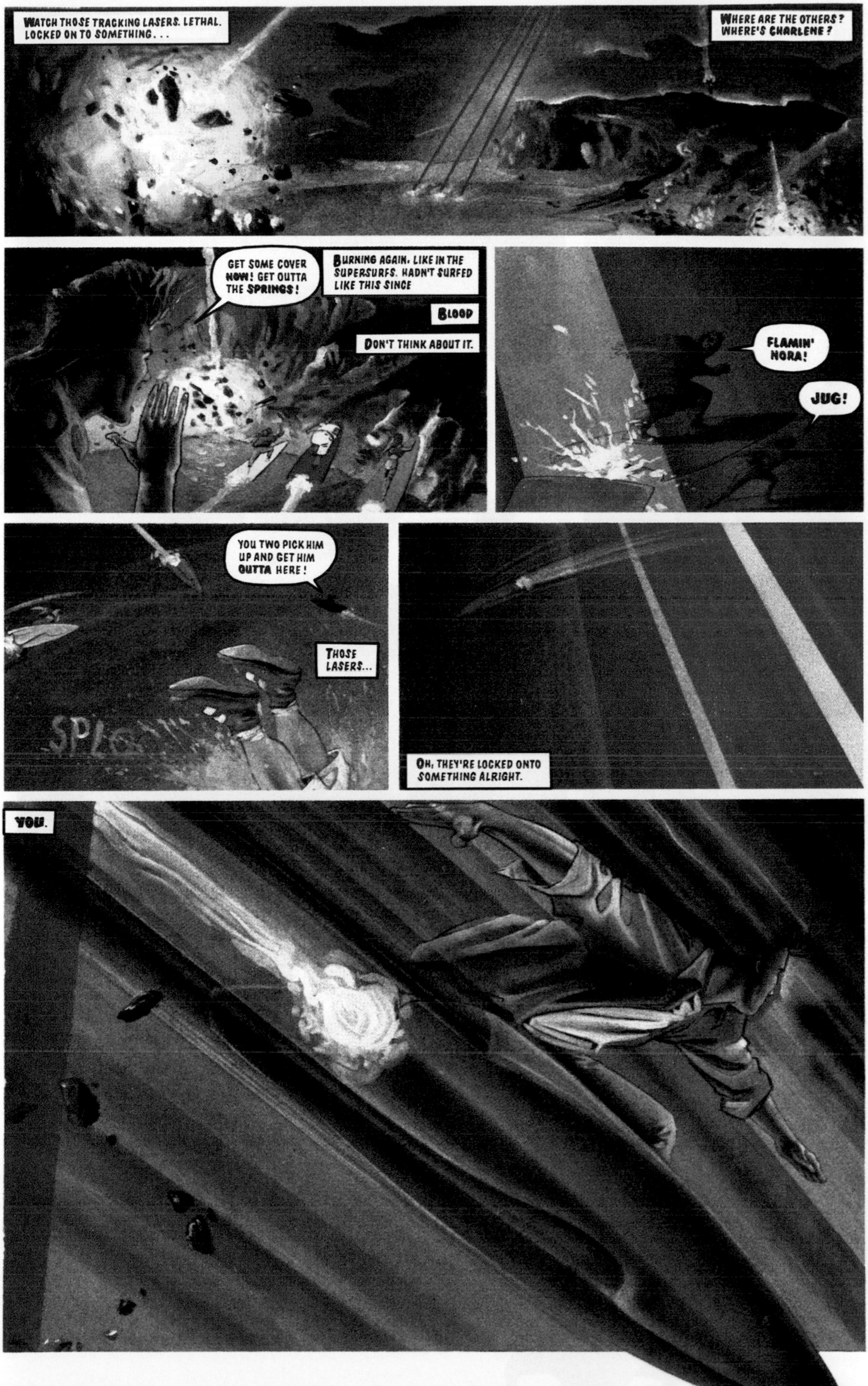
WATCH THOSE TRACKING LASERS. LETHAL. LOCKED ON TO SOMETHING . . .
WHERE ARE THE OTHERS? WHERE'S CHARLENE?
GET SOME COVER NOW! GET OUTTA THE SPRINGS!
BURNING AGAIN. LIKE IN THE SUPERSURFS. HADN'T SURFED LIKE THIS SINCE
BLOOD
DON'T THINK ABOUT IT.
FLAMIN' NORA!
JUG!
YOU TWO PICK HIM UP AND GET HIM OUTTA HERE!
THOSE LASERS...
OH, THEY'RE LOCKED ONTO SOMETHING ALRIGHT.
YOU.

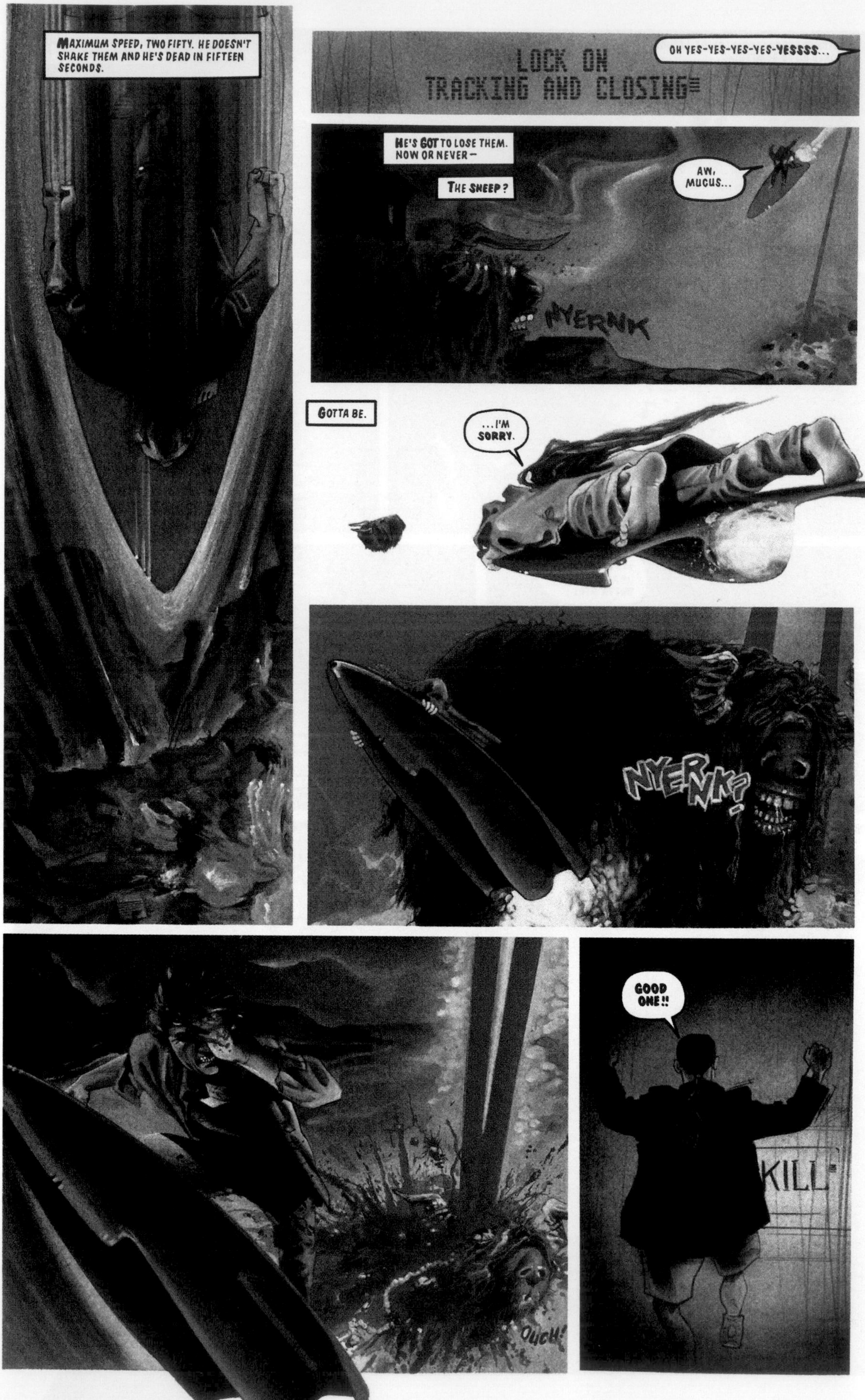
MAXIMUM SPEED, TWO FIFTY. HE DOESN'T SHAKE THEM AND HE'S DEAD IN FIFTEEN SECONDS.
LOCK ON
TRACKING AND CLOSING
OH YES-YES-YES-YES-YESSSS...
HE'S GOT TO LOSE THEM. NOW OR NEVER—
THE SHEEP?
AW, MUCUS...
NYERNK
GOTTA BE.
...I'M SORRY.
NYERNK?
OUCH!
GOOD ONE!!
KILL

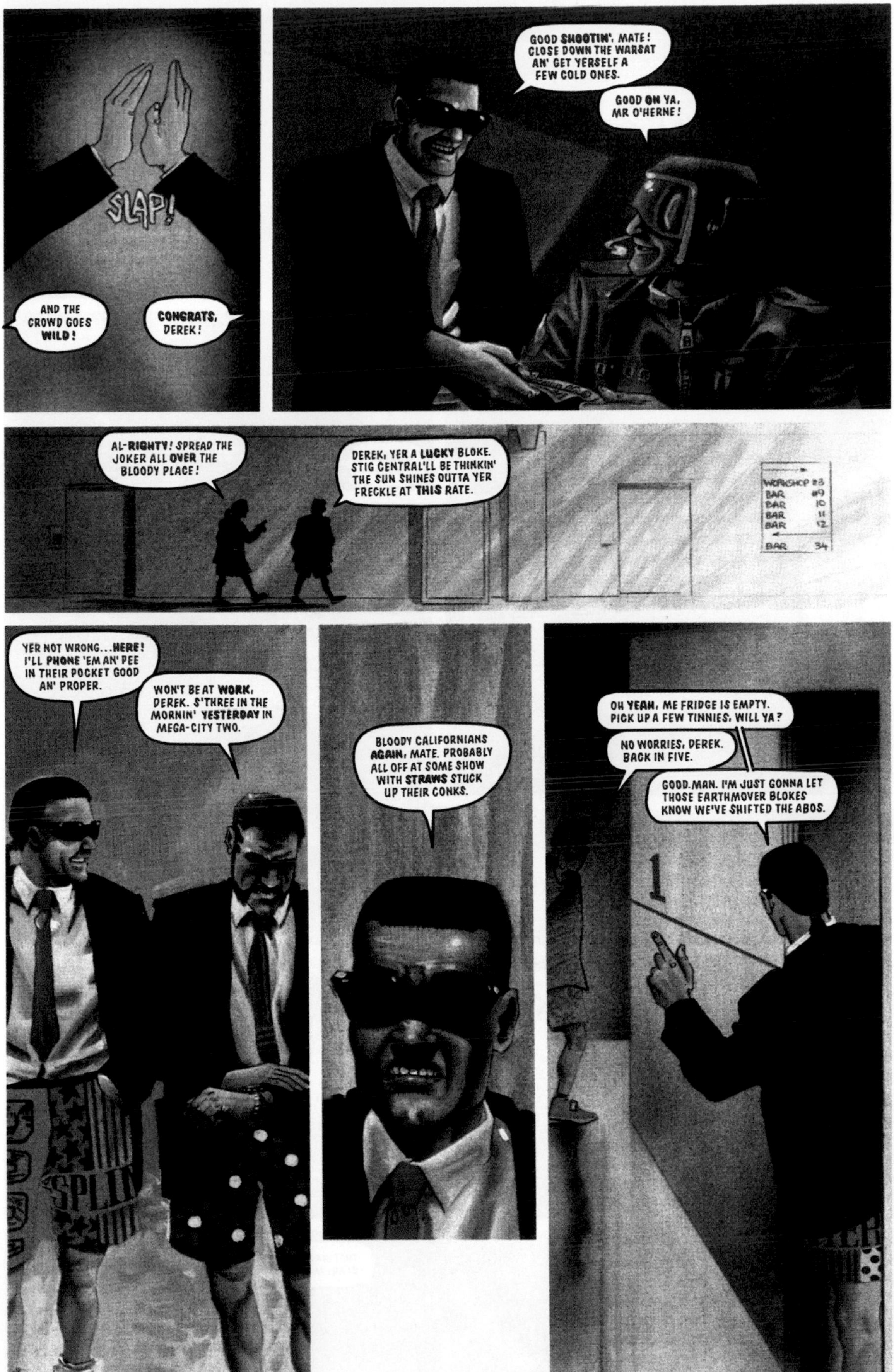
SLAP!
AND THE CROWD GOES WILD!
CONGRATS, DEREK!
GOOD SHOOTIN', MATE! CLOSE DOWN THE WARSAT AN' GET YERSELF A FEW COLD ONES.
GOOD ON YA, MR O'HERNE!
AL-RIGHTY! SPREAD THE JOKER ALL OVER THE BLOODY PLACE!
DEREK, YER A LUCKY BLOKE. STIG CENTRAL'LL BE THINKIN' THE SUN SHINES OUTTA YER FRECKLE AT THIS RATE.
WORKSHOP #8
BAR #9
BAR 10
BAR 11
BAR 12
BAR 34
YER NOT WRONG... HERE! I'LL PHONE 'EM AN' PEE IN THEIR POCKET GOOD AN' PROPER.
WON'T BE AT WORK, DEREK. S'THREE IN THE MORNIN' YESTERDAY IN MEGA-CITY TWO.
BLOODY CALIFORNIANS AGAIN, MATE. PROBABLY ALL OFF AT SOME SHOW WITH STRAWS STUCK UP THEIR CONKS.
OH YEAH, ME FRIDGE IS EMPTY. PICK UP A FEW TINNIES, WILL YA?
NO WORRIES, DEREK. BACK IN FIVE.
GOOD.MAN. I'M JUST GONNA LET THOSE EARTHMOVER BLOKES KNOW WE'VE SHIFTED THE ABOS.
1

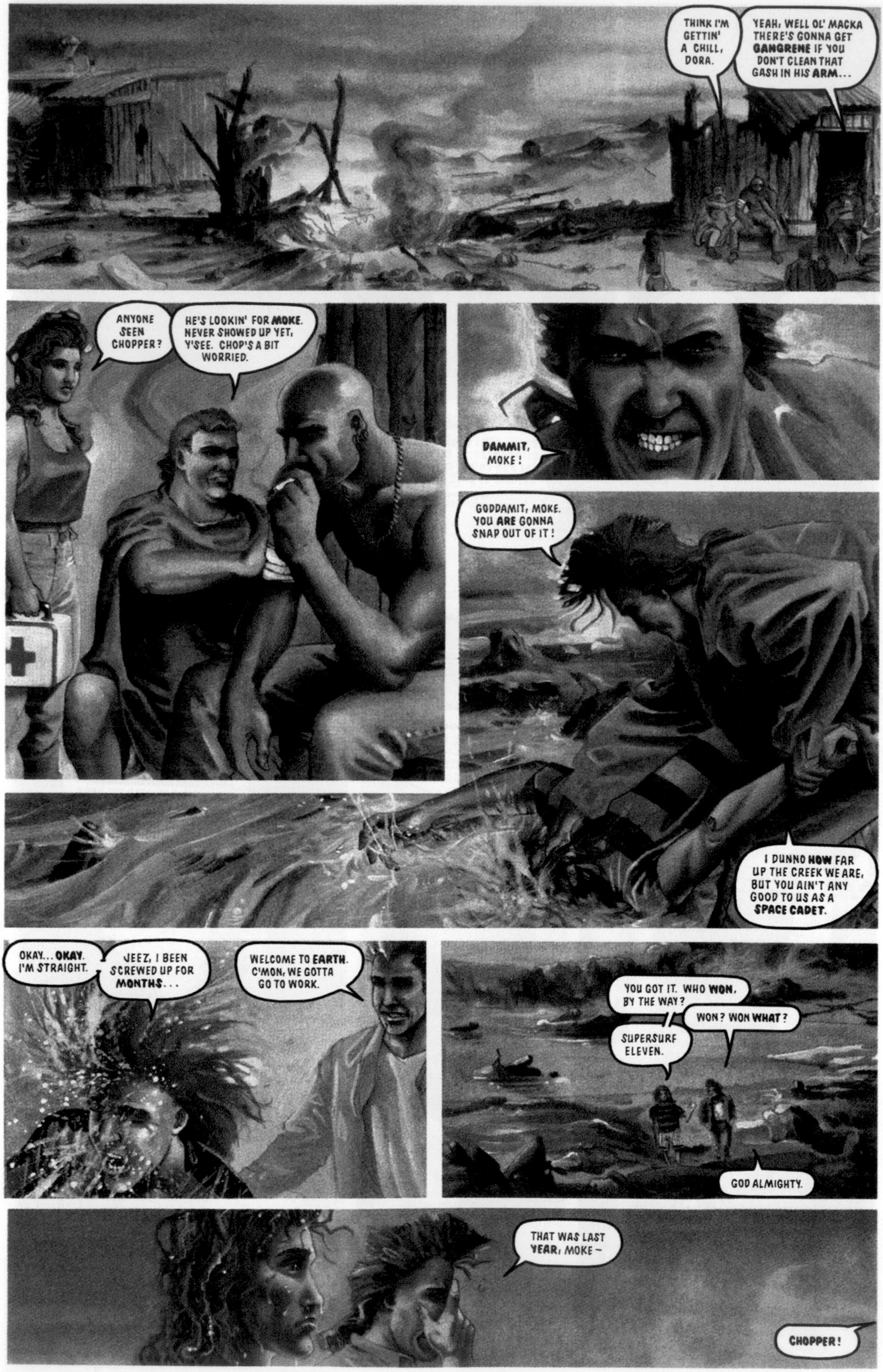
THINK I'M GETTIN' A CHILL, DORA.
YEAH, WELL OL' MACKA THERE'S GONNA GET **GANGRENE** IF YOU DON'T CLEAN THAT GASH IN HIS **ARM**...
ANYONE SEEN CHOPPER?
HE'S LOOKIN' FOR **MOKE**. NEVER SHOWED UP YET, Y'SEE. CHOP'S A BIT WORRIED.
DAMMIT, MOKE!
GODDAMIT, MOKE. YOU **ARE** GONNA SNAP OUT OF IT!
I DUNNO **HOW** FAR UP THE CREEK WE ARE, BUT YOU AIN'T ANY GOOD TO US AS A **SPACE CADET**.
OKAY... **OKAY**. I'M STRAIGHT.
JEEZ, I BEEN SCREWED UP FOR **MONTHS**...
WELCOME TO **EARTH**. C'MON, WE GOTTA GO TO WORK.
YOU GOT IT. WHO **WON**, BY THE WAY?
WON? WON **WHAT**?
SUPERSURF ELEVEN.
GOD ALMIGHTY.
THAT WAS LAST **YEAR**, MOKE —
CHOPPER!

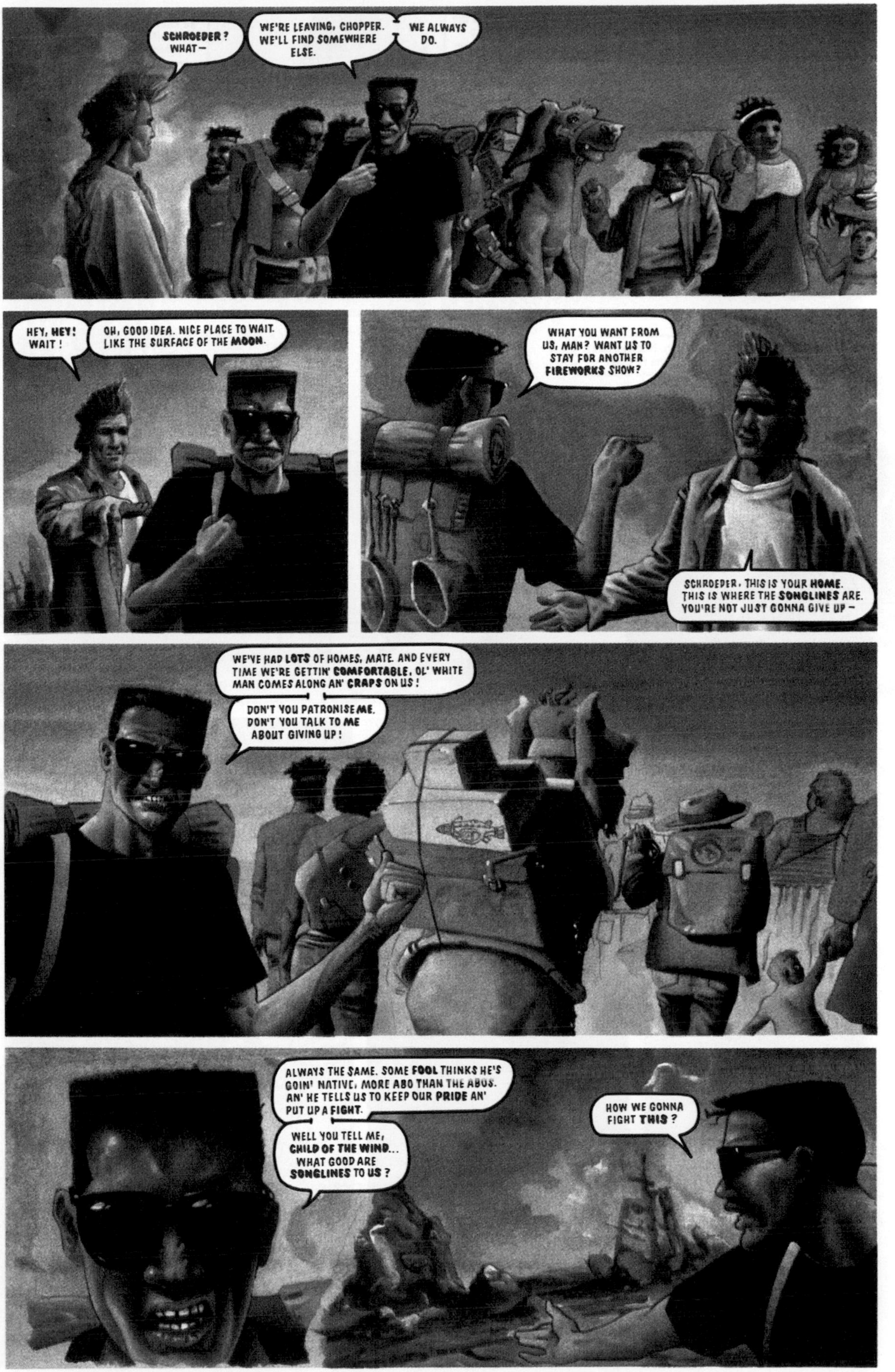
SCHROEDER? WHAT—
WE'RE LEAVING, CHOPPER. WE'LL FIND SOMEWHERE ELSE.
WE ALWAYS DO.
HEY, HEY! WAIT!
OH, GOOD IDEA. NICE PLACE TO WAIT. LIKE THE SURFACE OF THE MOON.
WHAT YOU WANT FROM US, MAN? WANT US TO STAY FOR ANOTHER FIREWORKS SHOW?
SCHROEDER, THIS IS YOUR HOME. THIS IS WHERE THE SONGLINES ARE. YOU'RE NOT JUST GONNA GIVE UP—
WE'VE HAD LOTS OF HOMES, MATE. AND EVERY TIME WE'RE GETTIN' COMFORTABLE, OL' WHITE MAN COMES ALONG AN' CRAPS ON US!
DON'T YOU PATRONISE ME. DON'T YOU TALK TO ME ABOUT GIVING UP!
ALWAYS THE SAME. SOME FOOL THINKS HE'S GOIN' NATIVE, MORE ABO THAN THE ABOS. AN' HE TELLS US TO KEEP OUR PRIDE AN' PUT UP A FIGHT.
WELL YOU TELL ME, CHILD OF THE WIND... WHAT GOOD ARE SONGLINES TO US?
HOW WE GONNA FIGHT THIS?

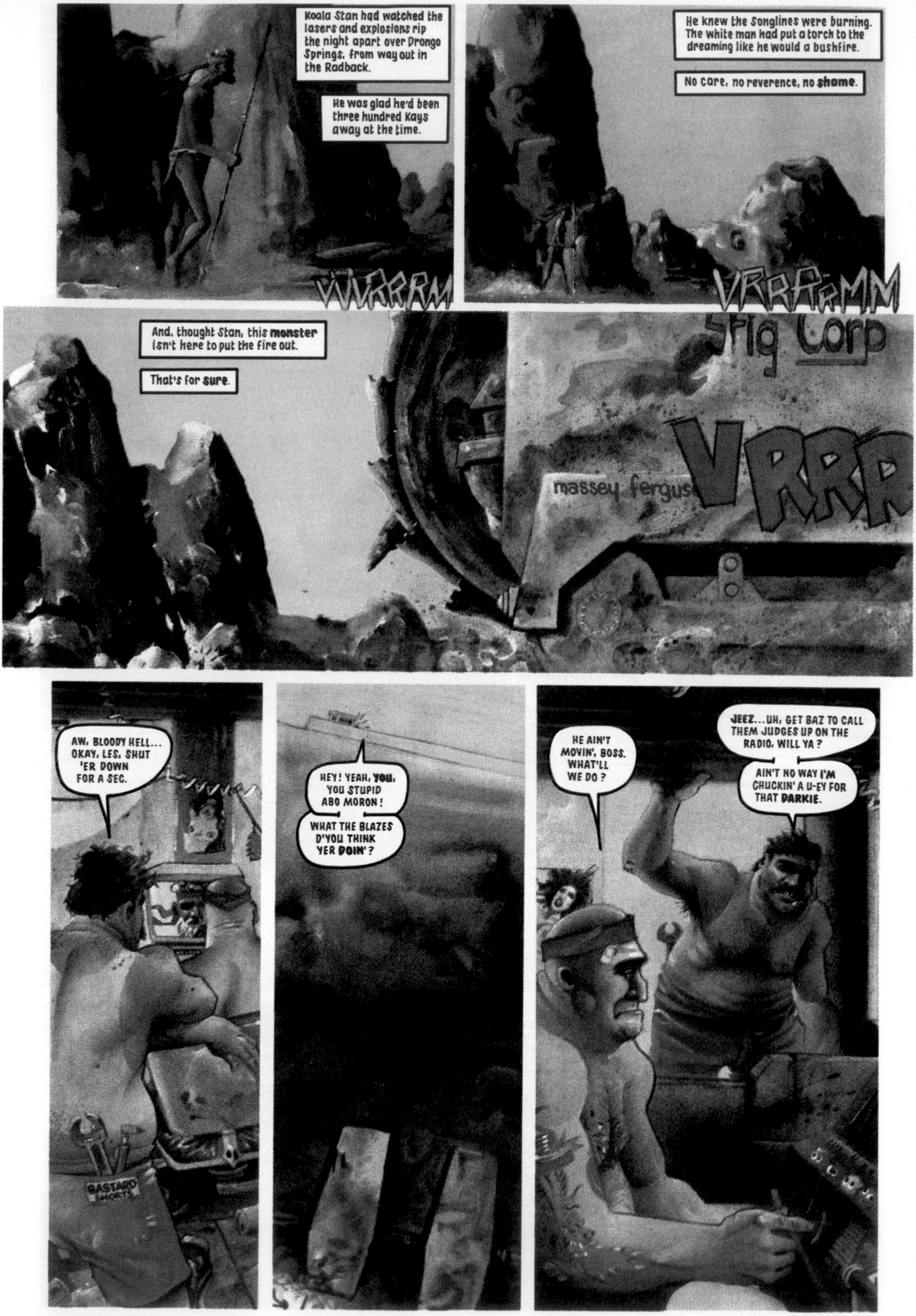
Koala Stan had watched the lasers and explosions rip the night apart over Drongo Springs, from way out in the Radback.
He was glad he'd been three hundred Kays away at the time.
VVVRRRM
He knew the Songlines were burning. The white man had put a torch to the dreaming like he would a bushfire.
No care, no reverence, no shame.
VRRRRMM
And, thought Stan, this monster isn't here to put the fire out.
That's for sure.
Stig Corp
massey fergus
VRRR
AW, BLOODY HELL... OKAY, LES, SHUT 'ER DOWN FOR A SEC.
BASTARD SHORTS
HEY! YEAH, YOU, YOU STUPID ABO MORON!
WHAT THE BLAZES D'YOU THINK YER DOIN'?
HE AIN'T MOVIN', BOSS. WHAT'LL WE DO?
JEEZ...UH, GET BAZ TO CALL THEM JUDGES UP ON THE RADIO, WILL YA?
AIN'T NO WAY I'M CHUCKIN' A U-EY FOR THAT DARKIE.

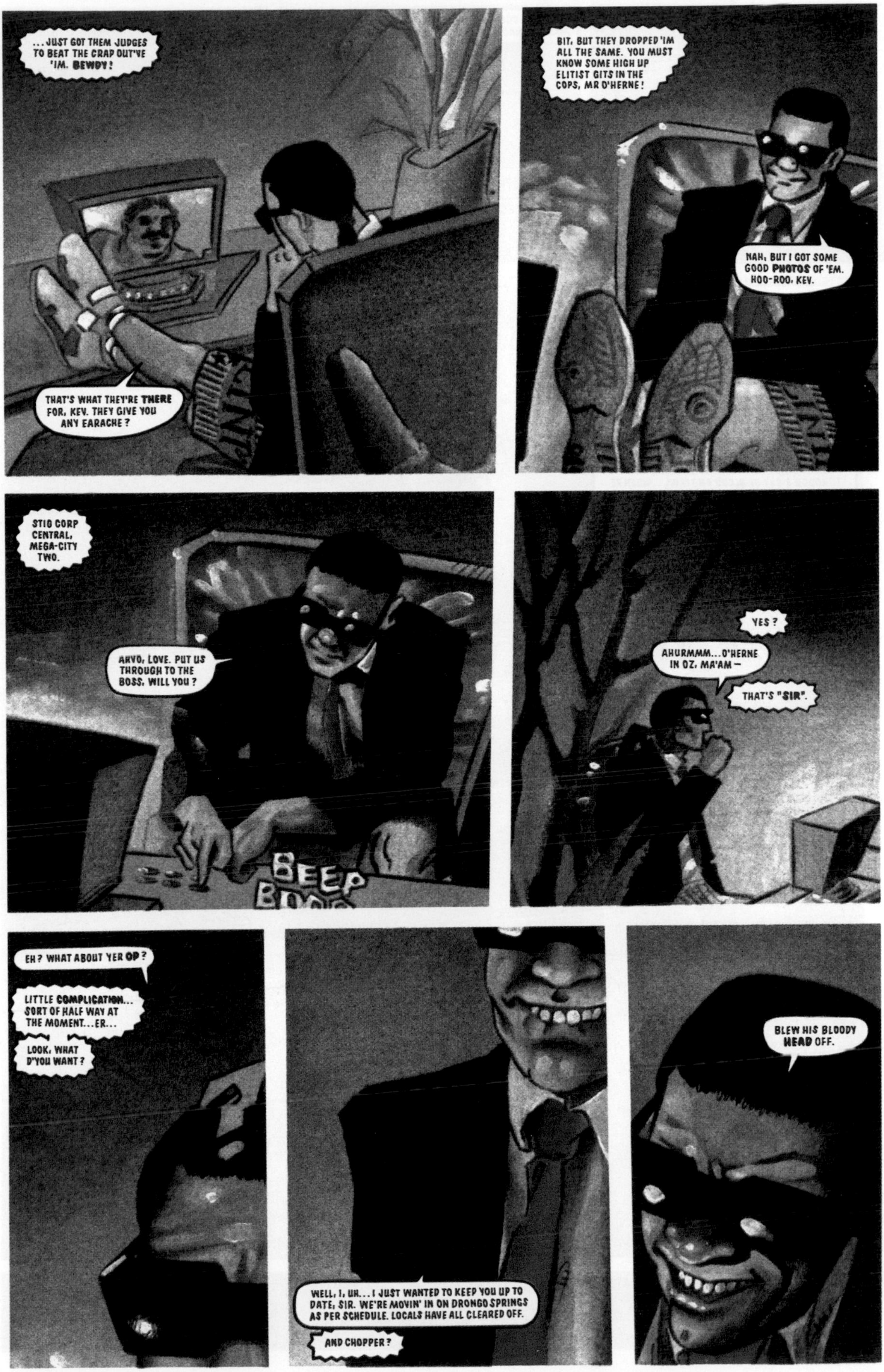
...JUST GOT THEM JUDGES TO BEAT THE CRAP OUT'VE 'IM. BEWDY!
THAT'S WHAT THEY'RE THERE FOR, KEV. THEY GIVE YOU ANY EARACHE?
BIT, BUT THEY DROPPED 'IM ALL THE SAME. YOU MUST KNOW SOME HIGH UP ELITIST GITS IN THE COPS, MR O'HERNE!
NAH, BUT I GOT SOME GOOD PHOTOS OF 'EM. HOO-ROO, KEV.
STIG CORP CENTRAL, MEGA-CITY TWO.
ARVO, LOVE. PUT US THROUGH TO THE BOSS, WILL YOU?
BEEP
YES?
AHURMMM...O'HERNE IN OZ, MA'AM—
THAT'S "SIR".
EH? WHAT ABOUT YER OP?
LITTLE COMPLICATION... SORT OF HALF WAY AT THE MOMENT...ER...
LOOK, WHAT D'YOU WANT?
WELL, I, UH... I JUST WANTED TO KEEP YOU UP TO DATE, SIR. WE'RE MOVIN' IN ON DRONGO SPRINGS AS PER SCHEDULE. LOCALS HAVE ALL CLEARED OFF.
AND CHOPPER?
BLEW HIS BLOODY HEAD OFF.

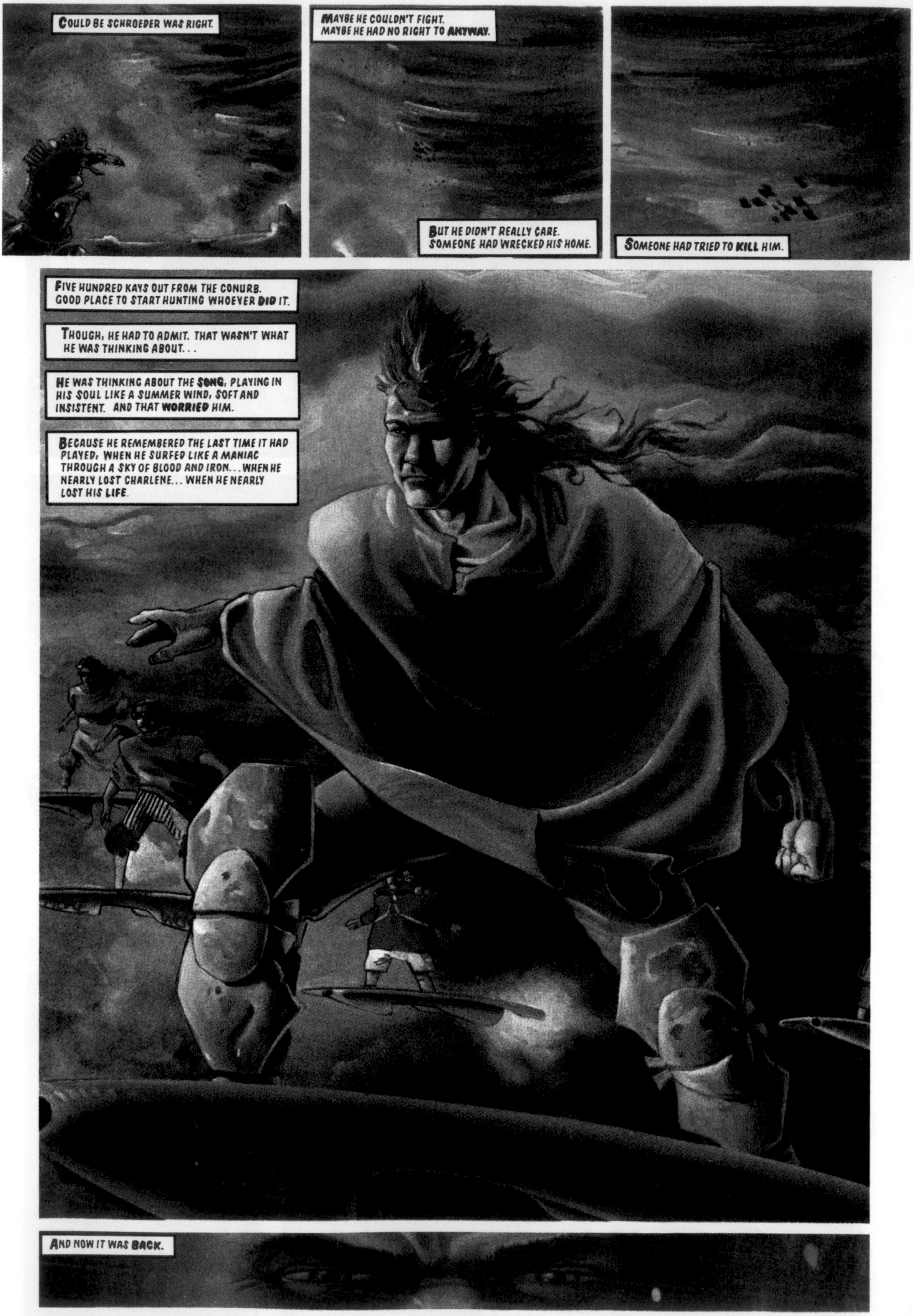
COULD BE SCHROEDER WAS RIGHT.
MAYBE HE COULDN'T FIGHT. MAYBE HE HAD NO RIGHT TO ANYWAY.
BUT HE DIDN'T REALLY CARE. SOMEONE HAD WRECKED HIS HOME.
SOMEONE HAD TRIED TO KILL HIM.
FIVE HUNDRED KAYS OUT FROM THE CONURB. GOOD PLACE TO START HUNTING WHOEVER DID IT.
THOUGH, HE HAD TO ADMIT, THAT WASN'T WHAT HE WAS THINKING ABOUT...
HE WAS THINKING ABOUT THE SONG, PLAYING IN HIS SOUL LIKE A SUMMER WIND, SOFT AND INSISTENT. AND THAT WORRIED HIM.
BECAUSE HE REMEMBERED THE LAST TIME IT HAD PLAYED, WHEN HE SURFED LIKE A MANIAC THROUGH A SKY OF BLOOD AND IRON... WHEN HE NEARLY LOST CHARLENE... WHEN HE NEARLY LOST HIS LIFE.
AND NOW IT WAS BACK.

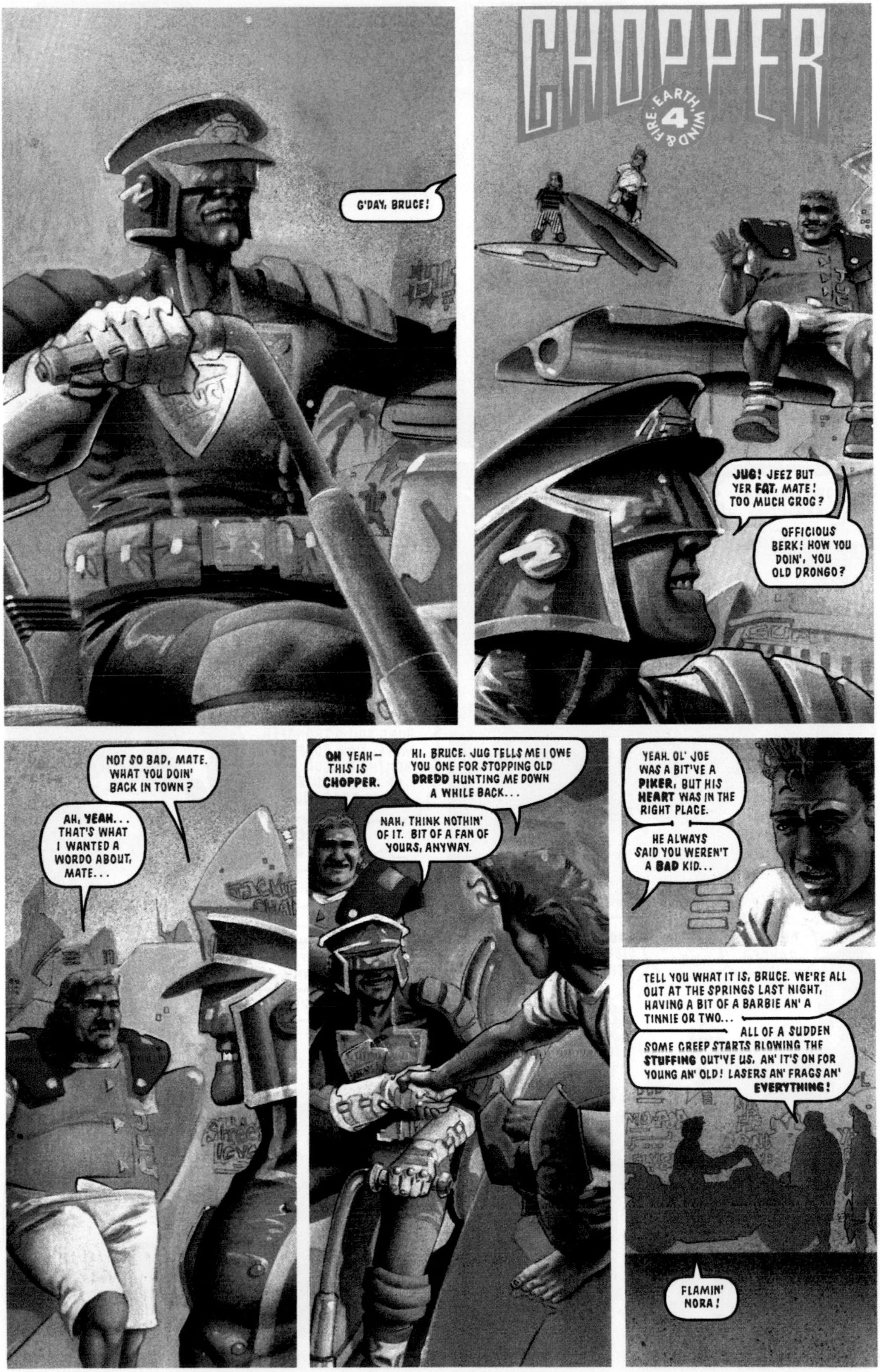
G'DAY, BRUCE!
CHOPPER
EARTH, WIND & FIRE 4
JUG! JEEZ BUT YER FAT, MATE! TOO MUCH GROG?
OFFICIOUS BERK! HOW YOU DOIN', YOU OLD DRONGO?
NOT SO BAD, MATE. WHAT YOU DOIN' BACK IN TOWN?
AH, YEAH... THAT'S WHAT I WANTED A WORDO ABOUT, MATE...
OH YEAH— THIS IS CHOPPER.
HI, BRUCE. JUG TELLS ME I OWE YOU ONE FOR STOPPING OLD DREDD HUNTING ME DOWN A WHILE BACK...
NAH, THINK NOTHIN' OF IT. BIT OF A FAN OF YOURS, ANYWAY.
YEAH. OL' JOE WAS A BIT'VE A PIKER, BUT HIS HEART WAS IN THE RIGHT PLACE.
HE ALWAYS SAID YOU WEREN'T A BAD KID...
TELL YOU WHAT IT IS, BRUCE. WE'RE ALL OUT AT THE SPRINGS LAST NIGHT, HAVING A BIT OF A BARBIE AN' A TINNIE OR TWO...
ALL OF A SUDDEN SOME CREEP STARTS BLOWING THE STUFFING OUT'VE US, AN' IT'S ON FOR YOUNG AN' OLD! LASERS AN' FRAGS AN' EVERYTHING!
FLAMIN' NORA!

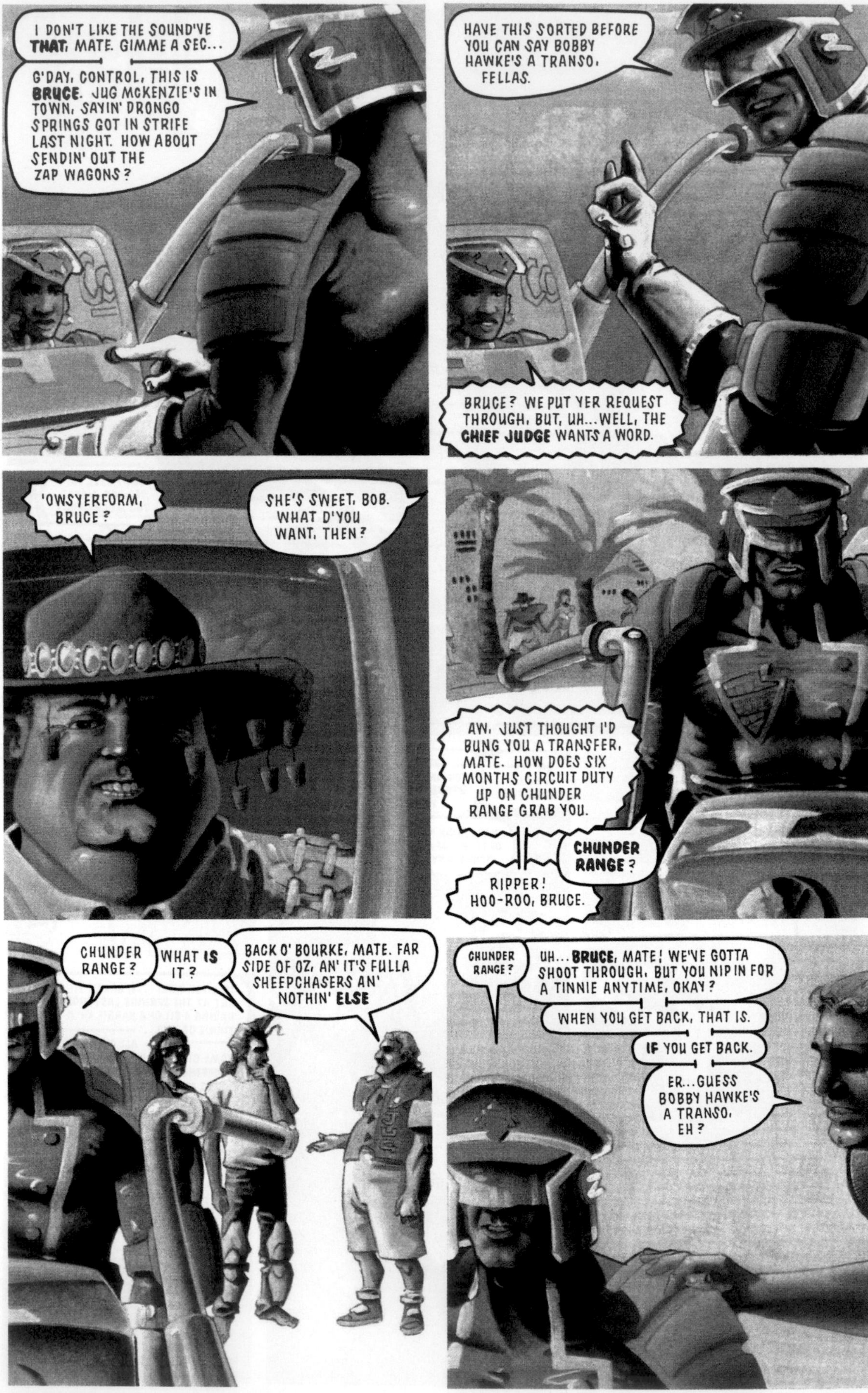
I DON'T LIKE THE SOUND'VE THAT, MATE. GIMME A SEC...
G'DAY, CONTROL, THIS IS BRUCE. JUG McKENZIE'S IN TOWN, SAYIN' DRONGO SPRINGS GOT IN STRIFE LAST NIGHT. HOW ABOUT SENDIN' OUT THE ZAP WAGONS?
HAVE THIS SORTED BEFORE YOU CAN SAY BOBBY HAWKE'S A TRANSO, FELLAS.
BRUCE? WE PUT YER REQUEST THROUGH, BUT, UH... WELL, THE CHIEF JUDGE WANTS A WORD.
'OWSYERFORM, BRUCE?
SHE'S SWEET, BOB. WHAT D'YOU WANT, THEN?
AW, JUST THOUGHT I'D BUNG YOU A TRANSFER, MATE. HOW DOES SIX MONTHS CIRCUIT DUTY UP ON CHUNDER RANGE GRAB YOU.
CHUNDER RANGE?
RIPPER! HOO-ROO, BRUCE.
CHUNDER RANGE?
WHAT IS IT?
BACK O' BOURKE, MATE. FAR SIDE OF OZ, AN' IT'S FULLA SHEEPCHASERS AN' NOTHIN' ELSE
CHUNDER RANGE?
UH... BRUCE, MATE! WE'VE GOTTA SHOOT THROUGH, BUT YOU NIP IN FOR A TINNIE ANYTIME, OKAY?
WHEN YOU GET BACK, THAT IS.
IF YOU GET BACK.
ER...GUESS BOBBY HAWKE'S A TRANSO, EH?

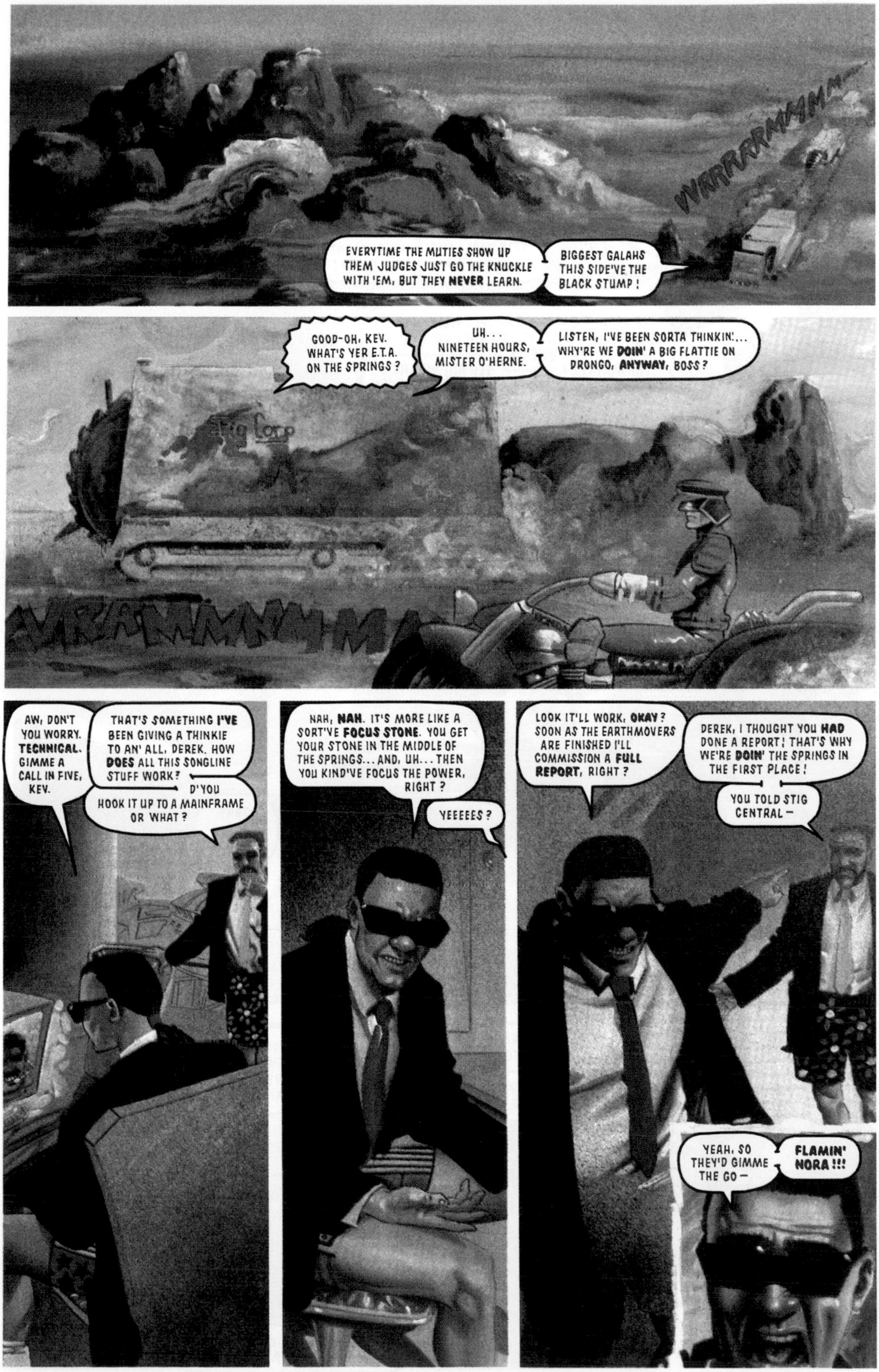
EVERYTIME THE MUTIES SHOW UP THEM JUDGES JUST GO THE KNUCKLE WITH 'EM, BUT THEY **NEVER** LEARN.
BIGGEST GALAHS THIS SIDE'VE THE BLACK STUMP!
GOOD-OH, KEV. WHAT'S YER E.T.A. ON THE SPRINGS?
UH... NINETEEN HOURS, MISTER O'HERNE.
LISTEN, I'VE BEEN SORTA THINKIN'... WHY'RE WE **DOIN'** A BIG FLATTIE ON DRONGO, **ANYWAY**, BOSS?
AW, DON'T YOU WORRY. **TECHNICAL**. GIMME A CALL IN FIVE, KEV.
THAT'S SOMETHING **I'VE** BEEN GIVING A THINKIE TO AN' ALL, DEREK. HOW **DOES** ALL THIS SONGLINE STUFF WORK?
D'YOU HOOK IT UP TO A MAINFRAME OR WHAT?
NAH, **NAH**. IT'S MORE LIKE A SORT'VE **FOCUS STONE**. YOU GET YOUR STONE IN THE MIDDLE OF THE SPRINGS... AND, UH... THEN YOU KIND'VE FOCUS THE POWER, RIGHT?
YEEEEES?
LOOK IT'LL WORK, **OKAY**? SOON AS THE EARTHMOVERS ARE FINISHED I'LL COMMISSION A **FULL REPORT**, RIGHT?
DEREK, I THOUGHT YOU **HAD** DONE A REPORT! THAT'S WHY WE'RE **DOIN'** THE SPRINGS IN THE FIRST PLACE!
YOU TOLD STIG CENTRAL—
YEAH, SO THEY'D GIMME THE GO—
FLAMIN' NORA!!!

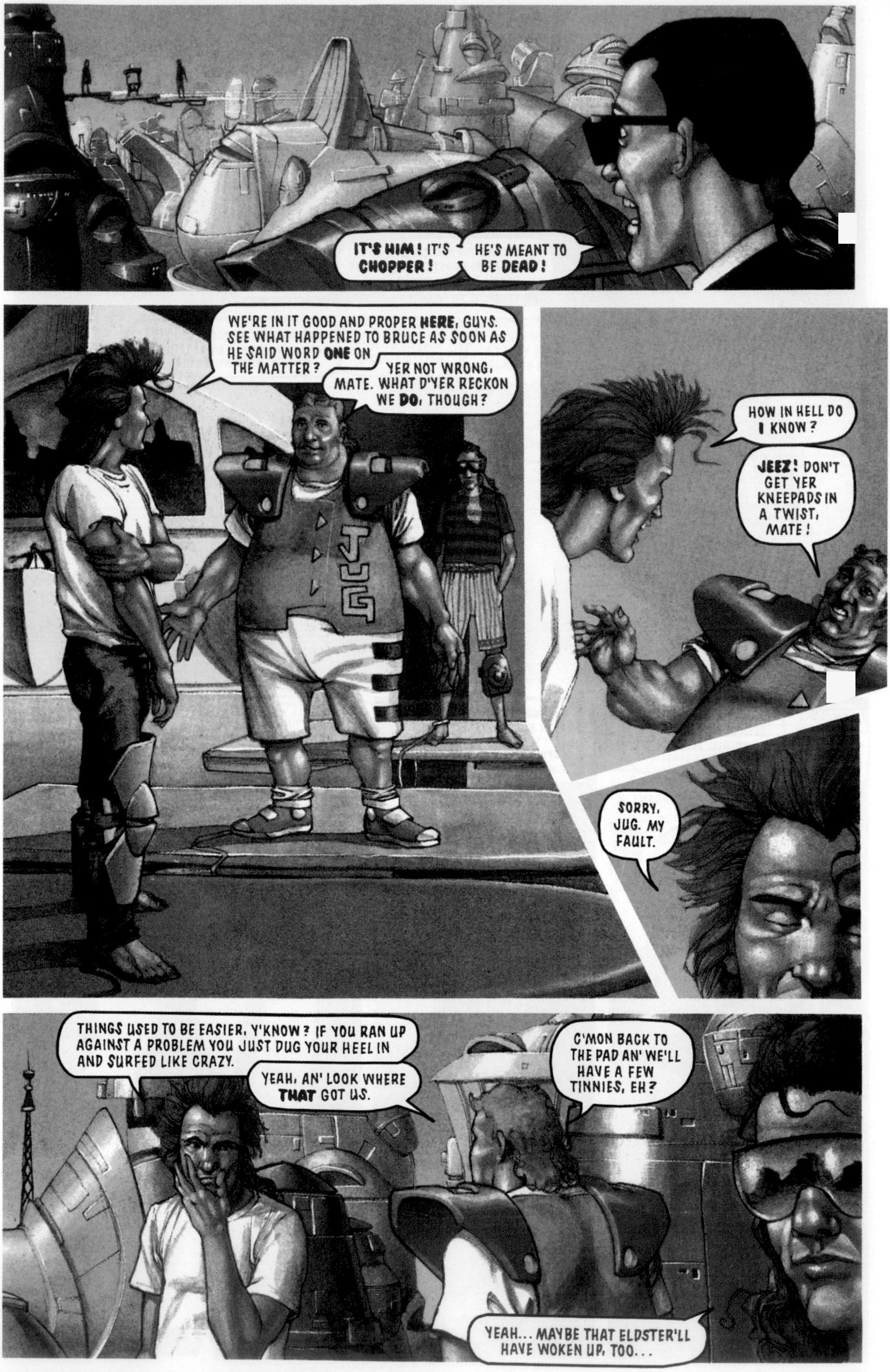
IT'S HIM! IT'S CHOPPER!
HE'S MEANT TO BE DEAD!
WE'RE IN IT GOOD AND PROPER HERE, GUYS. SEE WHAT HAPPENED TO BRUCE AS SOON AS HE SAID WORD ONE ON THE MATTER?
YER NOT WRONG, MATE. WHAT D'YER RECKON WE DO, THOUGH?
HOW IN HELL DO I KNOW?
JEEZ! DON'T GET YER KNEEPADS IN A TWIST, MATE!
SORRY, JUG. MY FAULT.
THINGS USED TO BE EASIER, Y'KNOW? IF YOU RAN UP AGAINST A PROBLEM YOU JUST DUG YOUR HEEL IN AND SURFED LIKE CRAZY.
YEAH, AN' LOOK WHERE THAT GOT US.
C'MON BACK TO THE PAD AN' WE'LL HAVE A FEW TINNIES, EH?
YEAH... MAYBE THAT ELDSTER'LL HAVE WOKEN UP, TOO...

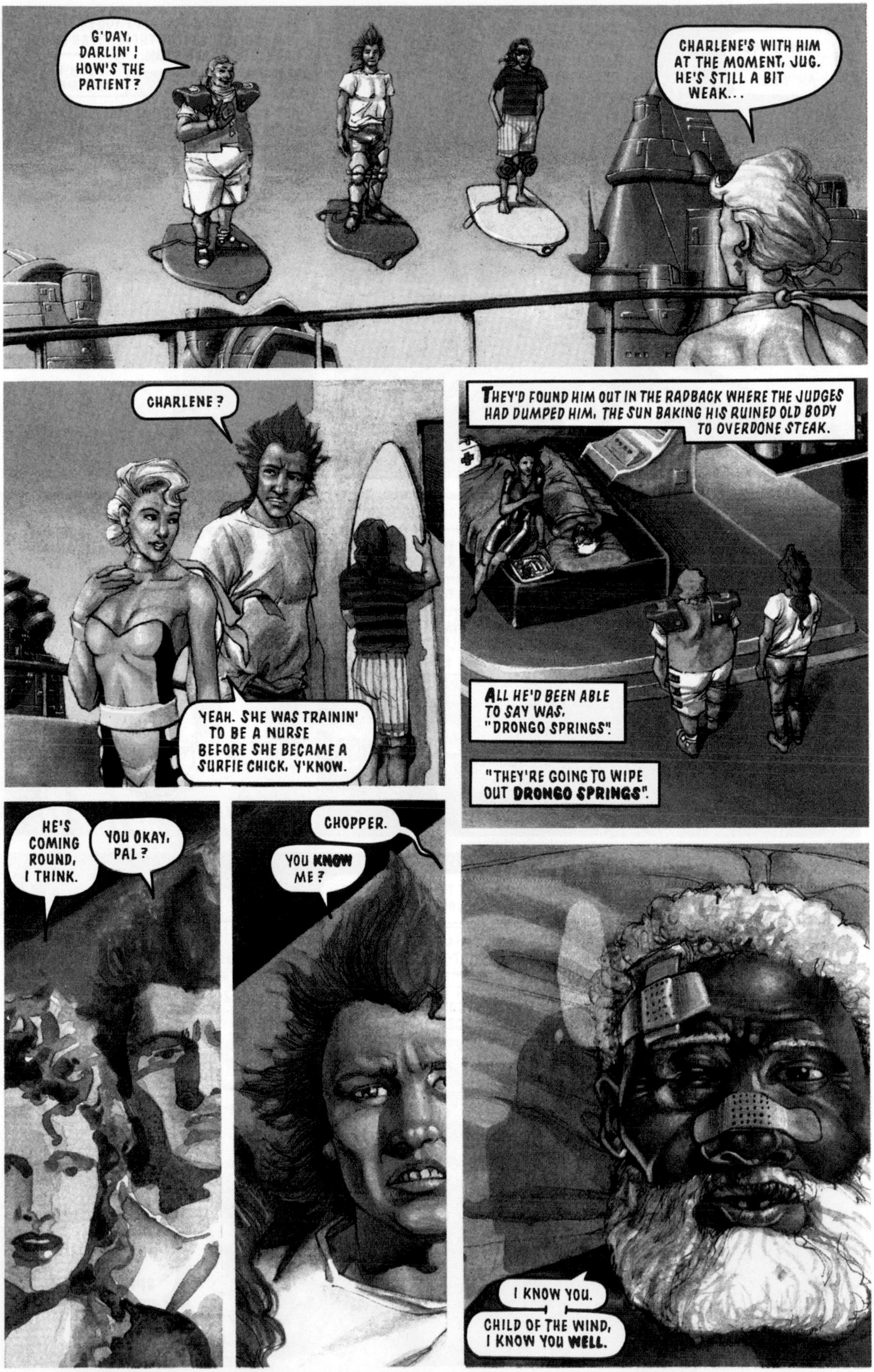
G'DAY, DARLIN'! HOW'S THE PATIENT?
CHARLENE'S WITH HIM AT THE MOMENT, JUG. HE'S STILL A BIT WEAK...
CHARLENE?
YEAH. SHE WAS TRAININ' TO BE A NURSE BEFORE SHE BECAME A SURFIE CHICK, Y'KNOW.
THEY'D FOUND HIM OUT IN THE RADBACK WHERE THE JUDGES HAD DUMPED HIM, THE SUN BAKING HIS RUINED OLD BODY TO OVERDONE STEAK.
ALL HE'D BEEN ABLE TO SAY WAS, "DRONGO SPRINGS".
"THEY'RE GOING TO WIPE OUT DRONGO SPRINGS".
HE'S COMING ROUND, I THINK.
YOU OKAY, PAL?
CHOPPER.
YOU KNOW ME?
I KNOW YOU.
CHILD OF THE WIND, I KNOW YOU WELL.

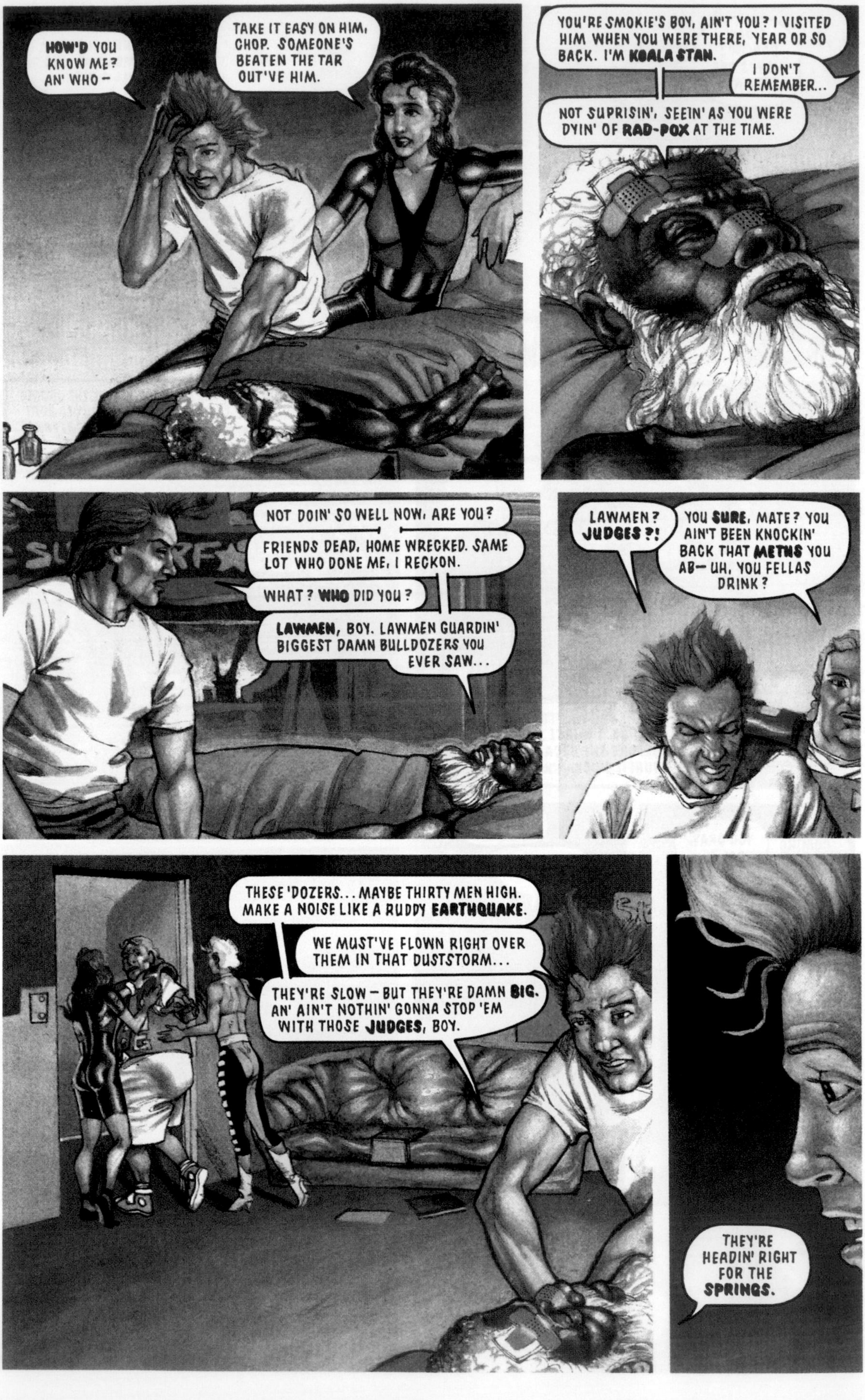
HOW'D YOU KNOW ME? AN' WHO –
TAKE IT EASY ON HIM, CHOP. SOMEONE'S BEATEN THE TAR OUT'VE HIM.
YOU'RE SMOKIE'S BOY, AIN'T YOU? I VISITED HIM WHEN YOU WERE THERE, YEAR OR SO BACK. I'M KOALA STAN.
I DON'T REMEMBER...
NOT SUPRISIN', SEEIN' AS YOU WERE DYIN' OF RAD-POX AT THE TIME.
NOT DOIN' SO WELL NOW, ARE YOU?
FRIENDS DEAD, HOME WRECKED. SAME LOT WHO DONE ME, I RECKON.
WHAT? WHO DID YOU?
LAWMEN, BOY. LAWMEN GUARDIN' BIGGEST DAMN BULLDOZERS YOU EVER SAW...
LAWMEN? JUDGES?!
YOU SURE, MATE? YOU AIN'T BEEN KNOCKIN' BACK THAT METHS YOU AB– UH, YOU FELLAS DRINK?
THESE 'DOZERS... MAYBE THIRTY MEN HIGH. MAKE A NOISE LIKE A RUDDY EARTHQUAKE.
WE MUST'VE FLOWN RIGHT OVER THEM IN THAT DUSTSTORM...
THEY'RE SLOW – BUT THEY'RE DAMN BIG. AN' AIN'T NOTHIN' GONNA STOP 'EM WITH THOSE JUDGES, BOY.
THEY'RE HEADIN' RIGHT FOR THE SPRINGS.

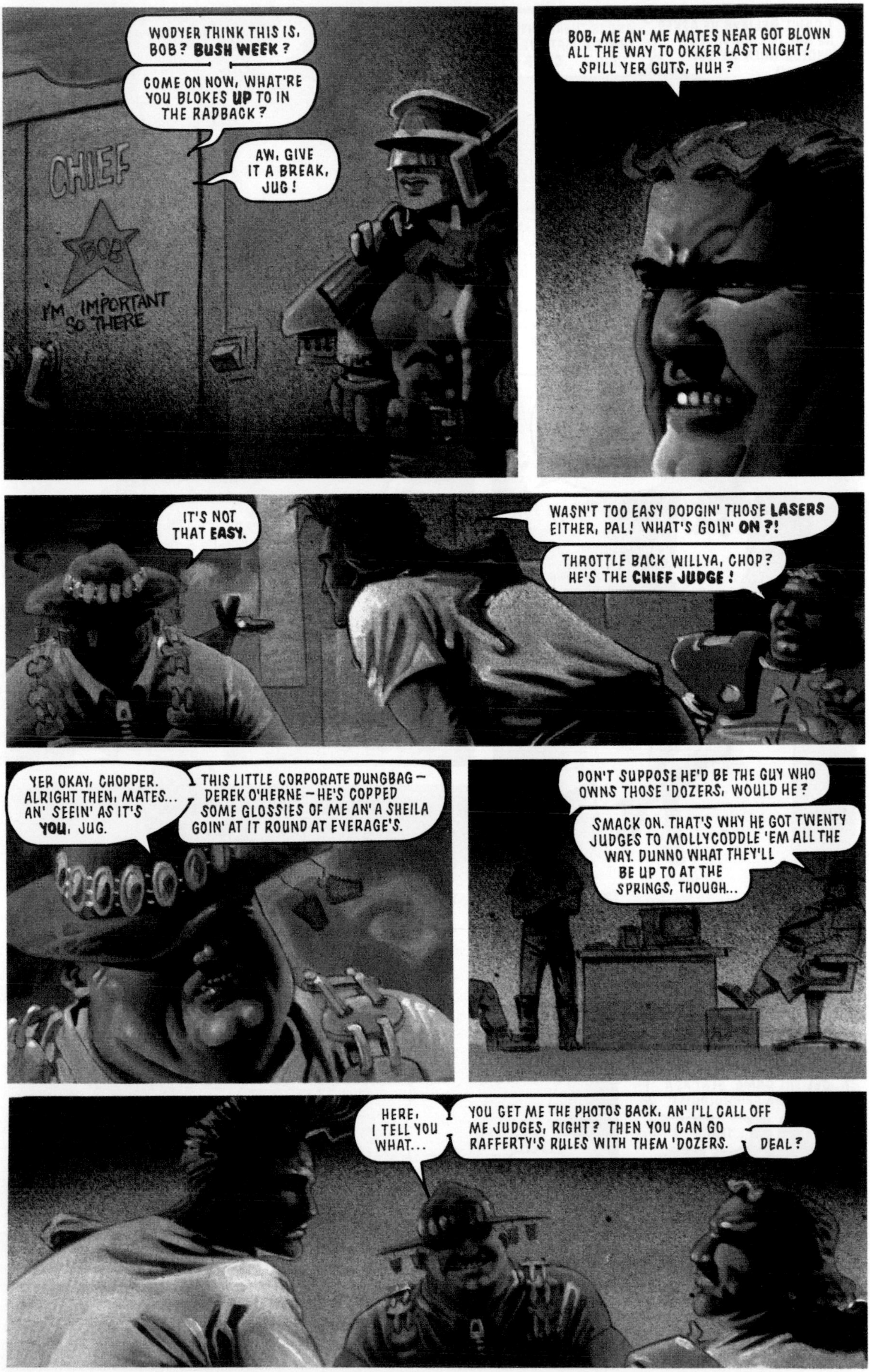

CHIEF
BOB
I'M IMPORTANT SO THERE
WODYER THINK THIS IS, BOB? BUSH WEEK?
COME ON NOW, WHAT'RE YOU BLOKES UP TO IN THE RADBACK?
AW, GIVE IT A BREAK, JUG!
BOB, ME AN' ME MATES NEAR GOT BLOWN ALL THE WAY TO OKKER LAST NIGHT! SPILL YER GUTS, HUH?
IT'S NOT THAT EASY.
WASN'T TOO EASY DODGIN' THOSE LASERS EITHER, PAL! WHAT'S GOIN' ON?!
THROTTLE BACK WILLYA, CHOP? HE'S THE CHIEF JUDGE!
YER OKAY, CHOPPER. ALRIGHT THEN, MATES... AN' SEEIN' AS IT'S YOU, JUG.
THIS LITTLE CORPORATE DUNGBAG — DEREK O'HERNE — HE'S COPPED SOME GLOSSIES OF ME AN' A SHEILA GOIN' AT IT ROUND AT EVERAGE'S.
DON'T SUPPOSE HE'D BE THE GUY WHO OWNS THOSE 'DOZERS, WOULD HE?
SMACK ON. THAT'S WHY HE GOT TWENTY JUDGES TO MOLLYCODDLE 'EM ALL THE WAY. DUNNO WHAT THEY'LL BE UP TO AT THE SPRINGS, THOUGH...
HERE, I TELL YOU WHAT...
YOU GET ME THE PHOTOS BACK, AN' I'LL CALL OFF ME JUDGES, RIGHT? THEN YOU CAN GO RAFFERTY'S RULES WITH THEM 'DOZERS.
DEAL?

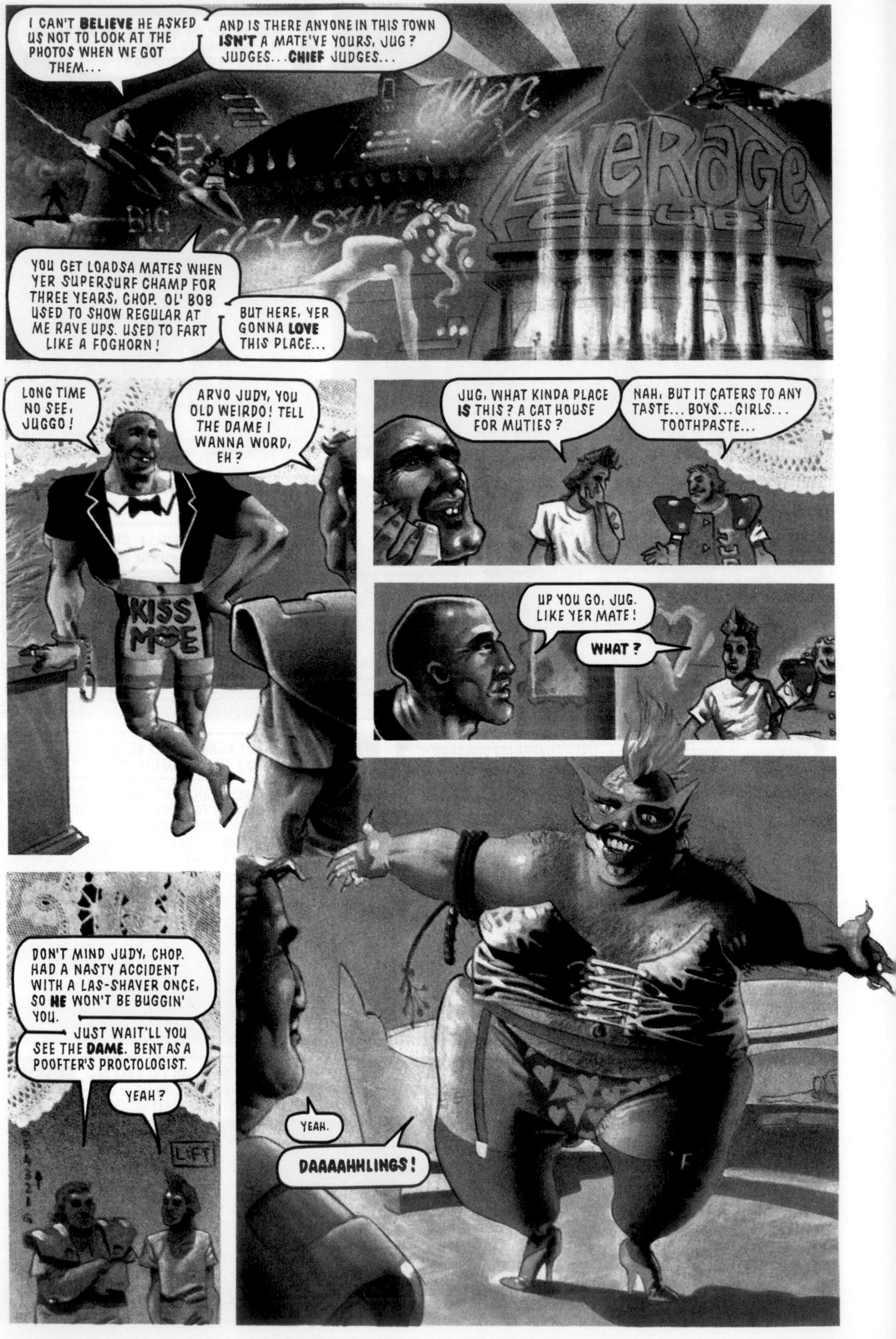

I CAN'T **BELIEVE** HE ASKED US NOT TO LOOK AT THE PHOTOS WHEN WE GOT THEM...
AND IS THERE ANYONE IN THIS TOWN **ISN'T** A MATE'VE YOURS, JUG? JUDGES... **CHIEF** JUDGES...
YOU GET LOADSA MATES WHEN YER SUPERSURF CHAMP FOR THREE YEARS, CHOP. OL' BOB USED TO SHOW REGULAR AT ME RAVE UPS. USED TO FART LIKE A FOGHORN!
BUT HERE, YER GONNA **LOVE** THIS PLACE...
LONG TIME NO SEE, JUGGO!
ARVO JUDY, YOU OLD WEIRDO! TELL THE DAME I WANNA WORD, EH?
KISS ME
JUG, WHAT KINDA PLACE **IS** THIS? A CAT HOUSE FOR MUTIES?
NAH, BUT IT CATERS TO ANY TASTE... BOYS... GIRLS... TOOTHPASTE...
UP YOU GO, JUG. LIKE YER MATE!
WHAT?
DON'T MIND JUDY, CHOP. HAD A NASTY ACCIDENT WITH A LAS-SHAVER ONCE, SO **HE** WON'T BE BUGGIN' YOU.
JUST WAIT'LL YOU SEE THE **DAME**. BENT AS A POOFTER'S PROCTOLOGIST.
YEAH?
LIFT
YEAH.
DAAAAHHLINGS!

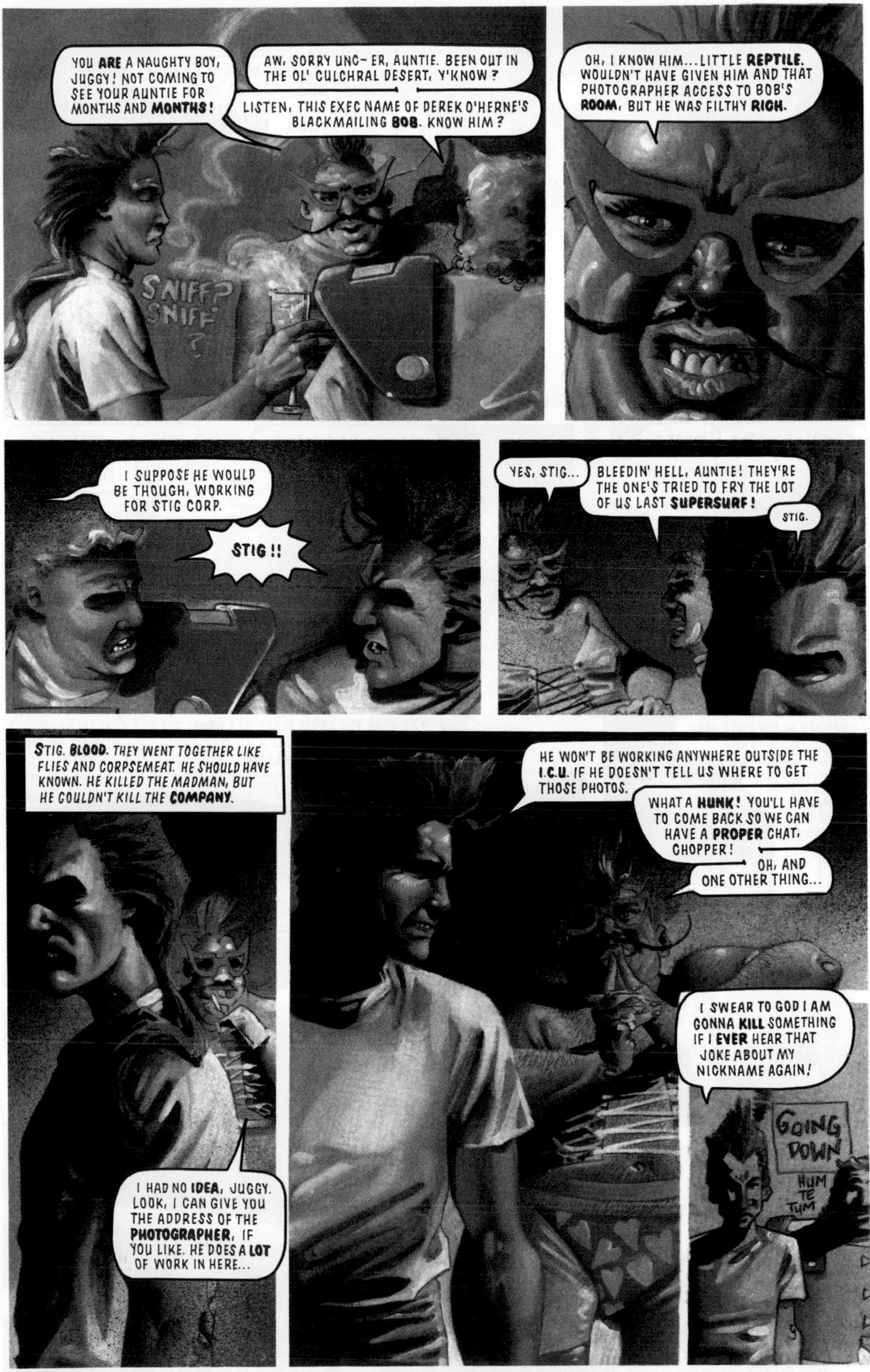
YOU **ARE** A NAUGHTY BOY, JUGGY! NOT COMING TO SEE YOUR AUNTIE FOR MONTHS AND **MONTHS**!
AW, SORRY UNC– ER, AUNTIE. BEEN OUT IN THE OL' CULCHRAL DESERT, Y'KNOW?
LISTEN, THIS EXEC NAME OF DEREK O'HERNE'S BLACKMAILING **BOB**. KNOW HIM?
SNIFF? SNIFF ?
OH, I KNOW HIM... LITTLE **REPTILE**. WOULDN'T HAVE GIVEN HIM AND THAT PHOTOGRAPHER ACCESS TO BOB'S **ROOM**, BUT HE WAS FILTHY **RICH**.
I SUPPOSE HE WOULD BE THOUGH, WORKING FOR STIG CORP.
STIG!!
YES, STIG...
BLEEDIN' HELL, AUNTIE! THEY'RE THE ONE'S TRIED TO FRY THE LOT OF US LAST **SUPERSURF**!
STIG.
STIG. **BLOOD**. THEY WENT TOGETHER LIKE FLIES AND CORPSEMEAT. HE SHOULD HAVE KNOWN. HE KILLED THE MADMAN, BUT HE COULDN'T KILL THE **COMPANY**.
I HAD NO **IDEA**, JUGGY. LOOK, I CAN GIVE YOU THE ADDRESS OF THE **PHOTOGRAPHER**, IF YOU LIKE. HE DOES A **LOT** OF WORK IN HERE...
HE WON'T BE WORKING ANYWHERE OUTSIDE THE **I.C.U.** IF HE DOESN'T TELL US WHERE TO GET THOSE PHOTOS.
WHAT A **HUNK**! YOU'LL HAVE TO COME BACK SO WE CAN HAVE A **PROPER** CHAT, CHOPPER!
OH, AND ONE OTHER THING...
I SWEAR TO GOD I AM GONNA **KILL** SOMETHING IF I **EVER** HEAR THAT JOKE ABOUT MY NICKNAME AGAIN!
GOING DOWN
HUM TE TUM

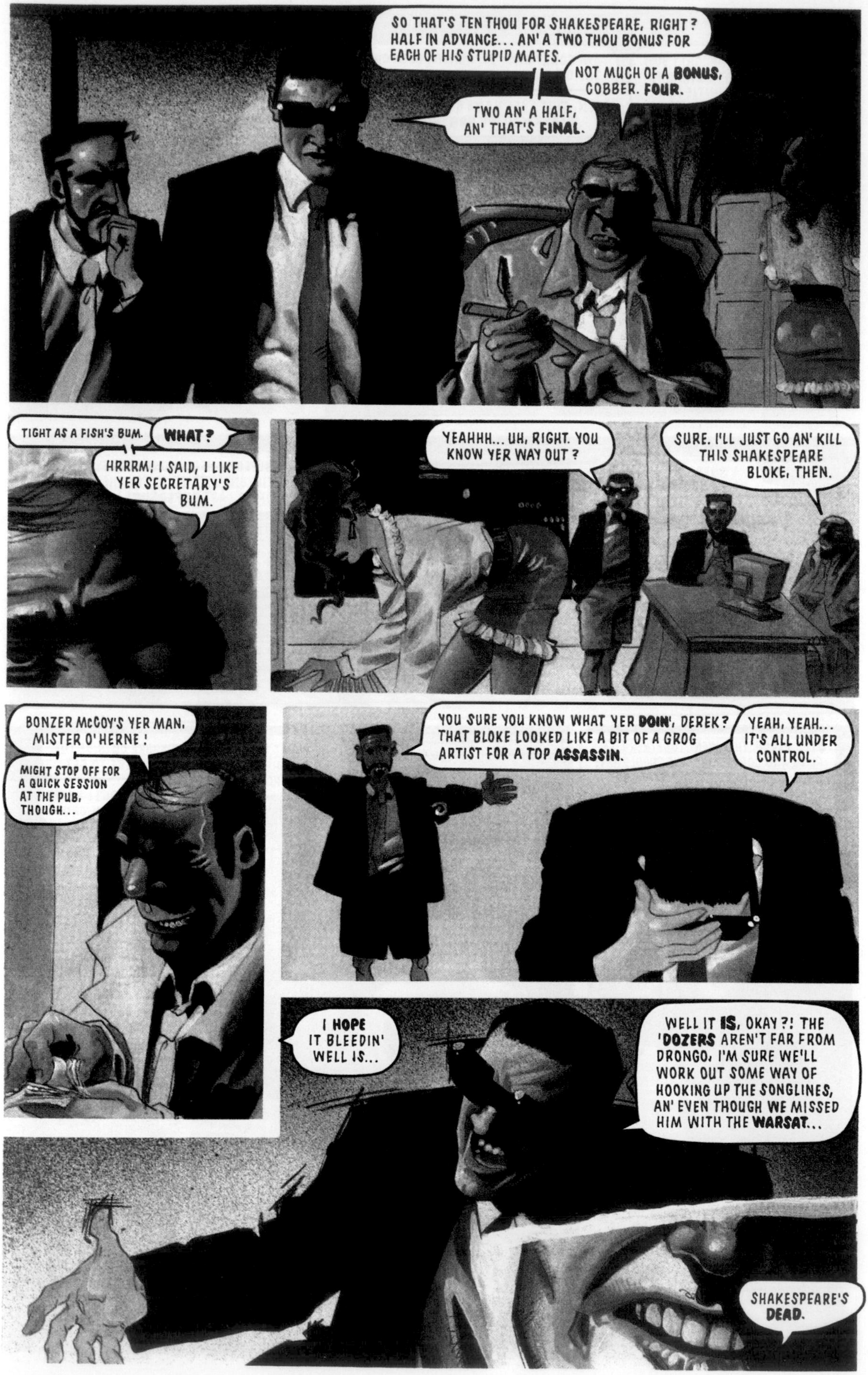
SO THAT'S TEN THOU FOR SHAKESPEARE, RIGHT? HALF IN ADVANCE... AN' A TWO THOU BONUS FOR EACH OF HIS STUPID MATES.
TWO AN' A HALF, AN' THAT'S FINAL.
NOT MUCH OF A BONUS, COBBER. FOUR.
TIGHT AS A FISH'S BUM.
WHAT?
HRRRM! I SAID, I LIKE YER SECRETARY'S BUM.
YEAHHH... UH, RIGHT. YOU KNOW YER WAY OUT?
SURE. I'LL JUST GO AN' KILL THIS SHAKESPEARE BLOKE, THEN.
BONZER McCOY'S YER MAN, MISTER O'HERNE!
MIGHT STOP OFF FOR A QUICK SESSION AT THE PUB, THOUGH...
YOU SURE YOU KNOW WHAT YER DOIN', DEREK? THAT BLOKE LOOKED LIKE A BIT OF A GROG ARTIST FOR A TOP ASSASSIN.
YEAH, YEAH... IT'S ALL UNDER CONTROL.
I HOPE IT BLEEDIN' WELL IS...
WELL IT IS, OKAY?! THE 'DOZERS AREN'T FAR FROM DRONGO, I'M SURE WE'LL WORK OUT SOME WAY OF HOOKING UP THE SONGLINES, AN' EVEN THOUGH WE MISSED HIM WITH THE WARSAT...
SHAKESPEARE'S DEAD.

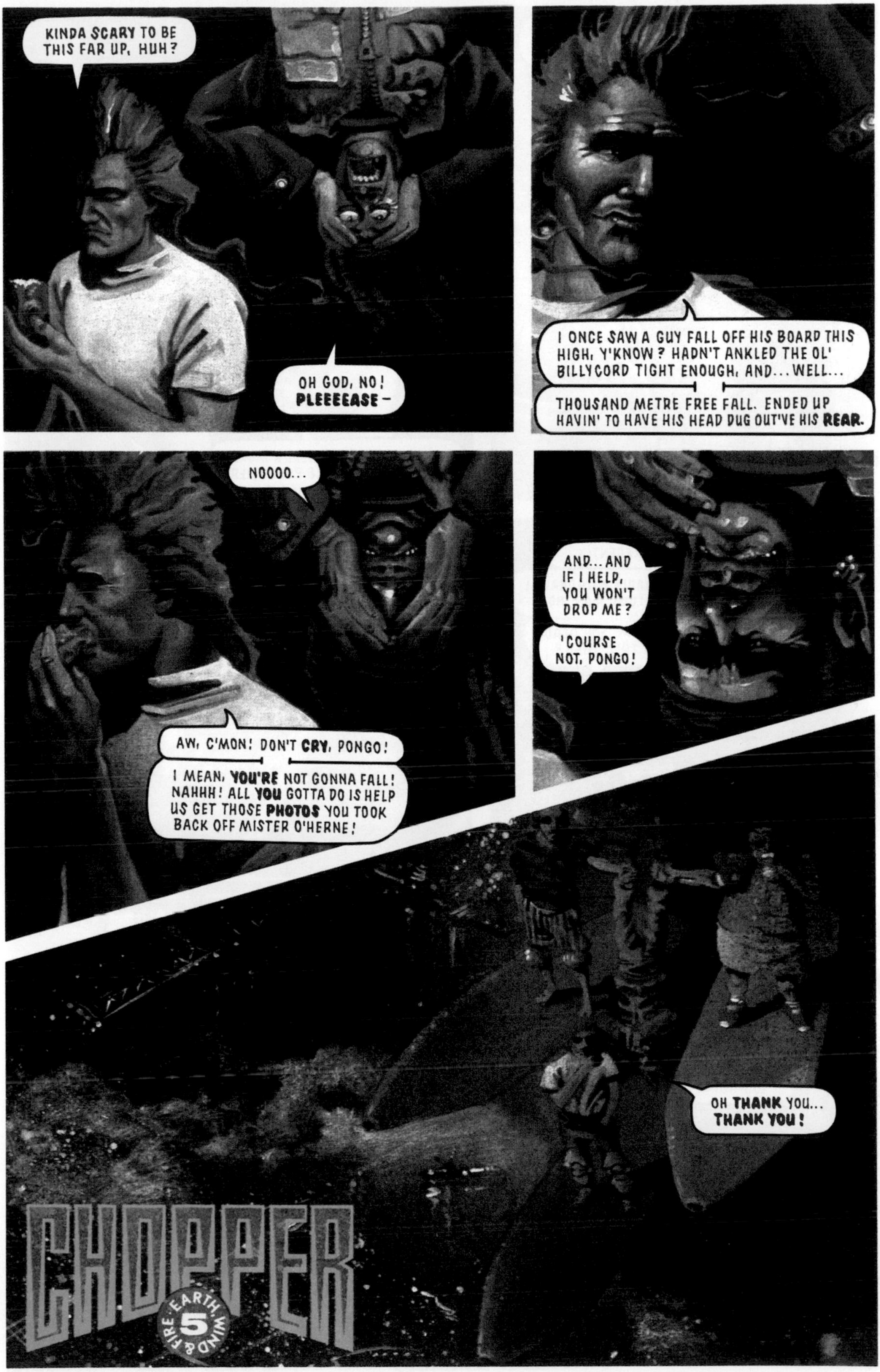
KINDA SCARY TO BE THIS FAR UP, HUH?
OH GOD, NO! PLEEEEASE—
I ONCE SAW A GUY FALL OFF HIS BOARD THIS HIGH, Y'KNOW? HADN'T ANKLED THE OL' BILLYCORD TIGHT ENOUGH, AND... WELL...
THOUSAND METRE FREE FALL. ENDED UP HAVIN' TO HAVE HIS HEAD DUG OUT'VE HIS REAR.
NOOOO...
AW, C'MON! DON'T CRY, PONGO!
I MEAN, YOU'RE NOT GONNA FALL! NAHHH! ALL YOU GOTTA DO IS HELP US GET THOSE PHOTOS YOU TOOK BACK OFF MISTER O'HERNE!
AND... AND IF I HELP, YOU WON'T DROP ME?
'COURSE NOT, PONGO!
OH THANK YOU... THANK YOU!
CHOPPER
EARTH, WIND & FIRE
5

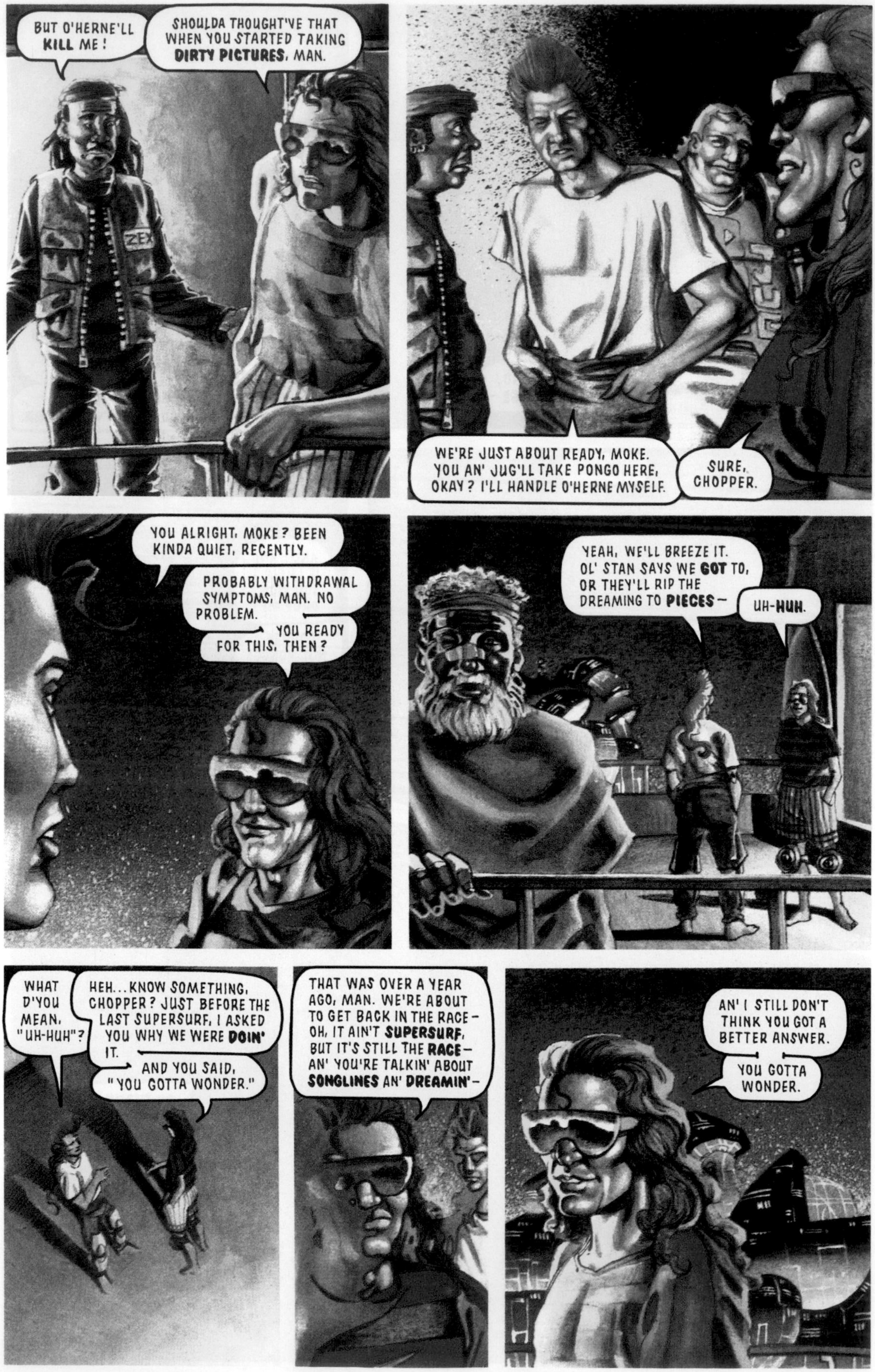
BUT O'HERNE'LL KILL ME!
SHOULDA THOUGHT'VE THAT WHEN YOU STARTED TAKING DIRTY PICTURES, MAN.
ZEX
WE'RE JUST ABOUT READY, MOKE. YOU AN' JUG'LL TAKE PONGO HERE, OKAY? I'LL HANDLE O'HERNE MYSELF.
SURE, CHOPPER.
YOU ALRIGHT, MOKE? BEEN KINDA QUIET, RECENTLY.
PROBABLY WITHDRAWAL SYMPTOMS, MAN. NO PROBLEM.
YOU READY FOR THIS, THEN?
YEAH, WE'LL BREEZE IT. OL' STAN SAYS WE GOT TO, OR THEY'LL RIP THE DREAMING TO PIECES—
UH-HUH.
WHAT D'YOU MEAN, "UH-HUH"?
HEH... KNOW SOMETHING, CHOPPER? JUST BEFORE THE LAST SUPERSURF, I ASKED YOU WHY WE WERE DOIN' IT.
AND YOU SAID, "YOU GOTTA WONDER."
THAT WAS OVER A YEAR AGO, MAN. WE'RE ABOUT TO GET BACK IN THE RACE— OH, IT AIN'T SUPERSURF, BUT IT'S STILL THE RACE— AN' YOU'RE TALKIN' ABOUT SONGLINES AN' DREAMIN'—
AN' I STILL DON'T THINK YOU GOT A BETTER ANSWER.
YOU GOTTA WONDER.

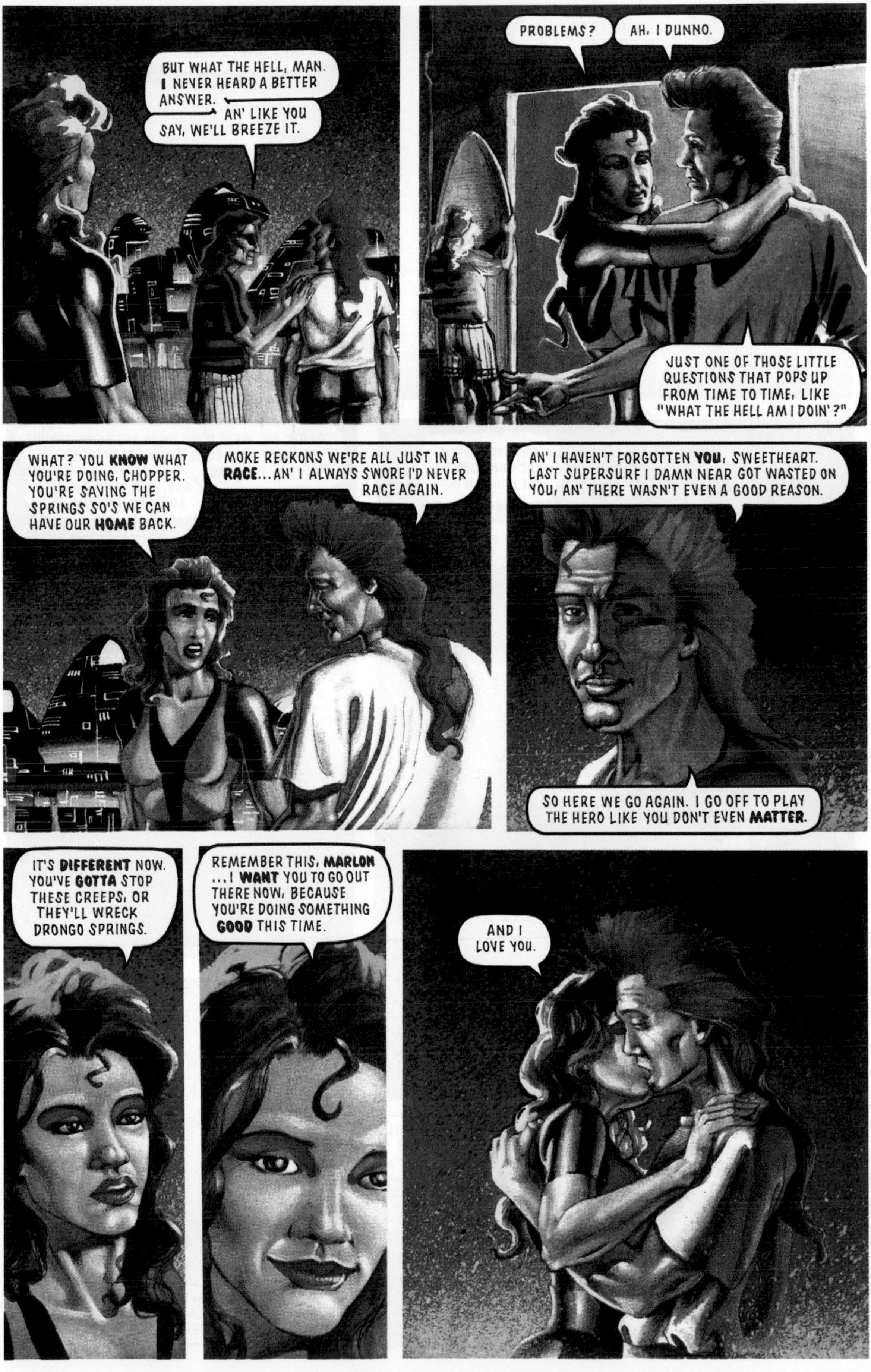
BUT WHAT THE HELL, MAN. I NEVER HEARD A BETTER ANSWER.
AN' LIKE YOU SAY, WE'LL BREEZE IT.
PROBLEMS?
AH, I DUNNO.
JUST ONE OF THOSE LITTLE QUESTIONS THAT POPS UP FROM TIME TO TIME, LIKE "WHAT THE HELL AM I DOIN'?"
WHAT? YOU **KNOW** WHAT YOU'RE DOING, CHOPPER. YOU'RE SAVING THE SPRINGS SO'S WE CAN HAVE OUR **HOME** BACK.
MOKE RECKONS WE'RE ALL JUST IN A **RACE**... AN' I ALWAYS SWORE I'D NEVER RACE AGAIN.
AN' I HAVEN'T FORGOTTEN **YOU**, SWEETHEART. LAST SUPERSURF I DAMN NEAR GOT WASTED ON YOU, AN' THERE WASN'T EVEN A GOOD REASON.
SO HERE WE GO AGAIN. I GO OFF TO PLAY THE HERO LIKE YOU DON'T EVEN **MATTER**.
IT'S **DIFFERENT** NOW. YOU'VE **GOTTA** STOP THESE CREEPS, OR THEY'LL WRECK DRONGO SPRINGS.
REMEMBER THIS, **MARLON** ...I **WANT** YOU TO GO OUT THERE NOW, BECAUSE YOU'RE DOING SOMETHING **GOOD** THIS TIME.
AND I LOVE YOU.

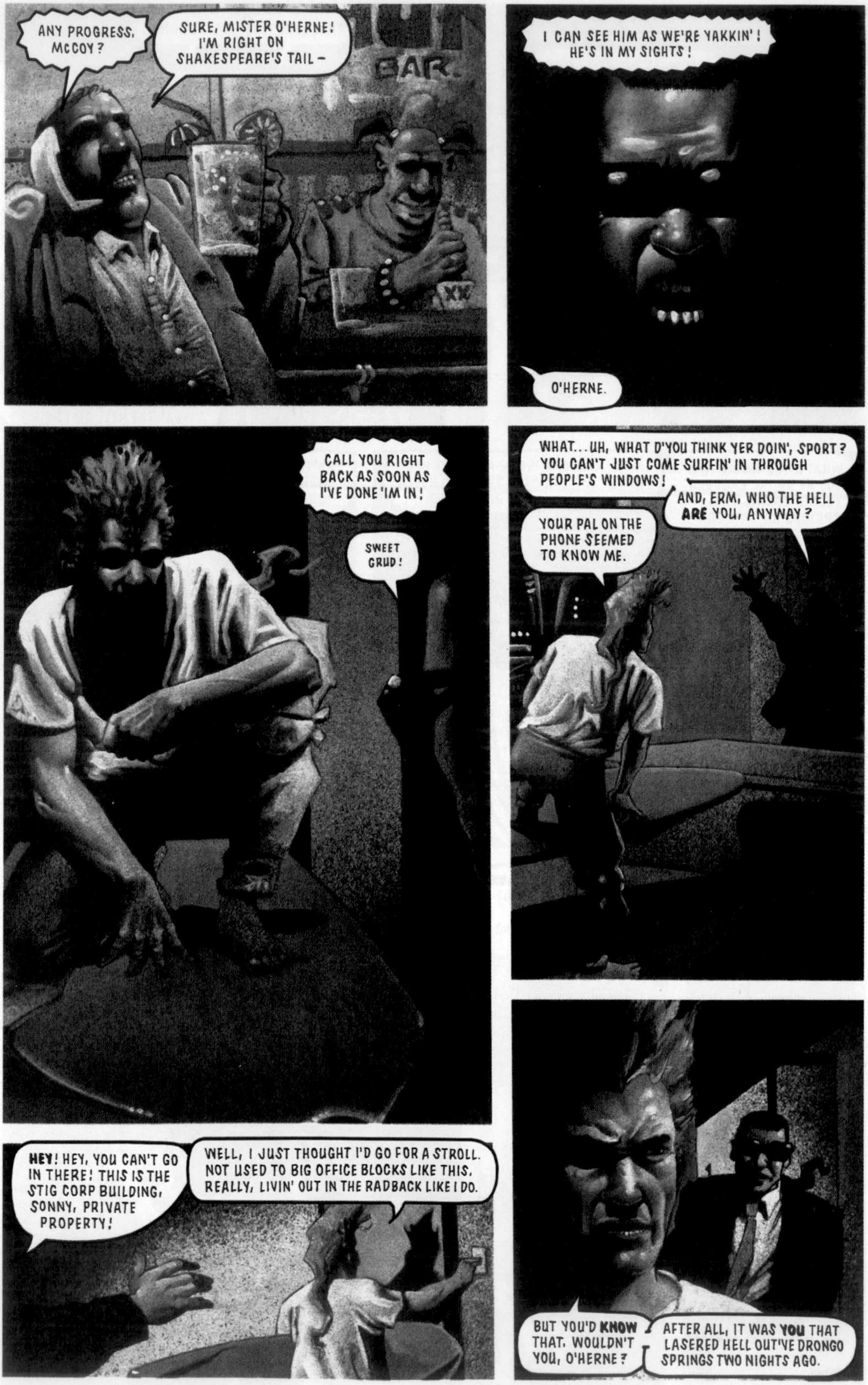
ANY PROGRESS, McCOY?
SURE, MISTER O'HERNE! I'M RIGHT ON SHAKESPEARE'S TAIL —
BAR
I CAN SEE HIM AS WE'RE YAKKIN'! HE'S IN MY SIGHTS!
O'HERNE.
CALL YOU RIGHT BACK AS SOON AS I'VE DONE 'IM IN!
SWEET GRUD!
HEY! HEY, YOU CAN'T GO IN THERE! THIS IS THE STIG CORP BUILDING, SONNY, PRIVATE PROPERTY!
WELL, I JUST THOUGHT I'D GO FOR A STROLL. NOT USED TO BIG OFFICE BLOCKS LIKE THIS, REALLY, LIVIN' OUT IN THE RADBACK LIKE I DO.
WHAT... UH, WHAT D'YOU THINK YER DOIN', SPORT? YOU CAN'T JUST COME SURFIN' IN THROUGH PEOPLE'S WINDOWS!
AND, ERM, WHO THE HELL ARE YOU, ANYWAY?
YOUR PAL ON THE PHONE SEEMED TO KNOW ME.
BUT YOU'D KNOW THAT, WOULDN'T YOU, O'HERNE?
AFTER ALL, IT WAS YOU THAT LASERED HELL OUT'VE DRONGO SPRINGS TWO NIGHTS AGO.

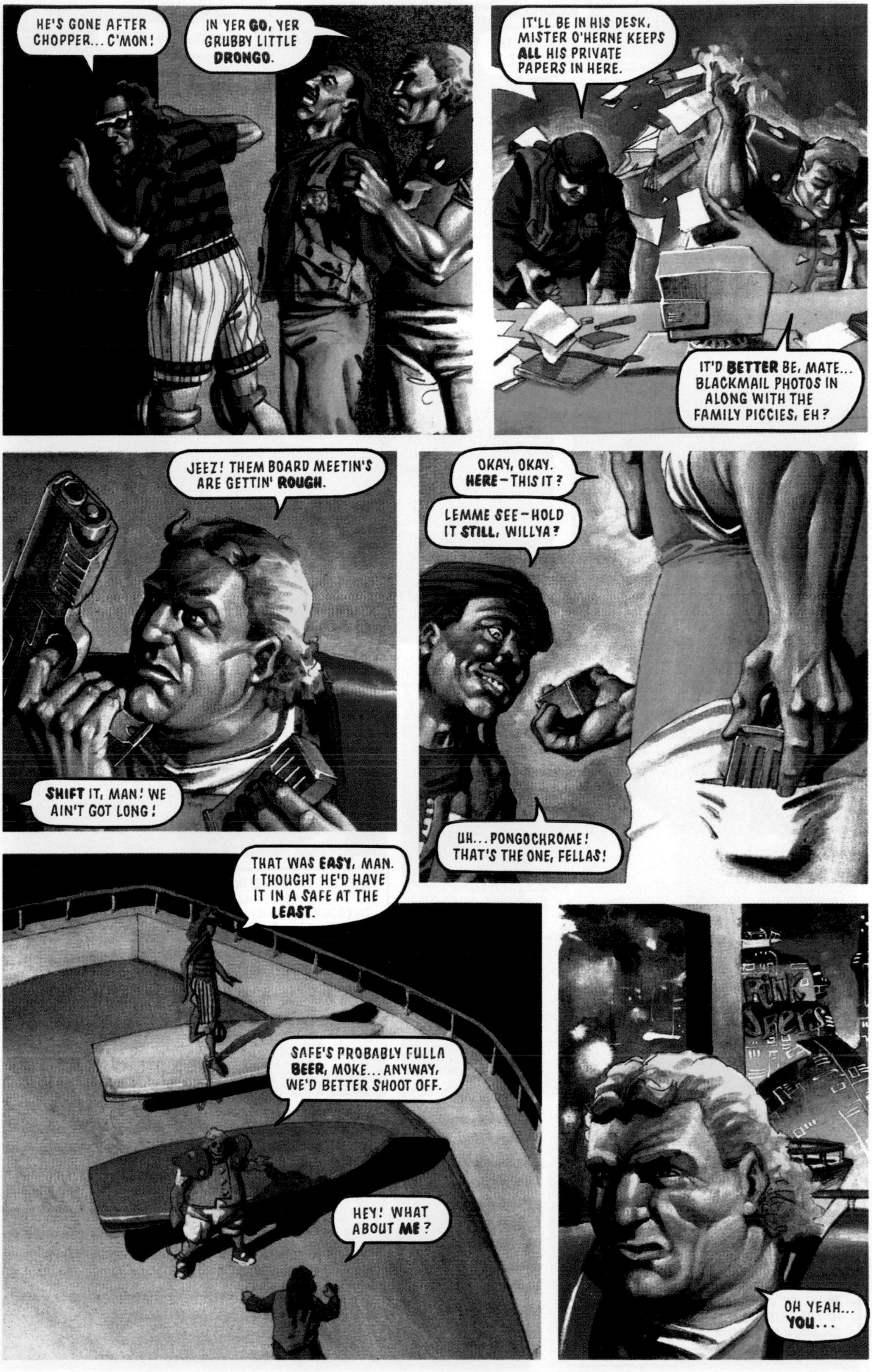

HE'S GONE AFTER CHOPPER... C'MON!
IN YER GO, YER GRUBBY LITTLE DRONGO.
IT'LL BE IN HIS DESK, MISTER O'HERNE KEEPS ALL HIS PRIVATE PAPERS IN HERE.
IT'D BETTER BE, MATE... BLACKMAIL PHOTOS IN ALONG WITH THE FAMILY PICCIES, EH?
JEEZ! THEM BOARD MEETIN'S ARE GETTIN' ROUGH.
SHIFT IT, MAN! WE AIN'T GOT LONG!
OKAY, OKAY. HERE—THIS IT?
LEMME SEE—HOLD IT STILL, WILLYA?
UH... PONGOCHROME! THAT'S THE ONE, FELLAS!
THAT WAS EASY, MAN. I THOUGHT HE'D HAVE IT IN A SAFE AT THE LEAST.
SAFE'S PROBABLY FULLA BEER, MOKE... ANYWAY, WE'D BETTER SHOOT OFF.
HEY! WHAT ABOUT ME?
OH YEAH... YOU...

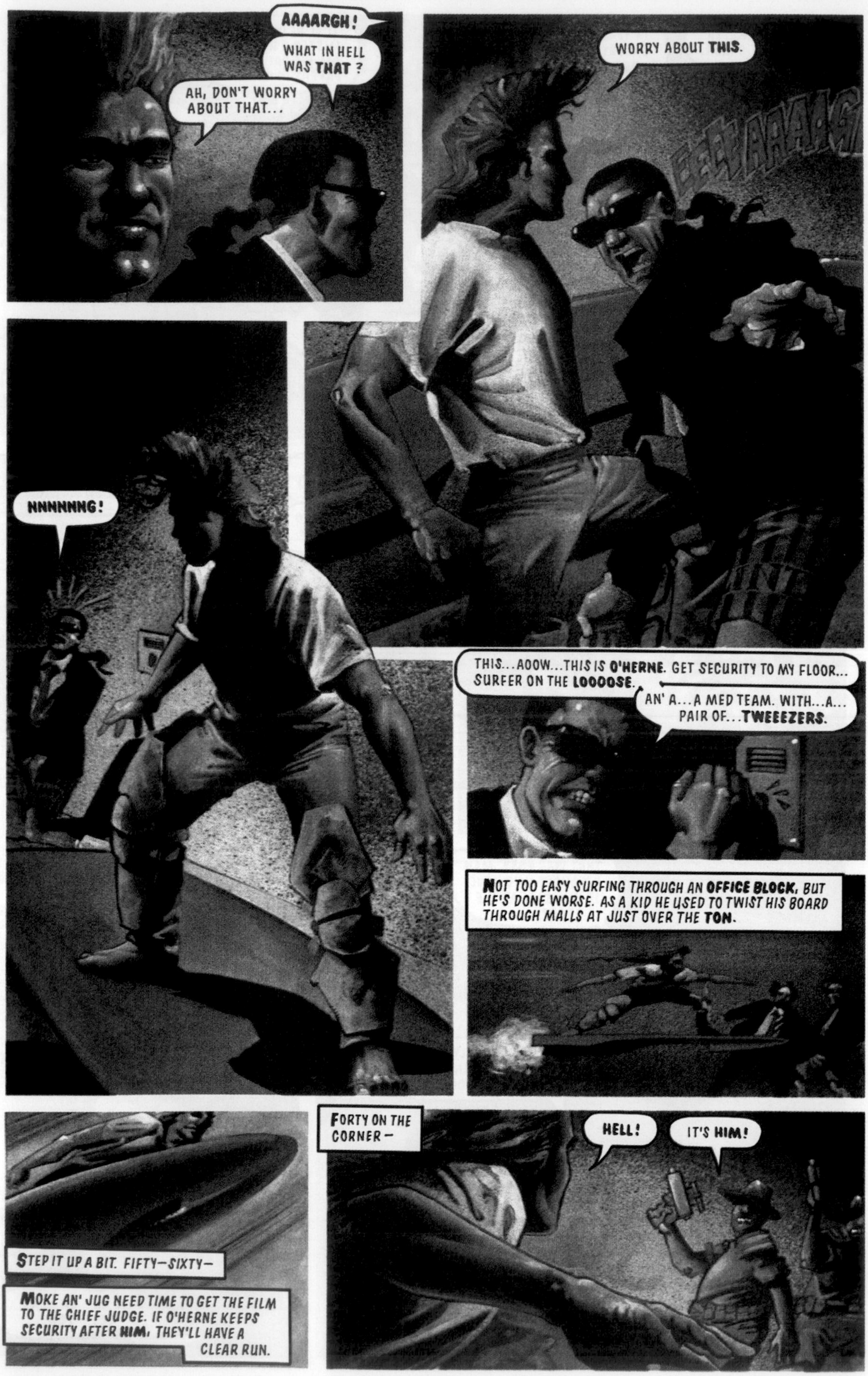
AAAARGH!
WHAT IN HELL WAS THAT?
AH, DON'T WORRY ABOUT THAT...
WORRY ABOUT THIS.
NNNNNNG!
THIS... AOOW... THIS IS O'HERNE. GET SECURITY TO MY FLOOR... SURFER ON THE LOOOOSE.
AN' A... A MED TEAM. WITH... A... PAIR OF... TWEEEZERS.
NOT TOO EASY SURFING THROUGH AN OFFICE BLOCK, BUT HE'S DONE WORSE. AS A KID HE USED TO TWIST HIS BOARD THROUGH MALLS AT JUST OVER THE TON.
STEP IT UP A BIT. FIFTY—SIXTY—
MOKE AN' JUG NEED TIME TO GET THE FILM TO THE CHIEF JUDGE. IF O'HERNE KEEPS SECURITY AFTER HIM, THEY'LL HAVE A CLEAR RUN.
FORTY ON THE CORNER—
HELL!
IT'S HIM!

THIS IS DALEY ON THE SOUTH SIDE! WE GOT HIM!

THE LIFTS? CRAZY. TRY IT ANYWAY — SLOW HER TO TWENTY—

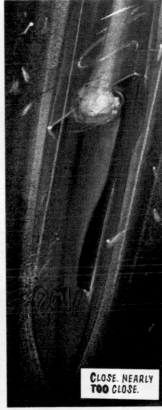

CLOSE. NEARLY TOO CLOSE.

LUCKY BOY — NOW, GET SOME SPEED OR YOU'LL LOSE IT—

NINETY—THE TON—ONE TEN—

ONE TWENTY—ONE THIRTY—

DAMMIT!

UPCOMING LIFT. THAT'S ALL YOU NEED.

THOSE TWO BOZOS UP ABOVE ARE STILL KEEN, SO NO GOING BACK.

AIM FOR THE WALL AND PRAY—

ONE FORTY — ONE FIFTY — ONE SIXTY—

YEEEEAAAHH!

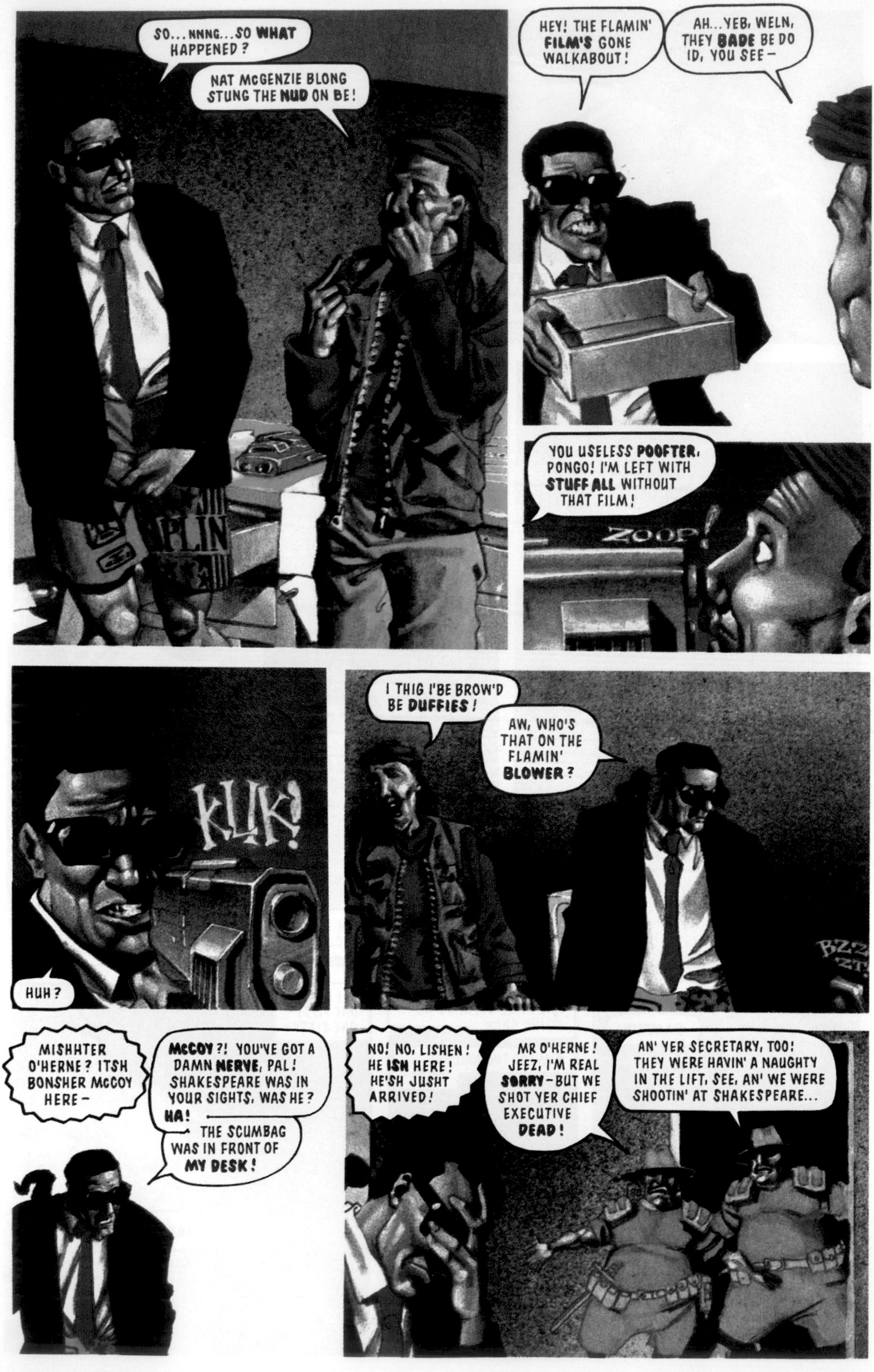
SO...NNNG...SO **WHAT** HAPPENED?
NAT McGENZIE BLONG STUNG THE **NUD** ON BE!
HEY! THE FLAMIN' **FILM'S** GONE WALKABOUT!
AH...YEB, WELN, THEY **BADE** BE DO ID, YOU SEE—
YOU USELESS **POOFTER**, PONGO! I'M LEFT WITH **STUFF ALL** WITHOUT THAT FILM!
ZOOP!
KLIK!
HUH?
I THIG I'BE BROW'D BE **DUFFIES**!
AW, WHO'S THAT ON THE FLAMIN' **BLOWER**?
MISHHTER O'HERNE? ITSH BONSHER McCOY HERE—
McCOY?! YOU'VE GOT A DAMN **NERVE**, PAL! SHAKESPEARE WAS IN YOUR SIGHTS, WAS HE? **HA!**
THE SCUMBAG WAS IN FRONT OF **MY DESK**!
NO! NO, LISHEN! HE **ISH** HERE! HE'SH JUSHT ARRIVED!
MR O'HERNE! JEEZ, I'M REAL **SORRY**—BUT WE SHOT YER CHIEF EXECUTIVE **DEAD**!
AN' YER SECRETARY, TOO! THEY WERE HAVIN' A NAUGHTY IN THE LIFT, SEE, AN' WE WERE SHOOTIN' AT SHAKESPEARE...

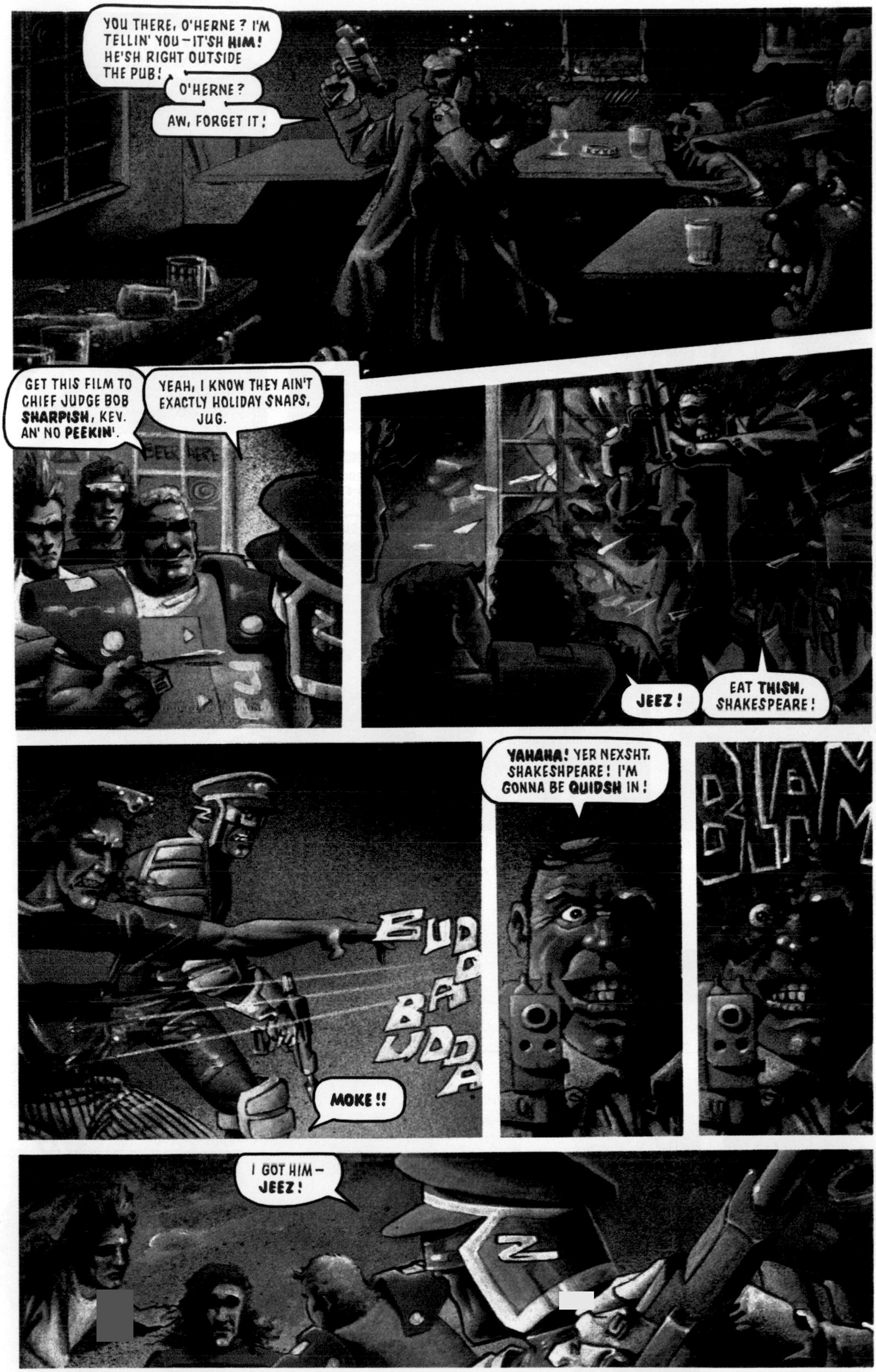
YOU THERE, O'HERNE? I'M TELLIN' YOU—IT'SH **HIM**! HE'SH RIGHT OUTSIDE THE PUB!
O'HERNE?
AW, FORGET IT!
GET THIS FILM TO CHIEF JUDGE BOB **SHARPISH**, KEV. AN' NO **PEEKIN'**.
YEAH, I KNOW THEY AIN'T EXACTLY HOLIDAY SNAPS, JUG.
JEEZ!
EAT **THISH**, SHAKESPEARE!
MOKE!!
YAHAHA! YER NEXSHT, SHAKESHPEARE! I'M GONNA BE **QUIDSH** IN!
BLAM
BLAM
I GOT HIM—
JEEZ!

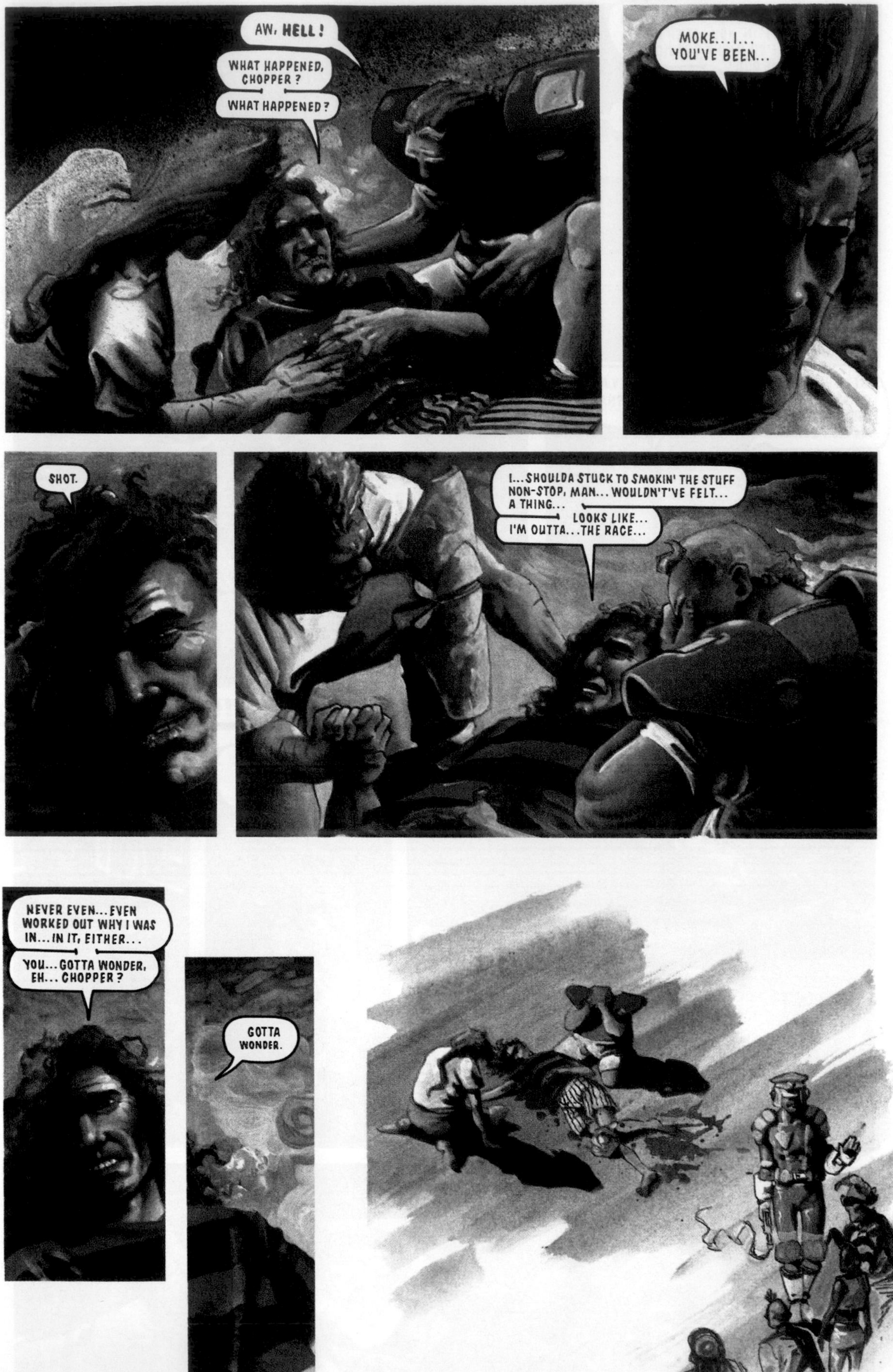
AW, HELL!
WHAT HAPPENED, CHOPPER?
WHAT HAPPENED?
MOKE... I... YOU'VE BEEN...
SHOT.
I...SHOULDA STUCK TO SMOKIN' THE STUFF NON-STOP, MAN... WOULDN'T'VE FELT... A THING...
LOOKS LIKE... I'M OUTTA... THE RACE...
NEVER EVEN... EVEN WORKED OUT WHY I WAS IN... IN IT, EITHER...
YOU... GOTTA WONDER, EH... CHOPPER?
GOTTA WONDER.

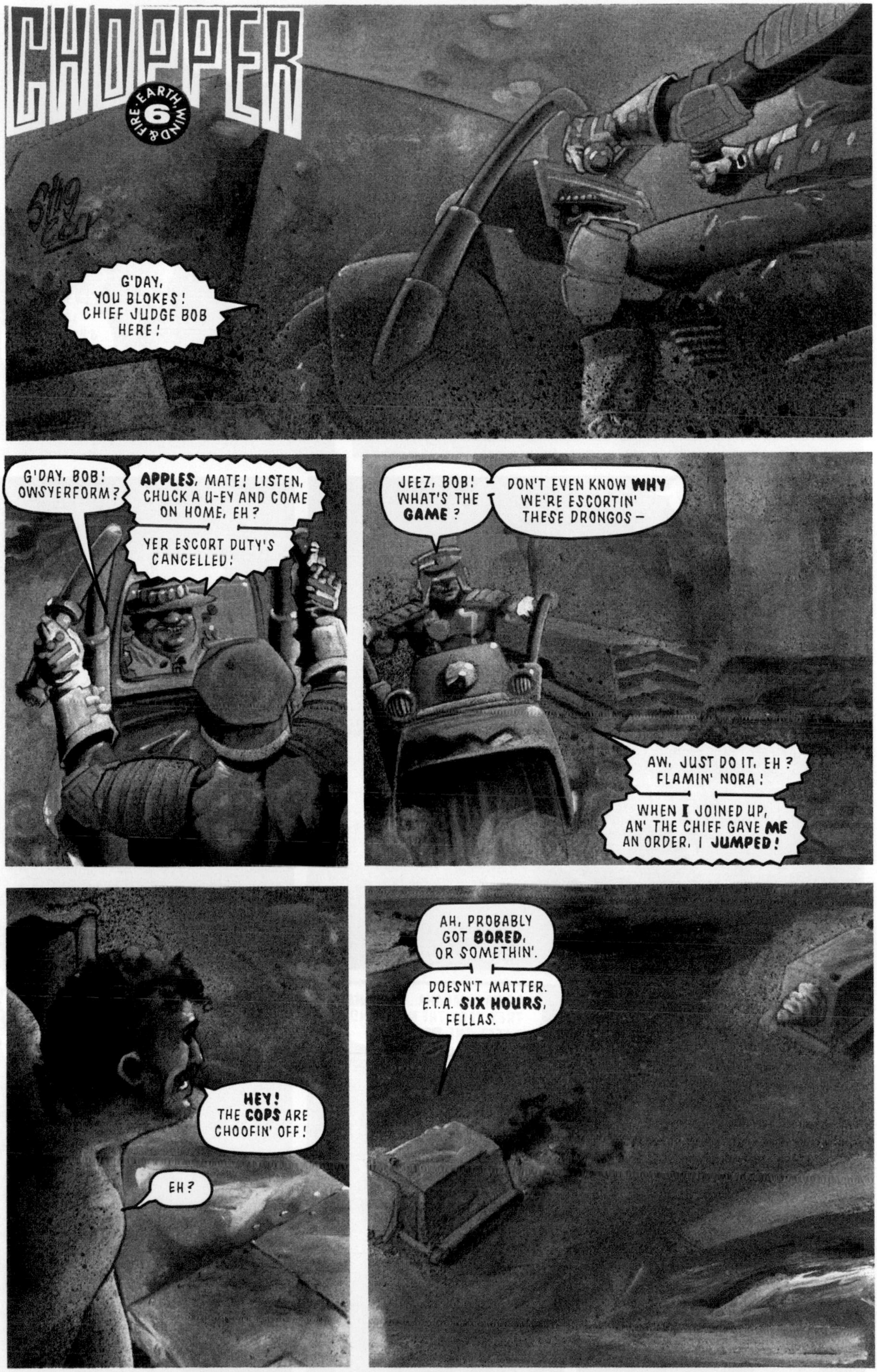
CHOPPER
EARTH, WIND & FIRE 6
G'DAY, YOU BLOKES! CHIEF JUDGE BOB HERE!
G'DAY, BOB! OWSYERFORM?
APPLES, MATE! LISTEN, CHUCK A U-EY AND COME ON HOME, EH?
YER ESCORT DUTY'S CANCELLED!
JEEZ, BOB! WHAT'S THE **GAME**?
DON'T EVEN KNOW **WHY** WE'RE ESCORTIN' THESE DRONGOS –
AW, JUST DO IT, EH? FLAMIN' NORA!
WHEN **I** JOINED UP, AN' THE CHIEF GAVE **ME** AN ORDER, I **JUMPED**!
HEY! THE **COPS** ARE CHOOFIN' OFF!
EH?
AH, PROBABLY GOT **BORED**, OR SOMETHIN'.
DOESN'T MATTER. E.T.A. **SIX HOURS**, FELLAS.

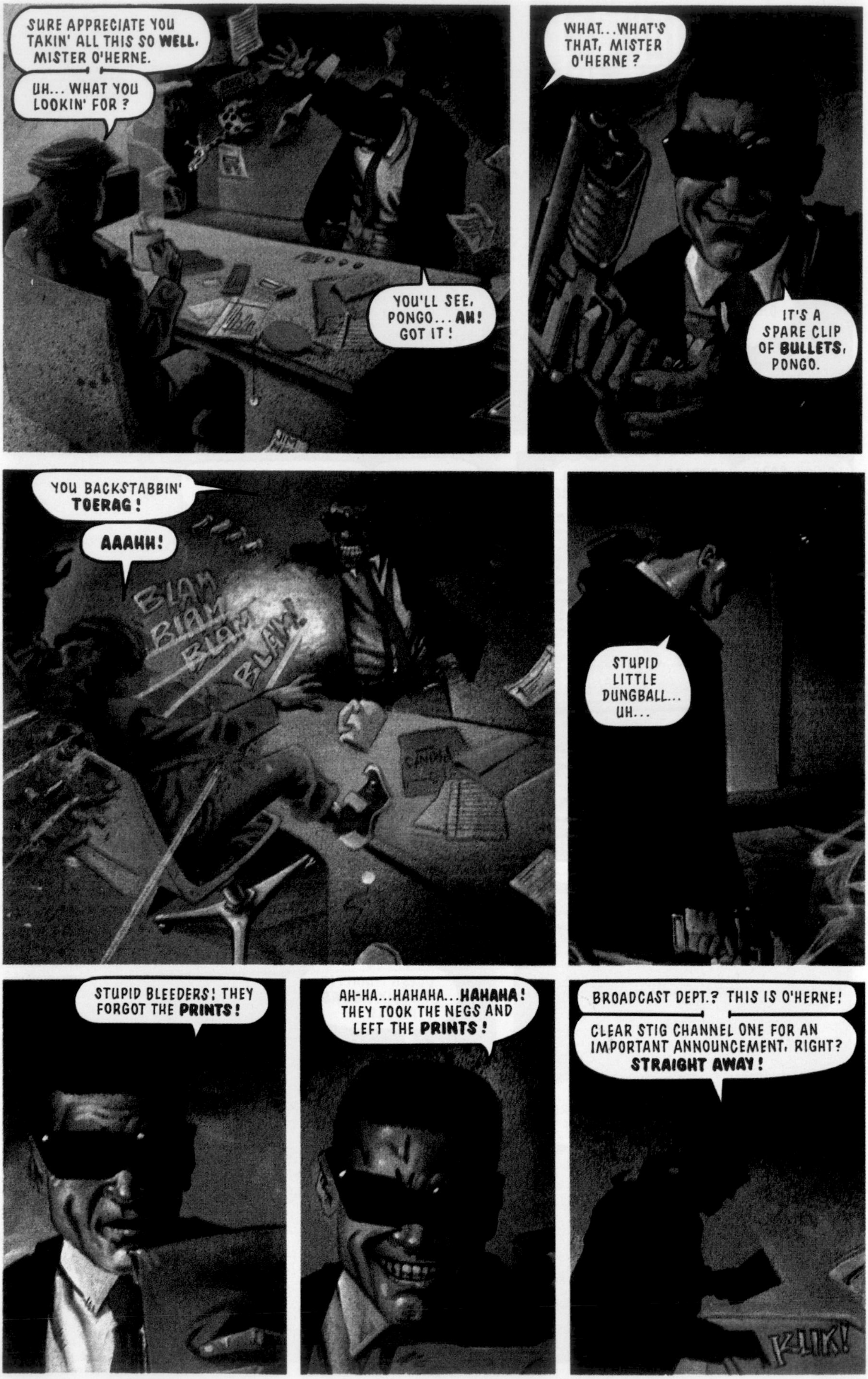
SURE APPRECIATE YOU TAKIN' ALL THIS SO WELL, MISTER O'HERNE.
UH... WHAT YOU LOOKIN' FOR?
YOU'LL SEE, PONGO... AH! GOT IT!
WHAT...WHAT'S THAT, MISTER O'HERNE?
IT'S A SPARE CLIP OF BULLETS, PONGO.
YOU BACKSTABBIN' TOERAG!
AAAHH!
BLAM BLAM BLAM BLAM!
STUPID LITTLE DUNGBALL... UH...
STUPID BLEEDERS! THEY FORGOT THE PRINTS!
AH-HA...HAHAHA...HAHAHA! THEY TOOK THE NEGS AND LEFT THE PRINTS!
BROADCAST DEPT.? THIS IS O'HERNE!
CLEAR STIG CHANNEL ONE FOR AN IMPORTANT ANNOUNCEMENT, RIGHT? STRAIGHT AWAY!
KLIK!

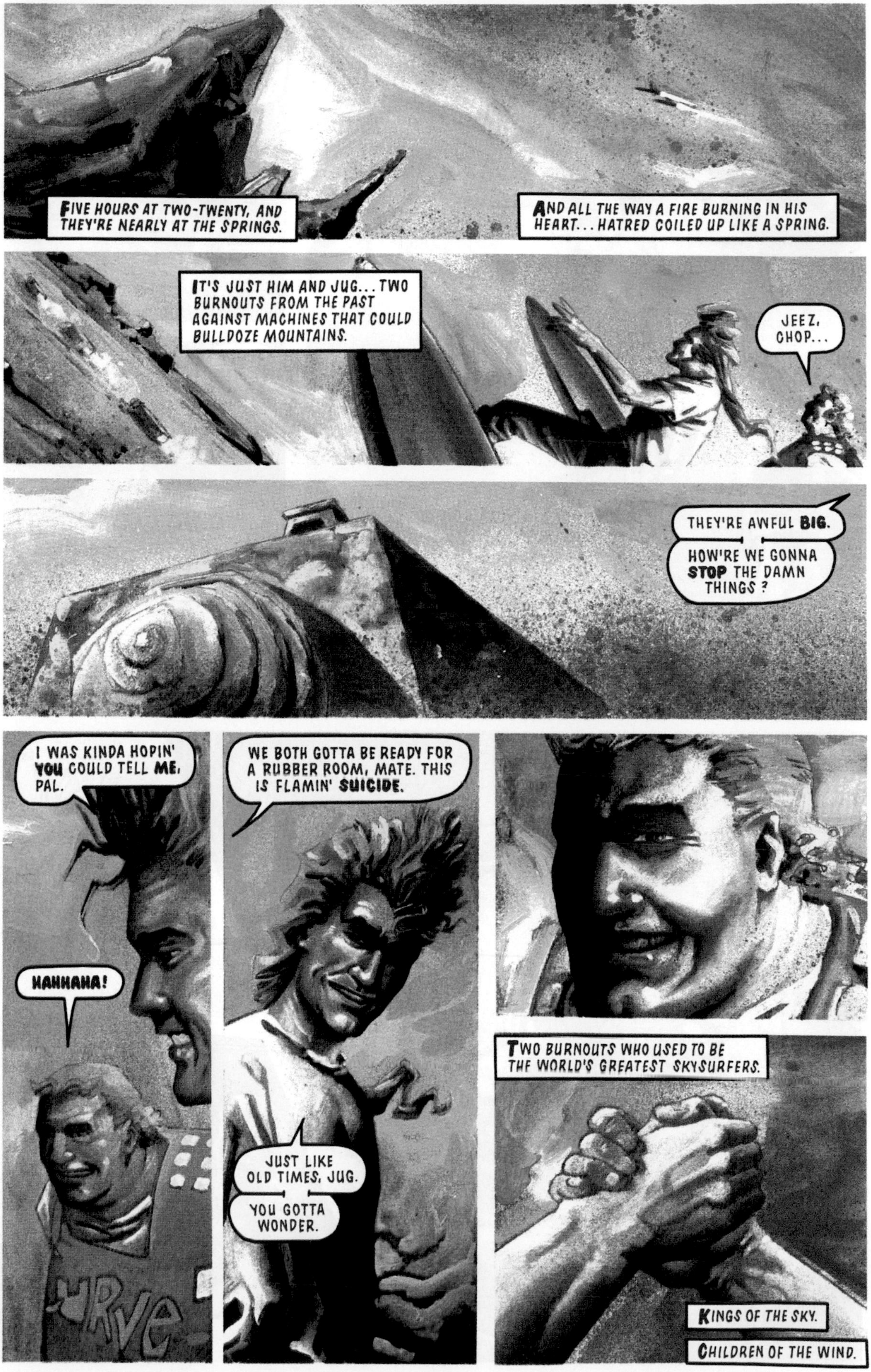
FIVE HOURS AT TWO-TWENTY, AND THEY'RE NEARLY AT THE SPRINGS.
AND ALL THE WAY A FIRE BURNING IN HIS HEART... HATRED COILED UP LIKE A SPRING.
IT'S JUST HIM AND JUG... TWO BURNOUTS FROM THE PAST AGAINST MACHINES THAT COULD BULLDOZE MOUNTAINS.
JEEZ, CHOP...
THEY'RE AWFUL BIG.
HOW'RE WE GONNA STOP THE DAMN THINGS?
I WAS KINDA HOPIN' YOU COULD TELL ME, PAL.
HAHHAHA!
WE BOTH GOTTA BE READY FOR A RUBBER ROOM, MATE. THIS IS FLAMIN' SUICIDE.
JUST LIKE OLD TIMES, JUG.
YOU GOTTA WONDER.
TWO BURNOUTS WHO USED TO BE THE WORLD'S GREATEST SKYSURFERS.
KINGS OF THE SKY.
CHILDREN OF THE WIND.

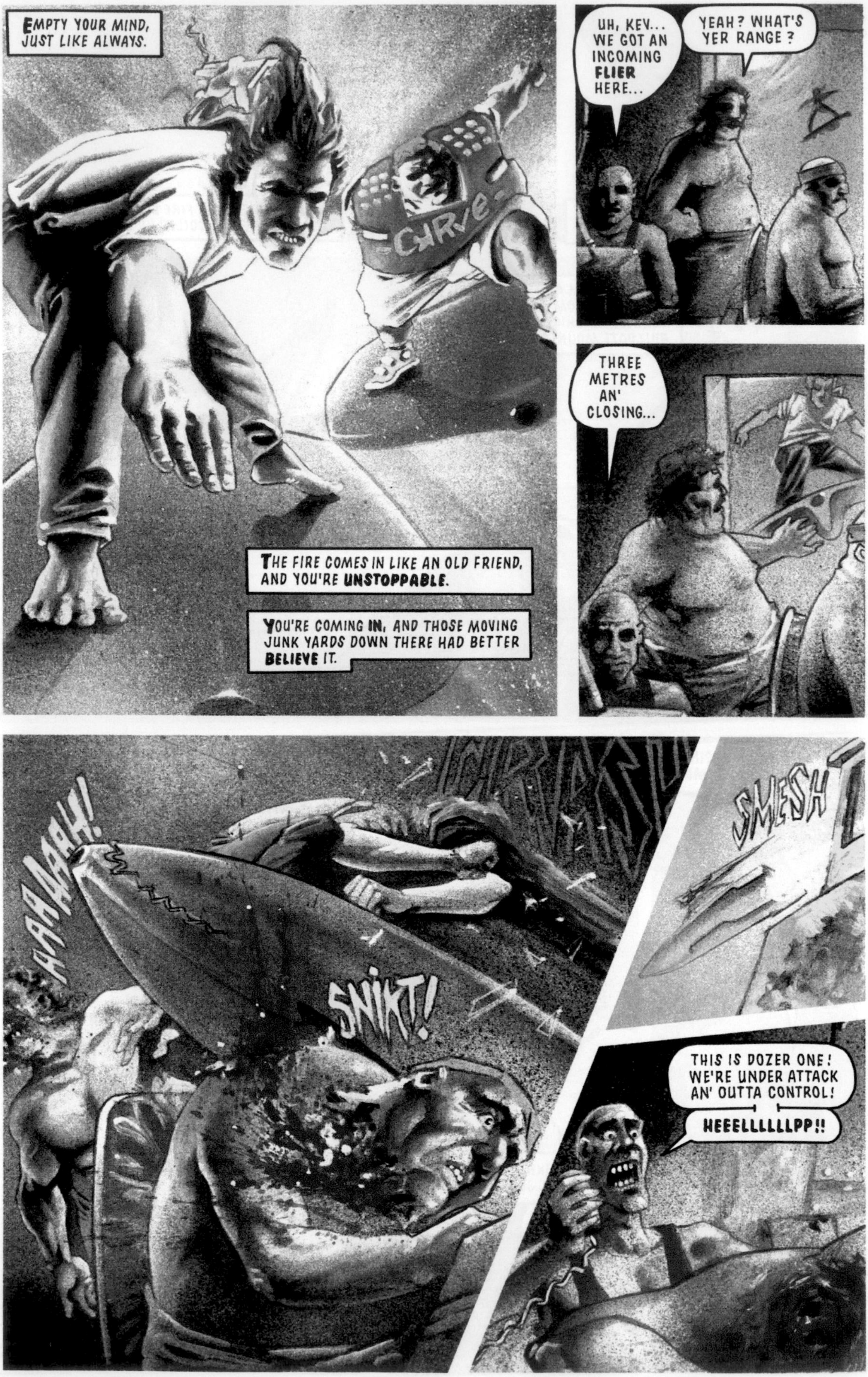
EMPTY YOUR MIND, JUST LIKE ALWAYS.
CARVE
THE FIRE COMES IN LIKE AN OLD FRIEND, AND YOU'RE **UNSTOPPABLE**.
YOU'RE COMING **IN**, AND THOSE MOVING JUNK YARDS DOWN THERE HAD BETTER **BELIEVE** IT.
UH, KEV... WE GOT AN INCOMING **FLIER** HERE...
YEAH? WHAT'S YER RANGE?
THREE METRES AN' CLOSING...
SNIKT!
SMESH
THIS IS DOZER ONE! WE'RE UNDER ATTACK AN' OUTTA CONTROL!
HEEELLLLLLLPP!!

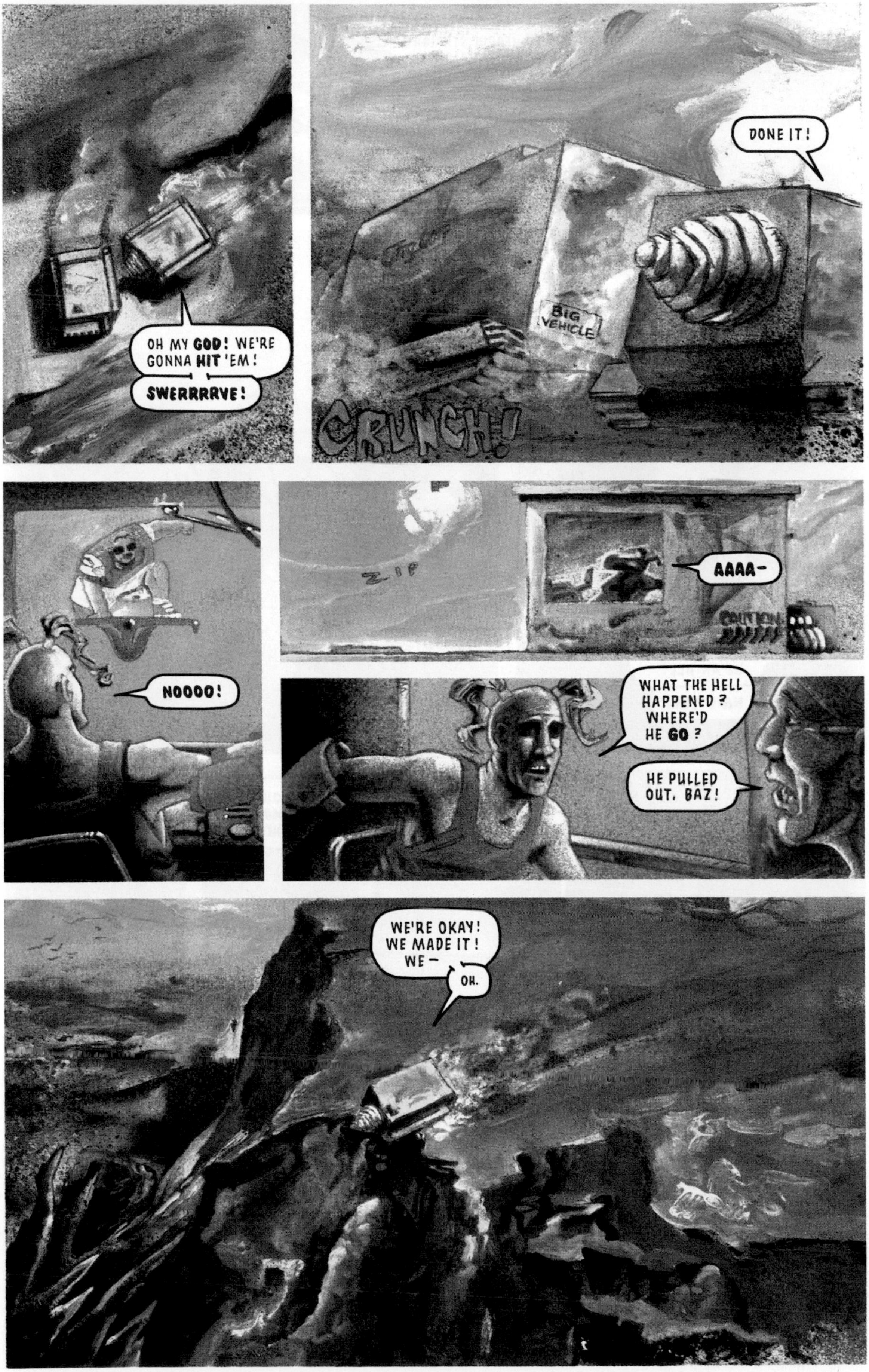
OH MY GOD! WE'RE GONNA HIT 'EM!
SWERRRRVE!
DONE IT!
BIG VEHICLE
CRUNCH!
NOOOO!
AAAA-
WHAT THE HELL HAPPENED? WHERE'D HE GO?
HE PULLED OUT, BAZ!
WE'RE OKAY! WE MADE IT! WE—
OH.

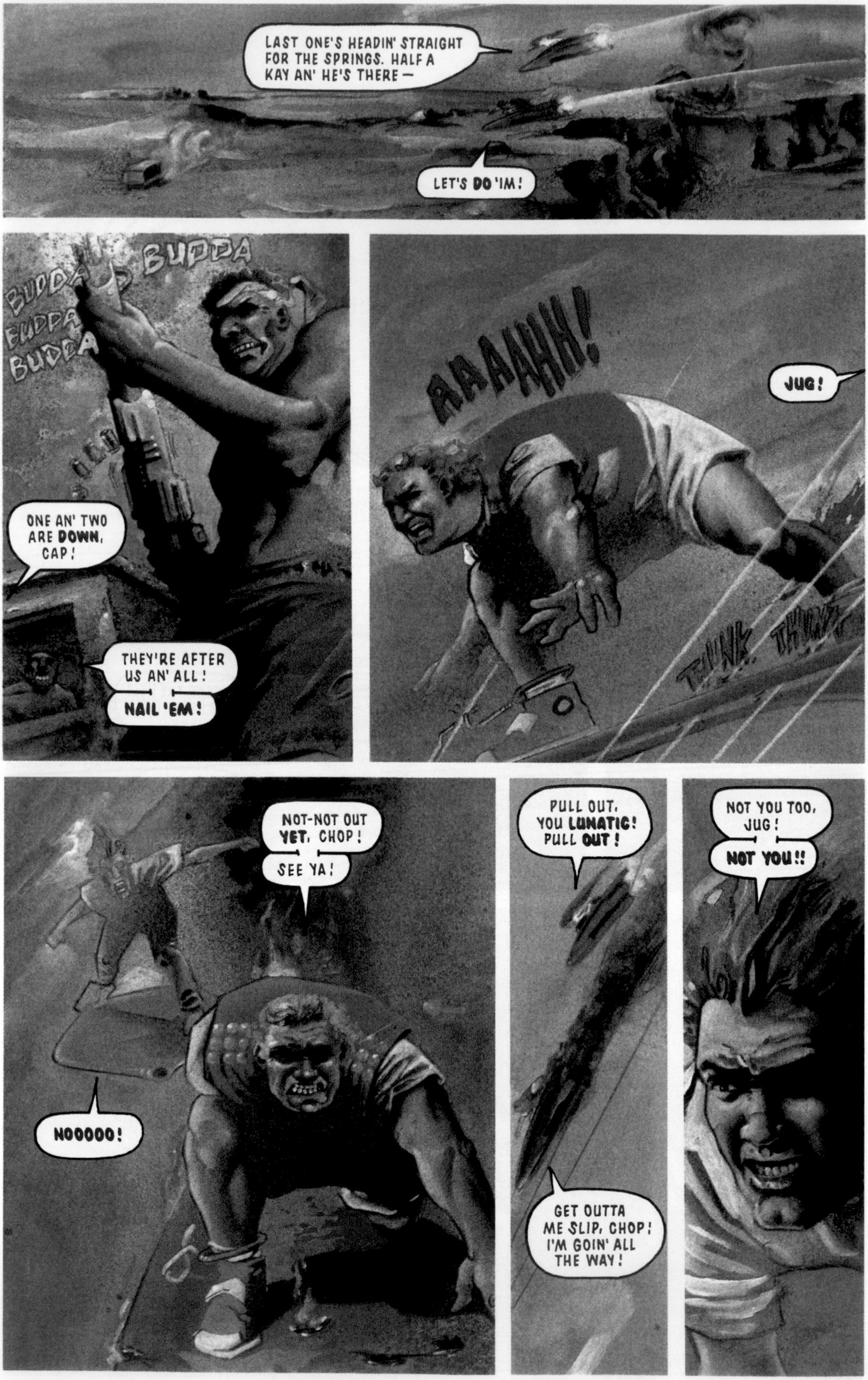
LAST ONE'S HEADIN' STRAIGHT FOR THE SPRINGS. HALF A KAY AN' HE'S THERE —
LET'S DO 'IM!
BUDDA BUDDA BUDDA BUDDA
ONE AN' TWO ARE DOWN, CAP!
THEY'RE AFTER US AN' ALL!
NAIL 'EM!
AAAAHH!
JUG!
NOT-NOT OUT YET, CHOP!
SEE YA!
NOOOOO!
PULL OUT, YOU LUNATIC! PULL OUT!
GET OUTTA ME SLIP, CHOP! I'M GOIN' ALL THE WAY!
NOT YOU TOO, JUG!
NOT YOU!!

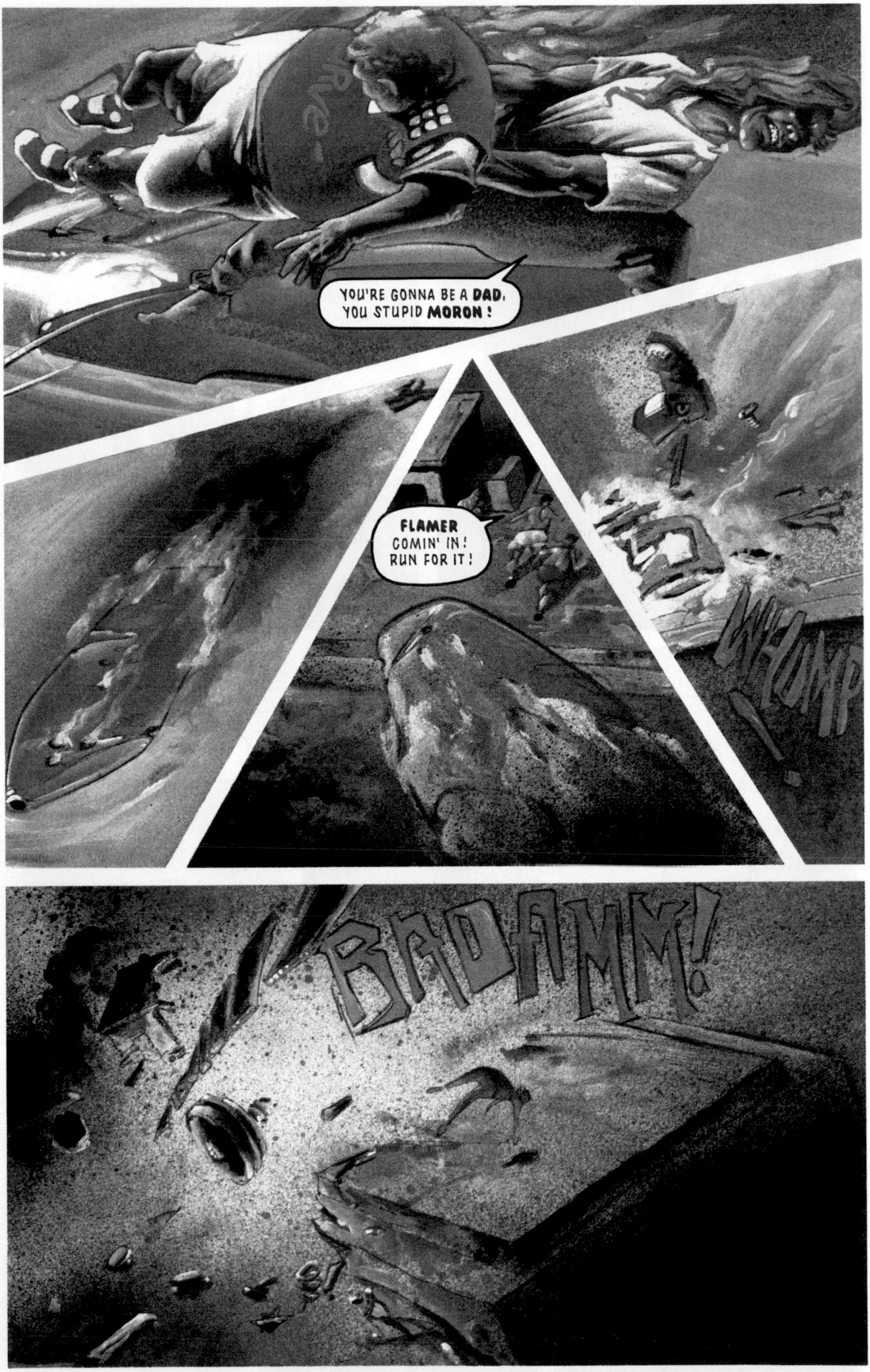
YOU'RE GONNA BE A DAD, YOU STUPID MORON!
FLAMER COMIN' IN! RUN FOR IT!
WHUMP!
BRDAMM!

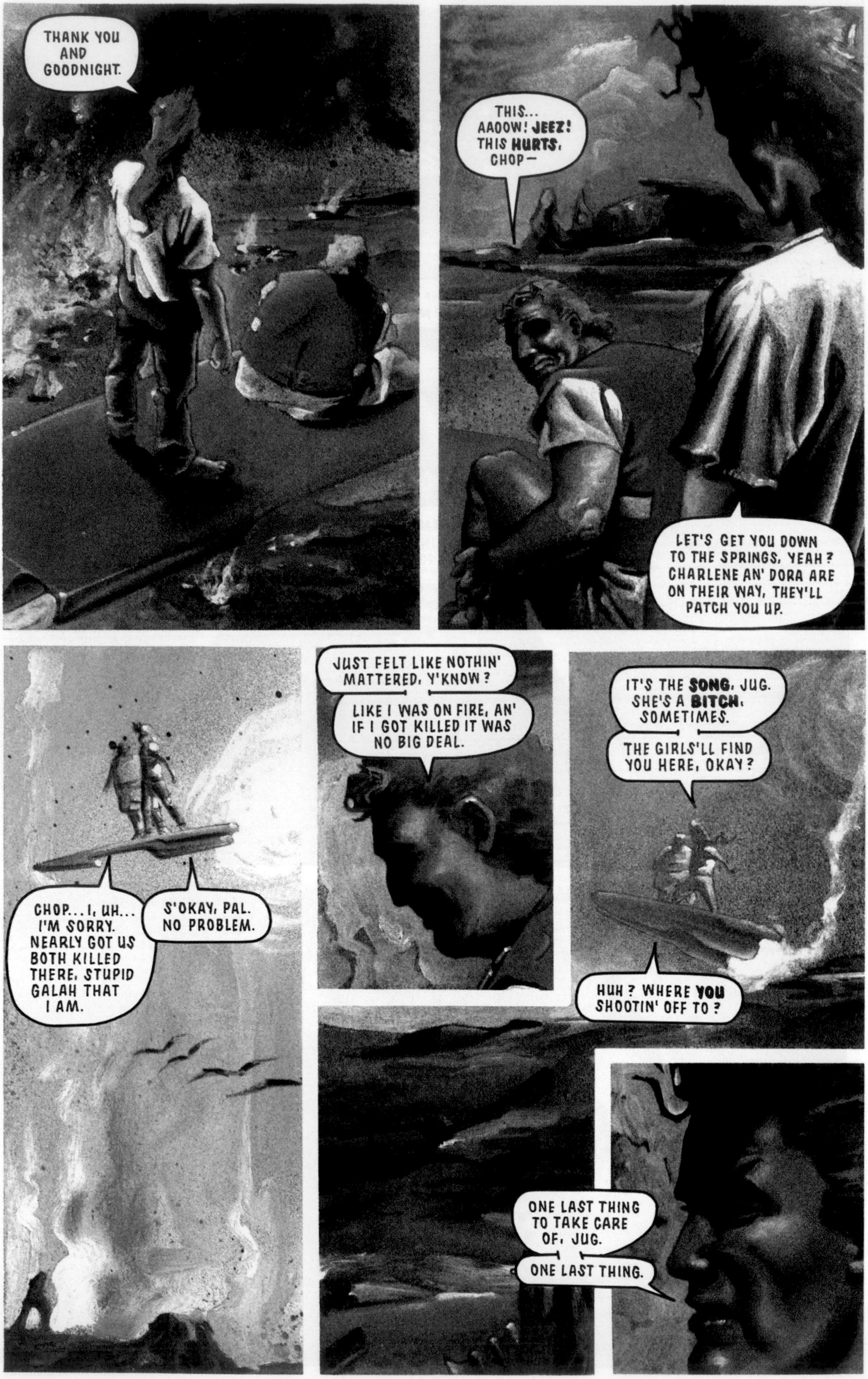
THANK YOU AND GOODNIGHT.
THIS... AAOOW! JEEZ! THIS HURTS, CHOP—
LET'S GET YOU DOWN TO THE SPRINGS, YEAH? CHARLENE AN' DORA ARE ON THEIR WAY, THEY'LL PATCH YOU UP.
CHOP... I, UH... I'M SORRY. NEARLY GOT US BOTH KILLED THERE, STUPID GALAH THAT I AM.
S'OKAY, PAL. NO PROBLEM.
JUST FELT LIKE NOTHIN' MATTERED, Y'KNOW?
LIKE I WAS ON FIRE, AN' IF I GOT KILLED IT WAS NO BIG DEAL.
IT'S THE SONG, JUG. SHE'S A BITCH, SOMETIMES.
THE GIRLS'LL FIND YOU HERE, OKAY?
HUH? WHERE YOU SHOOTIN' OFF TO?
ONE LAST THING TO TAKE CARE OF, JUG.
ONE LAST THING.

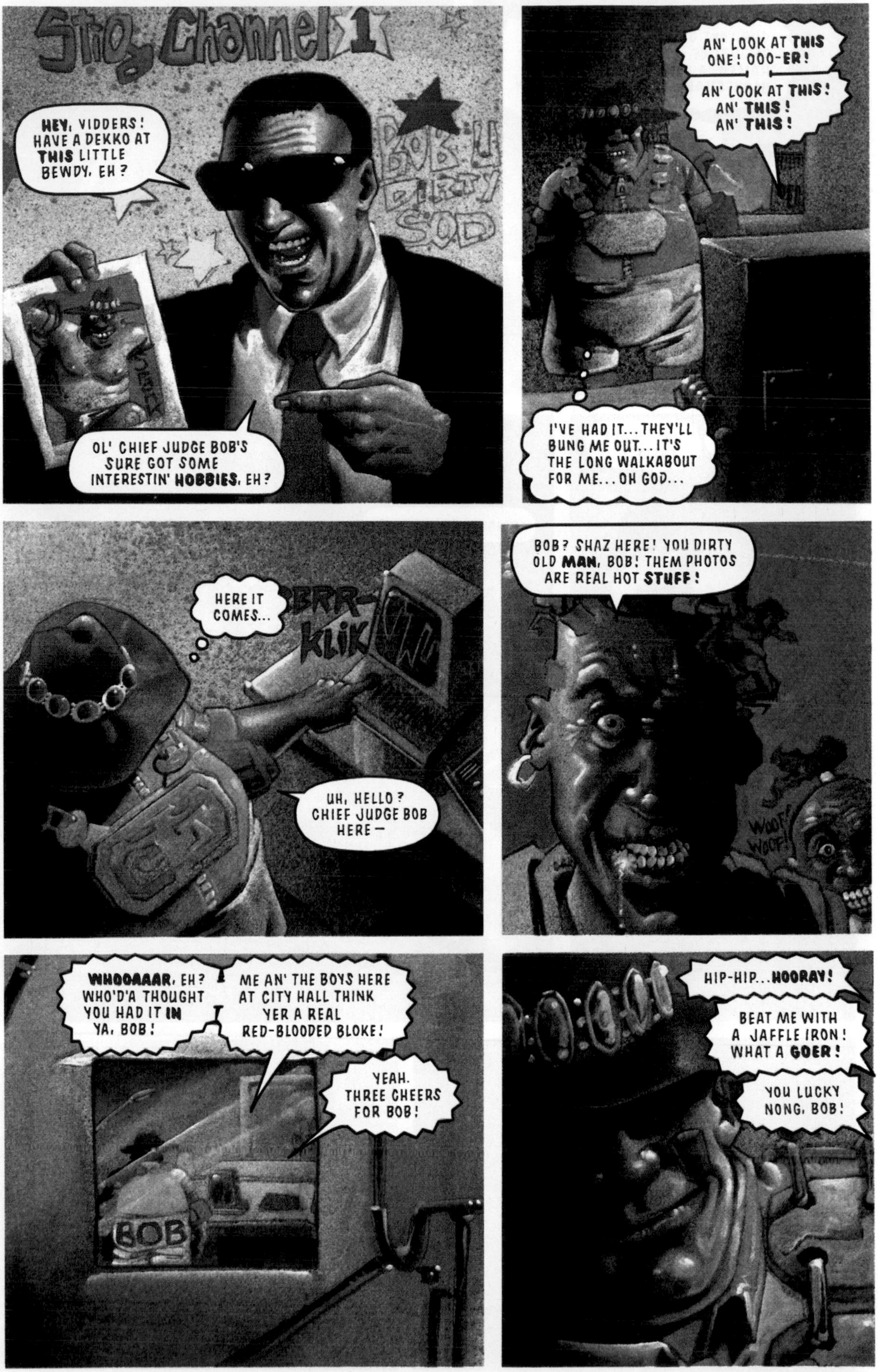
Strig Channel 1
BOB U DIRTY SOD
HEY, VIDDERS! HAVE A DEKKO AT THIS LITTLE BEWDY, EH?
OL' CHIEF JUDGE BOB'S SURE GOT SOME INTERESTIN' HOBBIES, EH?
AN' LOOK AT THIS ONE! OOO-ER!
AN' LOOK AT THIS! AN' THIS! AN' THIS!
I'VE HAD IT... THEY'LL BUNG ME OUT... IT'S THE LONG WALKABOUT FOR ME... OH GOD...
HERE IT COMES...
BRR-KLIK
UH, HELLO? CHIEF JUDGE BOB HERE—
BOB? SHAZ HERE! YOU DIRTY OLD MAN, BOB! THEM PHOTOS ARE REAL HOT STUFF!
WOOF! WOOF!
WHOOAAAR, EH? WHO'D'A THOUGHT YOU HAD IT IN YA, BOB!
ME AN' THE BOYS HERE AT CITY HALL THINK YER A REAL RED-BLOODED BLOKE!
YEAH. THREE CHEERS FOR BOB!
BOB
HIP-HIP... HOORAY!
BEAT ME WITH A JAFFLE IRON! WHAT A GOER!
YOU LUCKY NONG, BOB!

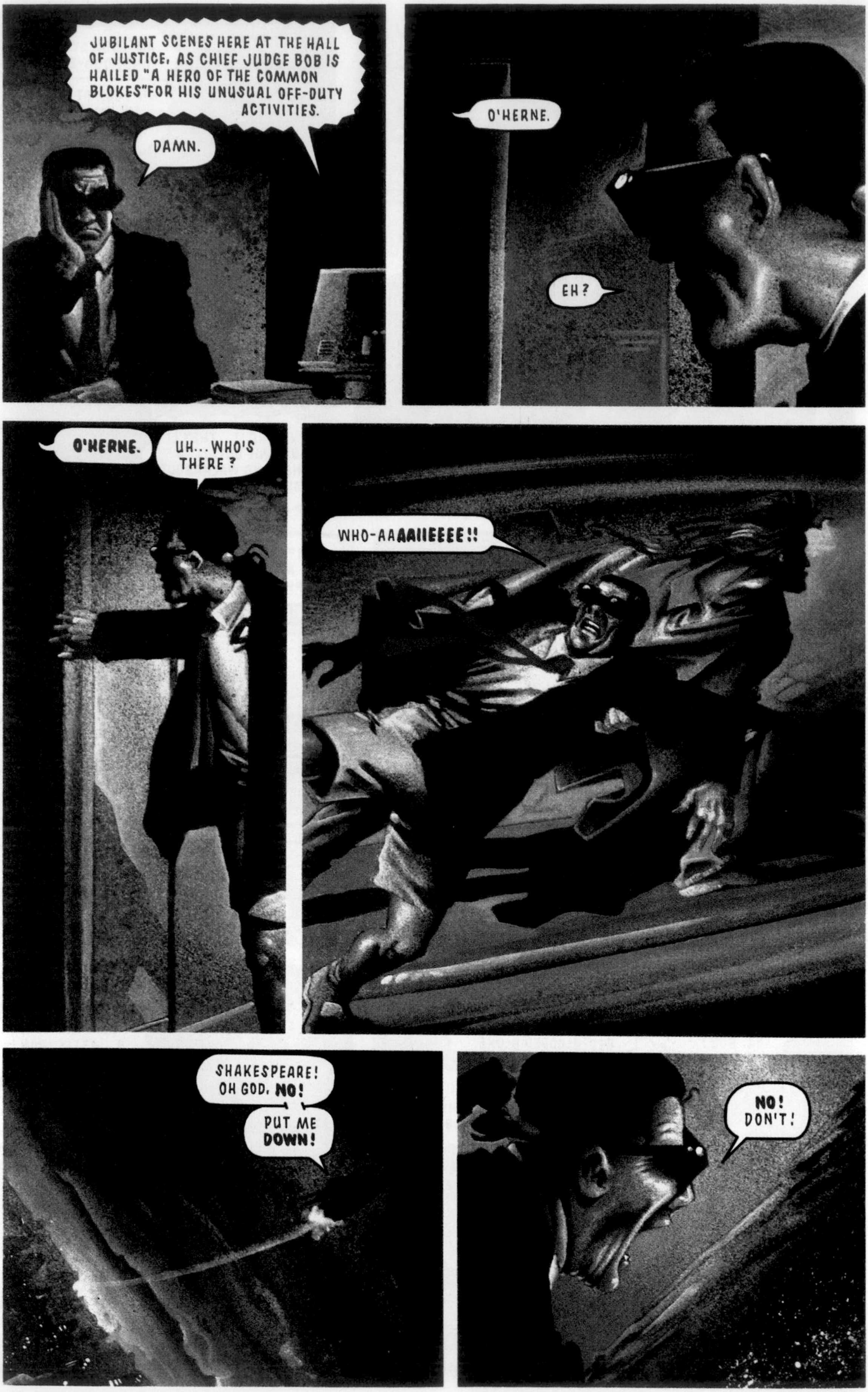
JUBILANT SCENES HERE AT THE HALL OF JUSTICE, AS CHIEF JUDGE BOB IS HAILED "A HERO OF THE COMMON BLOKES" FOR HIS UNUSUAL OFF-DUTY ACTIVITIES.
DAMN.
O'HERNE.
EH?
O'HERNE.
UH... WHO'S THERE?
WHO-AAAAIIEEEE!!
SHAKESPEARE! OH GOD, NO!
PUT ME DOWN!
NO! DON'T!

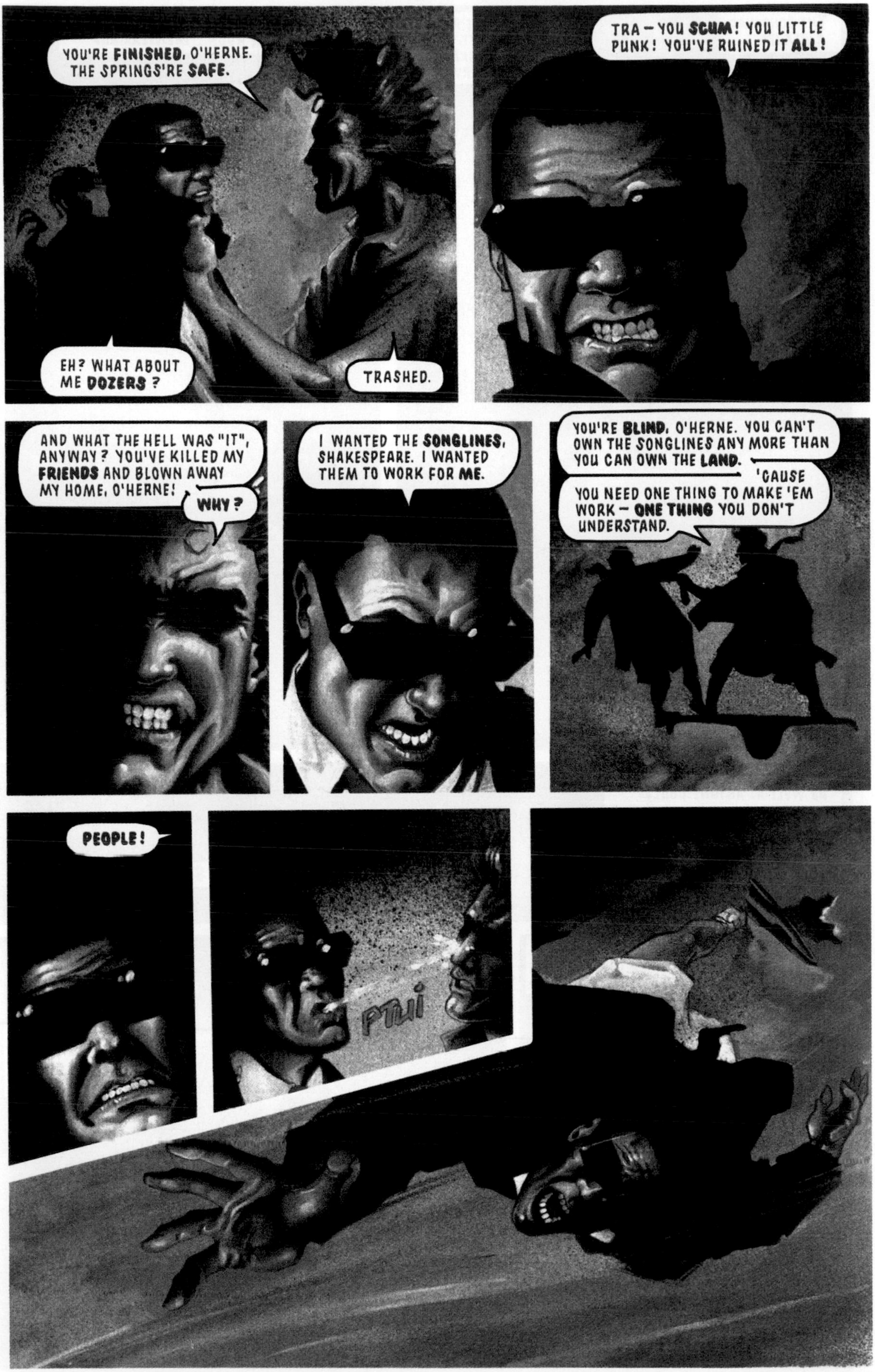
YOU'RE **FINISHED**, O'HERNE. THE SPRINGS'RE **SAFE**.
EH? WHAT ABOUT ME **DOZERS** ?
TRASHED.
TRA – YOU **SCUM**! YOU LITTLE PUNK! YOU'VE RUINED IT **ALL**!
AND WHAT THE HELL WAS "IT", ANYWAY? YOU'VE KILLED MY **FRIENDS** AND BLOWN AWAY MY HOME, O'HERNE!
WHY?
I WANTED THE **SONGLINES**, SHAKESPEARE. I WANTED THEM TO WORK FOR **ME**.
YOU'RE **BLIND**, O'HERNE. YOU CAN'T OWN THE SONGLINES ANY MORE THAN YOU CAN OWN THE **LAND**.
'CAUSE YOU NEED ONE THING TO MAKE 'EM WORK – **ONE THING** YOU DON'T UNDERSTAND.
PEOPLE!
PTUi

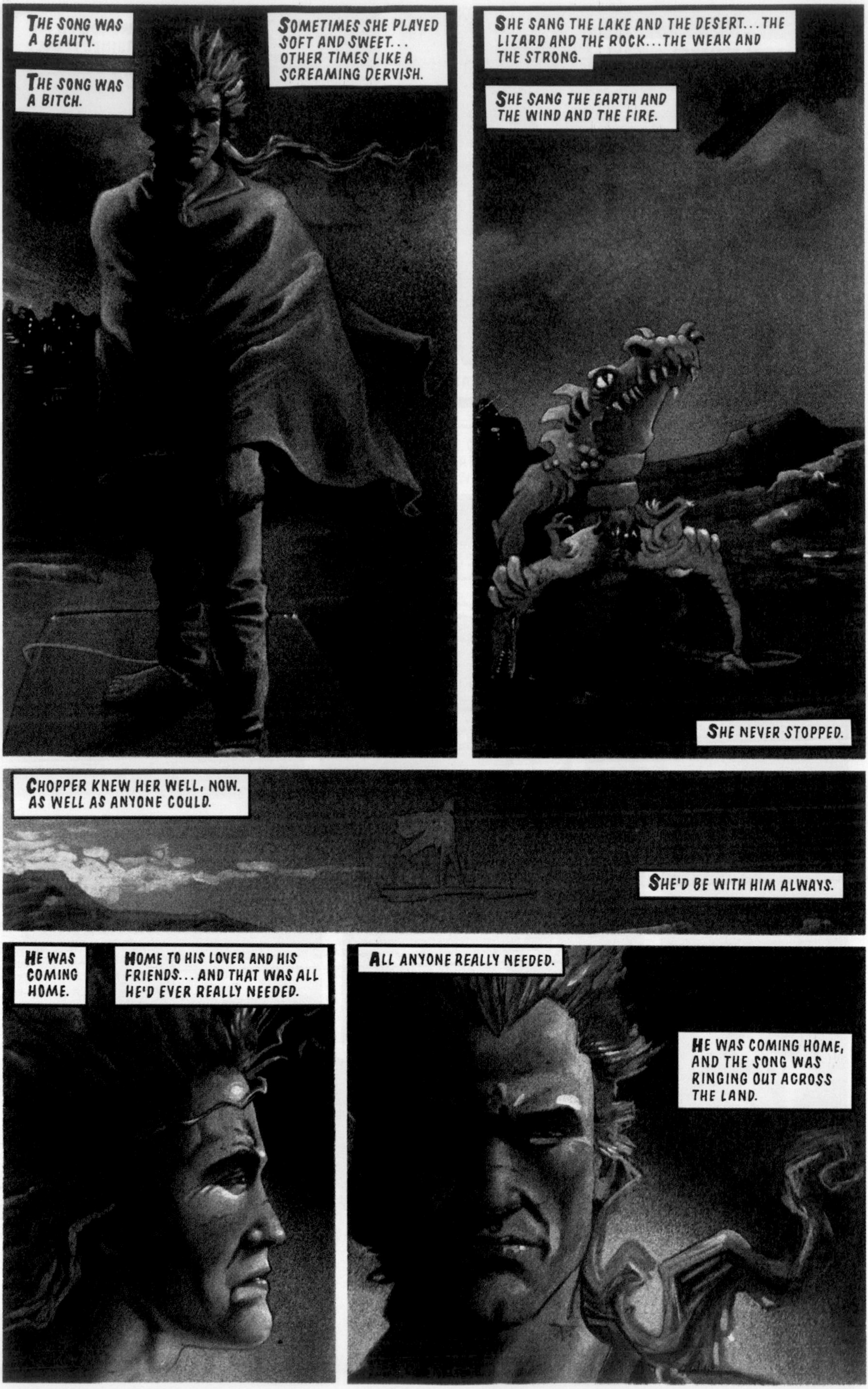
THE SONG WAS A BEAUTY.
THE SONG WAS A BITCH.
SOMETIMES SHE PLAYED SOFT AND SWEET... OTHER TIMES LIKE A SCREAMING DERVISH.
SHE SANG THE LAKE AND THE DESERT...THE LIZARD AND THE ROCK...THE WEAK AND THE STRONG.
SHE SANG THE EARTH AND THE WIND AND THE FIRE.
SHE NEVER STOPPED.
CHOPPER KNEW HER WELL, NOW. AS WELL AS ANYONE COULD.
SHE'D BE WITH HIM ALWAYS.
HE WAS COMING HOME.
HOME TO HIS LOVER AND HIS FRIENDS... AND THAT WAS ALL HE'D EVER REALLY NEEDED.
ALL ANYONE REALLY NEEDED.
HE WAS COMING HOME, AND THE SONG WAS RINGING OUT ACROSS THE LAND.

THE END

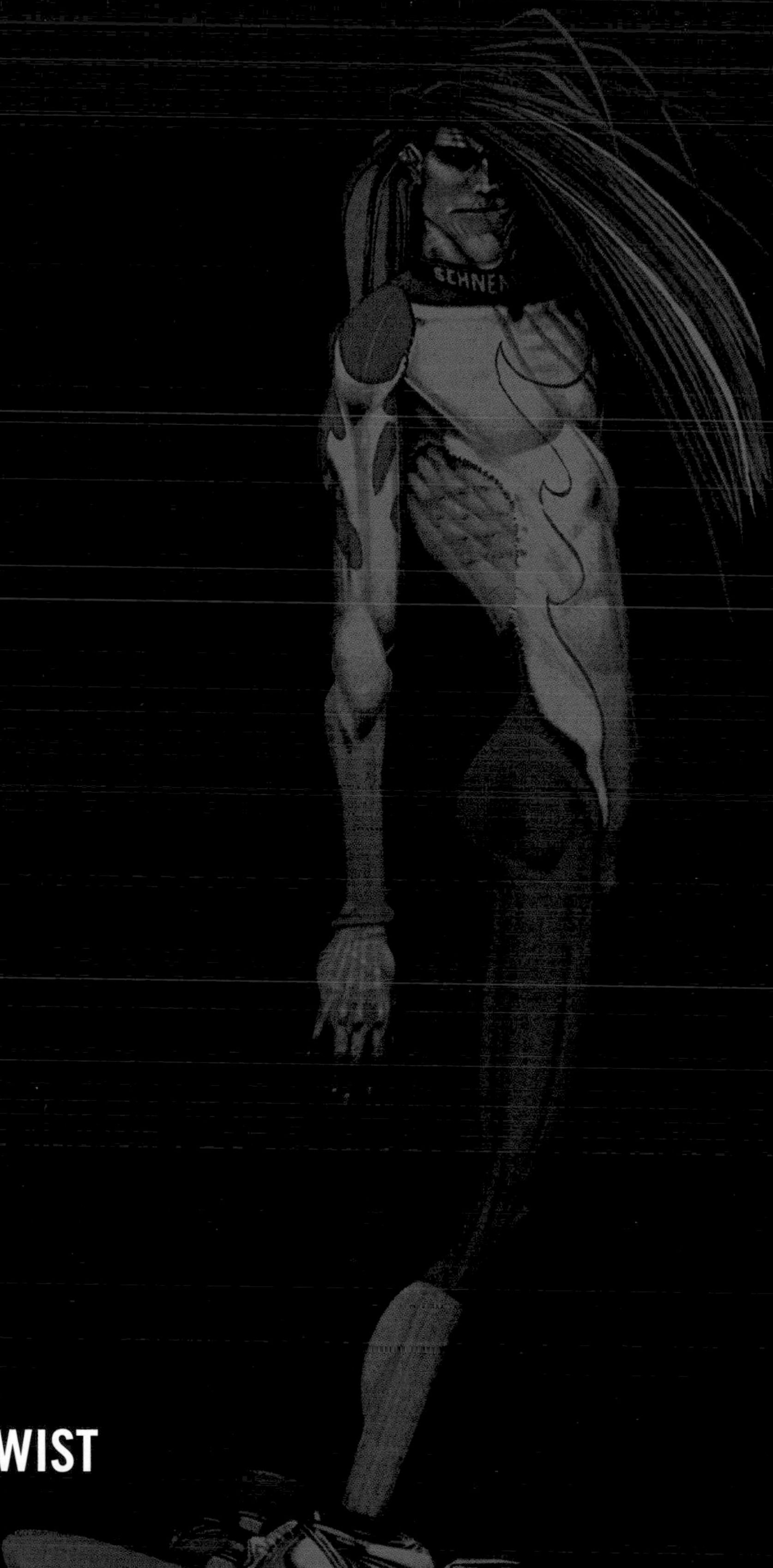

DEAD MAN'S TWIST

Script: Garth Ennis
Art: Martin Emond
Letters: Roger Langridge

Originally printed in *Judge Dredd* Megazine 2.36

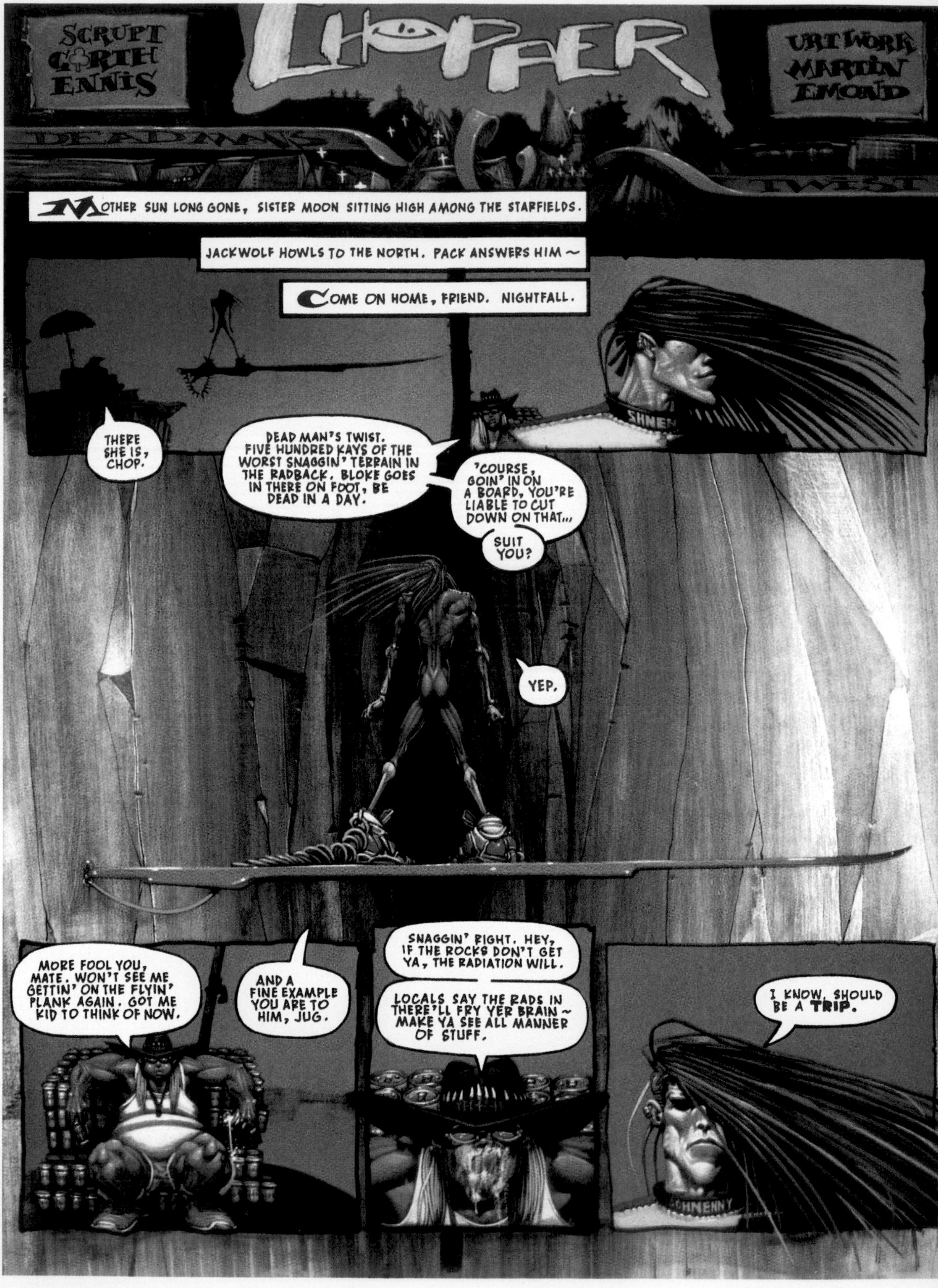

CHOPPER
SCRUPT GORTH ENNIS
URTWORK MARTIN EMOND
DEAD MAN'S TWIST
MOTHER SUN LONG GONE, SISTER MOON SITTING HIGH AMONG THE STARFIELDS.
JACKWOLF HOWLS TO THE NORTH. PACK ANSWERS HIM ~
COME ON HOME, FRIEND. NIGHTFALL.
THERE SHE IS, CHOP.
DEAD MAN'S TWIST. FIVE HUNDRED KAYS OF THE WORST SNAGGIN' TERRAIN IN THE RADBACK. BLOKE GOES IN THERE ON FOOT, BE DEAD IN A DAY.
'COURSE, GOIN' IN ON A BOARD, YOU'RE LIABLE TO CUT DOWN ON THAT...
SUIT YOU?
YEP.
MORE FOOL YOU, MATE. WON'T SEE ME GETTIN' ON THE FLYIN' PLANK AGAIN. GOT ME KID TO THINK OF NOW.
AND A FINE EXAMPLE YOU ARE TO HIM, JUG.
SNAGGIN' RIGHT. HEY, IF THE ROCKS DON'T GET YA, THE RADIATION WILL.
LOCALS SAY THE RADS IN THERE'LL FRY YER BRAIN ~ MAKE YA SEE ALL MANNER OF STUFF.
I KNOW. SHOULD BE A **TRIP**.

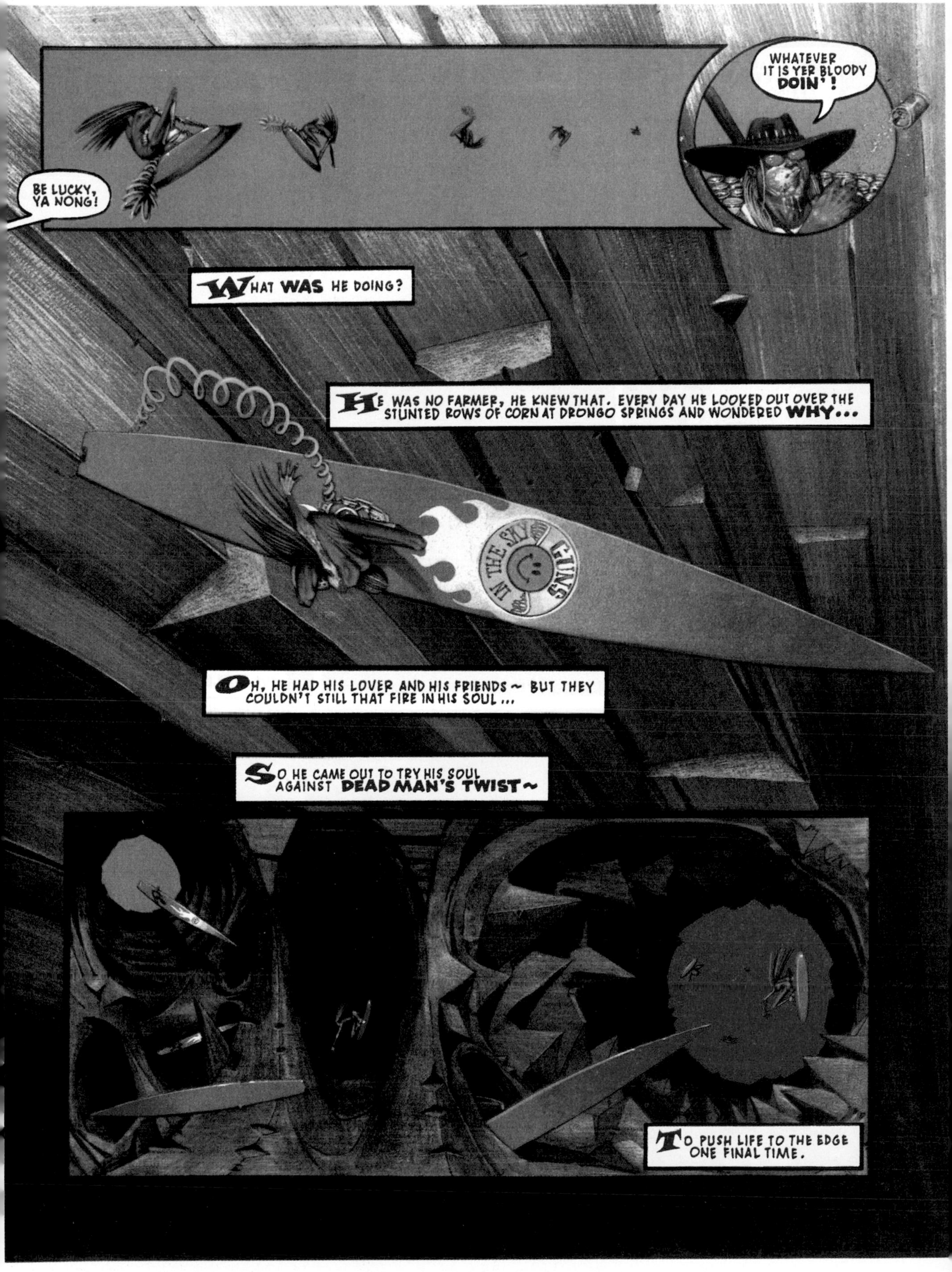
BE LUCKY, YA NONG!
WHATEVER IT IS YER BLOODY DOIN'!
WHAT WAS HE DOING?
HE WAS NO FARMER, HE KNEW THAT. EVERY DAY HE LOOKED OUT OVER THE STUNTED ROWS OF CORN AT DRONGO SPRINGS AND WONDERED WHY...
IN THE SKY GUNS
OH, HE HAD HIS LOVER AND HIS FRIENDS~ BUT THEY COULDN'T STILL THAT FIRE IN HIS SOUL...
SO HE CAME OUT TO TRY HIS SOUL AGAINST DEAD MAN'S TWIST~
TO PUSH LIFE TO THE EDGE ONE FINAL TIME.

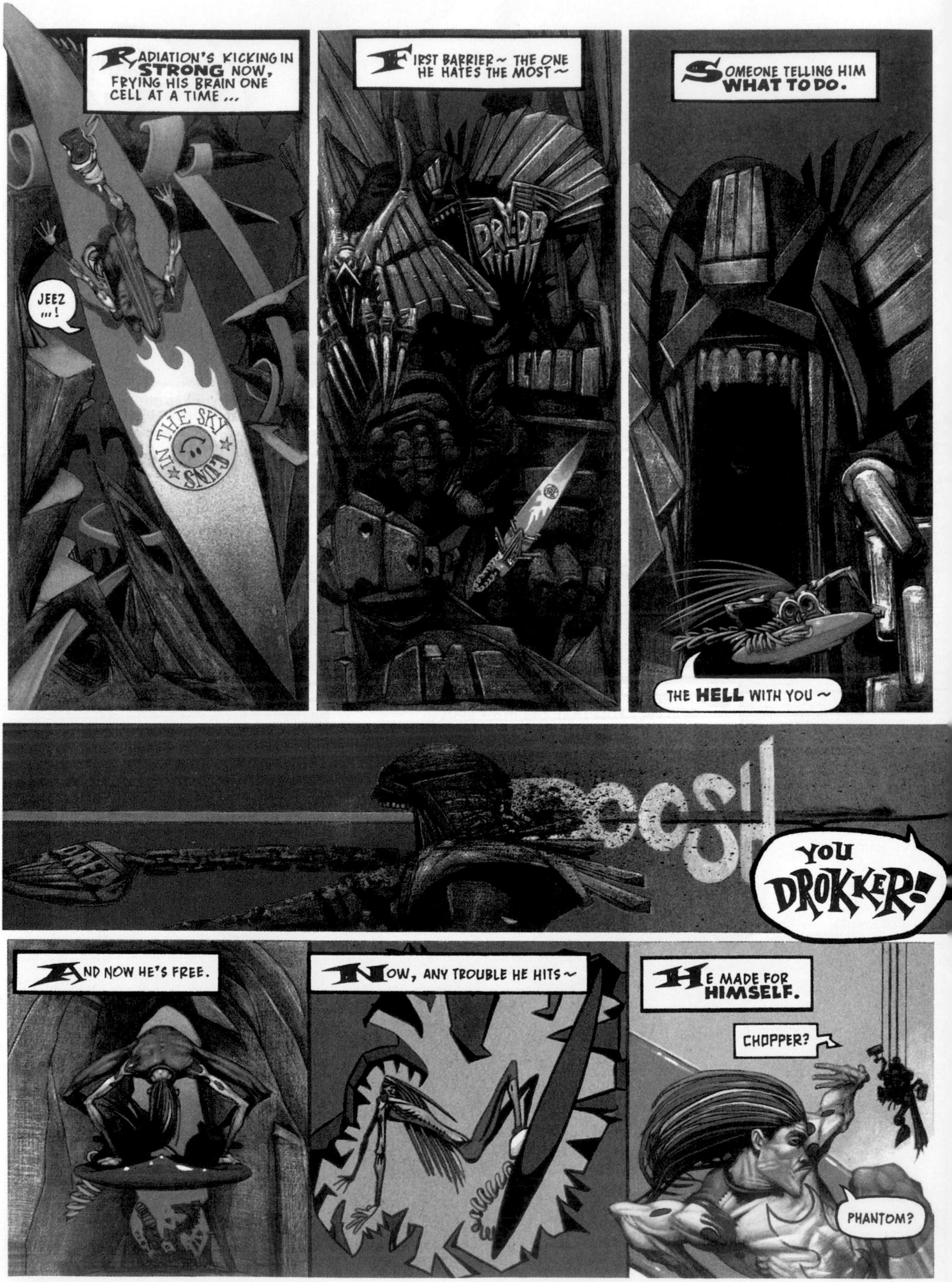
RADIATION'S KICKING IN STRONG NOW, FRYING HIS BRAIN ONE CELL AT A TIME ...
JEEZ ...!
IN THE SKY
GUNS
FIRST BARRIER ~ THE ONE HE HATES THE MOST ~
DREDD
SOMEONE TELLING HIM WHAT TO DO.
THE HELL WITH YOU ~
CCSH
YOU DROKKER!
AND NOW HE'S FREE.
NOW, ANY TROUBLE HE HITS ~
HE MADE FOR HIMSELF.
CHOPPER?
PHANTOM?

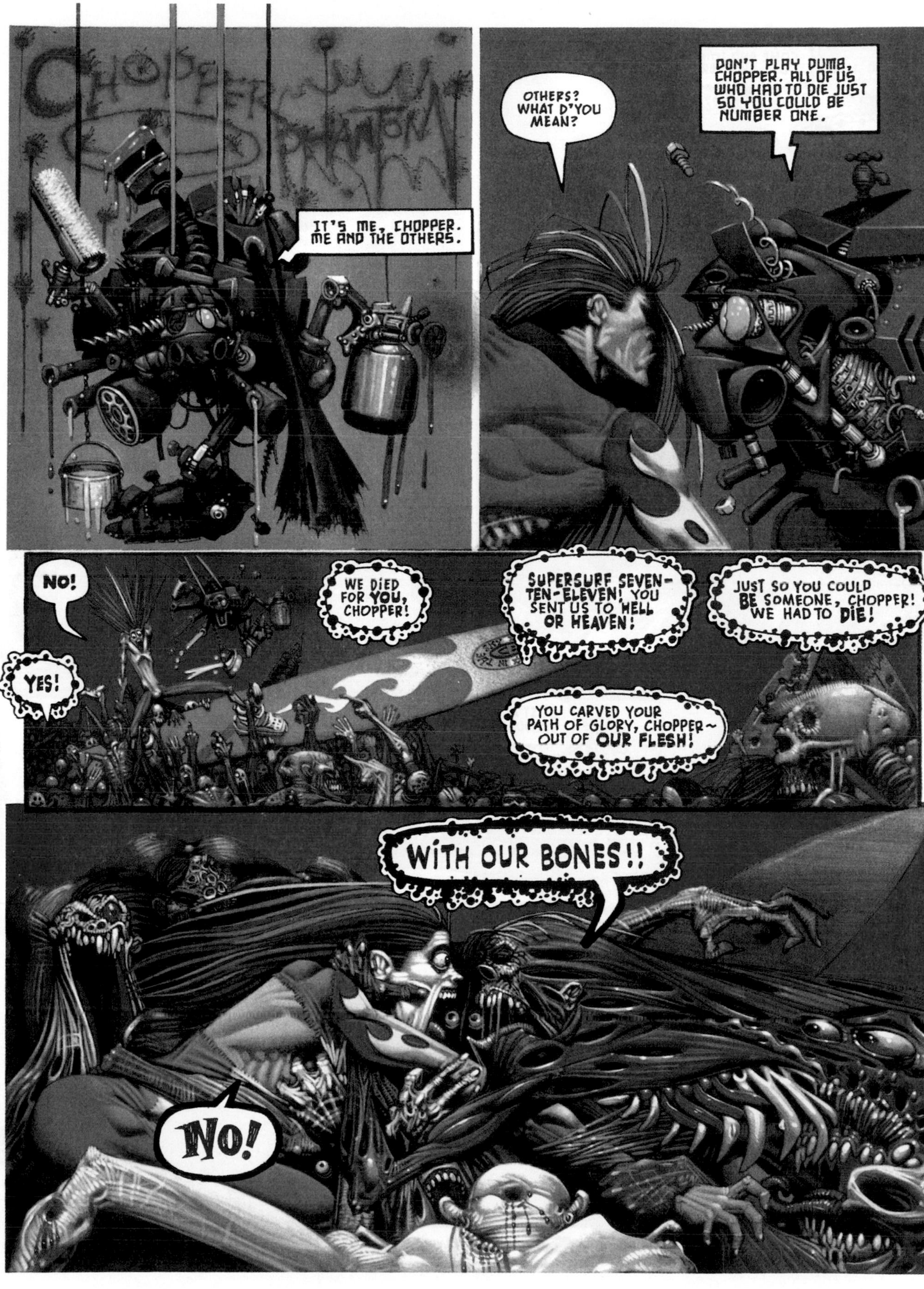
CHOPPER
PHANTOM
IT'S ME, CHOPPER. ME AND THE OTHERS.
OTHERS? WHAT D'YOU MEAN?
DON'T PLAY DUMB, CHOPPER. ALL OF US WHO HAD TO DIE JUST SO YOU COULD BE NUMBER ONE.
NO!
YES!
WE DIED FOR YOU, CHOPPER!
SUPERSURF SEVEN-TEN-ELEVEN! YOU SENT US TO HELL OR HEAVEN!
JUST SO YOU COULD BE SOMEONE, CHOPPER! WE HAD TO DIE!
YOU CARVED YOUR PATH OF GLORY, CHOPPER~ OUT OF OUR FLESH!
WITH OUR BONES!!
NO!

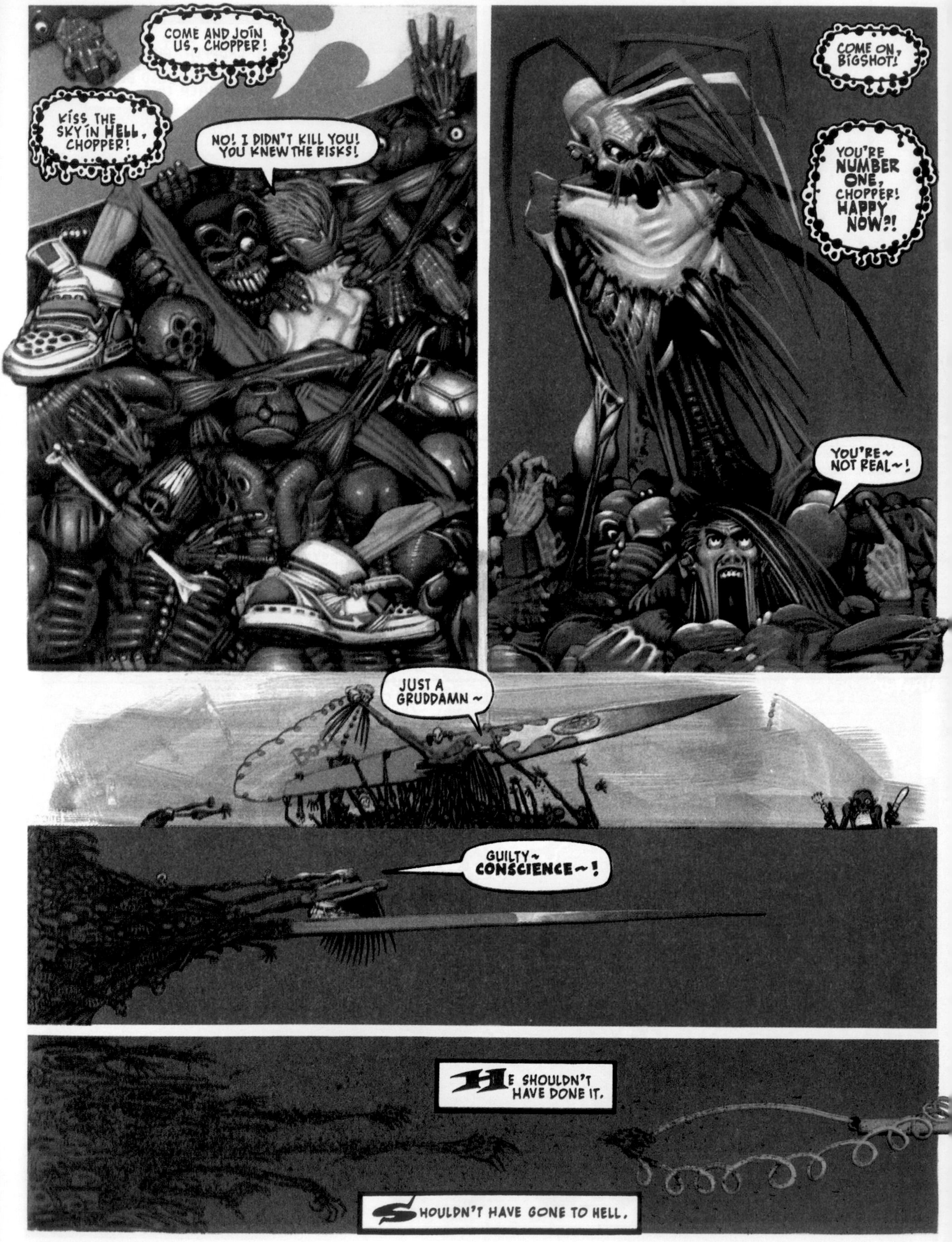
COME AND JOIN US, CHOPPER!
KISS THE SKY IN HELL, CHOPPER!
NO! I DIDN'T KILL YOU! YOU KNEW THE RISKS!
COME ON, BIGSHOT!
YOU'RE NUMBER ONE, CHOPPER! HAPPY NOW?!
YOU'RE~ NOT REAL~!
JUST A GRUDDAMN~
GUILTY~ CONSCIENCE~!
HE SHOULDN'T HAVE DONE IT.
SHOULDN'T HAVE GONE TO HELL.

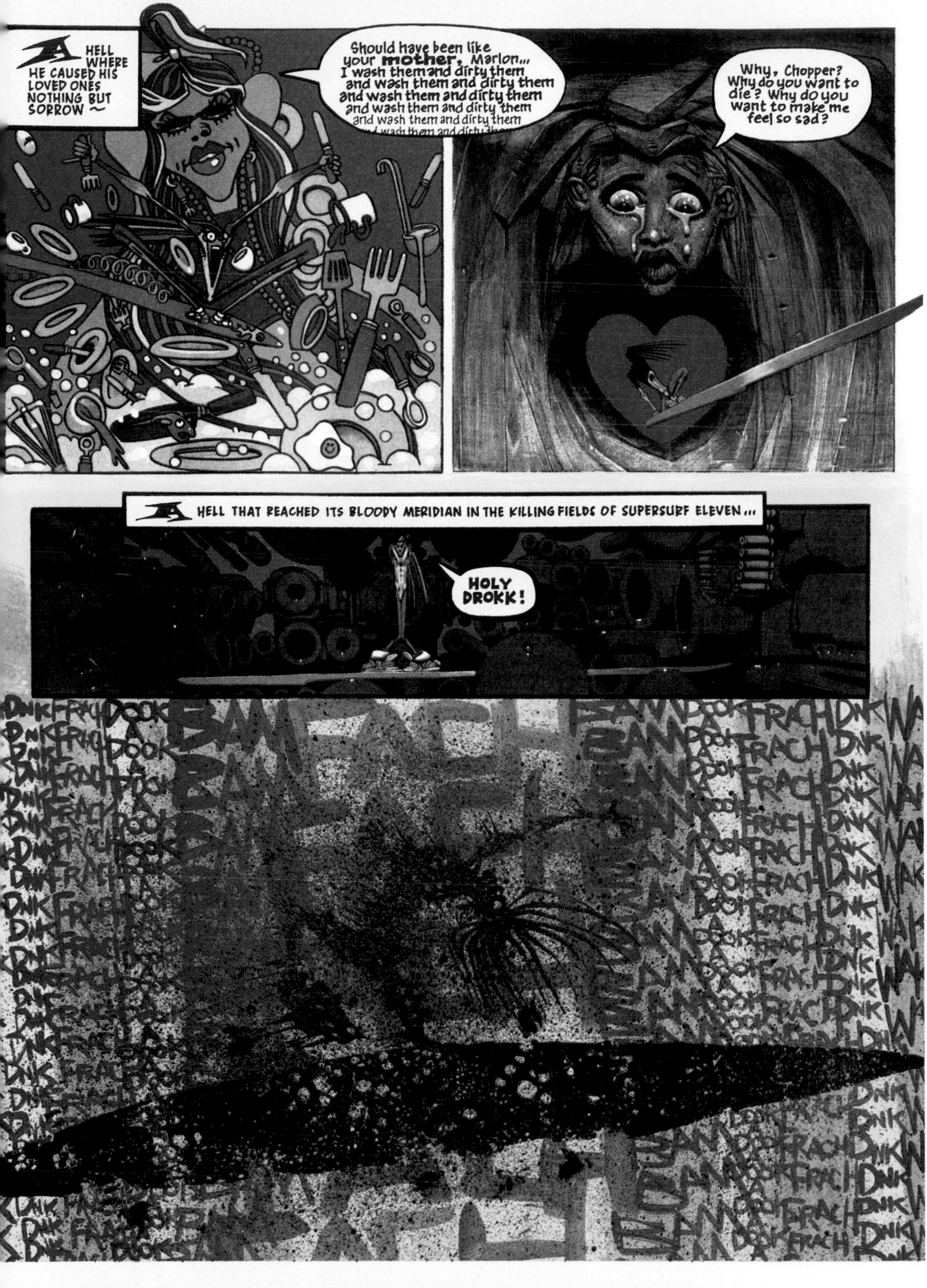
A HELL WHERE HE CAUSED HIS LOVED ONES NOTHING BUT SORROW ~
Should have been like your mother, Marlon... I wash them and dirty them and wash them and dirty them and wash them and dirty them and wash them and dirty them
Why, Chopper? Why do you want to die? Why do you want to make me feel so sad?
A HELL THAT REACHED ITS BLOODY MERIDIAN IN THE KILLING FIELDS OF SUPERSURF ELEVEN...
HOLY DROKK!
DNK FRACH DOOK A DOOK
BAM FACH
BAM DOOK A FRACH DNK
WAK

WHY DO YOU CHASE ME, CHOPPER?

WHY DO YOU WANT TO DIE SO BADLY?

I.... DON'T...

NO... IN A WORLD OF CONCRETE JUNGLES... AND BARREN DESERTS...

WHERE COWERING, BEATEN FOLK DO NOTHING MORE THAN CRAWL...

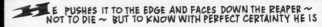

HE PUSHES IT TO THE EDGE AND FACES DOWN THE REAPER ~ NOT TO DIE ~ BUT TO KNOW WITH PERFECT CERTAINTY HE IS

ALIVE!

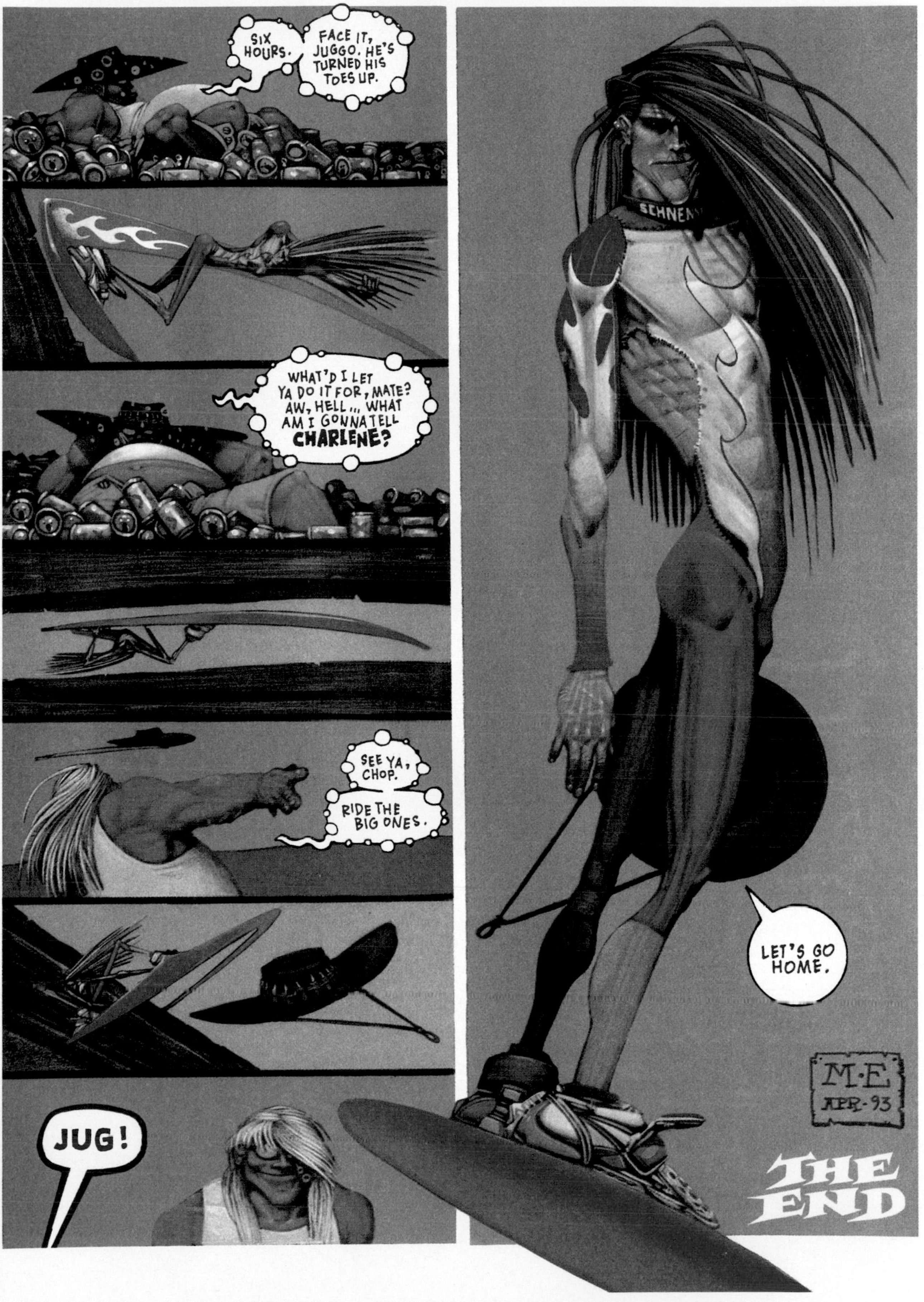
SIX HOURS.
FACE IT, JUGGO. HE'S TURNED HIS TOES UP.
WHAT'D I LET YA DO IT FOR, MATE? AW, HELL... WHAT AM I GONNA TELL CHARLENE?
SEE YA, CHOP.
RIDE THE BIG ONES.
JUG!
SCHNENS
LET'S GO HOME.
M·E APR-93
THE END

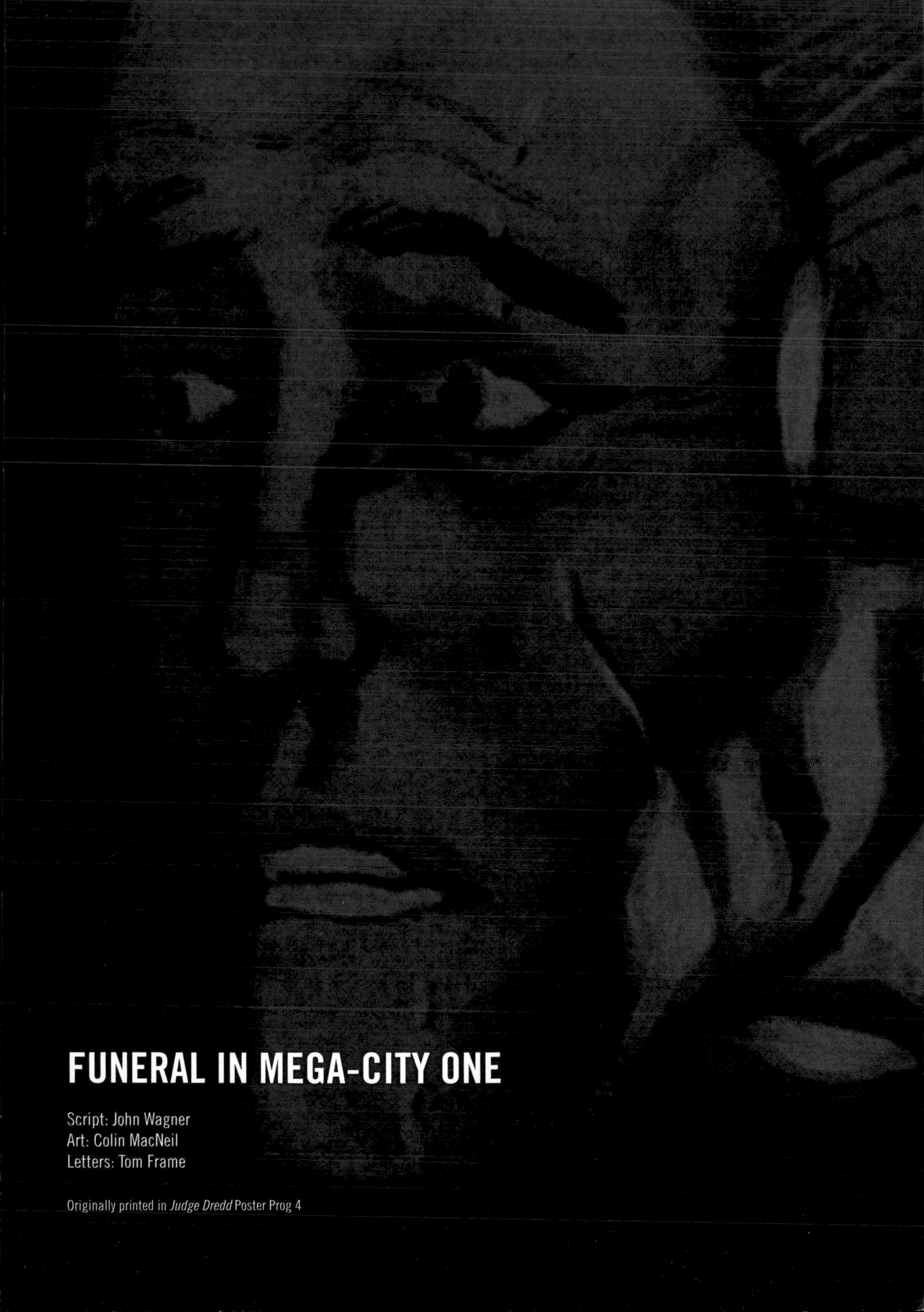

FUNERAL IN MEGA-CITY ONE

Script: John Wagner
Art: Colin MacNeil
Letters: Tom Frame

Originally printed in *Judge Dredd* Poster Prog 4

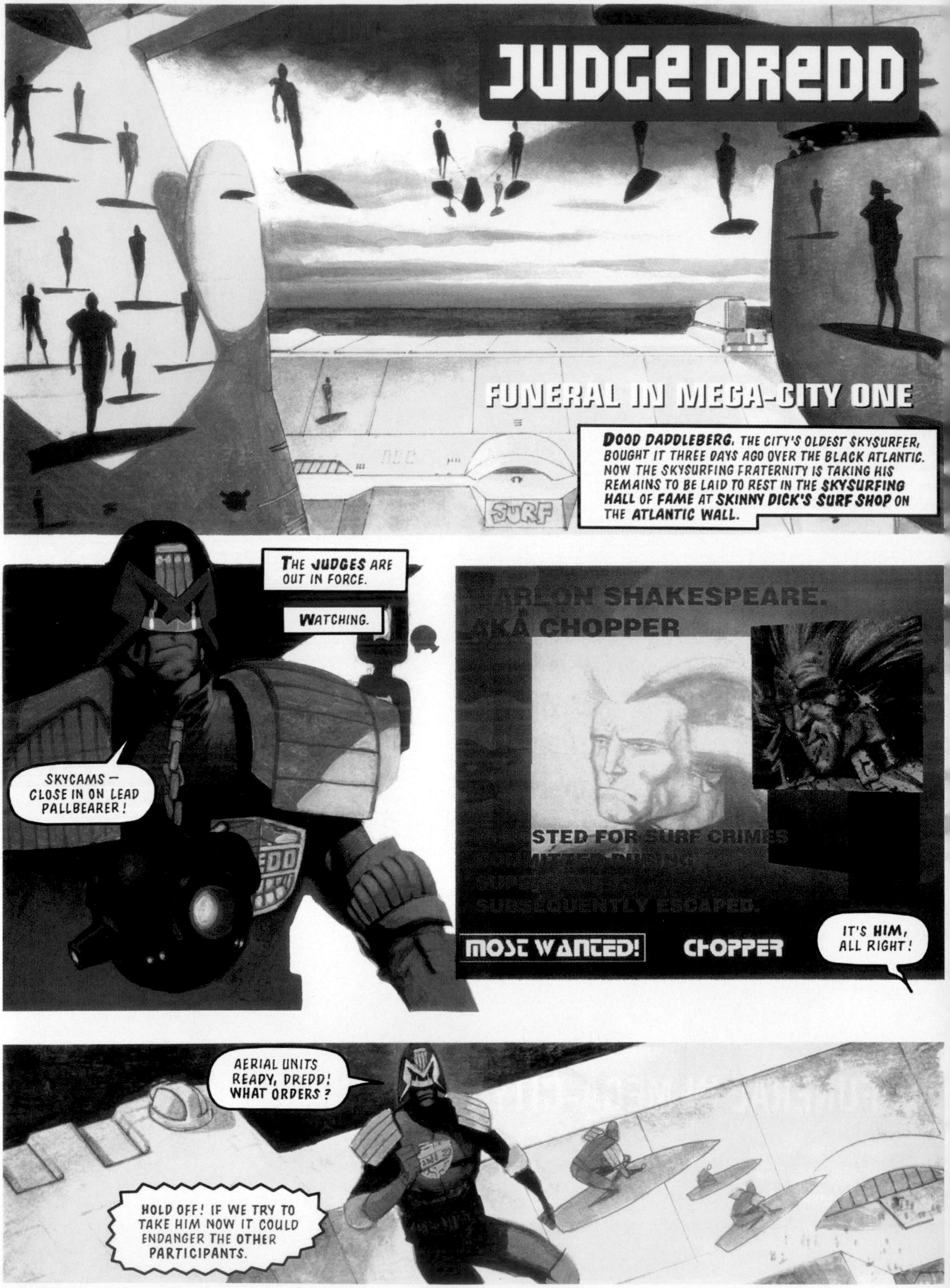

JUDGE DREDD
FUNERAL IN MEGA-CITY ONE
DOOD DADDLEBERG, THE CITY'S OLDEST SKYSURFER, BOUGHT IT THREE DAYS AGO OVER THE BLACK ATLANTIC. NOW THE SKYSURFING FRATERNITY IS TAKING HIS REMAINS TO BE LAID TO REST IN THE SKYSURFING HALL OF FAME AT SKINNY DICK'S SURF SHOP ON THE ATLANTIC WALL.
SURF
THE JUDGES ARE OUT IN FORCE.
WATCHING.
SKYCAMS — CLOSE IN ON LEAD PALLBEARER!
SHAKESPEARE.
CHOPPER
STED FOR SURF CRIMES
SUBSEQUENTLY ESCAPED.
MOST WANTED!
CHOPPER
IT'S HIM, ALL RIGHT!
AERIAL UNITS READY, DREDD! WHAT ORDERS?
HOLD OFF! IF WE TRY TO TAKE HIM NOW IT COULD ENDANGER THE OTHER PARTICIPANTS.

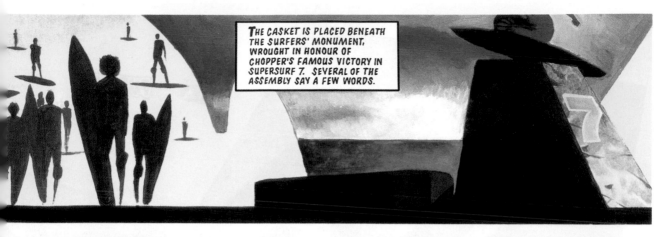

THE CASKET IS PLACED BENEATH THE SURFERS' MONUMENT, WROUGHT IN HONOUR OF CHOPPER'S FAMOUS VICTORY IN SUPERSURF 7. SEVERAL OF THE ASSEMBLY SAY A FEW WORDS.

MARLON SHAKESPEARE! THERE'S NO WAY OUT! I'M GIVING YOU ONE WARNING! SURRENDER OR YOU WILL BE SHOT DOWN!

YOU TOOK A REAL CHANCE COMIN' HERE, CHOPPER! JUDGES ARE HOLDING BACK FOR NOW, BUT AS SOON AS YOU SPLIT THEY'LL NAIL YOU!

I HAVE AN ESCAPE ROUTE PLANNED. ALL I NEED'S A LITTLE COVER--

GLAD TO OBLIGE! SCATTER!

AHHHH!

DANGEROUS SURFING! YOU'RE UNDER ARREST!

HE KNEW THE JUDGES WOULD BE WAITING FOR HIM. THERE'S A FAST HOVERSHIP STANDING BY FIFTY KAYS OFFSHORE, IF ONLY HE CAN REACH IT--

THE DOCK GATE'S OPENING! THAT'S HIS WAY!

DOCK LASERS WILL PICK HIM OFF! HE HASN'T GOT A CHANCE!

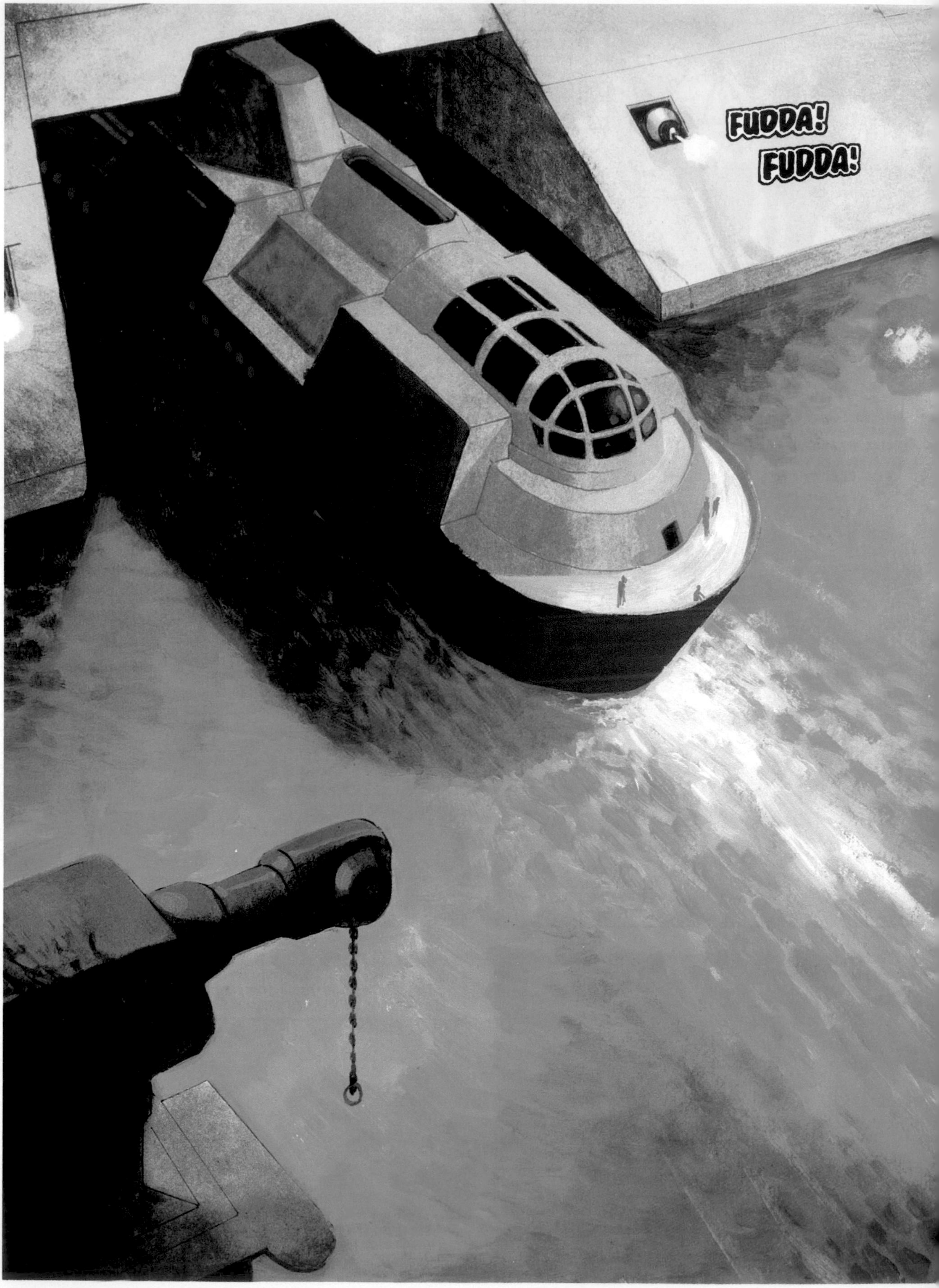
FUDDA!
FUDDA!

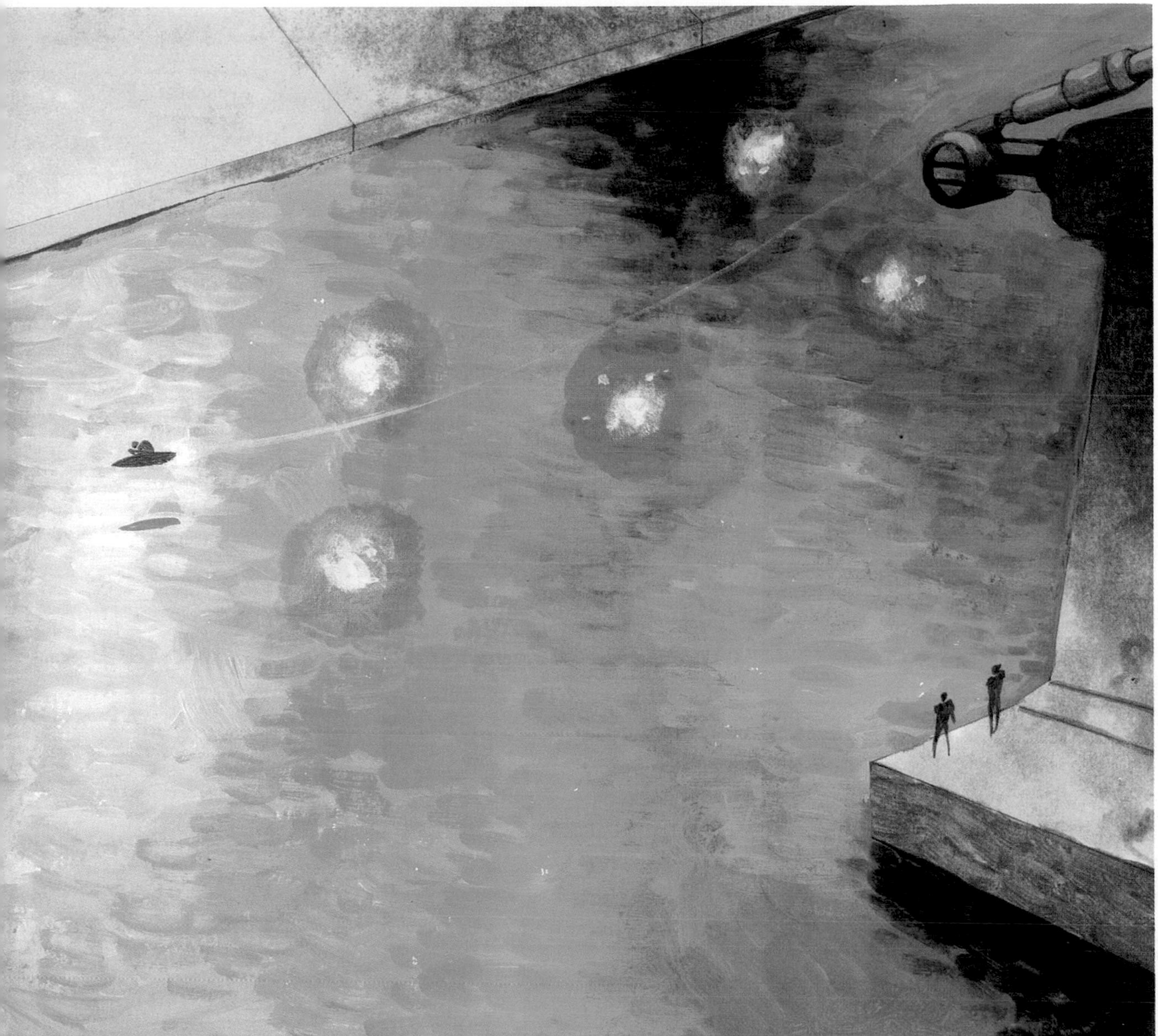
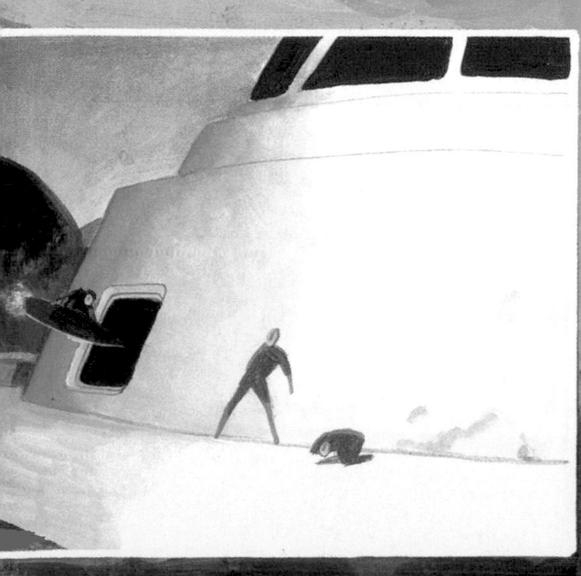
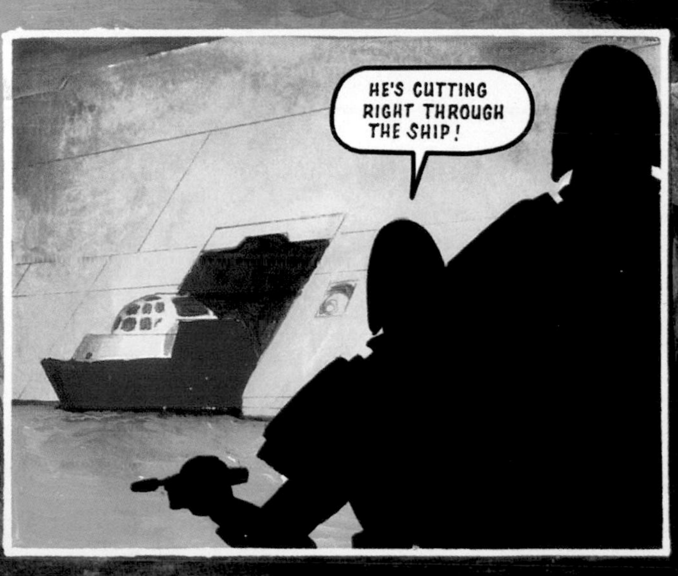
HE'S CUTTING RIGHT THROUGH THE SHIP!

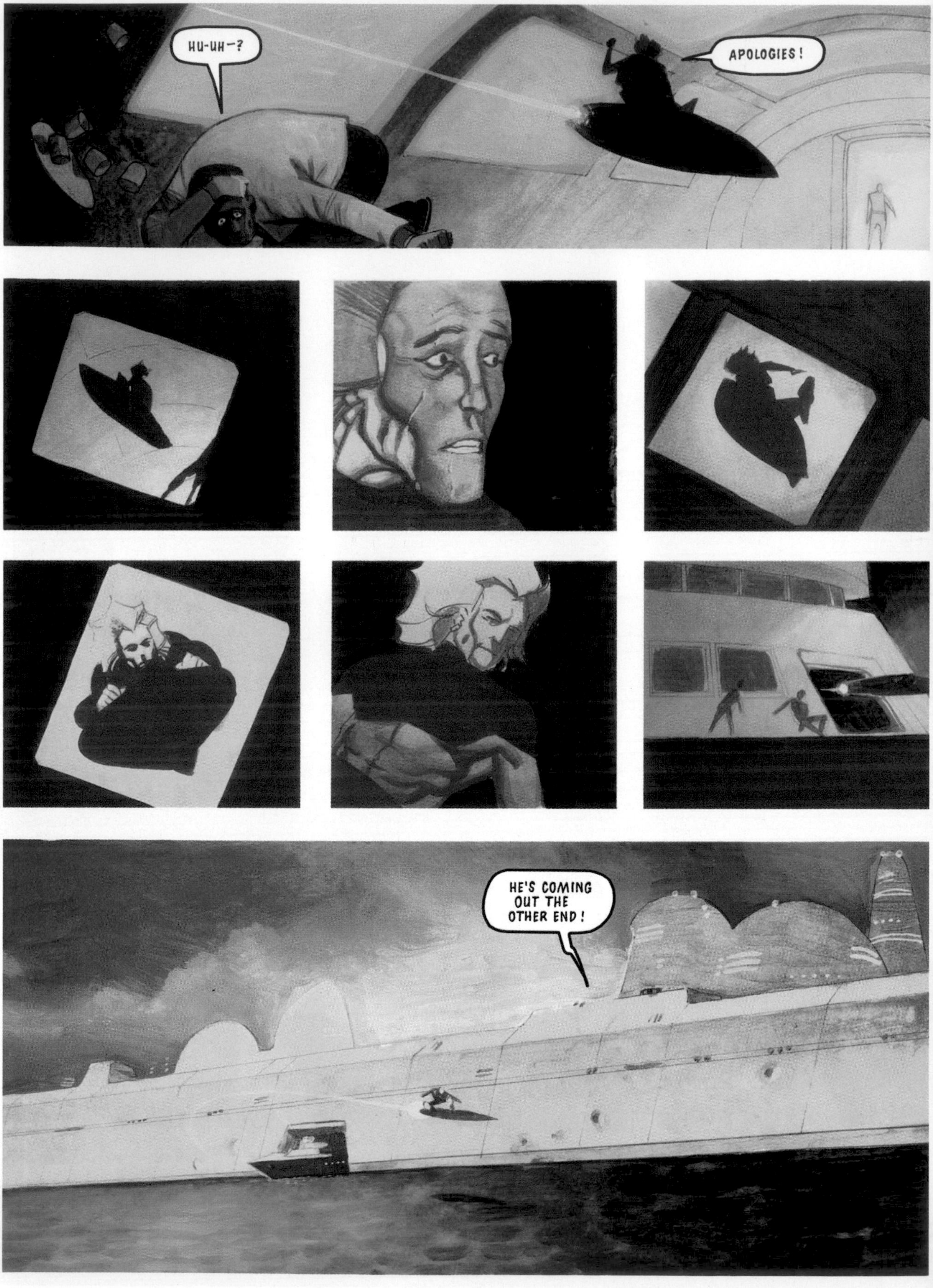
HU-UH-?
APOLOGIES!
HE'S COMING OUT THE OTHER END!

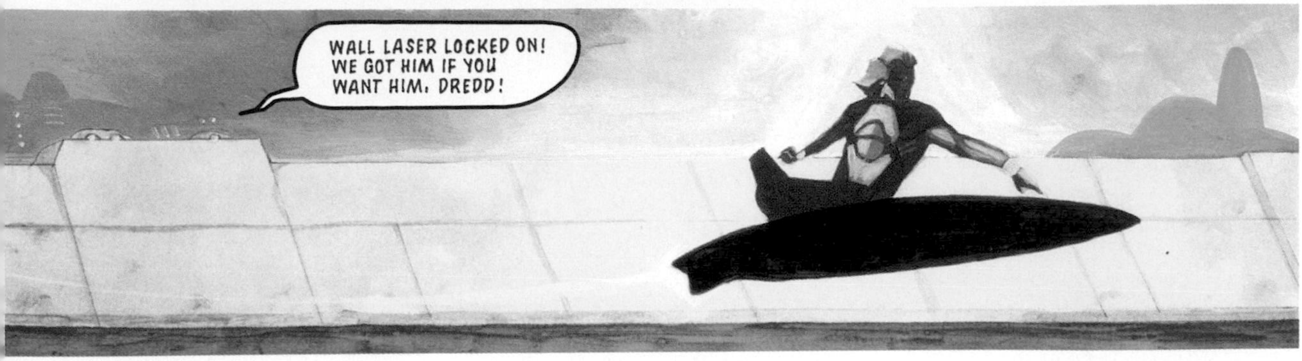
WALL LASER LOCKED ON! WE GOT HIM IF YOU WANT HIM, DREDD!
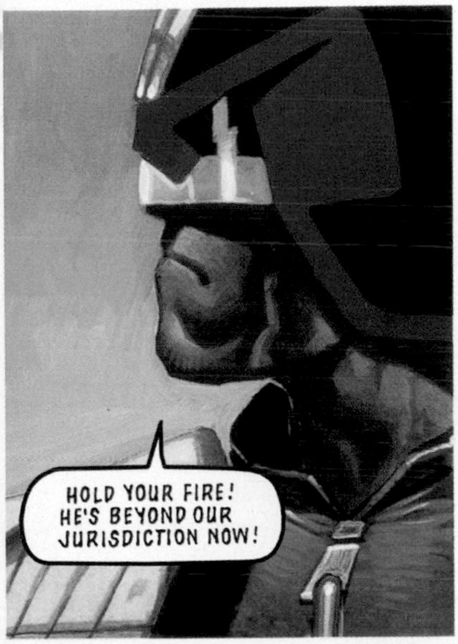
HOLD YOUR FIRE! HE'S BEYOND OUR JURISDICTION NOW!
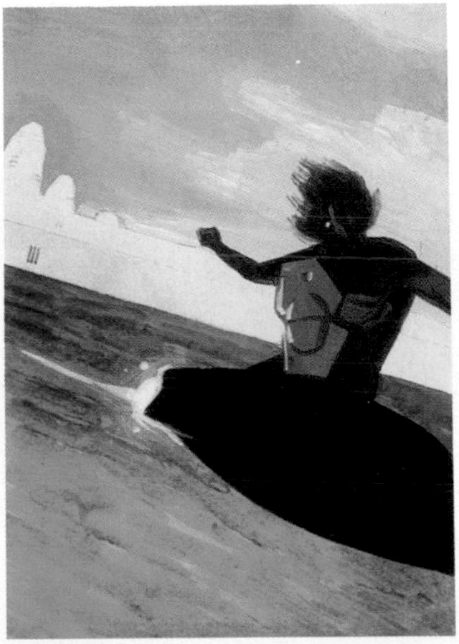
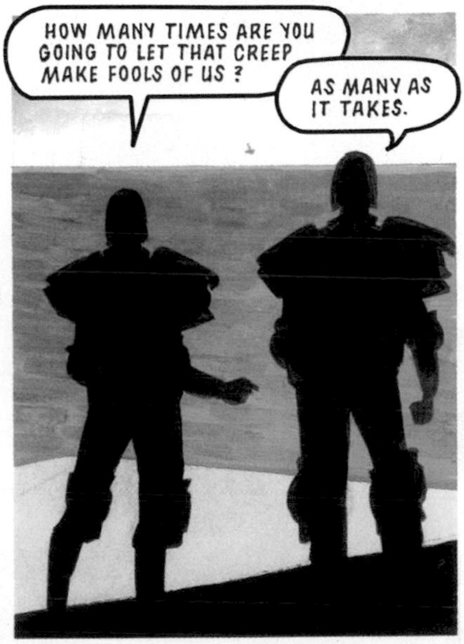
HOW MANY TIMES ARE YOU GOING TO LET THAT CREEP MAKE FOOLS OF US ?
AS MANY AS IT TAKES.
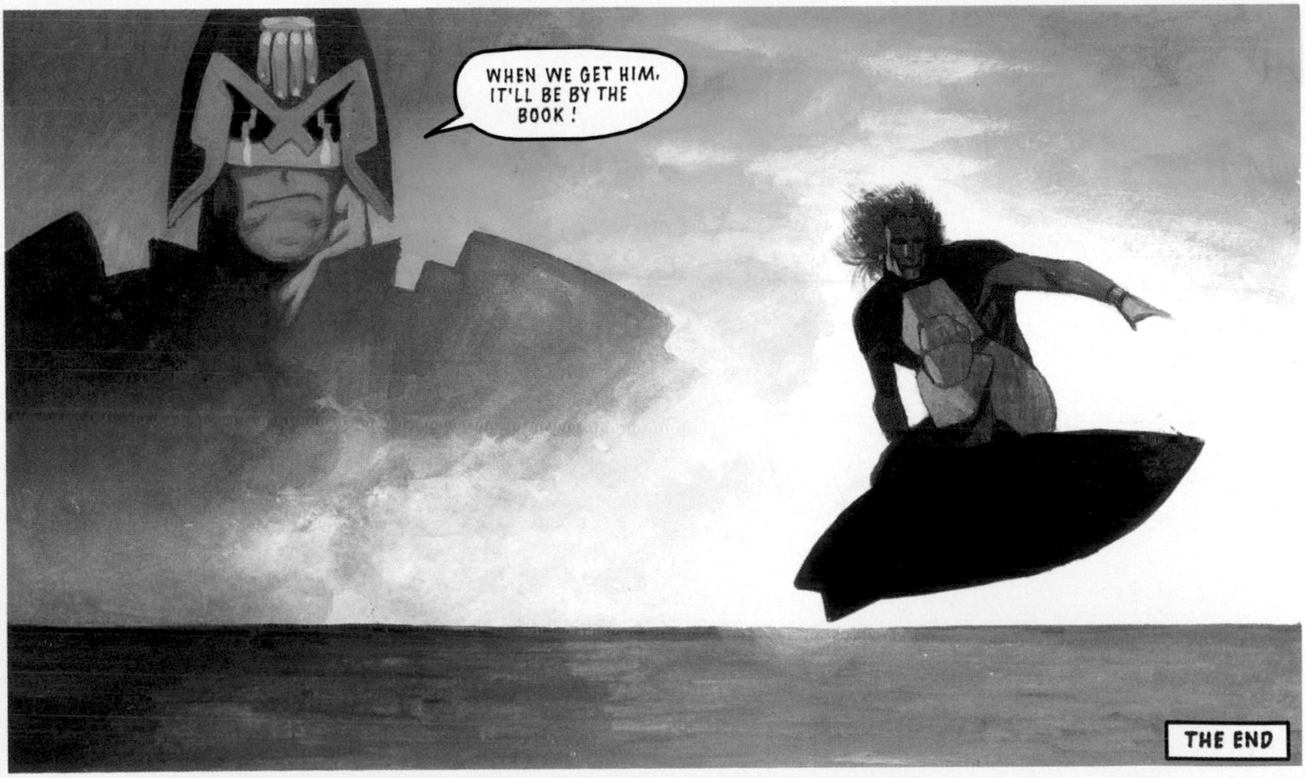
WHEN WE GET HIM, IT'LL BE BY THE BOOK!
THE END

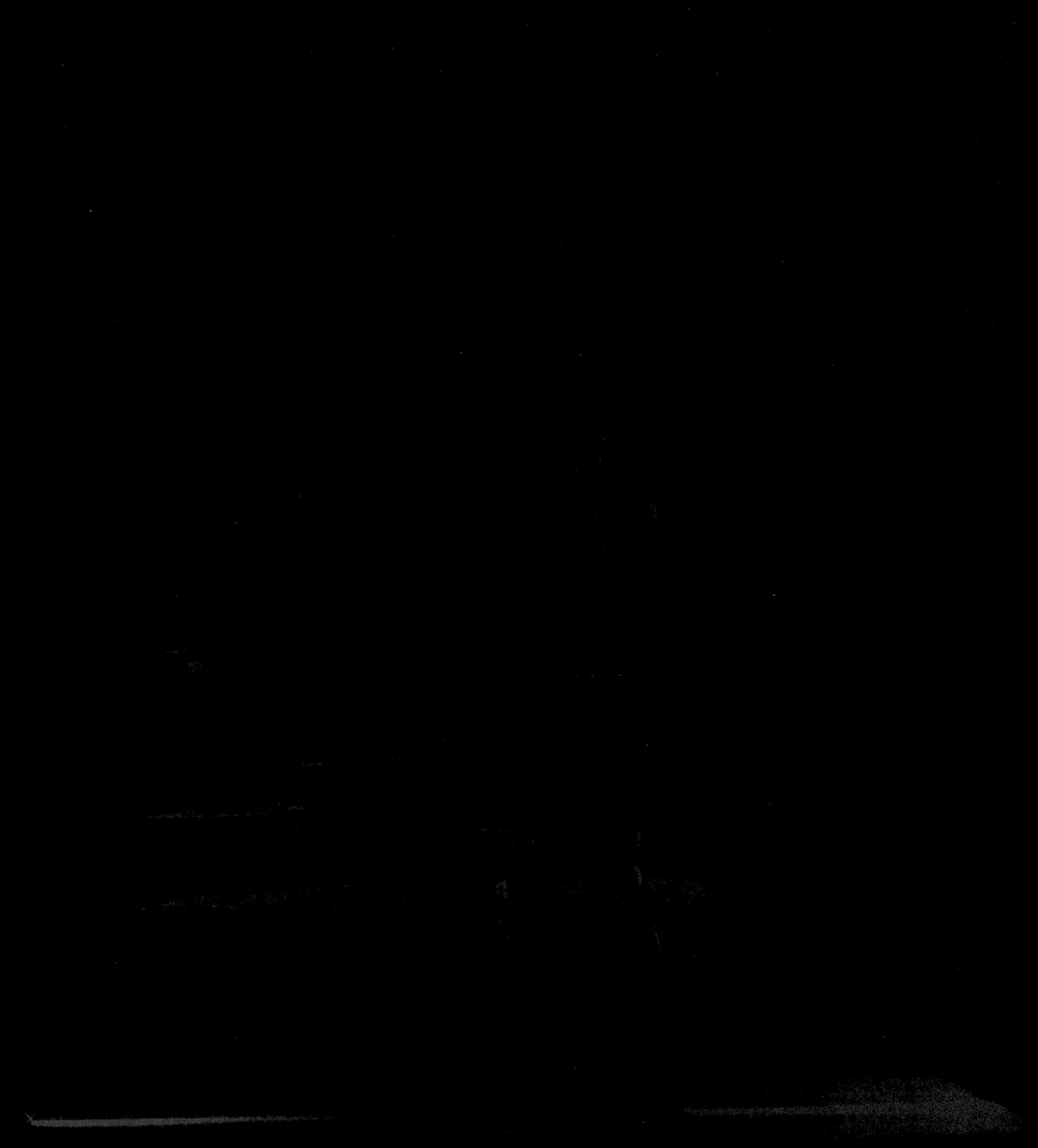

SUPERSURF 13

Script: Alan McKenzie
Art: John Higgins
Letters: Tom Frame

Originally printed in *2000 AD* Progs 964-971

SUPERSURF 13

PART 1

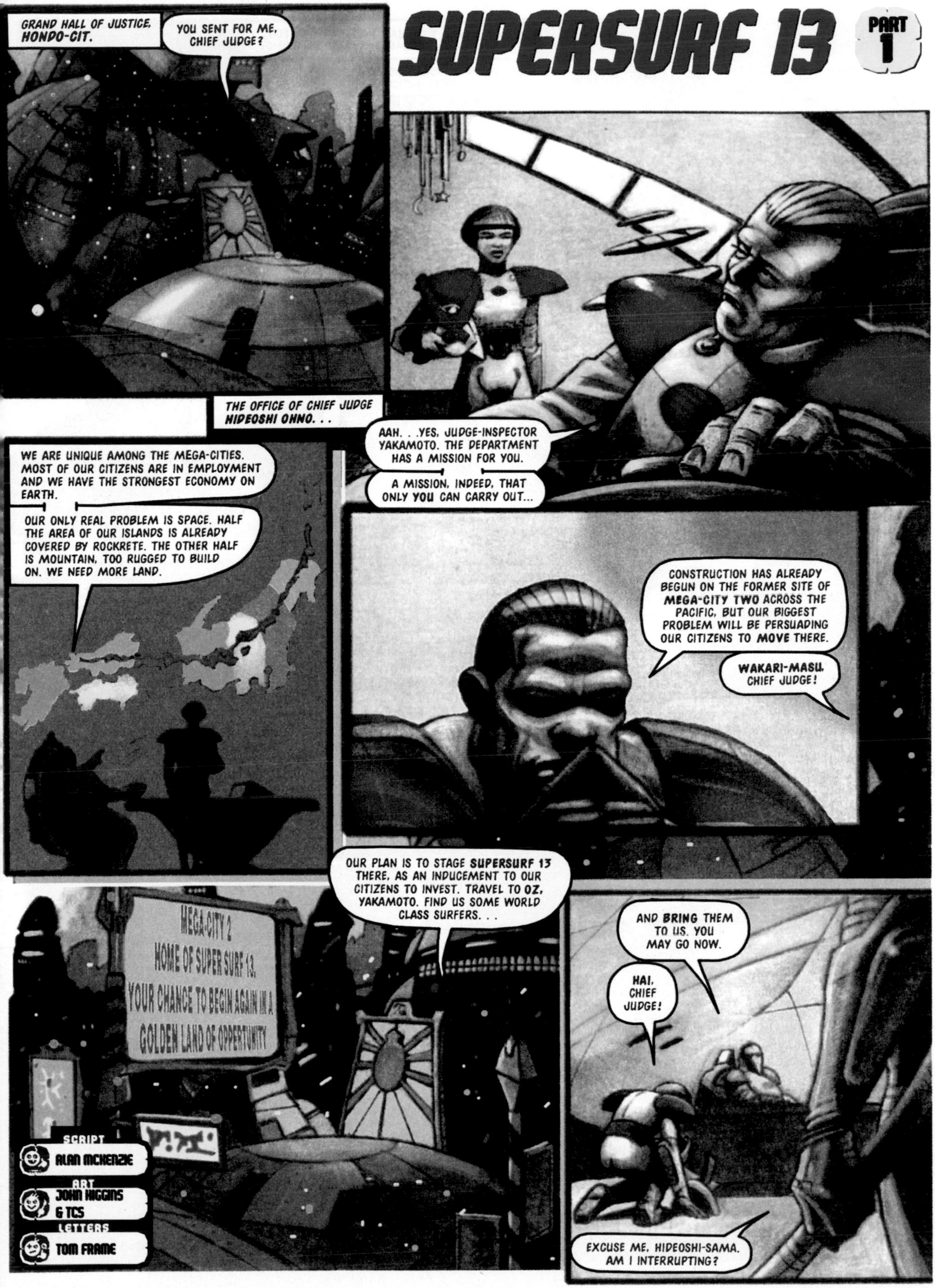

GRAND HALL OF JUSTICE, HONDO-CIT.
YOU SENT FOR ME, CHIEF JUDGE?
THE OFFICE OF CHIEF JUDGE HIDEOSHI OHNO. . .
AAH. . .YES, JUDGE-INSPECTOR YAKAMOTO. THE DEPARTMENT HAS A MISSION FOR YOU.
A MISSION, INDEED, THAT ONLY YOU CAN CARRY OUT...
WE ARE UNIQUE AMONG THE MEGA-CITIES. MOST OF OUR CITIZENS ARE IN EMPLOYMENT AND WE HAVE THE STRONGEST ECONOMY ON EARTH.
OUR ONLY REAL PROBLEM IS SPACE. HALF THE AREA OF OUR ISLANDS IS ALREADY COVERED BY ROCKRETE. THE OTHER HALF IS MOUNTAIN, TOO RUGGED TO BUILD ON. WE NEED MORE LAND.
CONSTRUCTION HAS ALREADY BEGUN ON THE FORMER SITE OF MEGA-CITY TWO ACROSS THE PACIFIC, BUT OUR BIGGEST PROBLEM WILL BE PERSUADING OUR CITIZENS TO MOVE THERE.
WAKARI-MASU, CHIEF JUDGE!
OUR PLAN IS TO STAGE SUPERSURF 13 THERE, AS AN INDUCEMENT TO OUR CITIZENS TO INVEST. TRAVEL TO OZ, YAKAMOTO. FIND US SOME WORLD CLASS SURFERS. . .
MEGA-CITY 2
HOME OF SUPER SURF 13.
YOUR CHANCE TO BEGIN AGAIN IN A GOLDEN LAND OF OPPERTUNITY
SCRIPT
ALAN MCKENZIE
ART
JOHN HIGGINS & TCS
LETTERS
TOM FRAME
AND BRING THEM TO US. YOU MAY GO NOW.
HAI, CHIEF JUDGE!
EXCUSE ME, HIDEOSHI-SAMA. AM I INTERRUPTING?

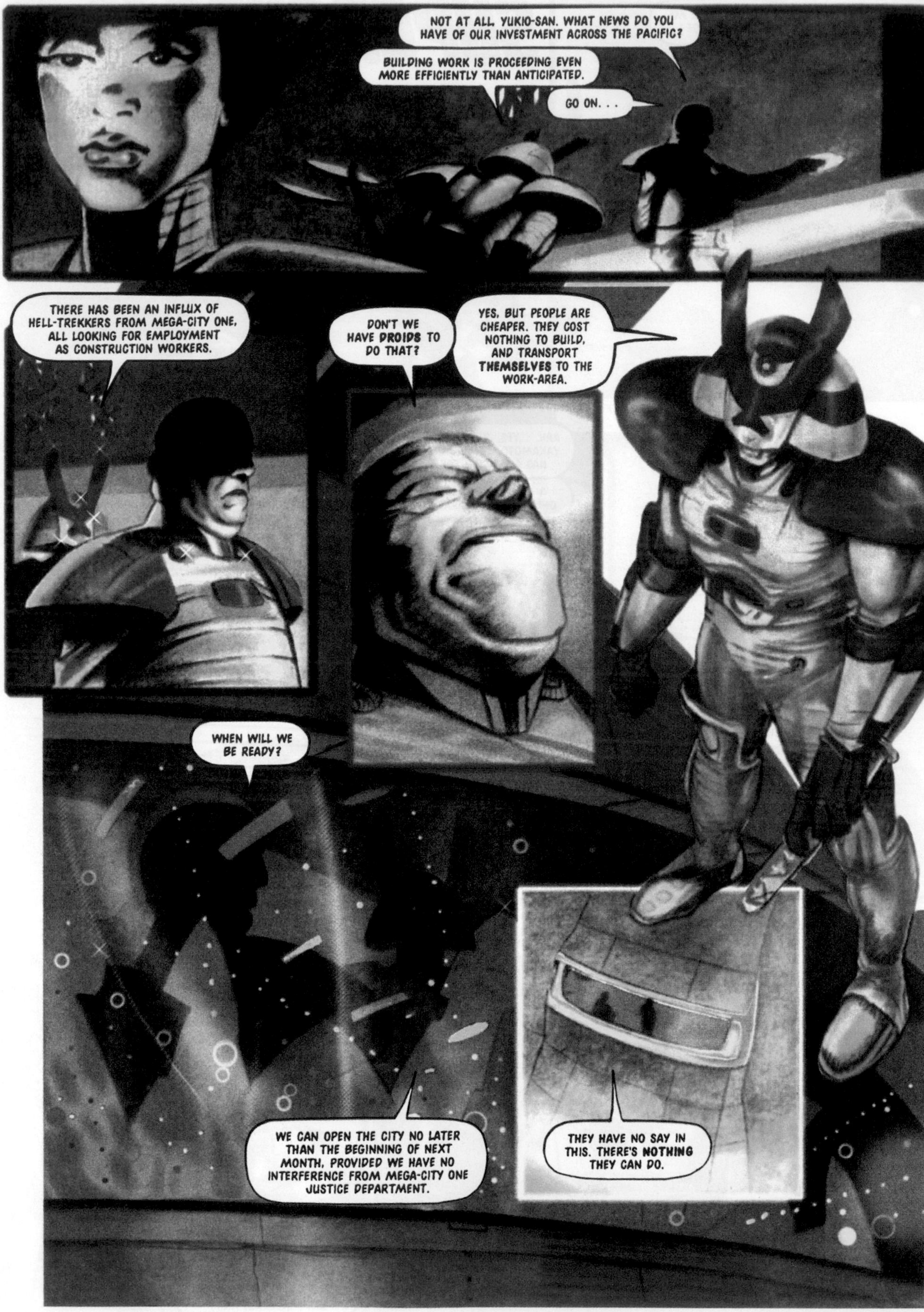
NOT AT ALL, YUKIO-SAN. WHAT NEWS DO YOU HAVE OF OUR INVESTMENT ACROSS THE PACIFIC?
BUILDING WORK IS PROCEEDING EVEN MORE EFFICIENTLY THAN ANTICIPATED.
GO ON. . .
THERE HAS BEEN AN INFLUX OF HELL-TREKKERS FROM MEGA-CITY ONE, ALL LOOKING FOR EMPLOYMENT AS CONSTRUCTION WORKERS.
DON'T WE HAVE DROIDS TO DO THAT?
YES, BUT PEOPLE ARE CHEAPER. THEY COST NOTHING TO BUILD, AND TRANSPORT THEMSELVES TO THE WORK-AREA.
WHEN WILL WE BE READY?
WE CAN OPEN THE CITY NO LATER THAN THE BEGINNING OF NEXT MONTH, PROVIDED WE HAVE NO INTERFERENCE FROM MEGA-CITY ONE JUSTICE DEPARTMENT.
THEY HAVE NO SAY IN THIS. THERE'S NOTHING THEY CAN DO.

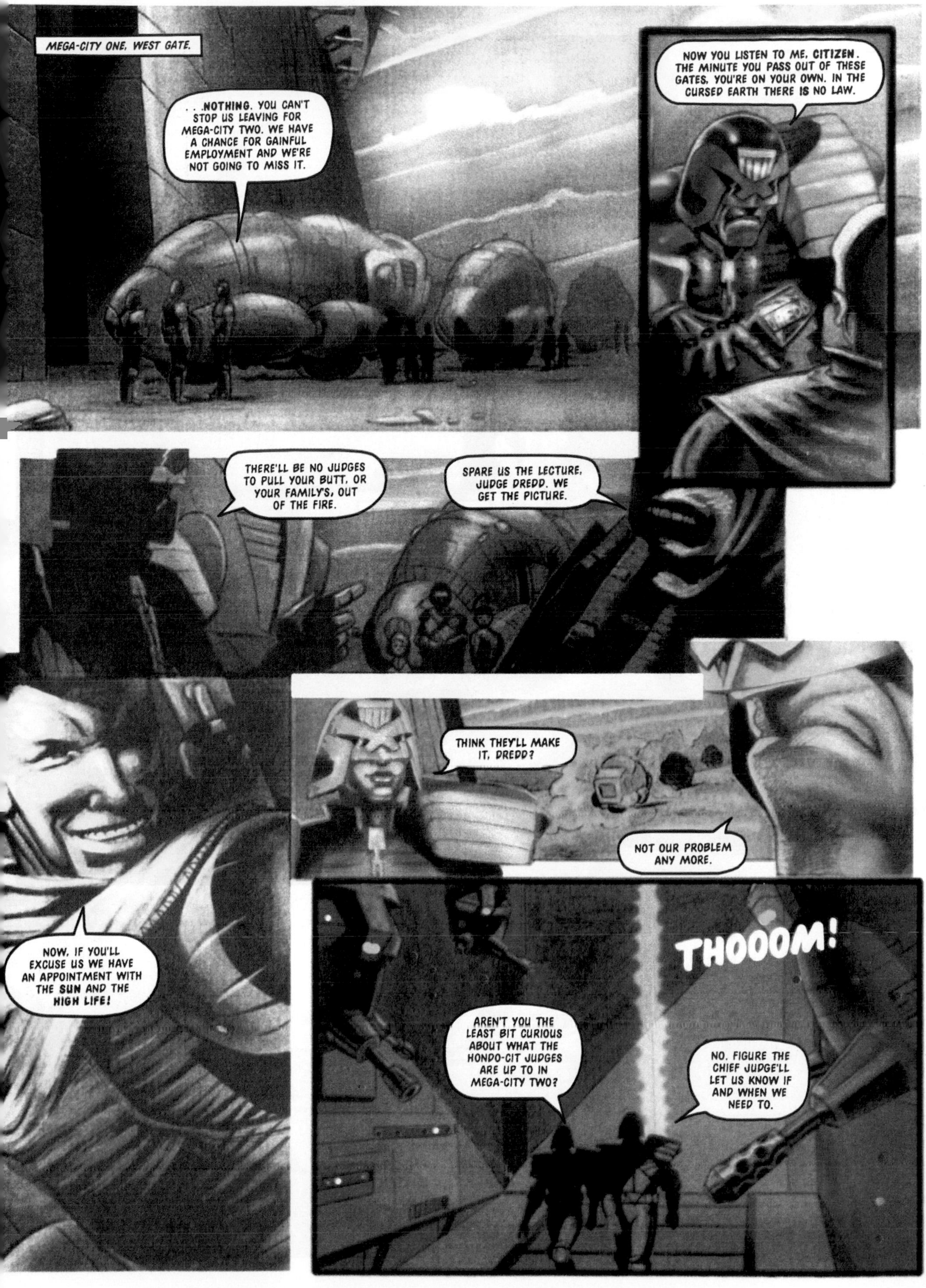
MEGA-CITY ONE, WEST GATE.
. . .NOTHING. YOU CAN'T STOP US LEAVING FOR MEGA-CITY TWO. WE HAVE A CHANCE FOR GAINFUL EMPLOYMENT AND WE'RE NOT GOING TO MISS IT.
NOW YOU LISTEN TO ME, CITIZEN. THE MINUTE YOU PASS OUT OF THESE GATES, YOU'RE ON YOUR OWN. IN THE CURSED EARTH THERE IS NO LAW.
THERE'LL BE NO JUDGES TO PULL YOUR BUTT, OR YOUR FAMILY'S, OUT OF THE FIRE.
SPARE US THE LECTURE, JUDGE DREDD. WE GET THE PICTURE.
NOW, IF YOU'LL EXCUSE US WE HAVE AN APPOINTMENT WITH THE SUN AND THE HIGH LIFE!
THINK THEY'LL MAKE IT, DREDD?
NOT OUR PROBLEM ANY MORE.
THOOOM!
AREN'T YOU THE LEAST BIT CURIOUS ABOUT WHAT THE HONDO-CIT JUDGES ARE UP TO IN MEGA-CITY TWO?
NO. FIGURE THE CHIEF JUDGE'LL LET US KNOW IF AND WHEN WE NEED TO.

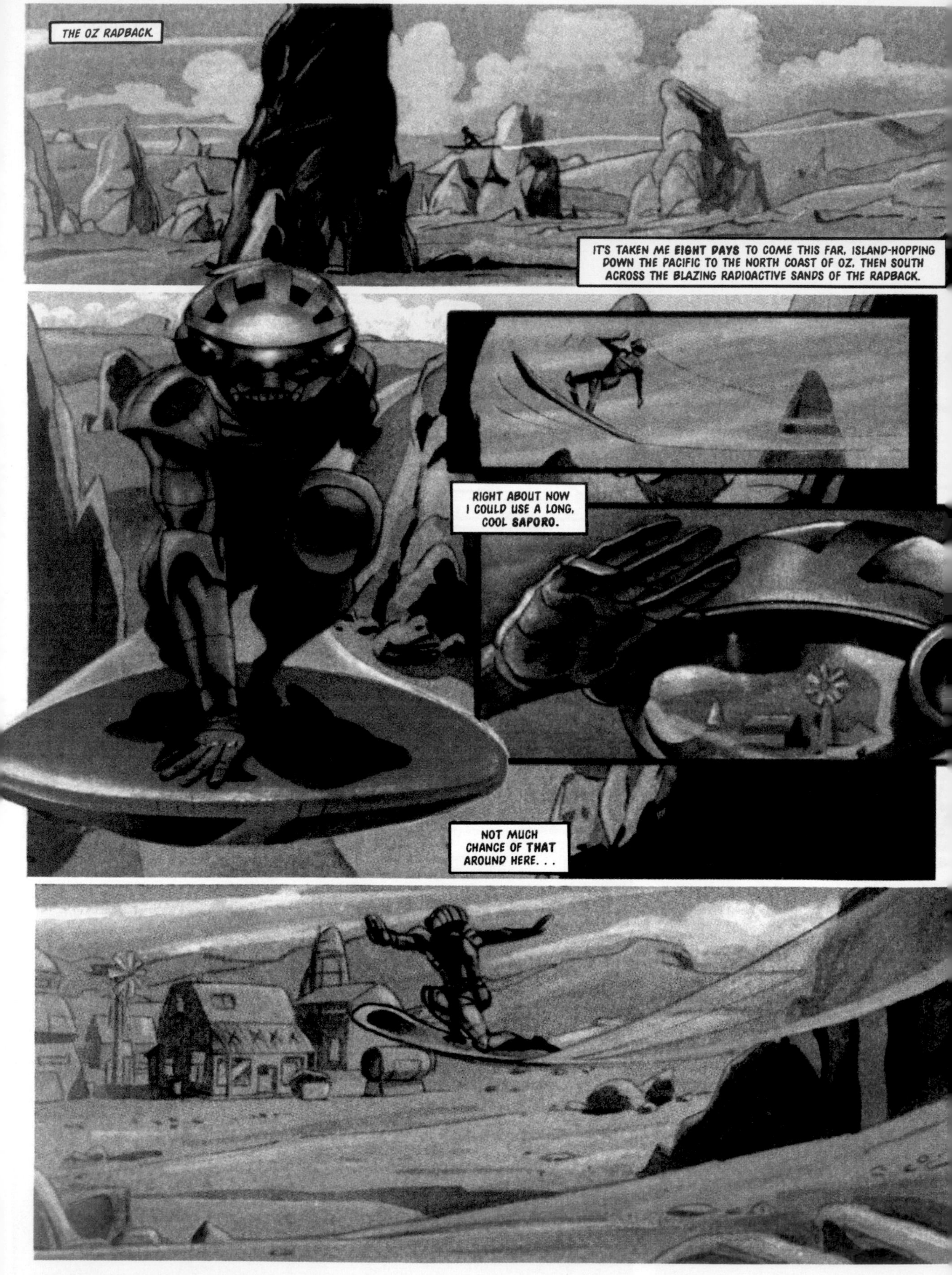
THE OZ RADBACK.
IT'S TAKEN ME EIGHT DAYS TO COME THIS FAR, ISLAND-HOPPING DOWN THE PACIFIC TO THE NORTH COAST OF OZ, THEN SOUTH ACROSS THE BLAZING RADIOACTIVE SANDS OF THE RADBACK.
RIGHT ABOUT NOW I COULD USE A LONG, COOL SAPORO.
NOT MUCH CHANCE OF THAT AROUND HERE. . .

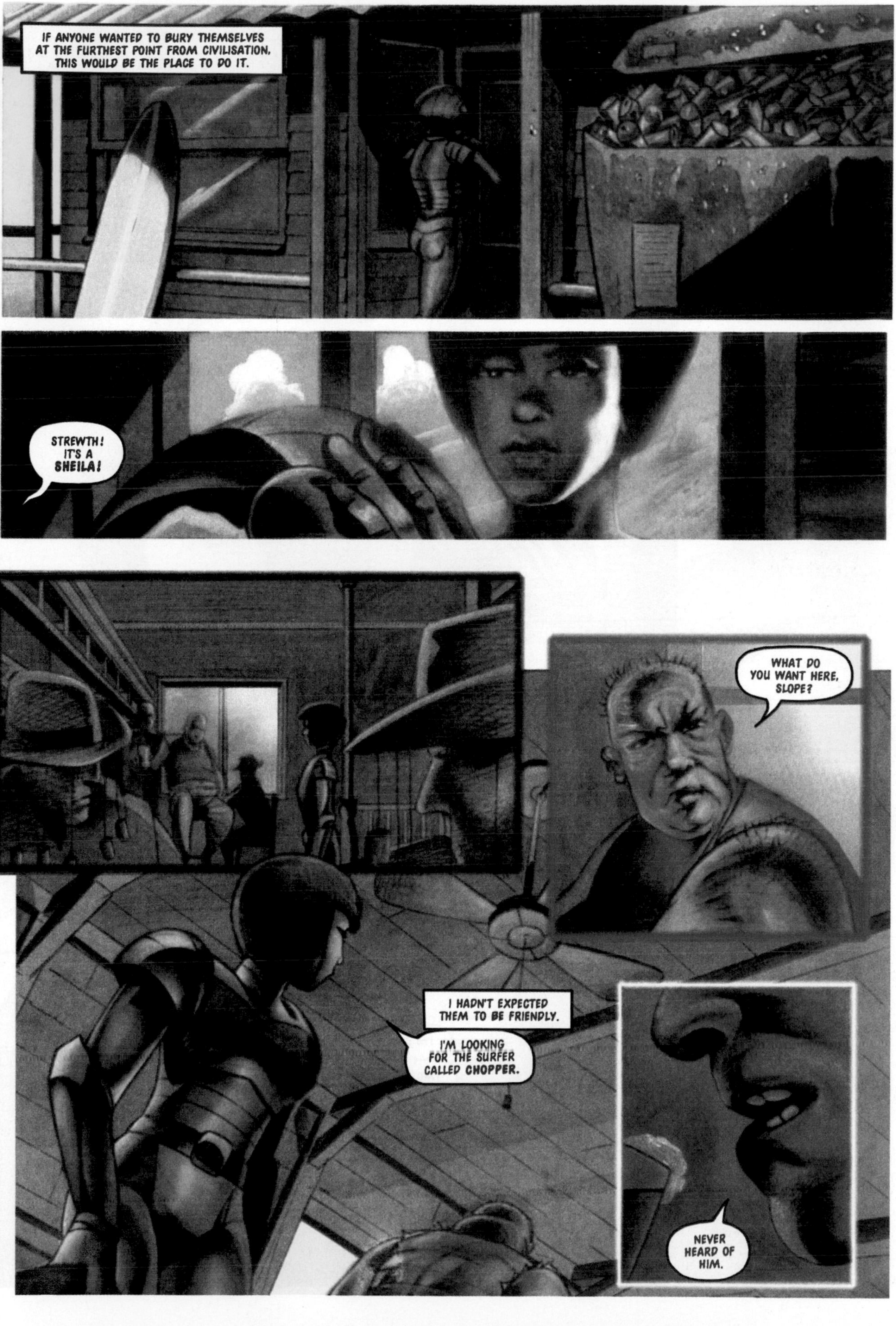
IF ANYONE WANTED TO BURY THEMSELVES AT THE FURTHEST POINT FROM CIVILISATION, THIS WOULD BE THE PLACE TO DO IT.
STREWTH! IT'S A SHEILA!
WHAT DO YOU WANT HERE, SLOPE?
I HADN'T EXPECTED THEM TO BE FRIENDLY.
I'M LOOKING FOR THE SURFER CALLED CHOPPER.
NEVER HEARD OF HIM.

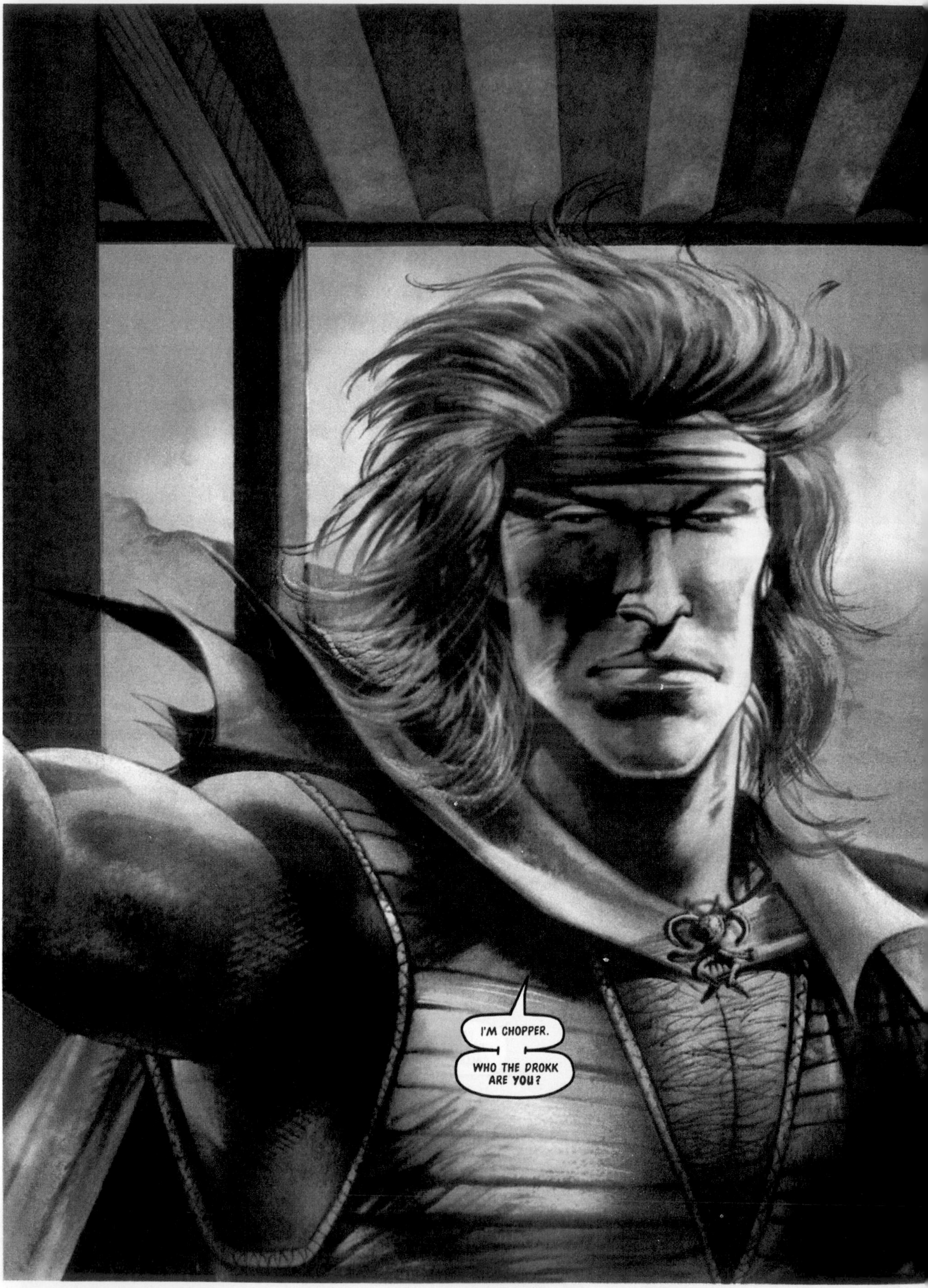
I'M CHOPPER.
WHO THE DROKK ARE YOU?

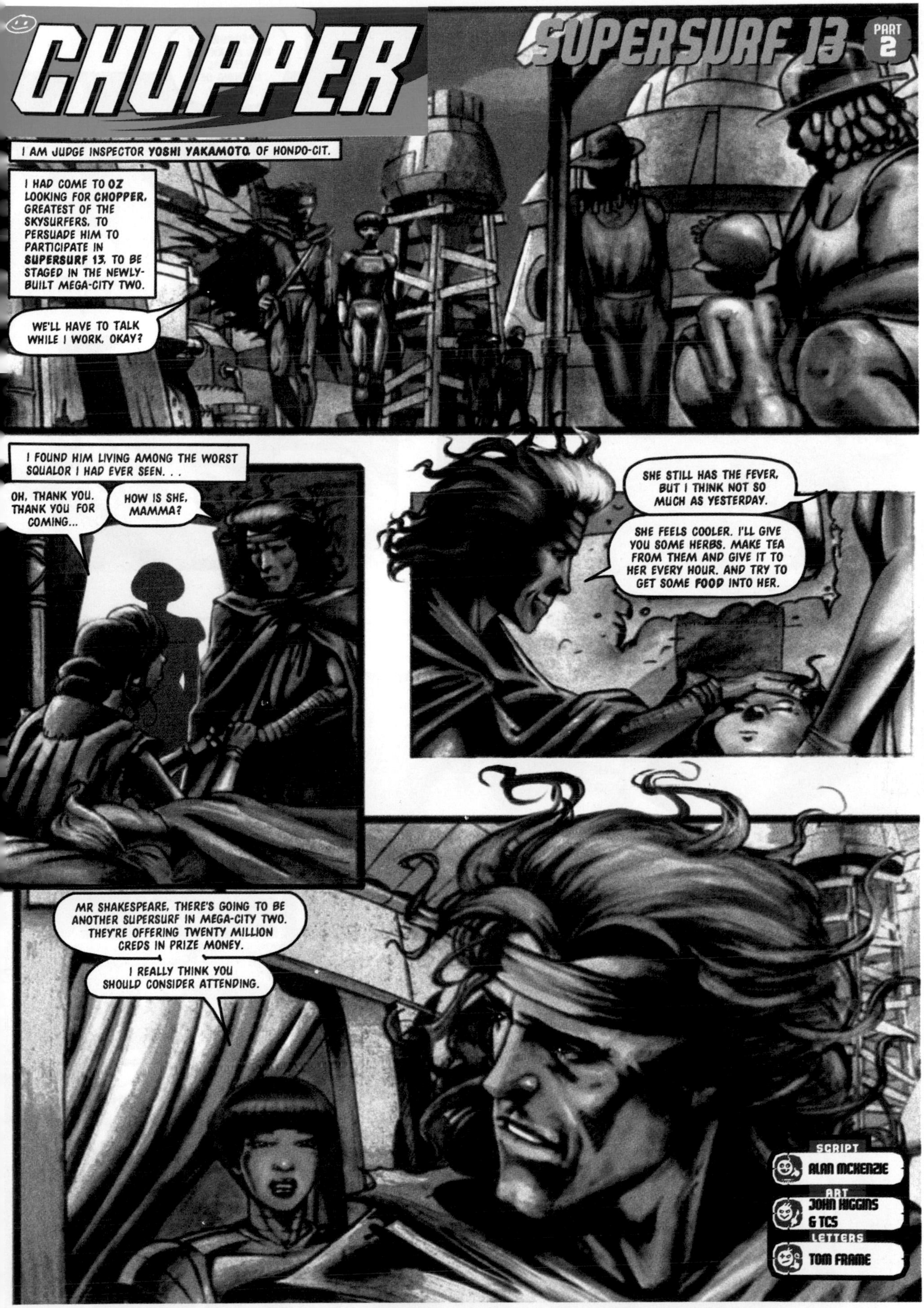
CHOPPER
SUPERSURF 13
PART 2
I AM JUDGE INSPECTOR YOSHI YAKAMOTO, OF HONDO-CIT.
I HAD COME TO OZ LOOKING FOR CHOPPER, GREATEST OF THE SKYSURFERS, TO PERSUADE HIM TO PARTICIPATE IN SUPERSURF 13, TO BE STAGED IN THE NEWLY-BUILT MEGA-CITY TWO.
WE'LL HAVE TO TALK WHILE I WORK, OKAY?
I FOUND HIM LIVING AMONG THE WORST SQUALOR I HAD EVER SEEN. . .
OH, THANK YOU. THANK YOU FOR COMING...
HOW IS SHE, MAMMA?
SHE STILL HAS THE FEVER, BUT I THINK NOT SO MUCH AS YESTERDAY.
SHE FEELS COOLER. I'LL GIVE YOU SOME HERBS. MAKE TEA FROM THEM AND GIVE IT TO HER EVERY HOUR. AND TRY TO GET SOME FOOD INTO HER.
MR SHAKESPEARE, THERE'S GOING TO BE ANOTHER SUPERSURF IN MEGA-CITY TWO. THEY'RE OFFERING TWENTY MILLION CREDS IN PRIZE MONEY.
I REALLY THINK YOU SHOULD CONSIDER ATTENDING.
SCRIPT
ALAN MCKENZIE
ART
JOHN HIGGINS
& TCS
LETTERS
TOM FRAME

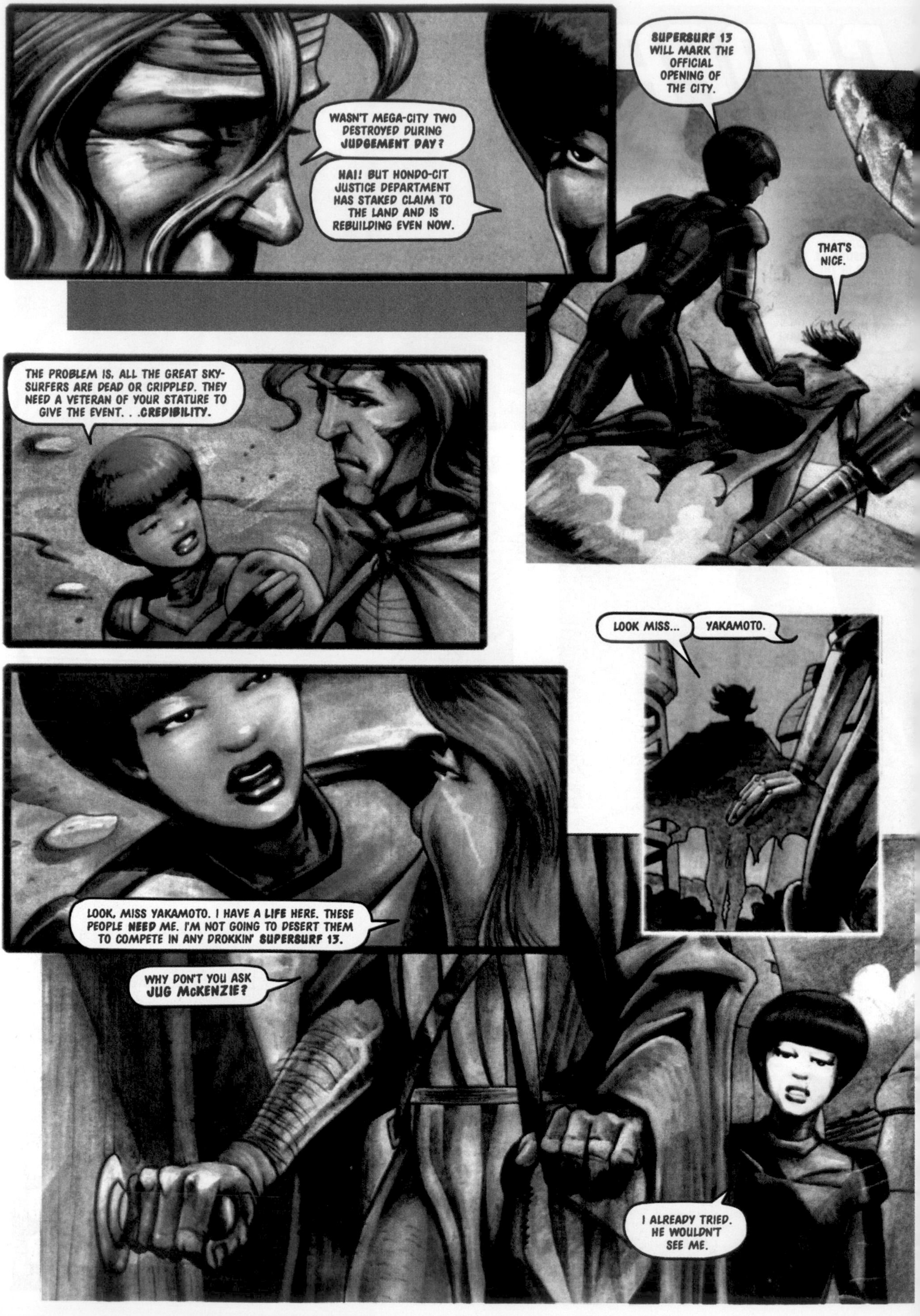
WASN'T MEGA-CITY TWO DESTROYED DURING JUDGEMENT DAY?
HAI! BUT HONDO-CIT JUSTICE DEPARTMENT HAS STAKED CLAIM TO THE LAND AND IS REBUILDING EVEN NOW.
SUPERSURF 13 WILL MARK THE OFFICIAL OPENING OF THE CITY.
THAT'S NICE.
THE PROBLEM IS, ALL THE GREAT SKY-SURFERS ARE DEAD OR CRIPPLED. THEY NEED A VETERAN OF YOUR STATURE TO GIVE THE EVENT. . .CREDIBILITY.
LOOK MISS...
YAKAMOTO.
LOOK, MISS YAKAMOTO. I HAVE A LIFE HERE. THESE PEOPLE NEED ME. I'M NOT GOING TO DESERT THEM TO COMPETE IN ANY DROKKIN' SUPERSURF 13.
WHY DON'T YOU ASK JUG McKENZIE?
I ALREADY TRIED. HE WOULDN'T SEE ME.

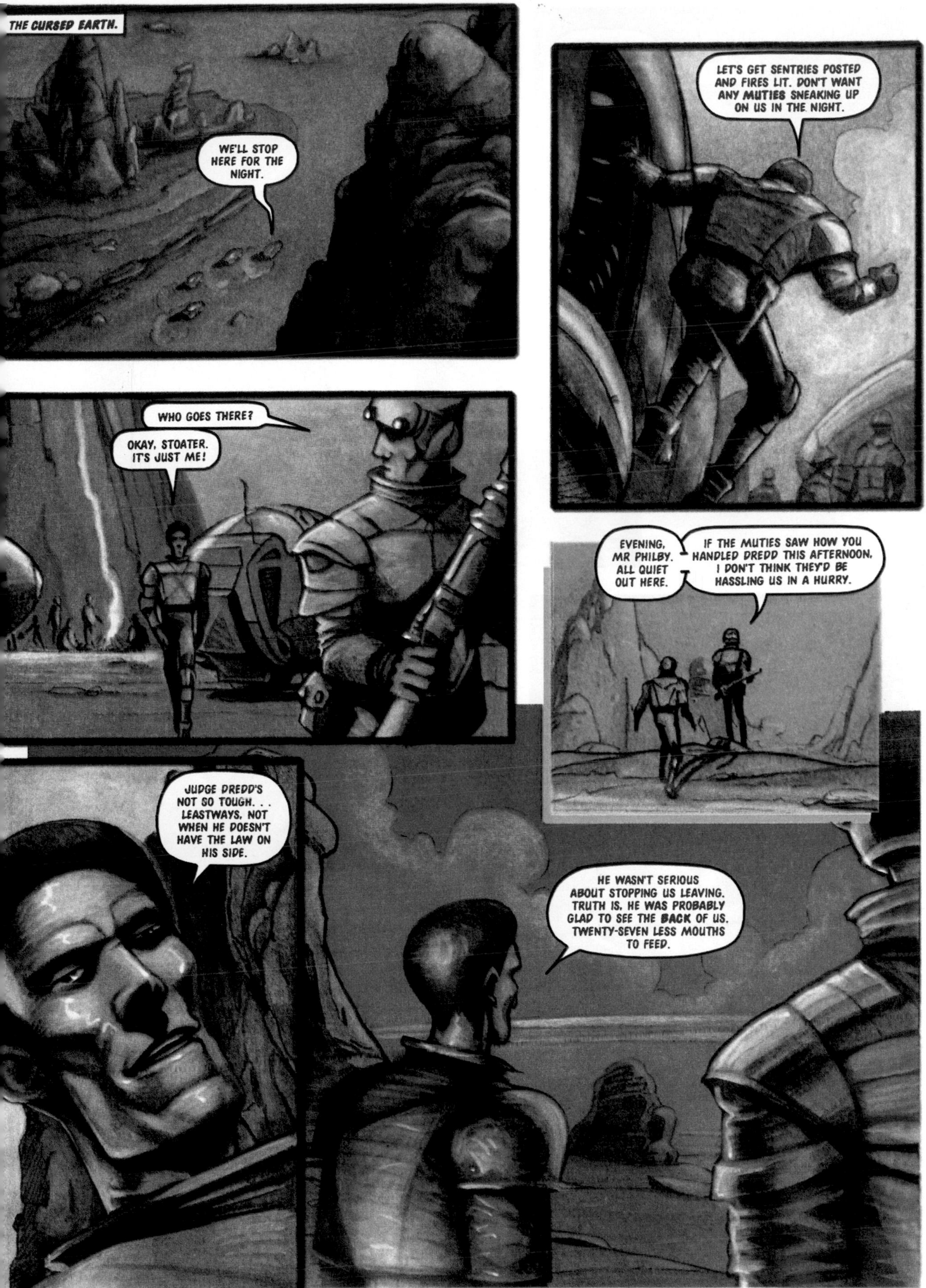
THE CURSED EARTH.
WE'LL STOP HERE FOR THE NIGHT.
LET'S GET SENTRIES POSTED AND FIRES LIT. DON'T WANT ANY MUTIES SNEAKING UP ON US IN THE NIGHT.
WHO GOES THERE?
OKAY, STOATER. IT'S JUST ME!
EVENING, MR PHILBY. ALL QUIET OUT HERE.
IF THE MUTIES SAW HOW YOU HANDLED DREDD THIS AFTERNOON, I DON'T THINK THEY'D BE HASSLING US IN A HURRY.
JUDGE DREDD'S NOT SO TOUGH. . . LEASTWAYS, NOT WHEN HE DOESN'T HAVE THE LAW ON HIS SIDE.
HE WASN'T SERIOUS ABOUT STOPPING US LEAVING. TRUTH IS, HE WAS PROBABLY GLAD TO SEE THE BACK OF US. TWENTY-SEVEN LESS MOUTHS TO FEED.

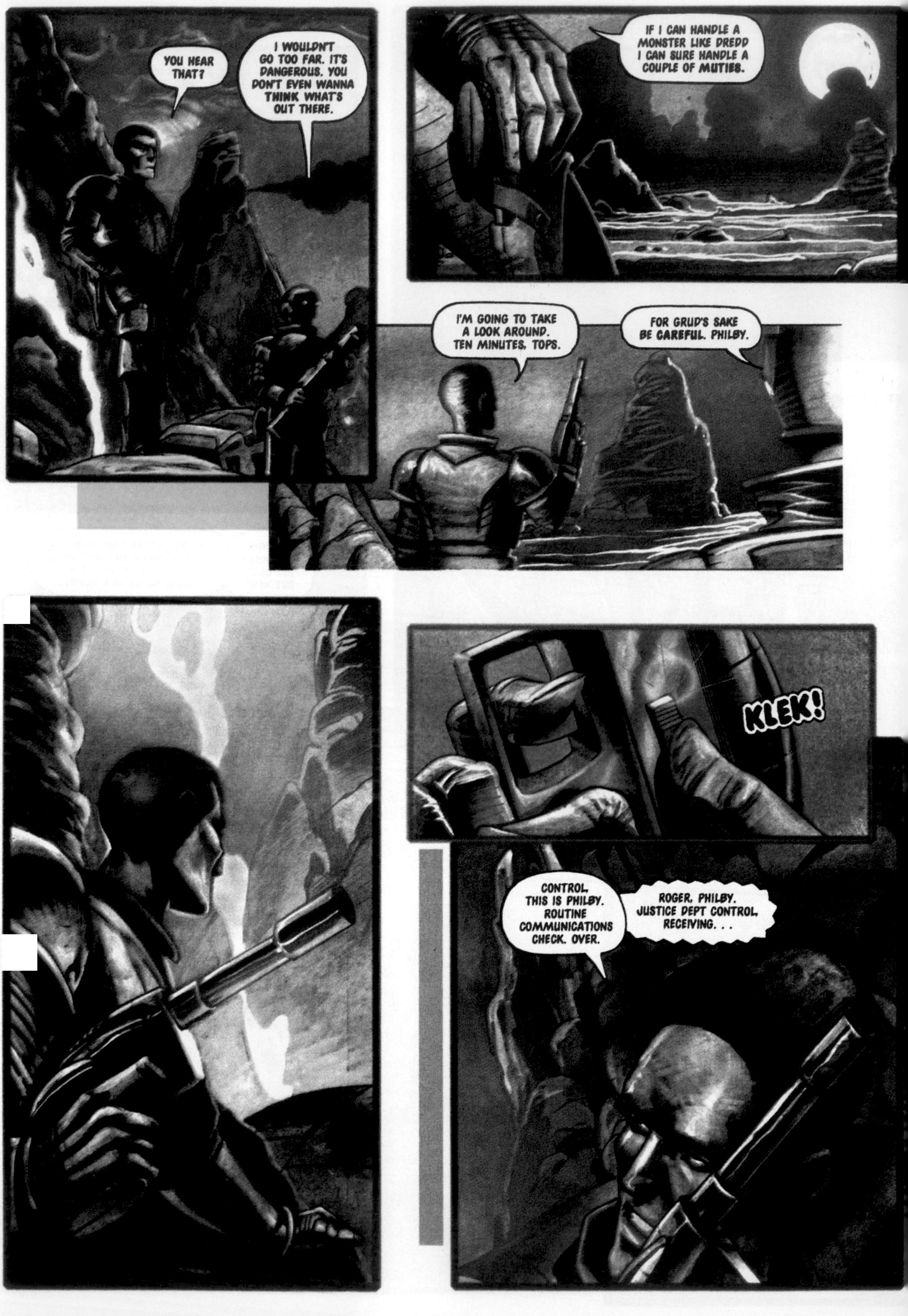
YOU HEAR THAT?
I WOULDN'T GO TOO FAR. IT'S DANGEROUS. YOU DON'T EVEN WANNA THINK WHAT'S OUT THERE.
IF I CAN HANDLE A MONSTER LIKE DREDD I CAN SURE HANDLE A COUPLE OF MUTIES.
I'M GOING TO TAKE A LOOK AROUND. TEN MINUTES, TOPS.
FOR GRUD'S SAKE BE CAREFUL, PHILBY.
KLEK!
CONTROL, THIS IS PHILBY. ROUTINE COMMUNICATIONS CHECK. OVER.
ROGER, PHILBY. JUSTICE DEPT CONTROL, RECEIVING. . .

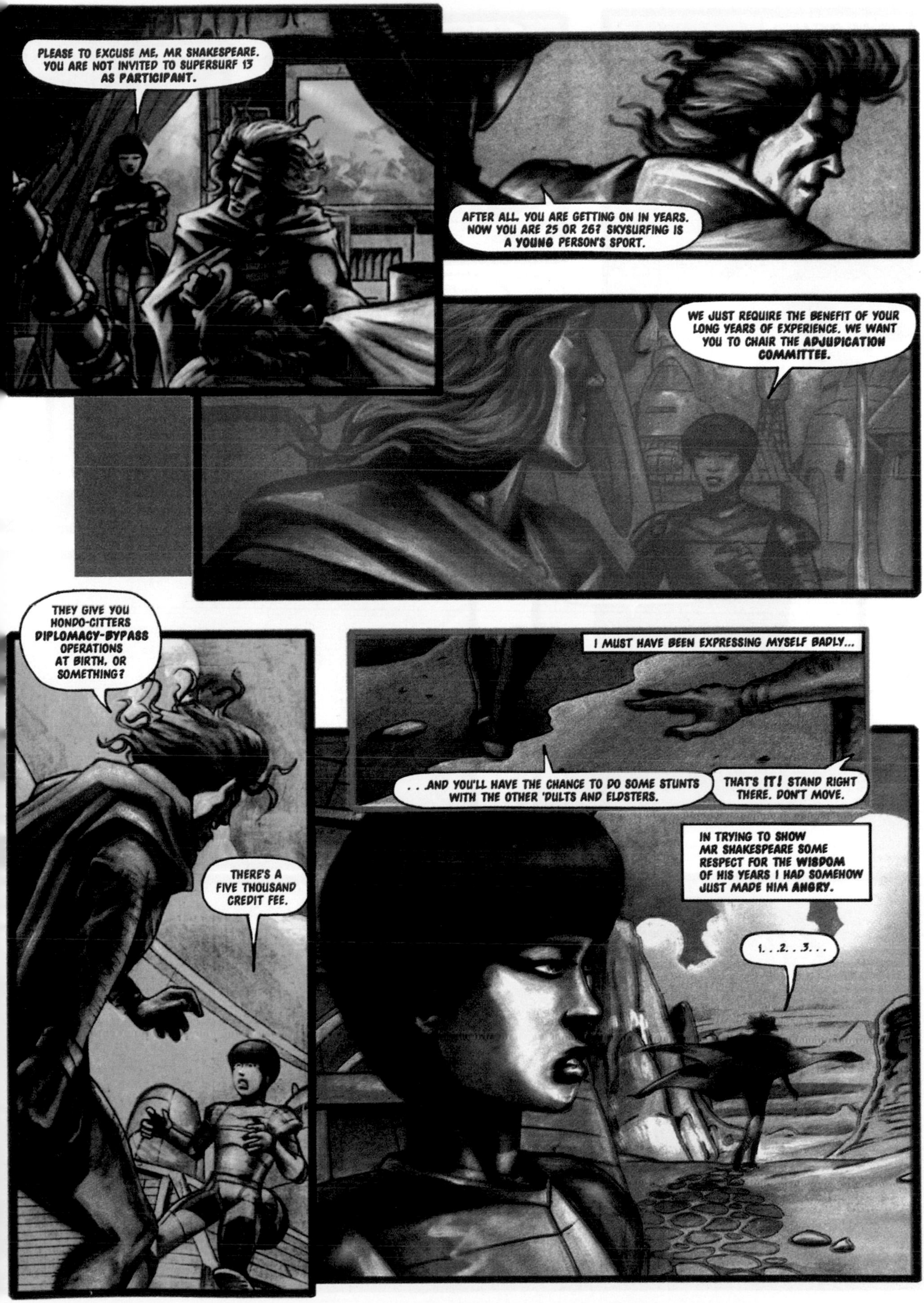

PLEASE TO EXCUSE ME, MR SHAKESPEARE. YOU ARE NOT INVITED TO SUPERSURF 13 AS PARTICIPANT.
AFTER ALL, YOU ARE GETTING ON IN YEARS. NOW YOU ARE 25 OR 26? SKYSURFING IS A YOUNG PERSON'S SPORT.
WE JUST REQUIRE THE BENEFIT OF YOUR LONG YEARS OF EXPERIENCE. WE WANT YOU TO CHAIR THE ADJUDICATION COMMITTEE.
THEY GIVE YOU HONDO-CITTERS DIPLOMACY-BYPASS OPERATIONS AT BIRTH, OR SOMETHING?
THERE'S A FIVE THOUSAND CREDIT FEE.
I MUST HAVE BEEN EXPRESSING MYSELF BADLY...
. . .AND YOU'LL HAVE THE CHANCE TO DO SOME STUNTS WITH THE OTHER 'DULTS AND ELDSTERS.
THAT'S IT! STAND RIGHT THERE. DON'T MOVE.
IN TRYING TO SHOW MR SHAKESPEARE SOME RESPECT FOR THE WISDOM OF HIS YEARS I HAD SOMEHOW JUST MADE HIM ANGRY.
1. . .2. . .3. . .

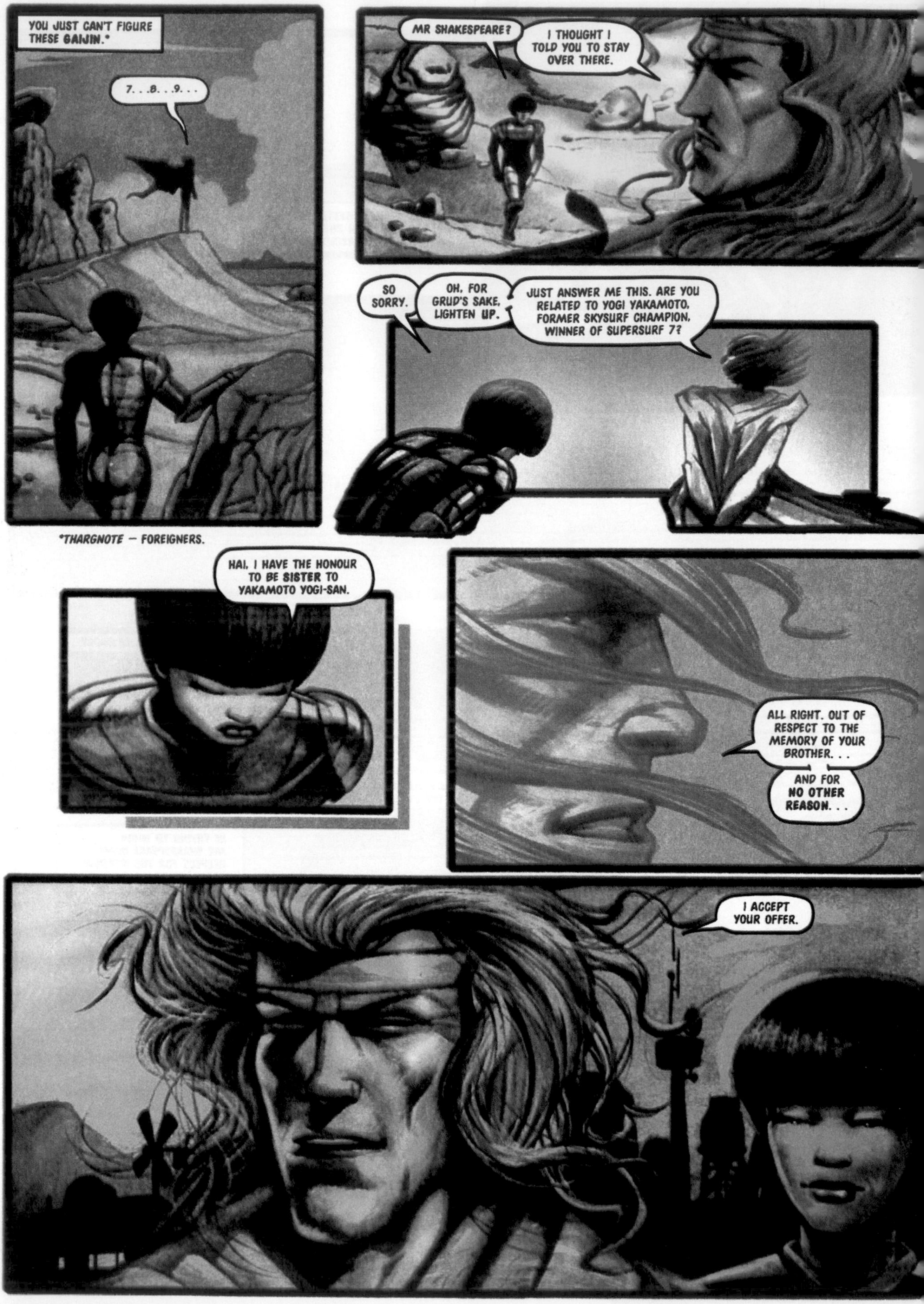
YOU JUST CAN'T FIGURE THESE GAIJIN.*
7. . .8. . .9. . .
MR SHAKESPEARE?
I THOUGHT I TOLD YOU TO STAY OVER THERE.
SO SORRY.
OH, FOR GRUD'S SAKE, LIGHTEN UP.
JUST ANSWER ME THIS. ARE YOU RELATED TO YOGI YAKAMOTO, FORMER SKYSURF CHAMPION, WINNER OF SUPERSURF 7?
*THARGNOTE — FOREIGNERS.
HAI, I HAVE THE HONOUR TO BE SISTER TO YAKAMOTO YOGI-SAN.
ALL RIGHT. OUT OF RESPECT TO THE MEMORY OF YOUR BROTHER. . .
AND FOR NO OTHER REASON. . .
I ACCEPT YOUR OFFER.

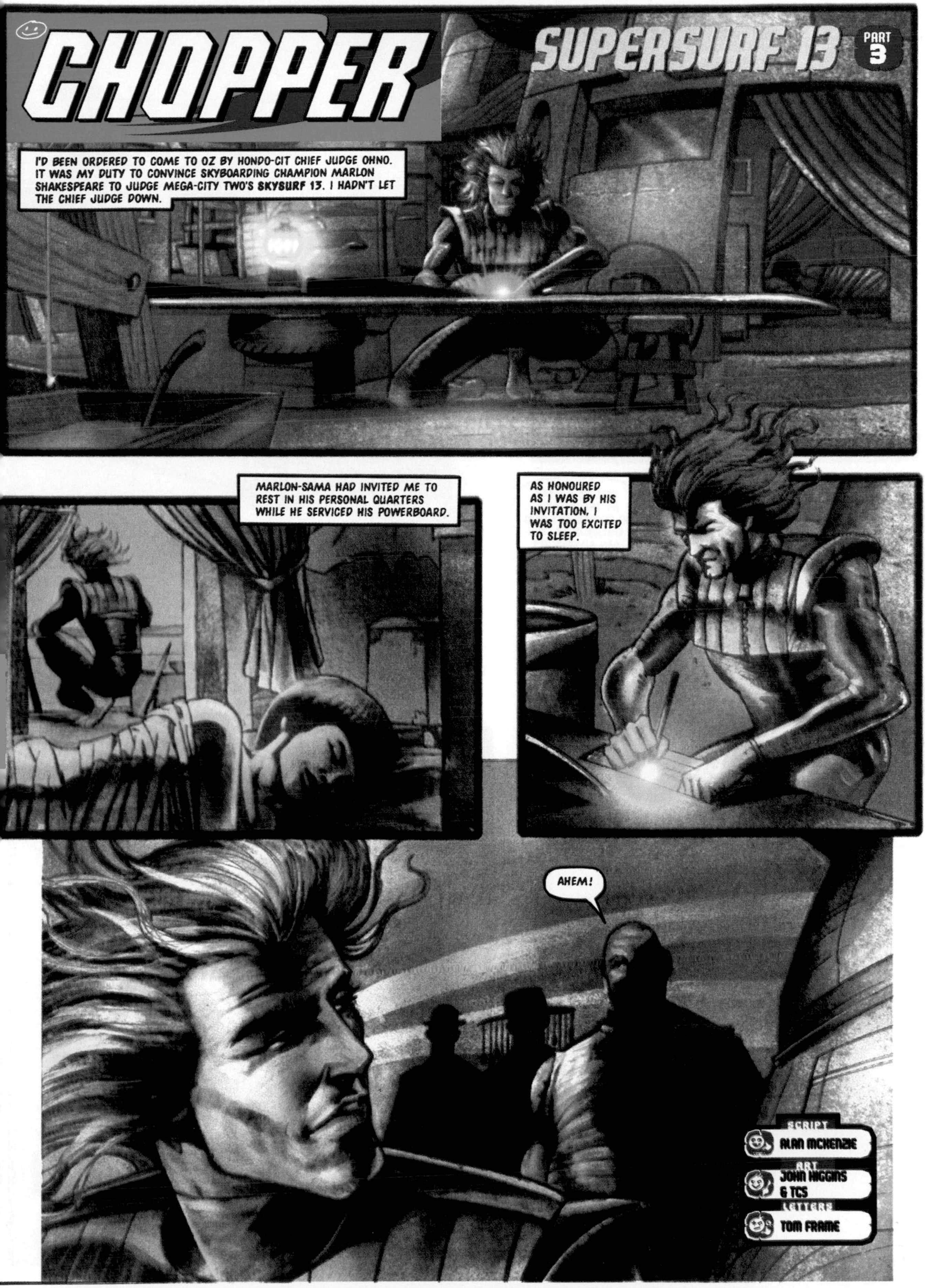
CHOPPER
SUPERSURF 13
PART 3
I'D BEEN ORDERED TO COME TO OZ BY HONDO-CIT CHIEF JUDGE OHNO. IT WAS MY DUTY TO CONVINCE SKYBOARDING CHAMPION MARLON SHAKESPEARE TO JUDGE MEGA-CITY TWO'S SKYSURF 13. I HADN'T LET THE CHIEF JUDGE DOWN.
MARLON-SAMA HAD INVITED ME TO REST IN HIS PERSONAL QUARTERS WHILE HE SERVICED HIS POWERBOARD.
AS HONOURED AS I WAS BY HIS INVITATION, I WAS TOO EXCITED TO SLEEP.
AHEM!
SCRIPT
ALAN MCKENZIE
ART
JOHN HIGGINS & TCS
LETTERS
TOM FRAME

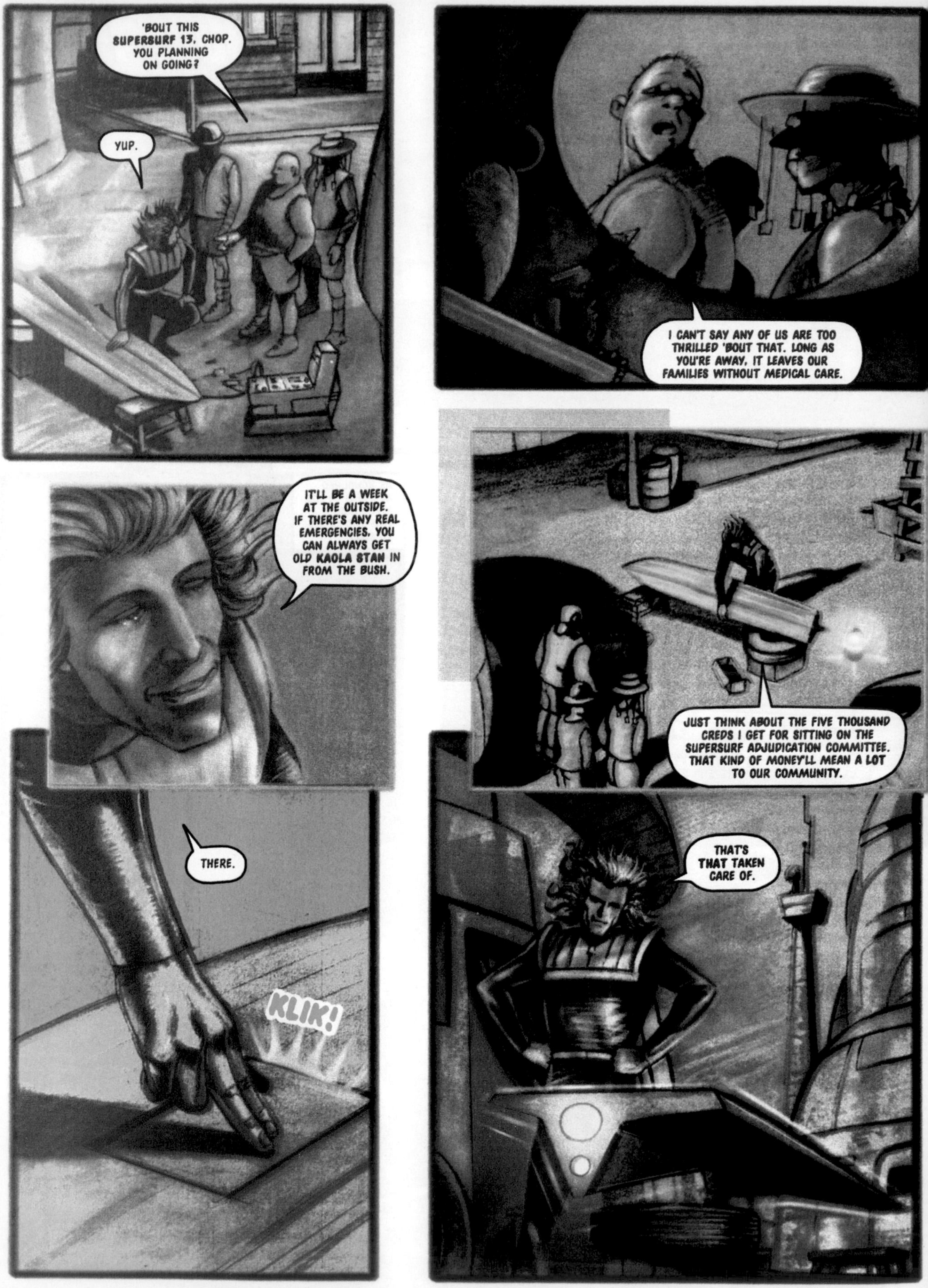
'BOUT THIS SUPERSURF 13, CHOP. YOU PLANNING ON GOING?
YUP.
I CAN'T SAY ANY OF US ARE TOO THRILLED 'BOUT THAT. LONG AS YOU'RE AWAY, IT LEAVES OUR FAMILIES WITHOUT MEDICAL CARE.
IT'LL BE A WEEK AT THE OUTSIDE. IF THERE'S ANY REAL EMERGENCIES, YOU CAN ALWAYS GET OLD KAOLA STAN IN FROM THE BUSH.
JUST THINK ABOUT THE FIVE THOUSAND CREDS I GET FOR SITTING ON THE SUPERSURF ADJUDICATION COMMITTEE. THAT KIND OF MONEY'LL MEAN A LOT TO OUR COMMUNITY.
THERE.
KLIK!
THAT'S THAT TAKEN CARE OF.

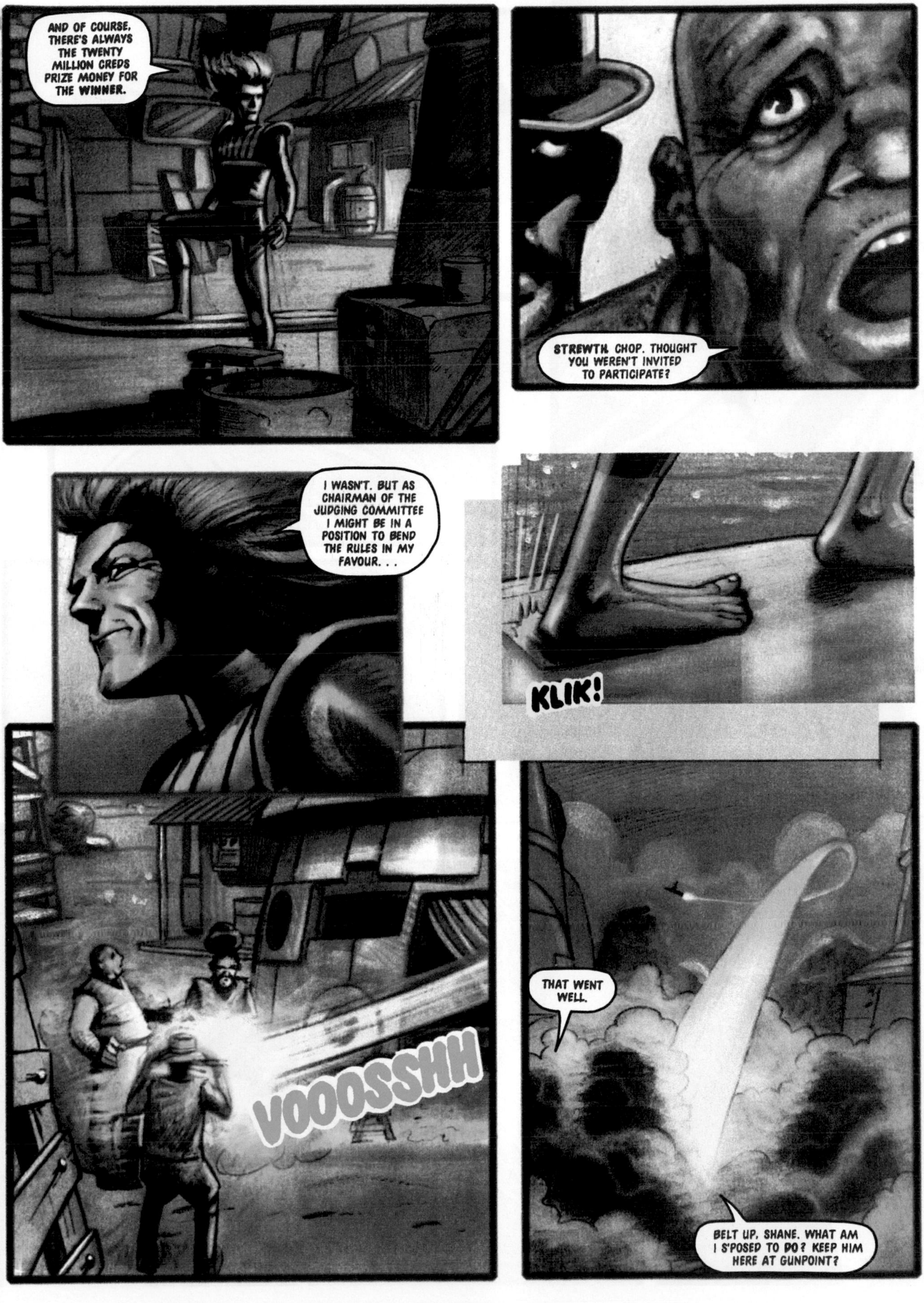
AND OF COURSE, THERE'S ALWAYS THE TWENTY MILLION CREDS PRIZE MONEY FOR THE WINNER.
STREWTH, CHOP. THOUGHT YOU WEREN'T INVITED TO PARTICIPATE?
I WASN'T. BUT AS CHAIRMAN OF THE JUDGING COMMITTEE I MIGHT BE IN A POSITION TO BEND THE RULES IN MY FAVOUR. . .
KLIK!
VOOOSSHH
THAT WENT WELL.
BELT UP, SHANE. WHAT AM I S'POSED TO DO? KEEP HIM HERE AT GUNPOINT?

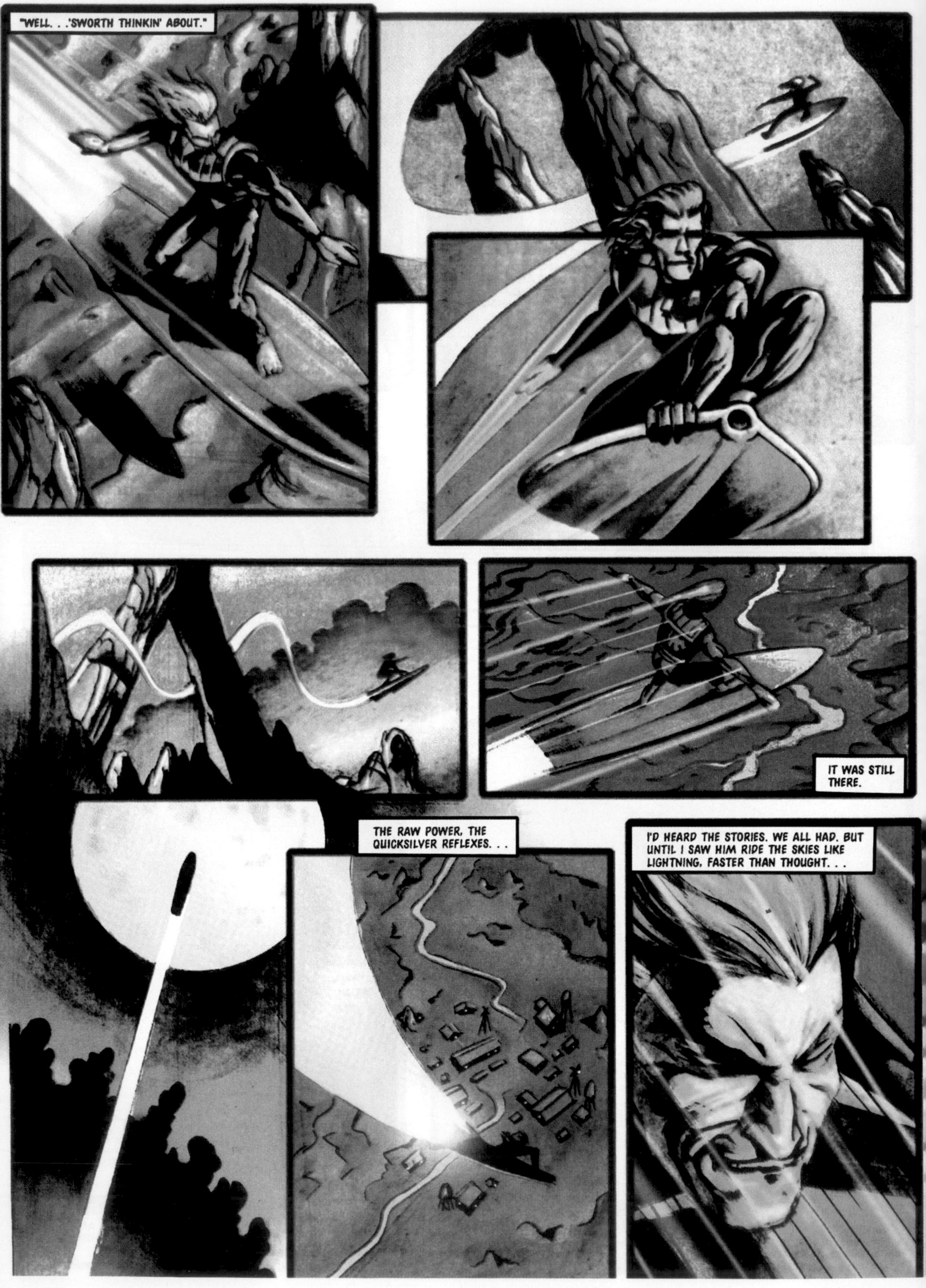
"WELL. . .'SWORTH THINKIN' ABOUT."
IT WAS STILL THERE.
THE RAW POWER, THE QUICKSILVER REFLEXES. . .
I'D HEARD THE STORIES. WE ALL HAD. BUT UNTIL I SAW HIM RIDE THE SKIES LIKE LIGHTNING, FASTER THAN THOUGHT. . .

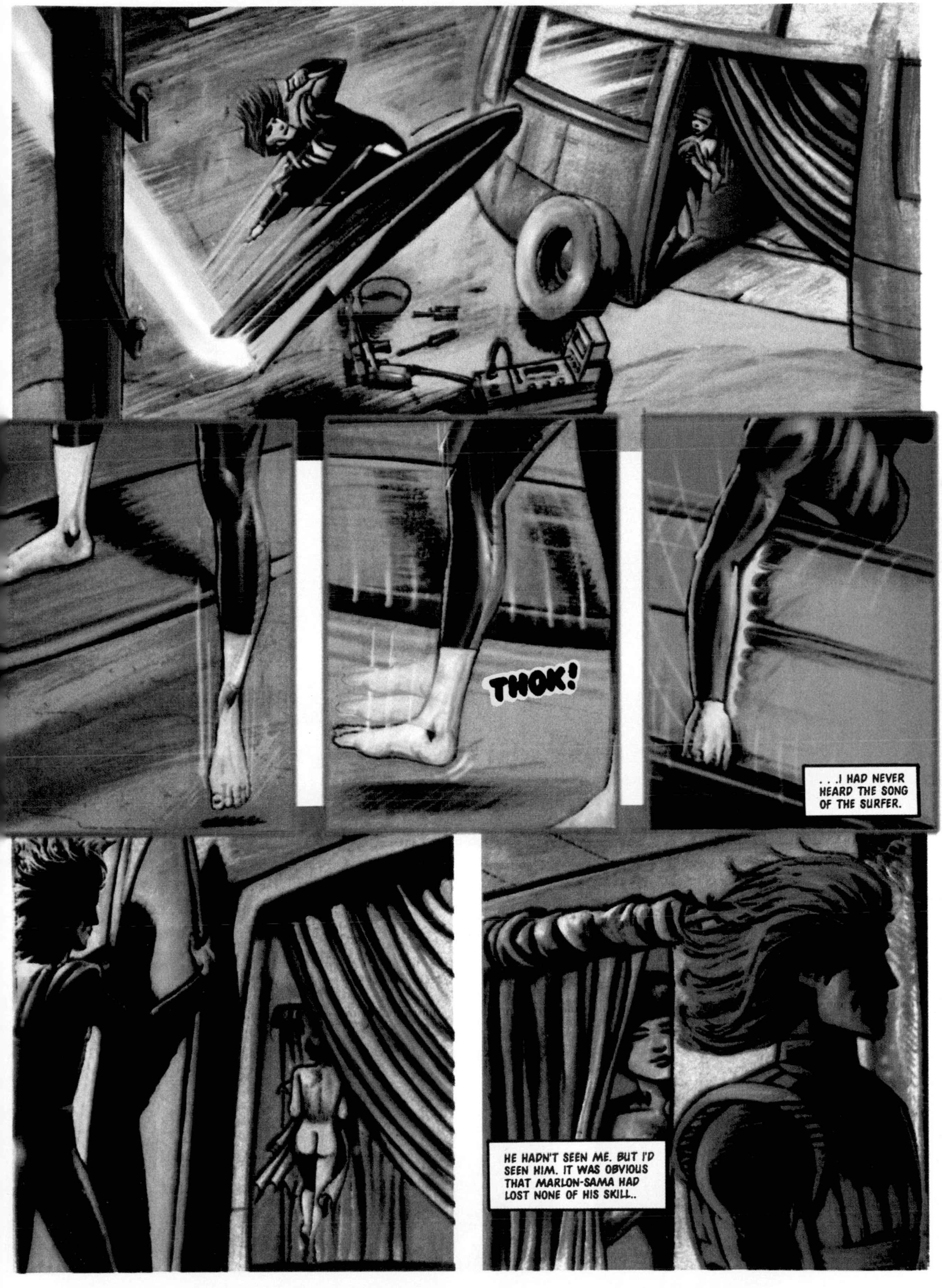
THOK!
. . .I HAD NEVER HEARD THE SONG OF THE SURFER.
HE HADN'T SEEN ME. BUT I'D SEEN HIM. IT WAS OBVIOUS THAT MARLON-SAMA HAD LOST NONE OF HIS SKILL..

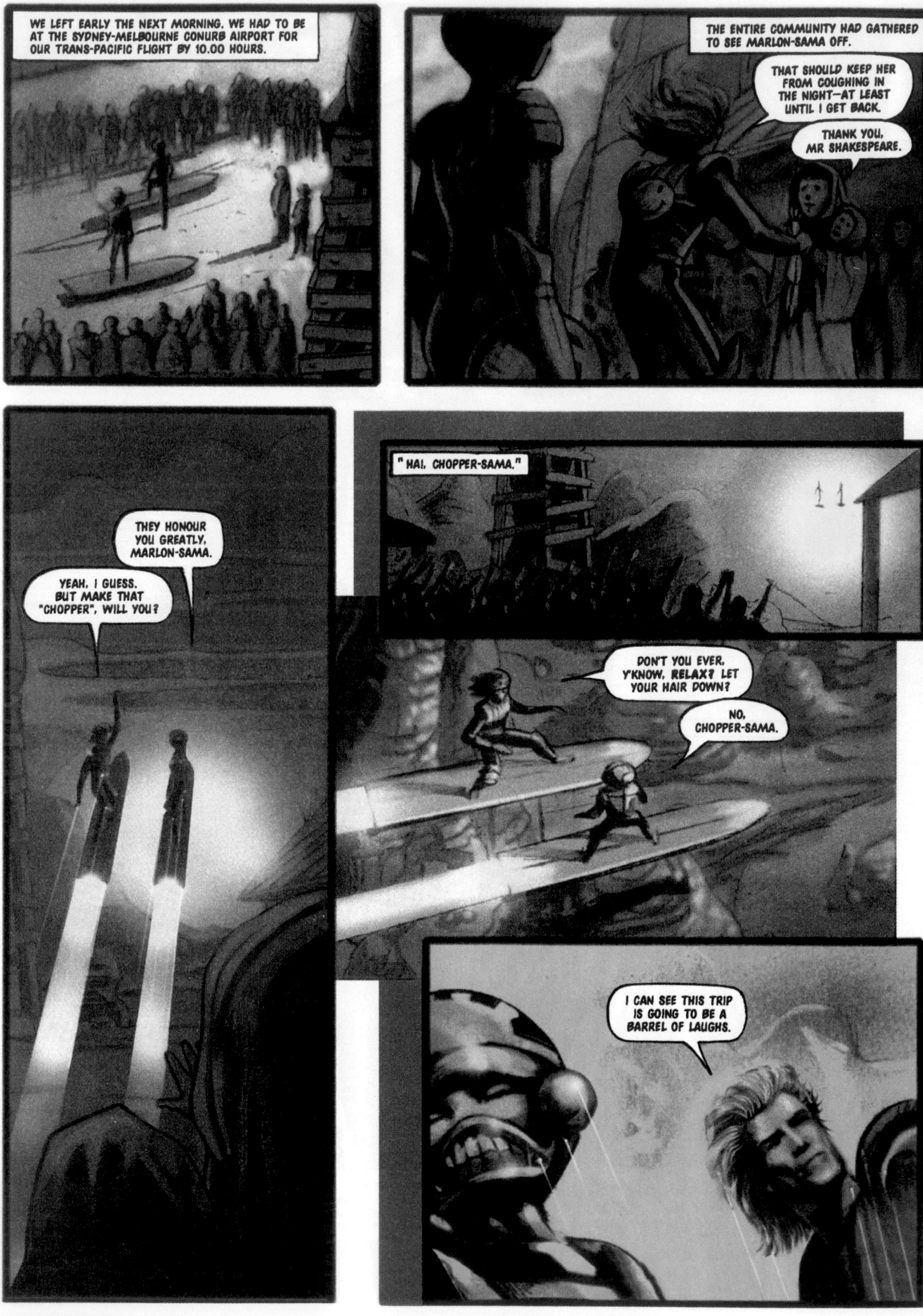

WE LEFT EARLY THE NEXT MORNING. WE HAD TO BE AT THE SYDNEY-MELBOURNE CONURB AIRPORT FOR OUR TRANS-PACIFIC FLIGHT BY 10.00 HOURS.
THE ENTIRE COMMUNITY HAD GATHERED TO SEE MARLON-SAMA OFF.
THAT SHOULD KEEP HER FROM COUGHING IN THE NIGHT—AT LEAST UNTIL I GET BACK.
THANK YOU, MR SHAKESPEARE.
THEY HONOUR YOU GREATLY, MARLON-SAMA.
YEAH, I GUESS. BUT MAKE THAT "CHOPPER", WILL YOU?
" HAI, CHOPPER-SAMA."
DON'T YOU EVER, Y'KNOW, RELAX? LET YOUR HAIR DOWN?
NO, CHOPPER-SAMA.
I CAN SEE THIS TRIP IS GOING TO BE A BARREL OF LAUGHS.

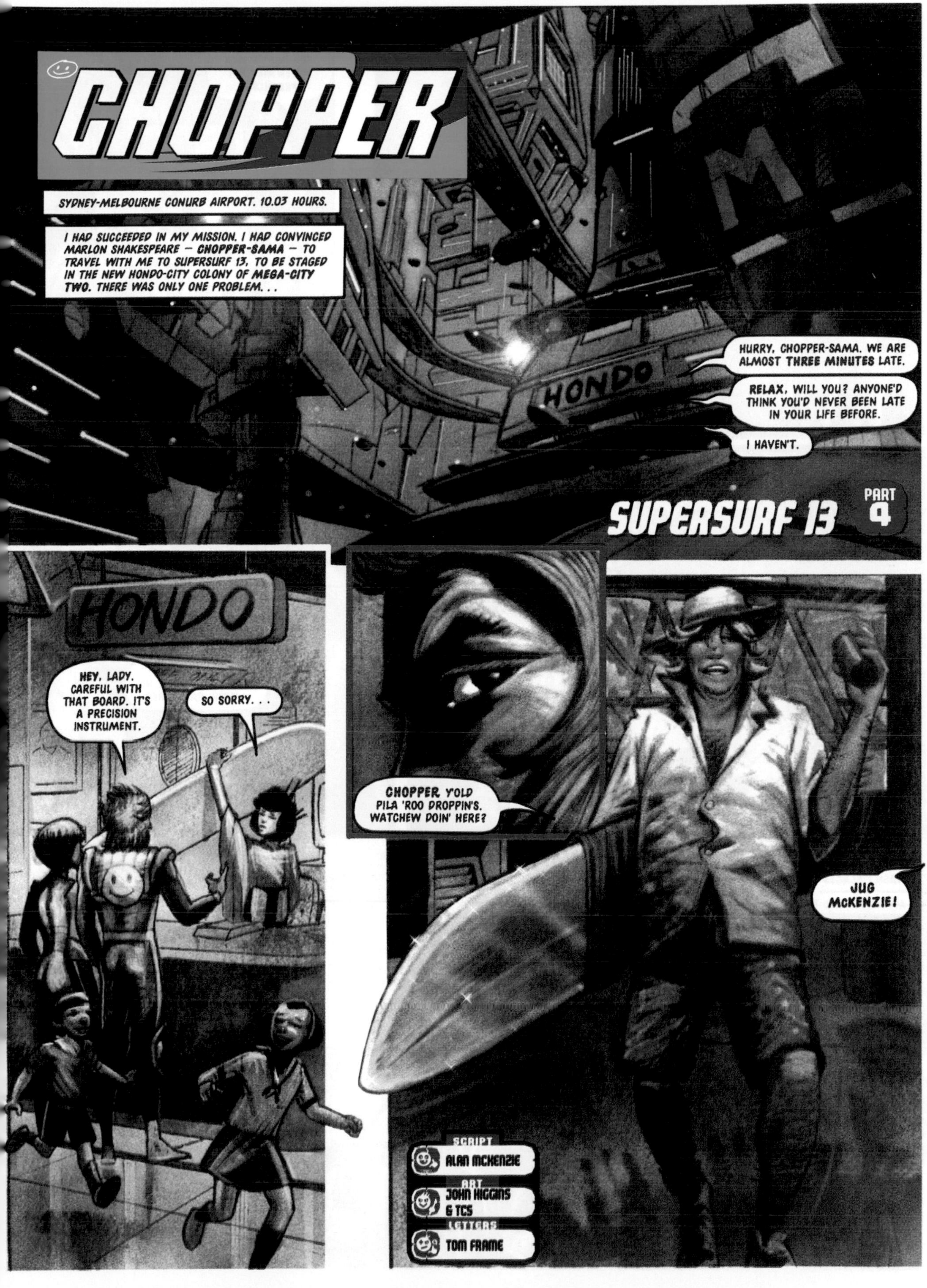
CHOPPER
SYDNEY-MELBOURNE CONURB AIRPORT. 10.03 HOURS.
I HAD SUCCEEDED IN MY MISSION. I HAD CONVINCED MARLON SHAKESPEARE — CHOPPER-SAMA — TO TRAVEL WITH ME TO SUPERSURF 13, TO BE STAGED IN THE NEW HONDO-CITY COLONY OF MEGA-CITY TWO. THERE WAS ONLY ONE PROBLEM. . .
HONDO
HURRY, CHOPPER-SAMA. WE ARE ALMOST THREE MINUTES LATE.
RELAX, WILL YOU? ANYONE'D THINK YOU'D NEVER BEEN LATE IN YOUR LIFE BEFORE.
I HAVEN'T.
SUPERSURF 13
PART 4
HONDO
HEY, LADY. CAREFUL WITH THAT BOARD. IT'S A PRECISION INSTRUMENT.
SO SORRY. . .
CHOPPER YOLD PILA 'ROO DROPPIN'S. WATCHEW DOIN' HERE?
JUG McKENZIE!
SCRIPT
ALAN McKENZIE
ART
JOHN HIGGINS & TCS
LETTERS
TOM FRAME

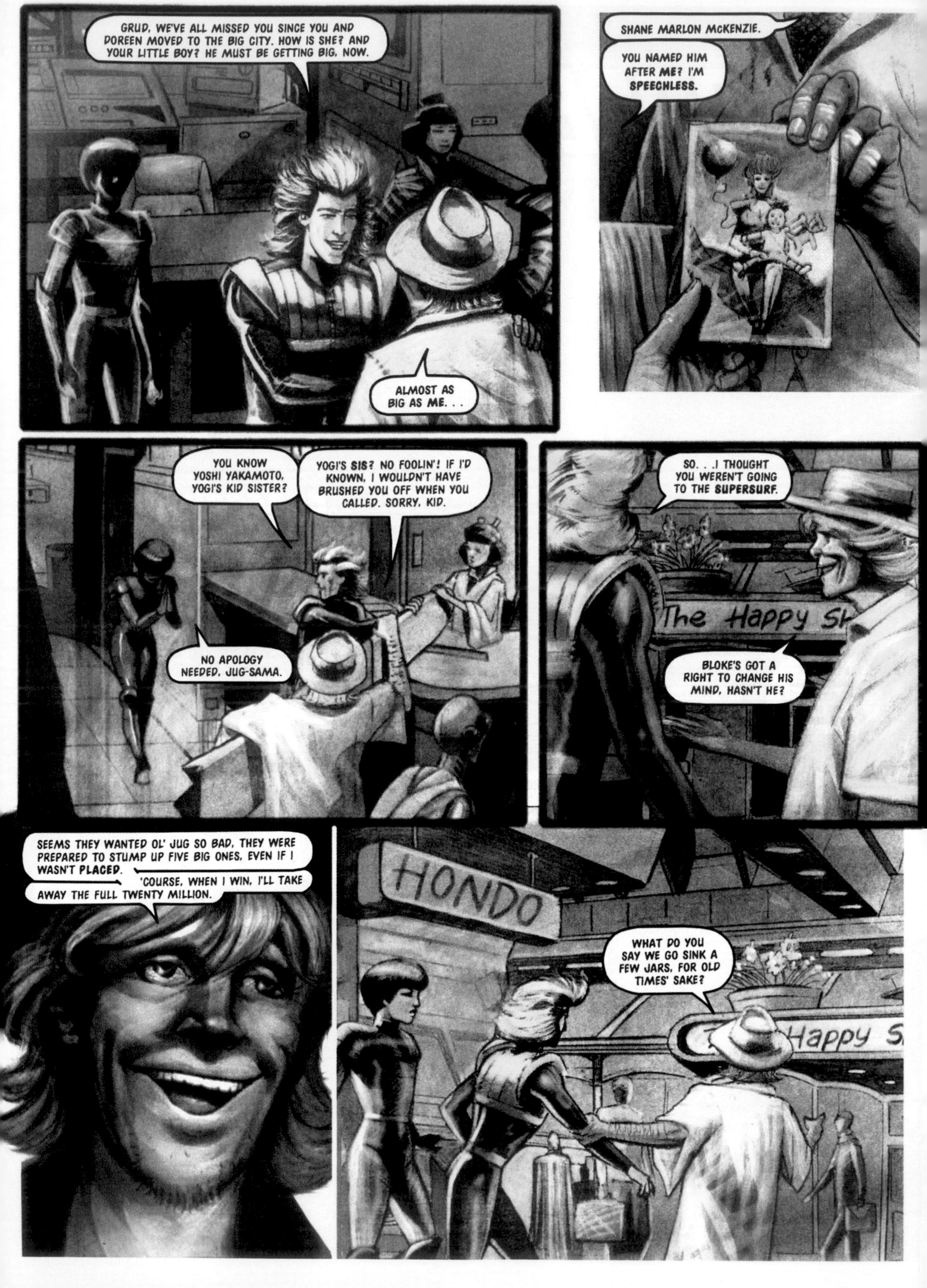
GRUD, WE'VE ALL MISSED YOU SINCE YOU AND DOREEN MOVED TO THE BIG CITY. HOW IS SHE? AND YOUR LITTLE BOY? HE MUST BE GETTING BIG, NOW.
ALMOST AS BIG AS ME. . .
SHANE MARLON McKENZIE.
YOU NAMED HIM AFTER ME? I'M SPEECHLESS.
YOU KNOW YOSHI YAKAMOTO, YOGI'S KID SISTER?
YOGI'S SIS? NO FOOLIN'! IF I'D KNOWN, I WOULDN'T HAVE BRUSHED YOU OFF WHEN YOU CALLED. SORRY, KID.
NO APOLOGY NEEDED, JUG-SAMA.
SO. . .I THOUGHT YOU WEREN'T GOING TO THE SUPERSURF.
The Happy S
BLOKE'S GOT A RIGHT TO CHANGE HIS MIND, HASN'T HE?
SEEMS THEY WANTED OL' JUG SO BAD, THEY WERE PREPARED TO STUMP UP FIVE BIG ONES, EVEN IF I WASN'T PLACED.
'COURSE, WHEN I WIN, I'LL TAKE AWAY THE FULL TWENTY MILLION.
HONDO
WHAT DO YOU SAY WE GO SINK A FEW JARS, FOR OLD TIMES' SAKE?
Happy S

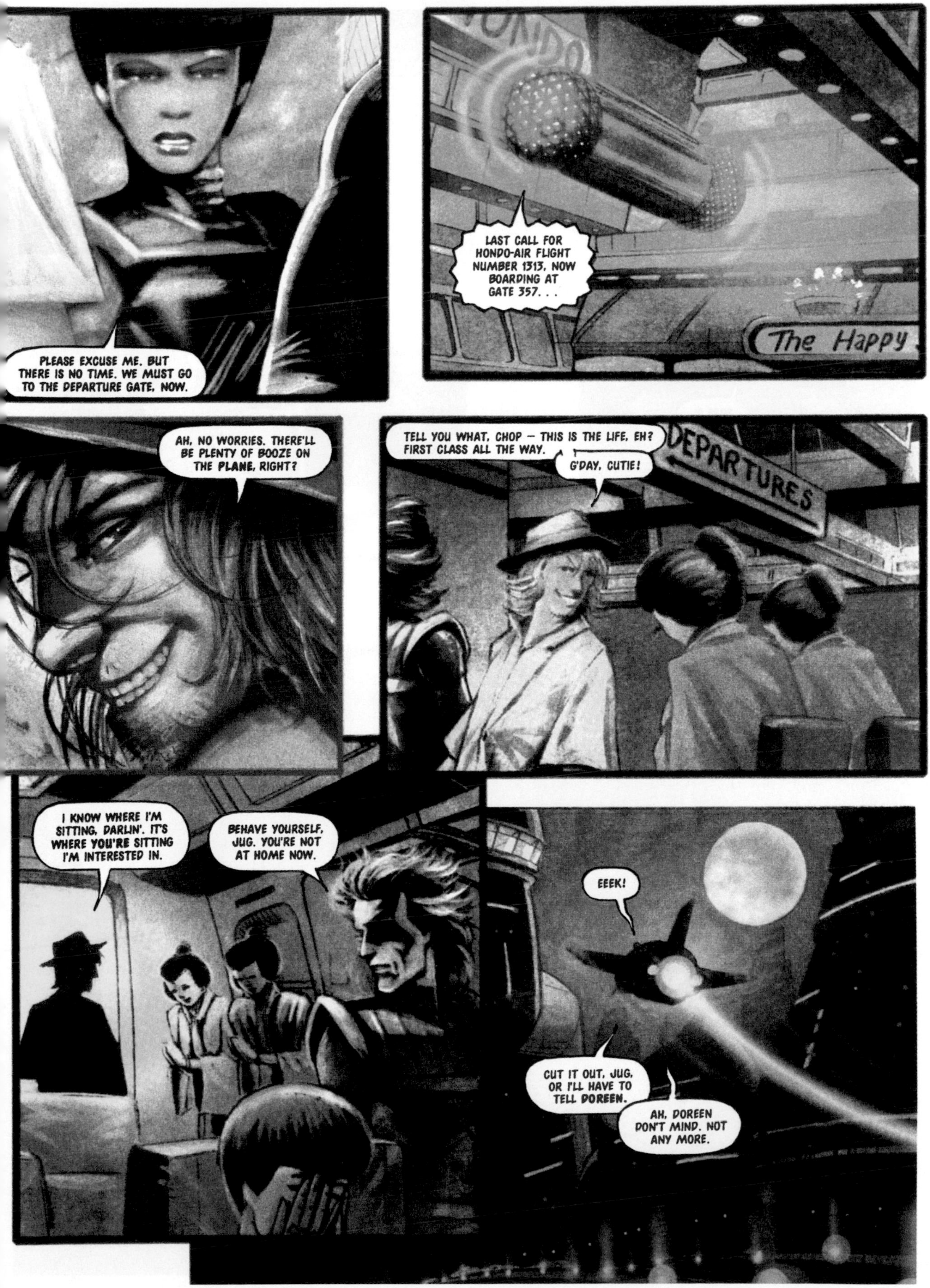
PLEASE EXCUSE ME. BUT THERE IS NO TIME. WE MUST GO TO THE DEPARTURE GATE, NOW.
LAST CALL FOR HONDO-AIR FLIGHT NUMBER 1313, NOW BOARDING AT GATE 357. . .
The Happy
AH, NO WORRIES. THERE'LL BE PLENTY OF BOOZE ON THE PLANE, RIGHT?
TELL YOU WHAT, CHOP — THIS IS THE LIFE, EH? FIRST CLASS ALL THE WAY.
G'DAY, CUTIE!
DEPARTURES
I KNOW WHERE I'M SITTING, DARLIN'. IT'S WHERE YOU'RE SITTING I'M INTERESTED IN.
BEHAVE YOURSELF, JUG. YOU'RE NOT AT HOME NOW.
EEEK!
CUT IT OUT, JUG, OR I'LL HAVE TO TELL DOREEN.
AH, DOREEN DON'T MIND. NOT ANY MORE.

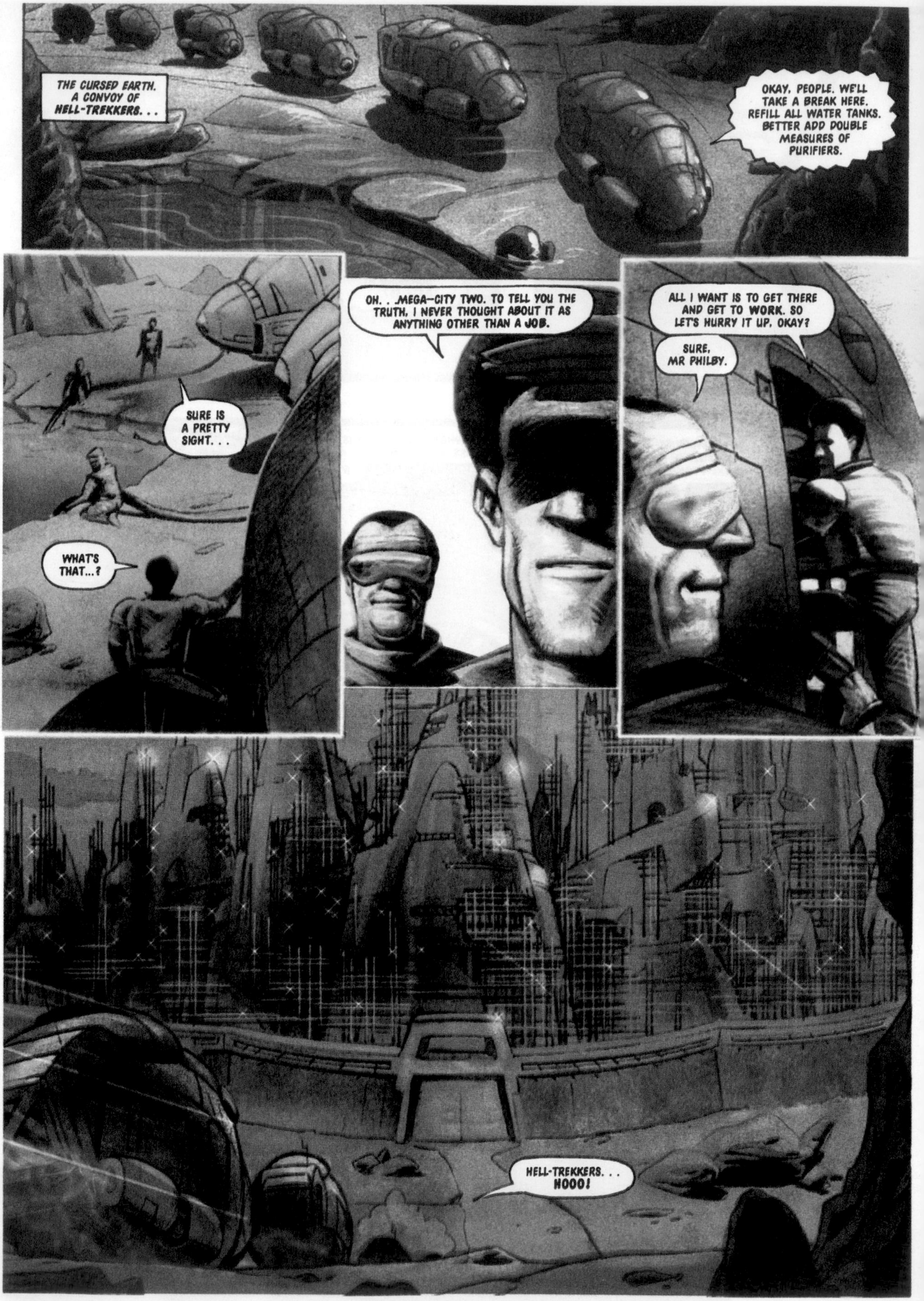
THE CURSED EARTH. A CONVOY OF HELL-TREKKERS. . .
OKAY, PEOPLE. WE'LL TAKE A BREAK HERE. REFILL ALL WATER TANKS. BETTER ADD DOUBLE MEASURES OF PURIFIERS.
SURE IS A PRETTY SIGHT. . .
WHAT'S THAT...?
OH. . .MEGA-CITY TWO. TO TELL YOU THE TRUTH, I NEVER THOUGHT ABOUT IT AS ANYTHING OTHER THAN A JOB.
ALL I WANT IS TO GET THERE AND GET TO WORK. SO LET'S HURRY IT UP, OKAY?
SURE, MR PHILBY.
HELL-TREKKERS. . . HOOO!

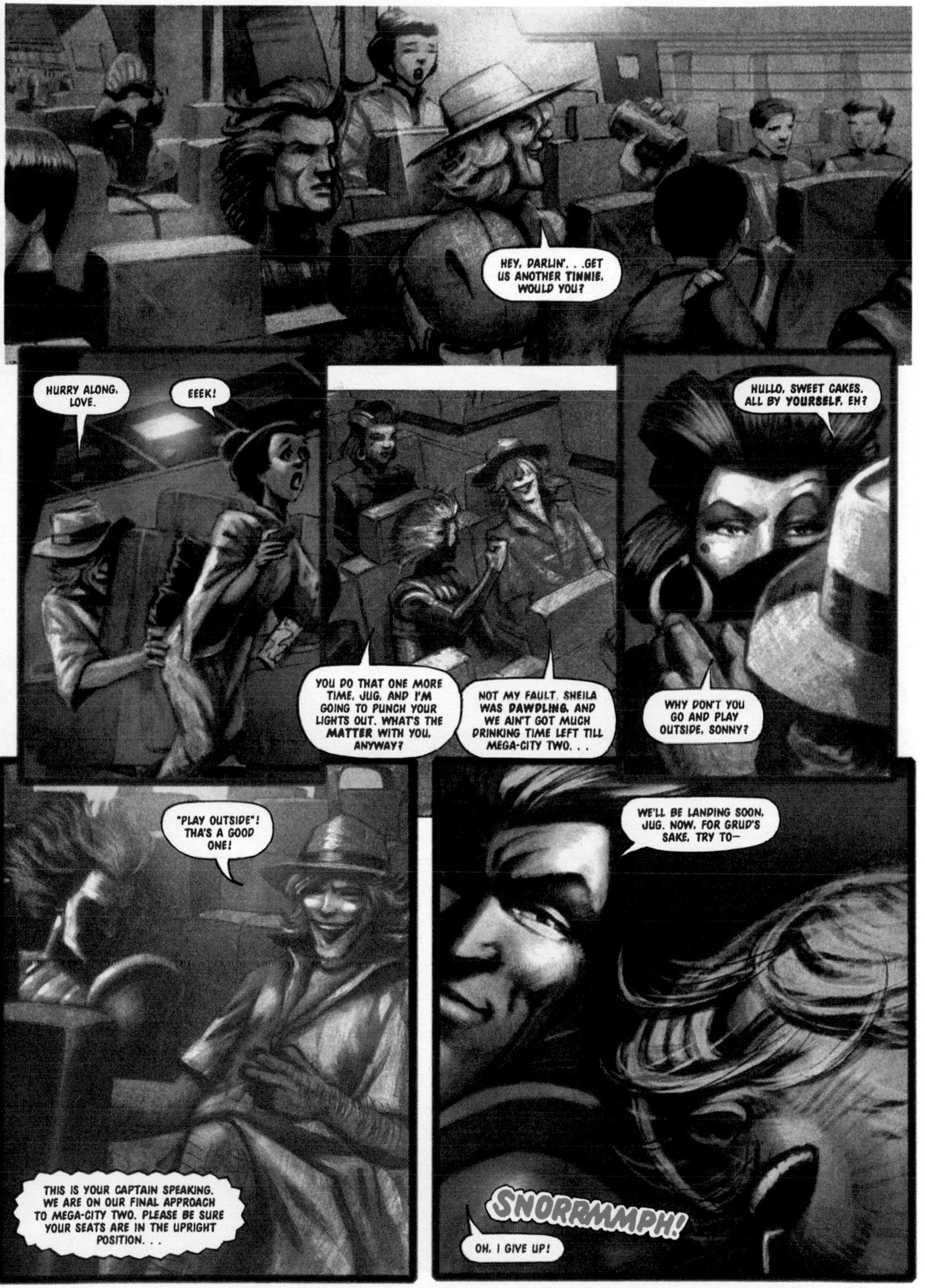
HEY, DARLIN'. . .GET US ANOTHER TINNIE, WOULD YOU?
HURRY ALONG, LOVE.
EEEK!
YOU DO THAT ONE MORE TIME, JUG, AND I'M GOING TO PUNCH YOUR LIGHTS OUT. WHAT'S THE MATTER WITH YOU, ANYWAY?
NOT MY FAULT. SHEILA WAS DAWDLING, AND WE AIN'T GOT MUCH DRINKING TIME LEFT TILL MEGA-CITY TWO. . .
HULLO, SWEET CAKES. ALL BY YOURSELF, EH?
WHY DON'T YOU GO AND PLAY OUTSIDE, SONNY?
"PLAY OUTSIDE"! THA'S A GOOD ONE!
THIS IS YOUR CAPTAIN SPEAKING. WE ARE ON OUR FINAL APPROACH TO MEGA-CITY TWO. PLEASE BE SURE YOUR SEATS ARE IN THE UPRIGHT POSITION. . .
WE'LL BE LANDING SOON, JUG. NOW, FOR GRUD'S SAKE, TRY TO—
SNORRMMPH!
OH, I GIVE UP!

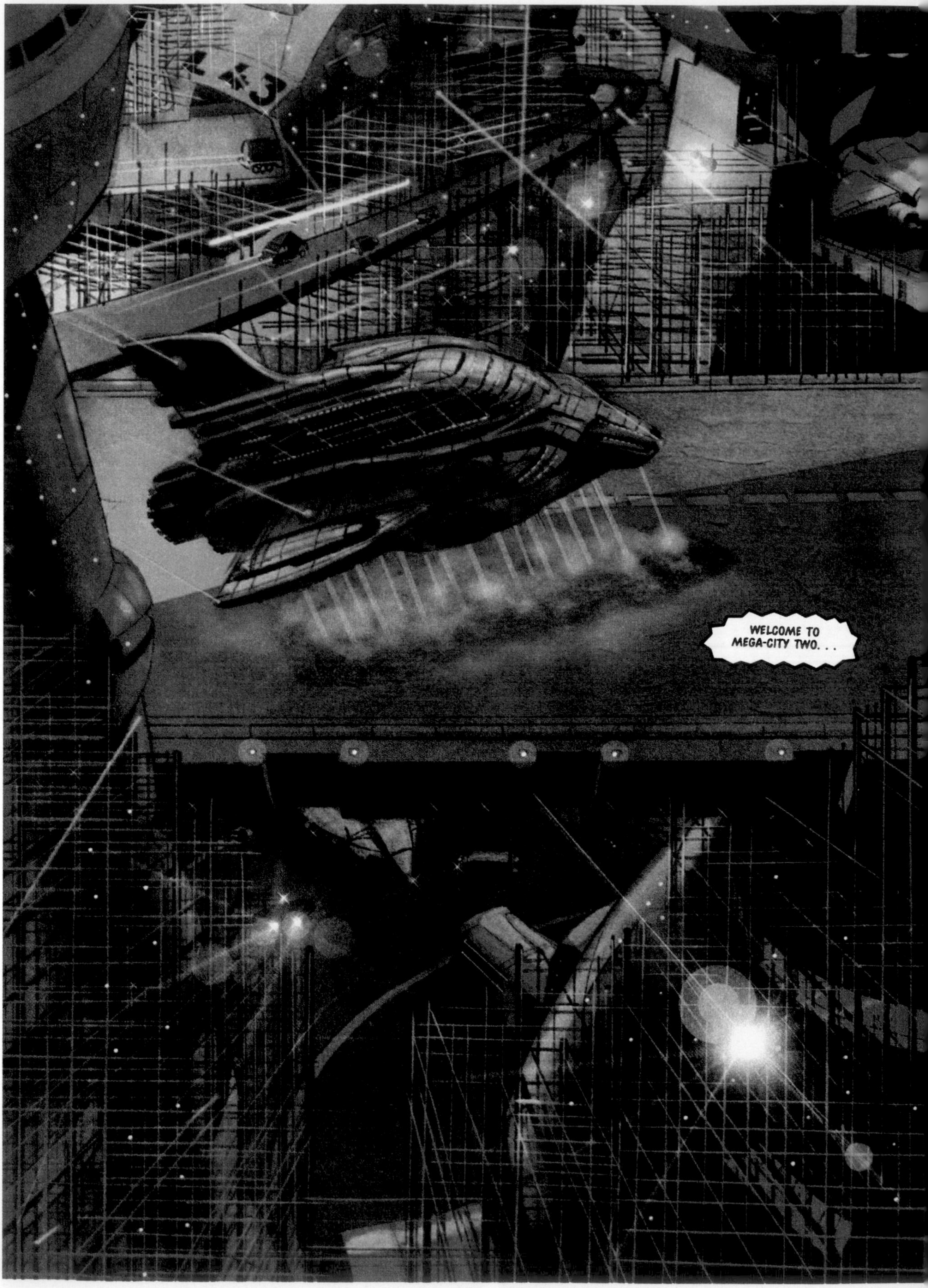
WELCOME TO MEGA-CITY TWO. . .

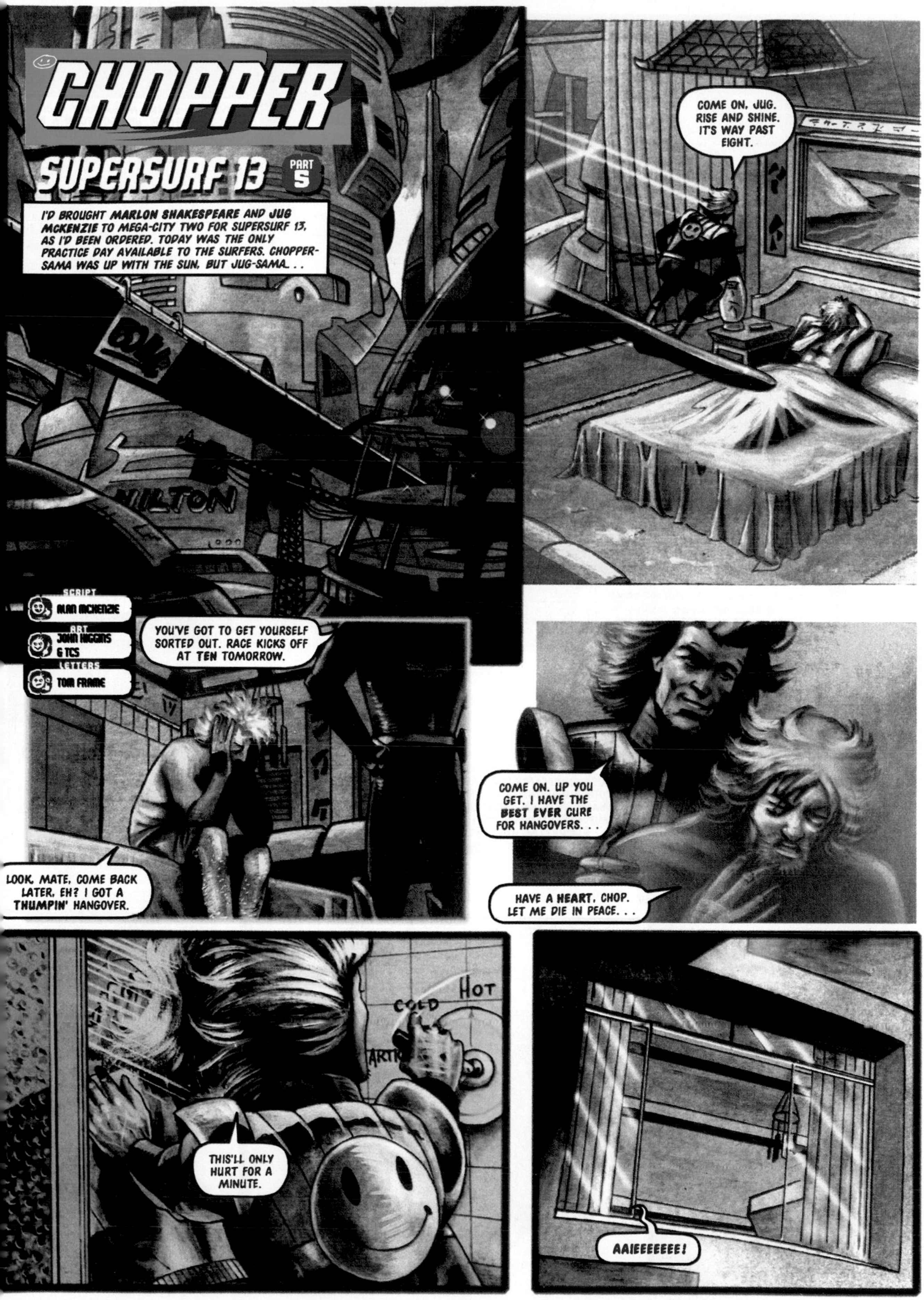
CHOPPER
SUPERSURF 13 PART 5
I'D BROUGHT MARLON SHAKESPEARE AND JUG McKENZIE TO MEGA-CITY TWO FOR SUPERSURF 13, AS I'D BEEN ORDERED. TODAY WAS THE ONLY PRACTICE DAY AVAILABLE TO THE SURFERS. CHOPPER-SAMA WAS UP WITH THE SUN, BUT JUG-SAMA. . .
HILTON
COME ON, JUG. RISE AND SHINE. IT'S WAY PAST EIGHT.
SCRIPT ALAN McKENZIE
ART JOHN HIGGINS & TCS
LETTERS TOM FRAME
YOU'VE GOT TO GET YOURSELF SORTED OUT. RACE KICKS OFF AT TEN TOMORROW.
LOOK, MATE, COME BACK LATER, EH? I GOT A THUMPIN' HANGOVER.
COME ON. UP YOU GET. I HAVE THE BEST EVER CURE FOR HANGOVERS. . .
HAVE A HEART, CHOP. LET ME DIE IN PEACE. . .
HOT
COLD
THIS'LL ONLY HURT FOR A MINUTE.
AAIEEEEEEE!

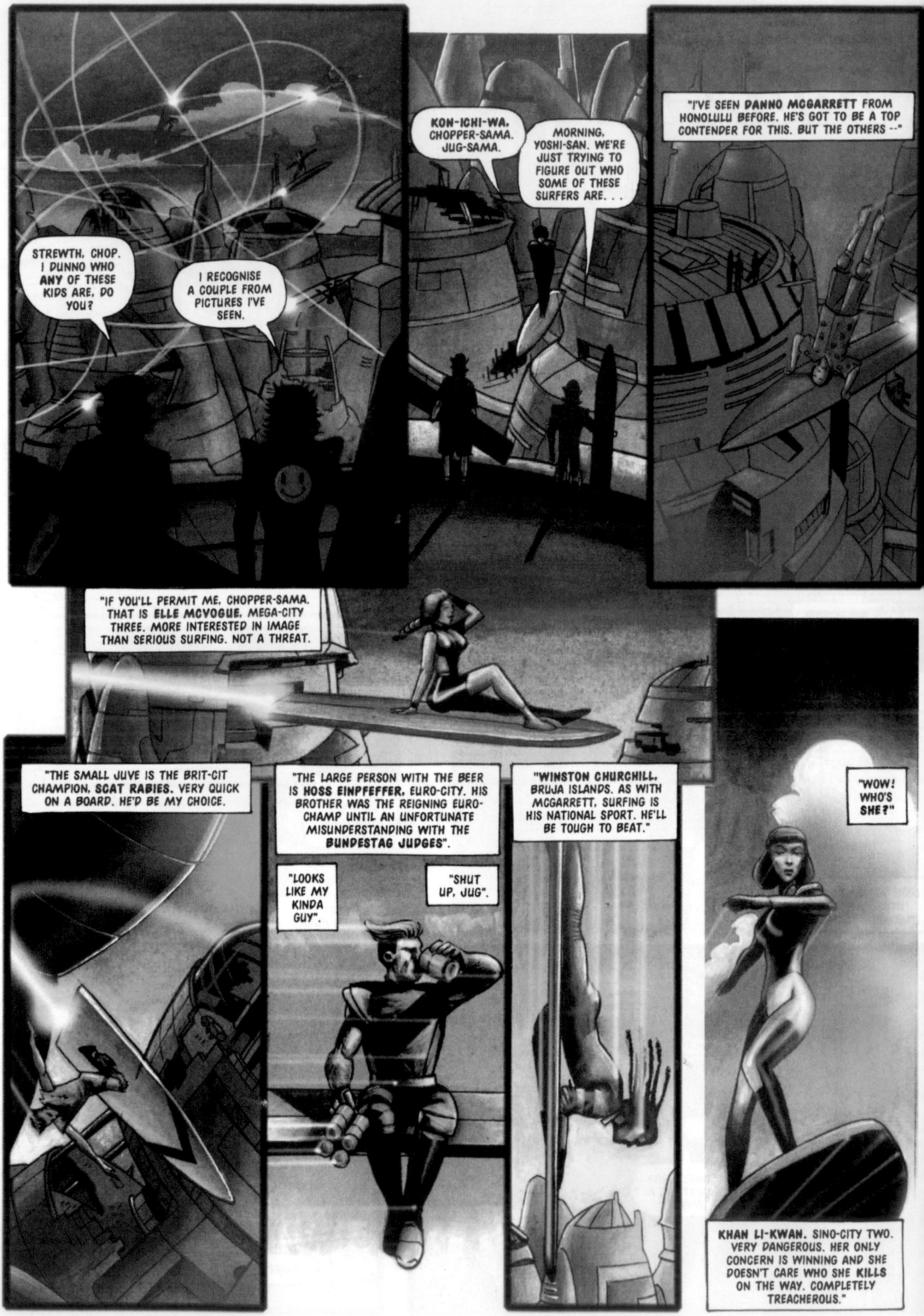
STREWTH, CHOP. I DUNNO WHO ANY OF THESE KIDS ARE, DO YOU?
I RECOGNISE A COUPLE FROM PICTURES I'VE SEEN.
KON-ICHI-WA, CHOPPER-SAMA. JUG-SAMA.
MORNING, YOSHI-SAN. WE'RE JUST TRYING TO FIGURE OUT WHO SOME OF THESE SURFERS ARE. . .
"I'VE SEEN DANNO McGARRETT FROM HONOLULU BEFORE. HE'S GOT TO BE A TOP CONTENDER FOR THIS. BUT THE OTHERS --"
"IF YOU'LL PERMIT ME, CHOPPER-SAMA. THAT IS ELLE McVOGUE, MEGA-CITY THREE. MORE INTERESTED IN IMAGE THAN SERIOUS SURFING. NOT A THREAT.
"THE SMALL JUVE IS THE BRIT-CIT CHAMPION, SCAT RABIES. VERY QUICK ON A BOARD. HE'D BE MY CHOICE.
"THE LARGE PERSON WITH THE BEER IS HOSS EINPFEFFER, EURO-CITY. HIS BROTHER WAS THE REIGNING EURO-CHAMP UNTIL AN UNFORTUNATE MISUNDERSTANDING WITH THE BUNDESTAG JUDGES".
"LOOKS LIKE MY KINDA GUY".
"SHUT UP, JUG".
"WINSTON CHURCHILL, BRUJA ISLANDS. AS WITH McGARRETT, SURFING IS HIS NATIONAL SPORT. HE'LL BE TOUGH TO BEAT."
"WOW! WHO'S SHE?"
KHAN LI-KWAN. SINO-CITY TWO. VERY DANGEROUS. HER ONLY CONCERN IS WINNING AND SHE DOESN'T CARE WHO SHE KILLS ON THE WAY. COMPLETELY TREACHEROUS."

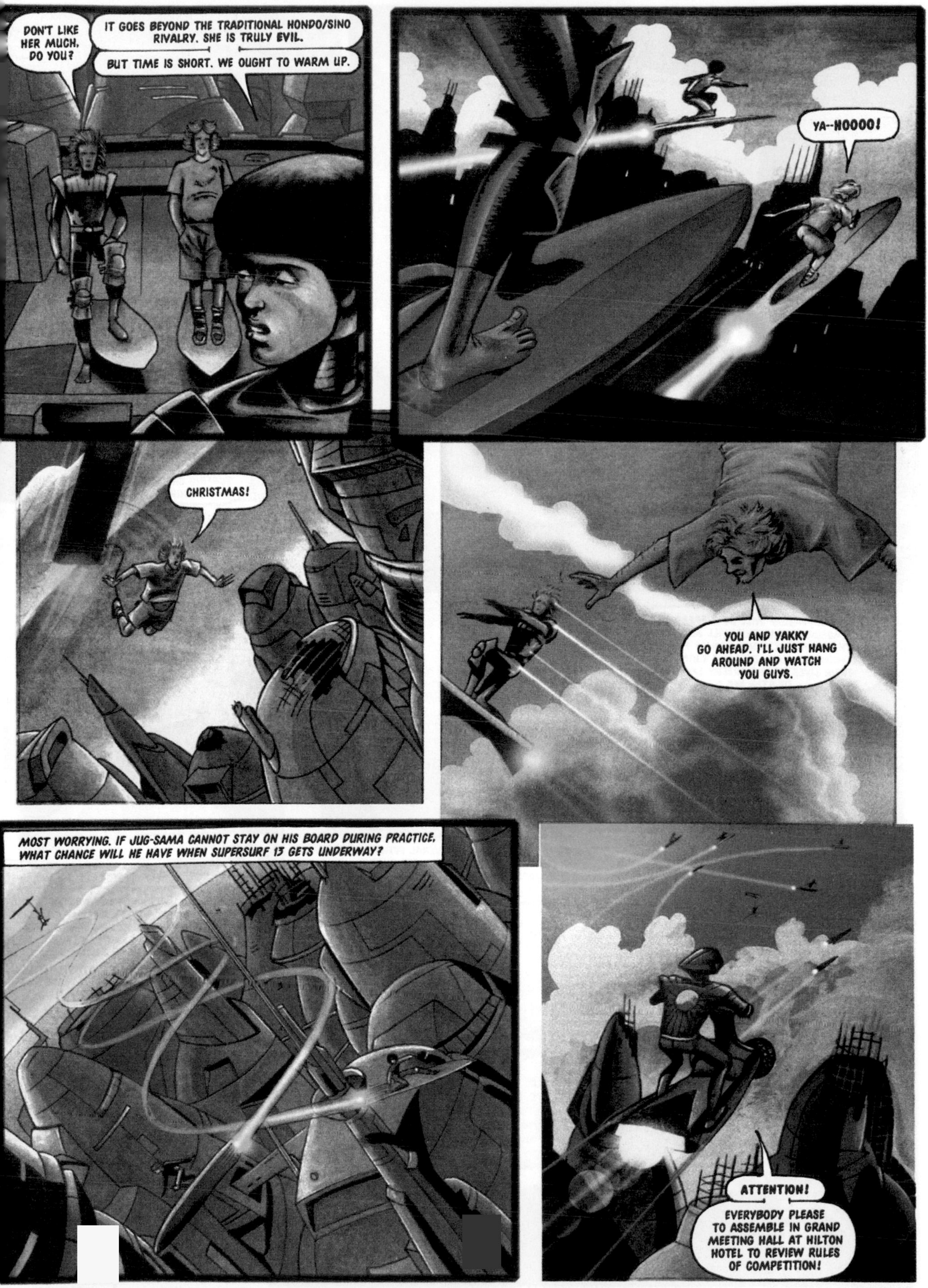
DON'T LIKE HER MUCH, DO YOU?
IT GOES BEYOND THE TRADITIONAL HONDO/SINO RIVALRY. SHE IS TRULY EVIL.
BUT TIME IS SHORT. WE OUGHT TO WARM UP.
YA--HOOOO!
CHRISTMAS!
YOU AND YAKKY GO AHEAD. I'LL JUST HANG AROUND AND WATCH YOU GUYS.
MOST WORRYING. IF JUG-SAMA CANNOT STAY ON HIS BOARD DURING PRACTICE, WHAT CHANCE WILL HE HAVE WHEN SUPERSURF 13 GETS UNDERWAY?
ATTENTION!
EVERYBODY PLEASE TO ASSEMBLE IN GRAND MEETING HALL AT HILTON HOTEL TO REVIEW RULES OF COMPETITION!

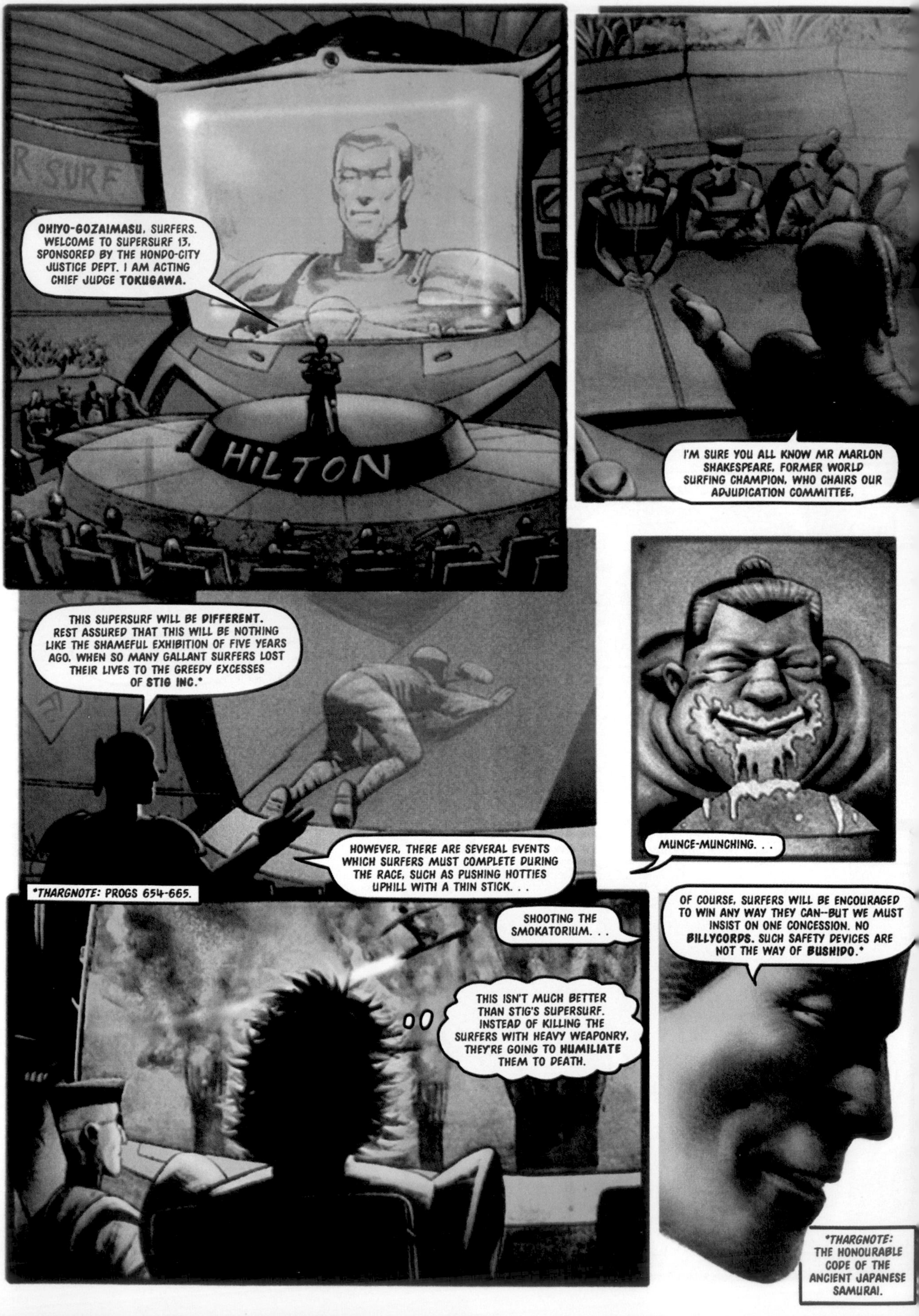
ONIYO-GOZAIMASU, SURFERS. WELCOME TO SUPERSURF 13, SPONSORED BY THE HONDO-CITY JUSTICE DEPT. I AM ACTING CHIEF JUDGE TOKUGAWA.
R SURF
HILTON
I'M SURE YOU ALL KNOW MR MARLON SHAKESPEARE, FORMER WORLD SURFING CHAMPION, WHO CHAIRS OUR ADJUDICATION COMMITTEE.
THIS SUPERSURF WILL BE DIFFERENT. REST ASSURED THAT THIS WILL BE NOTHING LIKE THE SHAMEFUL EXHIBITION OF FIVE YEARS AGO, WHEN SO MANY GALLANT SURFERS LOST THEIR LIVES TO THE GREEDY EXCESSES OF STIG INC.*
HOWEVER, THERE ARE SEVERAL EVENTS WHICH SURFERS MUST COMPLETE DURING THE RACE, SUCH AS PUSHING HOTTIES UPHILL WITH A THIN STICK. . .
*THARGNOTE: PROGS 654-665.
MUNCE-MUNCHING. . .
SHOOTING THE SMOKATORIUM. . .
THIS ISN'T MUCH BETTER THAN STIG'S SUPERSURF. INSTEAD OF KILLING THE SURFERS WITH HEAVY WEAPONRY, THEY'RE GOING TO HUMILIATE THEM TO DEATH.
OF COURSE, SURFERS WILL BE ENCOURAGED TO WIN ANY WAY THEY CAN--BUT WE MUST INSIST ON ONE CONCESSION. NO BILLYCORDS. SUCH SAFETY DEVICES ARE NOT THE WAY OF BUSHIDO.*
*THARGNOTE: THE HONOURABLE CODE OF THE ANCIENT JAPANESE SAMURAI.

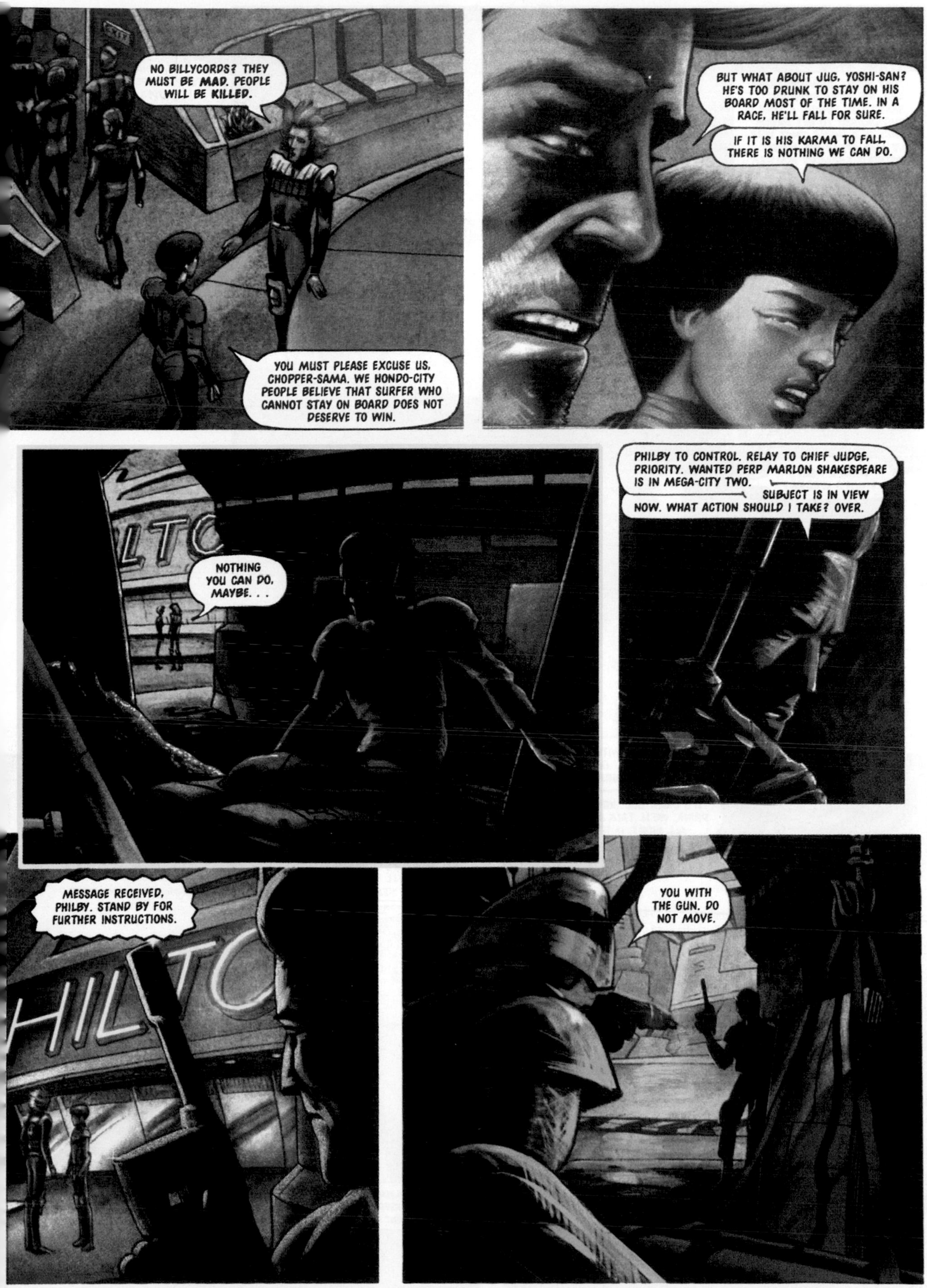
NO BILLYCORDS? THEY MUST BE MAD. PEOPLE WILL BE KILLED.
YOU MUST PLEASE EXCUSE US, CHOPPER-SAMA. WE HONDO-CITY PEOPLE BELIEVE THAT SURFER WHO CANNOT STAY ON BOARD DOES NOT DESERVE TO WIN.
BUT WHAT ABOUT JUG, YOSHI-SAN? HE'S TOO DRUNK TO STAY ON HIS BOARD MOST OF THE TIME. IN A RACE, HE'LL FALL FOR SURE.
IF IT IS HIS KARMA TO FALL, THERE IS NOTHING WE CAN DO.
NOTHING YOU CAN DO, MAYBE. . .
PHILBY TO CONTROL. RELAY TO CHIEF JUDGE, PRIORITY. WANTED PERP MARLON SHAKESPEARE IS IN MEGA-CITY TWO.
SUBJECT IS IN VIEW NOW. WHAT ACTION SHOULD I TAKE? OVER.
MESSAGE RECEIVED, PHILBY. STAND BY FOR FURTHER INSTRUCTIONS.
YOU WITH THE GUN. DO NOT MOVE.

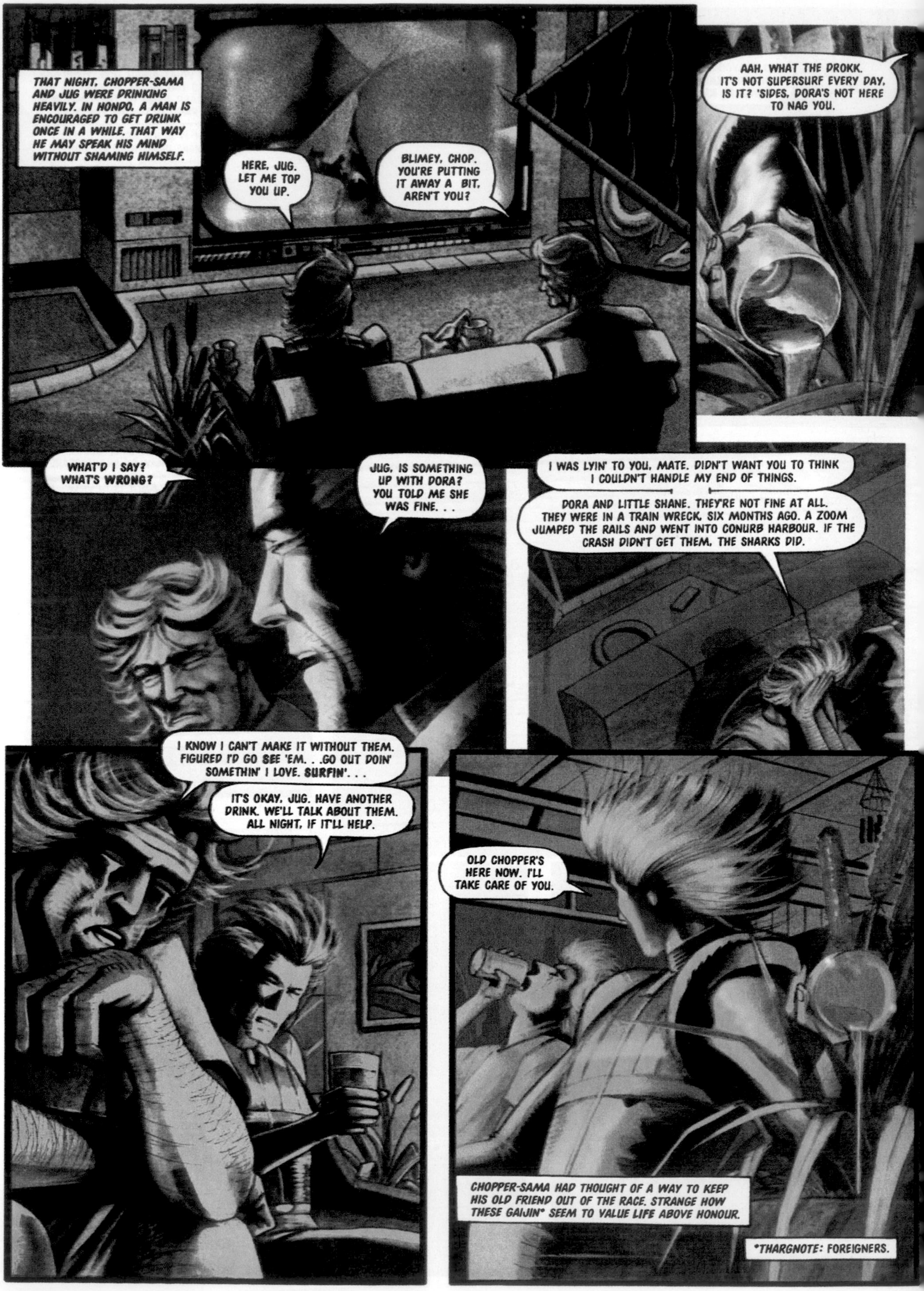
THAT NIGHT, CHOPPER-SAMA AND JUG WERE DRINKING HEAVILY. IN HONDO, A MAN IS ENCOURAGED TO GET DRUNK ONCE IN A WHILE. THAT WAY HE MAY SPEAK HIS MIND WITHOUT SHAMING HIMSELF.
HERE, JUG. LET ME TOP YOU UP.
BLIMEY, CHOP. YOU'RE PUTTING IT AWAY A BIT, AREN'T YOU?
AAH, WHAT THE DROKK. IT'S NOT SUPERSURF EVERY DAY, IS IT? 'SIDES, DORA'S NOT HERE TO NAG YOU.
WHAT'D I SAY? WHAT'S WRONG?
JUG, IS SOMETHING UP WITH DORA? YOU TOLD ME SHE WAS FINE. . .
I WAS LYIN' TO YOU, MATE. DIDN'T WANT YOU TO THINK I COULDN'T HANDLE MY END OF THINGS.
DORA AND LITTLE SHANE. THEY'RE NOT FINE AT ALL. THEY WERE IN A TRAIN WRECK, SIX MONTHS AGO. A ZOOM JUMPED THE RAILS AND WENT INTO CONURB HARBOUR. IF THE CRASH DIDN'T GET THEM, THE SHARKS DID.
I KNOW I CAN'T MAKE IT WITHOUT THEM. FIGURED I'D GO SEE 'EM. . .GO OUT DOIN' SOMETHIN' I LOVE. SURFIN'. . .
IT'S OKAY, JUG. HAVE ANOTHER DRINK. WE'LL TALK ABOUT THEM. ALL NIGHT, IF IT'LL HELP.
OLD CHOPPER'S HERE NOW. I'LL TAKE CARE OF YOU.
CHOPPER-SAMA HAD THOUGHT OF A WAY TO KEEP HIS OLD FRIEND OUT OF THE RACE. STRANGE HOW THESE GAIJIN* SEEM TO VALUE LIFE ABOVE HONOUR.
*THARGNOTE: FOREIGNERS.

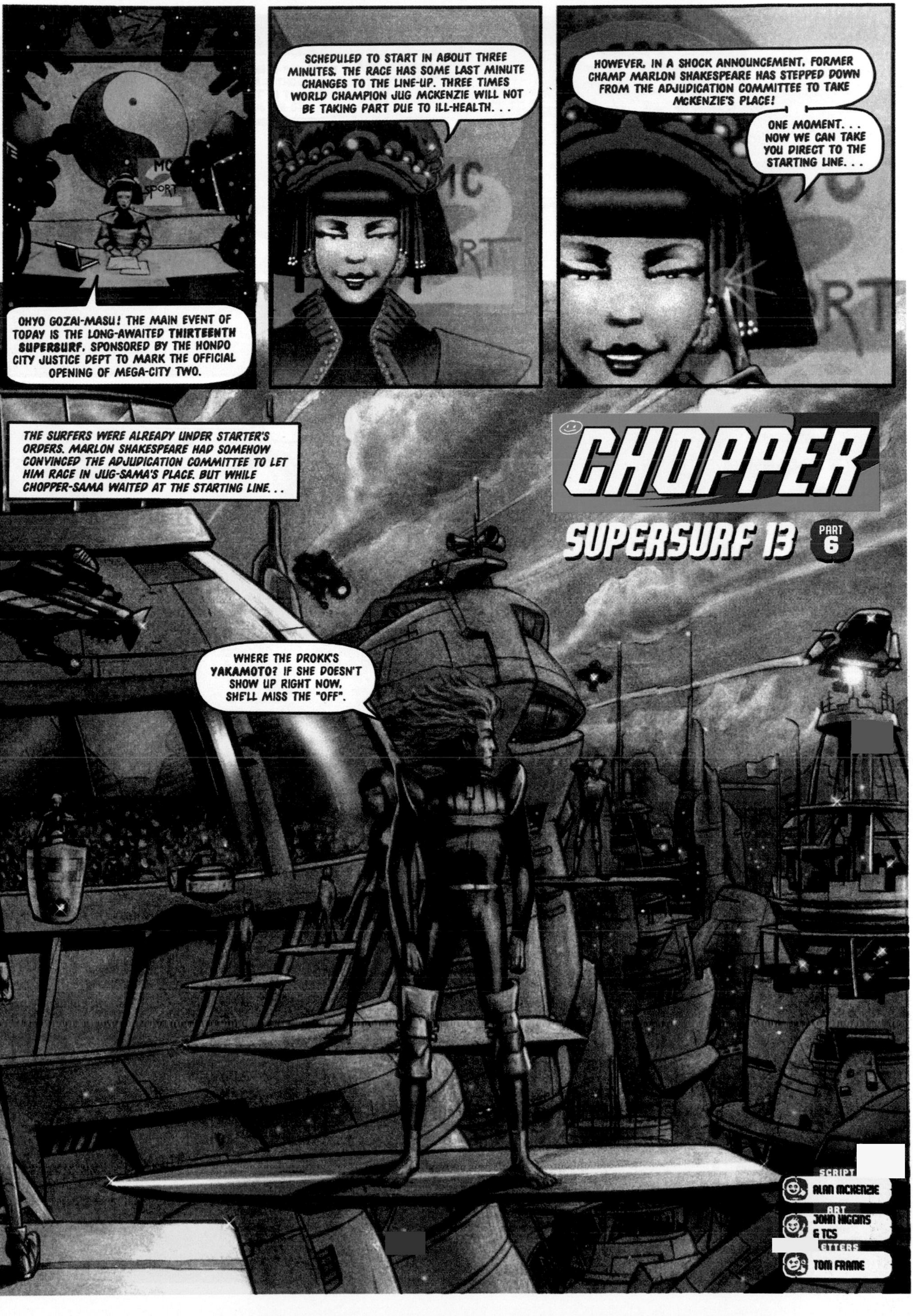

OHYO GOZAI-MASU! THE MAIN EVENT OF TODAY IS THE LONG-AWAITED THIRTEENTH SUPERSURF, SPONSORED BY THE HONDO CITY JUSTICE DEPT TO MARK THE OFFICIAL OPENING OF MEGA-CITY TWO.
SCHEDULED TO START IN ABOUT THREE MINUTES, THE RACE HAS SOME LAST MINUTE CHANGES TO THE LINE-UP. THREE TIMES WORLD CHAMPION JUG MCKENZIE WILL NOT BE TAKING PART DUE TO ILL-HEALTH. . .
HOWEVER, IN A SHOCK ANNOUNCEMENT, FORMER CHAMP MARLON SHAKESPEARE HAS STEPPED DOWN FROM THE ADJUDICATION COMMITTEE TO TAKE McKENZIE'S PLACE!
ONE MOMENT. . . NOW WE CAN TAKE YOU DIRECT TO THE STARTING LINE. . .
THE SURFERS WERE ALREADY UNDER STARTER'S ORDERS. MARLON SHAKESPEARE HAD SOMEHOW CONVINCED THE ADJUDICATION COMMITTEE TO LET HIM RACE IN JUG-SAMA'S PLACE. BUT WHILE CHOPPER-SAMA WAITED AT THE STARTING LINE. . .
CHOPPER
SUPERSURF 13 PART 6
WHERE THE DROKK'S YAKAMOTO? IF SHE DOESN'T SHOW UP RIGHT NOW, SHE'LL MISS THE "OFF".
SCRIPT
ALAN MCKENZIE
ART
JOHN HIGGINS & TCS
ETTERS
TOM FRAME

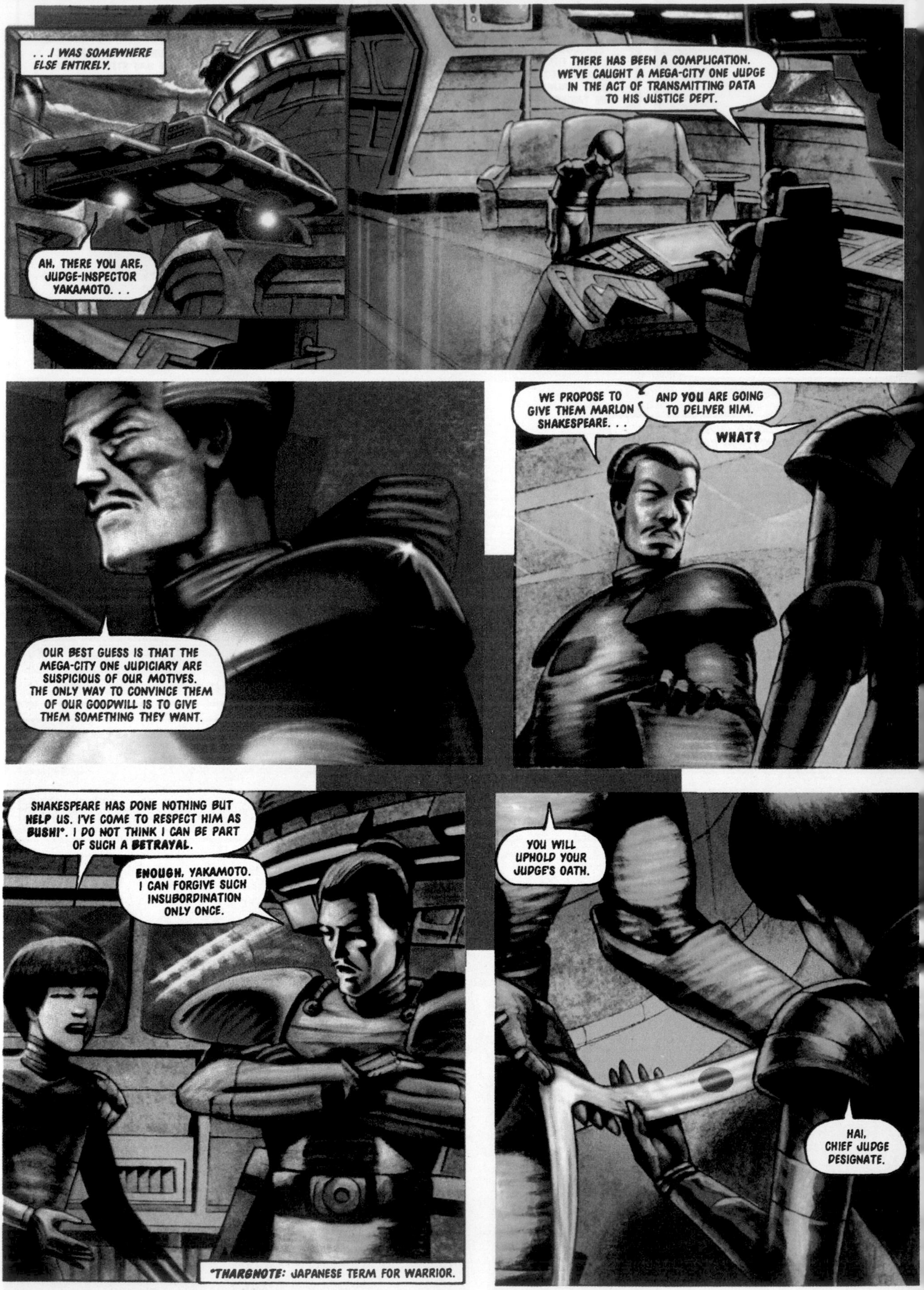
. . .I WAS SOMEWHERE ELSE ENTIRELY.
AH, THERE YOU ARE, JUDGE-INSPECTOR YAKAMOTO. . .
THERE HAS BEEN A COMPLICATION. WE'VE CAUGHT A MEGA-CITY ONE JUDGE IN THE ACT OF TRANSMITTING DATA TO HIS JUSTICE DEPT.
OUR BEST GUESS IS THAT THE MEGA-CITY ONE JUDICIARY ARE SUSPICIOUS OF OUR MOTIVES. THE ONLY WAY TO CONVINCE THEM OF OUR GOODWILL IS TO GIVE THEM SOMETHING THEY WANT.
WE PROPOSE TO GIVE THEM MARLON SHAKESPEARE. . .
AND YOU ARE GOING TO DELIVER HIM.
WHAT?
SHAKESPEARE HAS DONE NOTHING BUT HELP US. I'VE COME TO RESPECT HIM AS BUSHI*. I DO NOT THINK I CAN BE PART OF SUCH A BETRAYAL.
ENOUGH, YAKAMOTO. I CAN FORGIVE SUCH INSUBORDINATION ONLY ONCE.
*THARGNOTE: JAPANESE TERM FOR WARRIOR.
YOU WILL UPHOLD YOUR JUDGE'S OATH.
HAI, CHIEF JUDGE DESIGNATE.

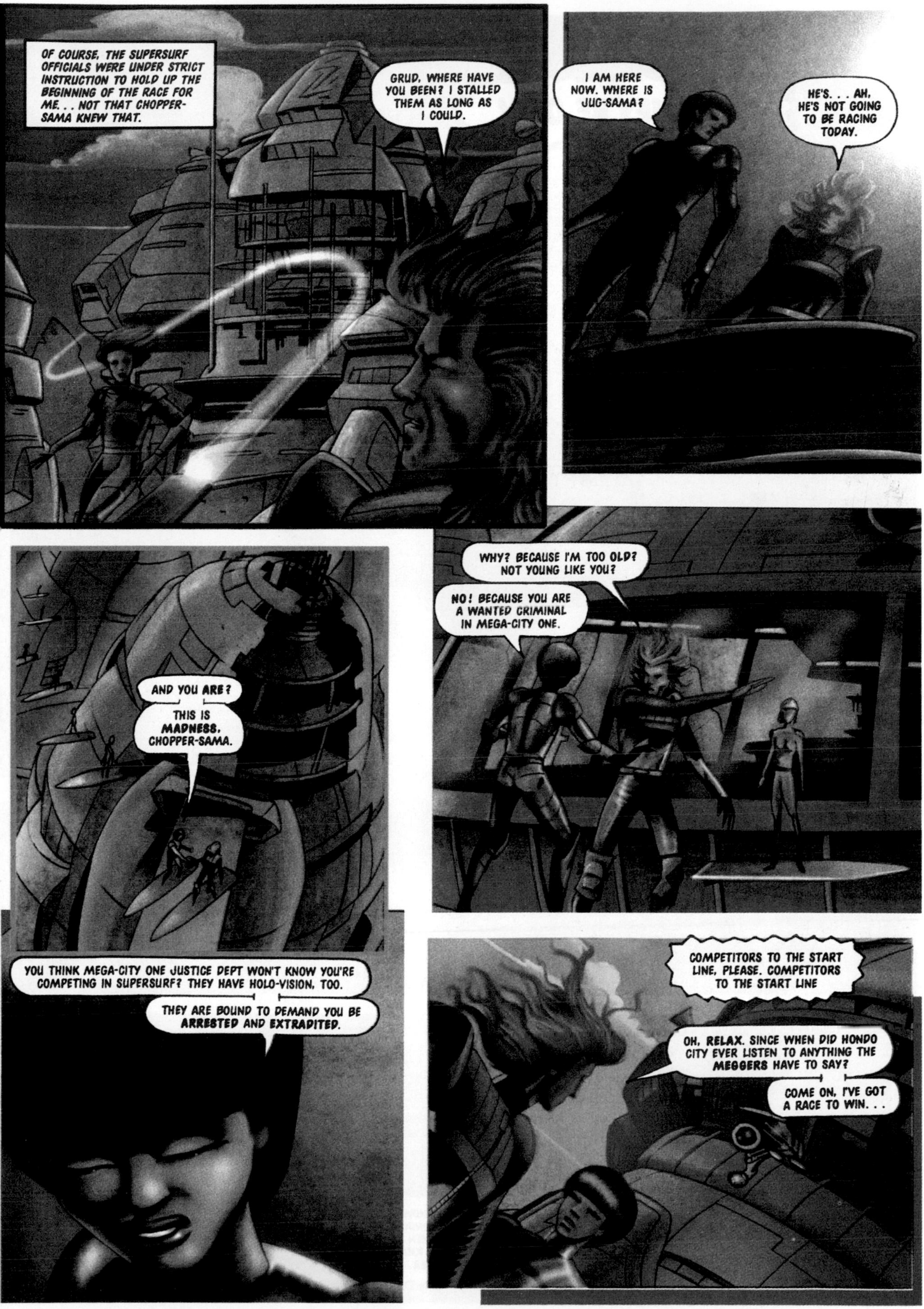
OF COURSE, THE SUPERSURF OFFICIALS WERE UNDER STRICT INSTRUCTION TO HOLD UP THE BEGINNING OF THE RACE FOR ME. . . NOT THAT CHOPPER-SAMA KNEW THAT.
GRUD, WHERE HAVE YOU BEEN? I STALLED THEM AS LONG AS I COULD.
I AM HERE NOW. WHERE IS JUG-SAMA?
HE'S. . . AH, HE'S NOT GOING TO BE RACING TODAY.
AND YOU ARE?
THIS IS MADNESS, CHOPPER-SAMA.
WHY? BECAUSE I'M TOO OLD? NOT YOUNG LIKE YOU?
NO! BECAUSE YOU ARE A WANTED CRIMINAL IN MEGA-CITY ONE.
YOU THINK MEGA-CITY ONE JUSTICE DEPT WON'T KNOW YOU'RE COMPETING IN SUPERSURF? THEY HAVE HOLO-VISION, TOO.
THEY ARE BOUND TO DEMAND YOU BE ARRESTED AND EXTRADITED.
COMPETITORS TO THE START LINE, PLEASE. COMPETITORS TO THE START LINE
OH, RELAX. SINCE WHEN DID HONDO CITY EVER LISTEN TO ANYTHING THE MEGGERS HAVE TO SAY?
COME ON, I'VE GOT A RACE TO WIN. . .

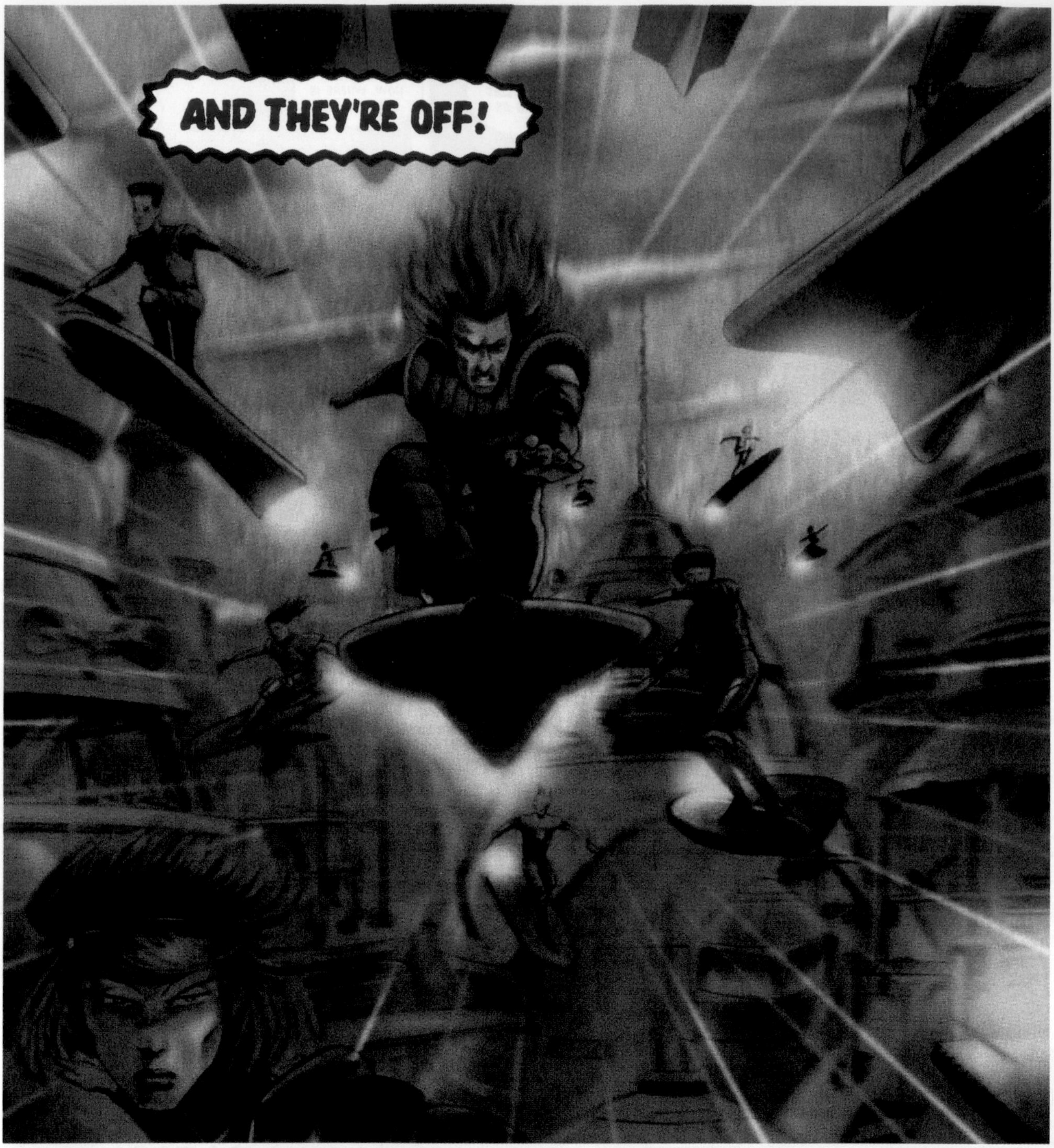
AND THEY'RE OFF!

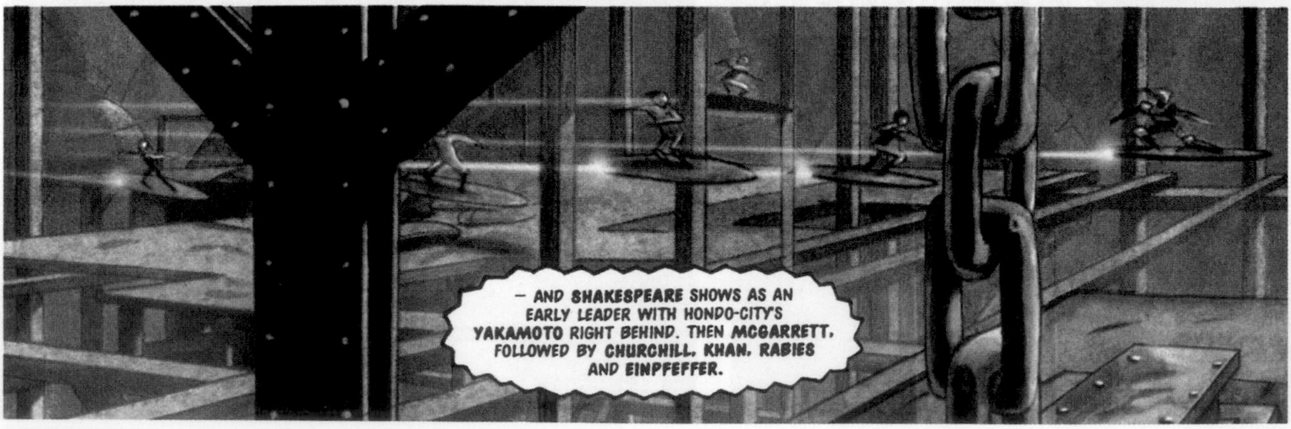
– AND SHAKESPEARE SHOWS AS AN EARLY LEADER WITH HONDO-CITY'S YAKAMOTO RIGHT BEHIND. THEN MCGARRETT, FOLLOWED BY CHURCHILL, KHAN, RABIES AND EINPFEFFER.

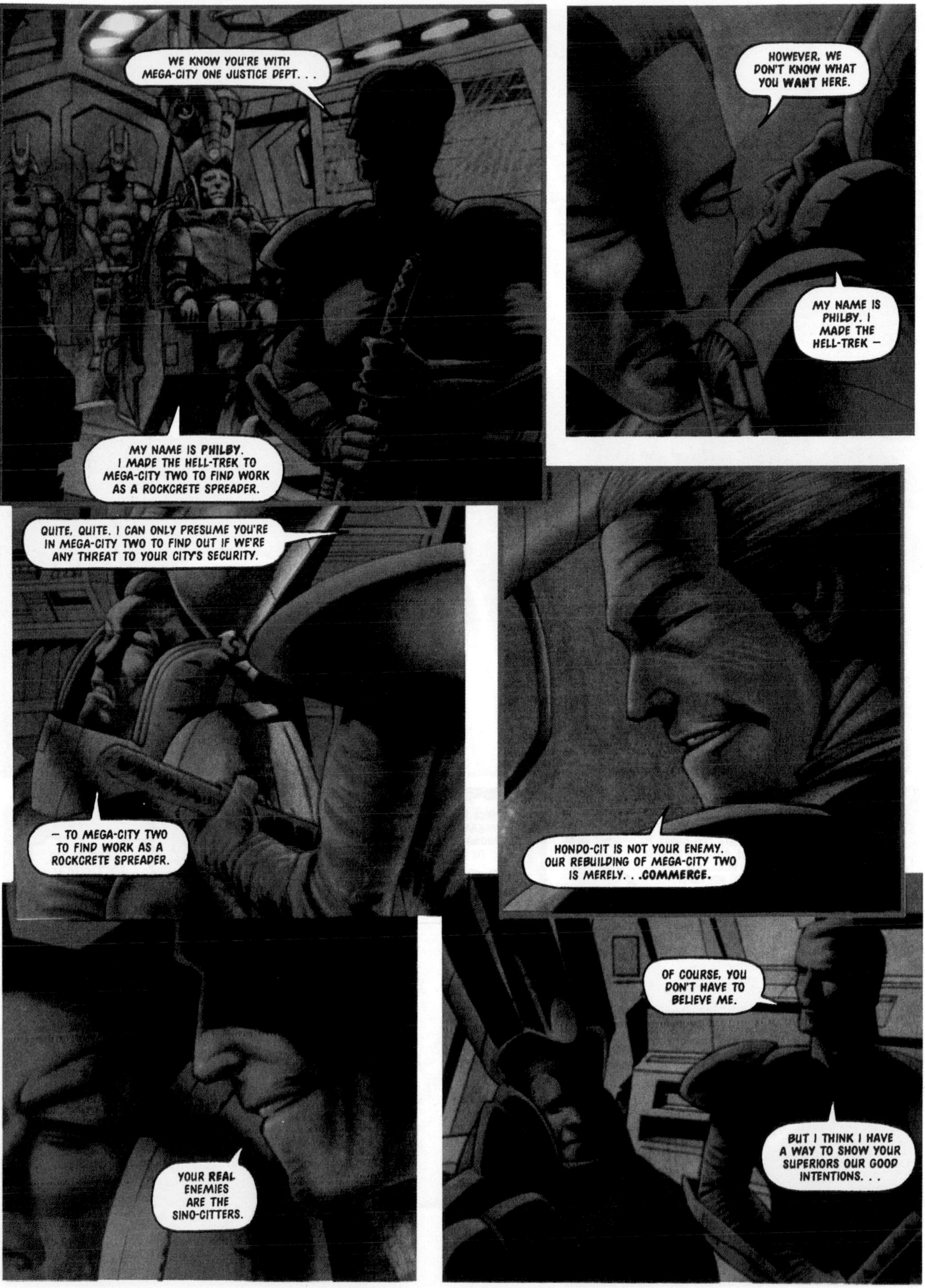
WE KNOW YOU'RE WITH MEGA-CITY ONE JUSTICE DEPT. . .
MY NAME IS PHILBY. I MADE THE HELL-TREK TO MEGA-CITY TWO TO FIND WORK AS A ROCKCRETE SPREADER.
HOWEVER, WE DON'T KNOW WHAT YOU WANT HERE.
MY NAME IS PHILBY. I MADE THE HELL-TREK —
QUITE, QUITE. I CAN ONLY PRESUME YOU'RE IN MEGA-CITY TWO TO FIND OUT IF WE'RE ANY THREAT TO YOUR CITY'S SECURITY.
— TO MEGA-CITY TWO TO FIND WORK AS A ROCKCRETE SPREADER.
HONDO-CIT IS NOT YOUR ENEMY. OUR REBUILDING OF MEGA-CITY TWO IS MERELY. . .COMMERCE.
YOUR REAL ENEMIES ARE THE SINO-CITTERS.
OF COURSE, YOU DON'T HAVE TO BELIEVE ME.
BUT I THINK I HAVE A WAY TO SHOW YOUR SUPERIORS OUR GOOD INTENTIONS. . .

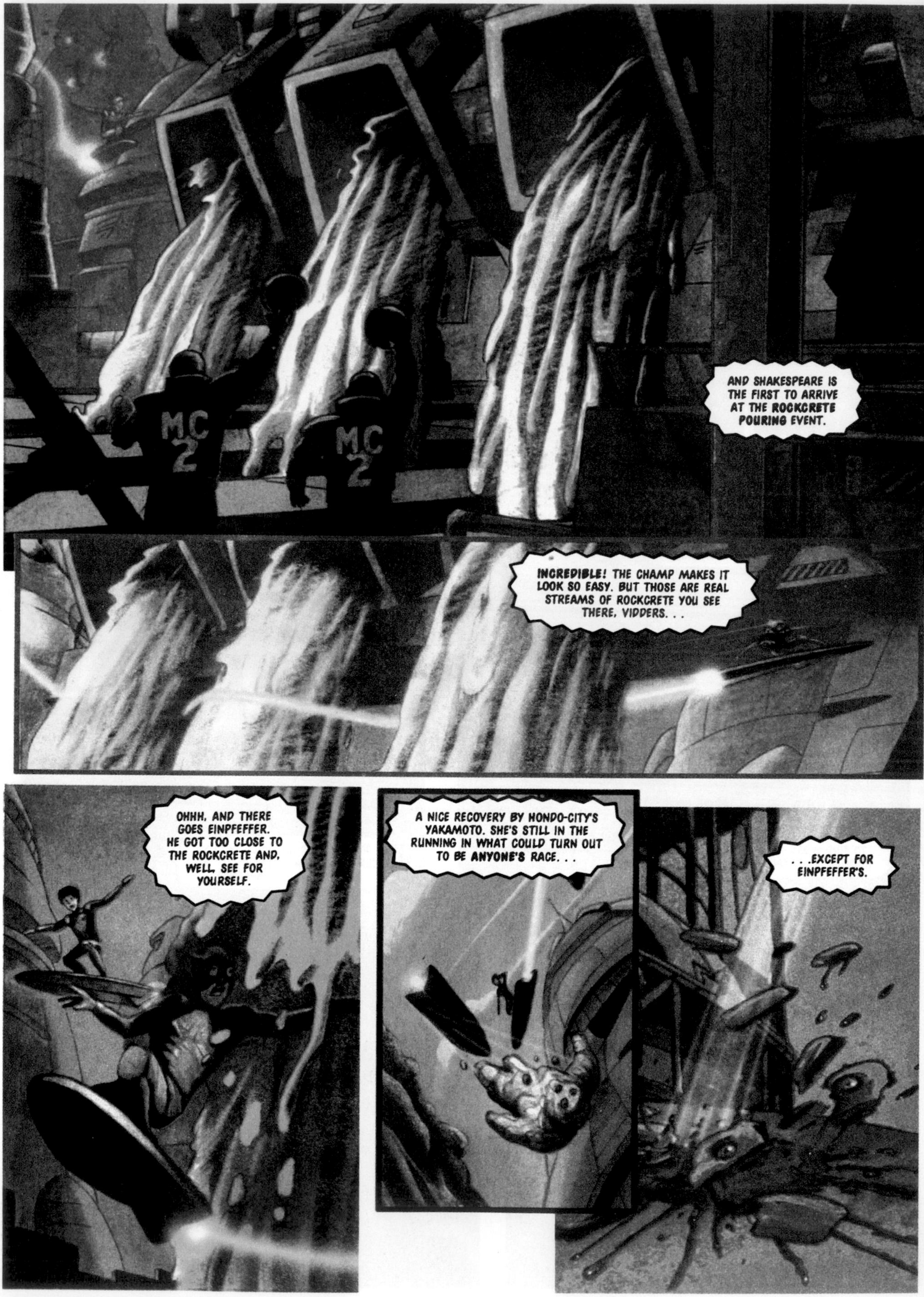

MC 2
MC 2
AND SHAKESPEARE IS THE FIRST TO ARRIVE AT THE ROCKCRETE POURING EVENT.
INCREDIBLE! THE CHAMP MAKES IT LOOK SO EASY. BUT THOSE ARE REAL STREAMS OF ROCKCRETE YOU SEE THERE, VIDDERS. . .
OHHH, AND THERE GOES EINPFEFFER. HE GOT TOO CLOSE TO THE ROCKCRETE AND, WELL, SEE FOR YOURSELF.
A NICE RECOVERY BY HONDO-CITY'S YAKAMOTO. SHE'S STILL IN THE RUNNING IN WHAT COULD TURN OUT TO BE ANYONE'S RACE. . .
. . .EXCEPT FOR EINPFEFFER'S.

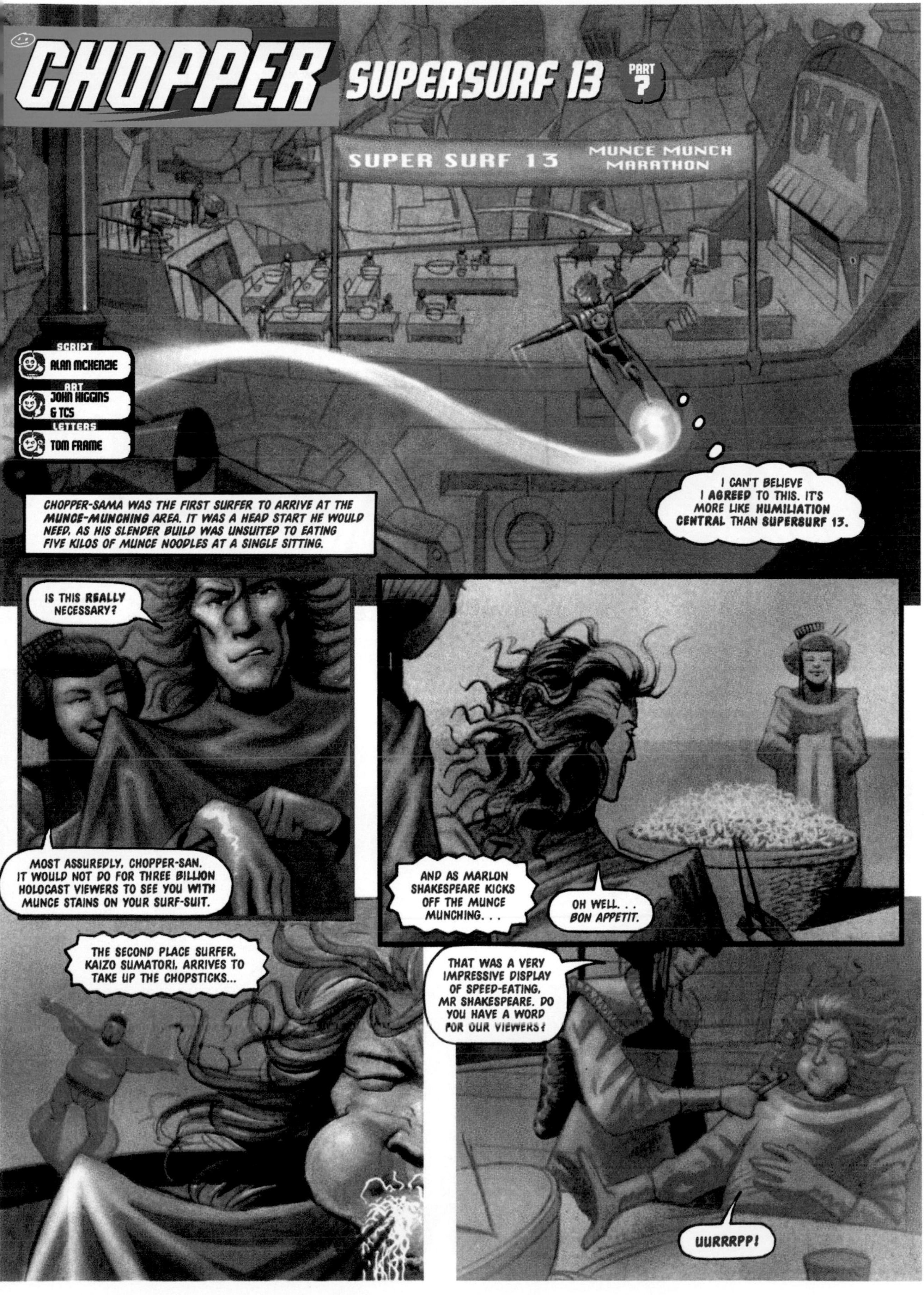
CHOPPER
SUPERSURF 13 PART 7
SUPER SURF 13
MUNCE MUNCH MARATHON
BAR
SCRIPT
ALAN MCKENZIE
ART
JOHN HIGGINS & TCS
LETTERS
TOM FRAME
CHOPPER-SAMA WAS THE FIRST SURFER TO ARRIVE AT THE MUNCE-MUNCHING AREA. IT WAS A HEAD START HE WOULD NEED, AS HIS SLENDER BUILD WAS UNSUITED TO EATING FIVE KILOS OF MUNCE NOODLES AT A SINGLE SITTING.
I CAN'T BELIEVE I AGREED TO THIS. IT'S MORE LIKE HUMILIATION CENTRAL THAN SUPERSURF 13.
IS THIS REALLY NECESSARY?
MOST ASSUREDLY, CHOPPER-SAN. IT WOULD NOT DO FOR THREE BILLION HOLOCAST VIEWERS TO SEE YOU WITH MUNCE STAINS ON YOUR SURF-SUIT.
AND AS MARLON SHAKESPEARE KICKS OFF THE MUNCE MUNCHING. . .
OH WELL. . . BON APPETIT.
THE SECOND PLACE SURFER, KAIZO SUMATORI, ARRIVES TO TAKE UP THE CHOPSTICKS...
THAT WAS A VERY IMPRESSIVE DISPLAY OF SPEED-EATING, MR SHAKESPEARE. DO YOU HAVE A WORD FOR OUR VIEWERS?
UURRRPP!

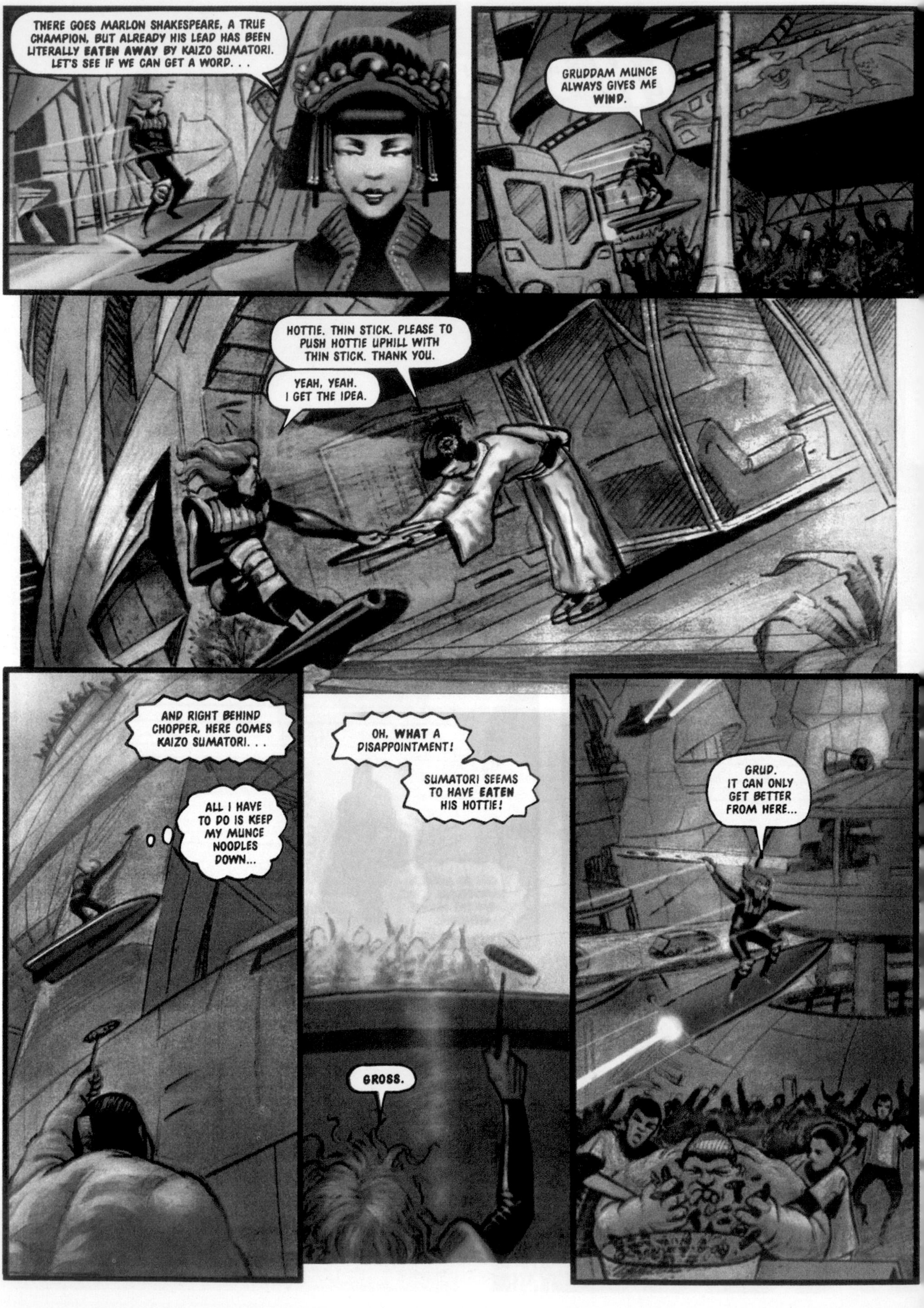
THERE GOES MARLON SHAKESPEARE, A TRUE CHAMPION, BUT ALREADY HIS LEAD HAS BEEN LITERALLY **EATEN AWAY** BY KAIZO SUMATORI. LET'S SEE IF WE CAN GET A WORD. . .
GRUDDAM MUNCE ALWAYS GIVES ME **WIND**.
HOTTIE. THIN STICK. PLEASE TO PUSH HOTTIE UPHILL WITH THIN STICK. THANK YOU.
YEAH, YEAH. I GET THE IDEA.
AND RIGHT BEHIND CHOPPER, HERE COMES KAIZO SUMATORI. . .
ALL I HAVE TO DO IS KEEP MY MUNCE NOODLES DOWN...
OH, **WHAT** A DISAPPOINTMENT!
SUMATORI SEEMS TO HAVE **EATEN** HIS HOTTIE!
GROSS.
GRUD. IT CAN ONLY GET BETTER FROM HERE...

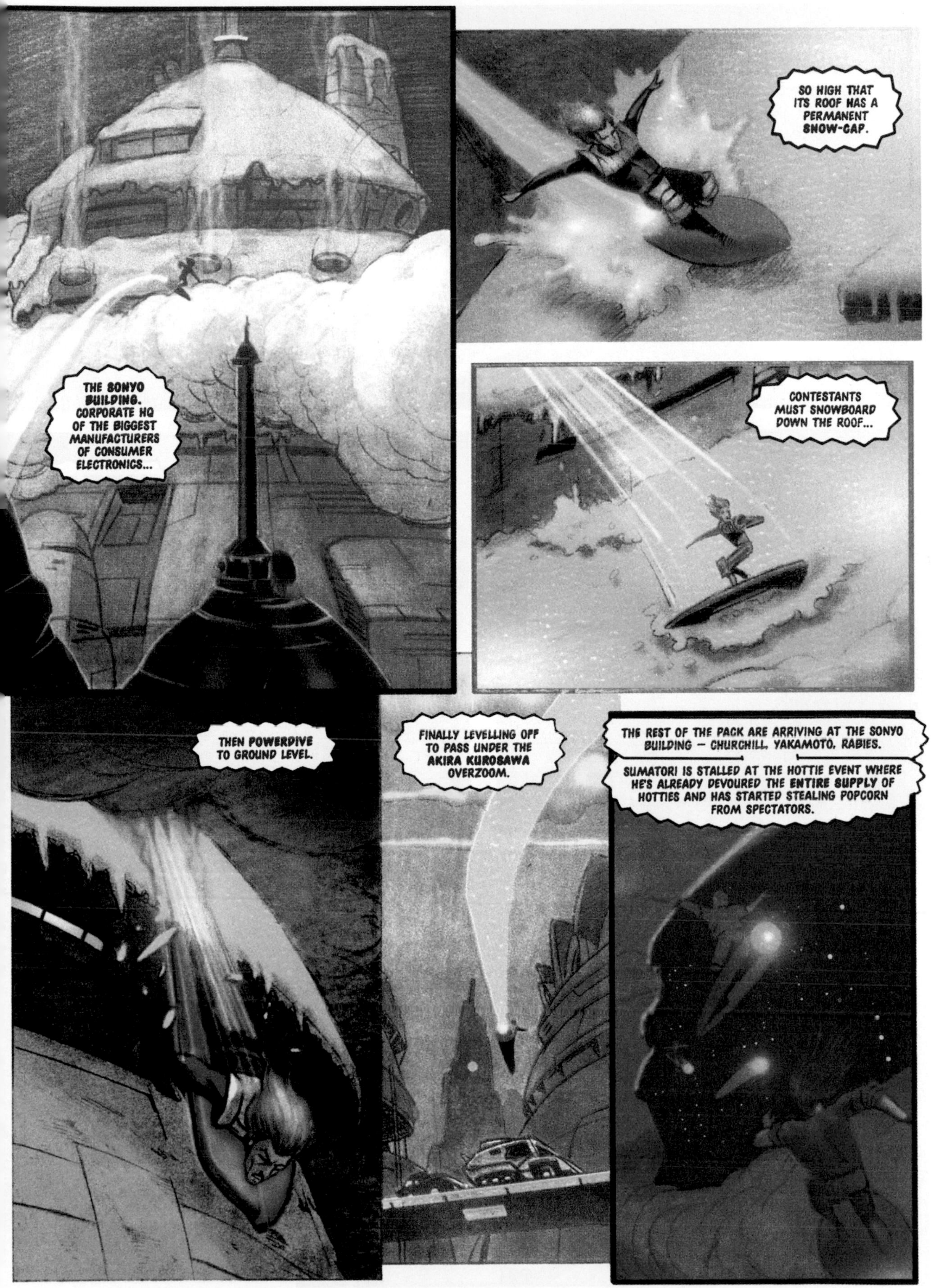
THE SONYO BUILDING. CORPORATE HQ OF THE BIGGEST MANUFACTURERS OF CONSUMER ELECTRONICS...
SO HIGH THAT ITS ROOF HAS A PERMANENT SNOW-CAP.
CONTESTANTS MUST SNOWBOARD DOWN THE ROOF...
THEN POWERDIVE TO GROUND LEVEL.
FINALLY LEVELLING OFF TO PASS UNDER THE AKIRA KUROSAWA OVERZOOM.
THE REST OF THE PACK ARE ARRIVING AT THE SONYO BUILDING – CHURCHILL, YAKAMOTO, RABIES.
SUMATORI IS STALLED AT THE HOTTIE EVENT WHERE HE'S ALREADY DEVOURED THE ENTIRE SUPPLY OF HOTTIES AND HAS STARTED STEALING POPCORN FROM SPECTATORS.

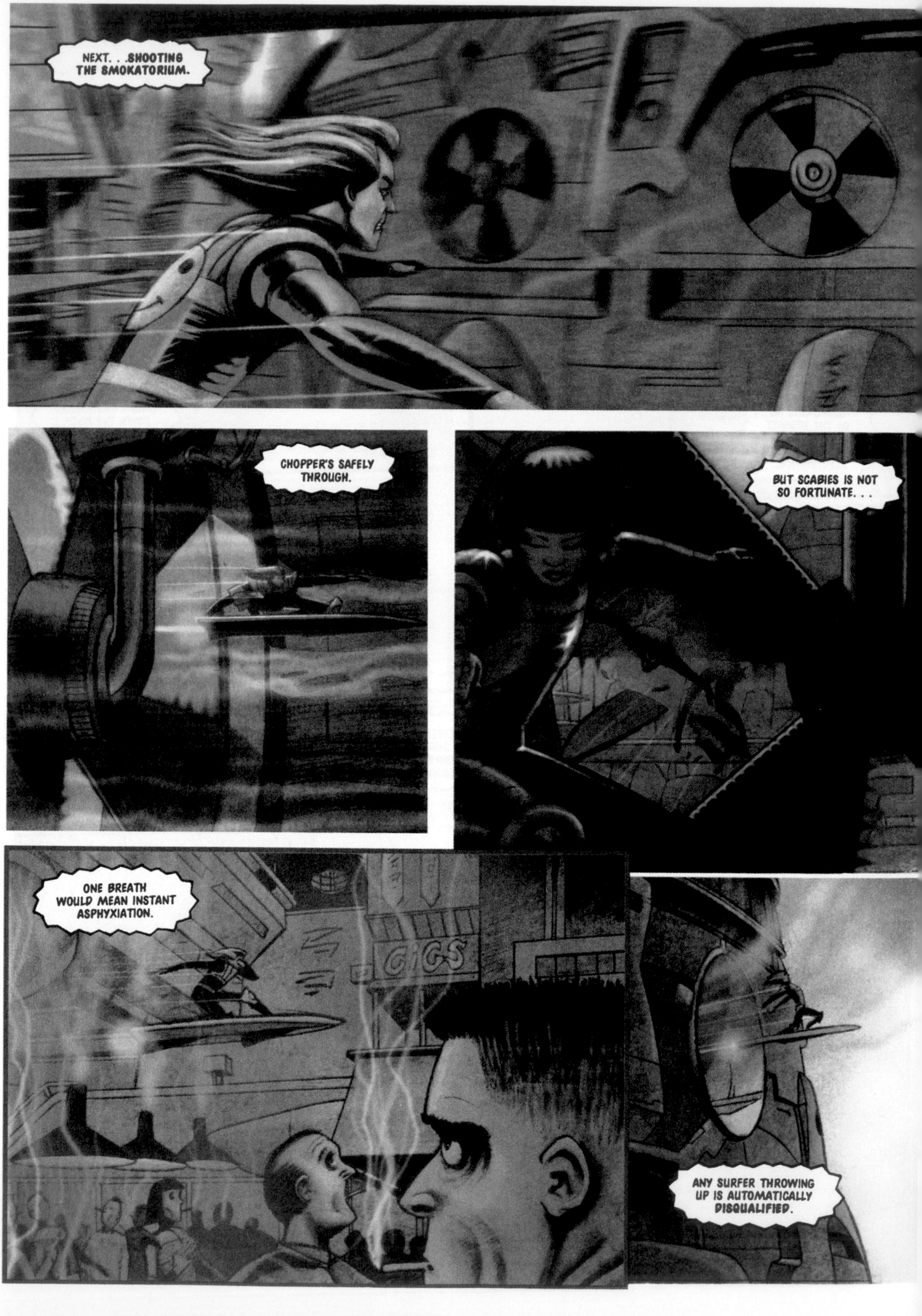
NEXT. . .SHOOTING THE SMOKATORIUM.
CHOPPER'S SAFELY THROUGH.
BUT SCABIES IS NOT SO FORTUNATE. . .
ONE BREATH WOULD MEAN INSTANT ASPHYXIATION.
GIGS
ANY SURFER THROWING UP IS AUTOMATICALLY DISQUALIFIED.

OOH—DISASTER. MCGARRETT AND CHURCHILL HAVE COLLIDED!

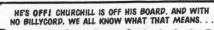

HE'S OFF! CHURCHILL IS OFF HIS BOARD. AND WITH NO BILLYCORD, WE ALL KNOW WHAT THAT MEANS. . .

WHAT'S THIS? SHAKESPEARE'S GOING THE WRONG WAY!

INCREDIBLE! CHURCHILL HAS BEEN SAVED BY SHAKESPEARE. . .

OH, MY GRUD!

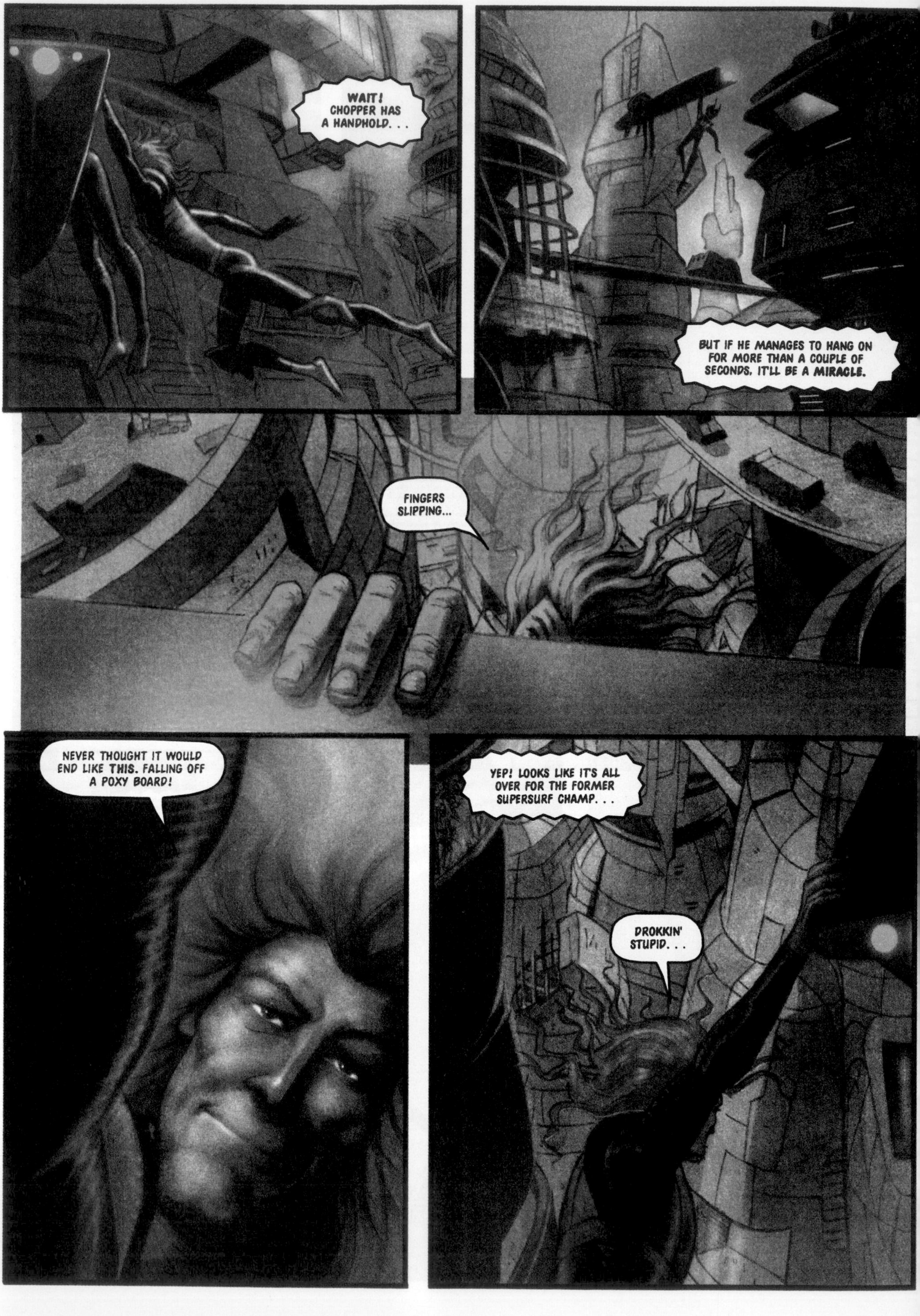
WAIT! CHOPPER HAS A HANDHOLD. . .
BUT IF HE MANAGES TO HANG ON FOR MORE THAN A COUPLE OF SECONDS, IT'LL BE A MIRACLE.
FINGERS SLIPPING...
NEVER THOUGHT IT WOULD END LIKE THIS. FALLING OFF A POXY BOARD!
YEP! LOOKS LIKE IT'S ALL OVER FOR THE FORMER SUPERSURF CHAMP. . .
DROKKIN' STUPID. . .

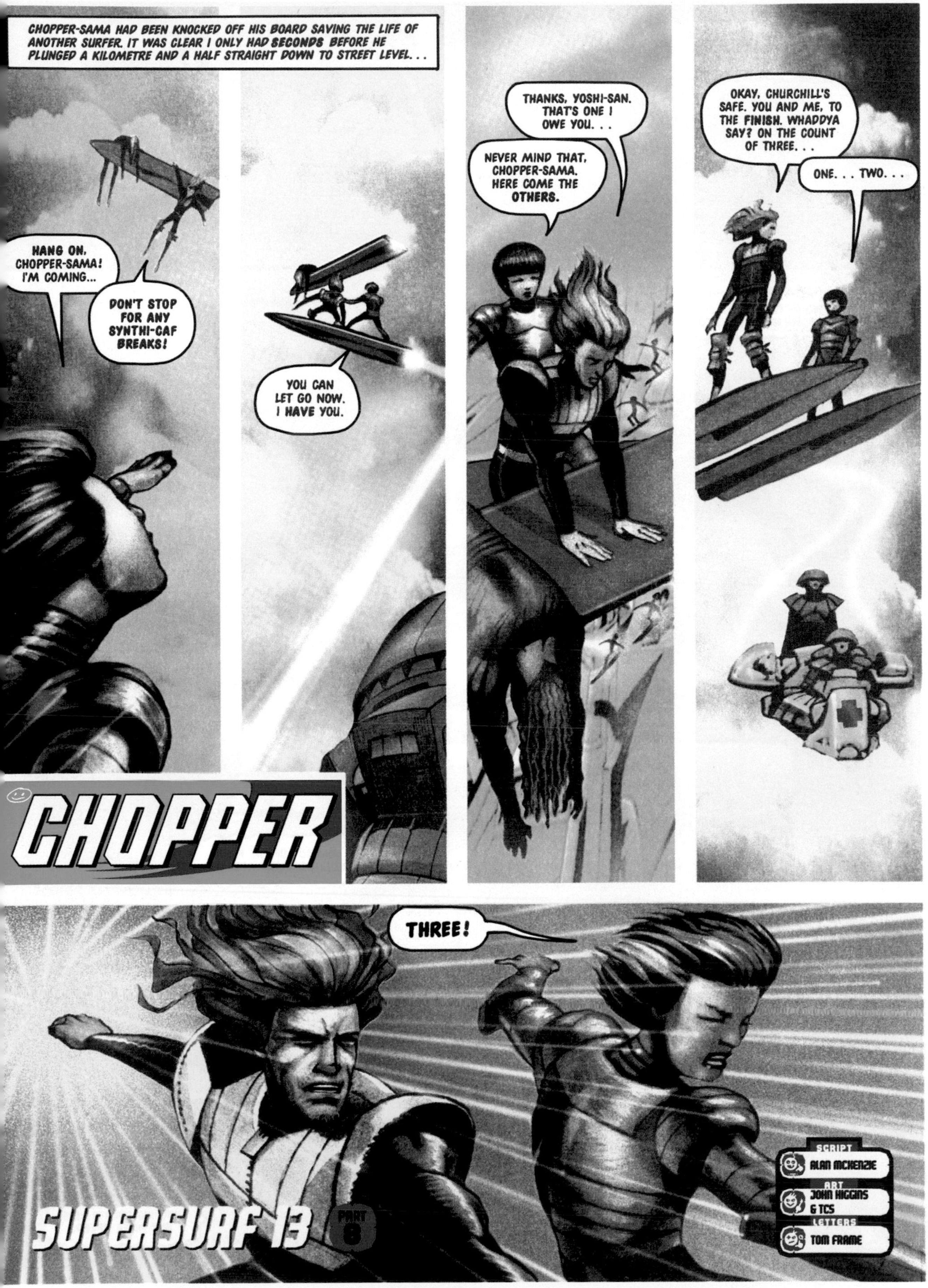

CHOPPER-SAMA HAD BEEN KNOCKED OFF HIS BOARD SAVING THE LIFE OF ANOTHER SURFER. IT WAS CLEAR I ONLY HAD SECONDS BEFORE HE PLUNGED A KILOMETRE AND A HALF STRAIGHT DOWN TO STREET LEVEL. . .
HANG ON, CHOPPER-SAMA! I'M COMING...
DON'T STOP FOR ANY SYNTHI-CAF BREAKS!
YOU CAN LET GO NOW. I HAVE YOU.
THANKS, YOSHI-SAN. THAT'S ONE I OWE YOU. . .
NEVER MIND THAT, CHOPPER-SAMA. HERE COME THE OTHERS.
OKAY, CHURCHILL'S SAFE. YOU AND ME, TO THE FINISH. WHADDYA SAY? ON THE COUNT OF THREE. . .
ONE. . . TWO. . .
CHOPPER
THREE!
SUPERSURF 13
PART 8
SCRIPT
ALAN MCKENZIE
ART
JOHN HIGGINS & TCS
LETTERS
TOM FRAME

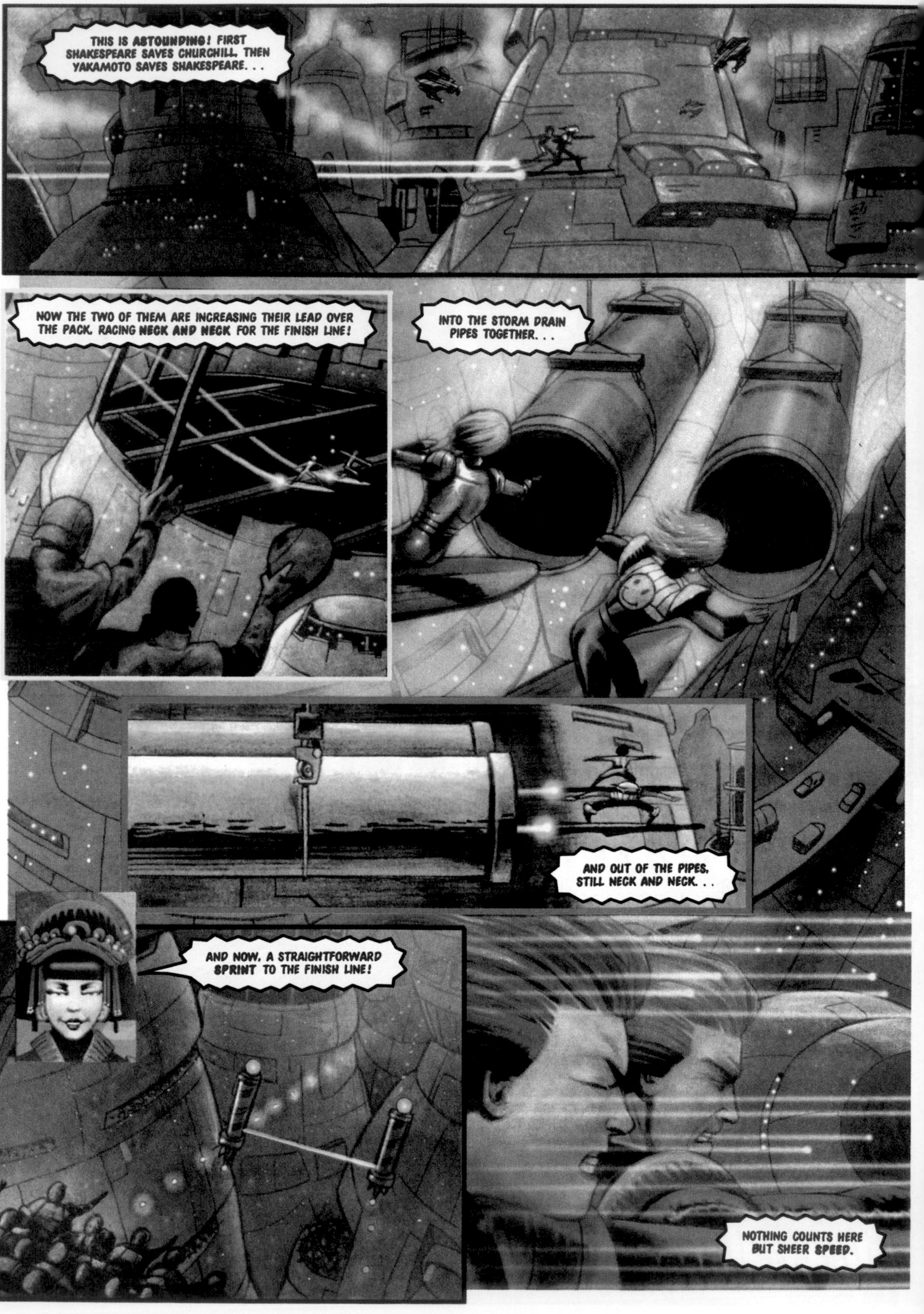
THIS IS ASTOUNDING! FIRST SHAKESPEARE SAVES CHURCHILL, THEN YAKAMOTO SAVES SHAKESPEARE. . .
NOW THE TWO OF THEM ARE INCREASING THEIR LEAD OVER THE PACK, RACING NECK AND NECK FOR THE FINISH LINE!
INTO THE STORM DRAIN PIPES TOGETHER. . .
AND OUT OF THE PIPES, STILL NECK AND NECK. . .
AND NOW, A STRAIGHTFORWARD SPRINT TO THE FINISH LINE!
NOTHING COUNTS HERE BUT SHEER SPEED.

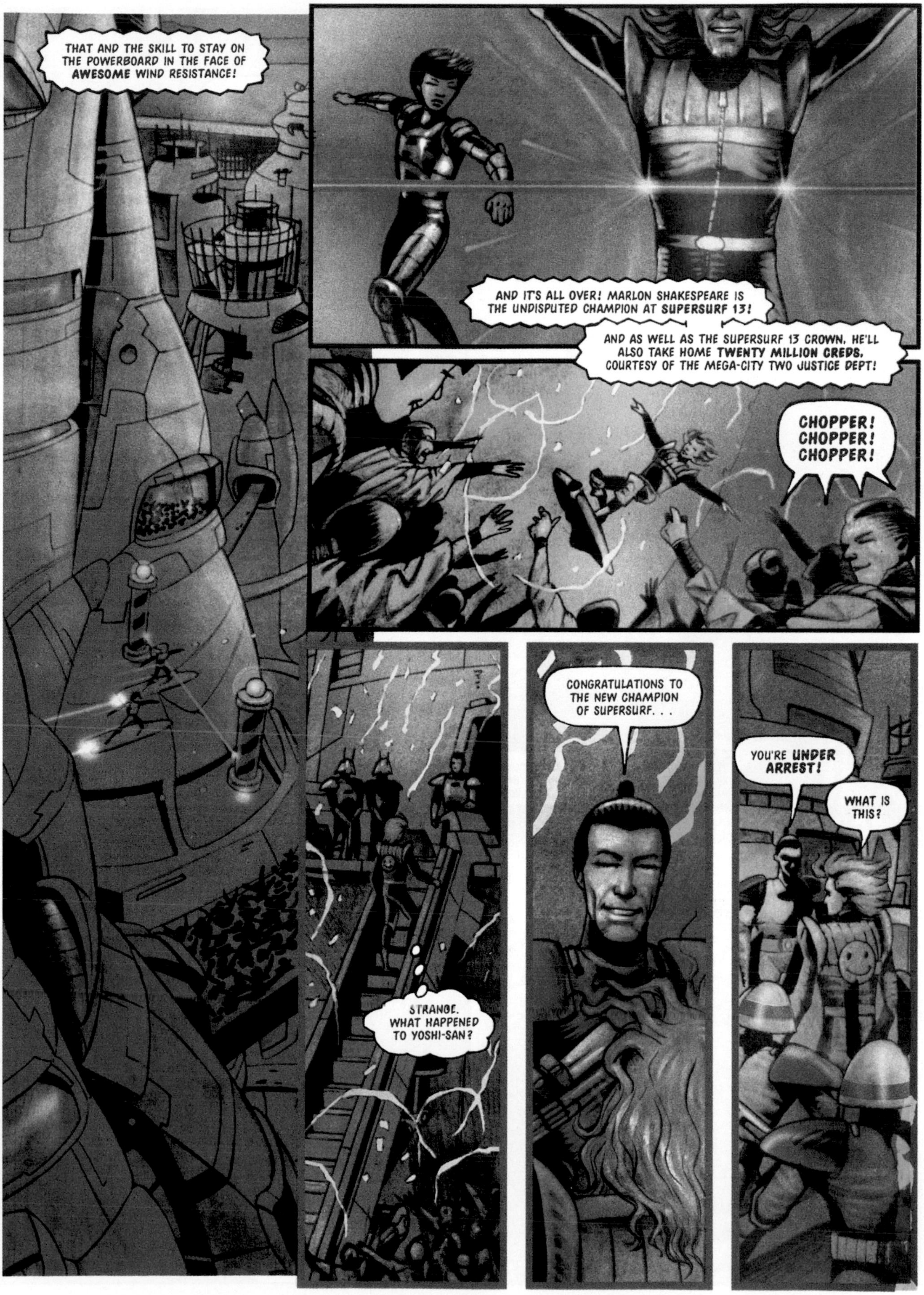

THAT AND THE SKILL TO STAY ON THE POWERBOARD IN THE FACE OF AWESOME WIND RESISTANCE!
AND IT'S ALL OVER! MARLON SHAKESPEARE IS THE UNDISPUTED CHAMPION AT SUPERSURF 13!
AND AS WELL AS THE SUPERSURF 13 CROWN, HE'LL ALSO TAKE HOME TWENTY MILLION CREDS, COURTESY OF THE MEGA-CITY TWO JUSTICE DEPT!
CHOPPER! CHOPPER! CHOPPER!
STRANGE. WHAT HAPPENED TO YOSHI-SAN?
CONGRATULATIONS TO THE NEW CHAMPION OF SUPERSURF. . .
YOU'RE UNDER ARREST!
WHAT IS THIS?

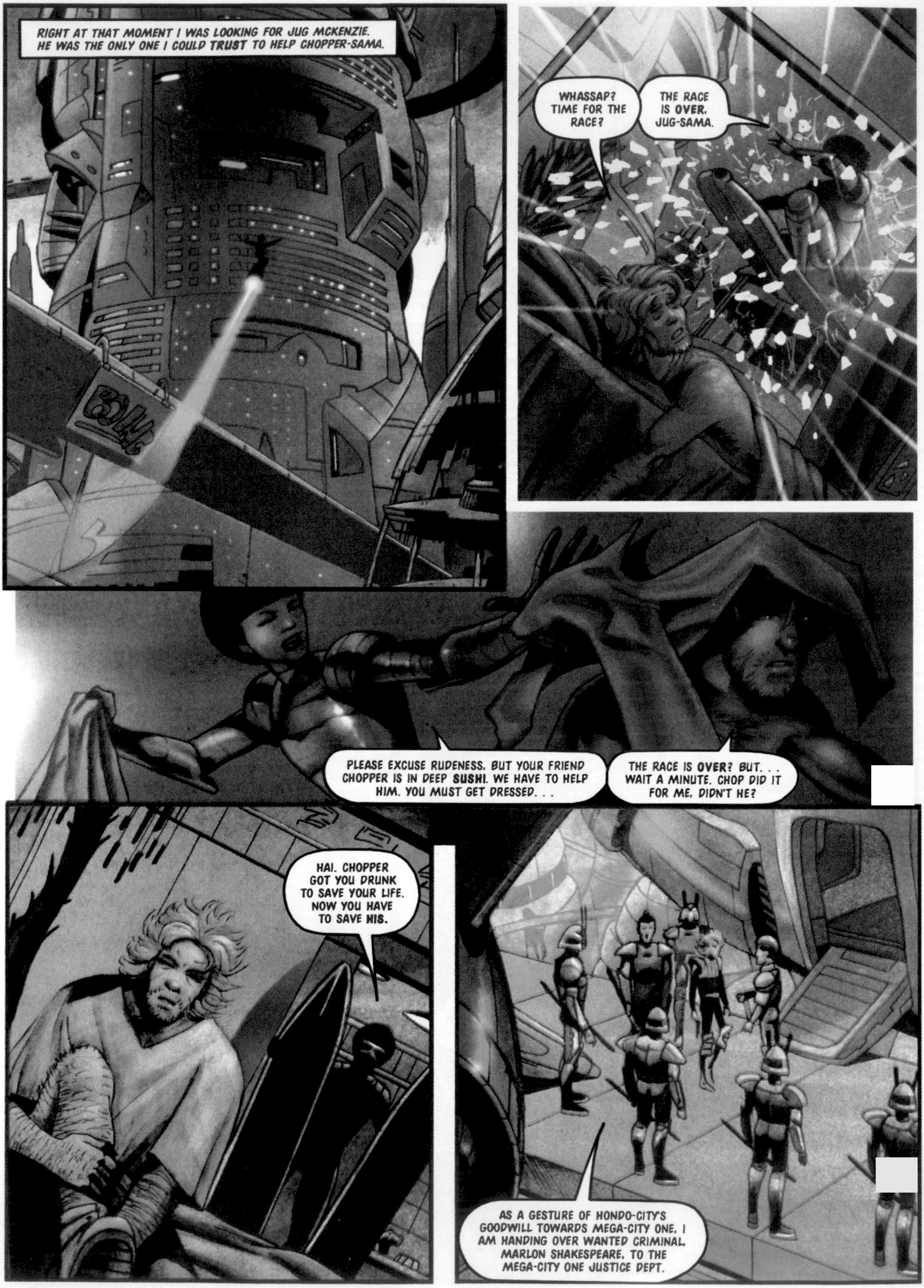

RIGHT AT THAT MOMENT I WAS LOOKING FOR JUG MCKENZIE. HE WAS THE ONLY ONE I COULD TRUST TO HELP CHOPPER-SAMA.
WHASSAP? TIME FOR THE RACE?
THE RACE IS OVER, JUG-SAMA.
PLEASE EXCUSE RUDENESS, BUT YOUR FRIEND CHOPPER IS IN DEEP SUSHI. WE HAVE TO HELP HIM. YOU MUST GET DRESSED. . .
THE RACE IS OVER? BUT. . . WAIT A MINUTE. CHOP DID IT FOR ME, DIDN'T HE?
HAI. CHOPPER GOT YOU DRUNK TO SAVE YOUR LIFE. NOW YOU HAVE TO SAVE HIS.
AS A GESTURE OF HONDO-CITY'S GOODWILL TOWARDS MEGA-CITY ONE, I AM HANDING OVER WANTED CRIMINAL, MARLON SHAKESPEARE, TO THE MEGA-CITY ONE JUSTICE DEPT.

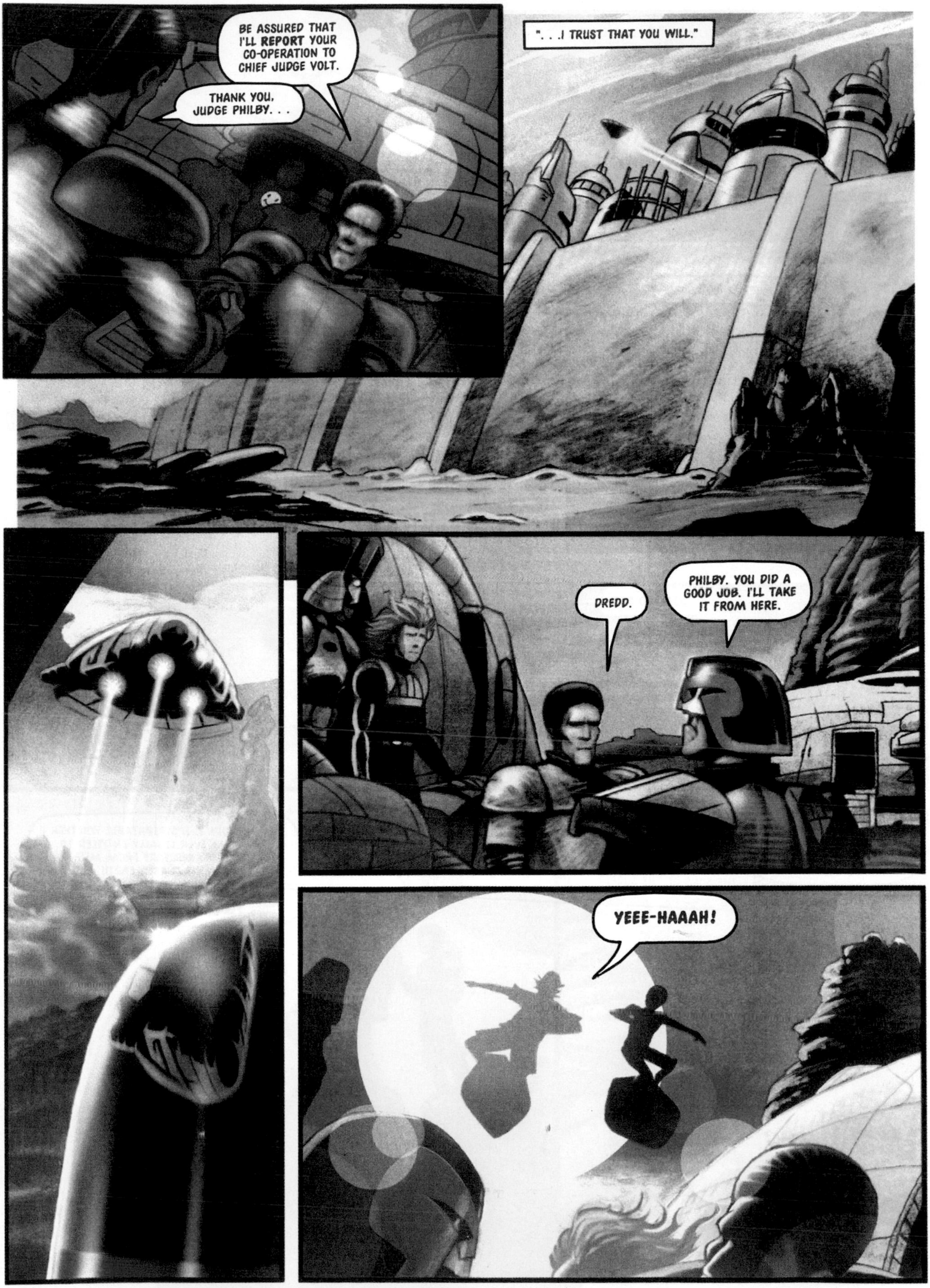
BE ASSURED THAT I'LL REPORT YOUR CO-OPERATION TO CHIEF JUDGE VOLT.
THANK YOU, JUDGE PHILBY. . .
". . .I TRUST THAT YOU WILL."
DREDD.
PHILBY. YOU DID A GOOD JOB. I'LL TAKE IT FROM HERE.
YEEE-HAAAH!

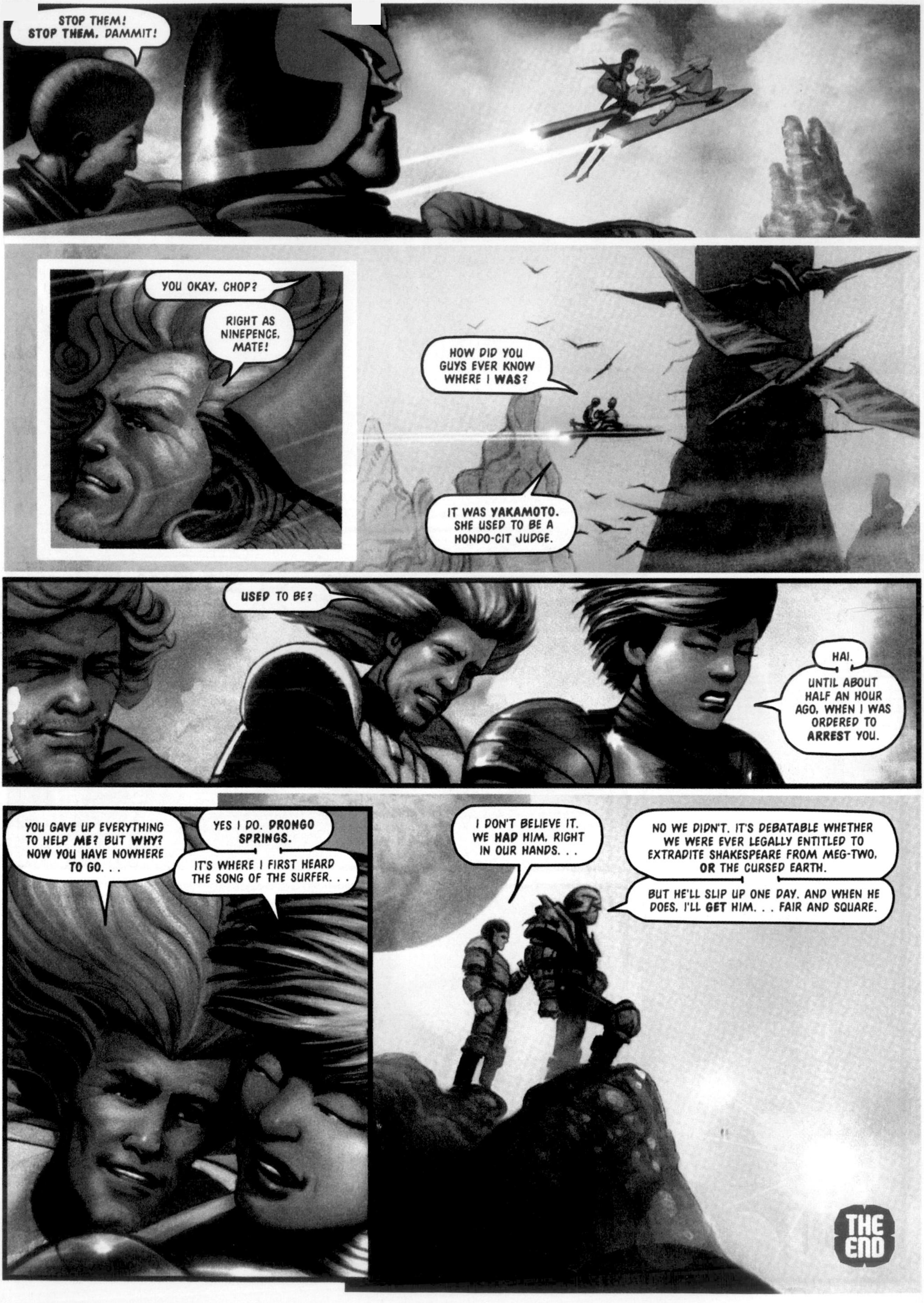
STOP THEM! STOP THEM, DAMMIT!
YOU OKAY, CHOP?
RIGHT AS NINEPENCE, MATE!
HOW DID YOU GUYS EVER KNOW WHERE I WAS?
IT WAS YAKAMOTO. SHE USED TO BE A HONDO-CIT JUDGE.
USED TO BE?
HAI.
UNTIL ABOUT HALF AN HOUR AGO, WHEN I WAS ORDERED TO ARREST YOU.
YOU GAVE UP EVERYTHING TO HELP ME? BUT WHY? NOW YOU HAVE NOWHERE TO GO. . .
YES I DO. DRONGO SPRINGS.
IT'S WHERE I FIRST HEARD THE SONG OF THE SURFER. . .
I DON'T BELIEVE IT. WE HAD HIM, RIGHT IN OUR HANDS. . .
NO WE DIDN'T. IT'S DEBATABLE WHETHER WE WERE EVER LEGALLY ENTITLED TO EXTRADITE SHAKESPEARE FROM MEG-TWO, OR THE CURSED EARTH.
BUT HE'LL SLIP UP ONE DAY. AND WHEN HE DOES, I'LL GET HIM. . . FAIR AND SQUARE.
THE END

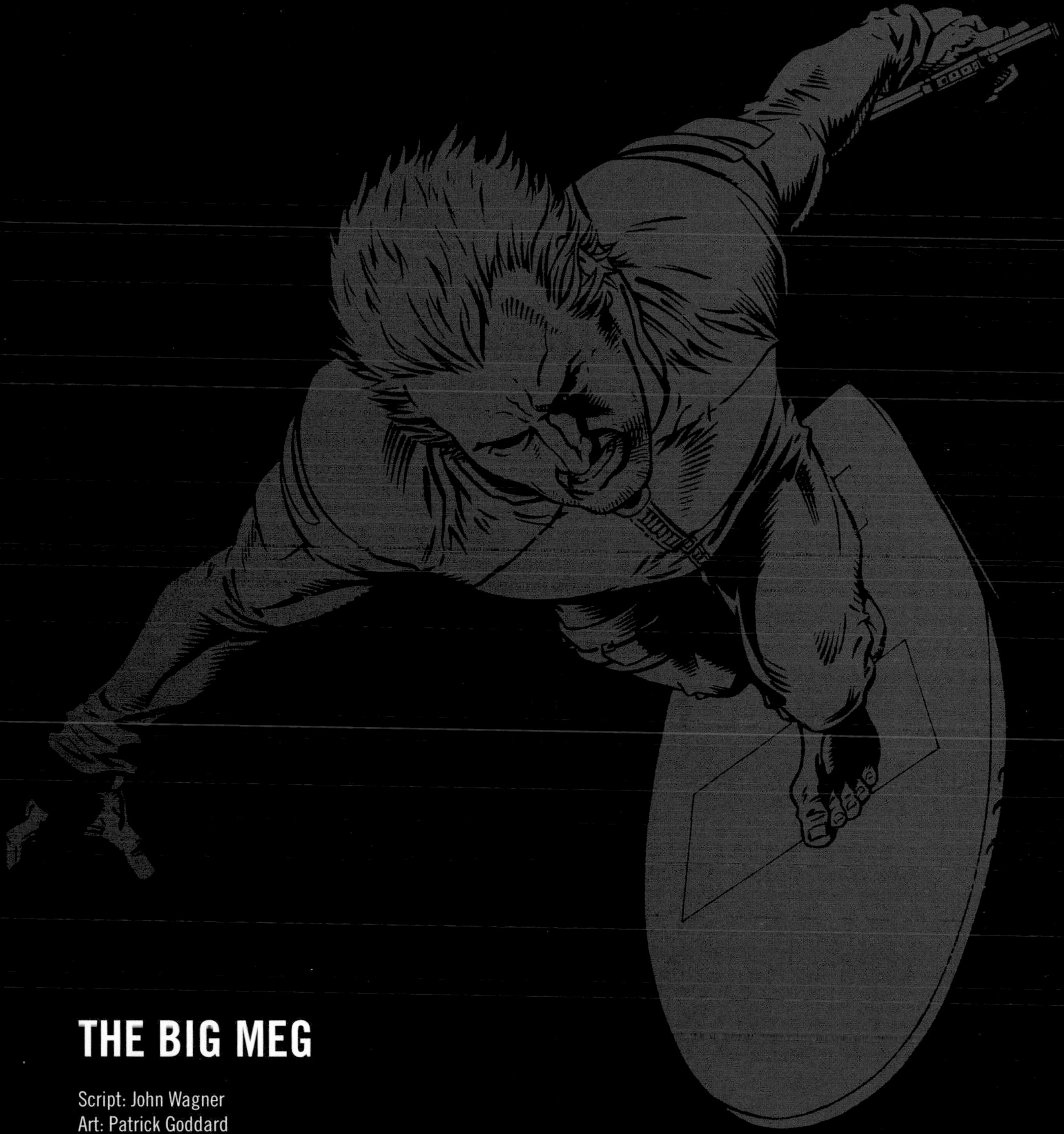

THE BIG MEG

Script: John Wagner
Art: Patrick Goddard
Pencils: Dylan Teague
Colours: Chris Blythe
Letters: Tom Frame

Originally printed in *2000 AD* Progs 1387-1394

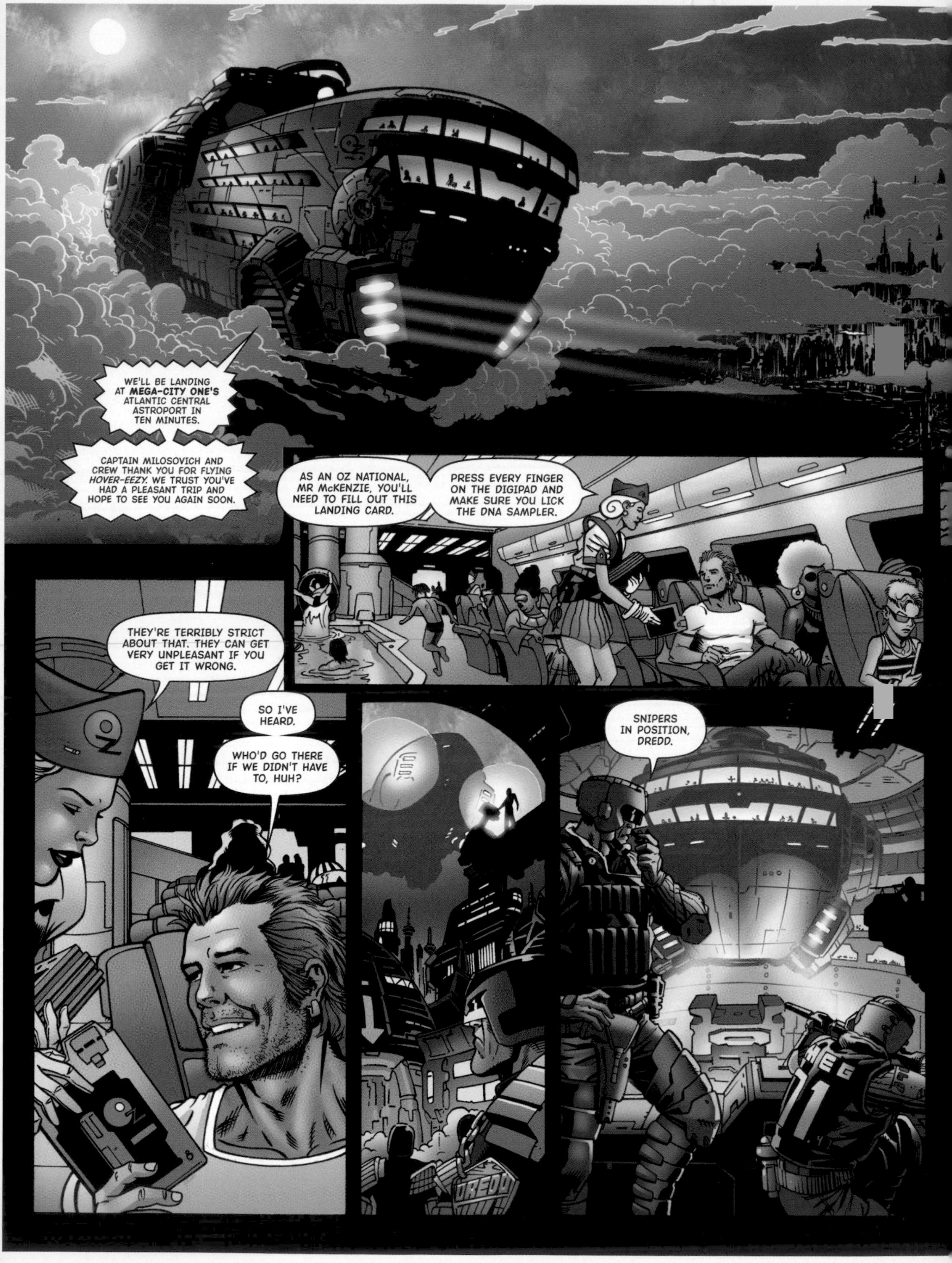

WE'LL BE LANDING AT MEGA-CITY ONE'S ATLANTIC CENTRAL ASTROPORT IN TEN MINUTES.
CAPTAIN MILOSOVICH AND CREW THANK YOU FOR FLYING HOVER-EEZY. WE TRUST YOU'VE HAD A PLEASANT TRIP AND HOPE TO SEE YOU AGAIN SOON.
AS AN OZ NATIONAL, MR McKENZIE, YOU'LL NEED TO FILL OUT THIS LANDING CARD.
PRESS EVERY FINGER ON THE DIGIPAD AND MAKE SURE YOU LICK THE DNA SAMPLER.
THEY'RE TERRIBLY STRICT ABOUT THAT. THEY CAN GET VERY UNPLEASANT IF YOU GET IT WRONG.
SO I'VE HEARD.
WHO'D GO THERE IF WE DIDN'T HAVE TO, HUH?
SNIPERS IN POSITION, DREDD.

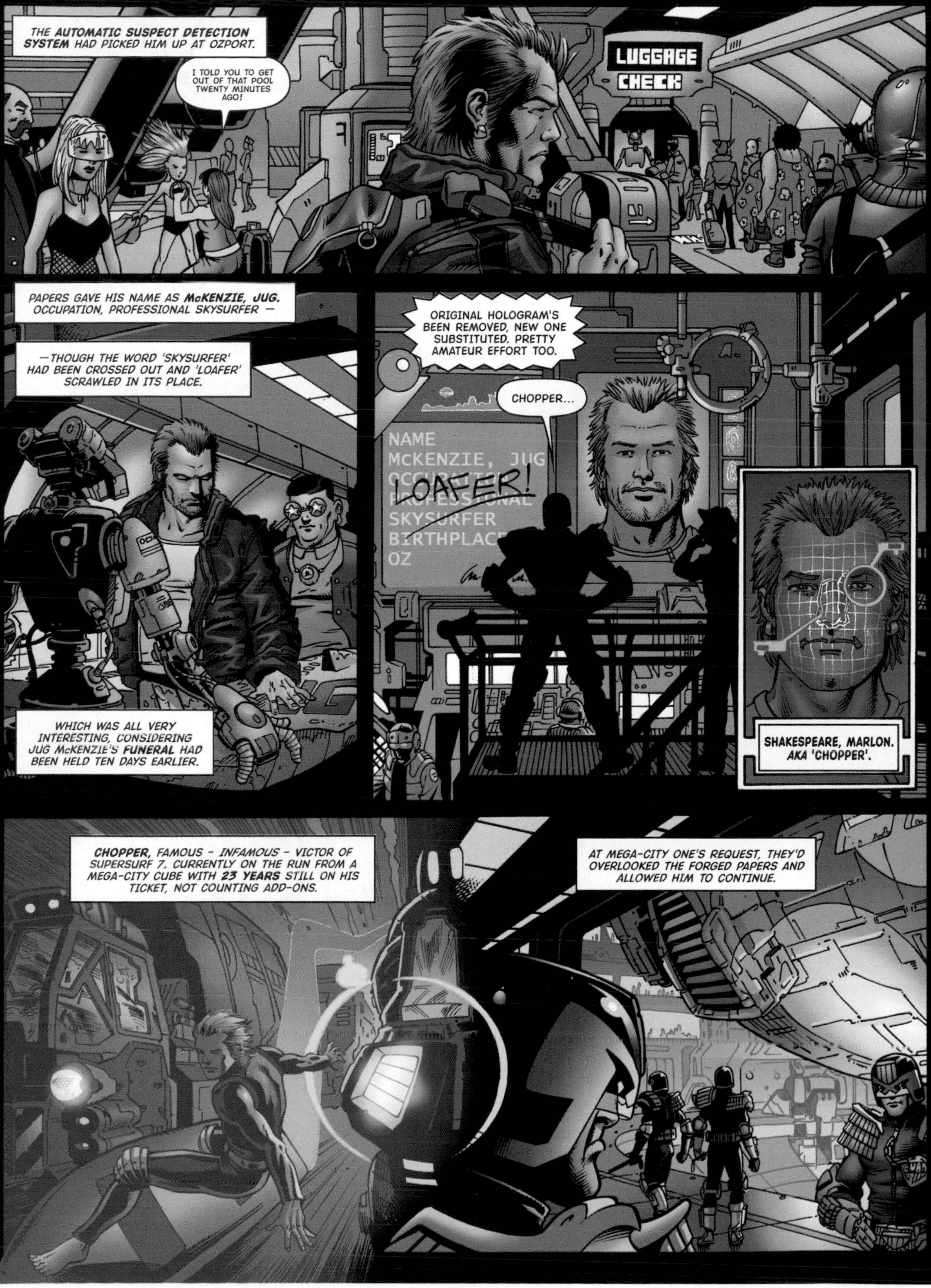
THE AUTOMATIC SUSPECT DETECTION SYSTEM HAD PICKED HIM UP AT OZPORT.
I TOLD YOU TO GET OUT OF THAT POOL TWENTY MINUTES AGO!
LUGGAGE CHECK
PAPERS GAVE HIS NAME AS McKENZIE, JUG. OCCUPATION, PROFESSIONAL SKYSURFER —
—THOUGH THE WORD 'SKYSURFER' HAD BEEN CROSSED OUT AND 'LOAFER' SCRAWLED IN ITS PLACE.
WHICH WAS ALL VERY INTERESTING, CONSIDERING JUG McKENZIE'S FUNERAL HAD BEEN HELD TEN DAYS EARLIER.
ORIGINAL HOLOGRAM'S BEEN REMOVED, NEW ONE SUBSTITUTED. PRETTY AMATEUR EFFORT TOO.
CHOPPER...
NAME
McKENZIE, JUG
LOAFER!
SKYSURFER
OZ
SHAKESPEARE, MARLON. AKA 'CHOPPER'.
CHOPPER, FAMOUS - INFAMOUS - VICTOR OF SUPERSURF 7. CURRENTLY ON THE RUN FROM A MEGA-CITY CUBE WITH 23 YEARS STILL ON HIS TICKET, NOT COUNTING ADD-ONS.
AT MEGA-CITY ONE'S REQUEST, THEY'D OVERLOOKED THE FORGED PAPERS AND ALLOWED HIM TO CONTINUE.

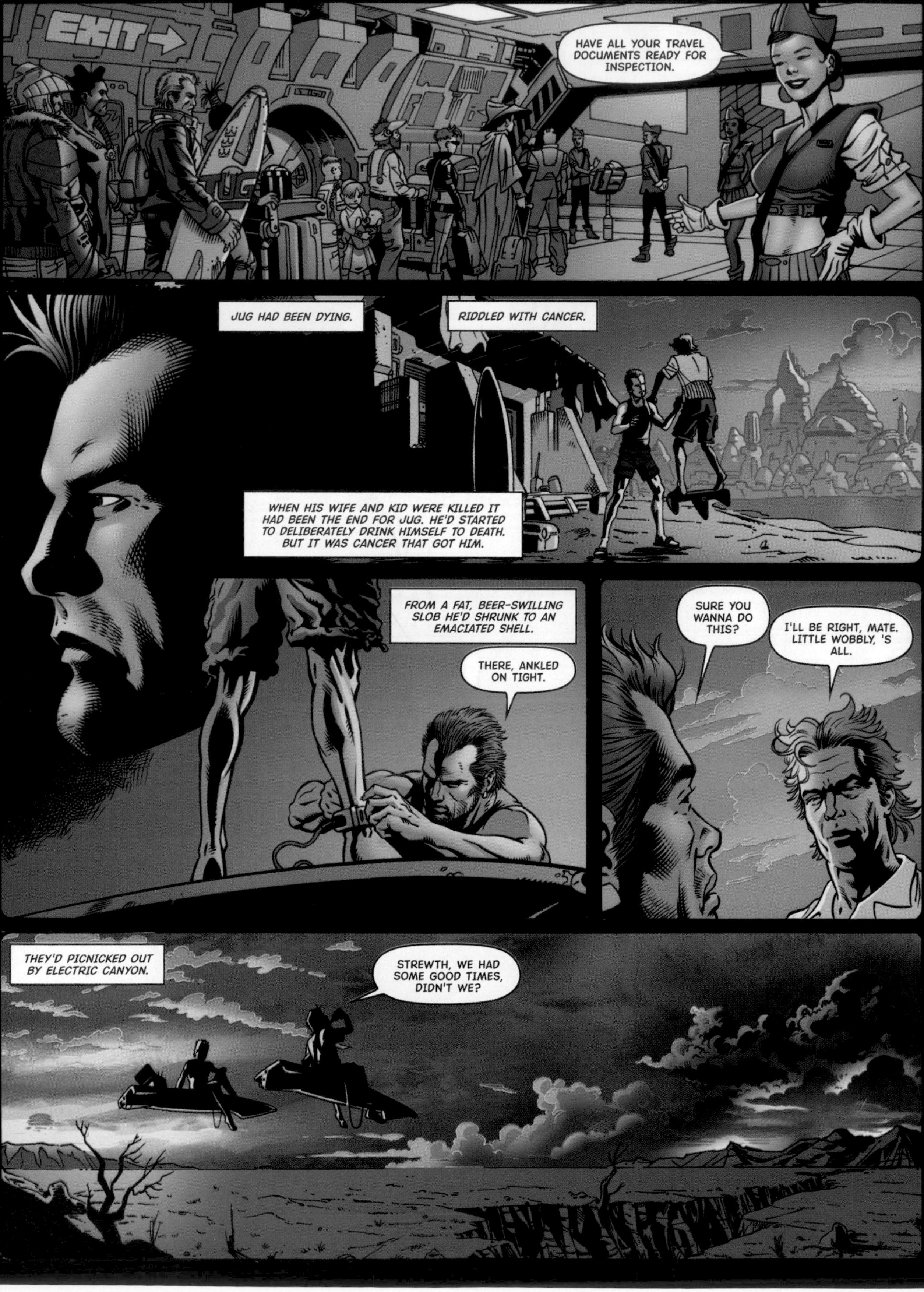
EXIT
HAVE ALL YOUR TRAVEL DOCUMENTS READY FOR INSPECTION.
JUG HAD BEEN DYING.
RIDDLED WITH CANCER.
WHEN HIS WIFE AND KID WERE KILLED IT HAD BEEN THE END FOR JUG. HE'D STARTED TO DELIBERATELY DRINK HIMSELF TO DEATH. BUT IT WAS CANCER THAT GOT HIM.
FROM A FAT, BEER-SWILLING SLOB HE'D SHRUNK TO AN EMACIATED SHELL.
THERE, ANKLED ON TIGHT.
SURE YOU WANNA DO THIS?
I'LL BE RIGHT, MATE. LITTLE WOBBLY, 'S ALL.
THEY'D PICNICKED OUT BY ELECTRIC CANYON.
STREWTH, WE HAD SOME GOOD TIMES, DIDN'T WE?

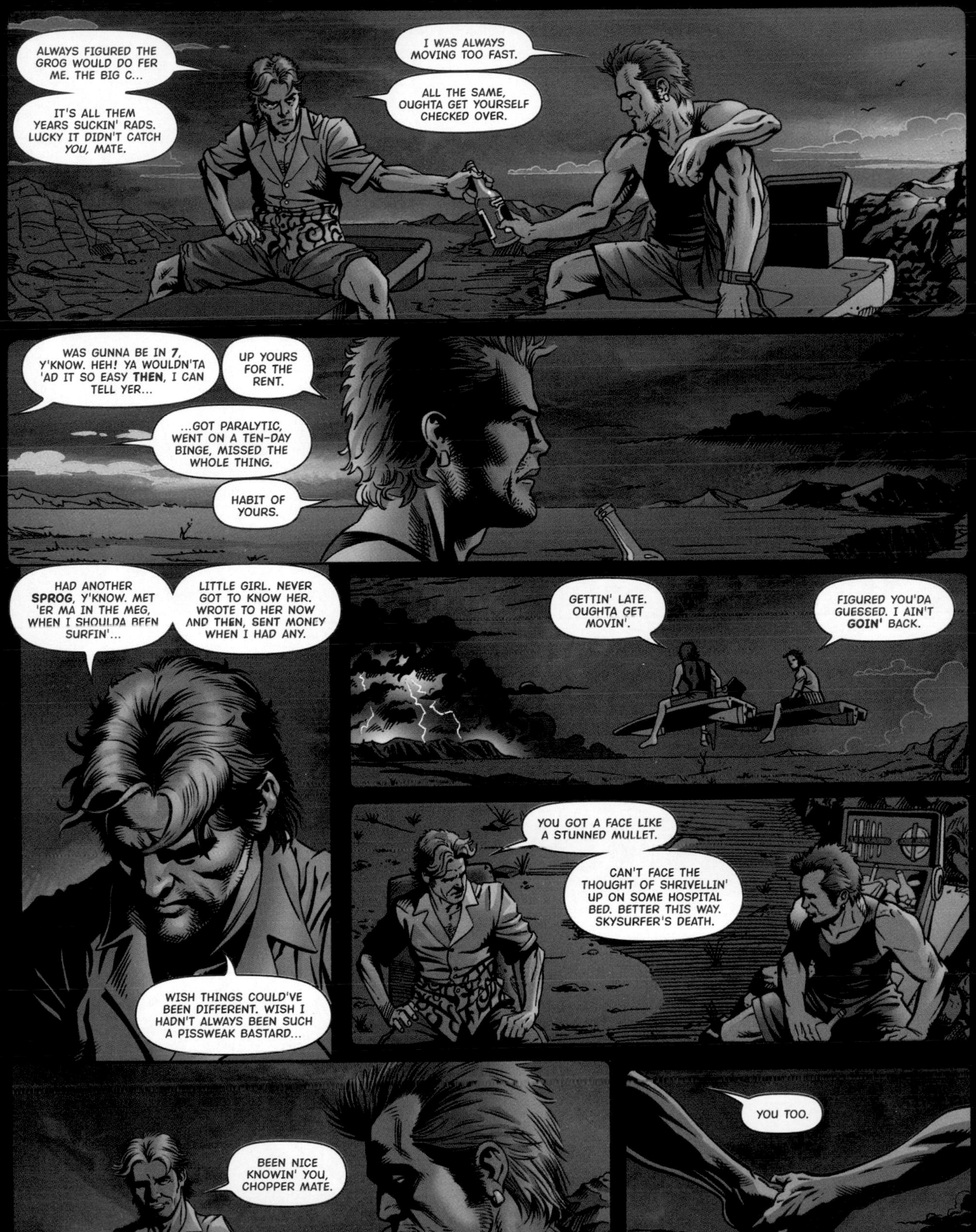
ALWAYS FIGURED THE GROG WOULD DO FER ME. THE BIG C...
I WAS ALWAYS MOVING TOO FAST.
IT'S ALL THEM YEARS SUCKIN' RADS. LUCKY IT DIDN'T CATCH *YOU,* MATE.
ALL THE SAME, OUGHTA GET YOURSELF CHECKED OVER.
WAS GUNNA BE IN **7**, Y'KNOW. HEH! YA WOULDN'TA 'AD IT SO EASY **THEN**, I CAN TELL YER...
UP YOURS FOR THE RENT.
...GOT PARALYTIC, WENT ON A TEN-DAY BINGE, MISSED THE WHOLE THING.
HABIT OF YOURS.
HAD ANOTHER **SPROG**, Y'KNOW. MET 'ER MA IN THE MEG, WHEN I SHOULDA BEEN SURFIN'...
LITTLE GIRL. NEVER GOT TO KNOW HER. WROTE TO HER NOW AND THEN, SENT MONEY WHEN I HAD ANY.
WISH THINGS COULD'VE BEEN DIFFERENT. WISH I HADN'T ALWAYS BEEN SUCH A PISSWEAK BASTARD...
GETTIN' LATE. OUGHTA GET MOVIN'.
FIGURED YOU'DA GUESSED. I AIN'T **GOIN'** BACK.
YOU GOT A FACE LIKE A STUNNED MULLET.
CAN'T FACE THE THOUGHT OF SHRIVELLIN' UP ON SOME HOSPITAL BED. BETTER THIS WAY. SKYSURFER'S DEATH.
BEEN NICE KNOWIN' YOU, CHOPPER MATE.
YOU TOO.

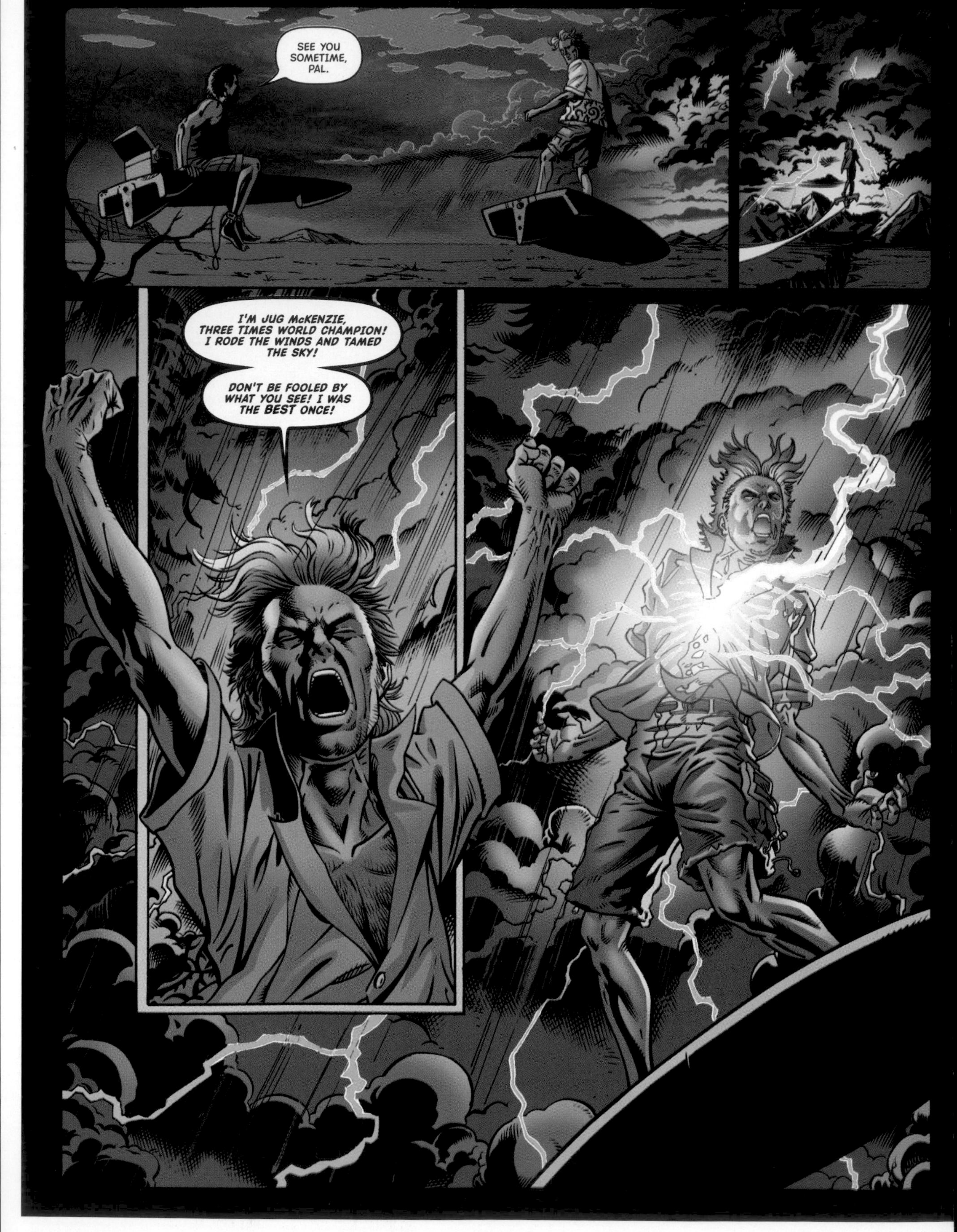
SEE YOU SOMETIME, PAL.
I'M JUG McKENZIE, THREE TIMES WORLD CHAMPION! I RODE THE WINDS AND TAMED THE SKY!
DON'T BE FOOLED BY WHAT YOU SEE! I WAS THE BEST ONCE!

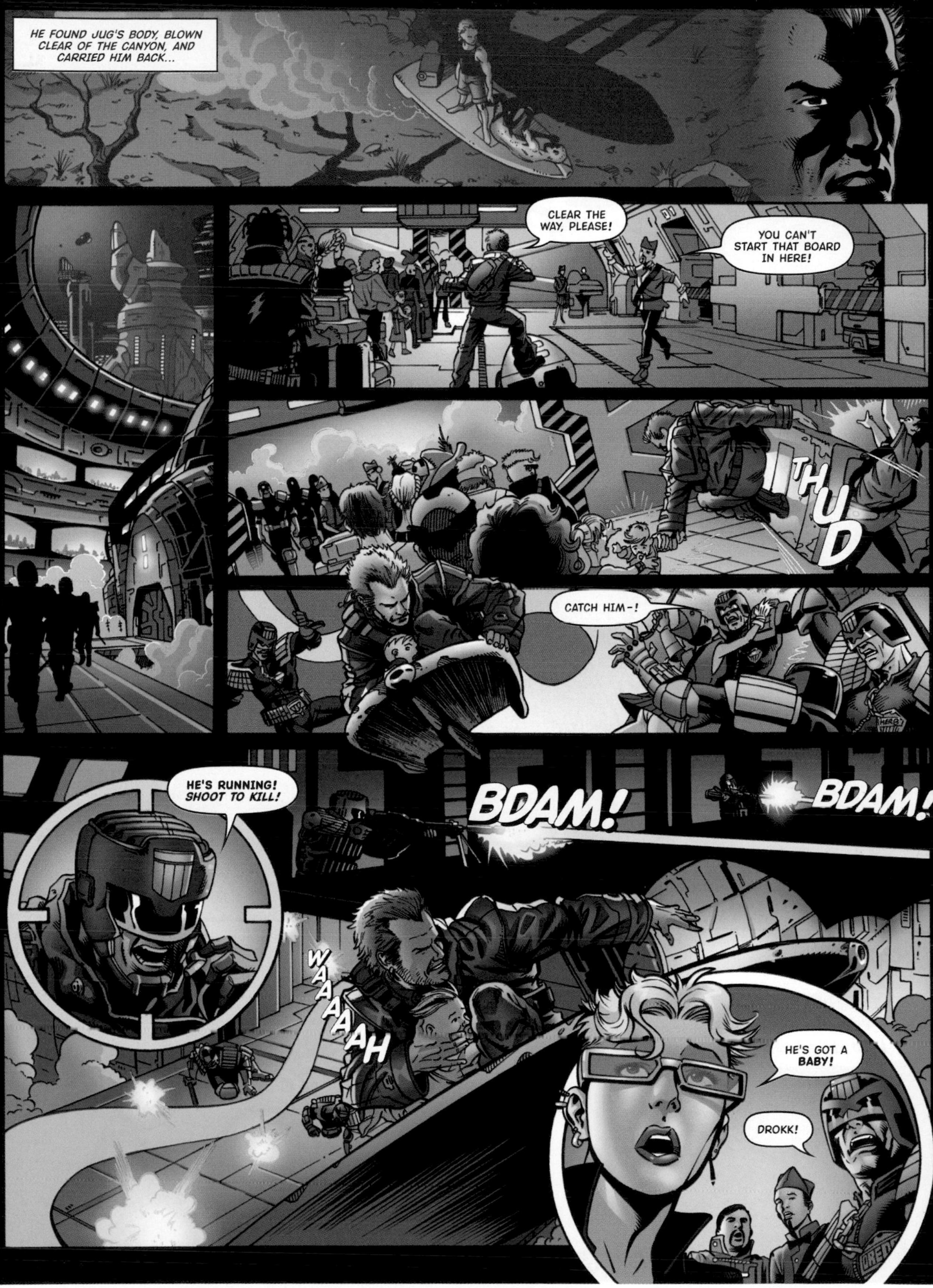
HE FOUND JUG'S BODY, BLOWN CLEAR OF THE CANYON, AND CARRIED HIM BACK...
CLEAR THE WAY, PLEASE!
YOU CAN'T START THAT BOARD IN HERE!
THUD
CATCH HIM-!
HE'S RUNNING! SHOOT TO KILL!
BDAM!
BDAM!
WAAAAAH
HE'S GOT A BABY!
DROKK!

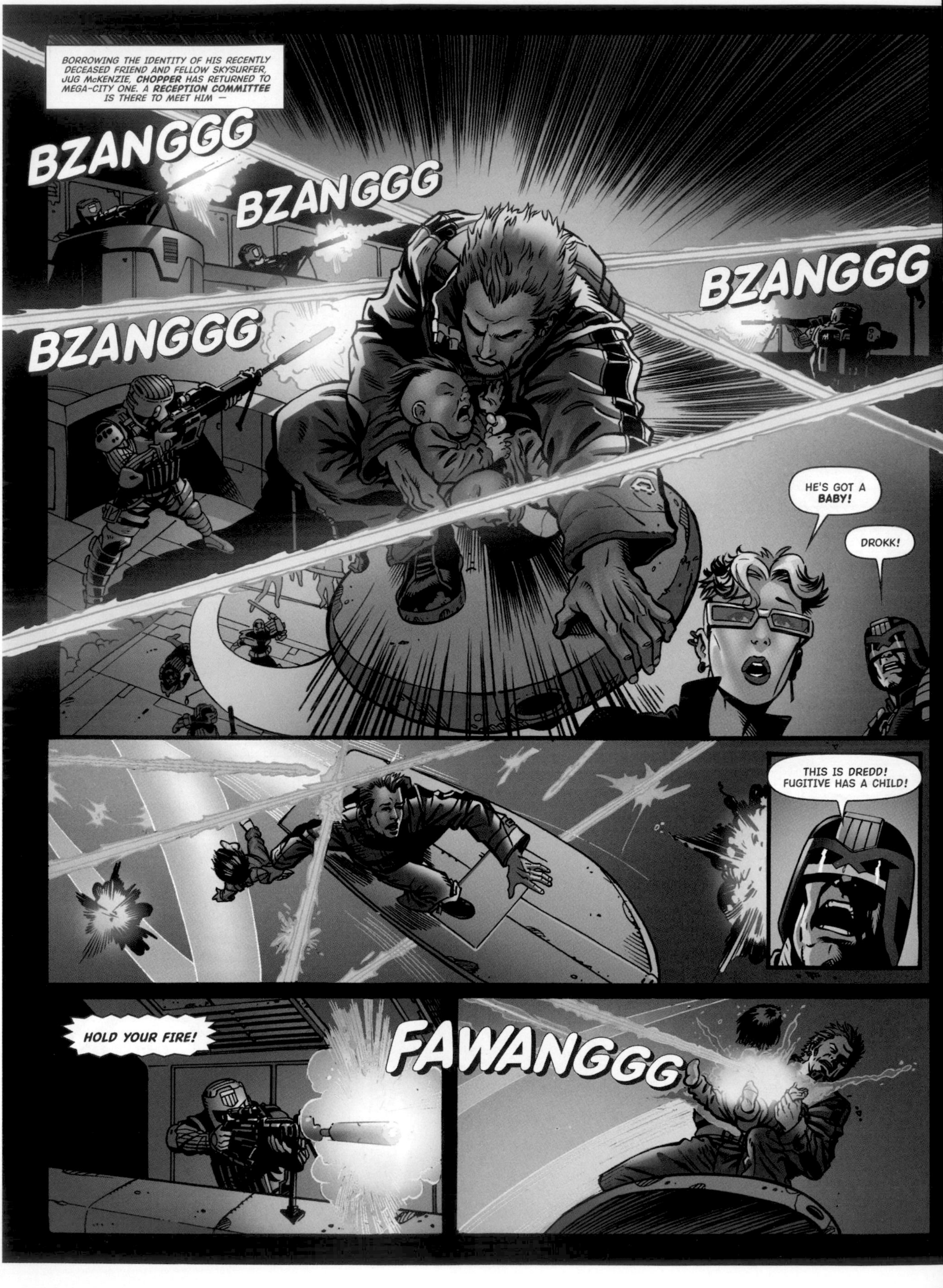
BORROWING THE IDENTITY OF HIS RECENTLY DECEASED FRIEND AND FELLOW SKYSURFER, JUG McKENZIE, CHOPPER HAS RETURNED TO MEGA-CITY ONE. A RECEPTION COMMITTEE IS THERE TO MEET HIM —
BZANGGG
BZANGGG
BZANGGG
BZANGGG
HE'S GOT A BABY!
DROKK!
THIS IS DREDD! FUGITIVE HAS A CHILD!
HOLD YOUR FIRE!
FAWANGGG

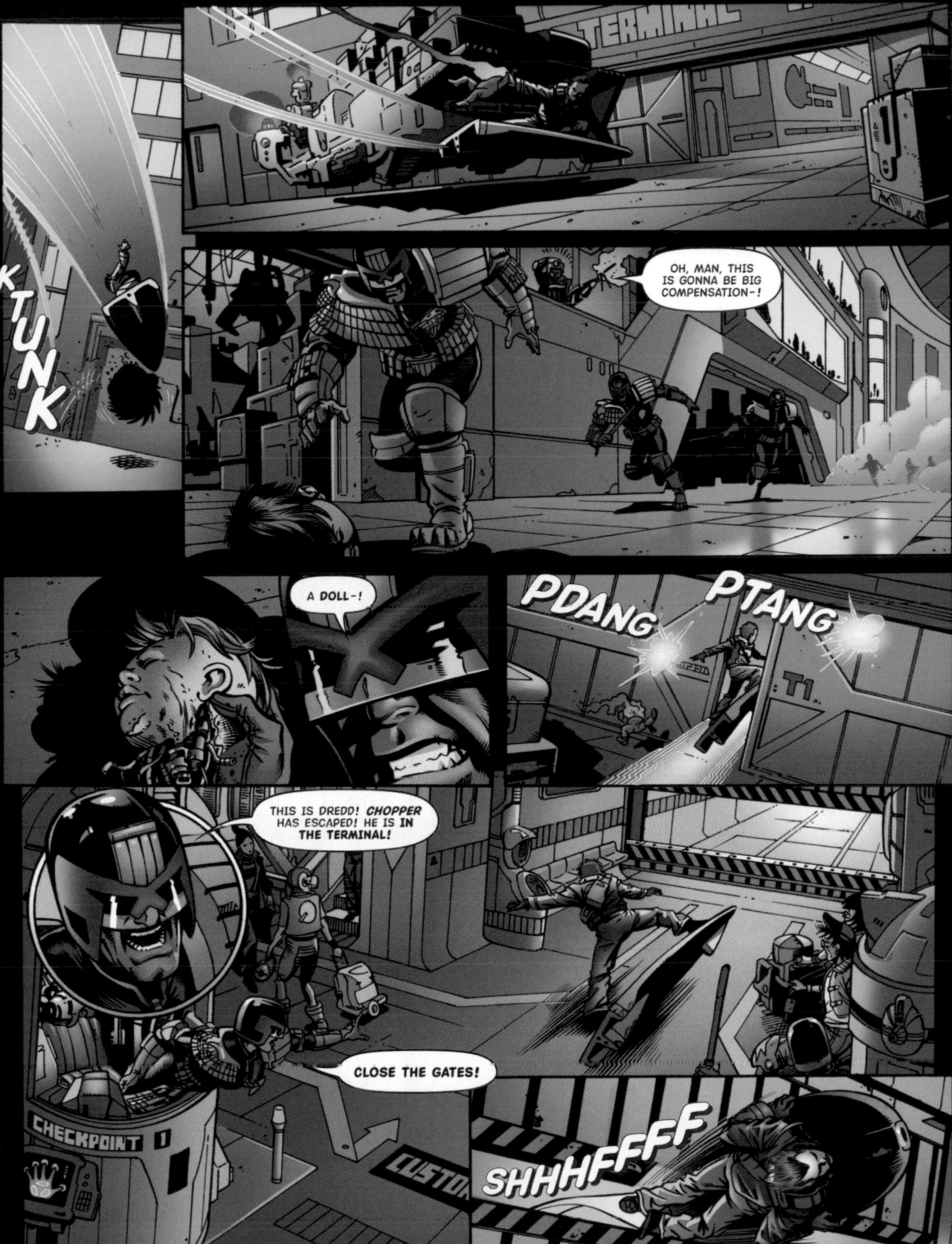
KTUNK
OH, MAN, THIS IS GONNA BE BIG COMPENSATION-!
A DOLL-!
PDANG
PTANG
THIS IS DREDD! CHOPPER HAS ESCAPED! HE IS IN THE TERMINAL!
CLOSE THE GATES!
CHECKPOINT 1
SHHHFFFFF

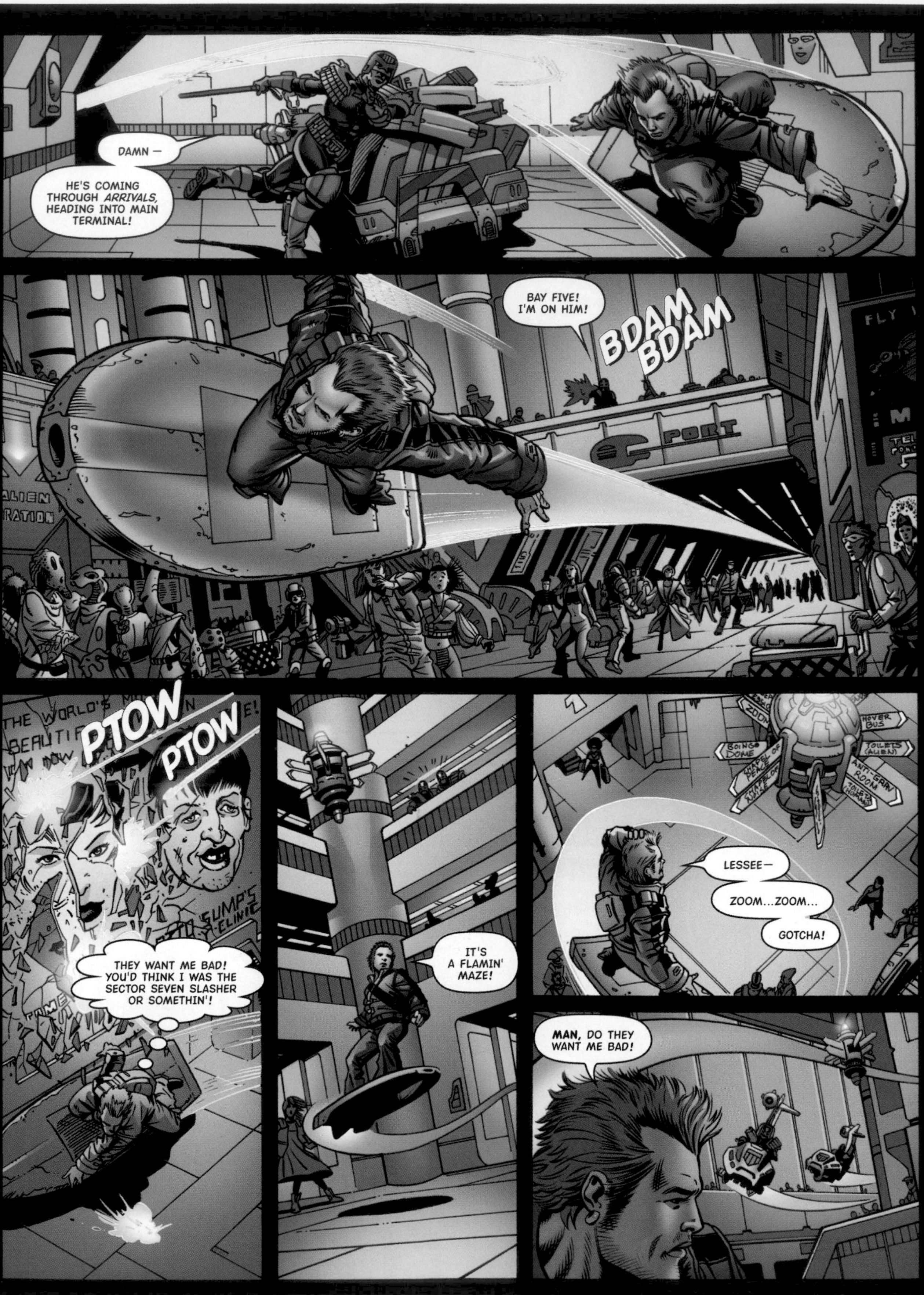
DAMN —
HE'S COMING THROUGH *ARRIVALS*, HEADING INTO MAIN TERMINAL!
BAY FIVE! I'M ON HIM!
BDAM BDAM
PTOW PTOW
THEY WANT ME BAD! YOU'D THINK I WAS THE SECTOR SEVEN SLASHER OR SOMETHIN'!
IT'S A FLAMIN' MAZE!
LESSEE—
ZOOM...ZOOM...
GOTCHA!
MAN, DO THEY WANT ME BAD!

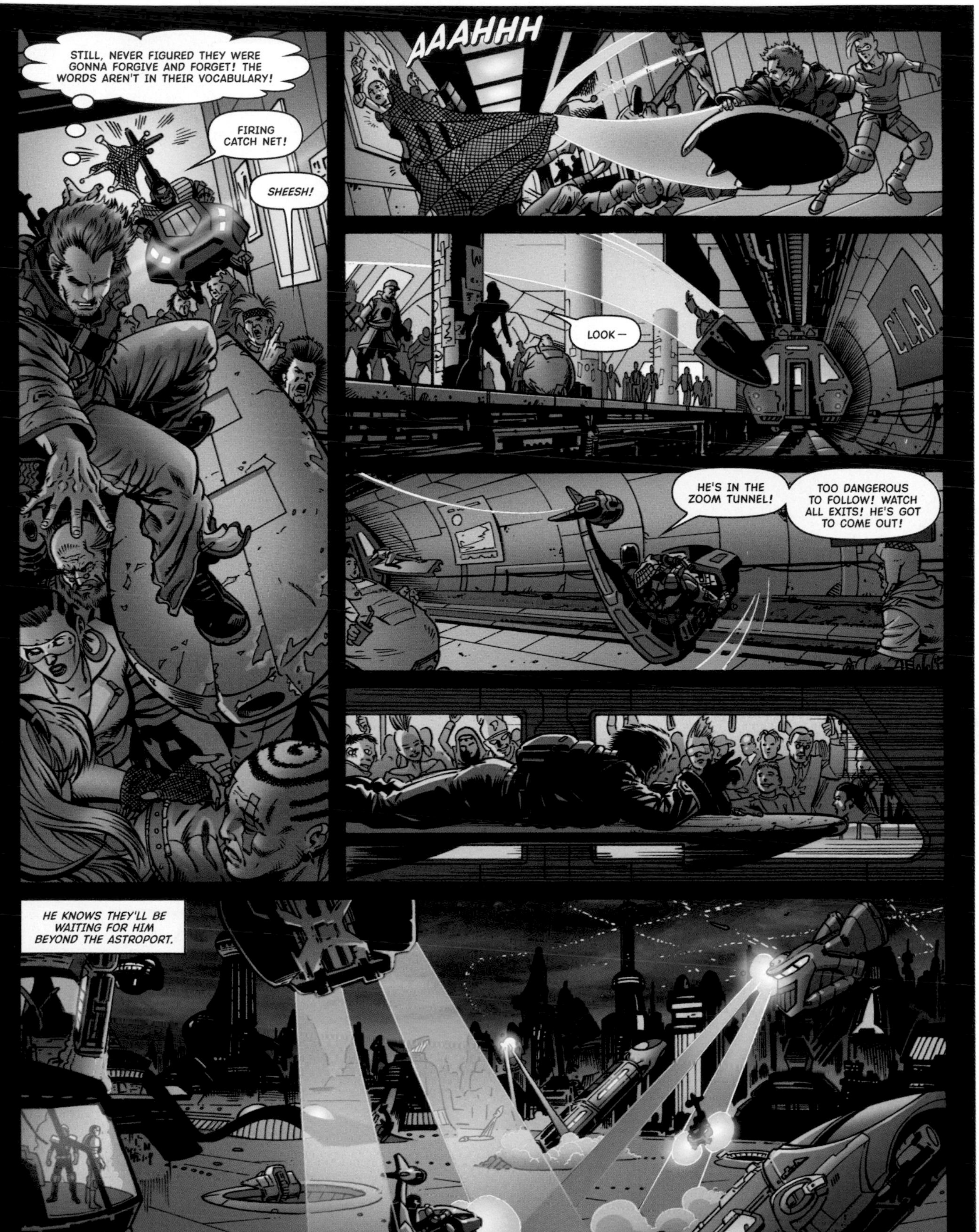
STILL, NEVER FIGURED THEY WERE GONNA FORGIVE AND FORGET! THE WORDS AREN'T IN THEIR VOCABULARY!
FIRING CATCH NET!
SHEESH!
AAAHHH
LOOK—
C.L.A.P.
HE'S IN THE ZOOM TUNNEL!
TOO DANGEROUS TO FOLLOW! WATCH ALL EXITS! HE'S GOT TO COME OUT!
HE KNOWS THEY'LL BE WAITING FOR HIM BEYOND THE ASTROPORT.

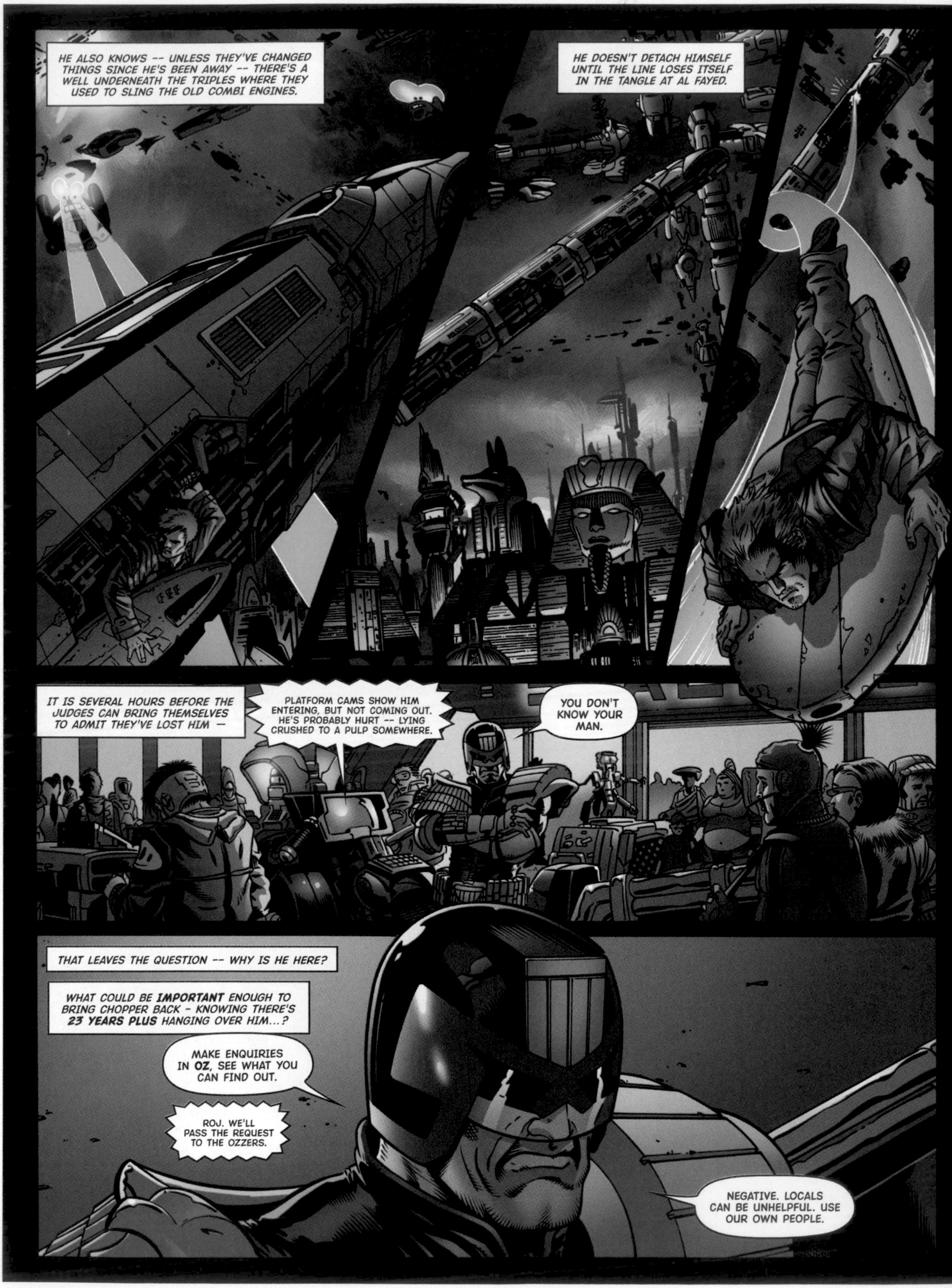
HE ALSO KNOWS -- UNLESS THEY'VE CHANGED THINGS SINCE HE'S BEEN AWAY -- THERE'S A WELL UNDERNEATH THE TRIPLES WHERE THEY USED TO SLING THE OLD COMBI ENGINES.
HE DOESN'T DETACH HIMSELF UNTIL THE LINE LOSES ITSELF IN THE TANGLE AT AL FAYED.
IT IS SEVERAL HOURS BEFORE THE JUDGES CAN BRING THEMSELVES TO ADMIT THEY'VE LOST HIM —
PLATFORM CAMS SHOW HIM ENTERING, BUT NOT COMING OUT. HE'S PROBABLY HURT -- LYING CRUSHED TO A PULP SOMEWHERE.
YOU DON'T KNOW YOUR MAN.
THAT LEAVES THE QUESTION -- WHY IS HE HERE?
WHAT COULD BE IMPORTANT ENOUGH TO BRING CHOPPER BACK - KNOWING THERE'S 23 YEARS PLUS HANGING OVER HIM...?
MAKE ENQUIRIES IN OZ, SEE WHAT YOU CAN FIND OUT.
ROJ. WE'LL PASS THE REQUEST TO THE OZZERS.
NEGATIVE. LOCALS CAN BE UNHELPFUL. USE OUR OWN PEOPLE.

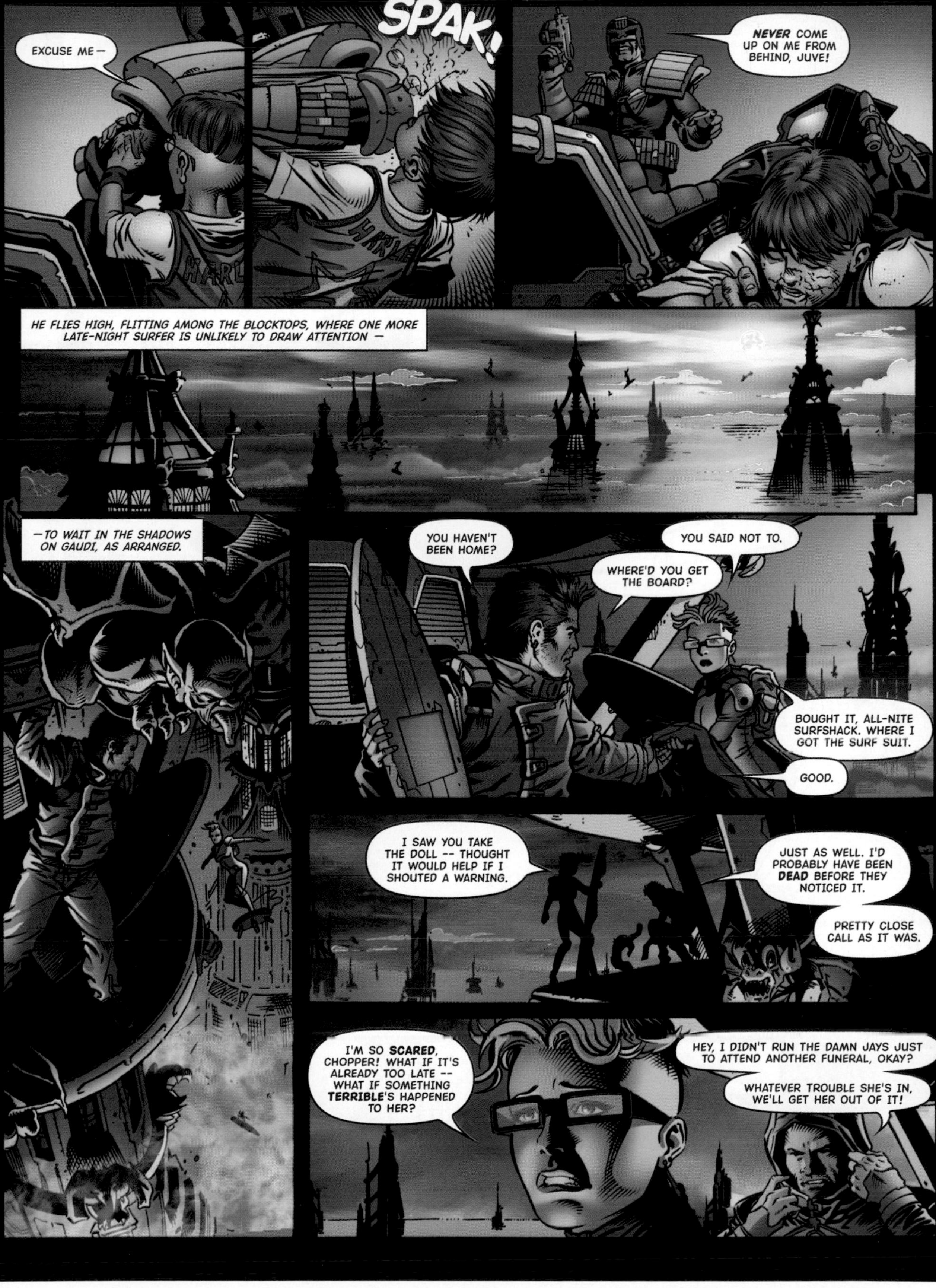
EXCUSE ME—
SPAK!
NEVER COME UP ON ME FROM BEHIND, JUVE!
HE FLIES HIGH, FLITTING AMONG THE BLOCKTOPS, WHERE ONE MORE LATE-NIGHT SURFER IS UNLIKELY TO DRAW ATTENTION —
—TO WAIT IN THE SHADOWS ON GAUDI, AS ARRANGED.
YOU HAVEN'T BEEN HOME?
YOU SAID NOT TO.
WHERE'D YOU GET THE BOARD?
BOUGHT IT, ALL-NITE SURFSHACK. WHERE I GOT THE SURF SUIT.
GOOD.
I SAW YOU TAKE THE DOLL -- THOUGHT IT WOULD HELP IF I SHOUTED A WARNING.
JUST AS WELL. I'D PROBABLY HAVE BEEN DEAD BEFORE THEY NOTICED IT.
PRETTY CLOSE CALL AS IT WAS.
I'M SO SCARED, CHOPPER! WHAT IF IT'S ALREADY TOO LATE -- WHAT IF SOMETHING TERRIBLE'S HAPPENED TO HER?
HEY, I DIDN'T RUN THE DAMN JAYS JUST TO ATTEND ANOTHER FUNERAL, OKAY?
WHATEVER TROUBLE SHE'S IN, WE'LL GET HER OUT OF IT!

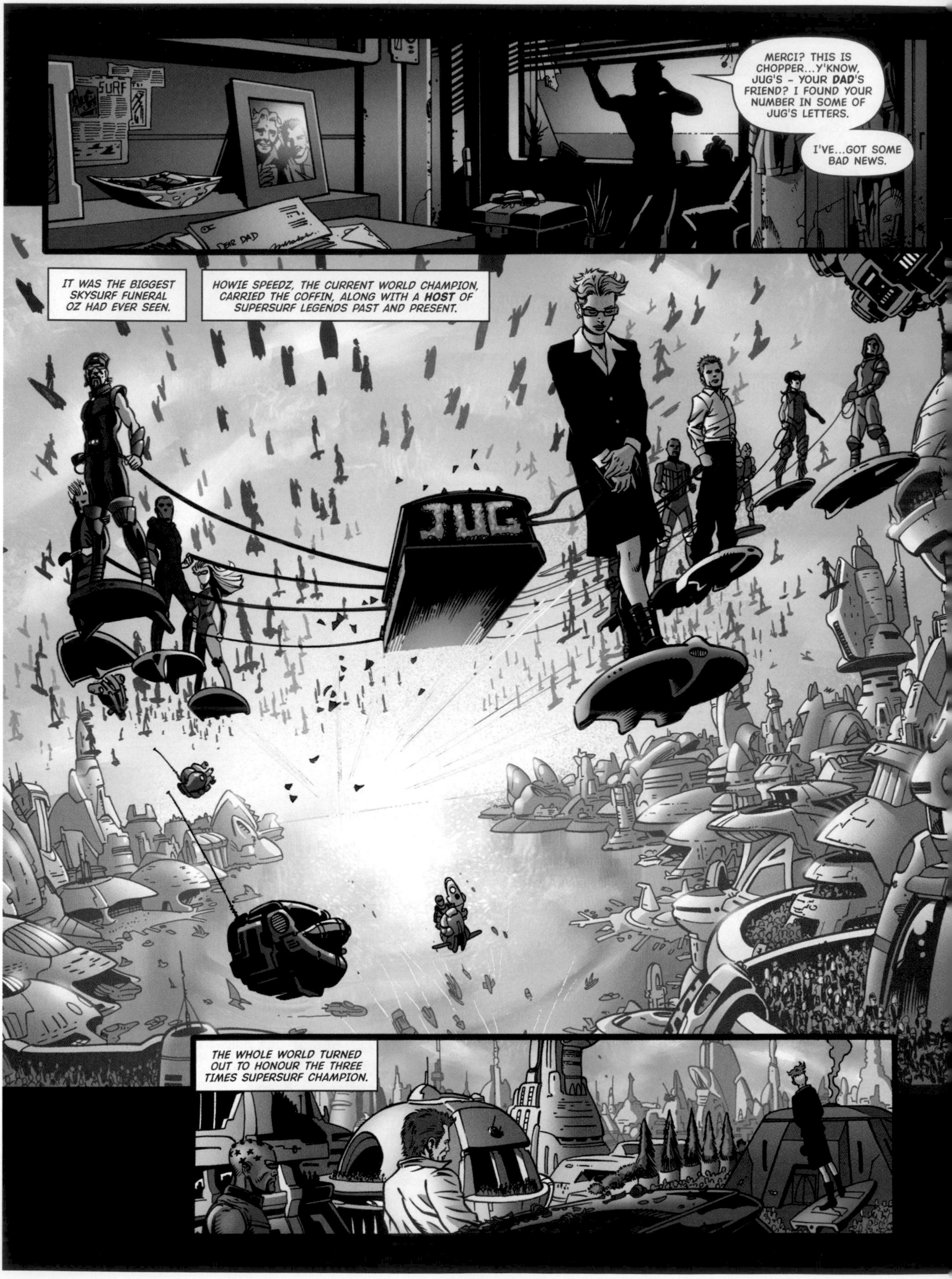
SURF
DEAR DAD
MERCI? THIS IS CHOPPER...Y'KNOW, JUG'S - YOUR DAD'S FRIEND? I FOUND YOUR NUMBER IN SOME OF JUG'S LETTERS.
I'VE...GOT SOME BAD NEWS.
IT WAS THE BIGGEST SKYSURF FUNERAL OZ HAD EVER SEEN.
HOWIE SPEEDZ, THE CURRENT WORLD CHAMPION, CARRIED THE COFFIN, ALONG WITH A HOST OF SUPERSURF LEGENDS PAST AND PRESENT.
JUG
THE WHOLE WORLD TURNED OUT TO HONOUR THE THREE TIMES SUPERSURF CHAMPION.

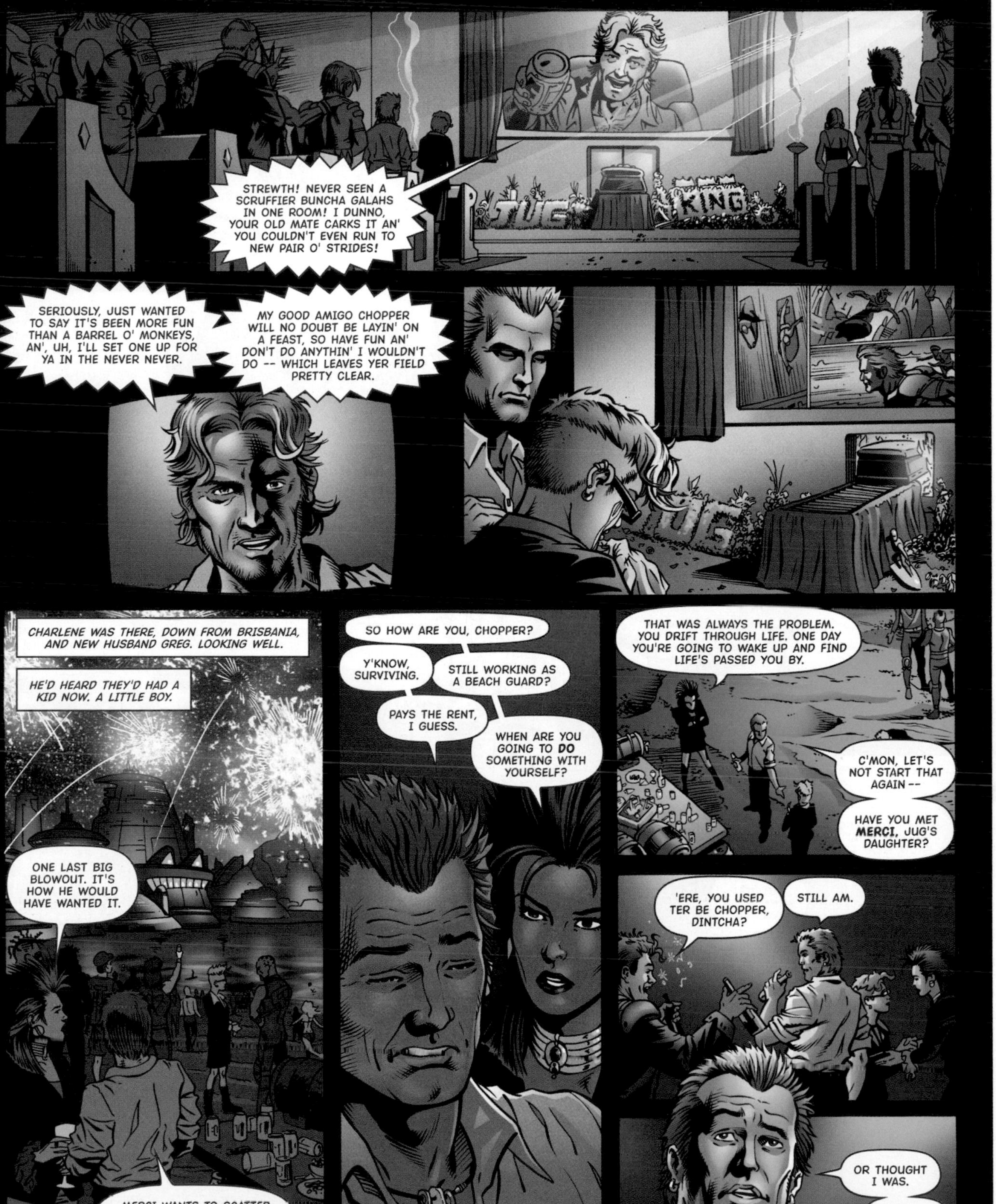

STREWTH! NEVER SEEN A SCRUFFIER BUNCHA GALAHS IN ONE ROOM! I DUNNO, YOUR OLD MATE CARKS IT AN' YOU COULDN'T EVEN RUN TO NEW PAIR O' STRIDES!
JUG
KING
SERIOUSLY, JUST WANTED TO SAY IT'S BEEN MORE FUN THAN A BARREL O' MONKEYS, AN', UH, I'LL SET ONE UP FOR YA IN THE NEVER NEVER.
MY GOOD AMIGO CHOPPER WILL NO DOUBT BE LAYIN' ON A FEAST, SO HAVE FUN AN' DON'T DO ANYTHIN' I WOULDN'T DO -- WHICH LEAVES YER FIELD PRETTY CLEAR.
JUG
CHARLENE WAS THERE, DOWN FROM BRISBANIA, AND NEW HUSBAND GREG. LOOKING WELL.
HE'D HEARD THEY'D HAD A KID NOW. A LITTLE BOY.
ONE LAST BIG BLOWOUT. IT'S HOW HE WOULD HAVE WANTED IT.
MERCI WANTS TO SCATTER HIS ASHES IN THE RADBACK. DIDN'T HAVE THE HEART TO TELL HER DOOLAN'S BAR MIGHT BE MORE APPROPRIATE.
SO HOW ARE YOU, CHOPPER?
Y'KNOW, SURVIVING.
STILL WORKING AS A BEACH GUARD?
PAYS THE RENT, I GUESS.
WHEN ARE YOU GOING TO **DO** SOMETHING WITH YOURSELF?
THAT WAS ALWAYS THE PROBLEM. YOU DRIFT THROUGH LIFE. ONE DAY YOU'RE GOING TO WAKE UP AND FIND LIFE'S PASSED YOU BY.
C'MON, LET'S NOT START THAT AGAIN --
HAVE YOU MET **MERCI**, JUG'S DAUGHTER?
'ERE, YOU USED TER BE CHOPPER, DINTCHA?
STILL AM.
OR THOUGHT I WAS.
MAYBE I'M NOT.

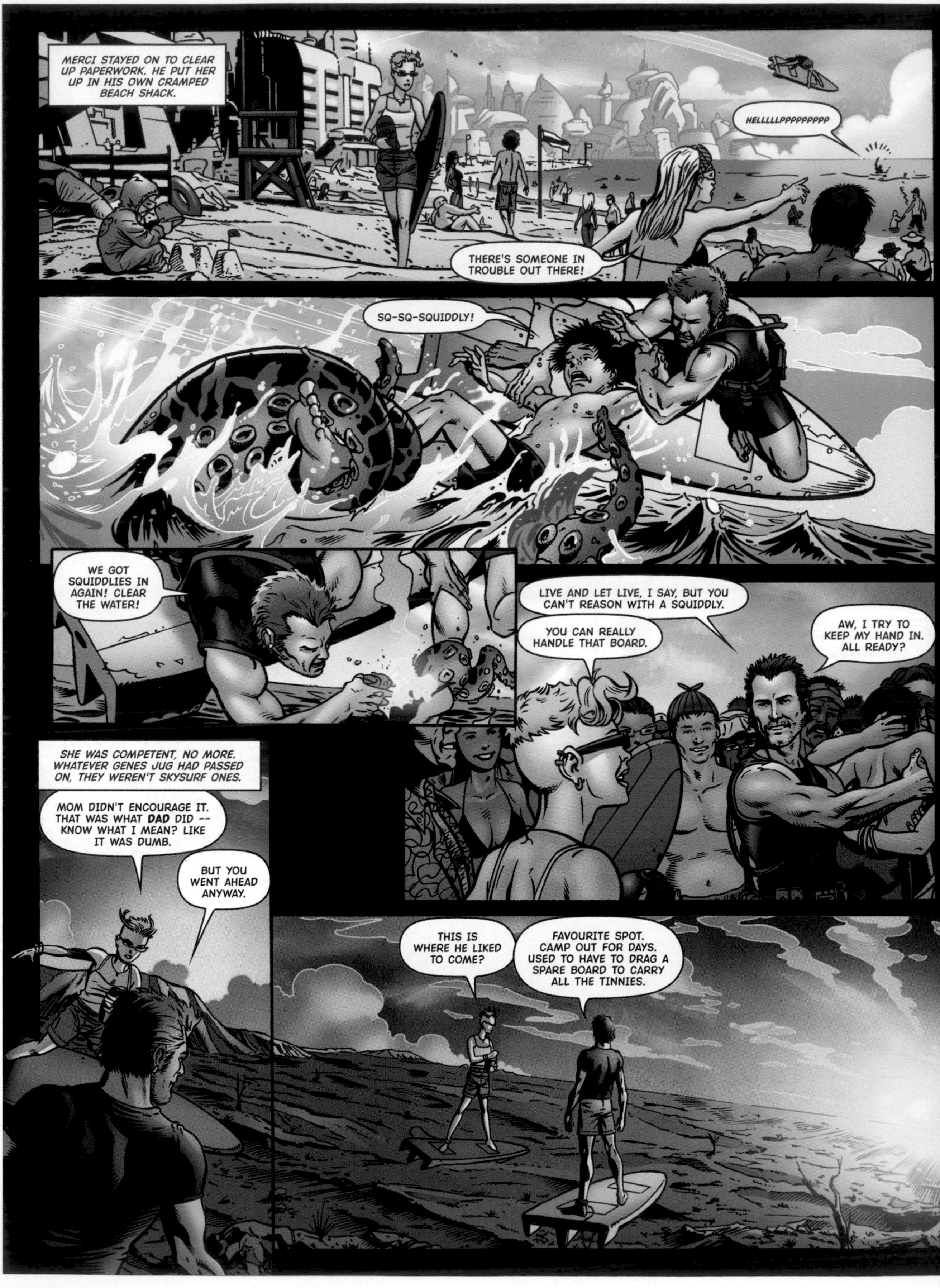
MERCI STAYED ON TO CLEAR UP PAPERWORK. HE PUT HER UP IN HIS OWN CRAMPED BEACH SHACK.
HELLLLLLPPPPPPPPP
THERE'S SOMEONE IN TROUBLE OUT THERE!
SQ-SQ-SQUIDDLY!
WE GOT SQUIDDLIES IN AGAIN! CLEAR THE WATER!
LIVE AND LET LIVE, I SAY, BUT YOU CAN'T REASON WITH A SQUIDDLY.
YOU CAN REALLY HANDLE THAT BOARD.
AW, I TRY TO KEEP MY HAND IN. ALL READY?
SHE WAS COMPETENT, NO MORE. WHATEVER GENES JUG HAD PASSED ON, THEY WEREN'T SKYSURF ONES.
MOM DIDN'T ENCOURAGE IT. THAT WAS WHAT DAD DID -- KNOW WHAT I MEAN? LIKE IT WAS DUMB.
BUT YOU WENT AHEAD ANYWAY.
THIS IS WHERE HE LIKED TO COME?
FAVOURITE SPOT. CAMP OUT FOR DAYS. USED TO HAVE TO DRAG A SPARE BOARD TO CARRY ALL THE TINNIES.

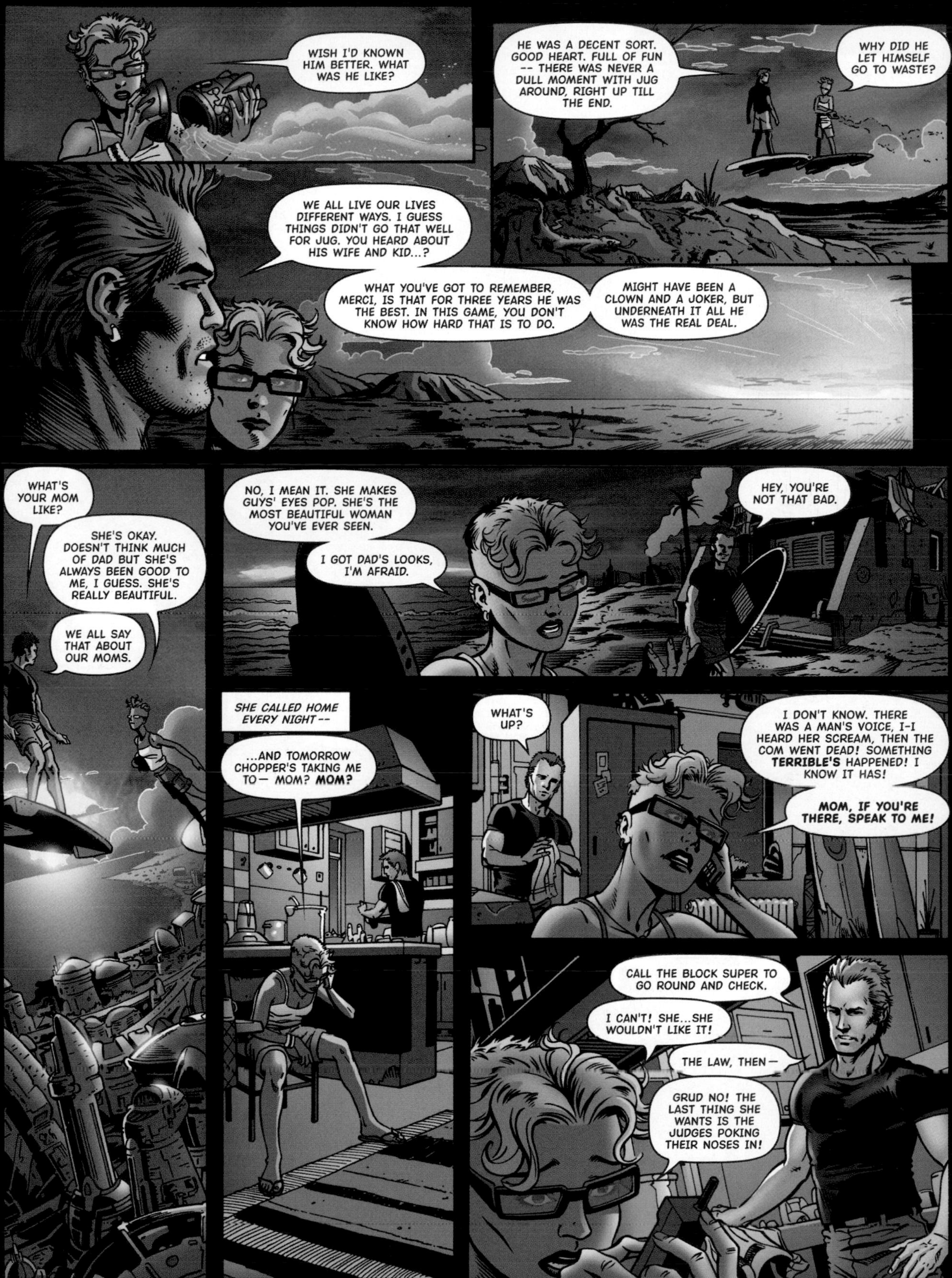
WISH I'D KNOWN HIM BETTER. WHAT WAS HE LIKE?
HE WAS A DECENT SORT. GOOD HEART. FULL OF FUN -- THERE WAS NEVER A DULL MOMENT WITH JUG AROUND, RIGHT UP TILL THE END.
WHY DID HE LET HIMSELF GO TO WASTE?
WE ALL LIVE OUR LIVES DIFFERENT WAYS. I GUESS THINGS DIDN'T GO THAT WELL FOR JUG. YOU HEARD ABOUT HIS WIFE AND KID...?
WHAT YOU'VE GOT TO REMEMBER, MERCI, IS THAT FOR THREE YEARS HE WAS THE BEST. IN THIS GAME, YOU DON'T KNOW HOW HARD THAT IS TO DO.
MIGHT HAVE BEEN A CLOWN AND A JOKER, BUT UNDERNEATH IT ALL HE WAS THE REAL DEAL.
WHAT'S YOUR MOM LIKE?
SHE'S OKAY. DOESN'T THINK MUCH OF DAD BUT SHE'S ALWAYS BEEN GOOD TO ME, I GUESS. SHE'S REALLY BEAUTIFUL.
WE ALL SAY THAT ABOUT OUR MOMS.
NO, I MEAN IT. SHE MAKES GUYS' EYES POP. SHE'S THE MOST BEAUTIFUL WOMAN YOU'VE EVER SEEN.
I GOT DAD'S LOOKS, I'M AFRAID.
HEY, YOU'RE NOT THAT BAD.
SHE CALLED HOME EVERY NIGHT --
...AND TOMORROW CHOPPER'S TAKING ME TO— MOM? **MOM?**
WHAT'S UP?
I DON'T KNOW. THERE WAS A MAN'S VOICE, I-I HEARD HER SCREAM, THEN THE COM WENT DEAD! SOMETHING **TERRIBLE'S** HAPPENED! I KNOW IT HAS!
MOM, IF YOU'RE THERE, SPEAK TO ME!
CALL THE BLOCK SUPER TO GO ROUND AND CHECK.
I CAN'T! SHE...SHE WOULDN'T LIKE IT!
THE LAW, THEN—
GRUD NO! THE LAST THING SHE WANTS IS THE JUDGES POKING THEIR NOSES IN!

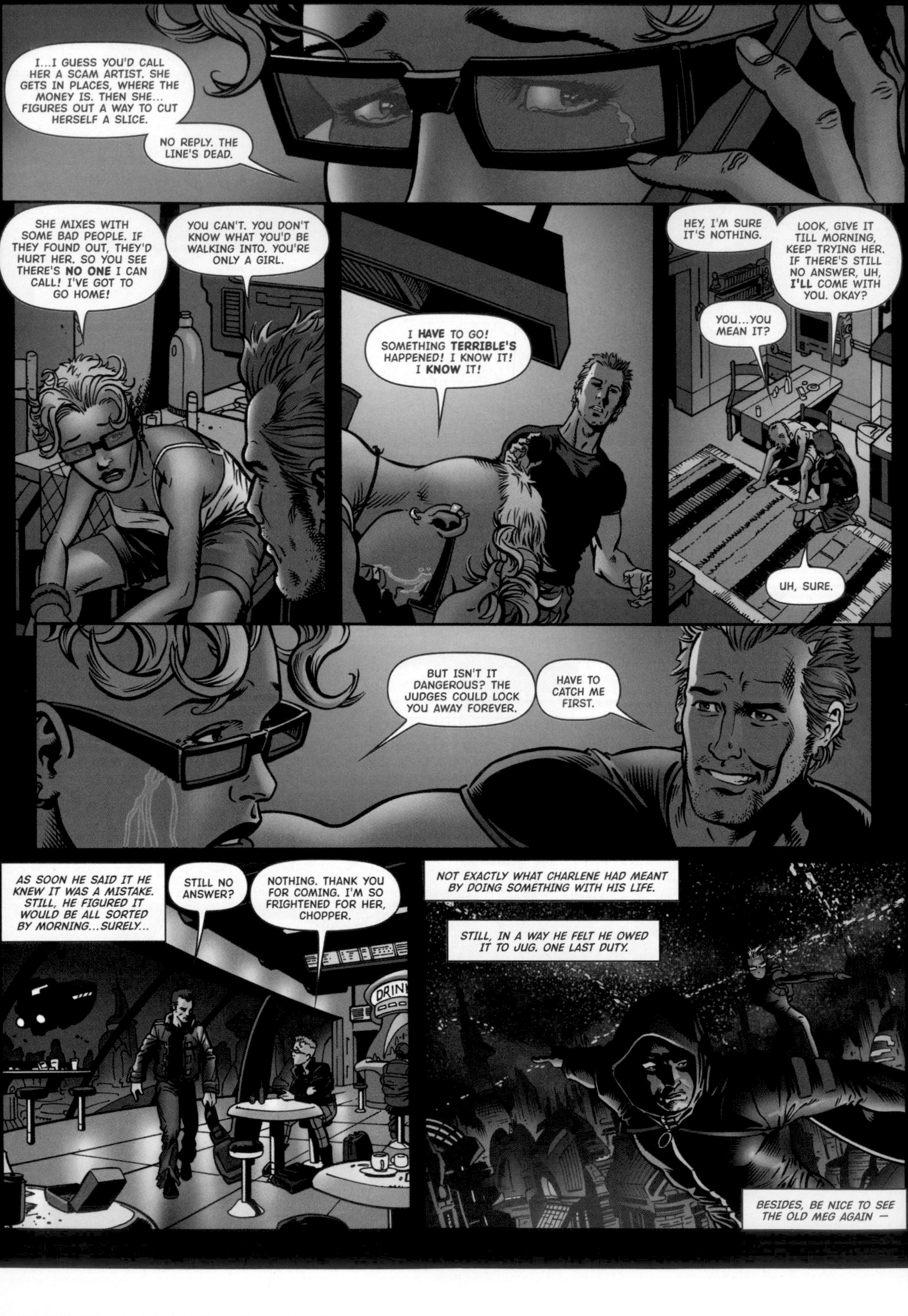
I...I GUESS YOU'D CALL HER A SCAM ARTIST. SHE GETS IN PLACES, WHERE THE MONEY IS. THEN SHE... FIGURES OUT A WAY TO CUT HERSELF A SLICE.
NO REPLY. THE LINE'S DEAD.
SHE MIXES WITH SOME BAD PEOPLE. IF THEY FOUND OUT, THEY'D HURT HER. SO YOU SEE THERE'S **NO ONE** I CAN CALL! I'VE GOT TO GO HOME!
YOU CAN'T. YOU DON'T KNOW WHAT YOU'D BE WALKING INTO. YOU'RE ONLY A GIRL.
I **HAVE** TO GO! SOMETHING **TERRIBLE'S** HAPPENED! I KNOW IT! I **KNOW** IT!
HEY, I'M SURE IT'S NOTHING.
LOOK, GIVE IT TILL MORNING, KEEP TRYING HER. IF THERE'S STILL NO ANSWER, UH, **I'LL** COME WITH YOU. OKAY?
YOU...YOU MEAN IT?
UH, SURE.
BUT ISN'T IT DANGEROUS? THE JUDGES COULD LOCK YOU AWAY FOREVER.
HAVE TO CATCH ME FIRST.
AS SOON HE SAID IT HE KNEW IT WAS A MISTAKE. STILL, HE FIGURED IT WOULD BE ALL SORTED BY MORNING...SURELY...
STILL NO ANSWER?
NOTHING. THANK YOU FOR COMING. I'M SO FRIGHTENED FOR HER, CHOPPER.
NOT EXACTLY WHAT CHARLENE HAD MEANT BY DOING SOMETHING WITH HIS LIFE.
STILL, IN A WAY HE FELT HE OWED IT TO JUG. ONE LAST DUTY.
BESIDES, BE NICE TO SEE THE OLD MEG AGAIN —

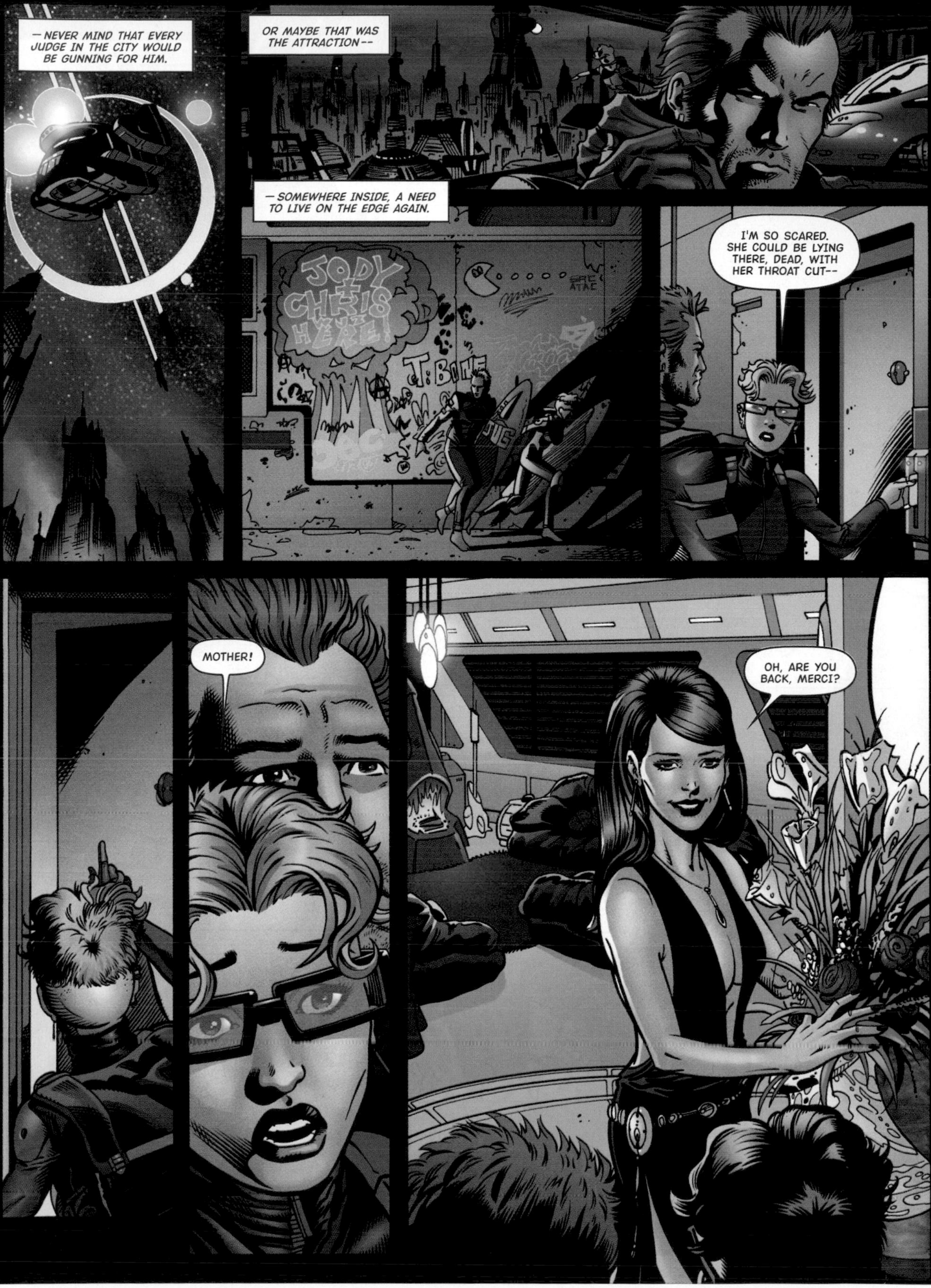
—NEVER MIND THAT EVERY JUDGE IN THE CITY WOULD BE GUNNING FOR HIM.
OR MAYBE THAT WAS THE ATTRACTION--
—SOMEWHERE INSIDE, A NEED TO LIVE ON THE EDGE AGAIN.
JODY + CHRIS HERE!
T. BONE
I'M SO SCARED. SHE COULD BE LYING THERE, DEAD, WITH HER THROAT CUT--
MOTHER!
OH, ARE YOU BACK, MERCI?

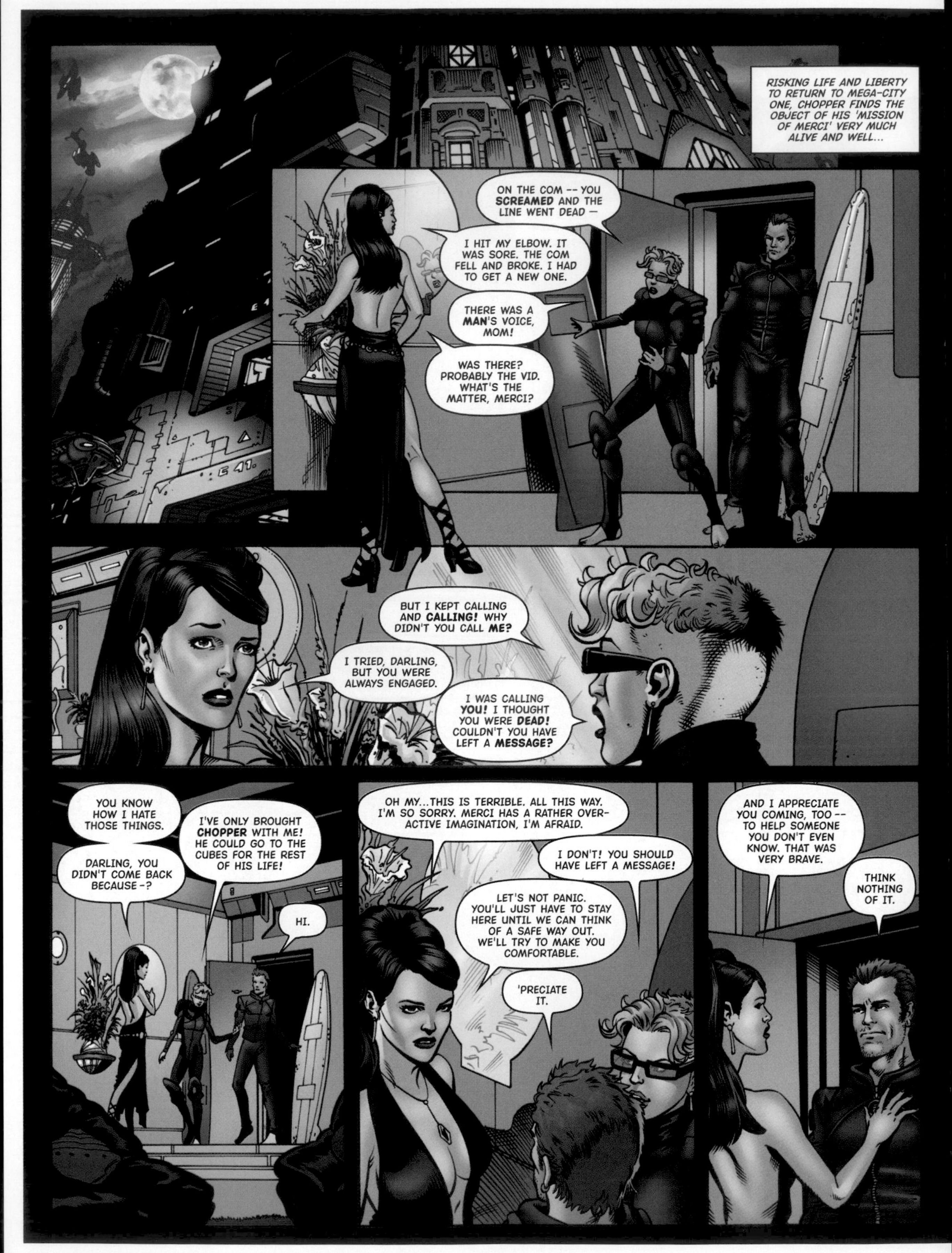
RISKING LIFE AND LIBERTY TO RETURN TO MEGA-CITY ONE, CHOPPER FINDS THE OBJECT OF HIS 'MISSION OF MERCI' VERY MUCH ALIVE AND WELL...
ON THE COM -- YOU SCREAMED AND THE LINE WENT DEAD —
I HIT MY ELBOW. IT WAS SORE. THE COM FELL AND BROKE. I HAD TO GET A NEW ONE.
THERE WAS A MAN'S VOICE, MOM!
WAS THERE? PROBABLY THE VID. WHAT'S THE MATTER, MERCI?
BUT I KEPT CALLING AND CALLING! WHY DIDN'T YOU CALL ME?
I TRIED, DARLING, BUT YOU WERE ALWAYS ENGAGED.
I WAS CALLING YOU! I THOUGHT YOU WERE DEAD! COULDN'T YOU HAVE LEFT A MESSAGE?
YOU KNOW HOW I HATE THOSE THINGS.
DARLING, YOU DIDN'T COME BACK BECAUSE -?
I'VE ONLY BROUGHT CHOPPER WITH ME! HE COULD GO TO THE CUBES FOR THE REST OF HIS LIFE!
HI.
OH MY...THIS IS TERRIBLE. ALL THIS WAY. I'M SO SORRY. MERCI HAS A RATHER OVER-ACTIVE IMAGINATION, I'M AFRAID.
I DON'T! YOU SHOULD HAVE LEFT A MESSAGE!
LET'S NOT PANIC. YOU'LL JUST HAVE TO STAY HERE UNTIL WE CAN THINK OF A SAFE WAY OUT. WE'LL TRY TO MAKE YOU COMFORTABLE.
'PRECIATE IT.
AND I APPRECIATE YOU COMING, TOO -- TO HELP SOMEONE YOU DON'T EVEN KNOW. THAT WAS VERY BRAVE.
THINK NOTHING OF IT.

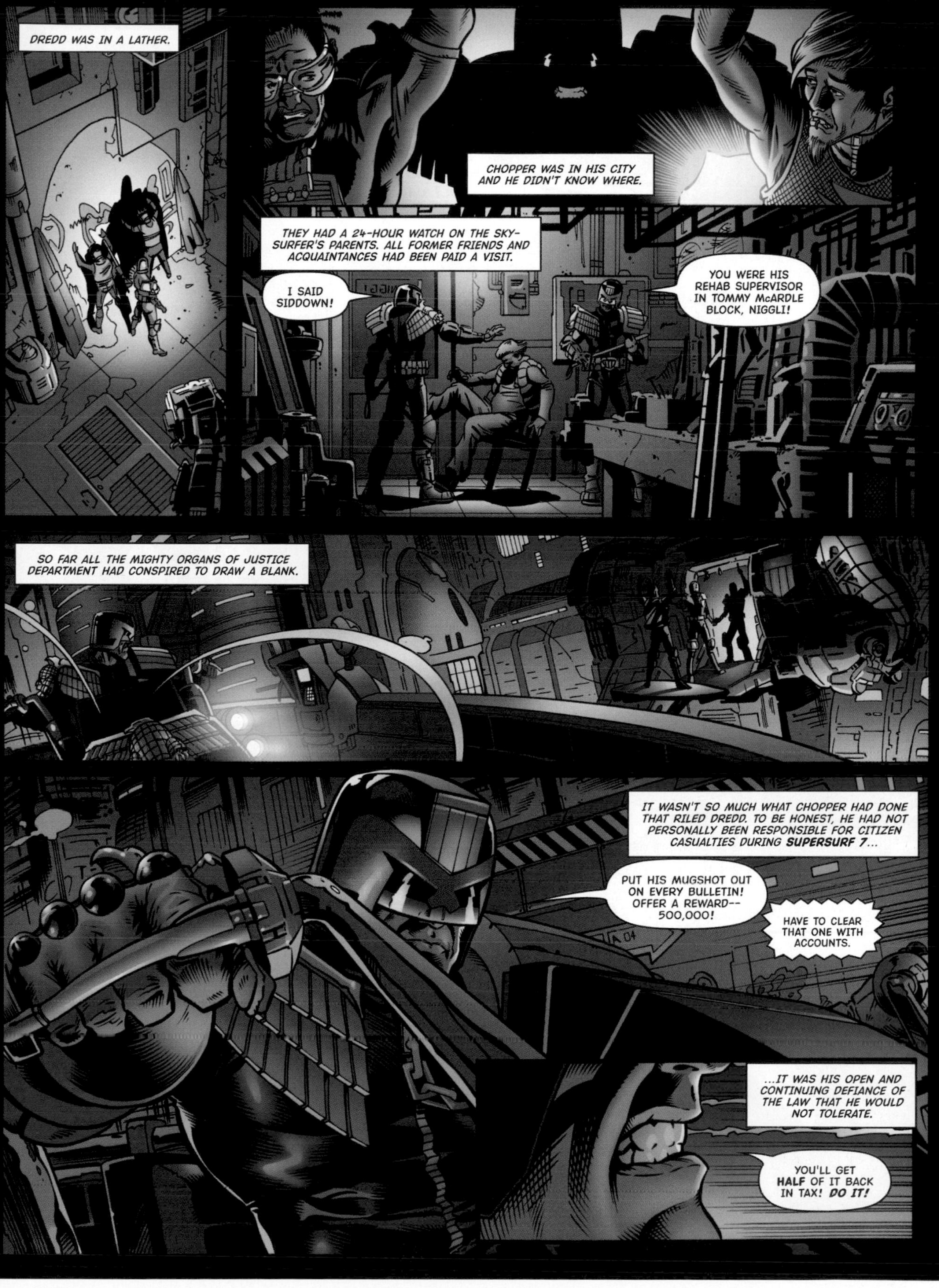
DREDD WAS IN A LATHER.
CHOPPER WAS IN HIS CITY AND HE DIDN'T KNOW WHERE.
THEY HAD A 24-HOUR WATCH ON THE SKY-SURFER'S PARENTS. ALL FORMER FRIENDS AND ACQUAINTANCES HAD BEEN PAID A VISIT.
I SAID SIDDOWN!
YOU WERE HIS REHAB SUPERVISOR IN TOMMY McARDLE BLOCK, NIGGLI!
SO FAR ALL THE MIGHTY ORGANS OF JUSTICE DEPARTMENT HAD CONSPIRED TO DRAW A BLANK.
IT WASN'T SO MUCH WHAT CHOPPER HAD DONE THAT RILED DREDD. TO BE HONEST, HE HAD NOT PERSONALLY BEEN RESPONSIBLE FOR CITIZEN CASUALTIES DURING SUPERSURF 7...
PUT HIS MUGSHOT OUT ON EVERY BULLETIN! OFFER A REWARD-- 500,000!
HAVE TO CLEAR THAT ONE WITH ACCOUNTS.
...IT WAS HIS OPEN AND CONTINUING DEFIANCE OF THE LAW THAT HE WOULD NOT TOLERATE.
YOU'LL GET HALF OF IT BACK IN TAX! DO IT!

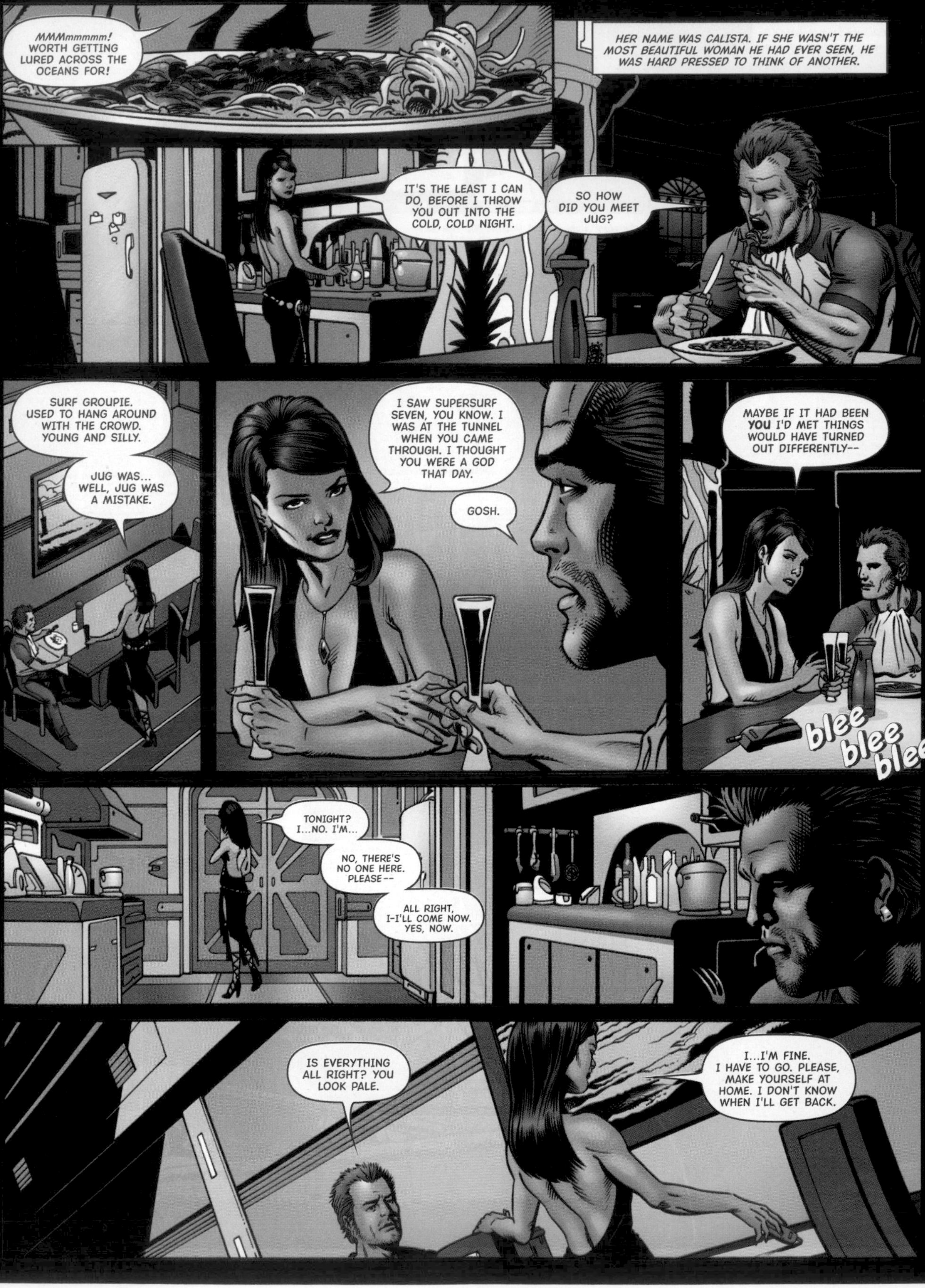
MMMmmmmm! WORTH GETTING LURED ACROSS THE OCEANS FOR!
IT'S THE LEAST I CAN DO, BEFORE I THROW YOU OUT INTO THE COLD, COLD NIGHT.
HER NAME WAS CALISTA. IF SHE WASN'T THE MOST BEAUTIFUL WOMAN HE HAD EVER SEEN, HE WAS HARD PRESSED TO THINK OF ANOTHER.
SO HOW DID YOU MEET JUG?
SURF GROUPIE. USED TO HANG AROUND WITH THE CROWD. YOUNG AND SILLY.
JUG WAS... WELL, JUG WAS A MISTAKE.
I SAW SUPERSURF SEVEN, YOU KNOW. I WAS AT THE TUNNEL WHEN YOU CAME THROUGH. I THOUGHT YOU WERE A GOD THAT DAY.
GOSH.
MAYBE IF IT HAD BEEN YOU I'D MET THINGS WOULD HAVE TURNED OUT DIFFERENTLY--
blee blee blee
TONIGHT? I...NO. I'M...
NO, THERE'S NO ONE HERE. PLEASE--
ALL RIGHT, I-I'LL COME NOW. YES, NOW.
IS EVERYTHING ALL RIGHT? YOU LOOK PALE.
I...I'M FINE. I HAVE TO GO. PLEASE, MAKE YOURSELF AT HOME. I DON'T KNOW WHEN I'LL GET BACK.

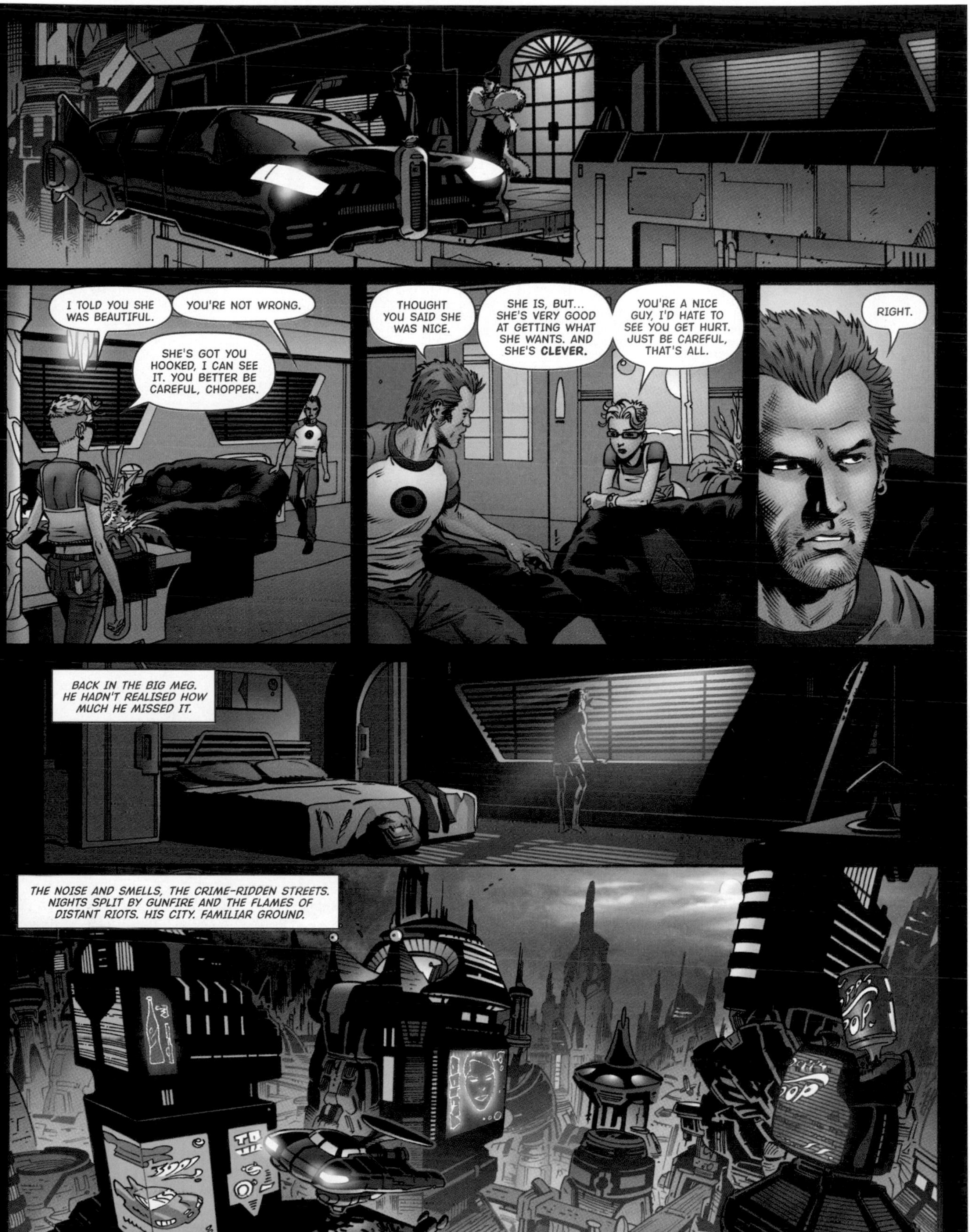
I TOLD YOU SHE WAS BEAUTIFUL.
YOU'RE NOT WRONG.
SHE'S GOT YOU HOOKED, I CAN SEE IT. YOU BETTER BE CAREFUL, CHOPPER.
THOUGHT YOU SAID SHE WAS NICE.
SHE IS, BUT... SHE'S VERY GOOD AT GETTING WHAT SHE WANTS. AND SHE'S **CLEVER.**
YOU'RE A NICE GUY, I'D HATE TO SEE YOU GET HURT. JUST BE CAREFUL, THAT'S ALL.
RIGHT.
BACK IN THE BIG MEG. HE HADN'T REALISED HOW MUCH HE MISSED IT.
THE NOISE AND SMELLS, THE CRIME-RIDDEN STREETS. NIGHTS SPLIT BY GUNFIRE AND THE FLAMES OF DISTANT RIOTS. HIS CITY. FAMILIAR GROUND.

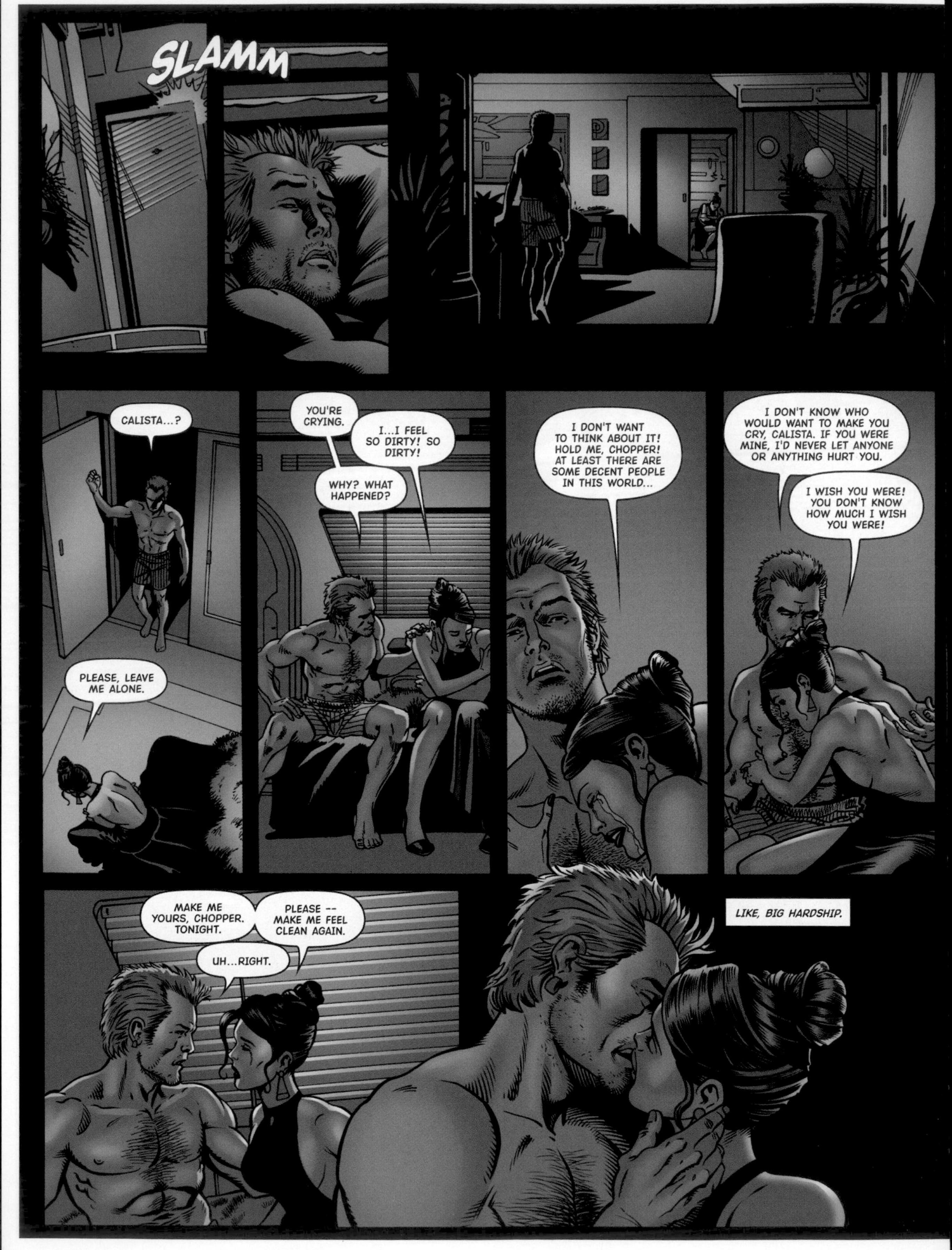
SLAMM
CALISTA...?
PLEASE, LEAVE ME ALONE.
YOU'RE CRYING.
I...I FEEL SO DIRTY! SO DIRTY!
WHY? WHAT HAPPENED?
I DON'T WANT TO THINK ABOUT IT! HOLD ME, CHOPPER! AT LEAST THERE ARE SOME DECENT PEOPLE IN THIS WORLD...
I DON'T KNOW WHO WOULD WANT TO MAKE YOU CRY, CALISTA. IF YOU WERE MINE, I'D NEVER LET ANYONE OR ANYTHING HURT YOU.
I WISH YOU WERE! YOU DON'T KNOW HOW MUCH I WISH YOU WERE!
MAKE ME YOURS, CHOPPER. TONIGHT.
PLEASE -- MAKE ME FEEL CLEAN AGAIN.
UH...RIGHT.
LIKE, BIG HARDSHIP.

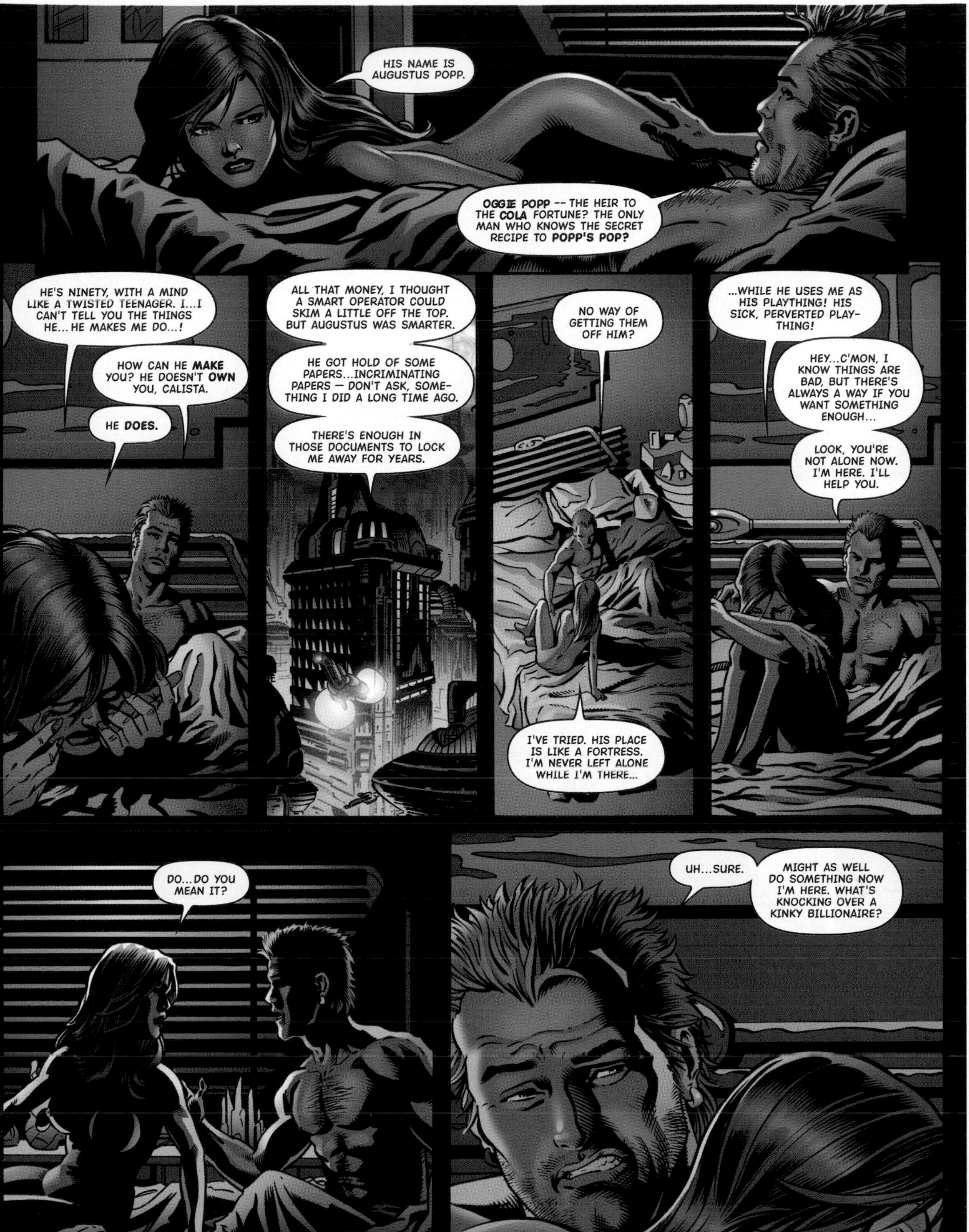
HIS NAME IS AUGUSTUS POPP.
OGGIE POPP -- THE HEIR TO THE COLA FORTUNE? THE ONLY MAN WHO KNOWS THE SECRET RECIPE TO POPP'S POP?
HE'S NINETY, WITH A MIND LIKE A TWISTED TEENAGER. I...I CAN'T TELL YOU THE THINGS HE... HE MAKES ME DO...!
HOW CAN HE MAKE YOU? HE DOESN'T OWN YOU, CALISTA.
HE DOES.
ALL THAT MONEY, I THOUGHT A SMART OPERATOR COULD SKIM A LITTLE OFF THE TOP. BUT AUGUSTUS WAS SMARTER.
HE GOT HOLD OF SOME PAPERS...INCRIMINATING PAPERS — DON'T ASK, SOMETHING I DID A LONG TIME AGO.
THERE'S ENOUGH IN THOSE DOCUMENTS TO LOCK ME AWAY FOR YEARS.
NO WAY OF GETTING THEM OFF HIM?
I'VE TRIED. HIS PLACE IS LIKE A FORTRESS. I'M NEVER LEFT ALONE WHILE I'M THERE...
...WHILE HE USES ME AS HIS PLAYTHING! HIS SICK, PERVERTED PLAYTHING!
HEY...C'MON, I KNOW THINGS ARE BAD, BUT THERE'S ALWAYS A WAY IF YOU WANT SOMETHING ENOUGH...
LOOK, YOU'RE NOT ALONE NOW. I'M HERE. I'LL HELP YOU.
DO...DO YOU MEAN IT?
UH...SURE.
MIGHT AS WELL DO SOMETHING NOW I'M HERE. WHAT'S KNOCKING OVER A KINKY BILLIONAIRE?

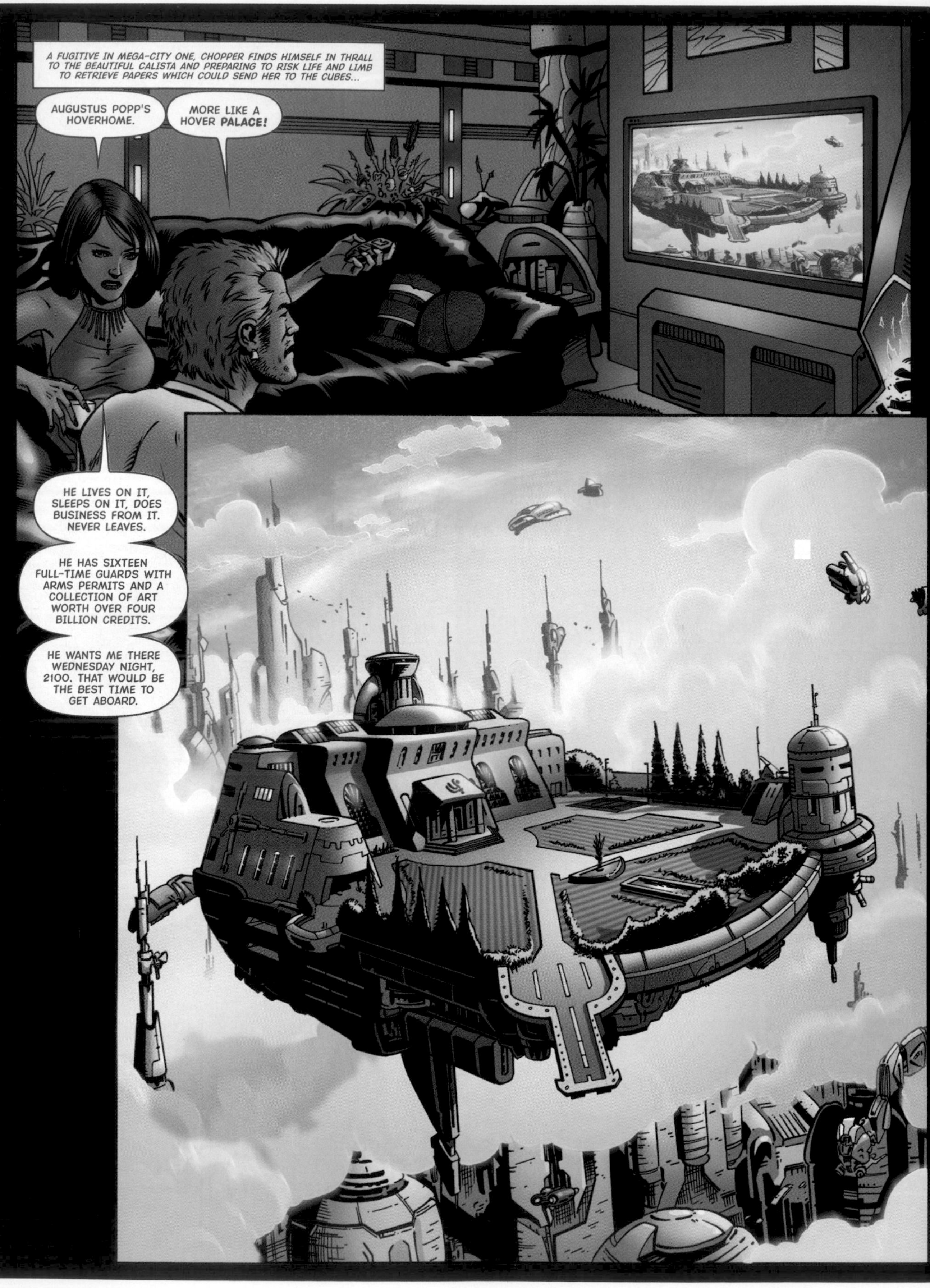
A FUGITIVE IN MEGA-CITY ONE, CHOPPER FINDS HIMSELF IN THRALL TO THE BEAUTIFUL CALISTA AND PREPARING TO RISK LIFE AND LIMB TO RETRIEVE PAPERS WHICH COULD SEND HER TO THE CUBES...
AUGUSTUS POPP'S HOVERHOME.
MORE LIKE A HOVER PALACE!
HE LIVES ON IT, SLEEPS ON IT, DOES BUSINESS FROM IT. NEVER LEAVES.
HE HAS SIXTEEN FULL-TIME GUARDS WITH ARMS PERMITS AND A COLLECTION OF ART WORTH OVER FOUR BILLION CREDITS.
HE WANTS ME THERE WEDNESDAY NIGHT, 2100. THAT WOULD BE THE BEST TIME TO GET ABOARD.

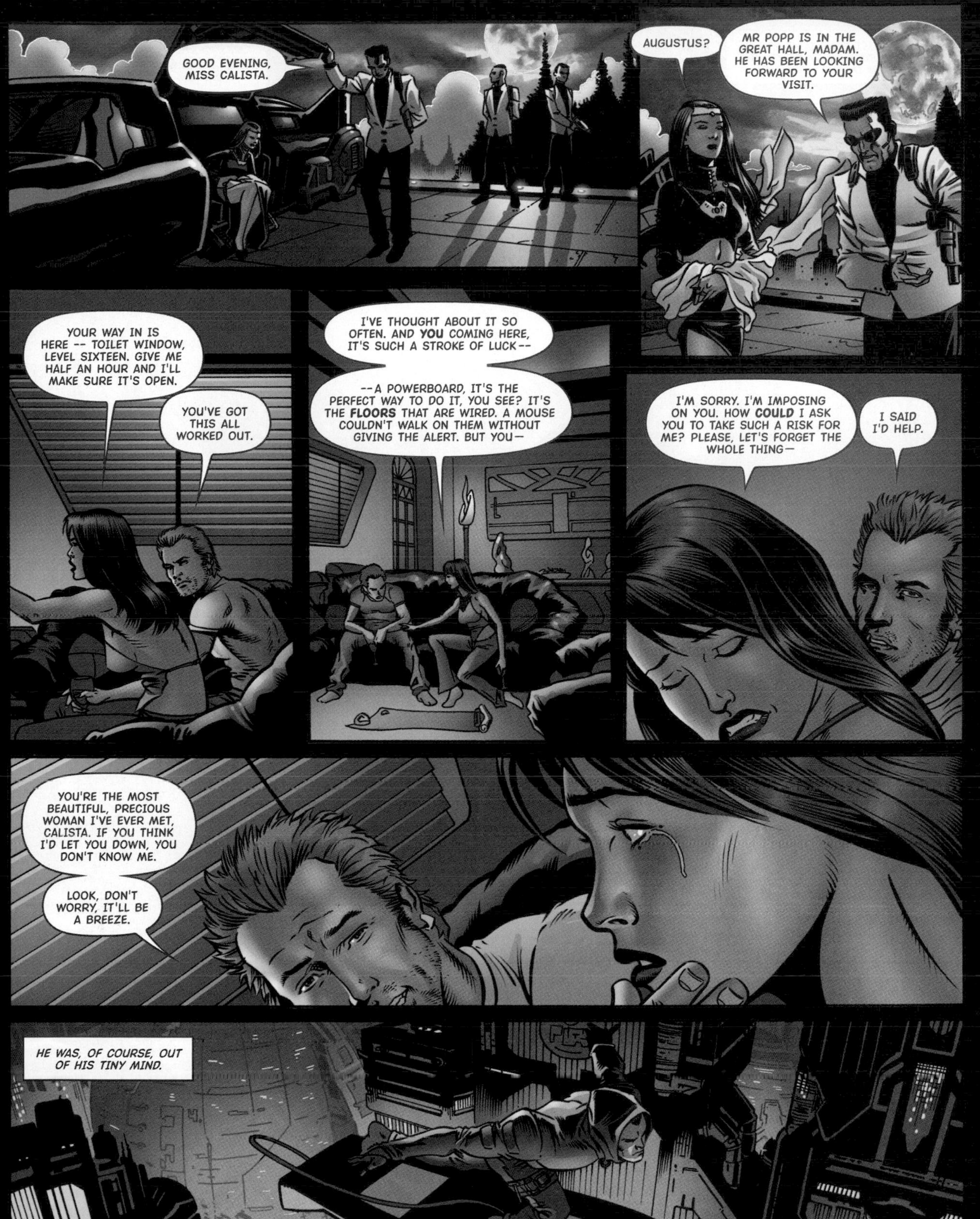
GOOD EVENING, MISS CALISTA.
AUGUSTUS?
MR POPP IS IN THE GREAT HALL, MADAM. HE HAS BEEN LOOKING FORWARD TO YOUR VISIT.
YOUR WAY IN IS HERE -- TOILET WINDOW, LEVEL SIXTEEN. GIVE ME HALF AN HOUR AND I'LL MAKE SURE IT'S OPEN.
YOU'VE GOT THIS ALL WORKED OUT.
I'VE THOUGHT ABOUT IT SO OFTEN. AND YOU COMING HERE, IT'S SUCH A STROKE OF LUCK--
--A POWERBOARD, IT'S THE PERFECT WAY TO DO IT, YOU SEE? IT'S THE FLOORS THAT ARE WIRED. A MOUSE COULDN'T WALK ON THEM WITHOUT GIVING THE ALERT. BUT YOU—
I'M SORRY. I'M IMPOSING ON YOU. HOW COULD I ASK YOU TO TAKE SUCH A RISK FOR ME? PLEASE, LET'S FORGET THE WHOLE THING—
I SAID I'D HELP.
YOU'RE THE MOST BEAUTIFUL, PRECIOUS WOMAN I'VE EVER MET, CALISTA. IF YOU THINK I'D LET YOU DOWN, YOU DON'T KNOW ME.
LOOK, DON'T WORRY, IT'LL BE A BREEZE.
HE WAS, OF COURSE, OUT OF HIS TINY MIND.

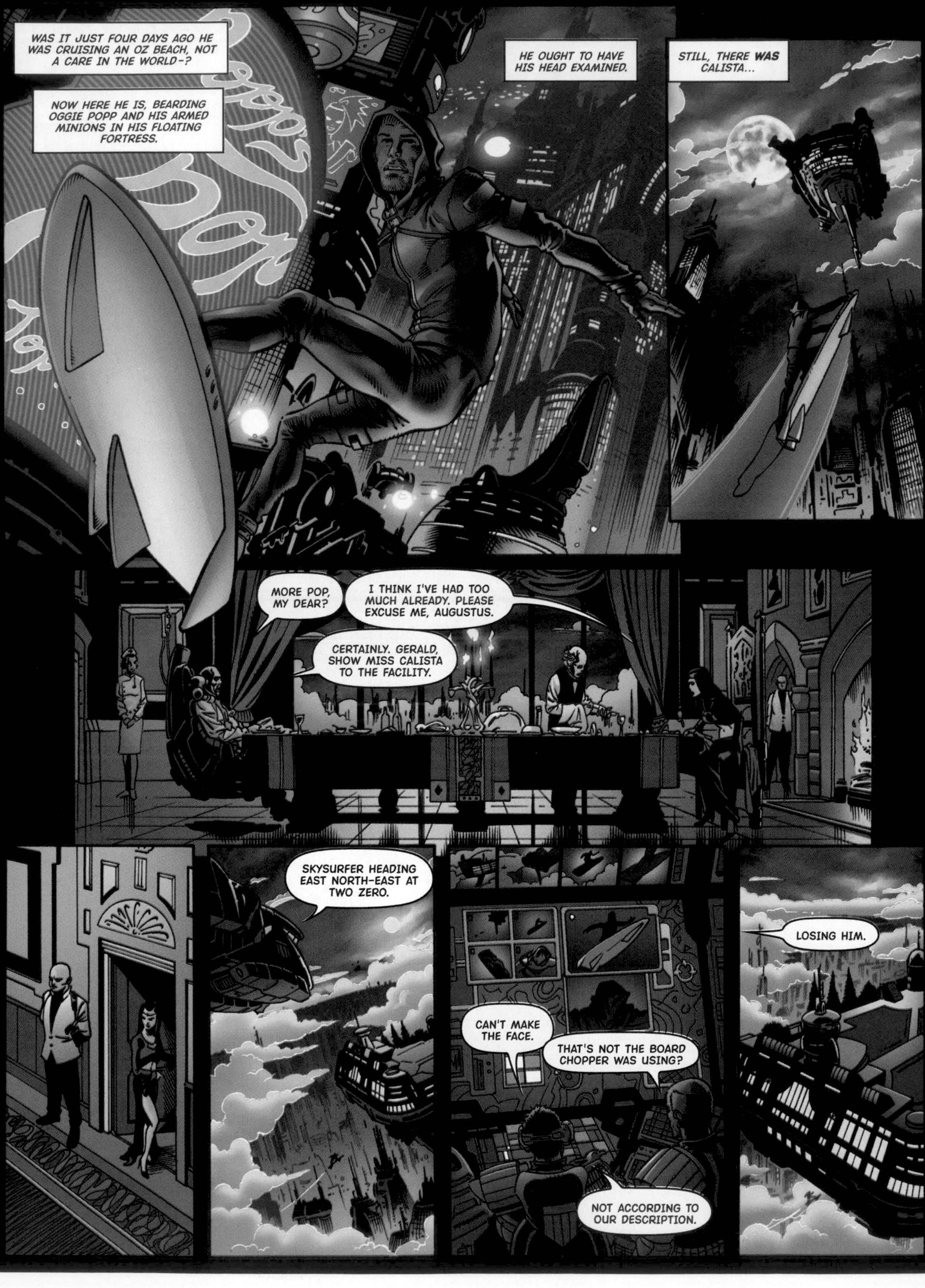
WAS IT JUST FOUR DAYS AGO HE WAS CRUISING AN OZ BEACH, NOT A CARE IN THE WORLD-?
NOW HERE HE IS, BEARDING OGGIE POPP AND HIS ARMED MINIONS IN HIS FLOATING FORTRESS.
HE OUGHT TO HAVE HIS HEAD EXAMINED.
STILL, THERE **WAS** CALISTA...
MORE POP, MY DEAR?
I THINK I'VE HAD TOO MUCH ALREADY. PLEASE EXCUSE ME, AUGUSTUS.
CERTAINLY. GERALD, SHOW MISS CALISTA TO THE FACILITY.
SKYSURFER HEADING EAST NORTH-EAST AT TWO ZERO.
CAN'T MAKE THE FACE.
THAT'S NOT THE BOARD CHOPPER WAS USING?
NOT ACCORDING TO OUR DESCRIPTION.
LOSING HIM.

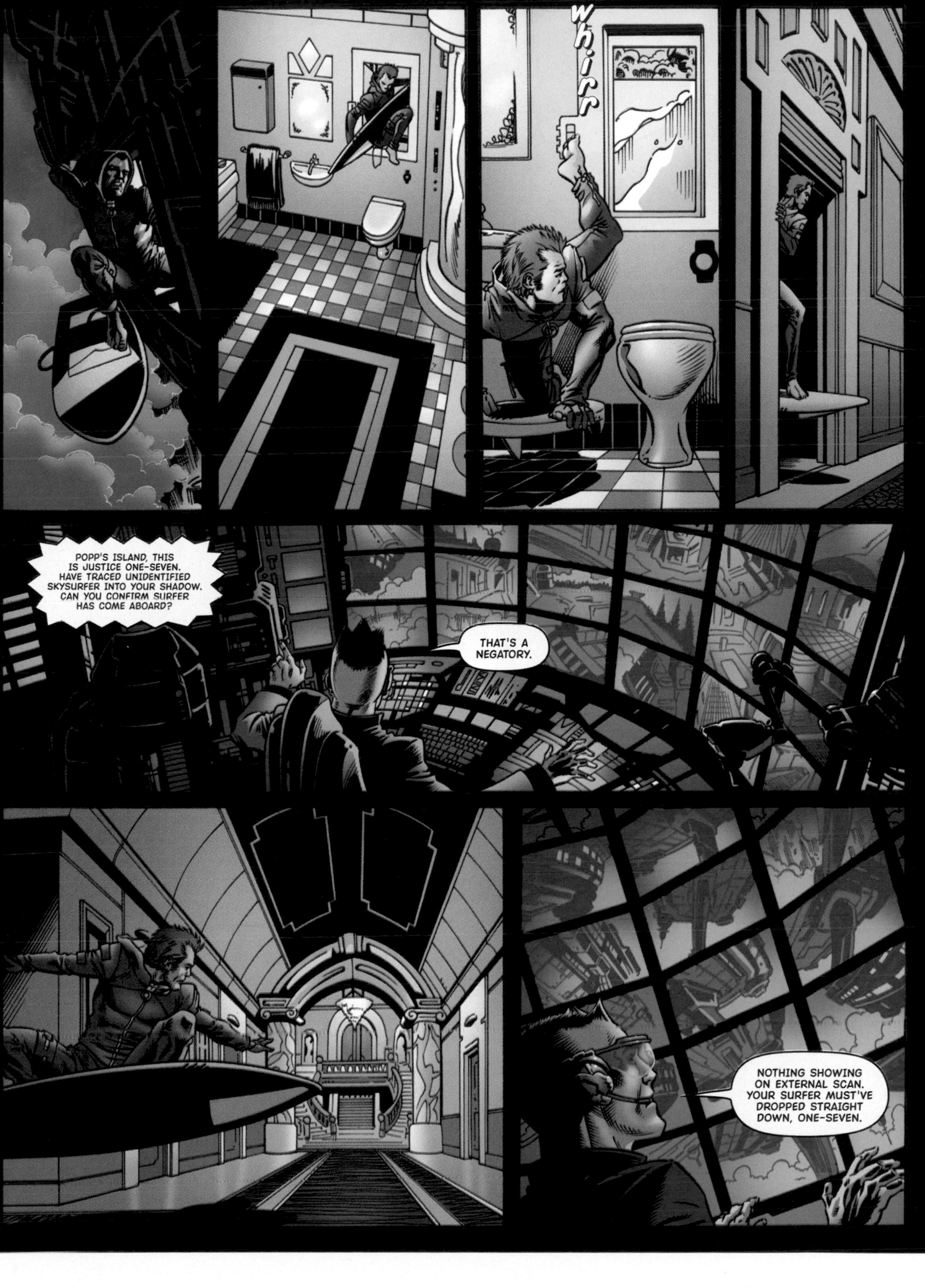
WHIRR
POPP'S ISLAND, THIS IS JUSTICE ONE-SEVEN. HAVE TRACED UNIDENTIFIED SKYSURFER INTO YOUR SHADOW. CAN YOU CONFIRM SURFER HAS COME ABOARD?
THAT'S A NEGATORY.
NOTHING SHOWING ON EXTERNAL SCAN. YOUR SURFER MUST'VE DROPPED STRAIGHT DOWN, ONE-SEVEN.

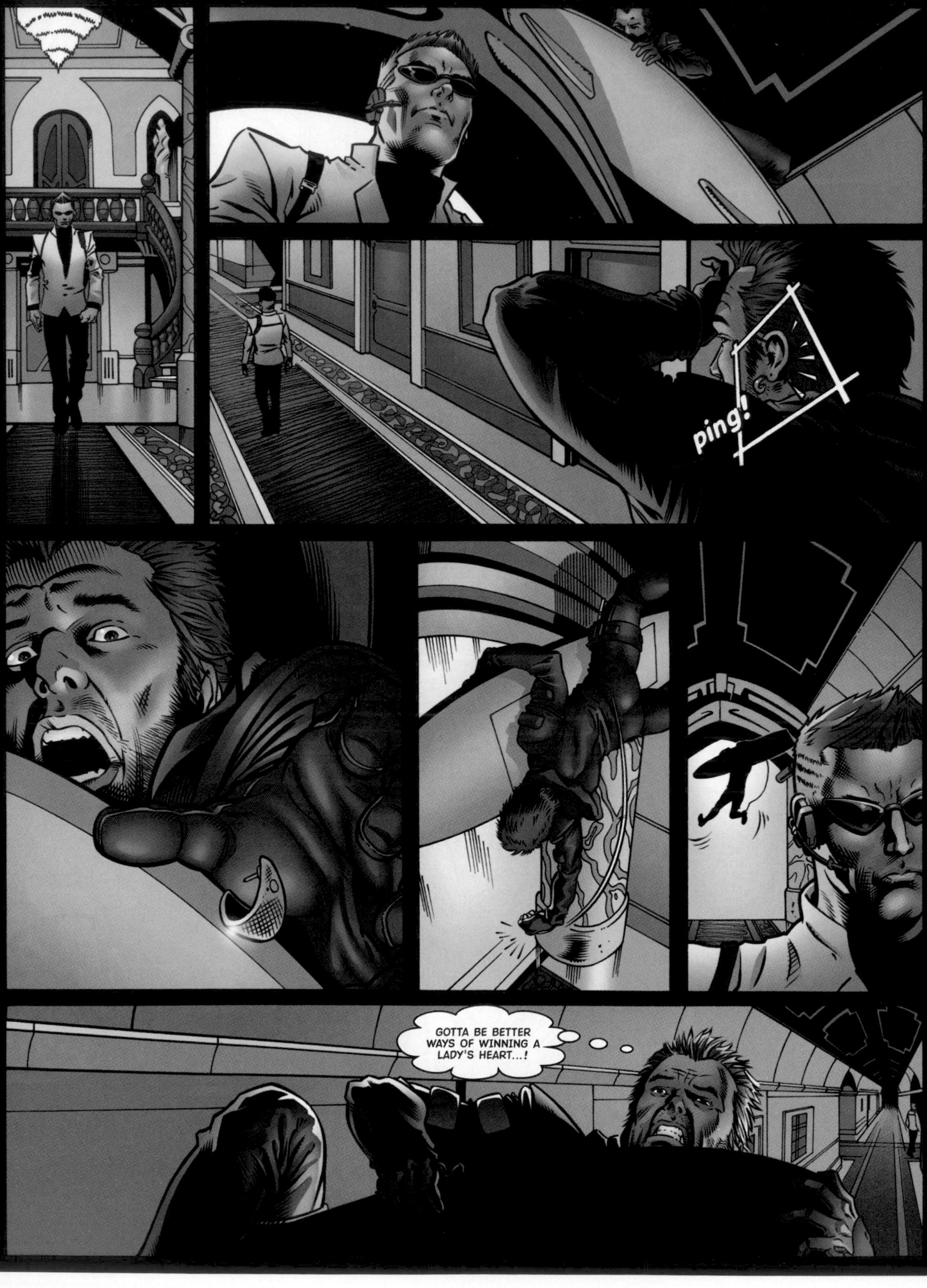
ping!
GOTTA BE BETTER WAYS OF WINNING A LADY'S HEART...!

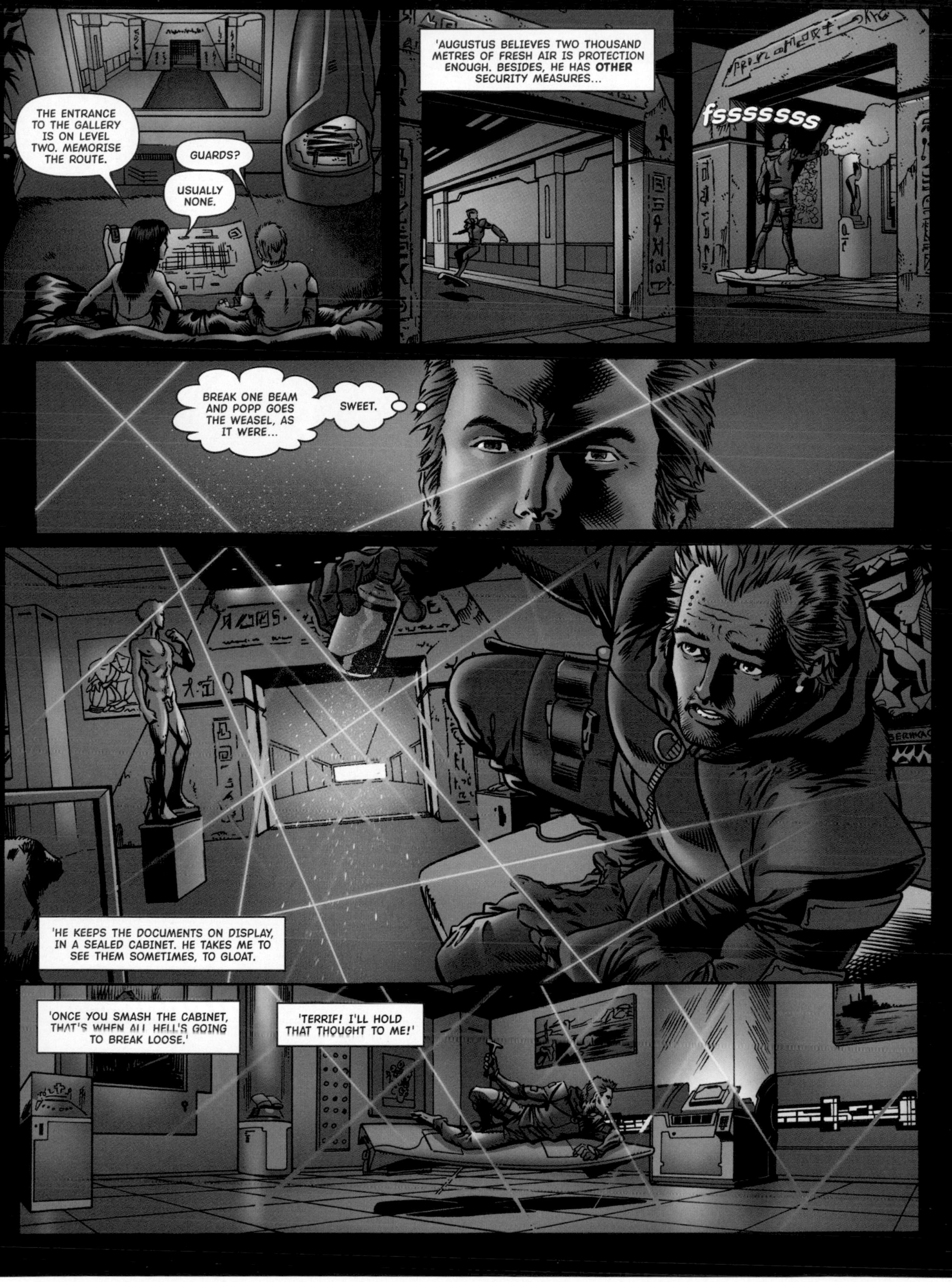
THE ENTRANCE TO THE GALLERY IS ON LEVEL TWO. MEMORISE THE ROUTE.
GUARDS?
USUALLY NONE.
'AUGUSTUS BELIEVES TWO THOUSAND METRES OF FRESH AIR IS PROTECTION ENOUGH. BESIDES, HE HAS **OTHER** SECURITY MEASURES...
fssssss
BREAK ONE BEAM AND POPP GOES THE WEASEL, AS IT WERE...
SWEET.
'HE KEEPS THE DOCUMENTS ON DISPLAY, IN A SEALED CABINET. HE TAKES ME TO SEE THEM SOMETIMES, TO GLOAT.
'ONCE YOU SMASH THE CABINET, THAT'S WHEN ALL HELL'S GOING TO BREAK LOOSE.'
'TERRIF! I'LL HOLD THAT THOUGHT TO ME!'

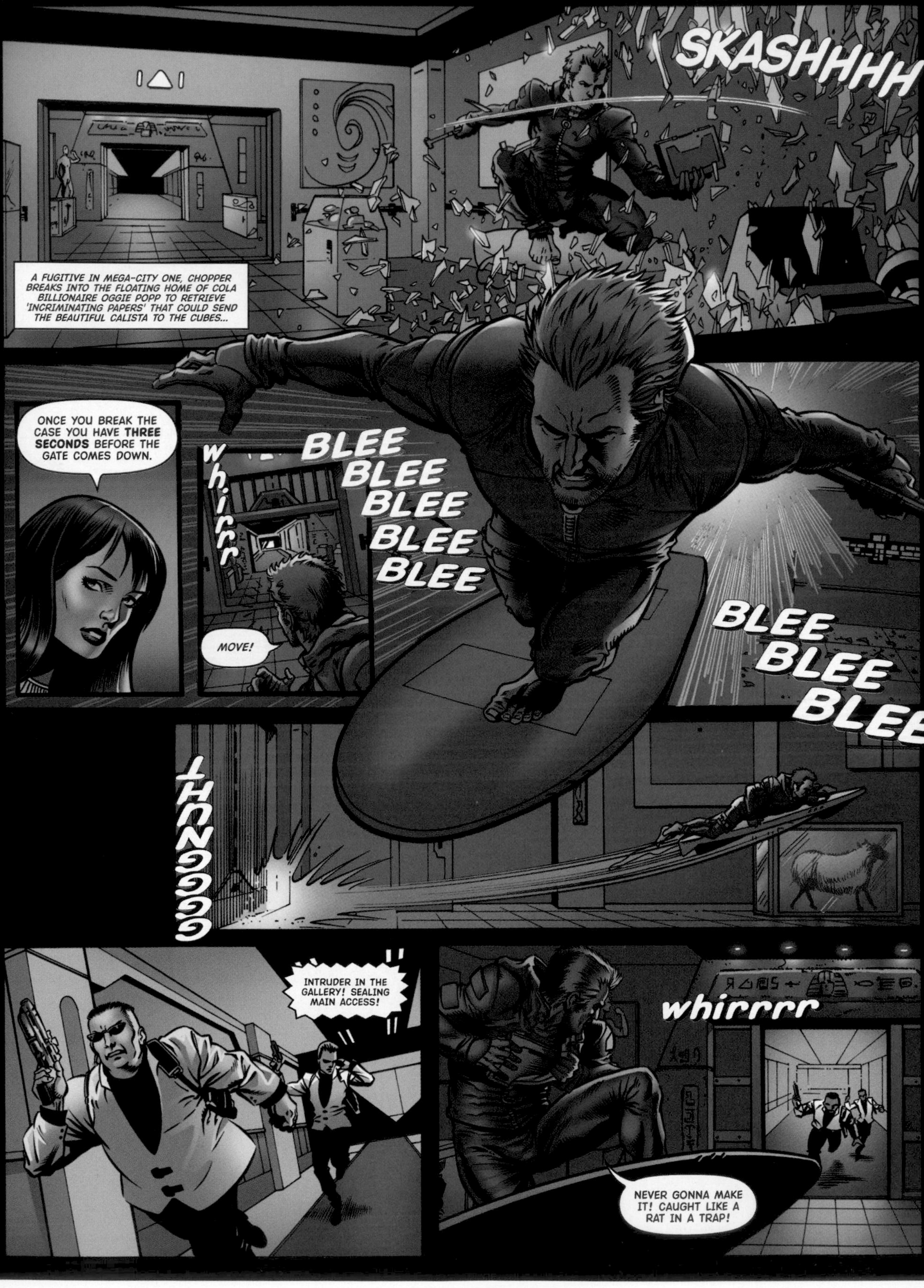
SKASHHHH
A FUGITIVE IN MEGA-CITY ONE, CHOPPER BREAKS INTO THE FLOATING HOME OF COLA BILLIONAIRE OGGIE POPP TO RETRIEVE 'INCRIMINATING PAPERS' THAT COULD SEND THE BEAUTIFUL CALISTA TO THE CUBES...
ONCE YOU BREAK THE CASE YOU HAVE **THREE SECONDS** BEFORE THE GATE COMES DOWN.
whirrr
BLEE BLEE BLEE BLEE BLEE
MOVE!
BLEE BLEE BLEE
THUNGGGG
INTRUDER IN THE GALLERY! SEALING MAIN ACCESS!
whirrrrr
NEVER GONNA MAKE IT! CAUGHT LIKE A RAT IN A TRAP!

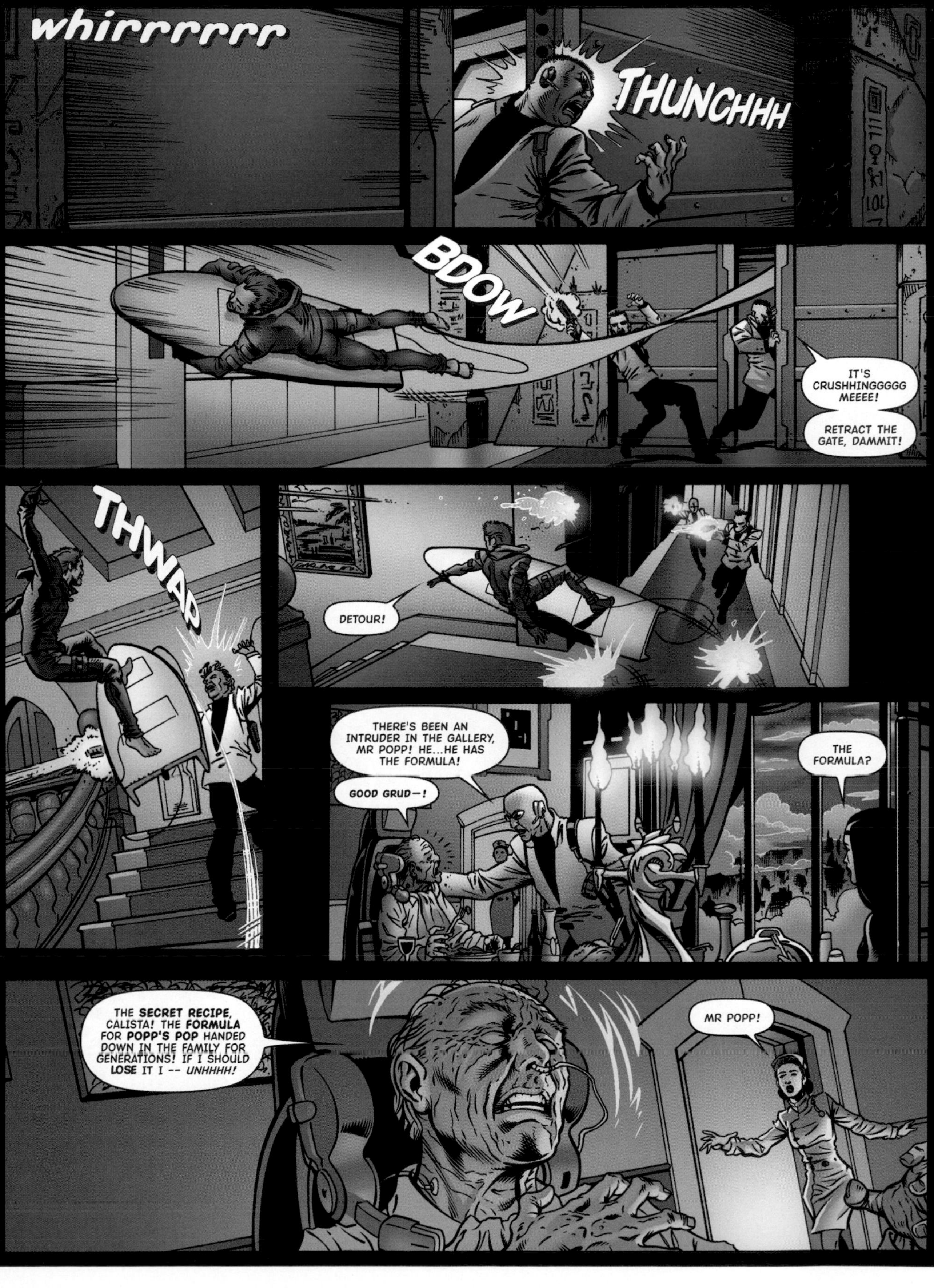
whirrrrrrr
THUNCHHH
BDOW
IT'S CRUSHHINGGGGG MEEEE!
RETRACT THE GATE, DAMMIT!
THWAP
DETOUR!
THERE'S BEEN AN INTRUDER IN THE GALLERY, MR POPP! HE...HE HAS THE FORMULA!
GOOD GRUD—!
THE FORMULA?
THE SECRET RECIPE, CALISTA! THE FORMULA FOR POPP'S POP HANDED DOWN IN THE FAMILY FOR GENERATIONS! IF I SHOULD LOSE IT I -- UNHHHH!
MR POPP!

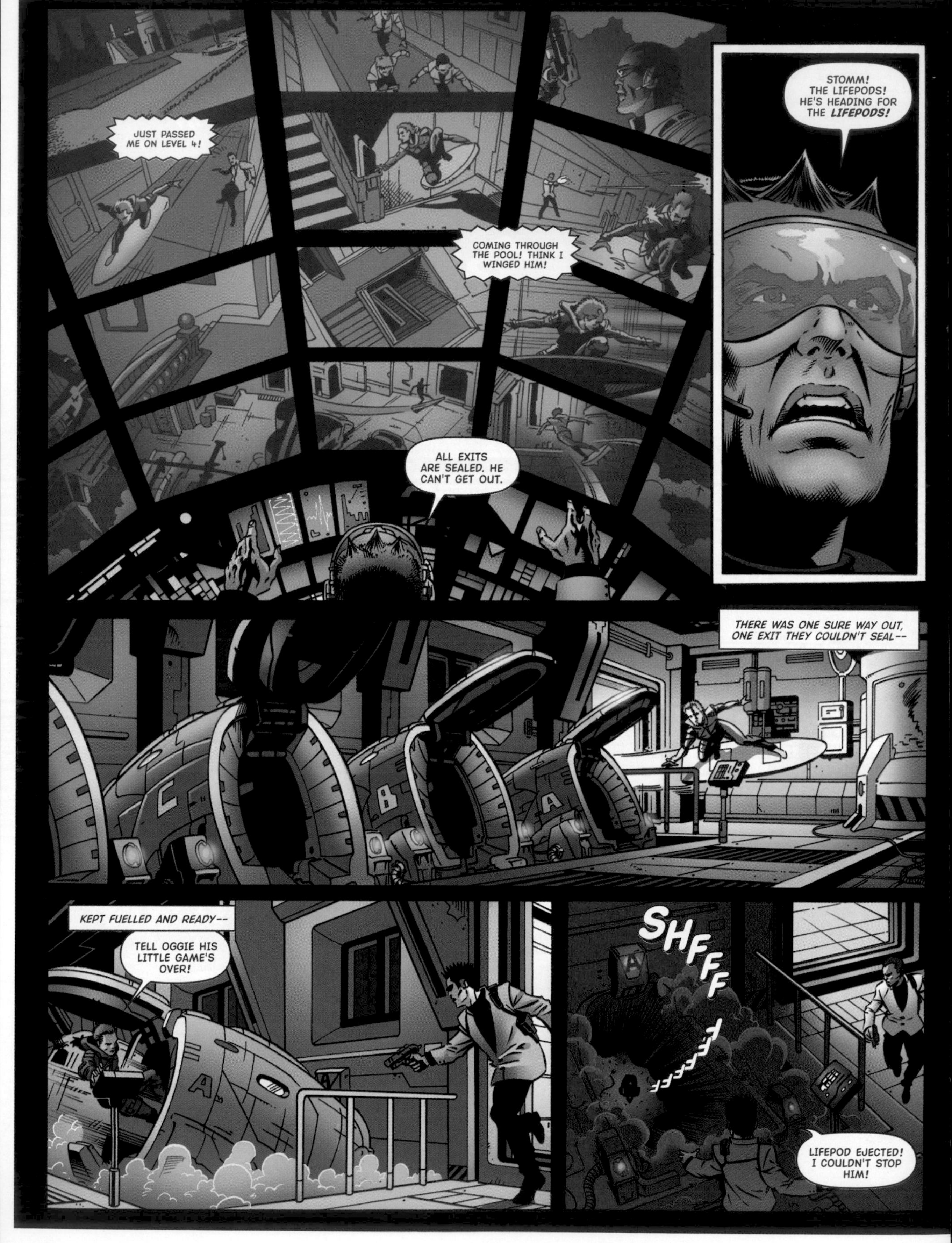
JUST PASSED ME ON LEVEL 4!
COMING THROUGH THE POOL! THINK I WINGED HIM!
ALL EXITS ARE SEALED. HE CAN'T GET OUT.
STOMM! THE LIFEPODS! HE'S HEADING FOR THE *LIFEPODS!*
THERE WAS ONE SURE WAY OUT, ONE EXIT THEY COULDN'T SEAL--
KEPT FUELLED AND READY--
TELL OGGIE HIS LITTLE GAME'S OVER!
SHFFF
LIFEPOD EJECTED! I COULDN'T STOP HIM!

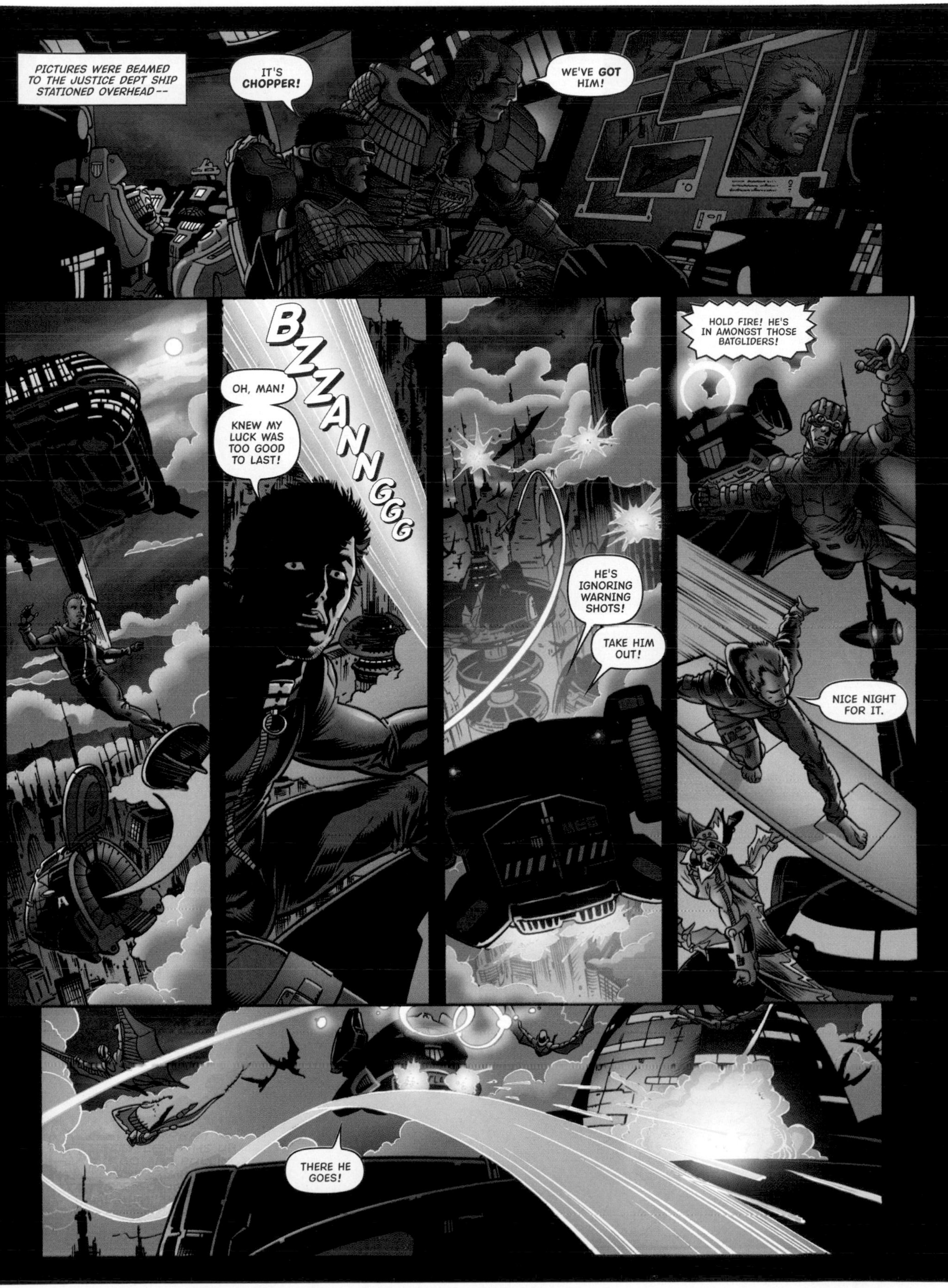
PICTURES WERE BEAMED TO THE JUSTICE DEPT SHIP STATIONED OVERHEAD--
IT'S **CHOPPER!**
WE'VE **GOT** HIM!
BZZANNGGG
OH, MAN!
KNEW MY LUCK WAS TOO GOOD TO LAST!
HE'S IGNORING WARNING SHOTS!
TAKE HIM OUT!
HOLD FIRE! HE'S IN AMONGST THOSE BATGLIDERS!
NICE NIGHT FOR IT.
THERE HE GOES!

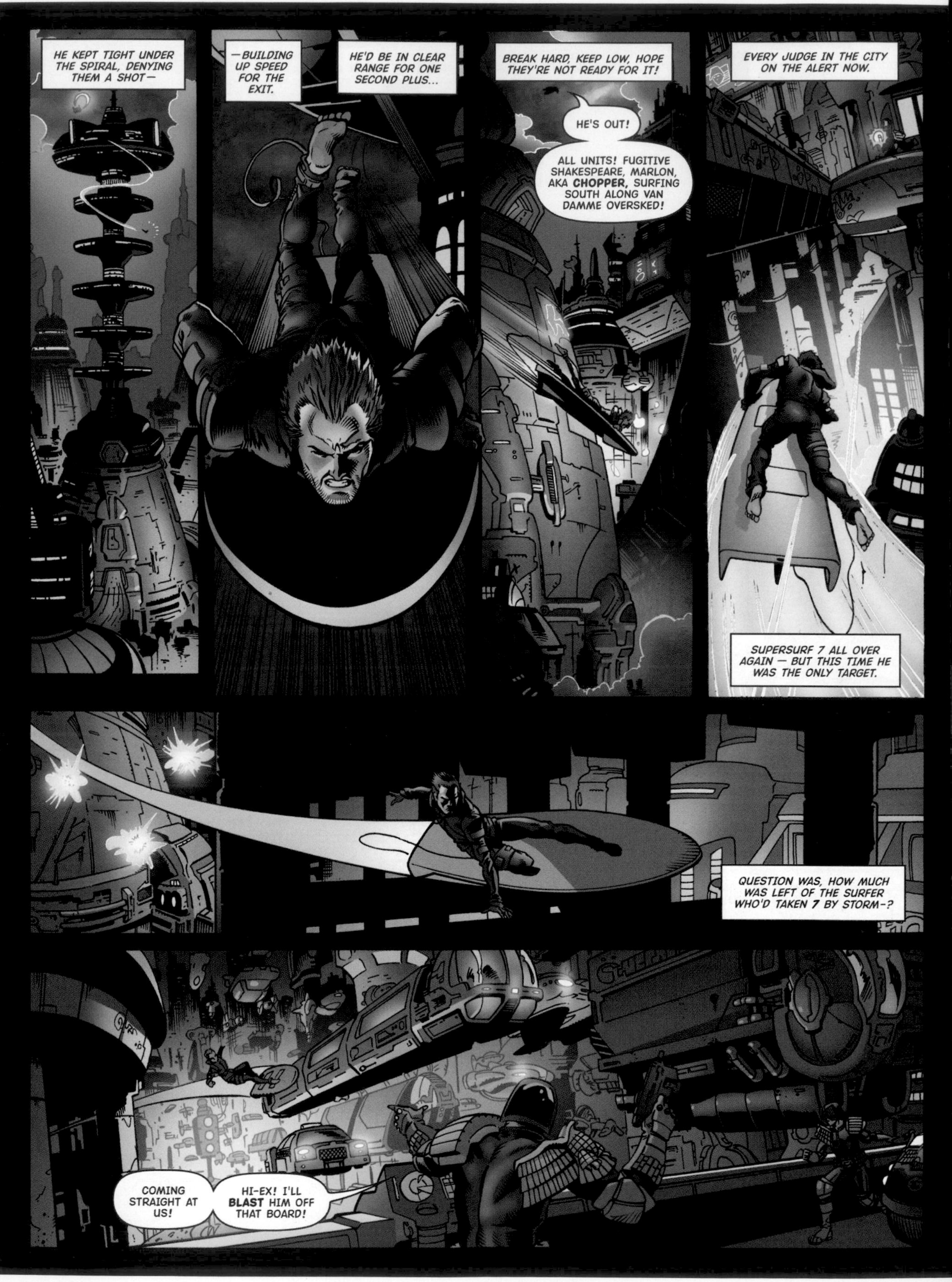
HE KEPT TIGHT UNDER THE SPIRAL, DENYING THEM A SHOT—
—BUILDING UP SPEED FOR THE EXIT.
HE'D BE IN CLEAR RANGE FOR ONE SECOND PLUS...
BREAK HARD, KEEP LOW, HOPE THEY'RE NOT READY FOR IT!
HE'S OUT!
ALL UNITS! FUGITIVE SHAKESPEARE, MARLON, AKA CHOPPER, SURFING SOUTH ALONG VAN DAMME OVERSKED!
EVERY JUDGE IN THE CITY ON THE ALERT NOW.
SUPERSURF 7 ALL OVER AGAIN — BUT THIS TIME HE WAS THE ONLY TARGET.
QUESTION WAS, HOW MUCH WAS LEFT OF THE SURFER WHO'D TAKEN 7 BY STORM-?
COMING STRAIGHT AT US!
HI-EX! I'LL BLAST HIM OFF THAT BOARD!

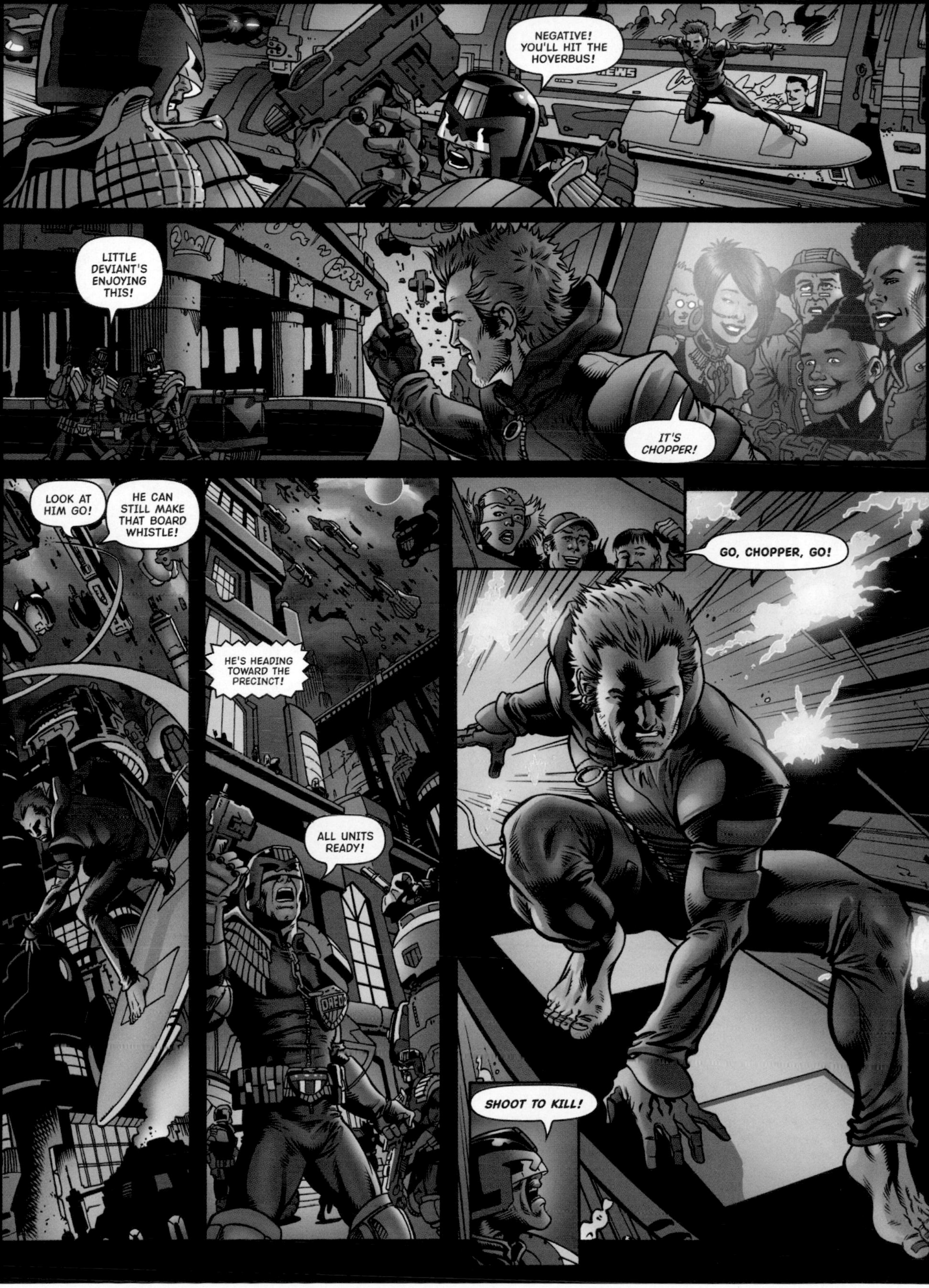
NEGATIVE! YOU'LL HIT THE HOVERBUS!
LITTLE DEVIANT'S ENJOYING THIS!
IT'S CHOPPER!
LOOK AT HIM GO!
HE CAN STILL MAKE THAT BOARD WHISTLE!
HE'S HEADING TOWARD THE PRECINCT!
ALL UNITS READY!
GO, CHOPPER, GO!
SHOOT TO KILL!

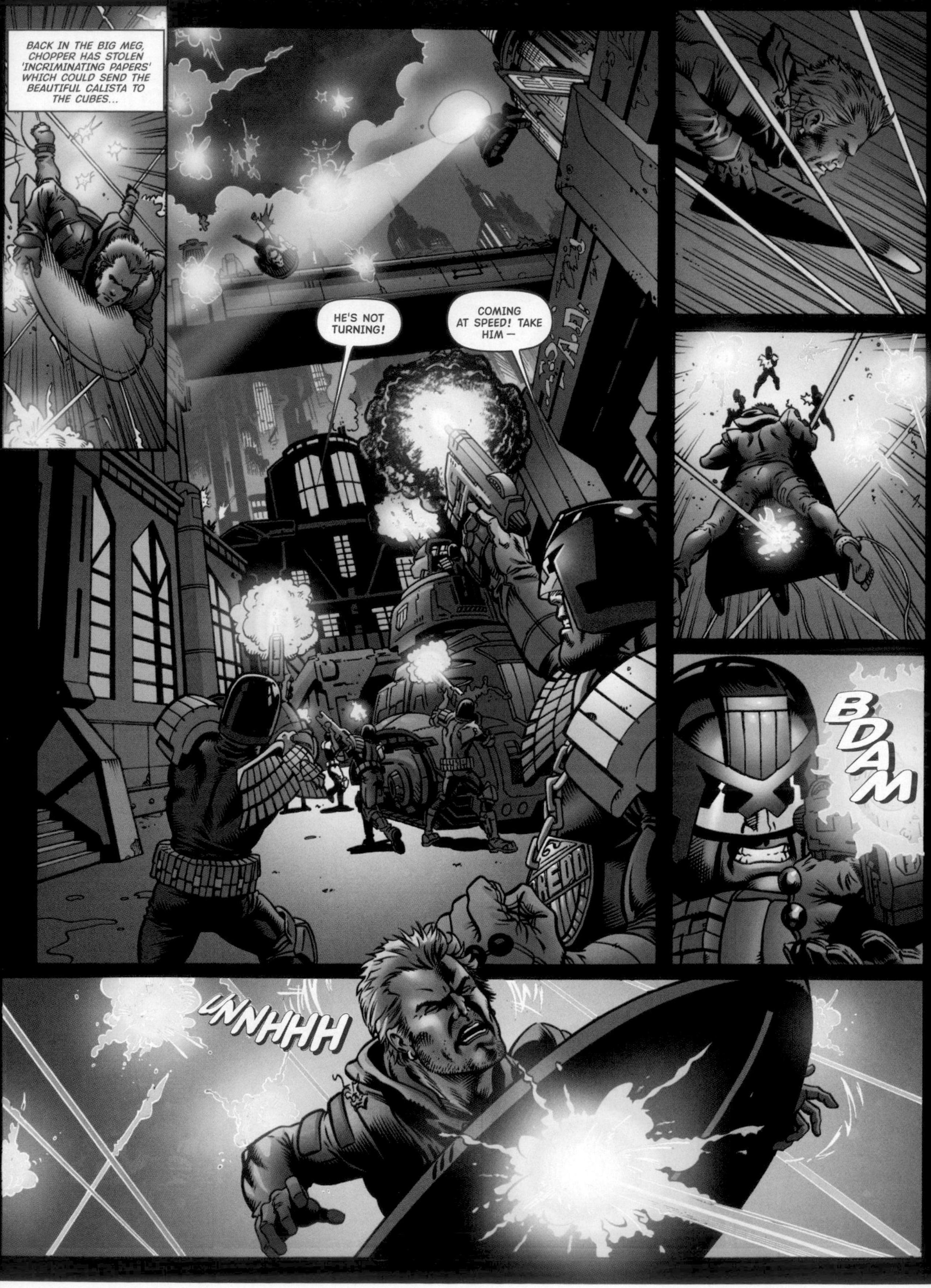
BACK IN THE BIG MEG, CHOPPER HAS STOLEN 'INCRIMINATING PAPERS' WHICH COULD SEND THE BEAUTIFUL CALISTA TO THE CUBES...
HE'S NOT TURNING!
COMING AT SPEED! TAKE HIM —
BDAM
UNNHHH

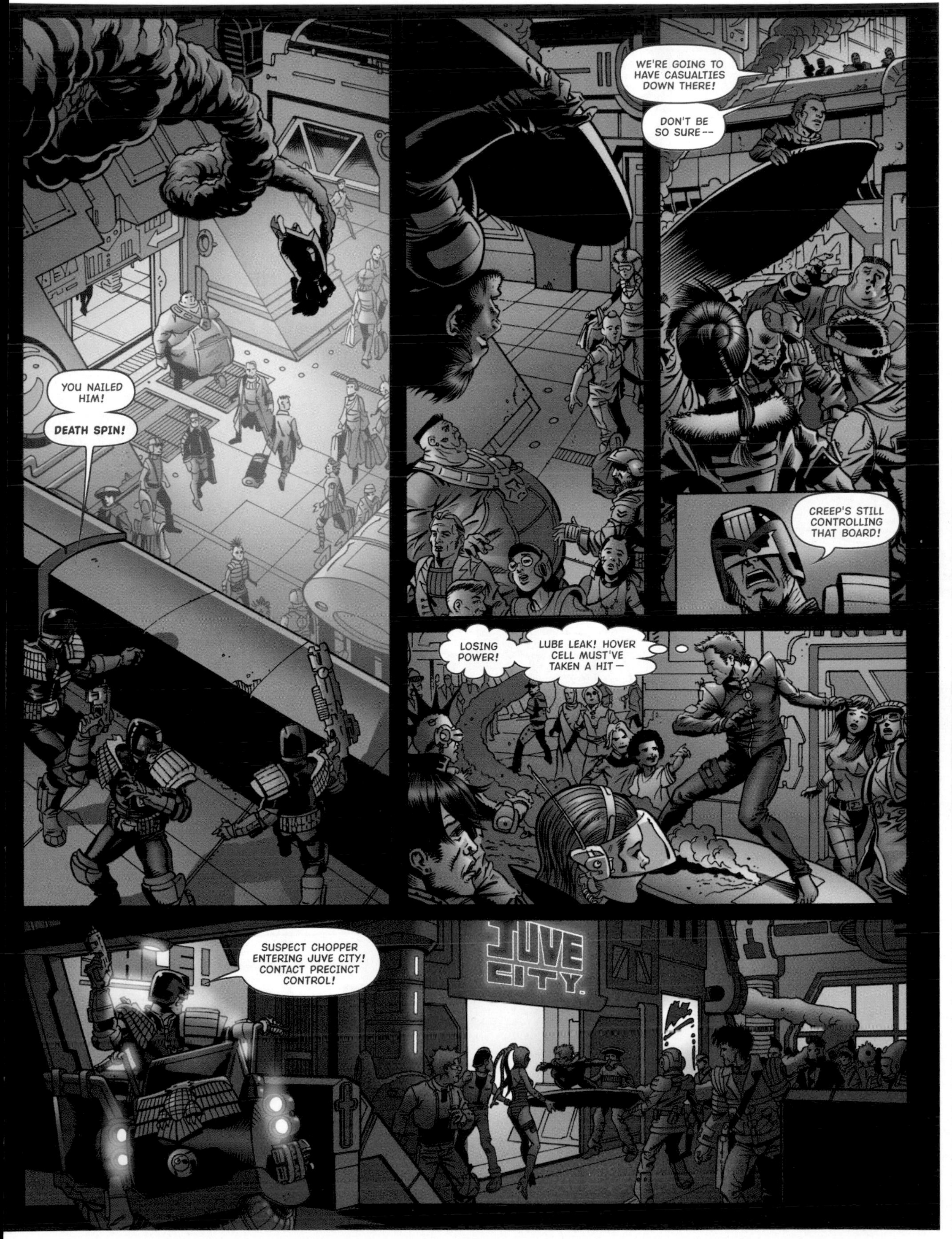
YOU NAILED HIM!
DEATH SPIN!
WE'RE GOING TO HAVE CASUALTIES DOWN THERE!
DON'T BE SO SURE--
CREEP'S STILL CONTROLLING THAT BOARD!
LOSING POWER!
LUBE LEAK! HOVER CELL MUST'VE TAKEN A HIT—
SUSPECT CHOPPER ENTERING JUVE CITY! CONTACT PRECINCT CONTROL!
JUVE CITY.

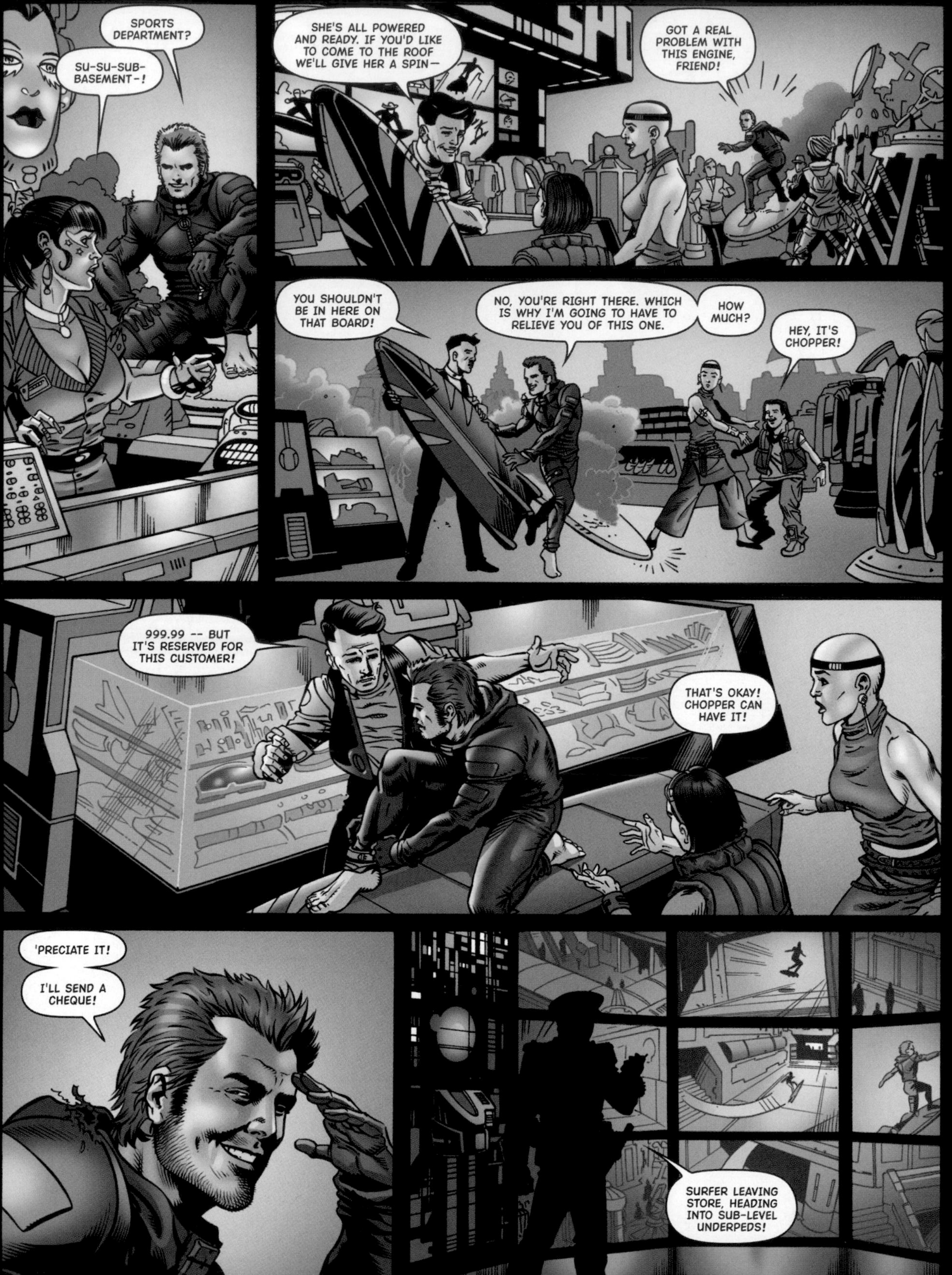
SPORTS DEPARTMENT?
SU-SU-SUB-BASEMENT-!
SHE'S ALL POWERED AND READY. IF YOU'D LIKE TO COME TO THE ROOF WE'LL GIVE HER A SPIN—
GOT A REAL PROBLEM WITH THIS ENGINE, FRIEND!
YOU SHOULDN'T BE IN HERE ON THAT BOARD!
NO, YOU'RE RIGHT THERE. WHICH IS WHY I'M GOING TO HAVE TO RELIEVE YOU OF THIS ONE.
HOW MUCH?
HEY, IT'S CHOPPER!
999.99 -- BUT IT'S RESERVED FOR THIS CUSTOMER!
THAT'S OKAY! CHOPPER CAN HAVE IT!
'PRECIATE IT!
I'LL SEND A CHEQUE!
SURFER LEAVING STORE, HEADING INTO SUB-LEVEL UNDERPEDS!

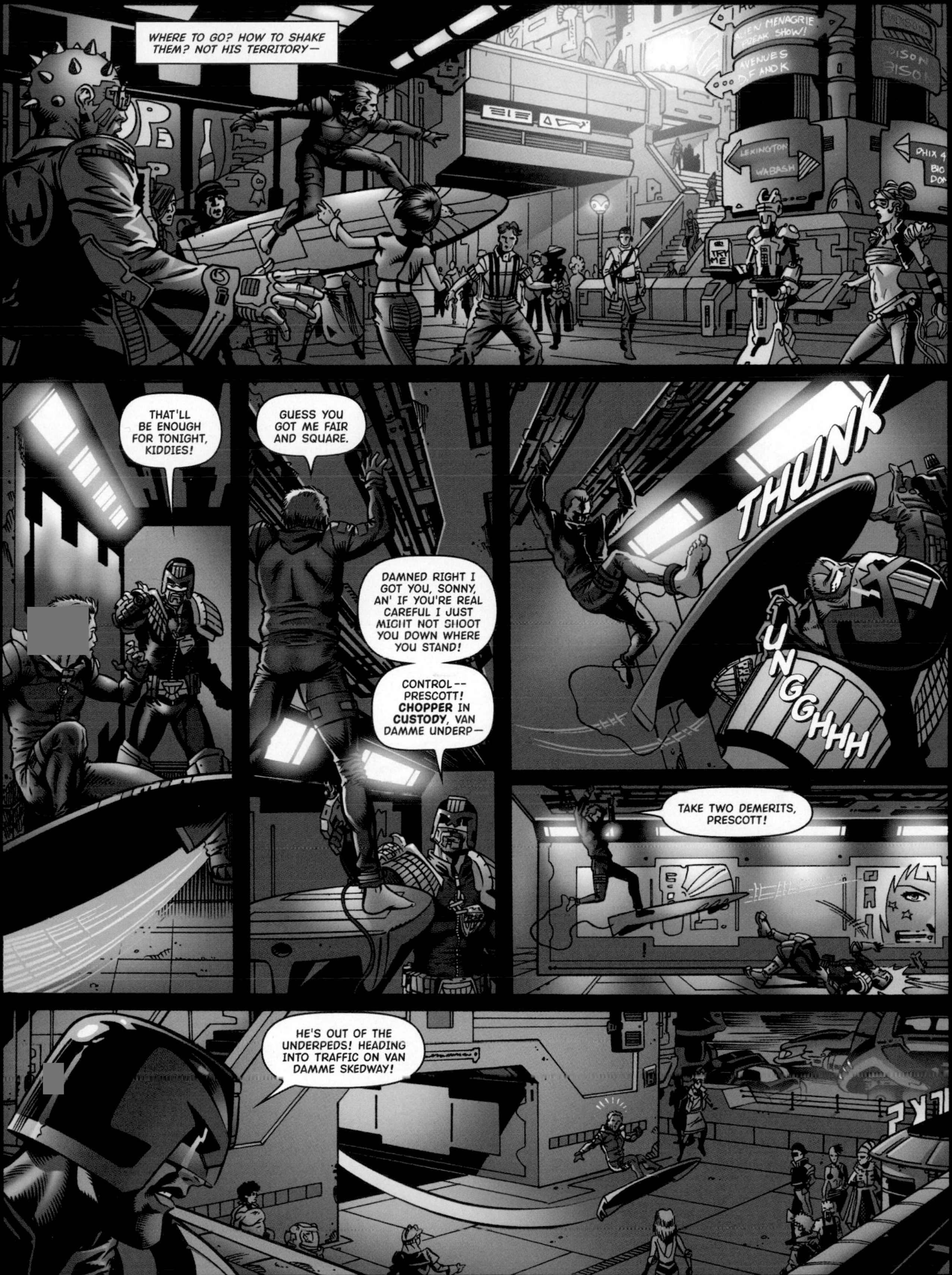
WHERE TO GO? HOW TO SHAKE THEM? NOT HIS TERRITORY—
ALIEN MENAGRIE FREAK SHOW!
LEXINGTON
WABASH
TRY ME
THAT'LL BE ENOUGH FOR TONIGHT, KIDDIES!
GUESS YOU GOT ME FAIR AND SQUARE.
DAMNED RIGHT I GOT YOU, SONNY, AN' IF YOU'RE REAL CAREFUL I JUST MIGHT NOT SHOOT YOU DOWN WHERE YOU STAND!
CONTROL-- PRESCOTT! **CHOPPER** IN **CUSTODY**, VAN DAMME UNDERP—
THUNK
UNGGHHH
TAKE TWO DEMERITS, PRESCOTT!
HE'S OUT OF THE UNDERPEDS! HEADING INTO TRAFFIC ON VAN DAMME SKEDWAY!

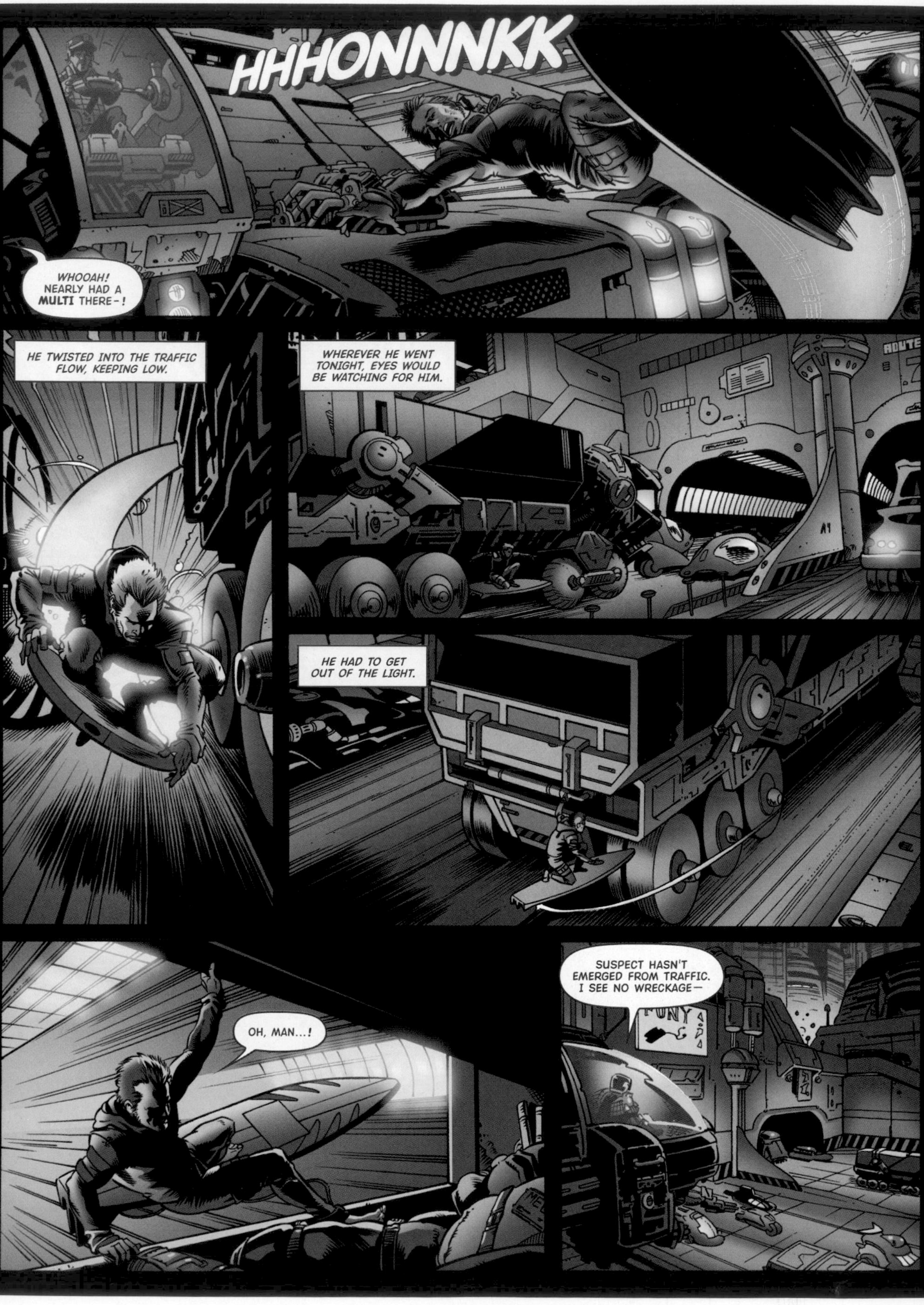
HHHONNNKK
WHOOAH! NEARLY HAD A **MULTI** THERE-!
HE TWISTED INTO THE TRAFFIC FLOW, KEEPING LOW.
WHEREVER HE WENT TONIGHT, EYES WOULD BE WATCHING FOR HIM.
HE HAD TO GET OUT OF THE LIGHT.
OH, MAN...!
SUSPECT HASN'T EMERGED FROM TRAFFIC. I SEE NO WRECKAGE—

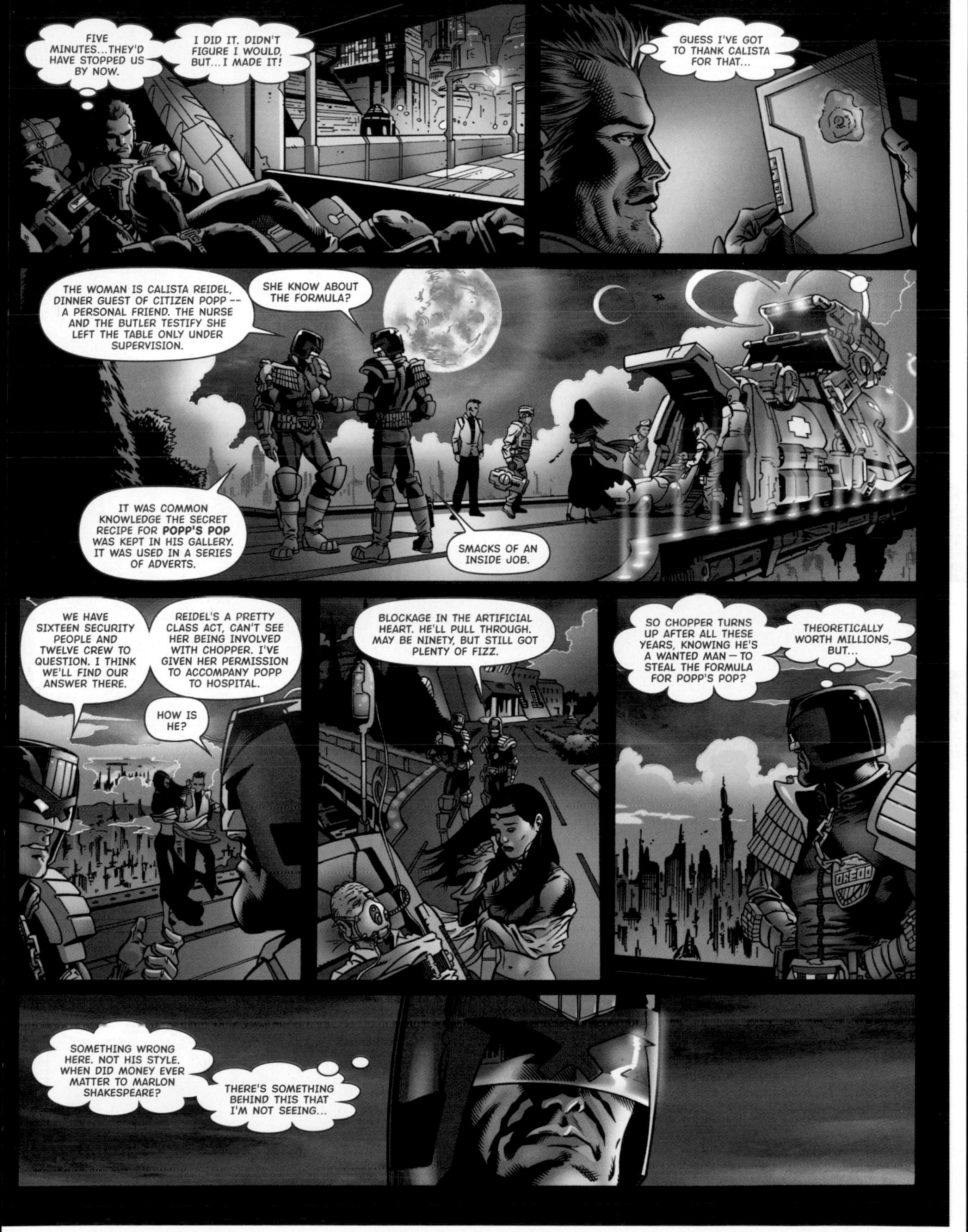

FIVE MINUTES...THEY'D HAVE STOPPED US BY NOW.
I DID IT. DIDN'T FIGURE I WOULD, BUT... I MADE IT!
GUESS I'VE GOT TO THANK CALISTA FOR THAT...
THE WOMAN IS CALISTA REIDEL, DINNER GUEST OF CITIZEN POPP -- A PERSONAL FRIEND. THE NURSE AND THE BUTLER TESTIFY SHE LEFT THE TABLE ONLY UNDER SUPERVISION.
SHE KNOW ABOUT THE FORMULA?
IT WAS COMMON KNOWLEDGE THE SECRET RECIPE FOR POPP'S POP WAS KEPT IN HIS GALLERY. IT WAS USED IN A SERIES OF ADVERTS.
SMACKS OF AN INSIDE JOB.
WE HAVE SIXTEEN SECURITY PEOPLE AND TWELVE CREW TO QUESTION. I THINK WE'LL FIND OUR ANSWER THERE.
REIDEL'S A PRETTY CLASS ACT, CAN'T SEE HER BEING INVOLVED WITH CHOPPER. I'VE GIVEN HER PERMISSION TO ACCOMPANY POPP TO HOSPITAL.
HOW IS HE?
BLOCKAGE IN THE ARTIFICIAL HEART. HE'LL PULL THROUGH. MAY BE NINETY, BUT STILL GOT PLENTY OF FIZZ.
SO CHOPPER TURNS UP AFTER ALL THESE YEARS, KNOWING HE'S A WANTED MAN — TO STEAL THE FORMULA FOR POPP'S POP?
THEORETICALLY WORTH MILLIONS, BUT...
DREDD
SOMETHING WRONG HERE. NOT HIS STYLE. WHEN DID MONEY EVER MATTER TO MARLON SHAKESPEARE?
THERE'S SOMETHING BEHIND THIS THAT I'M NOT SEEING...

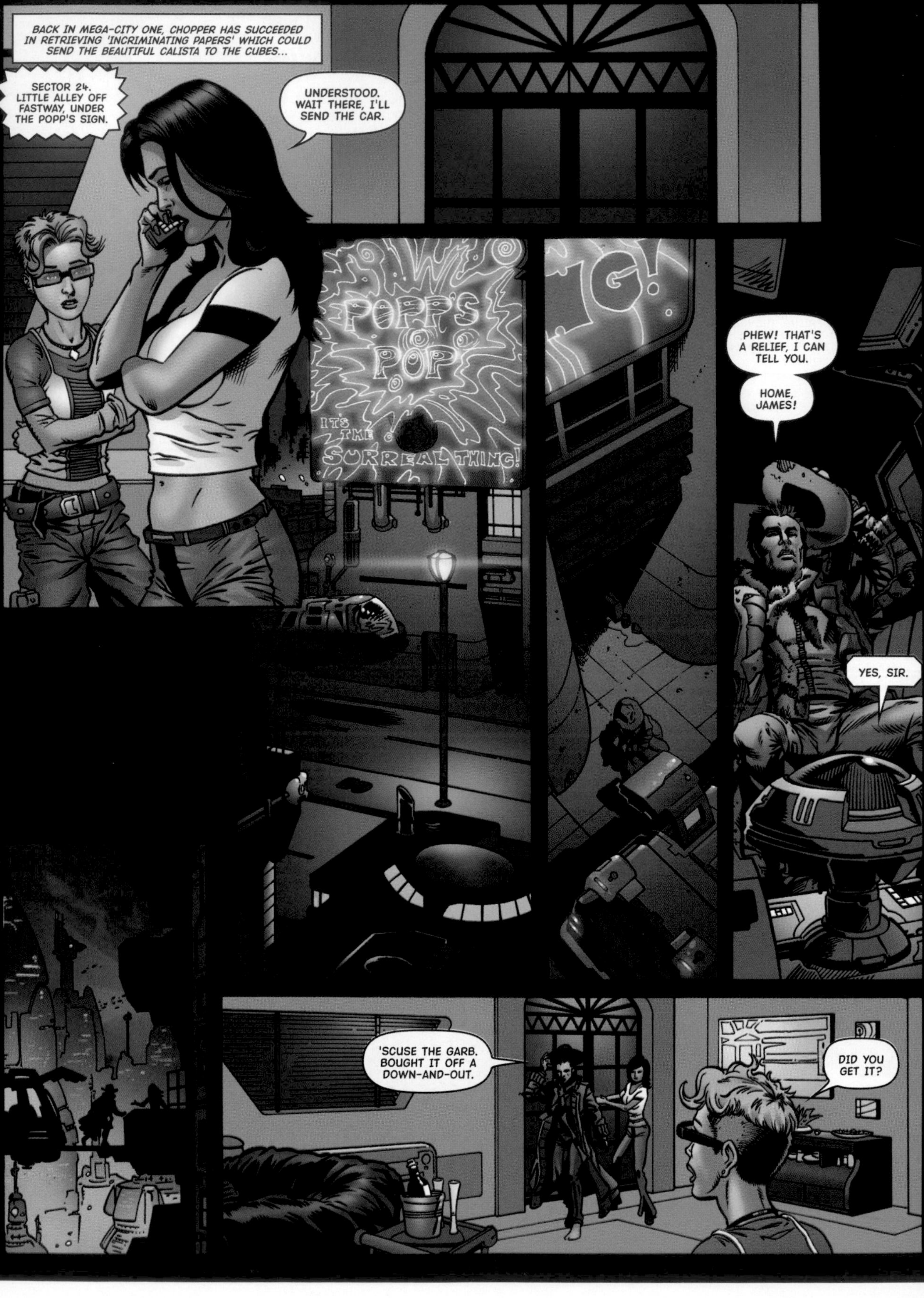
BACK IN MEGA-CITY ONE, CHOPPER HAS SUCCEEDED IN RETRIEVING 'INCRIMINATING PAPERS' WHICH COULD SEND THE BEAUTIFUL CALISTA TO THE CUBES...
SECTOR 24. LITTLE ALLEY OFF FASTWAY, UNDER THE POPP'S SIGN.
UNDERSTOOD. WAIT THERE, I'LL SEND THE CAR.
POPP'S POP
IT'S THE SURREAL THING!
PHEW! THAT'S A RELIEF, I CAN TELL YOU.
HOME, JAMES!
YES, SIR.
'SCUSE THE GARB. BOUGHT IT OFF A DOWN-AND-OUT.
DID YOU GET IT?

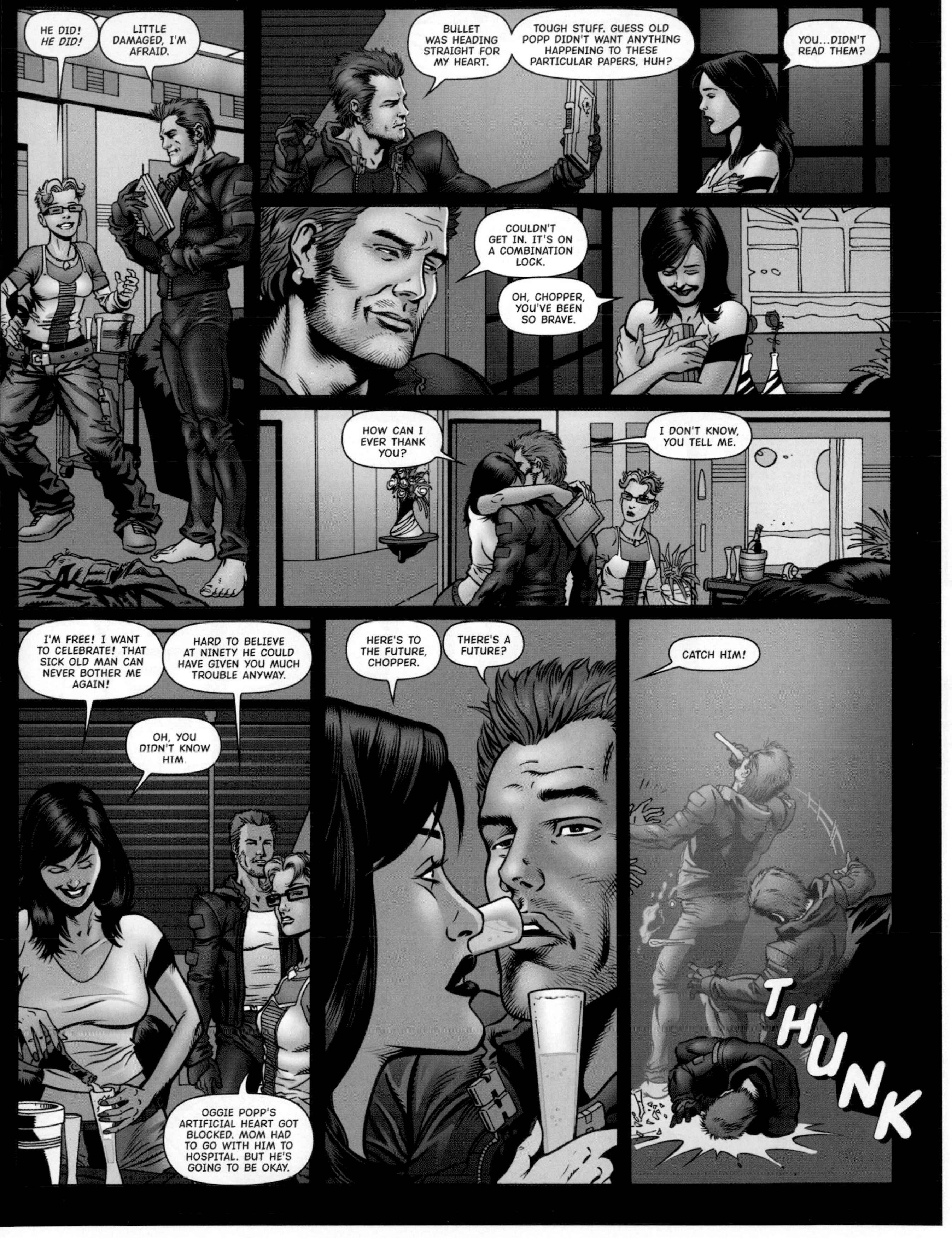
HE DID! *HE DID!*
LITTLE DAMAGED, I'M AFRAID.
BULLET WAS HEADING STRAIGHT FOR MY HEART.
TOUGH STUFF. GUESS OLD POPP DIDN'T WANT ANYTHING HAPPENING TO THESE PARTICULAR PAPERS, HUH?
YOU...DIDN'T READ THEM?
COULDN'T GET IN. IT'S ON A COMBINATION LOCK.
OH, CHOPPER, YOU'VE BEEN SO BRAVE.
HOW CAN I EVER THANK YOU?
I DON'T KNOW, YOU TELL ME.
I'M FREE! I WANT TO CELEBRATE! THAT SICK OLD MAN CAN NEVER BOTHER ME AGAIN!
HARD TO BELIEVE AT NINETY HE COULD HAVE GIVEN YOU MUCH TROUBLE ANYWAY.
OH, YOU DIDN'T KNOW HIM.
OGGIE POPP'S ARTIFICIAL HEART GOT BLOCKED. MOM HAD TO GO WITH HIM TO HOSPITAL. BUT HE'S GOING TO BE OKAY.
HERE'S TO THE FUTURE, CHOPPER.
THERE'S A FUTURE?
CATCH HIM!
THUNK

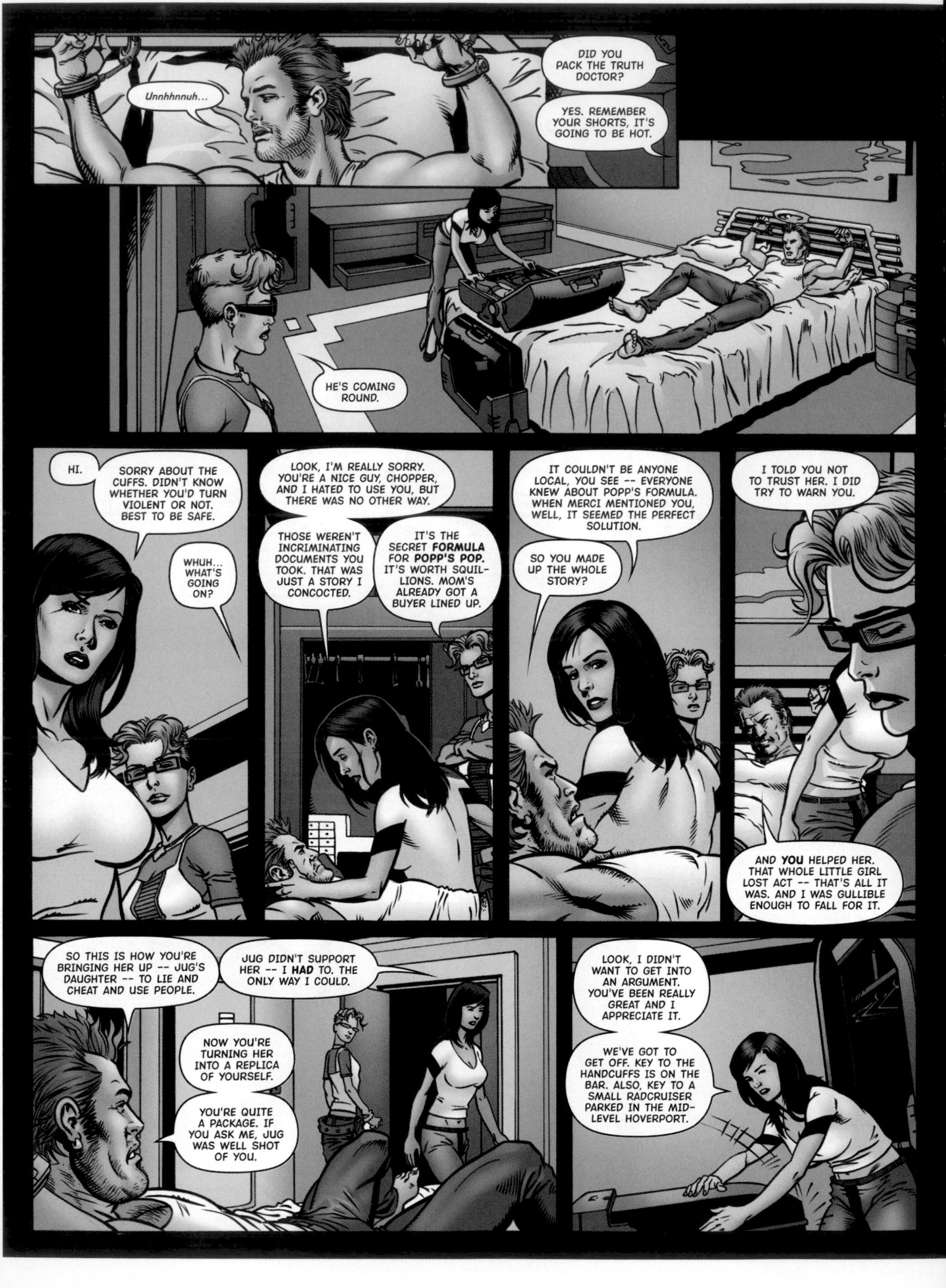
Unnhhnnuh...
DID YOU PACK THE TRUTH DOCTOR?
YES. REMEMBER YOUR SHORTS, IT'S GOING TO BE HOT.
HE'S COMING ROUND.
HI.
SORRY ABOUT THE CUFFS. DIDN'T KNOW WHETHER YOU'D TURN VIOLENT OR NOT. BEST TO BE SAFE.
WHUH... WHAT'S GOING ON?
LOOK, I'M REALLY SORRY. YOU'RE A NICE GUY, CHOPPER, AND I HATED TO USE YOU, BUT THERE WAS NO OTHER WAY.
THOSE WEREN'T INCRIMINATING DOCUMENTS YOU TOOK. THAT WAS JUST A STORY I CONCOCTED.
IT'S THE SECRET **FORMULA** FOR **POPP'S POP.** IT'S WORTH SQUIL-LIONS. MOM'S ALREADY GOT A BUYER LINED UP.
IT COULDN'T BE ANYONE LOCAL, YOU SEE -- EVERYONE KNEW ABOUT POPP'S FORMULA. WHEN MERCI MENTIONED YOU, WELL, IT SEEMED THE PERFECT SOLUTION.
SO YOU MADE UP THE WHOLE STORY?
I TOLD YOU NOT TO TRUST HER. I DID TRY TO WARN YOU.
AND **YOU** HELPED HER. THAT WHOLE LITTLE GIRL LOST ACT -- THAT'S ALL IT WAS. AND I WAS GULLIBLE ENOUGH TO FALL FOR IT.
SO THIS IS HOW YOU'RE BRINGING HER UP -- JUG'S DAUGHTER -- TO LIE AND CHEAT AND USE PEOPLE.
JUG DIDN'T SUPPORT HER -- I **HAD** TO. THE ONLY WAY I COULD.
NOW YOU'RE TURNING HER INTO A REPLICA OF YOURSELF.
YOU'RE QUITE A PACKAGE. IF YOU ASK ME, JUG WAS WELL SHOT OF YOU.
LOOK, I DIDN'T WANT TO GET INTO AN ARGUMENT. YOU'VE BEEN REALLY GREAT AND I APPRECIATE IT.
WE'VE GOT TO GET OFF. KEY TO THE HANDCUFFS IS ON THE BAR. ALSO, KEY TO A SMALL RADCRUISER PARKED IN THE MID-LEVEL HOVERPORT.

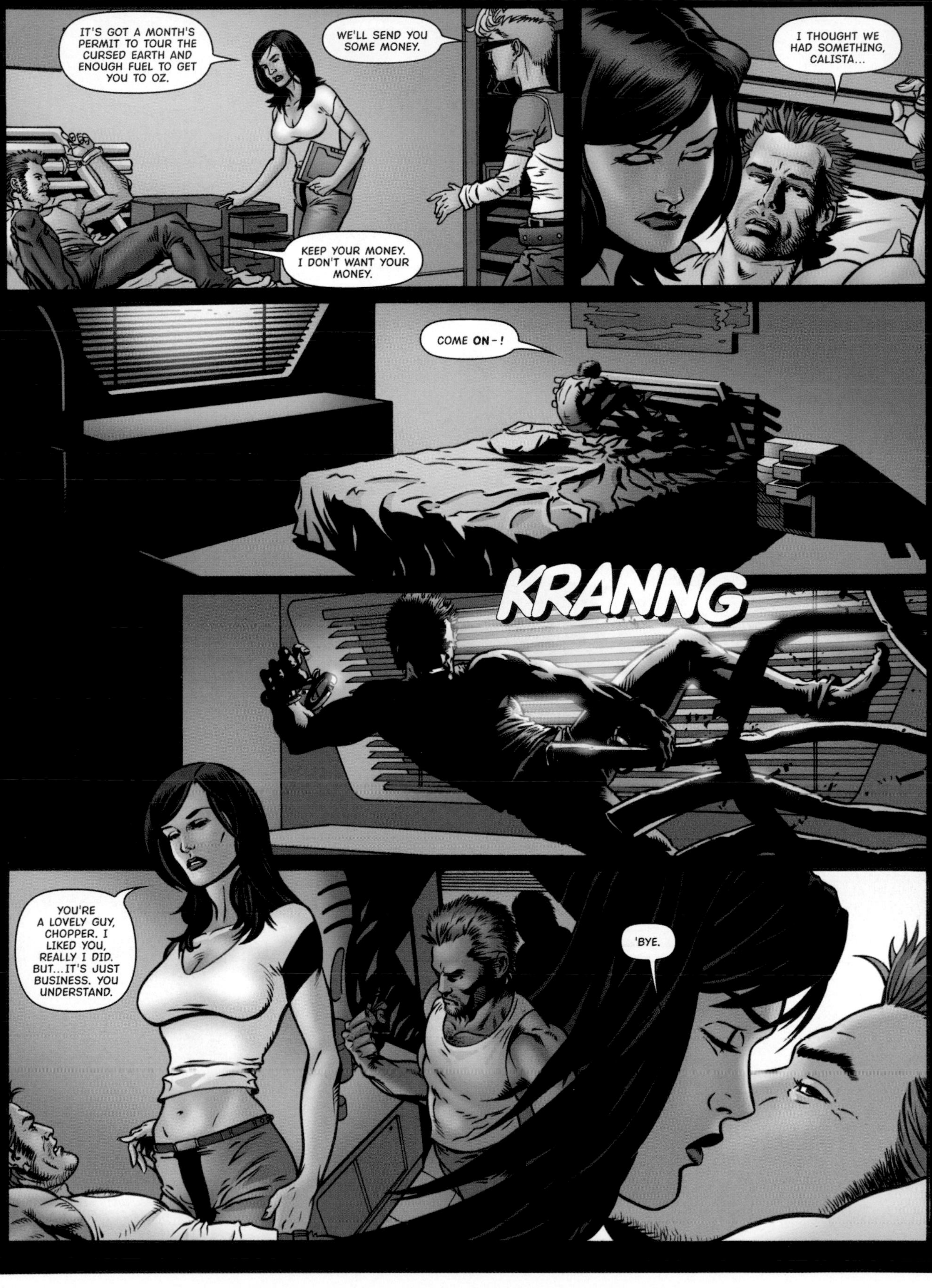
IT'S GOT A MONTH'S PERMIT TO TOUR THE CURSED EARTH AND ENOUGH FUEL TO GET YOU TO OZ.
WE'LL SEND YOU SOME MONEY.
KEEP YOUR MONEY. I DON'T WANT YOUR MONEY.
I THOUGHT WE HAD SOMETHING, CALISTA...
COME ON-!
KRANNG
YOU'RE A LOVELY GUY, CHOPPER. I LIKED YOU, REALLY I DID. BUT...IT'S JUST BUSINESS. YOU UNDERSTAND.
'BYE.

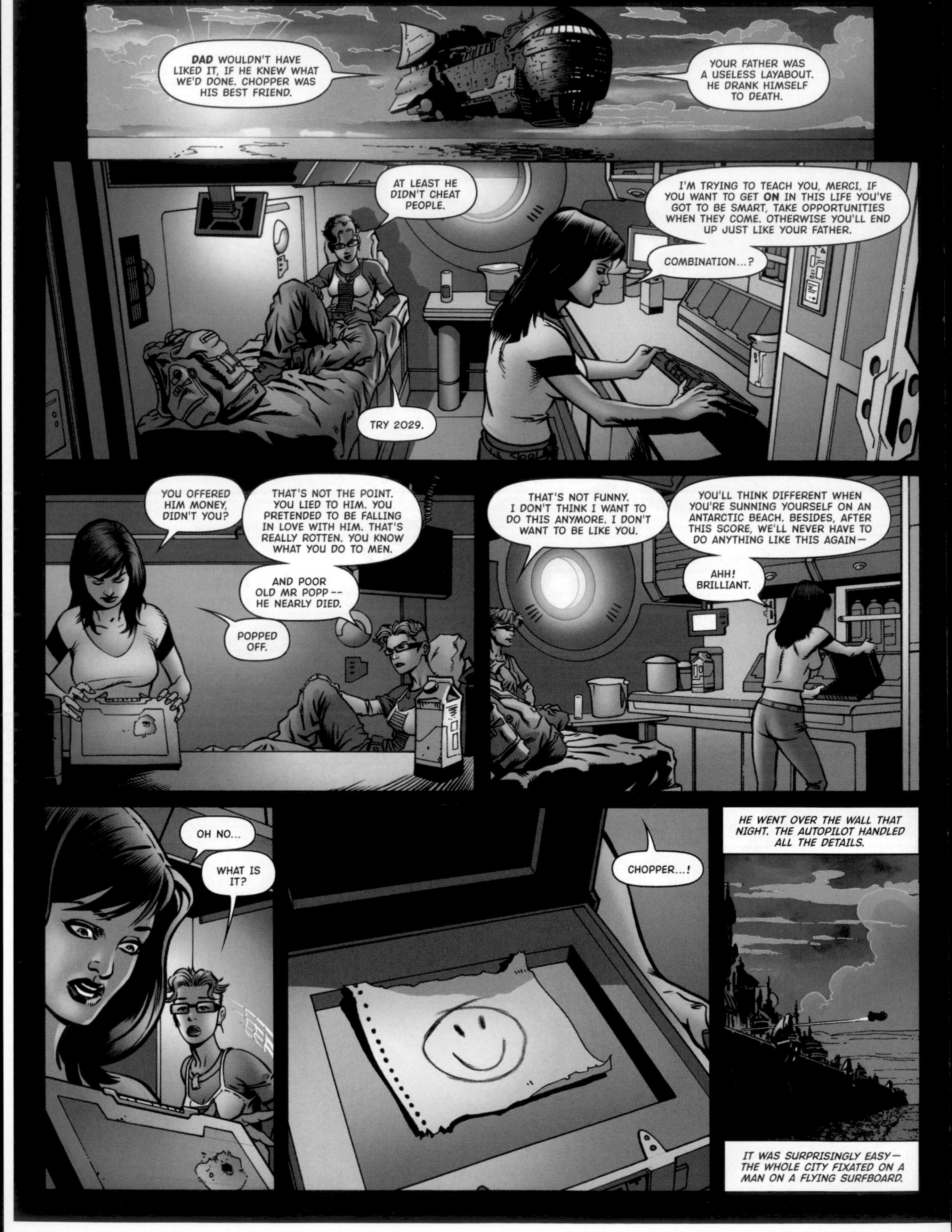

DAD WOULDN'T HAVE LIKED IT, IF HE KNEW WHAT WE'D DONE. CHOPPER WAS HIS BEST FRIEND.
YOUR FATHER WAS A USELESS LAYABOUT. HE DRANK HIMSELF TO DEATH.
AT LEAST HE DIDN'T CHEAT PEOPLE.
I'M TRYING TO TEACH YOU, MERCI, IF YOU WANT TO GET ON IN THIS LIFE YOU'VE GOT TO BE SMART, TAKE OPPORTUNITIES WHEN THEY COME. OTHERWISE YOU'LL END UP JUST LIKE YOUR FATHER.
COMBINATION...?
TRY 2029.
YOU OFFERED HIM MONEY, DIDN'T YOU?
THAT'S NOT THE POINT. YOU LIED TO HIM. YOU PRETENDED TO BE FALLING IN LOVE WITH HIM. THAT'S REALLY ROTTEN. YOU KNOW WHAT YOU DO TO MEN.
AND POOR OLD MR POPP -- HE NEARLY DIED.
POPPED OFF.
THAT'S NOT FUNNY. I DON'T THINK I WANT TO DO THIS ANYMORE. I DON'T WANT TO BE LIKE YOU.
YOU'LL THINK DIFFERENT WHEN YOU'RE SUNNING YOURSELF ON AN ANTARCTIC BEACH. BESIDES, AFTER THIS SCORE, WE'LL NEVER HAVE TO DO ANYTHING LIKE THIS AGAIN—
AHH! BRILLIANT.
OH NO...
WHAT IS IT?
CHOPPER...!
HE WENT OVER THE WALL THAT NIGHT. THE AUTOPILOT HANDLED ALL THE DETAILS.
IT WAS SURPRISINGLY EASY— THE WHOLE CITY FIXATED ON A MAN ON A FLYING SURFBOARD.

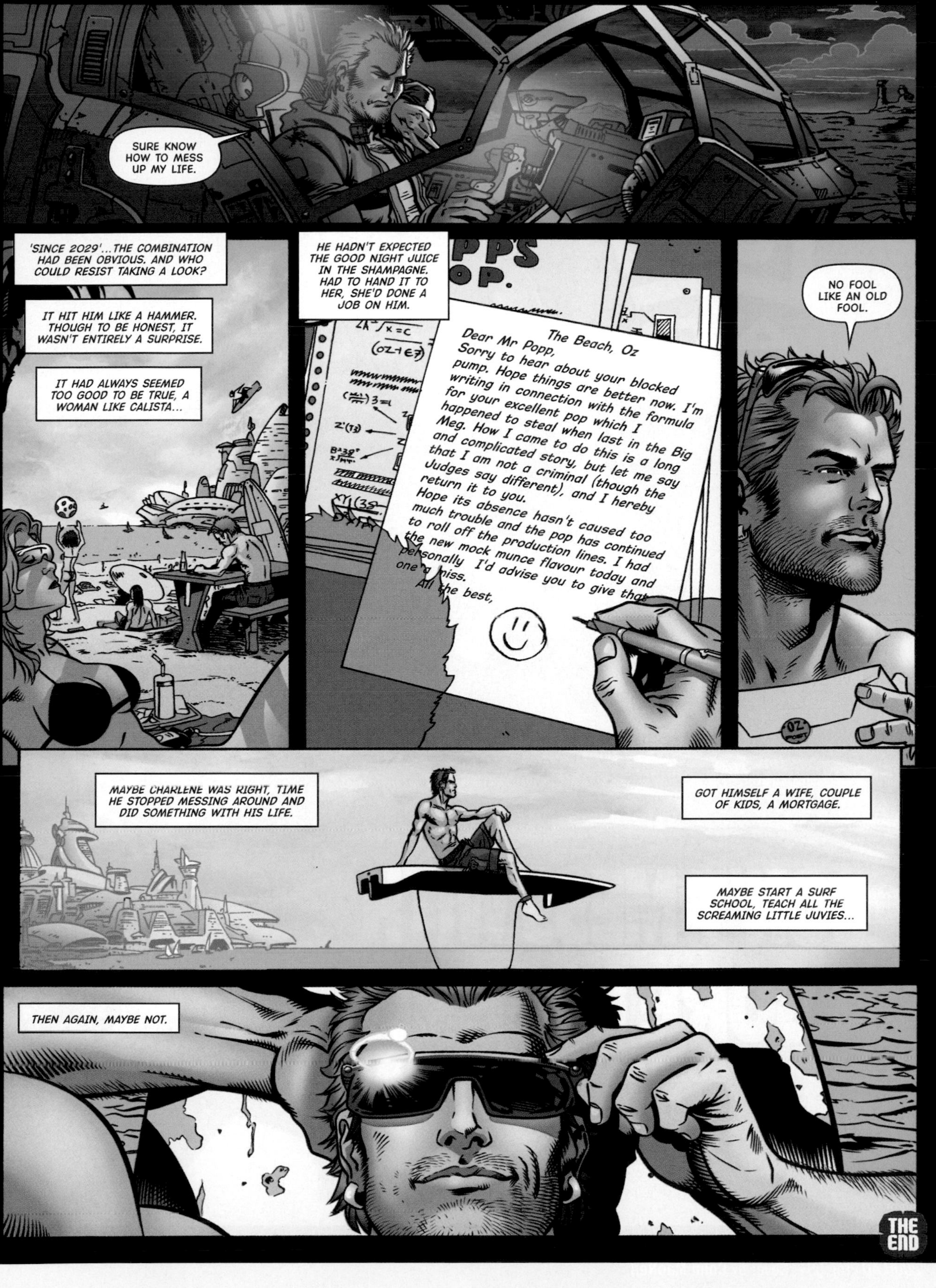
SURE KNOW HOW TO MESS UP MY LIFE.
'SINCE 2029'...THE COMBINATION HAD BEEN OBVIOUS. AND WHO COULD RESIST TAKING A LOOK?
IT HIT HIM LIKE A HAMMER. THOUGH TO BE HONEST, IT WASN'T ENTIRELY A SURPRISE.
IT HAD ALWAYS SEEMED TOO GOOD TO BE TRUE, A WOMAN LIKE CALISTA...
HE HADN'T EXPECTED THE GOOD NIGHT JUICE IN THE SHAMPAGNE. HAD TO HAND IT TO HER, SHE'D DONE A JOB ON HIM.
The Beach, Oz
Dear Mr Popp,
Sorry to hear about your blocked pump. Hope things are better now. I'm writing in connection with the formula for your excellent pop which I happened to steal when last in the Big Meg. How I came to do this is a long and complicated story, but let me say that I am not a criminal (though the Judges say different), and I hereby return it to you.
Hope its absence hasn't caused too much trouble and the pop has continued to roll off the production lines. I had the new mock munce flavour today and personally I'd advise you to give that one a miss.
All the best,
NO FOOL LIKE AN OLD FOOL.
OZ
MAYBE CHARLENE WAS RIGHT, TIME HE STOPPED MESSING AROUND AND DID SOMETHING WITH HIS LIFE.
GOT HIMSELF A WIFE, COUPLE OF KIDS, A MORTGAGE.
MAYBE START A SURF SCHOOL, TEACH ALL THE SCREAMING LITTLE JUVIES...
THEN AGAIN, MAYBE NOT.
THE END

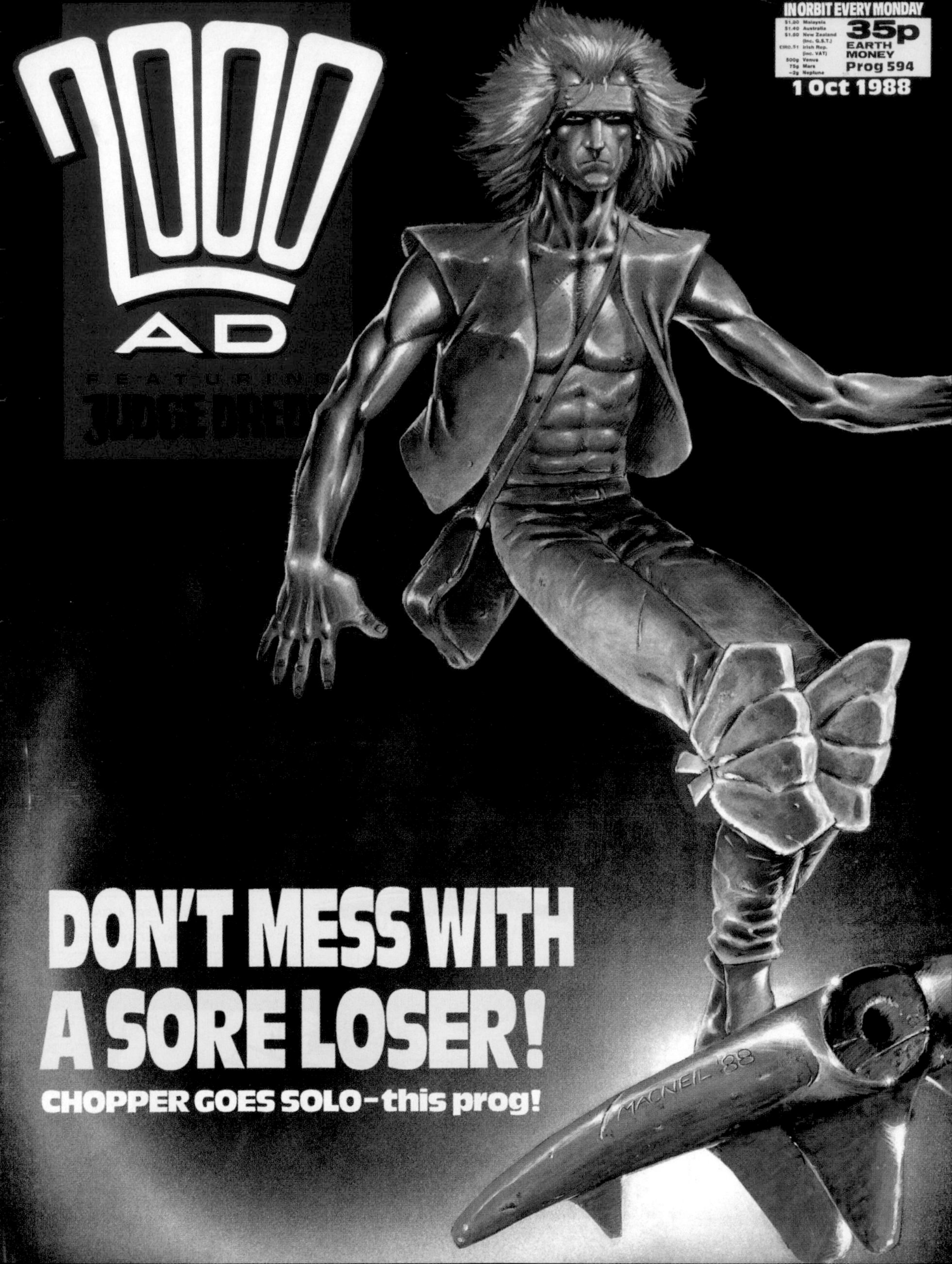

IN ORBIT EVERY MONDAY
$1.80 Malaysia
$1.40 Australia
$1.80 New Zealand (inc. G.S.T.)
EIR0.51 Irish Rep. (inc. VAT)
500g Venus
75g Mars
~2g Neptune
35p EARTH MONEY
Prog 594
1 Oct 1988
2000 AD
FEATURING
JUDGE DREDD
DON'T MESS WITH A SORE LOSER!
CHOPPER GOES SOLO-this prog!
MACNEIL '88

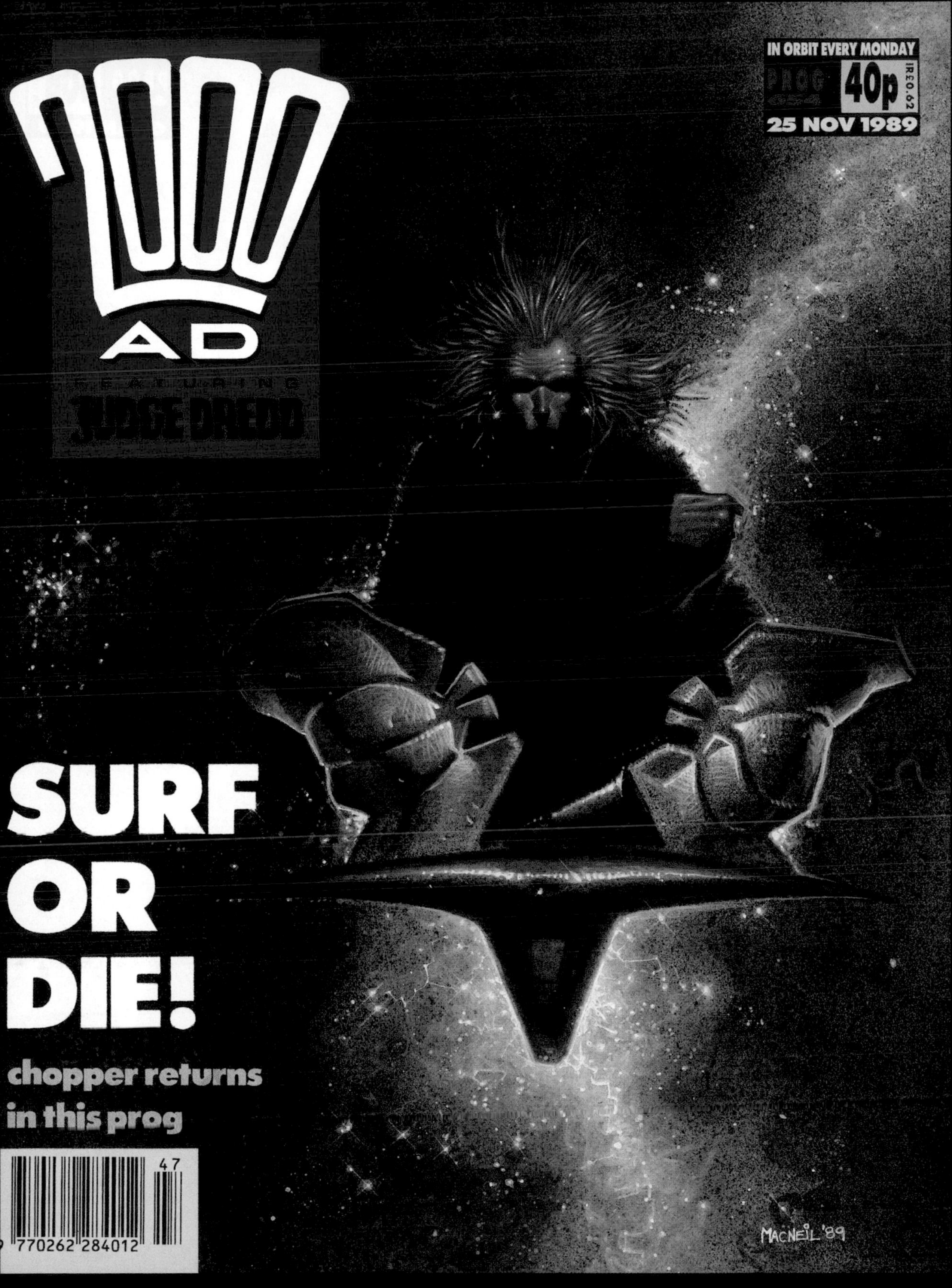
2000 AD
FEATURING
JUDGE DREDD
IN ORBIT EVERY MONDAY
PROG 654
40p
IR£0.62
25 NOV 1989
SURF OR DIE!
chopper returns in this prog
MACNEIL '89

2000 AD Prog 654: Cover by **Colin MacNeil**

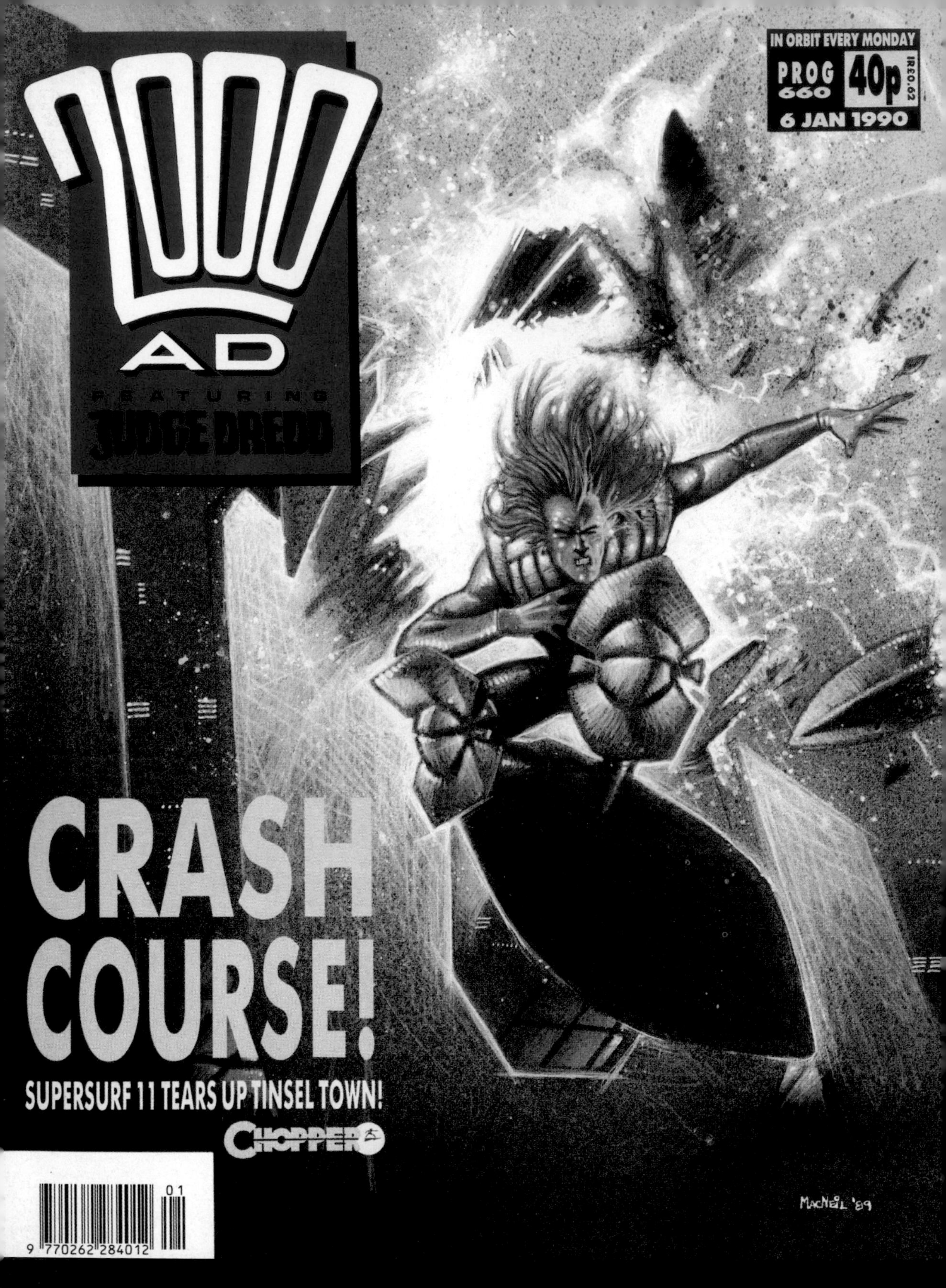
2000 AD
FEATURING
JUDGE DREDD
IN ORBIT EVERY MONDAY
PROG 660
40p
IR£0.62
6 JAN 1990
CRASH COURSE!
SUPERSURF 11 TEARS UP TINSEL TOWN!
CHOPPER
MacNeil '89
9 770262 284012
01

2000 AD Prog 660: Cover by **Colin MacNeil**

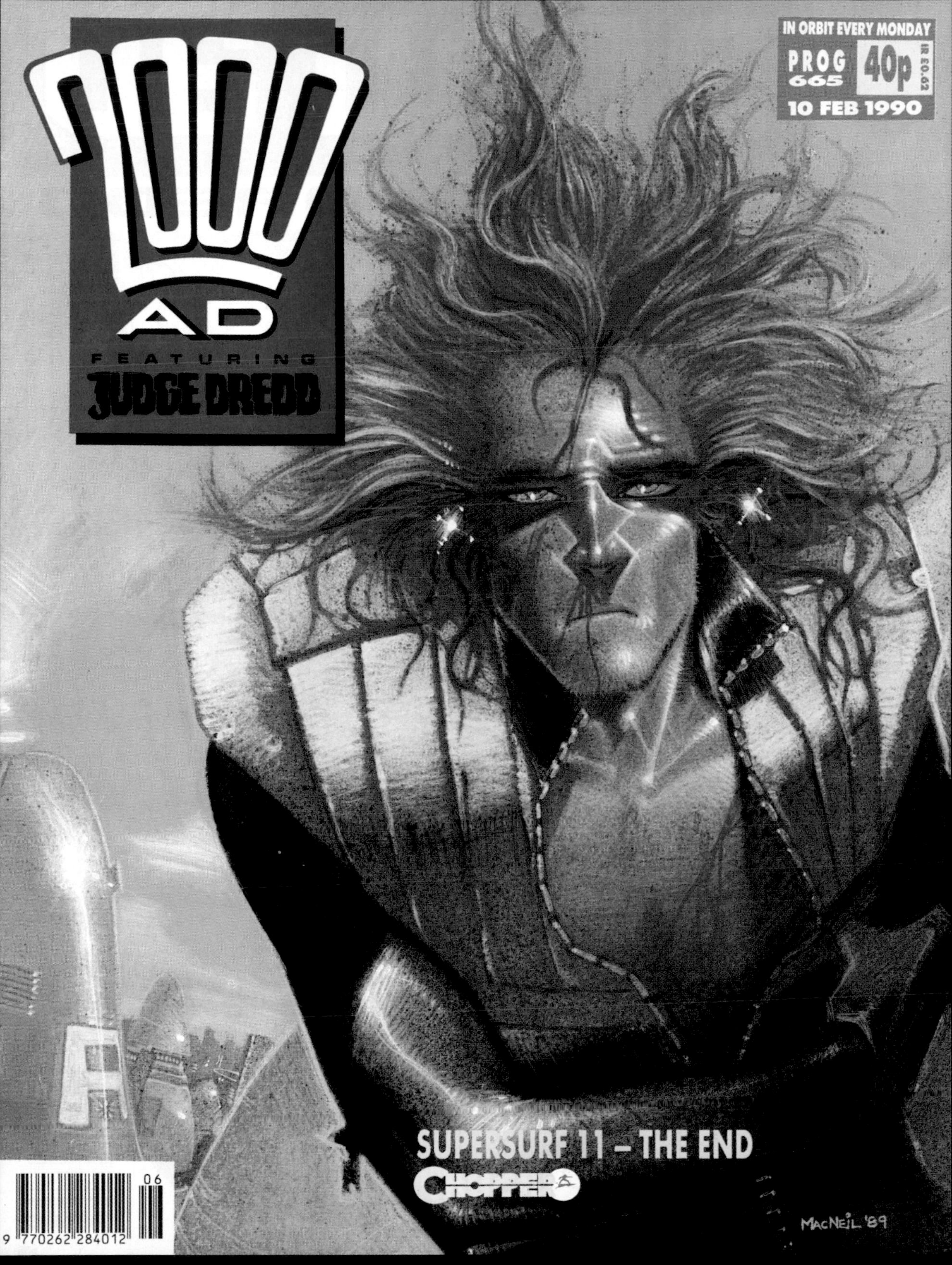
2000 AD
FEATURING
JUDGE DREDD
IN ORBIT EVERY MONDAY
PROG 665
40p
IR £0.62
10 FEB 1990
SUPERSURF 11 – THE END
CHOPPER
MACNEIL '89

2000 AD Prog 665: Cover by **Colin MacNeil**

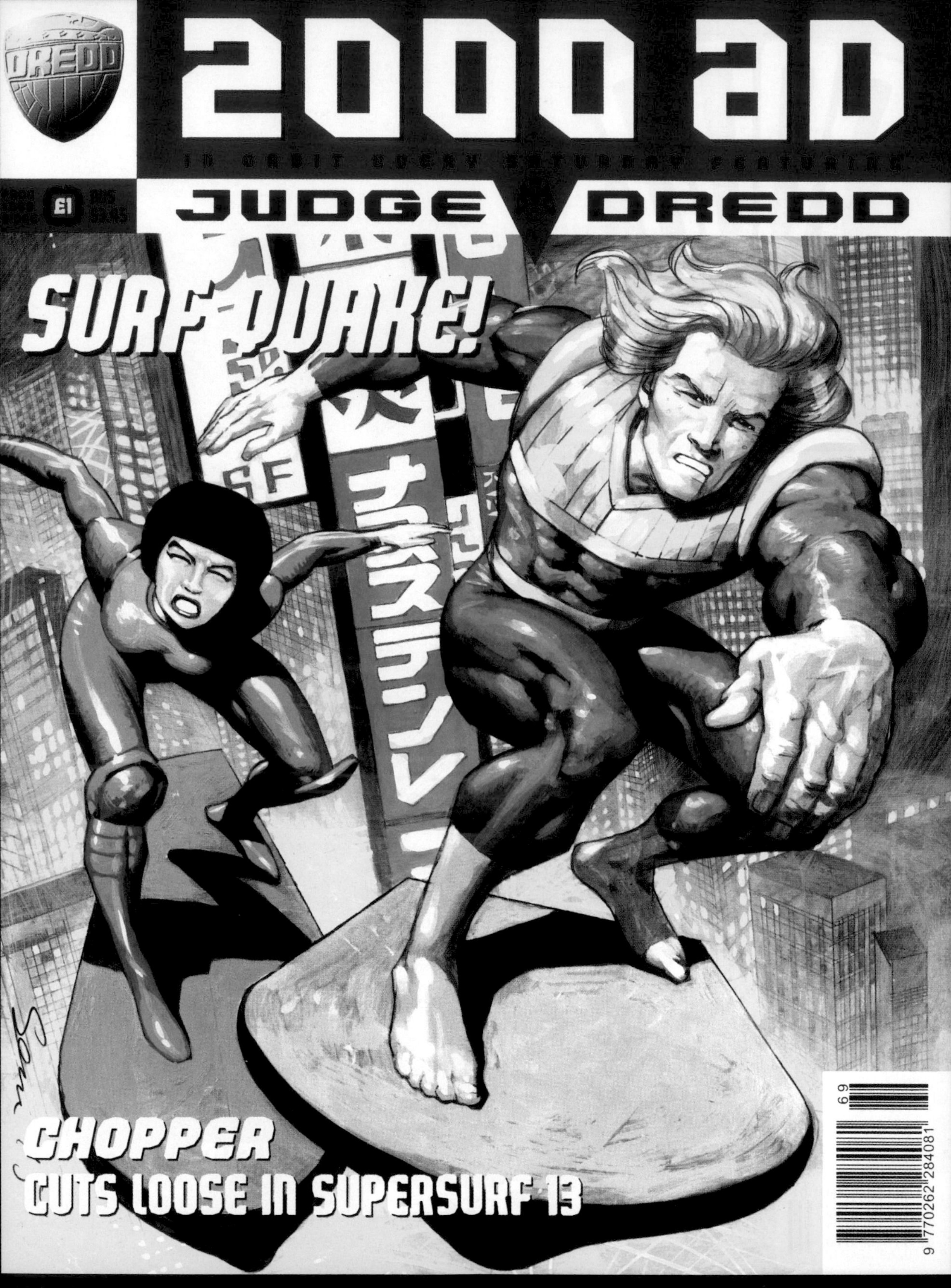
DREDD
2000 AD
IN ORBIT EVERY SATURDAY FEATURING
£1
JUDGE DREDD
SURF QUAKE!
CHOPPER
CUTS LOOSE IN SUPERSURF 13

2000 AD Prog 969: Cover by **Sean Phillips**

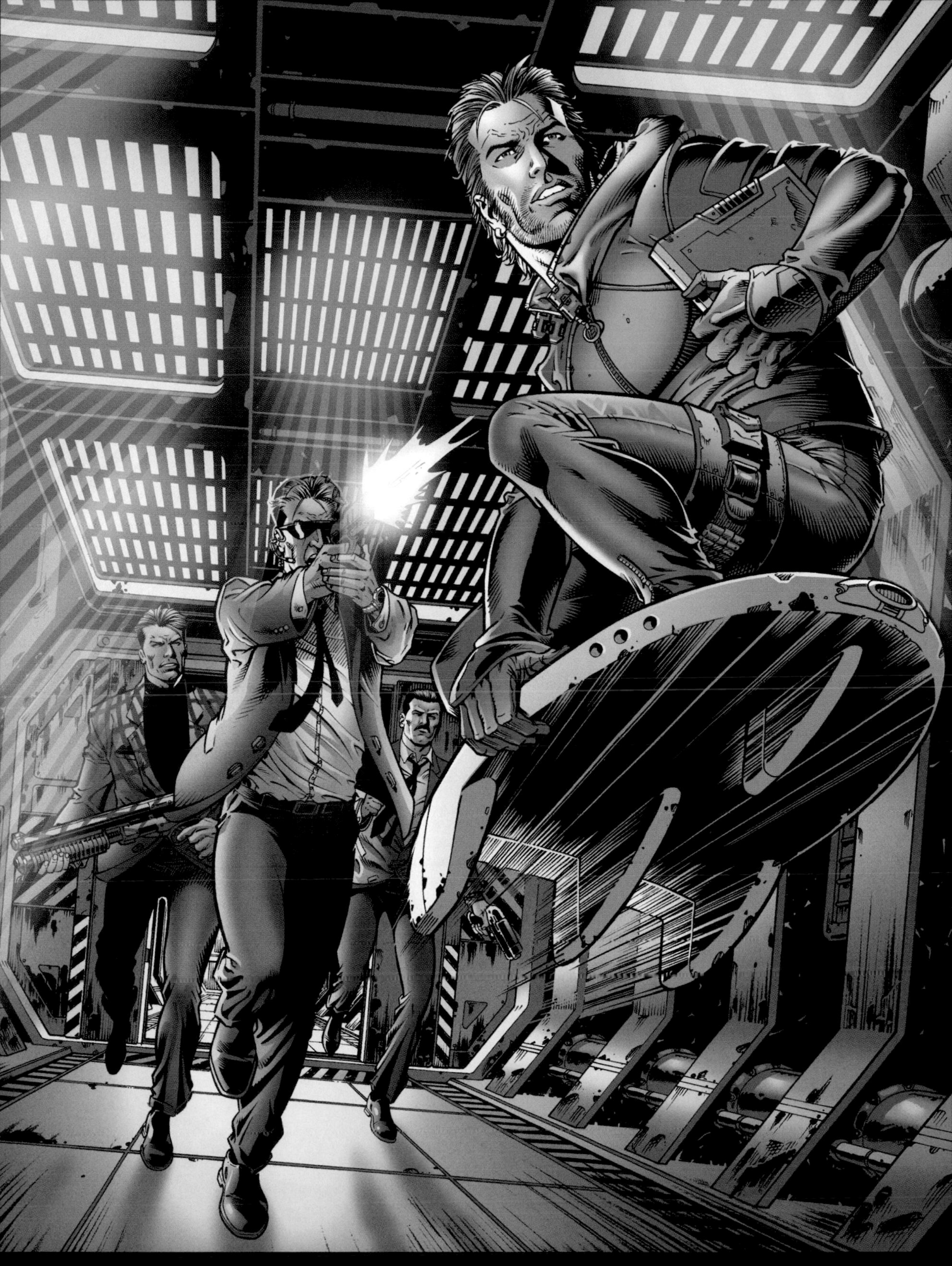

2000 AD Prog 1392: Cover by **Dylan Teague & Chris Blythe**

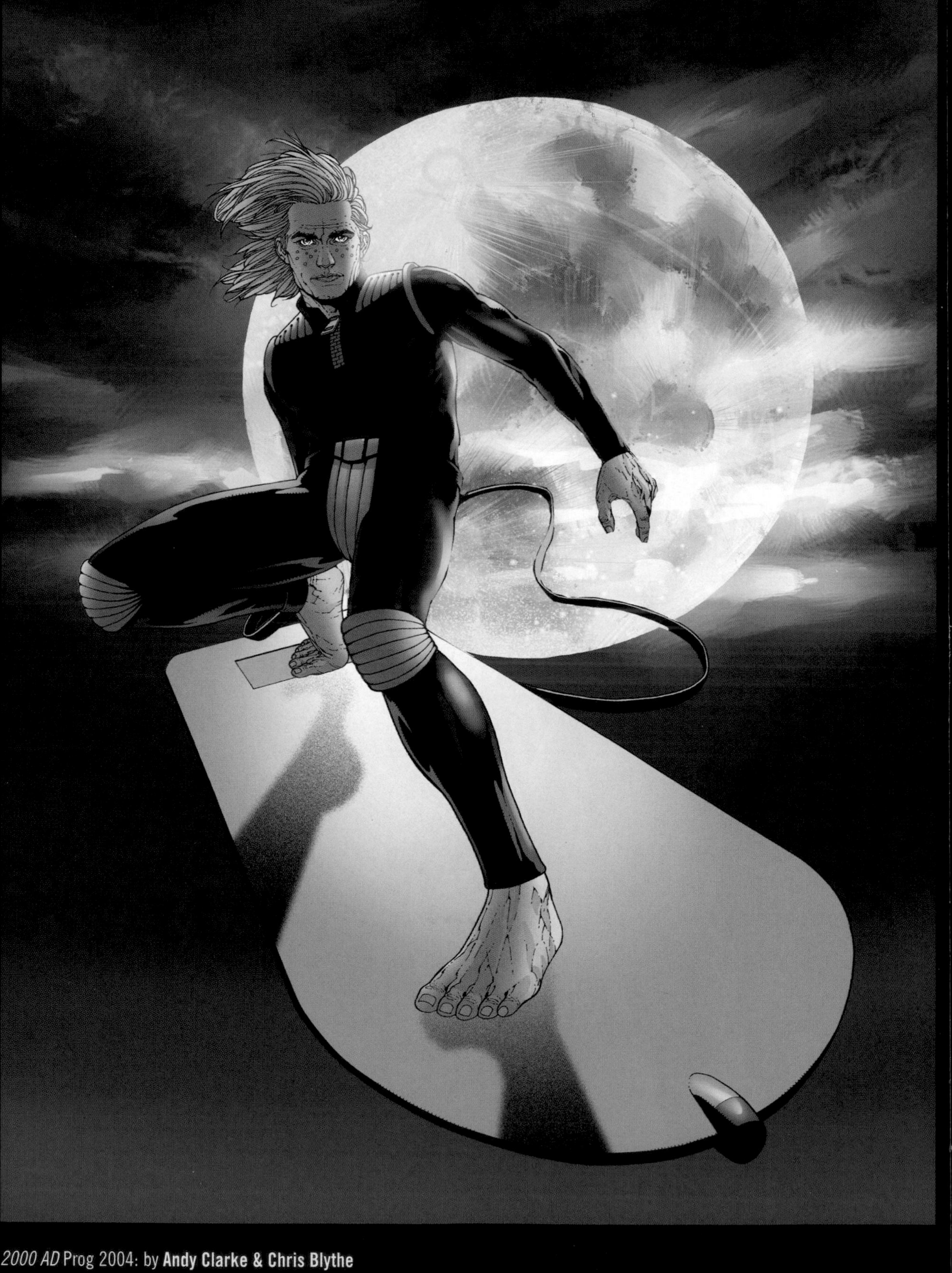

2000 AD Prog 2004: by **Andy Clarke & Chris Blythe**

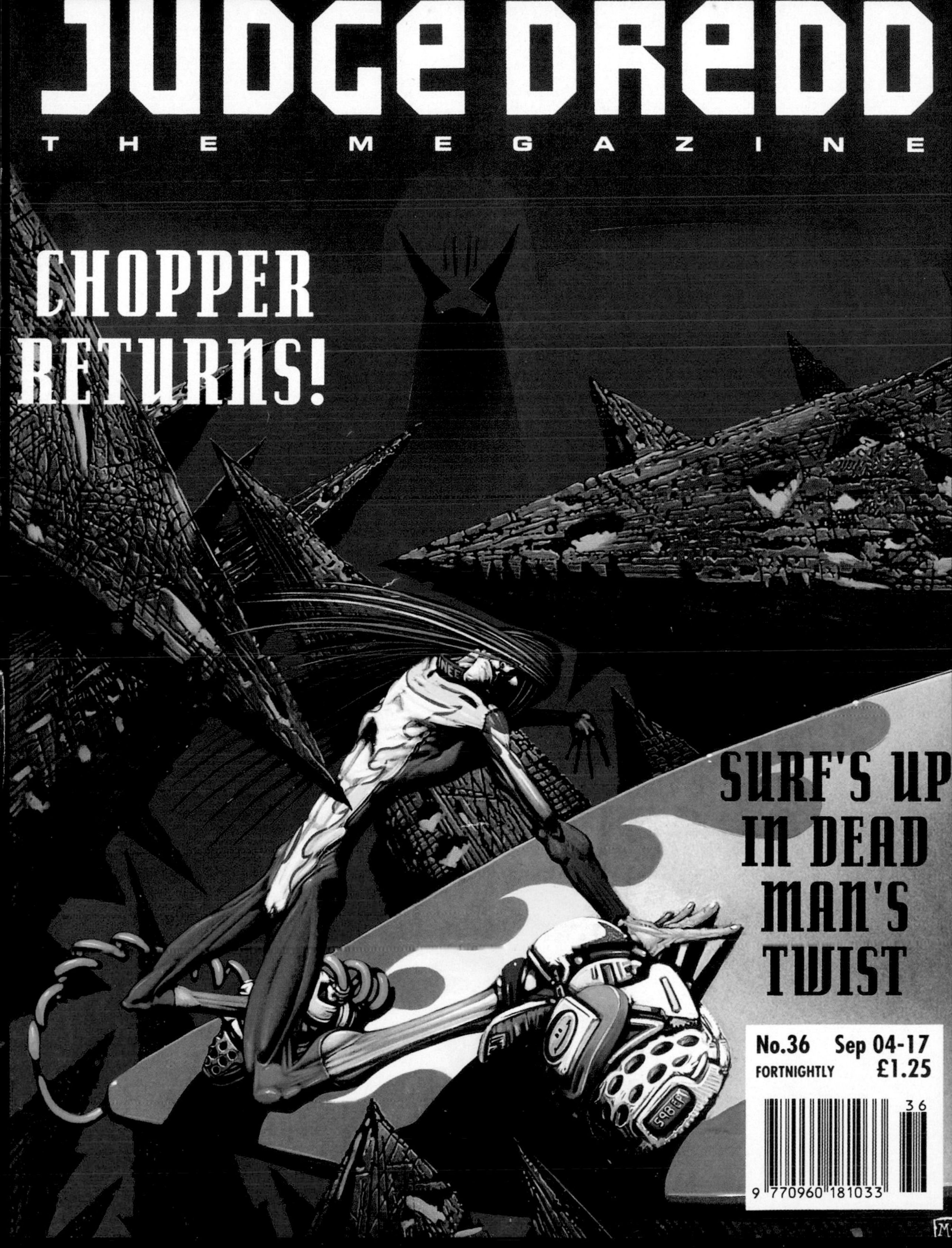
JUDGE DREDD
THE MEGAZINE
CHOPPER RETURNS!
SURF'S UP IN DEAD MAN'S TWIST
No.36 Sep 04-17
FORTNIGHTLY £1.25

Judge Dredd Megazine 2.36: Cover by **Martin Emond**

ARTISTS

Since joining *2000 AD* in 1986 **Colin MacNeil** has worked on many strips, including *Chopper — Song of the Surfer* and *Strontium Dog — The Final Solution*. He went on to collaborate with John Wagner on the award-winning *Judge Dredd — America* for the *Judge Dredd Megazine*. He has also worked on *Shimura, Maelstrom* and *Fiends of the Eastern Front — Stalingrad*. Recently he has worked on *Judge Dredd —Total War, Cadet, Mutants in Mega-City One* and *Emphatically Evil: The Life and Crimes of P J Maybe*. He also provided the atmospheric artwork on *Bloodquest* for Games Workshop. Away from comics, Colin enjoys creating large abstract paintings. He says its art therapy!

John Higgins is a multi-talented *2000 AD* artist and writer; as well as scripting a *Future Shock* and *Judge Dredd*, Higgins has illustrated *Chopper, Freaks,* One-Offs, *Tharg the Mighty* and *Time Twisters*. His work outside the Galaxy's Greatest Comic is also highly respected, and he has contributed to some of the most important series of recent times, including working as a colourist on the modern superhero classic *Watchmen*, and on *Vertigo's Animal Man, Hellblazer* and *Pride and Joy*.

John McCrea's striking art has graced various *2000 AD* strips including *Judge Dredd, Sinister Dexter* and *Chopper*. Outside of the Galaxy's Greatest he is well known for his work on *Hitman* with celebrated writer Garth Ennis.

Patrick Goddard's clean art style has graced many strips in the Galaxy's Greatest Comic. Co-creator of the *Megazine* series *Wardog*, he has penciled *Judge Dredd, Mean Machine, Middenface McNulty, Sinister Dexter* and took over the art duties on *Savage* from Charlie Adlard.

Kiwi artist **Martin Emond**'s unique artwork first came to prominence when he illustrated Gordon Rennie's *White Trash* for the short-lived British comic *Blast!* This led to Emond illustrating album covers for Glenn Danzig and working on high profile US comics such as *Lobo* and *The Punisher*. He also worked with Pat Mills on the ultra-violent *Accident Man* strip for *Toxic!*